READINGS IN

# EDUCATIONAL
# PSYCHOLOGY

# READINGS IN

# EDUCATIONAL PSYCHOLOGY

EDITED BY

### VICTOR H. NOLL
*Michigan State University*

### RACHEL P. NOLL
*Research Associate*

THE MACMILLAN COMPANY — NEW YORK

MACMILLAN NEW YORK, LONDON

A DIVISION OF THE CROWELL-COLLIER PUBLISHING COMPANY

Second Printing, 1964

Library of Congress catalog card number: 62-9296

The Macmillan Company, New York
Macmillan New York, London
Brett-Macmillan Ltd., Galt, Ontario

Printed in the United States of America

# PREFACE

Comparison of textbooks of today in educational psychology with those of a generation ago reveals many changes. The entire field of psychology has changed and inevitably particular areas like educational psychology have reflected such changes. Moreover, educational psychology has made progress in becoming a discipline in its own right. Leaders in the field have been committed to this viewpoint and have worked for its acceptance and implementation. The nature of this development and some of the important factors in it may be briefly mentioned.

Among the most important of these is the work in child growth and development, which has been led and carried on, not alone by psychologists, but often by educators and those who have become specialists in this field. The result has been a body of content and the development of methods and techniques for study of children that constitute a field of knowledge in themselves. Most of the work done impinges directly or indirectly on educational psychology and much of it has been absorbed into the content and the methods of that subject.

Another factor influencing educational psychology is the work in group dynamics by social psychologists, sociologists, anthropologists and educators. "No man is an island," said John Donne, and nowhere has this been taken to heart more earnestly than in this area. The functioning of the individual as a member of a class or group in school, the family, the community and its multitudinous organizations, or as a citizen of a country or even of the world is a matter of supreme importance to education. It is also of importance to the individual in terms of fulfilling certain basic human needs. In attention to this area, present-day textbooks in educational psychology are in marked contrast to those of twenty-five years ago. Most of the work along these lines had not been done or even begun at that time.

Another area whose importance and influence have increased greatly is that of mental health. Perhaps no area has a more prominent place in the thinking of those concerned with the preparation of teachers than this. It is possible that the responsibility of teachers for the mental health of their pupils has been overemphasized or sometimes misunderstood. At times teachers have come to think of themselves in a role of therapist first and teacher second which is, of course, putting the cart before the horse. Nevertheless, the impact of the work of mental hygienists is plainly visible in today's typical textbook in educational psychology. The effective functioning of the individual as an individual, the development of a wholesome personality, and the ability to meet the everyday problems of a complex civilization are among the major concerns of education.

Still another field of activity which has influenced educational psychology during the past twenty-five years is that of measurement and evaluation. Earlier textbooks in educational psychology might include a chapter on testing concerned mostly with standardized tests of intelligence and achievement. This was rather limited in its applicability to the work of the classroom teacher. The stereotyped nature of much of the earlier work with tests has been modified by broader concepts of measurement and an approach to more inclusive and extensive appraisal referred to as evaluation. This has had a salutary effect on the whole field of tests and measurements and in turn on the treatment of the topic in educational psychology.

A book of readings in educational psychology should, of course, reflect the influences and trends in the field. It has been our aim to do so in the selection of readings in this volume. The wealth of material in current educational, psychological, and sociological literature is so great as to defy complete coverage and analysis. In our search of this literature nearly one thousand articles or excerpts were read or at least scanned, usually by both editors. From this wealth of material a selection was made on the basis of certain criteria which seemed relevant and important. They included the following:

1. The selections should deal with significant problems and areas of educational psychology. The application of this criterion, as is true of the others also, is admittedly a somewhat subjective process. However, common content areas and emphases in educational psychology are rather generally agreed upon and the articles we chose seemed to us to meet the criterion stated.

2. The selections should be interesting, primarily to undergraduates in teacher education, though it is hoped that they would be found so by more advanced students as well. Many of the selections have been tried out with

students and reported by them to meet this criterion. With some, we have simply judged that most students would find them interesting.

3. Reading and understanding the selections should be possible without knowledge of an advanced statistical or technical nature. The typical undergraduate taking his first course in educational psychology has had no work in statistics or research methodology. Consequently, he could be baffled and discouraged by articles which depend for their understanding on the possession of such knowledge. On the other hand, many excellent studies depend heavily on such techniques and methods. Where reports of a somewhat technical nature were included, it seemed to us that the important points of procedure and the results could be gleaned from the report without the necessity of understanding the technicalities of statistical method or research design involved.

4. A criterion related to #3 was that the research studies included should exemplify sound procedures and techniques. Insofar as we were competent to judge and able to do so on the basis of the information given in the reports this criterion was rather well met. In some instances we included for other reasons, a study which did not satisfy this criterion as well as might have been desired.

5. The selections should represent a fair distribution in emphasis and concern between the fields of elementary and secondary education. In many institutions classes in educational psychology are mixed, enrolling both elementary and secondary education majors. In teaching such mixed classes the instructor must try to keep a balance between the interests and emphases of both groups. Even so, if the class concerns itself with problems of early elementary education the prospective high school teacher is likely to feel that time is being wasted. On the other hand, the elementary teacher is likely to have little interest in the problems that concern prospective high school teachers such as the characteristics of adolescence or the use of tests of interests, aptitudes, or achievement in high school subjects. In the choice of selections an attempt was made to represent the range from pre-school to late adolescence or maturity.

6. The selections should include some of the landmarks in the development of educational psychology. A small number of studies that seemed to meet this criterion was included even though what they brought out at the time of publication may have long since become part of the foundation of educational psychology. Many others could have been included on the same basis but were not for various reasons. Thorndike's monumental studies of transfer in high school subjects are a case in point. The reports of these are so long and so complicated that it seemed impractical to in-

clude them or to abridge them. Furthermore, the point they made so elo-
quently at the time seems no longer an issue today.

7. An attempt was made to avoid inclusion of studies often referred
to in widely-used textbooks in educational psychology. It was felt
that our selections should supplement rather than duplicate material frequently already available to the student. For this reason much important
work, widely known and referred to, does not appear in this volume.
Those included because of criterion #6 which may seem inconsistent with
this one, were generally older reports which are no longer so well-known.

A number of features of the collection may be briefly noted. It is believed that the questions following the introductory statement for each
selection will add to its usefulness. These are designed to serve at least
two purposes. One is to give the student some guidance in his reading of
the article and some idea of what to look for. The other is to serve him
and the instructor as a means of checking how well the selection has been
understood. Some questions were intended to be easy enough to give most
students a measure of success in interpreting and understanding the main
ideas of each selection; some difficult enough to be challenging and not
to be answered superficially. It is not easy to steer a true course between
these two points of reference. However, in most instances the questions
are likely to be more difficult for the student than the instructor thinks
they are or should be. Put in another way, questions that meet these two
criteria are likely to seem too easy rather than too difficult to the instructor.

Another feature that should make the volume useful for teaching purposes is the inclusion of a list of references following most of the readings.
These are ones cited by the authors in the original publication. Where more
background reading is desired related specifically to a particular report
they will provide a selection of materials for additional reading and study.

An extensive bibliography at the end of each section of the volume includes many additional selected references to source material.

Many persons have contributed to the preparation of this collection of
readings. We wish to acknowledge with sincere appreciation the generous
cooperation of the authors of the selections in giving permission to reprint
them. Such requests were granted in the case of every selection without
hesitancy. For this we are most grateful.

Acknowledgement should also be given for the many excellent suggestions and the editorial work of the publisher. These have added greatly to
whatever merit the volume may possess.

Thanks are expressed also to the staff of the library of Michigan State
University for their constant and patient assistance in locating materials.

The librarian and staff at the University of Arizona and at Teachers College, Columbia University, where some of the work was done, were also very helpful.

Finally, we acknowledge with thanks the granting of permission to reprint our selections from the following publishers: American Association for the Advancement of Science; American Psychological Association, Inc.; Association for Childhood Education International; The Bobbs-Merrill Company, Inc.; Bureau of Publications, Teachers College, Columbia University; Child Development Publications of the Society for Research in Child Development, Inc.; The Council of Exceptional Children; Dembar Publications, Inc.; Association for Supervision and Curriculum Development; Journal of the National Education Association; The Journal Press; The National Association of Secondary-School Principals; American Philosophical Society. Memoirs; The University of Chicago Press; Warwick and York, Inc.

VHN
RPN

# CONTENTS

## Part III Learning—The Major Concern of Educational Psychology

**Part IV   Mental Health, Personality and Adjustment—The Development
of Character**

# LIST OF TEXTBOOKS IN EDUCATIONAL PSYCHOLOGY

BLAIR, GLENN M., R. STEWART JONES, and RAY H. SIMPSON. *Educational Psychology*. New York: The Macmillan Company. Revised (1962).

COLE, LAWRENCE E. and WILLIAM F. BRUCE. *Educational Psychology*. New York: World Book Company. Revised (1958).

CRONBACH, LEE J. *Educational Psychology*. New York: Harcourt, Brace, and World. Revised (1963).

FRANDSEN, ARDEN N. *Educational Psychology: The Principles of Learning in Teaching*. New York: McGraw-Hill Book Company (1961).

KLAUSMEIER, HERBERT J. *Learning and Human Abilities: Educational Psychology*. New York: Harper and Row (1961).

LINDGREN, HENRY CLAY. *Educational Psychology in the Classroom*. New York: John Wiley and Sons, Inc. Revised (1962).

McDONALD, FREDERICK J. *Educational Psychology*. San Francisco: Wadsworth Publishing Company, Inc. (1959).

MOULY, GEORGE J. *Psychology for Effective Teaching*. New York: Holt, Rinehart and Winston, Inc. (1960).

PRESSEY, SIDNEY L., FRANCIS P. ROBINSON, and JOHN E. HORROCKS. *Psychology in Education*. New York: Harper and Brothers. Revised (1959).

SAWREY, JAMES M. and CHARLES W. TELFORD. *Educational Psychology*. Boston: Allyn and Bacon, Inc. (1958).

STEPHENS, J. M. *Educational Psychology: The Study of Educational Growth*. New York: Holt, Rinehart and Winston, Inc. Revised (1956).

THOMPSON, GEORGE G., ERIC F. GARDNER, and FRANCIS J. DiVESTA. *Educational Psychology*. New York: Appleton-Century-Crofts, Inc. (1959).

TROW, WILLIAM CLARK. *Psychology in Teaching and Learning*. Boston: Houghton Mifflin Company. Revised (1960).

In the table which follows, the readings in this volume are correlated by chapter with the textbooks in educational psychology listed above.

| Chapter Numbers | Blair, Jones, Simpson (1962 Revised) | Cole and Bruce (1958 Revised) | Cronbach (1963 Revised) | Frandsen (1961) | Lindgren (1962 Revised) |
|---|---|---|---|---|---|
| | Readings | Readings | Readings | Readings | Readings |
| Intro. | | | | | |
| 1 | 1, 2, 3 | 2, 33, 35, 36 | 1, 2 | 1, 2, 3, 18 | 1, 2, 3 |
| 2 | 4, 6, 36 | 4, 5 | 4, 5, 10 | 17, 18 | 17, 34, 35 |
| 3 | 4, 5, 6, 41 | 10, 11 | 17, 18 | 4, 5, 7, 8, 11, 16, 21 | 4, 6, 8, 10 |
| 4 | 6, 10, 11, 31, 37 | 6, 8, 26, 28 | 4, 5, 10, 11, 40 | 6, 9, 13, 44, 53 | 36, 37 |
| 5 | 17 | 32, 36, 42 | 36 | 12, 13, 14, 15, 25, 26, 29, 30 | 4, 10, 11, 25, 26, 35, 36, 38, 39, 41, 49 |
| 6 | 7, 8, 9, 12, 13, 16, 18, 27 | 8, 24, 36, 38 | 34, 39, 49 | 20, 22, 23, 24, 40 | 21, 32, 33, 37, 40, 42, 43 |
| 7 | 18, 20, 22, 24, 29, 35 | 10, 11, 34 | 9, 12, 15, 23, 41, 53 | 25, 26 | 17, 19, 22, 26, 30 |
| 8 | 23 | 17, 21, 22, 31 | 6, 7, 8, 13, 14, 21, 27, 28, 38 | 2, 17, 29 | 17, 18, 20, 24 |
| 9 | 18, 25, 26, 30 | 18, 19, 22, 29 | | 17, 18, 28 | 20, 22, 24 |
| 10 | 18, 19 | 24, 29 | 19, 26 | 19, 26 | 22, 23, 24, 35, 40 |
| 11 | 34, 36, 38, 39, 41, 49 | 18 | | 30 | 25, 26, 29, 30 |
| 12 | 14, 27, 28 | 19, 26 | 29, 30 | 10, 32, 34, 42 | 22, 35, 40, 43 |
| 13 | 34, 42 | 12, 20, 25, 26, 30, 35 | 31 | 32, 33, 37, 38, 39, 40, 42, 49 | 25. 26 |
| 14 | 43 | 49, 52, 53 | 20, 22, 24, 39 | 34, 36, 38, 39, 41, 43, 49 | 44, 45, 46, 47. 50, 51, 52 |
| 15 | 33, 42 | 44, 45, 46, 47, 48, 49, 50, 51, 52, 53 | 25, 26 | 44, 45, 46, 47, 48 | 6, 15, 44 |
| 16 | 15, 42 | 21, 23, 24 | 44, 45, 46, 47, 48, 50, 51, 52 | | 12, 13, 14, 15, 27, 28, 37, 53 |
| 17 | 12, 13, 44, 45, 53 | | 32, 33, 34, 35, 37, 42 | | 37 |

# CURRENT TEXTBOOKS IN EDUCATIONAL PSYCHOLOGY

| McDonald (1959) | Mouly (1960) | Pressey, Robinson, Horrocks (1959 Revised) | Klausmeier (1961) | Stephens (1956 Revised) | Thompson, Gardner, DiVesta (1959) | Trow (1960 Revised) |
|---|---|---|---|---|---|---|
| Readings | Readings | Readings | Readings | Readings | Readings | Readings |
| 1 | 1, 2, 3 | 1, 2, 3 | 2, 17, 18 | 1, 2, 3 | 4, 5 | 1, 2, 3 |
| 2, 3 | 1, 4, 34, 35 | 4, 5, 10 | | 1, 2, 3 | 4, 5 | 31, 33, 34, 35, 37 |
| 1, 2, 3 | 4, 5, 7, 8, | 4, 6, 7, 8, 9, 10 | 4, 8, 9, 11, 15 | | 20 | 7, 8 |
| 20, 22, 24 | 4, 10, 11 | 11, 31 | 23, 33, 35, 39, 40 | 4 | 44, 45 | 18, 23 |
| 17, 18 | 32, 33, 37, 42 | 1, 32, 33, 35, 37, 42 | 22, 23, 24, 32, 35, 40 | 6, 9, 12, 13, 14, 15, 16 | 44, 45, 47 | 4 |
| 17, 18 | 10, 11, 36, 37, 38, 39, 40, 41, 49 | 4, 10, 11, 34, 36, 38, 41, 42 | 17, 18 | 7, 8, 15, 16, 44, 45, 46, 47, 50, 51, 52 | 6, 8, 9, 15, 44 | 20, 44, 45, 46, 47, 50, 51, 52 |
| 10, 11, 23, 31, 43 | 6, 9, 12, 13, 16 | 7, 8, 18, 20, 22, 23, 24 | 25, 26 | 31, 36 | 11 | 4, 6, 9, 12, 13, 14, 15 |
| 23, 24, 31, 43 | 17, 18 | 17, 18, 29 | 4 | 17, 18 | 33, 34, 40 | 36, 39, 41, 49 |
| 19, 27, 29 | 23, 27, 28, 29 | 19, 29, 30 | 43 | 17, 18 | 36, 38, 39, 41, 49 | 5, 33, 36, 41, 42 |
| 19, 25, 26 | 17, 20, 21, 22, 23, 24 | 25, 26, 36, 37, 41, 43 | 34, 35, 36, 37, 38, 42, | 22, 24, 40 | | 19, 29 |
| 4, 5, 6, 11, 12, 13, 14, 15, 16 | 17, 19, 30 | 21, 22, 23, 24, 29, 35 | 43 17, 18, 20, 22, 24, 40 | 23, 24, 27, 28, 29 | 17, 18 | 19, 29 |
| 34, 35, 36, 42 | 25, 26 | 8, 9, 27, 28 | 19, 26, 30 | 25, 26 | 17, 18, 20, 21, 22, 23, 24 | 19, 25, 26, 27 |
| 23, 35, 37, 39, 40 | 4, 5, 10, 11, 23, 31 | 34, 44, 45, 46, 47, 49, 50, 51 | 7, 8, 9, 12, 13, 14, 15, 21, 27, 53 | 17, 29 | 17, 19 | 32, 33, 35, 37, 39, 40, 43 |
| 44, 46, 47, 48 | 44, 45, 46, 47, 48, 50, 51, 52 | | 29 | 19, 30 | 25, 26, 29 | 23, 25, 26, 30 |
| 44, 45, 47, 48, 49, 50, 51, 52 | 7, 8, 9, 12, 13, 14, 15, 27, 28, 29, 53 | 28 | 44, 46, 53 | 18, 21 | | |
| 6, 13, 15, 34, 44 | 10, 11, 32, 33, 34, 36, 37, 38, 39, 41 | 32, 33, 39 | 45, 47, 48, 49, 50, 51, 52 | 34, 35, 42, 44, 49 | 31 | |
| 36, 40, 41 | 32, 35, 40, 42, 43 | 12, 13, 16, 20 | 1 | 10, 11, 31, 33, 36, 42 | | |

| Chapter Numbers | Blair, Jones, Simpson (1962 Revised) | Cole and Bruce (1958 Revised) | Cronbach (1963 Revised) | Frandsen (1961) | Lindgren (1962 Revised) |
|---|---|---|---|---|---|
| | Readings | Readings | Readings | Readings | Readings |
| 18 | 23, 39, 44, 46, 53 | | 43 | | 32 |
| 19 | 15, 21, 47, 48, 50, 51, 52 | | | | |
| 20 | 48 | | | | |
| 21 | | | | | |
| 22 | 32, 42 | | | | |
| 23 | | | | | |
| 24 | | | | | |

# CURRENT TEXTBOOKS IN EDUCATIONAL PSYCHOLOGY

| McDonald (1959) | Mouly (1960) | Pressey, Robinson, Horrocks (1959 Revised) | Klausmeier (1961) | - Stephens (1956 Revised) | Thompson, Gardner, DiVesta (1959) | Trow (1960 Revised) |
|---|---|---|---|---|---|---|
| Readings | Readings | Readings | Readings | Readings | Readings | Readings |
| 1, 3, 17, 18 | 17, 18, 21, 25, 26, 29, 30 | | | 25, 26, 30 | 34, 42 | |
| | | 16 | | 33, 36, 38, 39, 40 | 32, 34, 35 | |
| | | | | 32, 35 | 10, 33, 37, 42 | |
| | | | | 32, 33, 34, 35, 36, 37, 42, 43 | 20, 23, 40 | |
| | | | | | 32, 33, 35, 36, 39, 43 | |
| | | | | | 32, 33 | |

# EDUCATIONAL
# PSYCHOLOGY

# PART I

---

# EDUCATIONAL PSYCHOLOGY— ITS DEFINITION AND SCOPE

For many students beginning the study of educational psychology it is the first course in psychology and sometimes even the first course in education. Consequently, it seems worthwhile to present some ideas at the outset on what psychology is and does, what education is and does, and how the two combined constitute the basis for a field of study which is different in a sense from either. Psychology is a science which takes for its province the study of human behavior in all its forms. It is concerned with the causes of human behavior and the principles by which behavior can be predicted, sustained, and/or modified. Education, while having some aspects of a science, is essentially a social process whose fundamental purpose is the modification of behavior. At this point psychology and education are one. The psychologist, however, is concerned primarily with methods of studying behavior and of developing a systematic body of knowledge and principles as a science; the educator, on the other hand, is concerned with getting a job done. The job is to change the behavior of children and adults in ways or directions which society has agreed are desirable. Needless to say, the distinction being drawn here is not a clear-cut, sharply defined one, but it does represent a generally accepted viewpoint and a useful basis for thinking about the two fields. In effect then, we are saying that educational psychology finds its influence and use as a bridge between psychology as a science and education as a process.

Educational psychology may be further defined and delimited in terms of areas of content. One way of stating them is represented by the major divisions of this book—human growth and development, learning, personality and adjustment, and measurement and evaluation.

Educational psychology may also be defined in terms of areas of operation, such as classroom teaching, educational research, personnel work, consulting, test development, and administration of psychological services. These different methods of delineation are not mutually exclusive but represent different ways of looking at the field in order to make its nature and sphere of influence clearer. For the prospective teacher beginning the study of educational psychology, the three articles in this section were chosen to provide an overview of the field.

# 1

# IMPLICATIONS OF RECENT ADVANCES IN PREDICTION AND CONTROL OF BEHAVIOR *

## Carl R. Rogers

In the public mind, psychology was for many years a kind of occult, mysterious pseudo-science which enabled the "psychologist" to read one's mind or the bumps on one's head. It was associated in the opinion of many persons with fortune telling, astrology, and hypnosis. In short, it may be said that most persons really did not know what psychology was, and many today probably still don't. Psychology has made great advances in the past fifty or sixty years. During this period understanding and acceptance of psychology as a science have greatly increased. Today there is no important activity in our lives—education, business, industry, scientific research, the military services—which does not benefit from the established principles of psychology or which does not employ psychologists as a matter of course. However, we do not always realize how varied and how significant the implications of psychological research are, especially in the field of education. In this thought-provoking article, Dr. Rogers lists and illustrates some of the well-founded psychological principles and their applications in education and other areas of activity.

*Questions:*

1. Give an illustration of an application of psychological research in improving instruction in your own field.

2. Psychology, like other sciences, may be used constructively or destructively. Give an example of application of psychological principles for destructive purposes.

3. As a future teacher or counselor, what appear to you to be some of the major contributions of psychology to education?

\* \* \*

* Reprinted from *Teachers College Record,* **57:**316–322 (February 1956) by permission of author and publisher.

The science of psychology, in spite of its immaturities and its brashness, has advanced mightily in recent decades. From a concern with observation and measurement, it has moved toward becoming an "if-then" science. By this I mean it has become more concerned with the discernment and discovery of lawful relationships such as that *if* certain conditions exist, *then* certain behaviors will predictably follow.

I believe that few people are aware of the breadth, depth, and extent of the advances in psychology and the behavioral sciences, and still fewer seem to be aware of the profound social, political, economic, ethical, philosophical, and educational problems posed by these advances. In this discussion I should like to focus on the educational implications of these advances in the science of psychology (which inevitably will involve me in some concern with the philosophical implications as well) and to review a few selected examples of what I mean by the increased ability of psychology to understand and predict or control behavior. Each illustration I will give is supported by reasonably rigorous and adequate research, though like all scientific findings, each is open to modification or correction through more exact or imaginative future studies.

What, then, are some of the behaviors or learnings for which we now know how to supply the antecedent conditions?

*We know how to set up the conditions under which many members of a group will report judgments which are contrary to the evidence of their senses.* They will, for example, report that Figure A covers a larger area than Figure B, when the evidence of their senses *plainly* indicates that the reverse is true. Experiments by Asch [2],* later refined and improved by Crutchfield [7], show that when a person is led to believe that everyone else in the group sees B as larger than A, then he has a strong tendency to go along with this judgment, and in many instances does so with a real belief in his false report.

*We know a great deal about how to establish conditions which will influence consumer responses and/or public opinion.* I refer you to the advertisements in any magazine, or to the TV program, "The $64,000 Question," and the sales of the sponsor's lipsticks.

*We know how to influence the buying behavior of individuals by setting up conditions which provide satisfaction for needs of which they are unconscious, but which we have been able to determine.* It has been shown that some women who do not buy instant coffee because of "a dislike for its flavor" actually dislike it at a subconscious level because it is associated in

* Figures in brackets apply to references at end of article.

their minds with laziness, spendthrift qualities, and being a poor house-keeper [12]. This type of study has led to sales campaigns based upon appealing to the unconscious motives of the individual—his unknown sexual, aggressive, or dependent desires.

*We know how to predict which members of an organization will be troublesome and delinquent.* On the basis of a paper and pencil test, Gough [11] has predicted which department store employees will be unreliable and dishonest or otherwise difficult. He freely states that it is quite possible to identify, with a good deal of accuracy, the potential troublemakers of any organized group.

This ability to identify troublemakers is only an extension of the knowledge we have about prediction in other fields—predicting which individual is most likely to become a good salesman, or typesetter, or physician, or student in college.

*We know how to provide conditions in a work group, whether in industry or in education, which will be followed by increased productivity, originality, and morale.* Conversely we know how to provide the conditions which lead to low productivity and low morale. Studies by Coch and French [5], and by Katz, Maccoby, and Morse [13] show in general that when workers in industry participate in planning and decisions, and when they are not supervised in a suspicious or authoritarian way, production and morale increase. The reverse conditions produce a reverse effect. A study reported by Corey [6] indicates that when the leader of a teacher group acts in a manner which is understanding, and which facilitates participation, the group is more productive in making and carrying through plans.

*We know how to provide the conditions of leadership which will be followed by personality growth in the members of the group, as well as by increased productivity and improved group spirit.* Richard [14], in his experience as manager of an industrial plant, and Gordon [10], in his study of leadership of a workshop, have shown that where the leader or leaders hold the attitudes customarily thought of as therapeutic, the results are good. In other words, if the leader is understanding, acceptant, and permissive toward his group and also acceptant of his own feelings in the situation, then the members of the group show evidence of personality growth and function more effectively and with better spirit.

*We know how to provide the psychological conditions in the classroom which will result not only in the usual learning of academic content, but in improved personal adjustment as well.* Studies by Asch [1] and Faw [8] show that if the attitudes of the teacher are similar to those described above for the leader, and hence responsible participation by the student is permitted and encouraged, then academic learning proceeds about as usual as measured by conventional tests, and personal growth and adjustment improve significantly.

*We know how to provide an interpersonal relationship with qualities such that it enables the individual to meet stress with more serenity, less anxiety.* Thetford [19], in an experiment with group therapy, and Faw [9], in a recent study of teacher-pupil relationships in the classroom, came to similar conclusions, though using very different methods and instruments. When individuals—clients or students—have experienced for a time a relationship of warmth, understanding, and acceptance, they are able to meet stress situations with less physiological upset and quicker recovery of physiological balance [Thetford] and are less upset psychologically by the stress [Faw].

*We know the attitudes which, if provided by a counselor or a therapist, will be predictably followed by certain constructive personality and behavior changes in the client.* Studies which in recent years have been completed in the field of psychotherapy justify this statement. [17, 15, 16] The findings from these studies may be very briefly summarized in the following terms:

If the therapist provides a relationship in which he is (*a*) genuine, internally consistent; (*b*) acceptant, prizing the client as a person of worth; (*c*) empathically understanding of the client's private world; then the client becomes (*a*) more realistic in his self-perceptions; (*b*) more confident and self-directing; (*c*) more positively valued by himself; (*d*) less likely to repress elements of his experience; (*e*) more mature, socialized, and adaptive in his behavior; (*f*) more like the healthy, integrated, well-functioning person in his personality structure.

It is obvious that the essence of these findings in the field of therapy is closely related to the three previous illustrations.

*We now know how, I believe, to disintegrate a man's personality structure, dissolving his self-confidence, destroying the concept he has of himself, and making him completely dependent upon another.* This example has not been, so far as I know, verified by objective research. I make this statement after having studied, as far as one is able, the methods used in preparing prisoners for confession in various purge trials in Russia, and the brainwashing procedures applied in Communist China. It seems rather evident that these methods use many of the principles of psychotherapy, but use them in reverse fashion to bring about the disintegration of the autonomous personality, rather than integration. In a curious and abhorrent way this tends to validate the principles of psychotherapy mentioned above, because it indicates that the lawfulness of the process of therapy may be used to build or destroy personality.

*We know how to provide psychological conditions which will produce vivid hallucinations and other abnormal reactions in the thoroughly normal individual in the waking state.* This knowledge came about as the unexpected by-product of research at McGill University [4]. It was discovered that if all channels of sensory stimulation are cut off or muffled, abnormal reactions follow. If healthy subjects lie relatively motionless, to reduce kinaesthetic stimuli, with eyes shielded by translucent goggles which do not permit perception, with hearing largely stifled by foam-rubber pillows as well as by being in a quiet cubicle, and with tactile sensations reduced by cuffs over the hands, then hallucinations and ideation bearing some resemblance to that of the psychotic occur within forty-eight hours in many of these subjects. What the results would be if the sensory stifling were continued longer is not known.

*We know how to influence psychological moods, attitudes, and behaviors through drugs.* For this illustration we have stepped over into the rapidly developing borderline area between chemistry and psychology. From "truth serum," to the chemotherapy now practiced in psychiatric wards, to drugs for the normal citizen there are many ways of changing psychological states. We may take a drug to mobilize our energy to cram for an exam, or a drug to allay our anxiety about the exam. Drugs have reportedly been given to soldiers before a battle to eliminate fear. While much is still unknown in this field, Dr. Skinner of Harvard states that "In the not-too-distant future, the motivational and emotional conditions of normal life will probably be maintained in any desired state through the use of drugs." [18]

*We know the psychological conditions of family life which, if established in a home, will tend to produce emotionally secure children with many socially valuable characteristics.* Here we go to a very different field, that of personality development in children, for our example. We can measure the attitudes and emotional climate which parents are creating for their children, and from these measurements we can predict that Home A will in all probability produce children who will grow somewhat brighter over the years, will be emotionally secure, original, relatively unexcitable; who will be liked by their peers, likely to be leaders, and well-adjusted to adults. On the other hand we can predict that Home B will be likely to produce emotional, excitable children, with little emotional control, and with less of originality than the children from Home A. The studies done by Baldwin

and others [3] at the Fels Research Institute are the basis for these statements. Home A is the home in which the parents' attitudes and behaviors
cluster in what the investigators have termed the "democratic" category,
and parental attitudes and behaviors in Home B cluster in what they term
the "actively rejectant" group.

My purpose in the above examples has been to point up the wide-ranging
power, the very diverse potentialities for control and prediction, which
psychological knowledge is giving us. When we project ourselves into the
future, and try to imagine the further developments which will inevitably
come, the prospect arouses uneasiness. Small wonder that Dr. Robert
Oppenheimer, in speaking of the points of similarity between his own profession, physics, and the profession of psychology, says that one of these
points "is the extent to which our progress will create profound problems
of decision in the public domain. The physicists have been quite noisy about
their contributions in the last decade. The time may well come—as psychology acquires a sound objective corpus of knowledge about human behavior
and feeling—when the powers of control thus made available will pose far
graver problems than any the physicists have posed."†

Inherent in this development of the psychological or behavioral sciences
are, I believe, two profound questions for educators. They are: How do
educators propose to use these rapidly increasing potentialities for influencing and altering human learning and human behavior? How shall we
prepare students to live in a world where the possibilities for such control
of human behavior exist?

I shall not attempt to answer either of these questions, but shall only
comment on each one. As to how educators propose to use this accumulat-
ing knowledge, I believe it is clear that it will depend entirely on their
philosophy of education, as that philosophy is operationally defined in
action. We are rapidly acquiring the knowledge and the skills which will
enable us to turn out passive followers or independent citizens. Many
teachers and educators, if we take account of their actions rather than their
words, have the former as their goal. They will be able to implement this
purpose much more adequately in the future. On the other hand, if the aim
is to turn out self-directing, inquiring minds which will form their own
judgments as to the truth, then knowledge exists which can facilitate this
purpose also. It will be up to the educators, and even more broadly, up to
the community, to choose the direction in which we shall go.

† From a speech to the American Psychological Association, San Francisco, September 5, 1955.

With regard to how we shall prepare students to live in this fearsome future world, I believe some of the research I have cited suggests possible answers.

In the investigation by Crutchfield [7], it was found that about one-third of the responses made by a group of individuals were strongly influenced by the majority opinion, even when that majority opinion was clearly false. However, not all individuals were equally influenced. Some persons were swayed on almost every item by what they thought to be a solid group opinion, but others were influenced scarcely at all. They "called the shots as they saw them," regardless of what others might think.

When Crutchfield analyzed the personality characteristics of these two groups on the basis of extensive personality assessment, the differences were sharp. The conforming group, who were swayed by the majority opinion, tended to be individuals who had little understanding of themselves, were defensive, had to put up a good "front." They were rigid, moralistic, and had great respect for authority. They were somewhat anxious, guilty, suggestible, and unable to tolerate ambiguity. They lacked self-confidence, were vacillating, and tended to become confused under stress.

The independent group, on the other hand, were active, effective, persuasive leaders. They were individuals in whom others felt confidence, and they had confidence in themselves. They were natural, unaffected, non-defensive, and expressive. They were unconventional and adventurous.

To generalize somewhat speculatively from Crutchfield's study to some of the others, I believe it may be tentatively said that the individuals who may be most easily "managed" through the psychological know-how I have tried to sketch in this paper are those who are passive, rigid, insecure, and authoritarian. On the other hand, those who resist being "managed," who are able to deal intelligently with these possible influences, are confident, open, secure, independent, and spontaneous.

But here again we face an exciting fact. The individuals who were not overwhelmed by the majority opinion in Crutchfield's experiment bear a very strong resemblance to individuals produced in a democratic home atmosphere, to workers who have developed in a group-centered industrial situation, to students who have been exposed to an acceptant teacher-pupil relationship, to clients who have experienced a warm and empathic relationship in therapy. In other words, we already know to a considerable degree how to provide the conditions in which such individuals develop. And though the reverse evidence is not quite so clear, I believe it may be said that in large measure we also know how to provide the conditions in which the passive, insecure followers develop.

What I have been trying to say is that the growing body of knowledge in the behavioral sciences gives to our modern culture an astonishing power of choice. We know how to influence and mold behavior and personality in a great many significant ways. We also have available the choice of whether to set the conditions which develop a suggestible, submissive, unsure individual who can be easily influenced to behave in any way that "we" think wise, or the conditions which will develop an open, adaptive, independent, free-thinking, self-respecting individual. It is this latter person who will perhaps be able to use with intelligence and sensitivity to human values the enormous powers which the physical and behavioral sciences are putting at his disposal. The issue of what choice to make in this regard constitutes, I believe, the challenge of tomorrow both for education and for our whole culture.

It might well be pointed out that with few exceptions the psychological know-how which I have sketched has not been widely used or exploited by society. Hence it might seem that the challenge as I have described it is greatly exaggerated.

It is quite true that this knowledge has not been widely used. In this respect the status of the physical sciences is very different from that of the behavioral sciences. The physical sciences have become so greatly respected that if scientists from these fields report that they can create a satellite in space, the only question in the public mind is, How soon will it be done? There is no tendency to scoff at the possibility, as the public in 1906 scoffed at the Wright brothers' "ridiculous" predictions that a machine could fly. As of 1955 the behavioral sciences occupy, in the public mind, a status similar to that of the physical sciences in 1906. The community does not as yet believe that the behavioral sciences can achieve results. Yet this attitude is changing with remarkable rapidity. Who would have supposed, a few years ago, that our military forces would invest millions of dollars in research in the behavioral sciences, that industrial leaders would employ consultants whose main task is to provide a therapeutic relationship for the executives, that research in consumer attitudes would be a big business?

So I conclude that knowledge in the science of psychology will in the near future be used and exploited as fully as knowledge in the physical sciences is used today. The challenge for educators is unreal only if we are looking a year or two ahead. From the long view I know of no problem holding greater potentiality of growth and of destruction than the question of how to live with the increasing power the behavioral sciences will place in our hands and the hands of our children.

## References

1. ASCH, MORTON J. "Nondirective Teaching in Psychology: An Experimental Study." *Psychological Monographs* (1951), **65:**4, 24 pp.

2. ASCH, SOLOMON E. *Social Psychology.* New York: Prentice-Hall (1952), 450–83.

3. BALDWIN, A. L., JOAN KALHORN, and F. H. BREESE. "Patterns of Parent Behavior." *Psychological Monographs.* No. 268, **58:**3, 1–75 (1945).

4. BESTON, W. H., WOODBURN HERON, and T. H. SCOTT. "Effects of Decreased Variation in the Sensory Environment." *Canadian Journal of Psychology,* **8:**70–76 (1954).

5. COCH, LESTER and J. R. P. FRENCH, JR. "Overcoming Resistance to Change." *Human Relations.* **1:**512–32 (1948).

6. COREY, S. M. *Action Research to Improve School Practices.* New York: Bureau of Publications, Teachers College, pp. 47–61 (1953).

7. CRUTCHFIELD, RICHARD S. "Conformity and Character." *American Psychology.* **10:**191–98 (1955).

8. FAW, VOLNEY E. "A Psychotherapeutic Method of Teaching Psychology." *American Psychology.* **4:**104–9 (1949).

9. FAW, VOLNEY E. Evaluation of Student-Centered Teaching. Unpublished manuscript.

10. GORDON, THOMAS. *Group-Centered Leadership,* Chapters 6 to 11. Boston: Houghton Mifflin (1955).

11. GOUGH, H. E. and D. R. PETERSON. "The Identification and Measurement of Predispositional Factors in Crime and Delinquency." *Journal of Consulting Psychology.* **16:**207–12 (1952).

12. HAIRE, M. "Projective Techniques in Marketing Research." *Journal of Marketing.* **14:**649–56 (April 1950).

13. KATZ, D., N. MACCOBY, and N. C. MORSE. *Productivity, Supervision, and Morale in an Office Situation.* Part I. Ann Arbor, Survey Research Center, University of Michigan (1950).

14. RICHARD, JAMES, in *Group-Centered Leadership,* by Thomas Gordon, Chapters 12 and 13. Boston: Houghton Mifflin (1955).

15. ROGERS, CARL R. *Client-Centered Therapy.* Boston: Houghton Mifflin (1951).

16. ROGERS, CARL R. and ROSALIND F. DYMOND (editors). *Psychotherapy and Personality Change*. Chicago: University of Chicago Press (1954).

17. SEEMAN, JULIUS and NATHANIEL J. RASKIN. "Research Perspectives in Client-Centered Therapy," in O. H. Mowrer (ed.), *Psychotherapy: Theory and Research*, Chapter 9. New York: Ronald Press (1953).

18. SKINNER, B. F. "The Control of Human Behavior." Paper presented to the New York Academy of Sciences, April 18, 1955, and published in the transactions of that body, pp. 547–51.

19. THETFORD, WILLIAM N. "An Objective Measure of Frustration Tolerance in Evaluating Psychotherapy," in W. Wolff (ed.), *Success in Psychotherapy*, Chapter 2. New York: Grune & Stratton (1952).

# 2

# THE RELEVANCY OF EDUCATIONAL PSYCHOLOGY *

## Arthur P. Coladarci

What is educational psychology? Is it education? Or is it psychology? Or is it both? Different writers and authorities answer these questions somewhat differently. In this article, the author defines educational psychology in terms of a body of information and as a method of solving educational problems. In the first instance, educational psychology helps the teacher to formulate intelligent hypotheses that can often be tested on the job. It provides the information upon which such hypotheses may be based. In the second instance, educational psychology provides the skills and attitudes necessary to the formulation and testing of hypotheses. These are sometimes referred to as the skills and attitudes of scientific problem solving. The author notes that educational psychology has other values also, but he chooses to confine himself in this article to the two mentioned.

*Questions:*

1. What information would be needed to formulate a sound hypothesis about teaching spelling by phonic methods?
2. What are some of the skills necessary in formulating hypotheses? What are some of the attitudes?
3. What is action research? Does it have any relevance to what Dr. Colardarci is saying here?

\* \* \*

The relevancy of an applied area depends in part upon the definition of the process, institution, or event to which it is applied. The contribution that can be made by *educational* psychology is partially a function of the particular meaning invested in "education." This statement is not merely

* Reprinted from *Educational Leadership,* **13:**489–492 (May 1956), by permission of author and publisher.

the usual innocuous preface to an extended discussion. Indeed, it is our major thesis. Too many teachers and administrators have thought of educational psychology as consisting only of an ordered catalogue of educational prescriptions, which, together with those provided by the other foundational fields in education, "tell" the teacher "how to teach" and the administrator "how to administer." The fallacy lies not only in the much too complimentary respect for the status of our knowledge in these areas but, more fundamentally, in the conception of education as a collection of successful recipes—the teacher or administrator is a person who has been armed with a bag-of-tricks into which he reaches for a decision regarding any given specific professional problem. Although this unfortunate orientation becomes an increasingly less frequent one, it still exists and may be partially attributable to the turn-of-the-century efforts to make education "scientific" by attempting to make it merely more *factual* [1].*

If one, however, thinks of the nature of the educator's role in another way, educational psychology, and education generally, become more powerful, exciting, and rigorous. The conception we have in mind can be described by beginning with a rather coarse but generally acceptable definition of the educator's role: to help the learner change his behavior in specified desirable directions. Although the definition is too ambiguous for detailed analysis, it serves to point out the two basic factors involved: a *process* ("behavior change") and a *criterion* ("specified desirable directions"). Suppose that the educator has clearly specified what he means by "desirable" behavior changes in the form of operationally stated educational goals [2]. It appears, now, that the focal task for the teacher is to so interact with his pupils, and to so arrange the conditions and materials, that these pupils will change in the hoped-for ways. Put in these terms, the teacher's task can be seen as one of manipulating the learning situation in such a way that the *predicted* behavior changes actually do occur. If, at this point, the educational psychologist could say that we now know which manipulations will produce the desired changes, no problem would exist— we have only to apply the correct recipe. However, educational psychology cannot do this. Any particular combination of teacher-pupil-class-group-community-available materials, etc., is somewhat different from any other combination. There is no general prescription that can be considered to be clearly valid for particular cases. The teacher, then, *must be an active, continuous inquirer into the validity of his own procedures.* As Corey puts it:

* Figures in brackets apply to references at end of article.

Most of the study of what should be kept in the schools and what should go and what should be added must be done in hundreds of thousands of classrooms and thousands of American communities. The studies must be understood by those who may have to change the way they do things as a result of the studies. Our schools cannot keep up with the life they are supposed to sustain and improve unless teachers, pupils, supervisors, administrators, and school patrons continuously examine what they are doing. Singly and in groups, they must use their imagination creatively and constructively to identify the practices that must be changed to meet the needs and demands of modern life, courageously to try out those practices that give better promise, and methodically and systematically gather evidence to test their worth [3].

At the risk of belaboring the point, let us put it in somewhat different form before considering the relevancy of educational psychology. The educator's decisions about methods, materials and curricular procedures should be thought of as *hypotheses* regarding the way in which the desired behavior changes can be brought about. These hypotheses must be *tested* continuously by inquiring into the degree to which the predicted behavior changes actually occurred. This view has been referred to elsewhere by the writer [4] as "teaching behavior defined as the-testing-of-hypotheses behavior." The crucial element is *tentativeness;* ideas and decisions about method and curriculum are to be held hypothetically, continuouly tested, and continuously revised if necessary.

### Contribution of Educational Psychology

Given this conception of the educator's role, how can educational psychology be brought to bear on it in helpful ways? The contribution can be broken down into two related categories. First, educational psychology, as a body of information and an arena of research activity, can help in the generation of the educational hypotheses. Intelligent hypotheses are not chosen randomly nor are they found full-blown. An intelligent hypothesizer thinks along the lines of the following model: "*On the basis of the best information now available to me, I* hypothesize that this procedure will produce this result." To translate this into the context of education, we might say, for instance: "*On the basis of what I now know* about individual differences and the reading process, I hypothesize that this kind of grouping-for-reading will lead to the kind of pupil progress in reading that I would like to bring about."

Educational psychology, as a source of information, contributes to the "on-the-basis-of-what-I-now-know" portion of the statement. It helps provide information on which to base hypotheses for particular purposes and particular children. The teacher or administrator who takes this point seriously will understand that one cannot merely "take a course in educational psychology," but that he must constantly keep informed about those developments in this area that are most relevant to his particular educational responsibilities. The reader may also note that this conception of the interaction between educational psychology and the teacher means that every teacher can *contribute to* educational psychology in the process of testing his hypotheses.

A second kind of contribution which educational psychology can make is that of helping teachers and administrators to acquire the attitudes and skills necessary to intelligent hypothesizing and the testing of hypotheses. Limitations of space preclude an explication of this. Generally, what is involved is learning such skills as how to interpret data intelligently, how to observe accurately, how to avoid common logical fallacies in making inferences, how to make adequate decisions regarding what data should be gathered, ways in which data can be gathered and recorded, etc.

Both of these contributions of educational psychology are shared by all the fields represented in this symposium. In the writer's view, this is the *raison d'être* of any field that purports to be "foundational" in professional education. Educational psychology, of course, has many additional and somewhat unique values for the educator. We have chosen to overlook those in this discussion since they are covered comprehensively and in detail in the available published literature. Those who are interested are invited to examine the published reports of a committee organized by the Executive Committee of the National Society of College Teachers of Education. The first report [5] discussed the ways in which educational psychology relates to curriculum development; the second [6] considers the nature of educational psychology and its general place in teacher education; the third [7] gives detailed attention to the ways in which specific areas of educational psychology can be helpful to the prospective teacher; the last report [8] describes present practices and developments in the teaching of educational psychology.

It is appropriate, in this case, that the final comment should be cautionary as well as benedictory. The writer has stated his position as though there are no responsible competing alternatives to it. Any dogmatic flavor in the statement is more a consequence of brevity than of intent. Many persons will hold that such a conception of education as we have presented here is both impractical and not valuable. Our response would be that the orientation is at least practical in the sense that many, many educators have learned to behave as inquirers; the orientation appears to be valuable in that where one finds such an educator he usually finds him to be valued by his colleagues, ego-involved in his profession, and able to criticize his procedures rationally. In short, such educators do exist and they appear to make the profession a better one by their membership in it.

## References

1. SMITH, B. OTHANEL. "Science of Education," in W. S. MONROE (editor), *Encyclopedia of Educational Research*. New York: Macmillan, pp. 1145–52 (1950).

2. TRAVERS, ROBERT M. W. *Educational Measurement*. New York: Macmillan, pp. 19–36 (1955).

3. COREY, STEPHEN M. *Action Research to Improve School Practices*. Bureau of Publications, Teachers College, Columbia University, p. viii (1953).

4. COLADARCI, ARTHUR P. "Are Educational Researchers Prepared to Do Meaningful Research." *California Journal of Educational Research*. **5**:3–6 (1954).

5. "The Psychological Basis of the Modern Curriculum," *Journal of Educational Psychology*. **39**:129–169 (1948).

6. "Educational Psychology in the Education of Teachers," *Journal of Educational Psychology*. **40**:257–94 (1949).

7. "Educational Psychology for Teachers," *Journal of Educational Psychology*. **41**:321–72 (1950).

8. "Current Practices and Innovations in the Teaching of Educational Psychology," *Journal of Educational Psychology*. **43**:1–30 (1952).

# 3

# THE FUNCTION OF THE DIVISION OF EDUCATIONAL PSYCHOLOGY OF THE AMERICAN PSYCHOLOGICAL ASSOCIATION: A COMMITTEE REPORT *

## Victor H. Noll, John E. Horrocks, and G. Lester Anderson

The report which follows, while written primarily for educational psychologists, may have some value for the prospective teacher or counselor. In it, the responsible committee outlines first what it believes the scope and limits of the field of educational psychology to be. Particular emphasis is given first to the concept of educational psychology as a bridge between education as a social process, on the one hand, and psychology as a science, on the other. Second, the field is described in terms of its major content areas. These are said to include human growth and development; learning, personality, and adjustment; measurement and evaluation; and techniques and methods in educational psychology. Third, educational psychology is defined in terms of areas of operation, such as teaching, research, personnel work, consulting, administration of psychological services, and development of tests. The article closes with re-emphasis on the function of educational psychology as integrator of education and psychology.

*Questions:*

1. Why should a prospective teacher or counselor be concerned with the definition and description of educational psychology? What reasons can you find in this article?

2. Educational psychology has sometimes been defined as psychology applied to education. Is this the point of view expressed here? Justify your answer.

3. Consider the five content areas said in the article to constitute the content of educational psychology. Would you delete any? Add any? If so, which one or ones?

* Abridged and reprinted from the *Journal of Educational Psychology,* **40**:361–370 (October 1949), by permission of the senior author and the publisher.

## What Educational Psychology Is

Educational psychology takes its form and gets its meaning from the two fields of education and psychology. Education is a social process. Psychology is a discipline, a body of knowledge, a social and natural science.

Psychology has usually been defined as the study of behavior, generally in its molar rather than its molecular aspects. Behavior is studied to the end that it may be predicted and controlled.

Education as a social process is concerned with the establishment of certain behavior patterns in men in order that they can adapt to a given environment, or in order that they may perform in certain ways so that the adaptation of other men is enhanced.

Educational psychology is concerned primarily with the study of human behavior as it is changed or directed under the social processes of education, and, secondarily, with those studies or processes that contribute to an increased understanding of how behavior is changed and directed through education.

Education is possible because humans can learn. Learning is a change in behavior which is correlated with experience. Education is concerned with learning as it is provided in a controlled environment. The educational psychologist is thus concerned primarily with learning. The psychology of human learning is the central core of educational psychology. Thus the function of the educational psychologist becomes specifically concerned with the study of human learning and functioning, to the end that they may be guided, directed, and carried out more successfully and efficiently.

It is not to be supposed, however, that educational psychology may properly confine itself only to the study of human learning as such. It must be remembered that this study and concern will take the educational psychologist into any aspect of psychology or education which contributes to his understanding of learning. Thus, everything he does has meaning as it relates to learning, whether it be measurement and evaluation, guidance and counseling, studying the psychology of school subjects, promoting social development, or performing a training function within industry. These areas are concerned with human beings in order to predict their capacity to learn —and hence, to be educated; to prepare them to learn efficiently, to evaluate the learning which has been presumed to occur in order to re-educate the learner who is deficient; or to improve teaching procedures, or to study certain specialized aspects of learning such as learning to read, or learning how to do a job.

Educational psychology is also concerned with non-learned types of behavior, (those which are maturational in origin) for two reasons. First, learned behavior and behavior which is maturational are closely related. Maturation must take place before certain processes of education can be effective. Those who attempt to guide or direct learning without an understanding of the maturational processes cannot help but be ineffective. Second, maturation normally progresses under a 'normal' environment. If, in a desire to produce certain kinds of learned behavior, the environment is too much disturbed, the normal growth processes will be disturbed and psychological harm may ensue.

## The Educational Psychologist as a Specialist

Because the guidance, direction, control, and evaluation of learning, and the understanding of the normal functions of the learner are complex matters, both at the levels of understanding and of study, the educational psychologist is often placed in a position of having to take a segment of the larger field as his special sphere of operation. Some choose to be primarily concerned with learning about and applying the methods of educational psychology to the child, or the adult; the brilliant, or the handicapped. Some choose to study learning which is school produced and so specialize in the psychology of reading or arithmetic, or the other school subjects. Still others are interested in segments of learned behavior such as personality or attitudes. Others, in their desire to promote adjustment, interest themselves in clinical psychology, or in guidance or counseling. However, whether he operates as a general educational psychologist or whether he espouses one or more specialties, the educational psychologist generally approaches his work with an over-all point of view based upon a somewhat common body of knowledge, and perception of the common problems of his profession. Despite the great diversity of activities which occupy the time of the educational psychologist, a frame of reference for his activities is supplied by the limits set by the two fields—education and psychology. That is, he is interested in studying some aspects of human behavior as it may be changed under the conditions of learning.

## Educational Psychology in Terms of Its Content

Another approach to an examination of educational psychology as a field would be an examination of the general fields or areas of psychology that must be part of the content and experience background of every educational psychologist. There would appear to be five such major areas: human growth and development, learning, personality and adjustment, measurement and evaluation, and techniques and methods in educational psychology. Looking at each area in turn, the more important subheadings under each division are as follows:

## Fields or Areas of Educational Psychology

I. Human Growth and Development—
   a) Heredity and Environment
   b) General Growth and Development
   c) Social and Emotional Development
   d) Motivation, Drives—Basic Theory
   e) Intelligence, Aptitudes, Interests
   f) Individual Differences

II. Learning—
   a) General Nature of Learning
   b) Factors Influencing Learning
   c) Motivation—Devices in Teaching
   d) Skills
   e) Reasoning and Problem-Solving
   f) Attitudes
   g) Learning of Particular School Subjects
   h) Transfer of Training

III. Personality and Adjustment—
   a) Emotions
   b) Mental Hygiene of the Pupil
   c) Mental Health of the Teacher
   d) Exceptional Children
   e) Character
   f) Social Interaction

IV. Measurement and Evaluation—
   a) Basic Principles of Measurement
   b) Measurement of Intelligence and Aptitudes
   c) Measurement of Learning
   d) Measurement of Adjustment
   e) Application of Results of Measurement

V. Techniques and Method in Educational Psychology—
   a) The Scientific Study of Educational Problems
   b) Statistical Techniques
   c) Implementation of Research for the Classroom Teacher

## Educational Psychology in Terms of Areas of Operation

The definition of the field of educational psychology may also be approached from the standpoint of the jobs held by those who are commonly designated as educational psychologists, and whose training has been particularly strong in those aspects of psychology designated previously as falling within the area of competence of the educational psychologist. An analysis would appear to indicate a number of types of activity, one or more of which usually fall within the duties of the person called an educational psychologist.

First is the teaching function at the college level. Ordinarily courses taught by educational psychologists are designed for teachers in training or in service, for persons studying to become educational psychologists, for persons entering other areas of psychology, and for persons electing the course for cultural reasons or as part of their training in an allied field such as sociology. Many, but not all of these courses are directly oriented toward the problems encountered in public school teaching and an understanding of school-age boys and girls.

Second is the research function. Nearly all educational psychologists actually do research in one aspect or another of their field. Some act as directors of research, while others take as their primary responsibility the integration and interpretation of existing research as it concerns or is of use in one or more of the various branches of educational psychology.

Third is the function of a personnel worker or expert. This may take the form of a training function in the preparation of guidance workers, and counselors or school psychologists. It may consist of student personnel services on the college or university level as a counselor or a remedial aids expert. It may take the form of a psychometrician or college guidance worker dealing among other things with selection, prognosis, placement, or transfer. The educational psychologist may also find himself fulfilling the capacity of a clinician, particularly where children are concerned.

Fourth is the consulting function. This may range from consultation on educational and psychological problems in industry or the armed forces to field work in the public schools.

Fifth is the function of psychological services administration. This function may range from a dean's office, or head of a psychological services center, to the administration of various psychological service programs.

Sixth is the function of test construction and the evaluation of measuring instruments.

**The Educational Psychologist Functions as a Scientist and an Integrator**

Implicit in the above discussion is the point of view that educational psychology is a science in its own right with a content as well as methods of procedure. The educational psychologist functions as a scientist among teachers of education and acts, both in psychology and education, as an intermediary between "pure" research and its application. His preoccupation is with a science of education, building his procedures and his points of view upon verified facts and research. He has, in a real sense, an integrative function that can be far-reaching service.

As has already been indicated, the study of human behavior under conditions that interest the educational psychologist is complex. There is an undeniable need for specialization. But there is also an undeniable need for an integration of the specialized tools and techniques, principles and generalizations, and knowledge and information that are produced by persons working at segments of the field.

An integration of education and psychology serves two purposes. It focuses the total outcomes upon the single objective of improved learning for more effective adaptation of human beings to the exigencies of life. Marshalled forces are more effective than are isolated forces. Educational psychology marshalls and integrates the forces of education and of psychology. Second, integration is mutually enriching to the integrated segments. It shows limitations or weaknesses and also strengths. It produces criteria for judgments of value or worth. It makes relative judgments possible. In this instance, it is mutually beneficial to education and psychology in obvious ways.

Unfortunately, at the present time, with clogged channels of communication between educational psychologists and educationists on the one hand, and among educational psychologists themselves on the other, it becomes increasingly difficult to fulfill the integrative or the facilitating function. The question as to how these channels may be opened is a vital one in the area of educational psychology—as vital to education, however, as to psychology because the histories of education and psychology abound with the contributions of educational psychology.

## Bibliography

*Educational Psychology—Its Definition and Scope*

1. AMATORA, MARY. "A Functional Approach to Educational Psychology." *Educ. Adm. Supp.* **43:**175–181 (March 1957).

2. ANDERSON, G. L. "Educational Psychology and Teacher Education." *J. Ed. Psychol.* **40:**275–284 (May 1949).

3. BLAIR, G. M. "The Vocabulary of Educational Psychology." *J. Educ. Psychol.* **32:**365–371 (May 1941).

4. ———. *Educational Psychology: Its Development and Present Status.* Urbana, Ill.: Bureau of Research and Service (1948).

5. ———. "The Content of Educational Psychology." *J. Educ. Psychol.* **40:**267–274 (May 1949).

6. BRUCE, W. F. "The Relations of Educational Psychology with General Psychology." *J. Educ. Psychol.* **40:**261–266 (May 1949).

7. DAVIS, R. A. "Applicability of Applications of Psychology with Particular Reference to Schoolroom Learning." *J. Educ. Res.* **37:**19–30 (September 1943).

8. FISKE, D. W. "Psychology and the Educative Process." *Sch. Rev.* **65:**317–329 (Autumn 1957).

9. FREEMAN, F. S. "The Need to Define and Re-Orient Educational Psychology." *J. Educ. Psychol.* **40:**257–260 (May 1949).

10. HAGGARD, E. A. "The Proper Concern of Educational Psychologists." *Amer. Psychol.* **9:**539–543 (September 1954).

11. HORROCKS, J. E. "Methodology and the Teaching of Educational Psychology. *J. Educ. Psychol.* **42:**277–284 (May 1951).

12. KLAUSMEIR, H., and D. SWANSON. "The Development of a Functional Course in Educational Psychology for Teachers." *J. Educ. Psychol.* **41:**449–472 (December 1950).

13. LYNCH, J. M. "The Applicability of Psychological Research to Education. *J. Educ. Psychol.* **36:**289–296 (May 1945).

14. MELTON, A. W. "The Science of Learning and the Technology of Educational Methods." *Harvard Educ. Rev.* **29:**96–106 (Spring 1959).

15. SPENCE, K. W. "The Relation of Learning Theory to the Technology of Education." *Harvard Educ. Rev.* **29:**84–95 (Spring 1959).

16. SYMONDS, P. M. "What Education Has to Learn from Psychology: I. Motivation." *Teach. Coll. Rec.* **56:**277–285 (February 1955).

17. ———. "What Education Has to Learn from Psychology: II. Reward." *Teach Coll. Rec.* **57:**15–25 (October 1955).

18. ———. "What Education Has to Learn from Psychology: III. Punishment." *Teach. Coll. Rec.* **57:**449–462 (April 1956).

19. ———. "What Education Has to Learn from Psychology: IV. Whole vs. Part Learning." *Teach. Coll. Rec.* **58:**329–339 (March 1957).

20. ———. "What Education Has to Learn from Psychology: V. Learning Is Reacting." *Teach. Coll. Rec.* **59**:89–100 (November 1957).

21. ———. "What Education Has to Learn from Psychology: VI. Emotion and Learning." *Teach. Coll. Rec.* **60**:9–22 (October 1958).

22. ———. "What Education Has to Learn from Psychology: VII. Transfer and Formal Discipline." *Teach. Coll. Rec.* **61**:30–45 (October, 1959).

23. ———. "What Education Has to Learn from Psychology: VIII. Individual Differences." *Teach. Coll. Rec.* **61**:86–98 (November 1959).

24. ———. "What Education Has to Learn from Psychology: IX. Origins of Personality." *Teach. Coll. Rec.* **61**:301–317 (March 1960).

25. SYMONDS, P. M., *et al.* "Psychologists in Teacher Training Institutions." *Amer. Psychol.* **7**:24–30 (January 1952).

26. TROW, WM. CLARK. "Educational Psychology Charts a Course." *J. Educ. Psychol.* **40**:285–294 (May 1949).

27. WATSON, GOODWIN. "What Psychology Can We Feel Sure About?" *Teach. Coll. Rec.* **61**:253–257 (February 1960).

28. WOLFLE, D. L. "The Sensible Organization of Courses in Psychology." *Amer. Psychol.* **2**:437–445 (October 1947).

PART II

# HUMAN GROWTH AND DEVELOPMENT— INDIVIDUAL DIFFERENCES

It has been said, "The most important, most helpful, most deceiving, most confusing, most neglected fact in education is growth." *

The statement is in no sense an exaggeration. Second in importance only to the phenomenon of growth is its concomitant, individual differences. Because individuals differ at the beginning of life and grow at different rates and in different ways, they will differ from each other at any and all times. The significance of this fact for education can hardly be over-emphasized.

Why do we use both the terms growth *and* development? Are they synonymous or is there a distinction? Some writers in the field use them interchangeably, others attempt to make a distinction. In the latter case, *development* is regarded as the broader term encompassing the over-all or comprehensive aspects of the process, whereas *growth* refers to particular aspects such as physical, mental or intellectual, social, and emotional growth.

In either case, growth and/or development are considered to be influenced by two sets of forces, namely heredity (nature) and environment (nurture). What one becomes or achieves is the product of these two working inextricably together. Heredity determines the potentialities of the organism; environment provides the opportunity, the stimulus, the nurture for the realization of the potentialities. In years past the question of the relative potency of heredity versus environment was a burning issue. One can still get a lively and often heated discussion of the question in almost any group. There are those who champion the importance of one and there are others equally convinced of the prepotency of the other. As far as education is concerned it would seem that our chief concern should be to take each child as he comes to us and help him to grow and develop as fully as possible to the extent of his potentialities.

As has already been mentioned, it is customary to study different aspects of growth separately. Physical growth may be measured in such aspects as height, weight, skeleton, and the like. Intellectual growth is measured in mental age or aptitudes. Emotional growth is measured by such indices as emotional control or freedom from such behavior as temper tantrums. Social growth may be measured in terms of effective participation in groups, harmonious relations with others, and character. Each of these is touched upon in some articles in the following group.

Reference was made above to the importance for education of the concept of individual differences. That individuals, and particularly in the present context, children, do differ in every conceivable way seems not to have been

* S. L. Pressey, *Psychology and the New Education.* New York: Harper and Brothers. 1933, p. 11.

a matter of any interest to educators of a century ago. Historians tell us that schoolmasters behaved as though all children were equally bright, equally prepared, and equal in every respect as far as learning was concerned excepting only industry. If one pupil did not learn as well as another it was because he was lazy. There was a cure for that, namely corporal punishment. Today "the rod" has practically disappeared from the educational scene, but our schools are still far from realizing the goal of providing for each pupil according to his needs and his abilities. Many types of provisions for individual differences are in use but none has proved to be a panacea. Probably none ever will. Some of the current attempts to solve the problem are discussed in this section.

# 4

## CHILD DEVELOPMENT AND THE GROWTH PROCESS *

### John E. Anderson

In this article Dr. Anderson, who has spent a lifetime in study and research in child development, presents a masterful summary of the status and trends in that field. Atlhough the yearbook in which this appeared as chapter one was published more than twenty years ago, the picture it portrays is still an accurate one. In the words of the author, it is an outline summary of the field, and as such it is a valuable addition to this collection of readings. In it the beginning student will find discussed in brief and lucid form major topics such as maturation and learning, physical growth and physiological development, development of motor skills, linguistic skills, intellectual development, development of problem solving ability, emotional growth, social development, the development of interests and activities, character and personality. The material presented will provide the beginner in this field with a good foundation for further study and research.

*Questions:*

1. Distinguish between learning and maturation. Give an illustration of each in human development.
2. Explain how different aspects of development are interrelated, *e.g.* physical growth and social development; intellectual development and emotional development; social development and linguistic development.

\* \* \*

### I. Introductory

. . . The child is a living being, moving from birth to maturity. Any particular moment of his life is a point of transition from an earlier to a

* Abridged and reprinted from "Child Development and the Curriculum," *38th Yearbook of the National Society for the Study of Education,* Part I (1939), by permission of the author and the University of Chicago Press. Copyright 1939 by the University of Chicago.

later level of development. The child, therefore, is dynamic, not static. He is engaged in going through a developmental course that will gradually carry him to maturity. He is moving from the dependency of infancy to the independence and self-reliance of adult life by building habits and skills and attitudes that will enable him to get along effectively in the world of his fellows and to meet the stresses and strains of adult living. The test of an educational program lies, then, in the effectiveness with which persons who as children have moved through that program meet the problems of adult living. In connection with each educational procedure we should ask ourselves whether it makes the child more dependent upon adults or whether it actually leads him forward toward an independent solution of his own problems.

Although the child's development is a continuous process that moves forward by small amounts, nevertheless it seems to have a saltatory character at some periods. When the appearance of any response is dependent upon the maturing of a number of processes or functions, the overt act will not appear until all these functions are at an appropriate level. The taking of the first step is such an act. Viewed as a process, it is dependent upon a number of maturing functions that develop gradually; viewed by parents or observers, it is a striking change in level of functioning.

The changes that take place in a short time are slight in amount. At the age of six years and three months, the child differs very little from what he was at age five years and nine months, even though in the intervening period he has reached the legal age for school entrance. If, however, a child is observed after an interval of three years or of six years, the changes that have taken place in his bodily structure and behavior are very marked, because the small changes that take place from day to day have accumulated over a relatively long period. Further, it is likely that each bodily organ, each body part, and each mental function has its own characteristic growth curve, with its own periods of rapid rise and its own point of maximal development, different from that of any other organ, part, or function. Development is, then, not a single uniform process that is general in character, but rather the sum of a whole series of specific growth processes, many of which are interrelated. It is quite possible, therefore, that the subject matter of the curriculum draws upon not one but many functions, and that no specific developmental process will be found correlated with any specific curricular material.

## II. Maturation and Learning

In discussing the relation of development to the curriculum, two inter-related processes must be distinguished, each of which makes its own contribution. The first may be called "maturation," the second, "learning."

By "maturation," we refer to the fact that during the developmental course all children follow a very similar order of development, irrespective of the environment to which they are exposed.

Approximately nine months after conception, the child is born. Fourteen months after birth he walks, and between twelve and fifteen years, depending on his sex and rate of development, he reaches puberty. The nine months' term from conception to birth shows some, but relatively little, variation. Babies in a wide variety of climates, of very different racial stocks, and under greatly varying conditions have been found to walk on the average at approximately the same age. Although there is somewhat more variation in the appearance of puberty, still this variation is relatively slight in comparison with the variation that would be possible if it were controlled only by environmental factors.

These are outstanding instances of the maturing process. But they can be paralleled by instances of many more specific responses that appear at their appropriate time and in a definite sequence of order in relation to other responses. Investigation has shown that many such responses are only slightly susceptible to training and that their time and order of appearance can be predicted for any group of children with a high accuracy. One can therefore describe the human being during the developmental period as going through an unwinding or unfolding process, in which the order of events is determined by internal factors.

There are, however, other types of responses that vary markedly with the environment and the opportunities afforded the child. For instance, because of the variation in state laws governing the age of school entrance, children in some regions do not learn to read until eight or nine years, while in others they learn at five or six. Some areas have only 10 percent literacy; others have 90 percent. Whether a population is literate or illiterate depends almost entirely upon the environmental background and the societal demands under which its members develop.

It is obvious that this distinction between maturing and learned responses is not a hard and fast one. For each system of responses and each phase of development there are variations in the extent to which the maturing factor and the learning factor determine its appearance. Thus, the appearance of some responses may be determined nine-tenths by internal factors and one-tenth by environmental factors; in other responses the internal factor may have a weight of 50 percent, and in still others a weight of only 10 percent.

In many instances a portion of a response system may be traced to one factor and another portion to other factors. Thus the time of appearance of talking seems to be determined by internal factors, while the form and content of language is determined by environmental factors. A boy's strength and coördination are determined by a combination of internal and environmental factors; whether he utilizes them in playing baseball or in playing cricket depends upon the particular environment in which he develops.

Moreover, the relation between maturation and learning may vary with developmental level and with the level of learning that the child has reached. For instance, retarded children show greater inadequacies in meeting life's demands as they become older. In the later stages of learning, the child approaches limits that seem to be set by his constitution.

In the subsequent discussion no consistent attempt will be made to distinguish between those response systems that are clearly to be traced to maturation and those to be traced to training. After all, the teacher or other worker with children takes the child as he is at any particular moment and deals with the skills, knowledge, and attitudes he possesses, regardless of their origin in internal process or external demand. . . .

## III. Outlines of Development

The complexity of the growth process has already been emphasized. It consists essentially of many functions that mature at different rates and that are tied together in a single individual, the child as we know him. When the growth process is broken down into its component parts, changes in the size and complexity of bodily organs and structures, *i.e.,* anatomical or physical growth, can first be distinguished. Next can be set off the changes that take place in the functioning of the great physiological processes, such as digestion, circulation, and elimination. Third can be distinguished the changes that take place in the functioning of the organism as a whole in relation to the environment; that is, changes in behavior. These involve increases in the range of stimulation to which the child reacts in the number and character of his skills, in his ability to solve problems, in the modification of his attitudes toward life, and in his capacity to coöperate with his fellowmen through social behavior.

These somewhat artificial divisions are made chiefly for purposes of classification and description. Actually, at any particular moment and in any particular situation there is only a child functioning in relationship to his environment. Sometimes in our concern with methods we forget that we are dealing with children and we erect fictions that increase our difficulties rather than simplify them. When, for instance, we regard learning, or emotions, or memory as separate and distinct processes, we may lose sight of the "whole" child. Actually, all his life processes, both physical and mental, are interrelated to some degree. A disturbance or a maladjustment in one area may reveal itself in a modification or change in another area. The child in poor health may learn less effectively than a well child; a handicapped child may not be able to make normal social adjustments; a child who comes from a nervous and tense home background may find it difficult to adjust to the school; and a child who suffers from excessive fatigue because of irregular sleep habits may show a nutritional disturbance. Such observations and experiences should lead us to be cautious in ascribing difficulties in adjustment to obvious and superficial relations. We need, in such cases, to make a thorough and careful evaluation of the child's relations with his entire environment. For, as teachers, our interest lies in the whole child, and our task is to utilize whatever potentialities and capacities he has for general adjustment to life.

## 1. Physical Growth and Physiological Development

The most obvious changes that take place in the growing individual are increases in size. On the average, the newborn infant is twenty and one-half inches long; the five-year-old is double that height; the average adult woman is five feet, four inches, tall, and the average adult man is five feet, nine inches, tall. The rate of increase in height is most rapid in early infancy. It becomes slower in childhood, is again accelerated just prior to and after puberty, becomes slower again during late adolescence, and finally ceases. Throughout, boys are taller than girls, except for a brief period between the ages of 10 and 13 years, when girls are likely to be taller and heavier than boys. The newborn infant weighs between six and eight pounds, doubles his weight during the first year, and during early adult life reaches the weight of 120 pounds if a girl, and 155 pounds if a boy. The curve for weight is somewhat like that for height. Except for the period just mentioned, when girls are both taller and heavier than boys, boys outweigh girls. Changes in height and weight take place gradually, whether individuals or groups are considered.

If growth is examined in detail, it is found that each body part has its own characteristic growth pattern. The head, which is relatively large in the newborn infant, grows slowly during childhood and has almost reached its adult size by six or seven years. The trunk, which is relatively long in infancy, grows rapidly during childhood and more slowly during adolescence. The extremities, however, are relatively short in infancy, grow very rapidly in childhood and early adolescence, and are proportionately much longer in the adult than in the infant. The smaller divisions of the body likewise have characteristic growth curves. In general, the parts of the body toward the head end and the point of attachment to the body are proportionately larger in infancy and grow more slowly, whereas the parts toward the extremities and farthest from the point of attachment are proportionately smaller in infancy and grow more rapidly during the period of childhood and youth.

This differential growth that is characteristic of external body parts is also characteristic of internal organs and structures. The muscles and skeleton, respectively, approximate in their growth the general form of the curve for the weight and height of the whole body. The brain and nervous system achieve 90 percent of their growth by the age of six years and grow relatively little in gross size from that point onward. The eye reaches adult size by 18 months; the sex organs grow very slowly during childhood and rapidly during adolescence. Lymph organs grow very rapidly during childhood and reach their maximal size and weight about puberty and then actually decrease in size during adolescence. There are not only changes in size and weight, but also changes in texture and structure. This fact is best exemplified in the growth of the skeleton, in which cartilage is replaced by bone and small masses of bone and cartilage, which are separated in the infant, but become joined together in the adult. Many more instances of the differential character of growth could be cited. Even this cursory summary shows how very complex is anatomical development.

Similar findings have been recorded for physiological development. The pulse and breathing rate in the infant are very rapid. With development they slow down and the blood pressure increases. The capacity of the lungs, however, steadily increases in spite of the slower breathing rate, so that the work done by the lungs is much greater in the adult than in the child. Digestive and eliminative processes likewise change with age.

The extent to which the entire developmental process, both physical and mental, is facilitated by an appropriate environment is one upon which few concrete data are available. There have been striking improvements in the height, weight, and general health of children as a result of the modern health program. Most of us would subscribe to the principle that the remedying of a defect, the improvement of physical status, the correction of a physiological deficiency, the improvement of an emotional or a mental adjustment will contribute substantially to the total adjustment of the child to his environment. It is not quite clear from existing data whether, in addition to the specific changes produced by a particular modification of the environment, such general changes in functioning facilitate the entire growth or developmental process. But it is reasonable to suppose that such an effect exists.

A group of important problems concerning training center about the control of various appetites and physiological processes. Normally, control of the eliminative processes is achieved during the first two years, control of the bowel coming first, and control of the bladder coming later. Control tends to develop slightly earlier in girls than in boys. Since this control is usually attained in the preschool years, it is not of primary concern to the teacher.

Many problems in the management of young children concern habits of eating. Usually by school age the child has learned to eat a wide variety of foods with relish and these problems have largely disappeared. There remain, however, occasional cases of retardation or maladjustment in nutrition that interfere with school work.

Sleeping, too, often becomes a matter of concern for the teacher in that inadequate rest may interfere with school adjustment. . . . Young children require more sleep than do older children. There is a rapid decrease from birth to five years in the amount of sleep taken. After that age the decline is slower up to the age of ten years. Thereafter, there is only a slight reduction with further age.

## 2. The Development of Motor Skills

At birth the range of motor acts is very limited. The infant moves his arms and legs, he turns from the dark side of the room to the light side, suckles, and so forth. During the first two years many reflexes and more complex acts appear in a definite sequence, largely under the control of internal processes. The child develops the ability to hold his head erect, to follow moving objects with his eyes, to kick or push with his feet, to grasp objects, and so on. In Figure 1 the age relations of some of the more out-standing reactions are presented.

The chief general motor response that develops in the first two years is locomotion. Although many think of locomotion as identical with the first step taken by the child at approximately 13 to 15 months, actually the processes involved are maturing for months prior to the first step. Normally

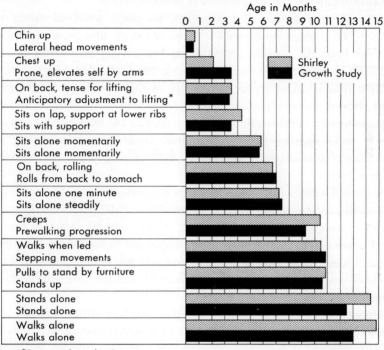

*From mental growth series

**Fig. 1.    The relation to age of twelve motor abilities is determined in two studies.**

the child goes through the following sequence: a phase of crawling in which the abdomen slides on the supporting surface, a phase of creeping in which the abdomen is lifted clear and cross coördination appears in the move-ment of arms and legs, a phase in which the child pulls himself to the standing position by taking hold of furniture or other objects, and finally the phase of stepping movements that terminates in walking. Once the capacity to move about has appeared, the pattern of the child's life changes. Instead of being a stationary object to which stimulation must come, he is now a free moving agent that can make contact with a very wide environment, and hence can have many new experiences. In the next three or four years he will establish many different locomotor skills. He will learn to run, jump, climb stairs, skip, walk a narrow rail or board, jump rope, and so forth. It is important that during this early period the child should have apparatus available that will encourage many types of locomotor play, for he develops control over his muscles through using them in a wide variety of situations and in the manipulation of many materials.

After the appearance of locomotion, no single universal motor skill appears. To a surprising degree the development of subsequent motor skills depends upon the specific opportunities the environment offers and the character of the skills for which social example is afforded. Large muscular coördinations seem to appear in advance of the small muscular coördinations. Hence, modern play equipment for young children is made up in large and easily manipulable units in contrast to the tendency a generation ago to make such equipment diminutive. Great interest in playing with miniature objects comes at the age of eight or nine years, rather than at three or four.

Some difference of opinion still exists with reference to the use of large and small play materials. While modern evidence and practice tend to support the principle of larger equipment, it must not be forgotten that the child's own readiness and interests are important factors in the determination of his activities. Thus, a good environment will not be composed exclusively of one type, one size, or one piece of material, but will contain a variety of materials and play objects.

Modern research also shows that there is very little intercorrelation among motor skills. One cannot predict high skill in one activity from high skill in another. A boy may throw a ball very well and yet be poor in manipulating a saw or a hammer. It follows, then, that the environment during the early school years should give the child a wide variety of opportunities for experience in many different situations, for otherwise he cannot explore his own potentialities. There is some indication, moreover, that early practice in motor skills possesses an advantage over later practice, probably not so much because of greater plasticity as because early practice gives the child so many more opportunities for later practice. The child who learns to swim at six will likely be swimming whenever opportunities offer, whereas the child who learns at fifteen or sixteen will almost inevitably get much less practice.

There are very wide differences among children with respect to their motor capacities and the ease with which they acquire the various manipulative skills. Even though motor ability is not related to intelligence, the intelligent child has some advantage because of his capacity to understand instructions and to envisage the situation in which the skill is to be used.

Because of the child's high degree of interest in motor activities and the tangible character of the activities themselves, the educational problem is essentially one of providing material and equipment rather than one of leading the child into new interests, as is the case with many intellectual and cultural skills. Since much of children's play is motor in its character, teachers and other workers have an excellent base upon which to build a program of guidance and instruction.

### 3. The Development of Linguistic Skills

In many respects the most striking feature of the development process is found in language, through which the human being develops those characteristics and activities that distinguish him most sharply from the animal and that make possible both the development of a social order and an educational program. . . .

The most striking characteristic of language is the use of a response of one modality, called a "symbol," to represent an experience or to take the place of a response of another modality. Thus, a flick of the throat comes to stand for the movements of arms or legs and a series of flicks of the throat is used to describe a sunset. Speech symbols appear first, followed in the school years by the written and printed symbols.

The newborn infant makes a wide variety of vowel and consonant sounds just as spontaneously and as naturally as he moves his arms and legs. The first sounds are single vowels; later, consonants are attached. At six or seven months of age the infant begins to babble; that is, to make sounds in sequences that have a superficial appearance of language but that lack meaning. Usually the first true language response or symbol used representatively occurs at about twelve months; in the next six months a few additional words appear. At about 18 months the child makes the discovery that symbols represent objects, and asks the names of objects. When this discovery is made, language development proceeds very rapidly. Soon the child is using simple sentences. Even in early infancy a distinction can be made between the language of understanding and the language of use; for at 15 months, when the child can use very few words symbolically, he will respond to a variety of commands, demands, and requests in verbal form.

Studies of sentence length and structure show that the child begins to use complex sentences early and that, by the age of five years, when he enters school, he uses every part of speech in sentences of complex structure. There is even some indication that, beyond eight years, there is relatively little further modification of spoken language. Thus the spoken language develops very early, at a very rapid rate, and has reached a very large proportion of the adult form before the child receives school instruction. There is some indication that written language involves skills somewhat different from those of spoken language. The developmental curves for written language show a uniform and steady progression from eight or nine years up to 16 or 17 years, and even by that age have probably not reached their terminal point.

The amount of practice had by the young child in speaking is so enormous that it is no wonder that by five years speech is already a highly developed skill. The fact that corrections in spoken speech tend to come well after speech is a smooth-running and automatic process raises the question whether written language should not be permitted to develop for some time, without too much effort at correction. Perhaps too early an emphasis upon correct usage and grammar may serve to reduce the motivation of the child for writing, whereas the same corrections, applied after writing has become a reasonably automatic process, may operate to improve its quality without reducing motivation.

The environment has a marked effect on language development. Children of higher socio-economic and cultural status are definitely advanced in this respect. The only child is more advanced than is the child with brothers and sisters, and he in turn is more advanced than are twins or triplets. Apparently the only child imitates the speech of adults who are far along in the linguistic process; the single child imitates the speech of older brothers and sisters, who are a little farther along; twins or triplets imitate each other and develop poor linguistic form as well as poor articulation. In the light of these facts one wonders whether the examples of language usage furnished by parents and associates in the home and play situation may not be of more importance as determiners of spoken language than is school instruction. In any event, the first-grade teacher works with children possessing highly developed language skills that have been fixated by much practice over several years. Improvement of home speech might lighten her task considerably.

There is a definite relationship between linguistic skill and intelligence, since children of higher intellectual levels show more linguistic skill than do children of low intelligence.

Almost from the outset the use of symbols fulfills a definite social need in the life of the child. Through symbols he can modify the behavior of other persons and can change the social pattern. Far too few studies of the function of language, as distinct from its structure, have been made; but there is clear indication of progression from accidental and superficial associations to logical thought, and evidence of growing capacity to express meanings and to adapt symbols to a wide variety of uses and functions in such a way that increased mastery of self and the external world is gained.

## 4. Intellectual Development

Ever since the days of Binet, intelligence tests have been widely used and have performed a very significant function in the guidance of children. Binet devised a scale that made possible the classification of any child in terms of the average, or typical, performance of a well-sampled group of children at each chronological age. For example, a child with a chronological age of fourteen years whose performance on the test is like that of typical ten-year-olds is said to have a mental age of ten years and an I.Q. of 10 divided by 14, or .71. An intelligence scale is composed of a number of items that involve the use of vocabulary, computation, problem-solving, range of information, interpretation of pictures, and so forth. Children classified as subnormal rarely adjust to the school curriculum or to life situations as effectively as do children classified as bright or superior. The reader is referred to the more technical literature for a detailed discussion of the significance of intelligence for the educational process. This literature shows that children develop in intelligence at varying rates and that there is a reasonable degree of consistency in their intellectual performances as measured by the scales from time to time. The child who at five years obtains a low rating is likely also to obtain a low rating at ten; the eight-year-old child with a high rating is likely to have a high rating when he is tested at 16 or at 17 years. Moreover, the tests have been found to be predictive in some degree of the adjustment of the child in school and in practical life. The measure, then, obtained from a battery of tests or a scale reflects a general underlying ability that is important for both learning and adjustment.

From the standpoint of mental growth, test results indicate that as the child grows older he increases in his ability to remember, to attend, to persist at an intellectual task, and to solve complicated problems. There is no precise way in which the growth curve for intelligence can be determined or plotted, because of the fact that the units are worked out on a chronological-age scale and are relative rather than absolute. But there is evidence that growth in intelligence proceeds gradually and continues from birth to maturity.

There is a definite relation between the intelligence of parents and that of children, and between children and their siblings. This suggests that there is a hereditary component in intelligence. There is difference of opinion as to the relative weight of this component. Some investigators give it almost one hundred percent, while others give it much less or even very little weight, but most investigators would weight the hereditary factor more than the environmental factor. Perhaps a conservative statement would be that, while intelligence is in large part determined by hereditary components, it is modified or changed in some degree by environmental factors. The environment determines in large part the extent, degree, and manner in which the innate potentialities of children are realized, and the manner in which hereditary capacities are put to work. In general, the more stimulating an environment is, short of extreme pressure, the better are potentialities realized.

So far as school experience is concerned, there is a definite relation between the child's intelligence level and the ability with which he handles school subject matter. This is perhaps more marked in the case of arithmetic and reading than it is in some of the other fields, possibly because it is much easier to obtain tangible evidence of performance for these subjects. Modern educational practice based upon many investigations supports the view that the school should make special provisions both for children of high intellectual level and for those who are much retarded. This may be accomplished either by appropriate advancement or delay in school progress, by the provision of an enriched or a simplified curriculum, or by the development of appropriate extra-curricular activities. The modern movement away from the educational lock-step of a grade per year of chronological age gives striking testimony to the better understanding both of individual differences and of developmental progress that has come with the scientific study of children. It is unfortunate that a trend has appeared in the reverse direction, seen, for instance, in the custom in some schools to promote all pupils in terms of chronological age.

There are a number of skills closely related to intellectual development. The child's capacity to memorize increases with age. The increase is most marked in the early years. The child's ability to attend increases rapidly during the preschool years and more slowly in the school years. It is difficult to keep a two-year-old child at a particular task or even interested in a toy for any length of time; the older child will show interest for long periods of time. In setting a program for very young children, some account must be taken of their attention and persistence span, since they cannot carry activities over from one day to another with any marked continuity of effort. At five years, when the child enters kindergarten, more emphasis can be placed upon remote goals, and projects can be developed that carry over from day to day. This prepares the child for the much longer projects of the early school years.

Drawing ability in its earliest years appears to be very definitely correlated with intelligence. The young child draws what he thinks rather than what he sees; after the age of ten or eleven years the child tries to draw what he sees.

Musical ability, which is not closely related to intelligence, appears early and to a high degree in some children, and not at all in others. Recent studies of younger children show, however, that many children previously thought lacking in capacity have some ability. The development of artistic and musical appreciation differs in some respects from that of the skills involved in the production of works of art and of music. The range of children with possibilities of appreciation is far wider than the range of those who can perform effectively; hence, a stimulating environment enables almost every child to develop some capacity for appreciation and enables children with ability to discover their own potentialities and secure appropriate training.

### 5. The Development of Problem-Solving Ability and Thoughts

Within recent years there have been two distinct methods of studying the development of thought processes in children, apart from the specific studies made in connection with curricular material. . . . The first, growing out of the animal experiments of Koehler, consists in presenting children with problems that can be solved only by the recognition of a principle or relationship, *i.e.,* not by pure trial and error. The results show that children at all age levels can solve problems of a degree of complexity appropriate to their developmental level and that, with increase in chronological and mental age, problems of greater complexity can be solved. The approach to a problem is very similar at all age levels and it ranges from pure trial and error, through exploration and elimination, which may be very systematic, to solutions without overt evidence of random behavior. With simple problems (for the particular age level) solution is likely to be immediate and may be called "insight"; with complex problems the process of exploration, elimination, and approximation to a solution takes place slowly; with very complex problems there is much trial-and-error behavior. In the studies of young children, cases of immediate insight have been found to occur in not over 4 percent of the trials. In the majority of children, the process of exploration, elimination, and successive approximations to the solution is characteristic. In a small proportion, blundering, ineffective, and purely random behavior seems to be typical. The whole process of problem-solving can be described as a series of approximations in which insight is shown in recognizing both the inappropriateness of some responses and the appropriateness of others. It is also of some interest that when either children or adults are confronted with a problem that is much too difficult, they struggle for a while in the attempt to solve it; then explain their failures in much the same way. Qualitatively, the types of excuses given for failure are the same, even though the adult has the advantage of being able to clothe his rationalizations in more language. While the form of the growth curve for problem-solving ability is not known, the literature suggests that the increase with age is very gradual and that experiential as well as maturity factors are significant in the development of this ability.

The second method of studying the development of thought processes in children, initiated by Piaget, involves the use of the language responses of the child, not so much for the analysis of form and content, as for the analysis of their meaning and function in the life of the child. Three tendencies in development have been described: first, a transition from egocentric responses characteristic of the young child to socialized language responses characteristic of the older child and the adult; second, a transition from an early stage, in which superficial associations are made among experiences characteristic of the young child and called "syncretic" thinking, to an intermediate stage characteristic of the elementary-school level, in which the child is able to reason in the presence of the objects of thought, and thence to a final stage characteristic of the adolescent and adult, in which the individual is able to engage in abstract thought; and third, a transition from mystical, animistic, and magical modes of thought characteristic of children and primitive peoples to the logical, mechanistic, and causal modes of thinking characteristic of adults. The experimental literature shows that, although these transitions describe the general course of the development of thought, the developmental process cannot be divided so sharply into stages as the continental investigators think, and that there is an intimate relation between the type of thinking and the situation that calls forth that thinking. Even young children show a high degree of socialized thinking, of abstract thinking, and of logical thinking in some situations and a low degree in others. Some four- and five-year-old children show quite as much capacity to make generalizations as do some fifteen- or sixteen-year-old children. Even adults who have developed mature types of thought revert to egocentric, syncretic, and primitive types of thought when presented with problems well beyond their level or lying outside the subject matter in which they have been trained or have had experience. The problem of the development of logical processes is, then, much more complex than was formerly supposed. There is, moreover, a strong suggestion in the literature that the social or environmental context has a marked influence upon the type of thinking revealed; thus, young American children show less egocentric and more logical thinking than do young French children, and in Poland rural children show much more primitive types of thinking than do city children.

It is clear, then, that no absolute generalizations can be made with respect to stages of development in thought, nor can we say that the capacity to generalize or to show insight is completely lacking at any level. The teacher should not approach the child with a concept of stages; rather she should evaluate her teaching techniques and material, in order to present to the child, from his very first experiences in school, opportunities for problem-solving or reasoning that are appropriate to his level and that will stimulate him to demonstrate the abilities he possesses.

### 6. Emotional Growth

Pervading all the reactions of the child and furnishing the background of many of the most important aspects of his personality and adjustment are the emotions and the feelings. . . . Here only a brief and general summary will be given.

At times the infant is calm and placid, at other times he is excited, on some occasions he gives every evidence of delight, and on others unmistakable evidence of distress. As he grows older, fear, anger, love, disgust, and a whole host of other emotions will be differentiated. He will show marked attachment for some persons and objects and dislike for others. He will meet some situations calmly; others, so tensely that his behavior will be disorganized. On some occasions he will be keyed up, enthusiastic, energetic, and on others even the most strenuous appeals on the part of parents and teachers will fail to move him.

We can distinguish between two types of emotion. First, there are the exciting emotions, such as fear, rage, jealousy, and so forth, which can be viewed as emergency reactions to situations that the child is not quite prepared to meet on the basis of his experience. Second, there are the milder emotions, attitudes, sentiments, and feelings that pervade the entire behavior of the child and grow out of his previous experience.

An exciting emotion arises whenever the child is blocked or thwarted. The internal tension created results in overt attempts to meet the blocking or thwarting situation by energetic behavior directed toward or away from the stimulus. The internal tension disappears when the child develops behavior that meets or avoids the situation. In infancy and early childhood the primitive and undifferentiated excitement is differentiated into a number of specific emotional reactions that are described by such terms as fear, anger, jealousy, negativism, love, and the like. By the time the child enters school he has developed characteristic emotional expressions and possesses varied methods of showing and controlling his emotions. Differentiation continues at a slower rate during later childhood and the adolescent period.

From the standpoint of training it is important to recognize that in an emotional reaction of the exciting type, the child is facing a situation for which an adequate response is lacking. Much of his behavior springs from an attempt to develop a solution by running through a repertoire of action in order to organize a method of meeting the situation. When such a method is acquired, the situation no longer produces excitement. A distinction must then be made between expert, smooth-running, non-emotional behavior, which indicates effective adaptation, and the tense, exciting, emotional behavior, which indicates that adjustment is in process.

Some emphasis must be placed on the manner in which emotions are affected by factors, both internal and external, other than those involving direct stimulation. Temper tantrums vary with the physical state of the child, with toxic conditions, and with the tenseness of the adults who are present. Often tantrums can be eliminated or reduced if a thorough-going analysis is made of the relation of the child to his environment, whereby the need of specific methods of control may be obviated.

From the practical standpoint the most significant emotional states are those of fear, anger, jealousy, negativism, and love. In anger the reactions of the child are directed toward the thwarting or blocking situation; in the case of the temper tantrum there is an undirected display of energy of a very primitive sort. Temper tantrums occur most frequently in two-year-olds, gradually decrease in frequency as the child grows older, and usually disappear by the time he enters school. The time of disappearance is determined by the type of training the child receives. Ignoring, isolating, or not giving in are more effective methods of eliminating temper tantrums than are spanking, threatening, or giving the child what he wants. Negativism, or refusals, are likewise marked in two- and three-year-old children and typically disappear by five or six years.

Fear reactions are present throughout the whole developmental period, but show some decrease in frequency as age increases. The infant shows marked fear of loud noises and of strangers. Young children are likely to show fear of dogs and strange animals. With development there is a change in the stimuli that characteristically elicit fear. The seven- or eight-year-old child is very responsive to the dangerous and thrilling situations of motion pictures, whereas the sixteen- or seventeen-year-old has developed more control and shows less emotional response. Fear reactions increase in frequency whenever the child is faced with a new situation or moves from a zone of life in which he has become habituated to one that presents new problems and relations. There is always a question whether or not it is the newness or strangeness of the stimulation, rather than its intrinsic character, that produces the fear reaction in children.

Fears may be set by a single intense experience, by repetition of many unfortunate experiences, or by examples of fear behavior shown by older persons in the presence of the child. Considerable care should be taken in developing techniques for removing fear. In general, the most satisfactory procedure is that of training the child in an effective mode of action that will reduce tension. It is not our task in this summary to describe in detail the methods for controlling fear. Readers are referred to longer and more adequate discussions of the subject.

Jealousy is an emotion that is displayed most frequently in the preschool years, though it is still present in some school children. Many children show no evidence of jealousy and in most instances it is the result of an unwise distribution of affection and attention among the members of the family.

The emotion of love shows a characteristic developmental pattern. In infancy the child's attachment centers about his parents. Gradually attachments for other members of the family appear. In the early school years, attachments are made largely with persons of the same sex; that is, boys become friendly with boys and girls with girls. In the period of adolescence both boys and girls develop a strong interest in the opposite sex as well as in their own.

So far we have emphasized the exciting emotions that further the adaptation of the child to emergencies. But the school is equally concerned with the sentiments, the attitudes, the enthusiasms, and the attachments of the child for all manner of objects, activities, skills, and situations. In general, these attachments are the product of the concrete experiences of the child, and become more specific with increasing age. It is not the function of the school to educate emotion out of the child, but rather to encourage positive attitudes and enthusiasms and to build up in the child a capacity to discriminate that will enable him to manifest emotion in socially desirable ways. With the question of values, we cannot here concern ourselves, but we can point out the importance of including in the educational program some provision for education of the emotions.

## 7. Social Development

The importance of social development and the establishment of an appropriate environment for developing the social reactions of the child are becoming of increasing concern, for it is obvious that an individual must live in close relationship with other persons and be dependent upon them in large measure for his success and happiness. The school is an organization in which many children are brought into social relations. The clear recognition of the socializing function of the school is important for the development of educational procedures and for meeting the child's basic needs.

In infancy the child is primarily concerned with himself. But he quickly learns to smile when his mother comes toward him, to distinguish between the sound of human voices and the sounds made by other objects, and to show more interest in the sounds made by human beings. If young children are brought together in groups at the age of two or three years, the striking characteristic of their social behavior is called "parallel, or solitary, play." Essentially the children go off by themselves and maintain independent activities without evidence of true social contacts. By the age of three and one-half years, interest in other children has developed to such a degree that many rudimentary social activities are appearing. The child becomes interested in what other children do to him and finds that other children will on occasion coöperate with him in a joint project. By the age of five years evidence of coöperative play is very marked and there is some tendency to form social groupings.

In connection with the child's progress from the parallel play of his early years, through the coöperative play of the early school years, to the socially organized activities of later childhood and early adolescence, it may be pointed out that the child gets an amazing amount of practice in social situations, for he is with other children and other persons much of the time. He not only becomes aware of his own social "stimulus value," but he also experiments with methods and techniques, some good and some poor, in meeting other people. This social trial-and-error process is important because any group of social reactions that persists into late maturity has been tried in a wide variety of situations and is the product of a long course of practice. Clear examples of this trial-and-error behavior and of this selective process are furnished not only in the studies of young children, but also in the studies of older children, particularly those dealing with the effects of motion pictures upon children's behavior.

In addition to opportunities for observing the effectiveness of his own social behavior in influencing the behavior of others, the child receives from other individuals much direct instruction in social behavior. This includes specific comments on his social acts, general precepts, and formal or informal instruction in the "rules of the game." To these must be added the examples furnished by older persons and the child's direct observations of the effects achieved by adults and by other children in their own social contacts.

In early childhood the *games* played by children are largely individual in character. At about the age of six they begin to exhibit rotation; each child in turn takes the responsibility of carrying through the activity by being "it," catching the other children, or doing a stunt, as in jumping rope. At about the age of nine or ten this rotating type of game is superseded by games in which there is some specificity of social function; one child is the captain, another the catcher, another the pitcher, and so on. Children come to recognize the capacity of their companions for various jobs, and encourage them in their attempts to compete for these positions. This increasing specificity in the selection of appropriate social tasks is carried still further in later adolescence and is a prominent feature of adult social adjustment. Involved in the recognition of this specificity of social function is also the recognition of the hierarchy of functions. While few specific data on the appearance of such recognition are available, casual observation indicates that differences in social status and position begin to be recognized in the early school period.

When the *friendships* of children are examined, it is found that in addition to the tendency of young children to associate with those of the same sex and in adolescence to form associations both with their own sex and with the opposite sex, there is a definite relation between the characteristics of the child and the friends and associates whom he chooses. Children of the same age level tend to play together. Within that particular age level there is a tendency for brighter children to choose as their chums other bright children, the duller children to have dull chums; the physically strong tend to associate with the strong, and the weaker to associate with the weak. Very bright and physically well-developed children cut across the age divisions upward and play with children chronologically older than themselves, while the retarded and physically undeveloped cut across these divisions downward and play with younger children.

As children become older, their associates tend to be determined, not only by age, ability, and physical development, but also by common interests and needs. In adult life most social groupings are based on common interests and experiences.

Studies of the choice of boy and girl friends in adolescence tend to support the general principle that like selects like rather than unlike. Studies of the resemblances and differences between marital partners show the same principle at work. It thus becomes clear that the associations formed by children, although partially determined by incidental and accidental factors, are to a great extent selective in their character.

The form that social activity takes depends in large part upon the environment. Thus, children in an area of high delinquency tend to accept delinquency as normal and even desirable, whereas children in an area of low delinquency look upon the same behavior as abnormal and undesirable.

Certain other findings in connection with social development are of interest. It is, for instance, very difficult to control three- and four-year-old children by holding up older children or other children as examples. But by the age of five years the appeal to the performance of others may be an effective method of motivating both the individual and the group. The evidence seems to be rather clear that competitive tendencies appear at about five years, and that competitive and coöperative tendencies develop together.

The studies of *leadership* in children show that almost every child has opportunities to be a leader in some situations and a follower in other situations. The amount of practice received by children in leading or following varies greatly from child to child and depends in large part upon the physical, mental, and social characteristics of the child. Even at a very early age certain children stand out distinctly from the group by virtue of their capacity to direct and control others, and these children receive an amazing amount of practice in exercising such control, while others receive relatively little. Recent work shows that leader-follower and ascendance-submission reactions in children can be modified through a considerable range by controlling the child's experience in the group.

Finally, it may be said that the social reactions the child shows are the products of his experience with adults and other children. They are set in part by example, demand, and instruction, and in part by the child's own experience in observing the manner in which other persons react to his social ventures and techniques.

## 8. The Development of Interests and Activities

In one sense, the course of development can be said to be a succession of interests, for the child comes gradually to direct his attention away from himself into an objective world and to manifest interest in one activity after another. At first these interests are fleeting; later they show more continuity; and finally, in late adolescence, they may become integrated into a permanent vocation or avocation.

The infant's interest is centered largely in the body and in objects that stimulate sensory surfaces. He plays with his toes and his fingers, and enjoys a rattle that can be fondled, bitten, pushed, pulled, and shaken. For several years he will be exploring all manner of objects, trying to take them to pieces, running his hands over them, manipulating them, getting into every nook and cranny. These activities not only train his developing sense organs but also build up motor skills. This display of manipulation and curiosity increases during early childhood. With the development of language there comes the ability to inquire about objects, their origins, meanings, and so forth. As a result the child indulges in much verbal play, asks many questions, and acquires much information concerning the world about him. He also shows a strong tendency toward dramatic play; he imitates the actions of older persons, plays doctor and patient, mother and child, and the like. He shows much imagination in his play, whether it takes an overt or a linguistic form.

With the entrance into school, interests developed around the school situation become more important. As the child gains skill in reading, he learns to like books, stories, and articles. Through contact with his fellows and older children, he learns the games played on the school playground. He develops a series of enthusiasms, spending much time for a few weeks on one hobby, and then turning suddenly to another. Sometimes parents and teachers become concerned over these sudden changes in interest. Such changes, however, are characteristic of the early years and, if children are watched for a period of years, it will be seen that with increasing age, interest in particular activities becomes more sustained.

Lehman and Witty found that children at the age of nine years have the widest range of interests and activities, and that with each succeeding year interests become more narrow and specialized. If they had measured the length of time that interests persisted, they would probably have found that, as age increased, each interest and activity persisted for a longer period of time. Gradually the child locates those activities from which he can secure some measure of satisfaction and in which he has some skill and can develop more. These he continues, while others that are neither satisfying nor productive of reasonable skill are dropped. The exploratory character of the child's ventures into the realm of interests and activities cannot be emphasized too strongly. He needs a broad base of opportunity, and he needs encouragement and patient treatment by adults, in order that he may find himself. It is well for us, then, to recognize the principle that a teacher who shows some capacity for enthusiasm and who has a rich background of interests of her own can do much to facilitate the child's process of self-discovery.

### 9. The Development of Character and Personality

The most general terms used to describe children's reactions are "character" and "personality," both of which are so difficult to define that there is much disagreement as to their exact connotation. We may define a person's character as the effectiveness of his habits and behavior in fulfilling his own potentialities, both individually and as a member of society. Thus "character" implies both continuity of action in working for remote, rather than immediate, goals, and the capacity to respond to social demands and to identify one's own purposes with those of others. When we describe a person as of strong character, we refer not only to his capacity to meet conventional moral situations, but also to the fact that a certain continuity of pattern runs through his reactions to such situations.

Formerly it was thought that character traits were broad and general in nature, so that, for example, children could be definitely classified as honest or dishonest, truthful or lying, and so forth. Modern studies, however, show wide variation in the behavior of individual children and of groups of children as the situation to which they are exposed varies. The same child may be honest in one situation and dishonest in another situation; he may be truthful in one situation and untruthful in another. Thus, there is little evidence to support the contention that predictions can be made with a high degree of accuracy from the child's behavior in one situation to his behavior in another situation that is distinctly different. From the standpoint of character education the importance of this principle lies in its calling attention to the specific acts of the child, rather than to mythical "character traits." If we wish the child to be honest, we must give him both the opportunity to be honest and the gratification that comes from being honest in a wide variety of specific situations.

The young child's reactions are neither bad nor good in the moral sense. He tests numerous responses to numerous different situations and learns from his experience to identify those responses that are condoned by society and those that are condemned. The process of acquiring moral standards extends over many years and involves the child's experiences at home, in church, in school, and in contact with extra-community agencies, such as the radio, the newspaper, and the movies. If the total environment is sound, the child's behavior is likely to be of a high character. It may depart from that high character when a considerable number of unfavorable factors are present. The task of analyzing, of teasing out, these undesirable factors is a difficult one and demands the services of specialists in child behavior.

Modern research on character education adds weight to the traditional distinction between verbal behavior and overt behavior in concrete situations. Many times children know the rules of conduct without being able to apply them. Moreover, a program of character education that is essentially verbal may not be as effective as one in which the child has the opportunity to profit by experience in actual situations. There is also some discussion regarding the extent to which the child can generalize from one situation to another and the age at which this capacity appears. Since the ability to generalize increases with age, we can expect the older child to make generalizations on moral conduct from isolated experiences more readily than the younger child. In any event, a broadly conceived program of character education approaches the child from many different angles. It involves some contact with precepts and codes, some experience in specific situations, and some training in generalizing.

If we observe the age trends in infraction of the moral code, it is clear that up to the age of nine or ten years infractions of legal significance seldom occur. But after this age there is a steady increase in the number of such infractions. It is not clear whether the increase at nine years is due to the fact that the child has matured to such an extent that his acts have social consequences to a much greater degree than formerly, or whether the tendencies to delinquency that have been shown mainly at home hitherto have gone undetected because they have not affected persons outside the home.

So far as practical procedures in the handling of children are concerned, it is clear that social sanctions and condemnations increase in efficacy as the child becomes mature. Obviously, more can be demanded and expected of older children than of younger children. A teacher can tolerate in a six-year-old child an amount of make-believe or imaginative lying that could not be tolerated in a ten-year-old child, and she can set a standard of truth-telling for a sixteen-year-old child that is higher than that for a ten-year-old.

So far as personality is concerned, we can say that its development is not entirely a matter of the individual, but depends upon the reciprocal relations between the individual and the group of which he is a part. We all contribute to each other's personality. There is a tendency among modern investigators to define personality as "the social stimulus value" of a person, thus indicating that personality appears in our relations with others rather than in inherent characteristics. Whatever may be our point of view on this problem, it is clear that personality is a structure the child builds up in the course of his life on the basis of the many skills, abilities, attitudes, and experiences that have been discussed in the earlier portions of this section. It is a continuously changing structure, with a certain continuity running through it because these experiences cluster about one's physical and psychological entity. In this respect each personality is unique because it is composed of different elements or basic capacities that have been exposed to a different environment from the beginning.

The central problem so far as the child is concerned is to organize the training program, which includes the school, the home, the church, and his associates, in such a way that the child may become an integrated and wholesome personality rather than one that is broken, disintegrated, or disheartened by his contacts with life. On the one hand, the child is to be made responsive to social demands; on the other hand, the energy and motivations arising out of internal impulse must be preserved so that he will be able continuously to make a fresh attack upon his life's problems. Here lie major problems of mental hygiene. The teacher bears an important part in this picture. She should not be so concerned with her own prestige and importance that she tears down the personality of the children with whom she comes in contact. Rather, she should be the kind of individual who enhances the personalities of the children who come under her supervision. Contact with young minds should carry her forward in her own personal process of self-discovery and growth. For her, as for the children, zest, enthusiasm, a positive approach to life, and an enjoyment of the process of learning offer the best hope for the development of a well-rounded and wholesome personality that, on the one hand, will enable her to meet the inevitable stresses and strains of living, and on the other, will furnish a basis for enduring satisfaction in personal accomplishment and in effective contribution to the lives of others.

# 5

## THE RELATIONSHIP OF EARLY INFANT REGULATION AND LATER BEHAVIOR IN PLAY INTERVIEWS *

### Mary Ellen Durrett

It has been hypothesized that aggressive behavior in young children is related to child-rearing practices and that the more restrictive and strict such practices are, the more aggressive behavior the child will exhibit. This interesting theory is investigated in the study reported here. Four- and five-year-olds are tested in two standardized dollplay interviews for aggressive behavior and their mothers are interviewed regarding the practices they followed with the children with respect to such matters as feeding, toilet training, punishment, and the like. The results are analyzed for relationship of practices reported by the mothers to aggressive behavior exhibited by the children. Differences between the use of punishment by fathers and mothers and relation of aggression to sex of the child are brought out. The findings are interesting and thought-provoking and cast some doubt on the validity of the hypothesis.

*Questions:*

1. Can you point out any weaknesses in the technique of the study reported here? If so, how could they be eliminated?
2. Do the findings, assuming them to be valid, have any implications for teacher or counselor? If so, what are they?

*　*　*

Experiences of early infancy and childhood are alleged to be crucial in the formation of personality and in the etiology of behavior deviations. Much attention has been paid to the infant's first social contacts, those with his parents, most of them involving the handling of his feeding, sleep, and elimination needs. Sewell and Mussen [6] * suggest that these relationships

* Reprinted from *Child Development*, **30**:211–216, by permission of author and the Society for Research in Child Development, Inc.

are probably the most important aspects of the infant's early environment, and that early treatment and care must somehow be influential in determining the course of the child's later personality development, although the relationship between specific techniques of child guidance and particular personality traits may not be as direct or as great as many psychoanalytically-oriented writers and others believe. The available data do not provide unequivocal evidence of the exact nature in which early life conditions are related to later development.

The present study was initiated to investigate the relationship between fantasy aggression of 4- and 5-year-old children and early child-rearing experiences. It was hypothesized that there is a positive relationship between such aggression and strictness of regulation during infancy so that, if a mother uses very strict child-rearing practices, the child will display a high level of aggression.

## Procedure

### Subjects

Sixty children ranging in age from 4 to 6 years, and their mothers, from white, native-born, urban, intact families living in Tallahassee where the father followed a profession, served as subjects for this study. Of the 60 families represented, 50 of the fathers were members of the faculty at Florida State University and 10 followed a profession such as law or medicine. According to the Index of Social Status—Short Form, as devised by McGuire and White [2], which is based on occupation, source of income and education, 58 of the families were in the upper middle class, and two were in the lower upper class.

The children were the biological offspring of both parents with whom they lived, i.e., families with either adopted or stepchildren were not included in the study. There were 15 male and 15 female 4-year-olds, and 15 male and 15 female 5-year-olds. The mean age was 4 years, 10 months, the range being 4 years to 5 years, 10 months, with a standard deviation of 6.6 months. None of the children had physical handicaps nor severe health problems; none showed signs of mental deficiency; none had had previous experience with the doll play interview.

### Measurement of Fantasy Aggression

Data were obtained in controlled, standardized doll play interviews, following the procedure described by P. S. Sears (4). Each child was given

* Figures in brackets apply to references at end of article.

two play interviews of 20 minutes each, never on consecutive days, but always within a 5-day period. The categories used were the same or a modification of those used in previous doll play studies [1, 4]. These aspects of behavior were recorded: (A) indicated physical aggression— an action that had the intent to irritate, hurt, injure, punish, frustrate, or destroy a doll or equipment. (a) indicated verbal aggression—a verbal expression that had the intent to irritate, hurt, injure, punish, frustrate, or destroy a doll or equipment; scolding, threats, and uncooperativeness were included as were instances in which discomfort was attributed to a doll ("the boy is sick, sad, lost, etc."); (–) indicated nonaggression—any behavior which was not included in the above categories. The child's behavior was recorded in terms of the above symbols every 15 seconds. If verbal aggression or physical aggression or both occurred within any 15-second interval, it was recorded. The measure used in the present study was the "percentage of intervals" in which aggression occurred as contrasted with intervals in which aggression did not occur.

After approximately 25 hours of preliminary practice with the recording procedure, reliability was computed on the basis of 15 20-minute sessions of doll play with two observers, using children from the nursery school and kindergarten who were not serving as subjects in the investigation. One observer sat behind a one-way vision mirror and recorded the children's behavior independently of the experimenter who conducted and recorded the experimental sessions. Reliability was computed by means of percentage of agreement between the two observers, using the formula: 2(number of agreements) / total number of observations. In order to constitute an agreement, not only the same symbol or symbols had to be recorded by the two observers, but also within the same 15-second interval. The percentage of agreement between the observers based on these 15 20-minute sessions for total aggression, physical aggression, verbal aggression, and nonaggression was 88, 83, 80, and 97, respectively.

**Measurement of Early Regulation**

After the completion of the doll play sessions, the children's mothers were interviewed in their homes and asked to rate themselves on five scales, modeled after those used by Sears and his collaborators [5]: one rating on the child's feeding schedule—the degree of strictness, from an exact clock schedule to complete self-regulation; two scales concerning toilet training—the age when it was begun, and the way toilet accidents were handled; and two ratings on discipline and guidance—the amount of obedience expected of the child, and the way of handling aggression toward parents. Each 5-point scale included responses ranging from very permissive to very strict, although the responses were not presented to the mother in this order. Later, the mother's ratings were converted into a scaled score, using a key which included the same responses found on the interview schedule, but arranged from very permissive to very strict.

Ten weeks after the interviews were completed, 15 of the mothers rated themselves a second time. The mean percentage of agreement between the two sets of responses was 92.

## Results

### Fantasy Aggression

When the difference in the number of 15-second intervals in which aggression was shown for session 1 and session 2 was tested for significance, a $t$ of 11.81 was found, significant at the .001 level. Forty-five of the differences were increases from the first to the second session, the children showing significantly more aggression in the second session. The correlations between session 1 and session 2 for the percentage of intervals in which aggression was shown for boys, girls, and total group, respectively, were .59, .60, and .66, all significant at the .001 level. The scores for the two sessions for each child were therefore combined to obtain an over-all measure of fantasy aggression. The results are presented in Table 1.

It will be noted that boys showed a significantly higher percentage of physical aggression, out of the total number of intervals in which aggression occurred, than did girls. However, girls showed a significantly higher percentage of verbal aggression than did boys. The percentage of intervals in which either verbal or physical aggression was shown was significantly higher for boys than for girls. For both sexes, there was a significant session-to-session increase in the number of intervals in which aggression, physical,

### Table 1

#### Sex Differences in Aggression

| | N | PERCENTAGE OF INTERVALS SHOWING AGGRESSION | |
| | | Physical | Verbal |
|---|---|---|---|
| Boys ................. | 30 | 82.0 | 49.7 |
| Girls ................. | 30 | 37.6 | 86.3 |
| | | $p < .01$ | $p < .01$ |

verbal, either or both, was shown. There was also a significantly higher percentage of intervals in which aggression occurred among 5-year-olds than among 4-year-olds.

## Early Regulation

Intercorrelations of measures of early regulation were low and positive with few exceptions. Only two of the coefficients were significant at the .05 level: between degree of regulation of feeding schedule and timing of toilet training for boys; and between degree of regulation of feeding schedule and way of handling toilet accidents for girls. The data also disclosed a significant sex difference in frequency of spanking by mother and by father, as shown in Tables 2 and 3.

## Fantasy Aggression and Early Regulation

None of the correlation coefficients between aggression and early regulation measures was significant. Only two of the coefficients were in the predicted direction; the highest was +.29, between aggression and way of handling aggression toward parents in boys.

## Discussion

The doll play aggression data revealed more physical aggression in boys and more verbal aggression in girls. Although the girls at these ages appeared to be nearly equal in size and strength to the boys, they did not exhibit as much fighting or violence in their doll play. They were more likely to use words to express their aggression; the aggression they did show tended to be in the form of disparagement, scolding, or other nonphysical punishments. It is therefore interesting to note that the boys were spanked more frequently by both the mother and the father than were the girls.

Boys exhibited reliably more total aggression than did girls, thus confirming previous studies [1, 4]. Since earlier investigations used populations of somewhat lower socioeconomic status than the present sample, it would appear that this is a reasonably stable finding.

For both sexes, there was a significant session-to-session increase in the number of intervals in which aggression occurred. This finding is also consistent with that of other studies [1, 4] and has been interpreted to mean that the deliberate permissiveness of the experimental procedure progressively acts to reduce inhibitions of aggression that the child has heretofore acquired.

**Table 2**

**Differences in Frequency of Spankings Given Boys and Girls by Father**

| Frequency | Boys N = 30 | Girls N = 30 |
|---|---|---|
| 1. About once a week, more than once a month, less than once a week | 9 | 4 |
| 2. More than twice a year, not more than once a month ... | 7 | 9 |
| 3. Rarely, once or twice a year | 11 | 5 |
| 4. Once, twice, or three times in lifetime, or never | 3 | 12 |
| $\chi^2 = 9.82$ | | $p < .05$ |

**Table 3**

**Differences in Frequency of Spankings Given Boys and Girls by Mother**

| Frequency | Boys N = 30 | Girls N = 30 |
|---|---|---|
| 1. Several times a week or about once a week | 9 | 2 |
| 2. More than once a month, less than once a week | 10 | 7 |
| 3. More than twice a year, not more than once a month or rarely (once or twice a year), more frequently when child was younger | 6 | 11 |
| 4. Rarely (once or twice a year), not more frequently when child was younger, or once, twice or three times in lifetime or never | 5 | 10 |
| $\chi^2 = 8.12$ | | $p < .05$ |

There are several possible sources of explanation for the failure to find a relation between early regulation measures and aggression. The definition and measurement of variables are subject to some of the criticisms presented by Martin [3]. For example, the antecedent variables may not have adequately accounted for the meaning of early regulation practices for a particular child. Other variables, such as family constellation, ordinal position, influence of siblings, and mothers' feelings about child training practices, were not measured and not controlled. It may be, also, that the mother is not the best informant about her practices and those of other family members. Most of the mothers in this sample had had a college education and were acquainted with popularized versions of child psychology. Possibly, they were aware of what was considered appropriate behavior and rated their practices accordingly. Furthermore, upper middle class mothers may not show enough range of behavior to produce marked differences in aggression in children. The mothers may not have been able to recall accurately what actually happened in the child training situation. Therefore, the actual practices of the mothers may have differed from what was believed or reported to have happened.

The low intercorrelations of the early regulation measures do indicate that the mothers studied were not consistent in the degree of permissiveness or severity used from one child-rearing situation to another and are similar to those reported by Sewell, Mussen, and Harris [7].

## Summary

The general aim of this study was to investigate the relationship between fantasy aggression in young children and the degree of regulation in their infant feeding schedules, the timing of and methods used in their toilet education, and the methods of discipline and guidance used in specific situations.

The subjects were 60 4- and 5-year-old children and their mothers from intact families in Tallahassee in which the fathers followed a profession. The frequency of aggression was measured in two 20-minute sessions of standard doll play interviews with each of the 30 boys and 30 girls. The early regulation data were ratings obtained in interviews with the children's mothers following the completion of two doll play sessions.

Boys exhibited significantly more physical aggression than did girls, while girls displayed significantly more verbal aggression than did boys. The frequency of spankings given boys by mothers and fathers was significantly greater than that given girls. The findings of earlier investigations were confirmed in that, in both doll play sessions, boys were more aggressive than girls, and for both sexes, there was an increase in the amount of aggression from the first to the second session. No statistically significant relationship was found between aggression and the early regulation measures. Intercorrelations among early regulation measures were, with few exceptions, low and positive.

## References

1. LEVIN, H. and R. R. SEARS. "Identification with Parents as a Determinant of Doll Play Aggression." *Child Develpm.* **27**:135–153 (1956).

2. McGUIRE, C. and G. D. WHITE. "The Measurement of Social Status." Research paper in human development no. 3 (rev.). Austin: Univer. of Texas (1955).

3. MARTIN, W. E. "Effects of Early Training on Personality." *Marriage Fam. Living.* **19:**39–45 (1957).

4. SEARS, PAULINE S. "Doll Play Aggression in Normal Young Children: Influence of Sex, Age, Sibling Status, Father's Absence." *Psychol. Monogr.* **65:**6 (1951).

5. SEARS, R. R., ELEANOR E. MACCOBY, and H. LEVIN. *Patterns of Child Rearing.* Evanston, Ill.: Row, Peterson (1957).

6. SEWELL, W. H. and P. H. MUSSEN. "Infant Training and the Personality of the Child." *Amer. J. Sociol.* **58:**150–159 (1952).

7. SEWELL, W. H., P. H. MUSSEN, and C. W. HARRIS. "Relationships Among Child Training Practices." *Amer. Social Rev.* **20:**137–148 (1955).

# 6

# THE STABILITY OF MENTAL TEST PERFORMANCE BETWEEN TWO AND EIGHTEEN YEARS *

## Marjorie P. Honzik, Jean MacFarlane, and L. Allen

In this noteworthy longitudinal study, repeated individual intelligence tests were administered to a group of children from age twenty-one months to eighteen years. The children were all tested annually to age nine. From that point, tests were given at two-year intervals to age fifteen. All were tested finally at age eighteen. Some were tested at thirteen, fifteen, and eighteen; the remainder at fourteen, fifteen, and eighteen. It was thus possible to study an individual's mental test performance as measured, in most instances, fourteen times between the ages stated. The findings will give comfort and support to those who are inclined to view with skepticism any claims made for the constancy of the I.Q. Many changes of fifty points or even more in I.Q. took place as measured in this study. On the other hand, many children maintained a high degree of constancy in test performance. More than forty per cent changed less than fifteen points during the period from six to eighteen years. Those inclined to stress stability will regard this finding as rather remarkable, all factors considered. Perhaps the most important conclusion to be drawn from the study is the re-emphasis on the caution that too much confidence should never be placed on the results of a single measurement of an individual's mental ability, no matter how good the test.

*Questions:*

1. If the same test had been used throughout this study, what would have been possible advantages? Would there have been disadvantages?

2. As a counselor or guidance teacher, of what practical value would the results of this study have for you?

* Reprinted and abridged from the *Journal of Experimental Education,* **17:**309–324 (December 1948), by permission of the senior author and Dembar Publications, Inc.

In an earlier study, the constancy of mental test performance was reported for a group of normal children during their preschool years [8].* These children are now young adults, and it is possible to show the relative stability or lability of their mental test scores over the entire period of testing, twenty-one months to eighteen years, inclusive. The contribution of the present study lies in the fact of repeated individual tests given at specified ages over a sixteen-year period to more than 150 children; and second, in the fact that this group of children was selected so as to be a representative sample of the children born in an urban community during the late 1920's. Furthermore, since the Guidance study has as its primary purpose the study of personality development and associated factors, it has been possible to note the relation of fluctuations or stability in rate of mental growth to physical ills, unusual environmental strains or supports, and to evidences of tension or serenity within the individual child.

## The Sample

The Guidance study has been described in detail in previous publications [10, 11, 12]. Suffice it to say here that the two groups, which are referred to as the Guidance and Control groups, constitute representative subsamples of the Berkeley survey. The names of every third child born in Berkeley between January 1, 1928, and June 30, 1929 were included in the Berkeley survey [15]. A total of 252 children from the Berkeley survey group were asked to come to the Institute for their first mental test at the age of twenty-one months. At this age level, the group of 252 children was divided into two matched subsamples of 126 children on the basis of socio-economic factors (parents' national derivation, income, father's occupation, socio-economic rating, neighborhood, and mother's age and education). One of these (of the Berkeley survey) has been called the "Guidance group" because of the program of intensive interviews had with the parents and children; the second group, which has had physical examinations and mental tests but fewer and less intensive interviews and these at a much later age of the child, has been called the "Control group." The children in both groups were given mental tests at the age of twenty-one months. At ages two and two and one-half years, only the children in the Guidance group were tested. Thereafter, the testing program was the same for the two groups.

* Figures in brackets apply to references at end of article.

Every effort was made to test the children as nearly as possible on or near their birthdays. Actually from 72 to 95 per cent of the children were tested within one month of their birthdates at the various ages up to and including eight years [8].

As was to be expected in a longitudinal study, a number of children were unable to come in for one or more of the mental tests. The most frequent cause of a missed test was the family being "out of town." Also, a number of families lost interest or became uncooperative as their children grew older; one child was killed in an automobile accident. A few were lost for other reasons. However, at eighteen years 153 of the 252 children were tested on the Wechsler-Bellevue test.

### The Testing Program

The testing program followed in the Guidance study is summarized in the following table:

| Ages | Test |
|------|------|
| 21 months—5 years | California Preschool Schedule I or II |
| 6 and 7 years | Stanford-Binet, 1916 Revision |
| 8 years | Stanford Revision Form L |
| 9—15 years | Stanford Revision (either Form L or M) |
| 18 years | Wechsler-Bellevue |

During the preschool years, twenty-one months to five years inclusive, each child was tested at successive age levels on the same test, either the California Preschool Schedule I or California Preschool Schedule II. Beginning at age nine, a program of test alternation was begun which was designed to show the effects of a change in the form of the test on mental test constancy. All the children in both groups were tested on either Form L or Form M of the Stanford Revision at age nine years. But at ages twelve and fourteen years, only two-thirds of the groups were given mental tests; the remaining one-third of the groups were tested at ages thirteen and fifteen years.

The I.Q.'s obtained in the Stanford tests and the Wechsler-Bellevue were converted into sigma or standard scores so that they would be in comparable form to the mental test sigma scores obtained between twenty-one months and five years.

Although these children were selected as a representative sample of urban children, their scores are considerably above the test norms. The average I.Q. on the Stanford-Binet at ages six and seven and on the Stanford Revision, Form L at eight years varied from 118.3 to 118.7. During the age period nine to thirteen years, the average I.Q. was approximately 120. The highest average I.Q. of 123 was obtained for the test period fourteen and fifteen years; and the lowest I.Q. average, 118.2, was earned on the Wechsler-Bellevue at eighteen years.

The percentage distributions of I.Q.'s are relatively normal at all ages at which the Stanford-Binet or Form L or M of the Stanford Revision were the tests given. But at eighteen years, the distribution of I.Q.'s on the Wechsler-Bellevue suggests that this test lacks "top" or at least does not differentiate between the children earning the highest scores at the earlier ages. Bayley [1] has another explanation for the decreased variability at maturity. She suggests that variability is greatest during the age periods when the children are acquiring the functions being tested and that variability becomes restricted with the approach to maturity of the particular processes being measured.

### Group Trends in Mental Test Stability

Pearsonian coefficients of correlations between test scores earned at specified ages are shown in Table 1. These correlation coefficients are based on the scores of the children in the combined Guidance and Control groups for all but two age levels (two and two and one-half years) when only the children in the Guidance group were tested.

Correlations for adjacent ages indicate a fair degree of mental test constancy when the interval between tests is at a minimum. The range of correlations for adjacent ages varies from $r = .71$ (21 months $\times$ 2 years; $2 \times 2\frac{1}{2}$ years; $3 \times 3\frac{1}{2}$ years; and $5 \times 6$ years) to $r = .92$ for the ages $12 \times 14$ years on the Stanford Revision, Form L. However, the correlations decrease markedly with the interval between tests but tend to increase with the age of the children when tested.

67

## Table 1

### Correlations between Test Scores Given at Different Ages

Column groups: **California Preschool Schedule I or II** (ages 2–4) · **Stanford-Binet** (ages 5–7) · **Stanford Revision Forms** (L/M at ages 8–14 or 15) · **W–B** (age 18)

| Test | Age | n | 2 | 2½ | 3 | 3½ | 4 | 5 | 6 | 7 | L 8 | L 9 | M 10 | L 12 | L (12 or 13) | M 13 | L 14 | M (14 or 15) | 18 |
|---|---|---|---|---|---|---|---|---|---|---|---|---|---|---|---|---|---|---|---|
| California Preschool Schedule I or II | 1¾ | 234. | .71 | .62 | .52 | .48 | .38 | .39 | .27 | .29 | .27 | .26 | .17 | .22 | .19 | .13 | .07 | .21 | .07 |
| | 2 | 113 | | .71 | .69 | .60 | .46 | .32 | .47 | .46 | .43 | .45 | .29 | .37 | | .26 | .21 | .34 | .31 |
| | 2½ | 114 | | | .73 | .64 | .57 | .46 | .37 | .38 | .37 | .53 | .32 | .36 | | | .26 | .31 | .24 |
| | 3 | 229 | | | | .71 | .58 | .57 | .57 | .55 | .49 | .59 | .32 | .36 | .36 | .42 | .35 | .37 | .35 |
| | 3½ | 215 | | | | | .76 | .71 | .64 | .60 | .50 | .59 | .49 | .59 | .51 | .52 | .49 | .46 | .42 |
| | 4 | 211 | | | | | | .72 | .62 | .59 | .61 | .68 | .60 | .66 | .48 | .63 | .54 | .44 | .42 |
| Stanford-Binet | 6 | 214 | | | | | | | | .82 | .77 | .80 | .67 | .71 | .74 | .65 | .67 | .70 | .61 |
| | 7 | 208 | | | | | | | | | .83 | .82 | .80 | .77 | .71 | .82 | .73 | .76 | .71 |
| Stanford Revision Forms: | L 8 | 199 | | | | | | | | | | .91 | .93 | .88 | .85 | .82 | .85 | .81 | .70 |
| | L 9 | 90 | | | | | | | | | | | .88 | .88 | .90 | .91 | .87 | | .76 |
| | M 9 | 104 | | | | | | | | | | | .90 | .88 | | .79 | .85 | | .66 |
| | L 10 | 107 | | | | | | | | | | | | .87 | .87 | .85 | | | .70 |
| | M 10 | 83 | | | | | | | | | | | | | .91 | | | | .76 |
| | L 12 | 92 | | | | | | | | | | | | | .92 | | .85 | .89 | .76 |
| | L (12 or 13) | 120 | | | | | | | | | | | | | | | .92 | .88 | .78 |
| | M (12 or 13) | 71 | | | | | | | | | | | | | | | | .87 | .84 |
| | L 14 | 51 | | | | | | | | | | | | | | | | .88 | .73 |
| | M (14 or 15) | 117 | | | | | | | | | | | | | | | | | .79 |

Comparison of the correlation coefficients for three-year intervals shows clearly the increase in mental test constancy with age:

$$2 \times 5 \text{ years, } r = .32 \pm .06$$
$$3 \times 6 \text{ years, } r = .57 \pm .05$$
$$4 \times 7 \text{ years, } r = .59 \pm .04$$
$$5 \times 8 \text{ years, } r = .70$$
$$7 \times 10 \text{ years, } r = .78$$
$$9 \times 12 \text{ or } 13 \text{ years, } r = .85$$
$$14 \text{ or } 15 \times 18 \text{ years, } r = .79$$

The correlation between tests given at 2 and at 5 years $(r = +.32)$ suggests a prediction which is not much better than chance, but the magnitude of the test-retest correlation increases markedly with age.

### Effect of Change of Form of Test on Mental Test Constancy

The correlation between eight- and nine-year tests for children tested on the same form of the Stanford Form L is .91; but the correlation is even higher for the remainder of the group who were tested on Form L at eight years and Form M at nine years $(r = .93)$. Comparison of the effect of change of form on the test-retest correlations is made for six age periods. In all these comparisons, the difference between the test-retest coefficients, when the same or different forms of the Stanford test were used, was negligible. Bayley obtained similar results in the Berkeley growth   study [1].

### Changes in Scores over Certain Age Periods

The correlation coefficients in Table 1 indicate the group trends with respect to the constancy of mental test performance. It is also of interest to know the extent of the changes in sigma scores or I.Q. which are occurring in individual children. Furthermore, the question arises as to whether the correlation between mental test scores is largely determined by a relatively small proportion of the cases or by the group as a whole. In a previous study [8], we published the distribution of changes in sigma scores which occurred between the six- and seven-year tests $(r = .82)$ for these children. This distribution was normal, with 80 per cent of the group showing sigma score changes of .5 or less. However, there were six children whose scores differed on these two tests by 1.5 sigma (approximately

20 I.Q. points since the standard deviation for ages six and seven years is approximately 13) or more. The average change in score between six and seven years was .5 sigma (6.5 I.Q. points).

If changes in I.Q. of 20 points can occur between the six- and seven-year tests, it would be reasonable to expect rather marked changes in scores over the entire test period, twenty-one months to eighteen years. We have, therefore, prepared distributions of the range of sigma score changes for the entire sixteen-year period of testing. We find that the scores of three children have increased between 4 and 4.5 sigma (roughly 70 and 79 I.Q. points, assuming an approximate standard deviation of 17.5 I.Q. points); and the scores of two children have decreased a similar amount. The sigma score curves for four of these five children are depicted in Figure 1D and Figure 1E. The most interesting aspect of these tremendous changes in scores is the fact that the changes are not made abruptly but consistently over a long period of time. However, the greatest changes do occur on the preschool tests. We have, therefore, prepared distributions showing the range of changes in sigma scores and I.Q.'s between six and eighteen years. No child's sigma scores change as much as 4 sigmas during the school years. But the scores of one child (case 764, Figure 1D) changes 3 sigmas; and those of four others between 2.5 and 2.9 sigmas.

Since educators and clinical workers use I.Q.'s rather than standard scores, we have prepared a distribution of the range of changes in I.Q. during the twelve-year period from six to eighteen years for the two groups—Guidance and Control:

### I.Q. Changes between 6 and 18 Years

| Variation | Guidance N = 114 (per cent) | Control N = 108 (per cent) | Total N = 222 (per cent) |
|---|---|---|---|
| 50 or more I.Q. pts. | 1 | – | .5 |
| 30 or more I.Q. pts. | 9 | 10 | 9 |
| 20 or more I.Q. pts. | 32 | 42 | 35 |
| 15 or more I.Q. pts. | 58 | 60 | 58 |
| 10 or more I.Q. pts. | 87 | 83 | 85 |
| 9 or less I.Q. pts. | 13 | 17 | 15 |

We are impressed not only by the extent of the changes in I.Q. during the school years but also by the fact that the results are so similar for the two groups, Guidance and Control. This finding suggests the reliability of these figures and that they would probably be duplicated under similar conditions of testing. Changes in I.Q. of 30 or more points of I.Q. are

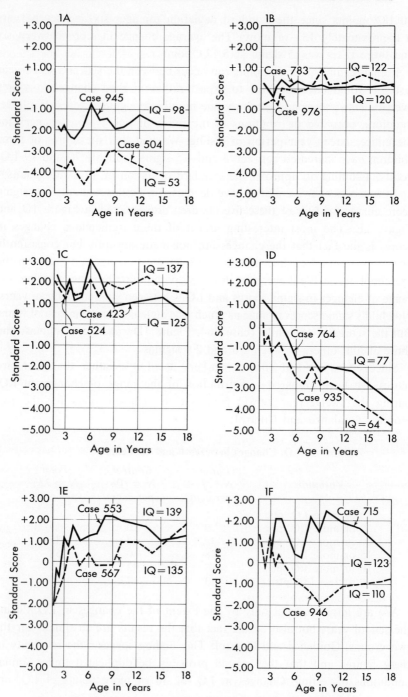

Fig. 1.    Stability of mental test scores in individual children.

shown by 9 per cent of the children in the Guidance group and 10 per cent in the Control group. The I.Q.'s of over half of the children showed a variation of 15 or more points of I.Q. at some time during the school years, and a third of the group varied as much as 20 points of I.Q.

Although it is extremely important to point out the possibility of marked changes in scores in individual cases, it is equally important to emphasize that the scores of many children change only slightly with respect to the group from one age period to the next. And it is only when the changes are consistently in one direction, or the other, over a period of years that the range of variation becomes as great as 3 or 4 sigmas (or over 50 I.Q. points).

## Stability and Instability in the Mental Test Scores
## of Individual Children **

Mental test sigma score curves have been drawn for all the children in the Guidance study. In this sample of 252 children, we have found individuals whose mental test scores have remained relatively stable at either a high, average, or low level over the entire period of testing (twenty-one months to eighteen years). Other children have shown highly inconsistent scores in their mental test performance. Examples of varying degrees of constancy of mental test performances are shown in Figure 1.

## Summary and Conclusions

A group of 252 children, who comprise a representative sample of the children living in an urban community, were given mental tests at specified ages between 21 months and 18 years. These data have been analyzed to show the extent of the stability of mental test performance for this age period. The results may be summarized as follows:

1. Mental test constancy for the age period twenty-one months to eighteen years is markedly dependent upon the age at testing and the interval between tests. That is, group prediction is good over short age periods, and mental test scores become increasingly predictive after the preschool years.
2. Test-retest correlations are as high for children tested on different forms (L or M) of the 1937 Stanford Revision as for children tested on the same form over the same age periods.

** For descriptions of individual case studies see the original article published in *J. of Exper. Educ.* **17:**312–315, 319–320; also Figures 1–4. December 1948.

3. Distributions of the extent of the changes in I.Q. for the age period six to eighteen years show that the I.Q.'s of almost 60 per cent of the group change 15 or more points; the I.Q.'s of one-third of the group change 20 or more points; and the I.Q.'s of 9 per cent of the group change 30 or more points. The I.Q.'s of 15 per cent of the group change *less* than 10 points of I.Q. The group averages, on the other hand, show a maximum shift in I.Q. over this age period of from 118 to 123.

4. Some individuals show consistent upward or downward trends in I.Q. over a long period resulting in changes of as much as 4.5 sigmas or 50 I.Q. points.

5. Inspection of the mental test curves of the individual children included in this paper indicates that changes in mental test scores tend to be in the direction of the family level, as judged by the parents' education and socio-economic status. (Group findings showing an increasing relationship of family status to the children's test scores were presented in an earlier study [6].)

6. Children whose mental test scores showed the most marked fluctuations had life histories which showed unusual variations with respect to disturbing and stabilizing factors. However, there were other children whose scores remained constant despite highly disturbing experiences.

In conclusion, it should be re-emphasized that, whereas the results for the group suggest mental test stability between 6 and 18 years, the observed fluctuations in the scores of individual children indicate the need for the utmost caution in the predictive use of a single test score, or even two such scores. This finding seems of especial importance since many plans for individual children are made by schools, juvenile courts, and mental hygiene clinics on the basis of a single mental test score. Specifically, it should be noted that a prediction based on a six-year test would be wrong to the extent of 20 I.Q. points for one out of three children by the age of 18 years, and to the extent of 15 I.Q. points for approximately six out of ten children.

## References

1. BAYLEY, NANCY. "Consistency and Variability in the Growth of Intelligence from Birth to Eighteen Years." *J. of Genet. Psychol.* (1948).

2. ————. "Factors Influencing the Growth of Intelligence in Young Children." *Yearbook of the National Society for the Study of Education.* pp. 47–79 (1940).

3. BRADWAY, KATHERINE P. "I. Q. Constancy on the Revised Stanford-Binet from the Preschool to the Junior High School Level." *J. of Genet. Psychol.* LXV, pp. 197–217 (1944).

4. GOODENOUGH, F. L. "Studies of the 1937 Revision of the Stanford-Binet Scale, I: Variability of the I.Q. at Successive Age Levels." *J. of Educ. Psychol.* XXXIII, pp. 241–251 (1942).

5. ———— and K. M. MAURER. *The Mental Growth of Children from Two to Fourteen Years.* Minneapolis: University of Minnesota Press, p. 130 (1942).

6. HONZIK, M. P. "Age Changes in the Relationship Between Certain Environmental Variables and Children's Intelligence." *Yearbook of the National Society for the Study of Education.* XXXIX, pp. 185–205 (1940).

7. ————. "The Constancy of Mental Test Performance During the Preschool Period." *J. of Genet. Psychol.* LII, pp. 285–302 (1938).

8. ———— and H. E. Jones. "Mental-Physical Relationships During the Preschool Period." *J. of Exper. Educ.* VII, pp. 139–146 (December 1937).

9. JAFFA, A. S. *The California Preschool Mental Scale (Form A).* Syllabus Series No. 251. Los Angeles: University of California, p. 66 (1934).

10. MACFARLANE, J. W. "Studies in Child Guidance: I. Methodology of Data Collection and Organization." *Monograph Society for Research in Child Development.* III, pp. 1–254 (1938).

11. ————. "The Guidance Study." *Sociometry.* II (1939).

12. ————. "Study of Personality Development." *Child Behavior and Development.* Barker, Kounin, and Wright, ch. XVIII.

13. TERMAN, L. M. and M. A. MERRILL. *Measuring Intelligence.* Boston: Houghton, Mifflin Co., 1937, p. 461.

14. WECHSLER, D. *The Measurement of Adult Intelligence.* Baltimore: Williams and Wilkins, 1944, p. 258.

15. WELCH, F. M. *The Berkeley Survey: A Study of the Socio-Economic Status of Four Hundred Berkeley Families in Years 1928–1929.* Manuscript. Berkeley, California: Institute of Child Welfare, University of California.

# 7

# EFFECT OF AGE OF ENTRANCE INTO GRADE I UPON ACHIEVEMENT IN ELEMENTARY SCHOOL *

## Inez B. King

Compulsory attendance laws generally require a child to enter school by the age of six. However, as a rule there is some variation in the actual age at entrance due to differences in dates of birth. Some children enter Grade I before they are six, others after their sixth birthday. In this study, two groups of children were compared on achievement, attendance, progress through the grades, and personal and social adjustment through the sixth grade. One group had entered Grade I at an average age of six years and seven months, the other at an average age of five years and ten months, a difference of nine months. The average I.Q. of the younger group exceeded that of the older by a small but statistically significant amount. Any advantage found to favor the younger group might then be related to superior intelligence while advantages found for the older group might therefore be regarded as even more significant in the light of the intellectual superiority of the younger children. The results of the study are consistent and worthy of most careful consideration. They lead to the conclusion that parents who insist on entering their children in Grade I at the earliest possible date may be doing them a genuine disservice.

*Questions:*

1. Calculate the average mental age of the two groups of children at entrance to Grade I. Do your results help explain the findings of the study?
2. What are some of the reasons why some parents try to have their children enter school at the earliest possible age? Are they sound?
3. Does this study throw any light on the problem of retentions? Explain.

* Reprinted from the *Elementary School Journal,* **55:**331–336 (February 1955), by permission of author and the University of Chicago Press. Copyright 1955 by the University of Chicago.

The purpose of this study is to determine some of the possible effects, qualitative as well as quantitative, that chronological age at the time of entrance to Grade I has on the achievement of pupils in their sixth year of school. More specifically, the problem is to compare the achievement of a group of children who entered Grade I before six years of age with the achievement of a group of children who entered after six years of age.

## Setting of the Study

The study was undertaken in the elementary schools of Oak Ridge, Tennessee. Since it was organized in 1943, the Oak Ridge school system has followed a type of program whereby the graded school organization is maintained as a basis for grouping children, but the instructional material is adapted to individual differences, and academic standards are modified as a criterion for promotion.

Children enter Grade I of the Oak Ridge schools in September if they are six years old by December 31.[1] The per cent of retentions is comparatively small, not more than 2 per cent. There are no subgroups within the grades, such as Grades I A and I B, and no midyear promotions. Teaching is directed toward meeting individual differences in the needs of children. Inevitably, however, the younger school entrants are frequently presented with situations that are beyond their developmental abilities, and as a result they are not able to realize their maximum achievement capacity and are likely to develop social and personal problems.

Standardized achievement tests and intelligence tests are given to each child so that the teacher may better understand his developmental needs. A cumulative guidance record system, giving the family, physical, mental, educational, and social history for each child, has been set up. At the sixth-grade level these cumulative records afford a rather complete summary of the children's elementary-school career, and they have provided the data for this study.

Under this system of grouping and promoting children and with the philosophy of adapting instruction to meet individual needs, it is important to know two things: (1) whether a child is achieving up to his ability and (2) whether he is achieving up to the level of his chronological age. Under the present plan of grouping and promotion, does the school meet the needs of the youngest school entrants? Do the typical children who enter Grade I

---

[1] Kindergartens are maintained as a part of the Oak Ridge public schools but were not considered in this study because kindergarten attendance is not compulsory.

before they are six years old "make up" during the first six years of school for the lack of chronological age readiness in Grade I? The present article reports a study which attempted to answer these questions.

Specifically, this study of the qualitative and quantitative aspects of achievement sought answers to the following questions:

1. How does the achievement of pupils who enter Grade I early in terms of chronological age compare with that of children who enter Grade I approximately eight months later (achievement to be measured on the basis of performance at the end of the sixth grade)?

2. Do younger entrants tend to be retained more often than older entrants?

3. Are boys more frequently retained than girls?

4. How does the average daily attendance for the younger entrants compare with that of the older entrants?

5. Are there more "problem children" among younger than among older entrants?

## Procedure

This study was based on the achievement records of one group of fifty-four children who entered Grade I when they were chronologically between five years and eight months old and five years and eleven months of age and the achievement records of another group of fifty children who entered Grade I when they were chronologically between six years and five months old and six years and eight months of age. All these children were born in the year 1940, entered Grade I in September, 1946, and attended the Oak Ridge schools for six years. The study used data in the cumulative folders of these children, where information concerning each child's school life had been recorded for six years.

Sufficient data had been accumulated to make possible a study of the children's achievement, which is based on (1) academic or grade standards attained, (2) average daily attendance, (3) progress through the grades, and (4) social or personal adjustment.

## Selection of Cases

The children who entered Grade I in 1946 were arbitrarily chosen by the writer as the group to be studied. The study was carried through the sixth year of school since Grade VI is the last year in the Oak Ridge elementary schools.

In addition to including in the study children born in 1940 and entering

Grade I in September, 1946, and remaining in the Oak Ridge schools for six years, a further control was the inclusion of only children whose intelligence quotients fell within the range of 90–110. This score was obtained by taking the average of the two or more intelligence-quotient scores recorded in each child's cumulative folder. Children within this range of intelligence quotients are considered in this study as typical or average children.

The children were divided into two groups according to their age at entrance to Grade I. The age of entrance in Grade I for the younger group ranged from five years and eight months to five years and eleven months; in the older group, from six years and five months to six years and eight months. A summary of the data with the statistical analysis, shown in Table 1, reveals that the mean age for the older group was six years and seven months. The mean age for the younger group was five years and ten months. The mean difference was nine months. The mean intelligence quotient for the older group was 100.08; that for the younger group was 102.04, with a mean difference of 1.96. The *t* test, when applied to the difference in intelligence quotients, indicated that the difference was significant at the 5 per cent level.

In addition to the criteria for inclusion stated above, children who had been homebound for one or more years were excluded from the study.

## Data Collected

The cumulative folder of each of the 104 pupils was reviewed, and a record was made of the following items:

1. The total average achievement scores in Grades VI (Grade V for retentions). These scores were earned by the children on the Stanford Achievement Test in March, 1952.

2. The number of days present for each of the six school years.

3. Referrals, if any had been made, to the school psychologist for special help.

4. Referrals, if any had been made, to corrective speech class.

5. Teachers' comments suggesting personal or social maladjustment in a child. Such comments indicated nervous manifestations, feelings of inadequacy, and emotional instability and behavioral immaturity.

6. Teachers' comments indicating good personal adjustment in the child and his ability to work with a group with wholesome social relationships. These comments indicated close personal relationships, interpersonal skills, and good school participation. Here, some of the frequently used expressions were: "good

thinker," "creative," "well adjusted," "good work habits," "favorite in the group," "good member of the group," and "able to follow through with plans."

**Table 1**

**Mean Chronological Age and Intelligence Quotient of Groups of Children Entering Grade I before and after Six Years of Age**

| Group | Chronological Age (in Years and Months) | Intelligence Quotient |
|---|---|---|
| Older group ........ | 6–7 | 100.08 |
| Younger group ...... | 5–10 | 102.04 |
| Difference ........ | 0–9 | 1.96 |

The intelligence quotients in these two established groups ranged from 90 to 110, with a small but significant difference in favor of the younger group. The two groups were fairly equal in the number for each sex, and both groups had similar school experiences for six years. There should be some basis, then, for thinking that any difference in their achievement could be explained either by difference in intelligence or by difference in their age. If the difference in achievement tended to favor the younger group, it seems reasonable to assume that the higher intelligence quotient in this group more than offset any disadvantage of early entrance. If the difference favored the older group, it seems reasonable to believe that the higher intelligence quotient of the younger group was not sufficient to offset the disadvantage of early entrance.

**Findings**

*Achievement*

Record was made of the achievement scores earned by the children on the Stanford Achievement Test near the end of the sixth year of school. These scores represent the total average achievement and are recorded in grade-equivalent terms. Table 2 lists the scores in descending order in each group. The reader will note that the scores of children in the older group range from Grade 11.3 to Grade 5.4. The scores of children in the younger group range from Grade 9.6 to Grade 3.8. The table shows that the majority of the children who entered Grade I before the chronological age of six years did not realize their optimum academic achievement (shown by a score of at least 6.8). A large per cent of the older group

### Table 2

**Total Achievement-Test Scores Made at End of Sixth Year of Schooling by
Children Who Entered Grade I before and after Six Years of Age**

*Younger Group*

| Pupil | Sex | Achievement Test Score | Pupil | Sex | Achievement Test Score |
|-------|-----|------------------------|-------|-----|------------------------|
| 1...... | F | 9.6 | 29...... | M | 6.0 |
| 2...... | M | 8.0 | 30...... | M | 6.0 |
| 3...... | M | 7.9 | *31...... | F | 6.0 |
| 4...... | M | 7.9 | 32...... | F | 6.0 |
| 5...... | M | 7.9 | 33...... | F | 5.9 |
| 6...... | F | 7.7 | 34...... | M | 5.8 |
| 7...... | M | 7.5 | *35...... | M | 5.8 |
| 8...... | F | 7.5 | 36...... | F | 5.8 |
| 9...... | F | 7.5 | 37...... | F | 5.7 |
| 10...... | F | 7.5 | 38...... | M | 5.7 |
| 11...... | F | 7.3 | 39...... | F | 5.6 |
| 12...... | M | 7.3 | 40...... | M | 5.4 |
| 13...... | F | 7.1 | *41...... | M | 5.3 |
| 14...... | M | 7.1 | 42...... | M | 5.3 |
| 15...... | M | 7.0 | *43...... | M | 5.0 |
| 16...... | F | 7.0 | 44...... | F | 5.0 |
| 17...... | F | 7.0 | *45...... | F | 4.8 |
| 18...... | M | 6.9 | 46...... | F | 4.8 |
| 19...... | F | 6.9 | 47...... | M | 4.7 |
| 20...... | F | 6.8 | *48...... | F | 4.7 |
| 21...... | F | 6.8 | *49...... | M | 4.3 |
| 22...... | M | 6.6 | *50...... | M | 4.3 |
| 23...... | M | 6.5 | 51...... | M | 4.3 |
| 24...... | M | 6.5 | *52...... | M | 4.2 |
| 25...... | F | 6.5 | 53...... | M | 4.1 |
| 26...... | F | 6.1 | *54...... | M | 3.8 |
| 27...... | F | 6.1 | | | |
| 28...... | M | 6.0 | Mean | ...... | 6.20 |

realized their potential in respect to academic achievement, and many of them overachieved.

The findings of this table were summarized, and the results were analyzed statistically by applying Fisher's *t* test to the differences in the scores of the two groups. It will be remembered that the younger group had a slightly higher intelligence quotient. Table 2 shows that the mean score of the older group was above Grade 7 as compared with slightly above Grade 6 for the younger group. The mean difference was slightly higher than one

*Older Group*

| Pupil | Sex | Achievement Test Score | Pupil | Sex | Achievement Test Score |
|-------|-----|------------------------|-------|-----|------------------------|
| 1...... | M | 11.3 | 27...... | M | 7.4 |
| 2...... | M | 10.8 | 28...... | F | 7.3 |
| 3...... | M | 10.8 | 29...... | F | 7.3 |
| 4...... | M | 9.9 | 30...... | F | 7.1 |
| 5...... | F | 9.9 | 31...... | M | 7.1 |
| 6...... | F | 9.6 | 32...... | M | 6.9 |
| 7...... | F | 9.6 | 33...... | M | 6.9 |
| 8...... | M | 9.3 | 34...... | F | 6.9 |
| 9...... | F | 9.3 | 35...... | M | 6.8 |
| 10...... | M | 9.2 | 36...... | M | 6.8 |
| 11...... | F | 8.6 | 37...... | F | 6.8 |
| 12...... | F | 8.5 | 38...... | F | 6.8 |
| 13...... | M | 8.4 | 39...... | F | 6.6 |
| 14...... | M | 8.3 | 40...... | F | 6.6 |
| 15...... | F | 8.3 | 41...... | F | 6.5 |
| 16...... | F | 8.1 | 42...... | F | 6.5 |
| 17...... | M | 8.1 | 43...... | F | 6.3 |
| 18...... | M | 7.9 | 44...... | F | 6.1 |
| 19...... | M | 7.9 | 45...... | M | 6.1 |
| 20...... | M | 7.7 | 46...... | M | 6.1 |
| 21...... | F | 7.7 | 47...... | M | 6.0 |
| 22...... | F | 7.7 | 48...... | M | 6.0 |
| 23...... | F | 7.5 | 49...... | F | 5.5 |
| 24...... | F | 7.5 | *50...... | M | 5.4 |
| 25...... | M | 7.5 | | | |
| 26...... | M | 7.4 | Mean | ...... | 7.68 |

* Pupils who were retained in one grade for more than a year.

year and four months. The *t* test indicated that the difference was significant at the 5 per cent level. Therefore, according to statistical treatment, there is a significant difference in achievement of the two groups.

## Retentions

Table 2 shows that, of the 104 children, 11 were retained. Only one child who had entered Grade I after six years of age was retained, while ten children who had entered before six years of age were retained.

Of the eleven retentions, only three were girls. This difference substantiates the findings of Pauley [2] that about half as many girls as boys are

[2] Frank R. Pauley, "Sex Differences and Legal School Entrance Age," *Journal of Educational Research,* XLV, September 1951, 1–9.

retained in the "primary grade" where immature children are given an extra year before entering Grade I. This finding indicates that chronological age at time of entrance to Grade I is of more significance for boys than for girls.

### Attendance

When the average daily attendance for the two groups was compared, it was found that there was a mean difference of 17.6 more days of attendance for the older group. This difference was found to be significant at the 5 per cent level of confidence.

### Personal and Social Adjustment

From the progress reports of the teachers and from the records of children who had received special help from the guidance department, there was a marked difference between the records of the children in the two groups. These differences were noticeable in the number having (1) speech defects, (2) nervous indications, and (3) personal and social maladjustments.

Seven children in the younger group attended a corrective-speech class for one or more years as compared with two in the older group. Again it is noticeable that seven of these nine were boys and two were girls.

Ten children in the younger group were described by their teachers with such phrases as "emotional problem," "facial tic," "bites nails," "cries often," "asthma," and "unduly nervous," while similar remarks were made about only three of the older group.

Undesirable growth characteristics were much more evident in the younger group. Nineteen boys and sixteen girls in the younger group were known to teachers to have been maladjusted in some way. Three of these had been referred to the school psychologist for special help. In the older group there were only three girls and three boys whose records indicated poor personal and social adjustments. Phrases most often used in describing these children were "rejected," "insecure," "stubborn," "sullen," "aggressive," "timid," "withdrawn," "needs a sense of belonging," and "immature." Of the children who had been referred to the school psychologist for special help, three were in the younger group while only one was in the older group.

All the retentions were said to have had personal and social maladjustments. However, six of these were said to have been better adjusted and happier in the year in which they repeated a grade.

## Conclusions

This study would seem to indicate that having attained a few additional months of chronological age at the beginning of Grade I is an important factor in a child's ability to meet imposed restrictions and tensions that the school necessarily presents.

With a group of children such as those included in this study, it appears likely that one can expect the following:

1. Younger entrants will have difficulty attaining up to grade level in academic skills, and a large portion of them may fall far below grade-level standards. Older entrants are more likely to achieve up to and beyond grade-level standards.

2. A larger number of the younger entrants will have to repeat a grade.

3. More boys than girls will repeat a grade.

4. Average daily attendance will be lower among younger entrants.

5. Younger entrants are likely to show more indications of poor personal and social adjustment in school.

# 8

# WHEN SHOULD CHILDREN BEGIN TO READ? *

## Mabel V. Morphett and Carleton Washburne

The experiment reported here was carried out in the schools of Winnetka, Illinois in 1928 and 1929. It has probably had more influence on thinking and practice in beginning the teaching of reading than any other. Clear, concise, and simple, it might serve as a model for the kind of experimentation which almost any teacher or school administrator could do.

When are children ready to learn to read? To answer the question, the authors tested 141 children entering first grade to determine mental age and I.Q. Progress in reading during the year was measured by twenty-one steps in first year reading and by sight-word scores. Normal reading progress was determined in relation to the number of steps completed and number of sight words learned by February. All the teachers had had previous experience with the reading materials used. After correlating the various measures used it was found that mental age showed the greatest degree of relationship to reading achievement and, accordingly, this was used as the criterion for measuring readiness. Scores were divided into groups according to half-year intervals of mental age and the percentage of children at each mental age level was determined. The results are still quoted today as the rule-of-thumb for predicting success in learning to read.

*Questions:*

1. What factors, not taken into account in this study, should be considered in judging readiness for reading, or lack of it? Can you cite evidence to support your answer?

2. If only 75 per cent of first grade children have the necessary mental maturity to begin reading, what should be done with the rest?

* Reprinted from the *Elementary School Journal,* **31:**496–503 (March 1931), by permission of Dr. Washburne and the University of Chicago Press. Copyright 1931 by the University of Chicago.

In tracing back to their origins the reading difficulties of some children and their distaste for the subject, the Department of Educational Counsel in Winnetka found that in several instances the children's mental ages on entering the first grade had been low and that discouragement had resulted from their first attempts to learn to read. This discouragement sometimes resulted in a mental set against reading, which lasted for years and which hampered all their school work. The research department, therefore, with the aid of the primary-grade teachers, set about the task of discovering the period in the mental development of children when, as a rule, there is the best chance of their learning to read readily.

In September, 1928, all Winnetka first-grade children, 141 in number, were given the Detroit First-Grade Intelligence Test. The eight first-grade teachers were not told the mental ages of the children and attempted to teach all of them to read. The method, in accordance with the Winnetka technique, was largely individual, so that the slow children did not retard the fast ones. In February, 1929, the reading progress of these children was measured for the purpose of determining the amount of progress made by children at each mental level.

In order that the reading progress might be measured, the first large teaching unit was divided into definite steps, which were measurable by the teachers. Twenty-one steps took the children through the beginning reading materials.[1] Each further step represented the reading of a primer or first reader. Reading progress was measured by the number of these steps which the child had completed by February.

In addition to these progress steps the sight-word score of each child was measured. Each child in Winnetka is required to know at least 139 words at sight before passing from first-grade reading to second-grade reading. These words are those most frequently used in primers and first readers. The children were tested individually with flash cards, and the number of words recognized by each child was recorded as his sight-word score. In some cases the children knew some of the second-grade sight words as well as the 139 first-grade words. In such cases the score was the total number of first- and second-grade words recognized.

The first-grade teachers, all of whom had had several years of experience with the reading materials, agreed that children who seemed ready for reading from the beginning of the year had usually completed at least thirteen progress steps and knew at least thirty-seven sight words by Feb-

[1] Livia Youngquist and Carleton Washburne, Winnetka Primary Reading Materials. Chicago: Rand McNally & Co., 1928.

ruary. Therefore, thirteen progress steps and thirty-seven sight words were accepted as the measure of the minimum degree of satisfactory progress.

The Detroit First-Grade Intelligence Test and the Stanford Revision of the Binet-Simon Scale were used to determine the mental ages of the children. The Detroit tests were given to all first-grade children entering in September. The Stanford-Binet test was given later in the year, and the mental ages were calculated as of September, 1928. In this way comparison between the mental ages determined by the Detroit and Stanford-Binet tests was made possible.

Table I gives the correlations which were found between the sight-word scores and intelligence and between reading progress and intelligence. Since

**Table I**

**Correlations between Achievement in Reading of 141 First-Grade Children and Their Intelligence as Measured by Detroit Test and Stanford-Binet Test**

| *Factors Correlated* | *Detroit Test* | *Stanford-Binet Test* |
|---|---|---|
| Sight-word score and mental age ..................... | .65 | .58 |
| Sight-word score and average of mental and chronological age as of September 1, 1928 ...................... | .57 | .49 |
| Sight-word score and intelligence quotient ............. | .56 | .54 |
| Reading progress and mental age .................... | .59 | .51 |
| Reading progress and average of mental and chronological age as of September 1, 1928 ...................... | .55 | .49 |
| Reading progress and intelligence quotient ............. | .50 | .53 |

the data proved to be non-linear, the correlation ratios rather than the correlation coefficients are given. When the relation between reading progress and intelligence was calculated, it was necessary to use the rank method of figuring correlations since the intervals of progress were not necessarily of equal difficulty. The correlations show that there is a fairly high degree of relationship between mental age and reading progress. The Detroit test shows more relation to progress than does the Stanford-Binet test. Of the three measures of intelligence—mental age, average of the mental and chronological ages, and intelligence quotient—mental age shows the greatest degree of relationship although the differences are slight. In all the calculations that follow, mental age alone is used as the method of figuring intelligence.

The scores were next divided into groups based on the children's mental ages in September. The percentage of children of each mental age making satisfactory progress (thirteen steps or more) and the percentage making satisfactory sight-word scores (thirty-seven or more) were determined. Tables II and III show the results.

Table II shows that a small percentage of children who began reading with a mental age of less than six years were able to achieve satisfactory reading progress but that for the group having a mental age between six

### Table II
#### Number of Children of Each Mental Age and Percentage Making Satisfactory Reading Progress

| Mental Age in Years and Months * | Number of Children † | | Percentage Making Satisfactory Reading Progress ‡ | |
|---|---|---|---|---|
| | Detroit Test | Stanford-Binet Test | Detroit Test | Stanford-Binet Test |
| 4–5 to 4–11 ........ | 1 | 1 | . . . . . . . . . . . | . . . . . . . . . . . |
| 5–0 to 5–5 ........ | 12 | 1 | 0 | . . . . . . . . . . . |
| 5–6 to 5–11 ........ | 12 | 12 | 0 | 8 |
| 6–0 to 6–5 ........ | 17 | 22 | 47 | 41 |
| 6–6 to 6–11 ........ | 23 | 38 | 78 | 68 |
| 7–0 to 7–5 ........ | 29 | 31 | 79 | 68 |
| 7–6 to 7–11 ........ | 16 | 15 | 75 | 87 |
| 8–0 to 8–5 ........ | 7 | 11 | . . . . . . . . . . . | 82 |
| 8–6 to 9–0 ........ | 8 | 2 | . . . . . . . . . . . | . . . . . . . . . . . |

* Intervals are half sigmas above and below the mean of the entire group as determined by the Detroit test.

† Because the tests were given on different dates, some children who were given the Detroit test were not given the Stanford-Binet test and vice versa.

‡ No percentages were figured for groups of less than ten children.

years and six years and six months there was a sharp rise in the percentage making satisfactory progress. This fact is shown graphically in Figure 1. The curves for the Stanford-Binet and the Detroit tests are essentially alike, although final flattening occurs later on the Stanford-Binet curve.

The curve of the results on the Stanford-Binet test seems to indicate that children would gain considerably in speed of learning if they could wait until they had attained a mental age of seven years and six months before beginning to read. However, the curve of the results of the Detroit test shows that the children with mental ages of six years and six months made progress practically as satisfactory as that of the children with higher mental ages. Since the results of the Detroit test show a higher correlation

## Table III
### Number of Children of Each Mental Age and Percentage Making Satisfactory Sight-Word Scores

| Mental Age in Years and Months | Number of Children * | | Percentage Making Satisfactory Sight-Word Scores | |
|---|---|---|---|---|
| | Detroit Test | Stanford-Binet Test | Detroit Test | Stanford-Binet Test |
| 4–5 to 4–11 ....... | 1 | 1 | ........... | ........... |
| 5–0 to 5–5 ........ | 12 | 1 | 0 | ........... |
| 5–6 to 5–11 ....... | 12 | 12 | 0 | 8 |
| 6–0 to 6–5 ........ | 17 | 25 | 71 | 52 |
| 6–6 to 6–11 ....... | 23 | 43 | 87 | 77 |
| 7–0 to 7–5 ........ | 31 | 35 | 84 | 89 |
| 7–6 to 7–11 ....... | 23 | 18 | 83 | 94 |
| 8–0 to 8–5 ........ | 10 | 11 | 90 | 91 |
| 8–6 to 9–0 ........ | 12 | 3 | 100 | ........... |

\* The numbers of children whose sight-word progress is compared differ from the numbers whose reading progress is compared in Table II because one group of children not taught by the individual method was omitted from the reading-progress group.

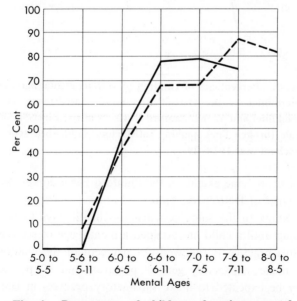

Fig. 1.   Percentages of children of various mental ages, as determined by the Detroit First-Grade Intelligence Test (solid line) and by the Stanford Revision of the Binet-Simon Scale (broken line), making satisfactory reading progress in school year 1928–29.

with reading progress than do the results of the Stanford-Binet test and since the Detroit test is more practicable to administer than the Stanford-Binet test, it seems reasonable to use the Detroit test as a basis for determining children's readiness for reading. The mental level of six years and six months is the breaking point in the curve, that is, the point beyond which there is very little gain in postponing the teaching of reading. This

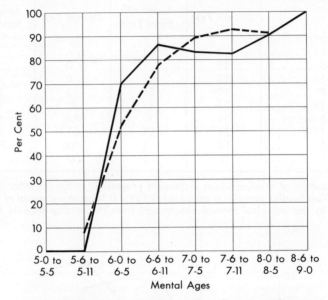

Fig. 2. Percentages of children of various mental ages, as determined by the Detroit First-Grade Intelligence Test (solid line) and by the Stanford Revision of the Binet-Simon Scale (broken line), making satisfactory sight-word scores in school year 1928–29.

break is evident to some extent on the Stanford-Binet curve and markedly true on the curve of Detroit test scores.

Figure 2 points to the same conclusion—that it pays to postpone beginning reading until a child has attained a mental age of six years and six months. If this practice is followed, 78 per cent of the children may be expected to make satisfactory general progress, and 87 per cent of the children may be expected to make satisfactory progress in learning sight words.

A similar study was carried on during the school year 1929–30 for the purpose of checking the results of the 1928–29 experiment.

All children who were mentally six years of age or more were taught reading from the beginning of the year. The previous study made it seem futile to try to teach younger children, but a few with lower mental ages were taught reading for the purpose of the experiment. Mental ages were determined this time by the Detroit First-Grade Intelligence Test and the Pintner-Cunningham Primary Mental Test.

**Table IV**

**Number of Children of Each Mental Age and Percentage Making Satisfactory Sight-Word Scores and Oral-Reading Scores**

| Mental Age in Years and Months * | Number of Children | | Percentage Making Satisfactory Progress | |
|---|---|---|---|---|
| | Sight-Word Test | Oral-Reading Test | Sight-Word Test | Oral-Reading Test |
| 5–0 to 5–5 ........ | 1 | 0 | ........... | ........... |
| 5–6 to 5–11 ....... | 10 | 9 | ........... | ........... |
| 6–0 to 6–5 ........ | 25 | 24 | 64 | 58 |
| 6–6 to 6–11 ....... | 23 | 23 | 87 | 83 |
| 7–0 to 7–5 ........ | 23 | 23 | 87 | 91 |
| 7–6 to 7–11 ....... | 12 | 12 | 83 | 92 |
| 8–0 to 8–5 ........ | 5 | 5 | ........... | ........... |
| 8–6 to 9–0 ........ | 1 | 1 | ........... | ........... |

* Average of scores on Detroit test and Pintner-Cunningham test.

At the end of the year (June, 1930) the children were tested on the sight-word list and the Gray Standardized Oral Reading Check Test. A child was considered to have made satisfactory progress if he knew the entire sight-word list (139 words) and read the Gray test in fifty seconds or less with three errors or less. This standard has been set by Gray for Grade I. Table IV gives the number of children of each mental age and the percentage of children at each mental level making satisfactory scores in both sight words and oral reading. Figure 3 makes the data of Table IV graphic. As in Figures 1 and 2, the percentage of children who learned to read satisfactorily is greatest at the mental ages of six years and six months and of seven years. The curve for sight-word scores breaks at the mental age of six years and six months, while the curve on the Gray Standardized Oral Reading Check Test breaks at the mental age of seven.

The second year's experiment, therefore, in which a different set of children, different teachers, a different method of determining mental age, and a different method of determining progress were used and in which a whole year's work instead of a half year's was taken as the measure of progress confirms the experiment of the first year.

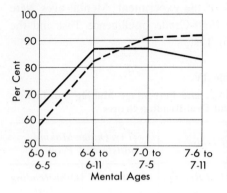

Fig. 3. Percentages of children of various mental ages who, in school year 1929–30, made satisfactory sight-word scores (solid line) and satisfactory scores on the Gray Standardized Oral Reading Check Test (broken line).

## Summary

1. Correlations between mental age and ability to learn to read, as measured by reading progress and sight-word scores, showed a fairly high degree of relationship. The correlations ranged from .50 to .65.

2. The correlations between mental age and reading progress were somewhat higher when mental age was measured by the Detroit First-Grade Intelligence Test than when mental age was measured by the Stanford Revision of the Binet-Simon Scale.

3. Mental age alone showed a larger degree of correlation with reading progress than did the intelligence quotient or the average of mental and chronological ages.

4. When the Detroit test was used as a basis for determining mental-age groups, the children who had a mental age of six years and six months made far better progress than did the less mature children and practically as satisfactory progress as did the children of a higher mental age.

5. When mental age was measured by the Stanford Revision of the Binet-Simon Scale, the children with a mental age of six years and six months again made very much better progress in reading than did those of less maturity, but they made less satisfactory progress than did those whose mental age was six months greater. The gain in ability up to six years and six months of mental age, however, was much greater than the subsequent gain.

6. A repetition of the experiment in 1929–30 with different teachers, different children, and different tests confirmed the earlier experiment in all its basic conclusions.

7. Consequently, it seems safe to state that, by postponing the teaching of reading until children reach a mental level of six and a half years, teachers can greatly decrease the chances of failure and discouragement and can correspondingly increase their efficiency.

## 9

# READING ABILITIES OF BRIGHT AND DULL CHILDREN OF COMPARABLE MENTAL AGES *

## Emery P. Bliesmer

Given two groups of children of the same mental age, one composed of older children with low I.Q.'s, the other of younger children with high I.Q.'s, how will the achievement of the two groups compare? In this study, two such groups were chosen and tested on the basic skills of reading speed and comprehension, vocabulary, and listening comprehension. All the test material consisted of, or was adapted from, standardized tests. All tests were administered by the author to insure uniformity of procedure. The bright children were selected from Grades 3 and 4, the dull from regular classes in Grades 8 and 9 and some special classes. There was nearly 50 points difference in average I.Q. favoring the bright group, while the dull group was, on the average, more than six years older. The original article includes a review of findings of earlier studies on this question, omitted here; we begin with the author's detailed presentation of procedures and results of this study and conclude with his discussion of its implications for teachers.

*Questions:*

1. What is the I.Q. of a fourteen-year-old whose mental age is twelve years? Of a ten-year-old with the same mental age? What differences would you employ in teaching them?

2. This article brings into sharp focus the importance of knowing and taking into account both mental age and I.Q. Discuss the significance of this point for the teacher.

* Abridged from the *Journal of Educational Psychology,* **45:**321–331 (October 1954), by permission of author and publisher.

**Procedure**

*Method of Sampling*

In order to measure a wide range of comprehension abilities, it was decided to employ test materials which are appropriate at the fourth- to fifth-grade level of reading ability. Considering the IQ criteria for "bright" and "dull" (lower and upper IQ limits of 116 and 84, respectively), and studying the overlap of MA's at various CA's for these bright and dull criteria, it was decided to use a mental age range of from ten years, seven months, through twelve years, six months, and to restrict the bright group to children with CA's of ten years or less and the dull group to children with CA's of fourteen years or above.

Children in the dull group were selected from regular eighth- and ninth-grade classes and some special education classes in two junior high schools, and children in the bright group from regular third- and fourth-grade classes in three elementary schools, in the public school system of a large Iowa city. For identification of pupils likely to meet sample specifications, the cumulative record folder of each child in the two junior high schools, and in third and fourth grades in the three elementary schools, was studied. A list was made of all the junior high pupils' who were fourteen years of age or older and for whom IQ's of 90 or below had been obtained with group intelligence tests which had been administered by the schools in previous years. In the elementary schools, a list was made of all third- and fourth-grade pupils who were ten years of age or younger and for whom IQ's of 110 or above had been obtained with group intelligence tests in previous years.

From the list of pupils indicated as likely to meet specifications for the dull group, pupils were selected randomly and the *Revised Sanford-Binet Scale,* Form L, was administered until there were obtained twenty-nine pupils who met the following specifications:

1. Estimated true IQ's of 84 or below.

2. Estimated true MA's of from ten years, seven months, through twelve years, six months.

From the list of third- and fourth-grade pupils indicated as likely to meet sample specifications for the bright group, pupils were selected randomly and the *Revised Stanford-Binet Scale,* Form L, was administered until there was obtained a sample of pupils meeting the following specifications:

1. Estimated true IQ's of 116 or above.

2. Estimated true MA's of from ten years, seven months, through twelve years, six months.

3. As many bright children in each of four six-months mental age intervals or levels (which constituted the two-year range indicated in the preceding specification) as there were dull children in that interval.

In the process of obtaining enough bright cases in each level to match the number of dull cases in that level, extra cases were obtained for some of the levels. For purposes of statistical analysis, extra cases in each level were later discarded randomly. The final sample contained twenty-eight children in each group, dull and bright, one case originally selected for the dull group having been lost because of incomplete data. In the dull group, there were fifteen boys and thirteen girls; thirteen in Grade 8, six in Grade 9, and nine in special classes. The bright group was composed of sixteen boys and twelve girls; fifteen in Grade 3 and thirteen in Grade 4. A summary of information relative to the dull and bright groups in the sample is presented in Table I.

**Table I**

**Characteristics of the Samples**

|  | Groups | |
|---|---|---|
|  | *Bright* | *Dull* |
| Range of CA's ........... | 8–7 through 9–10 | 14–2 through 16–3 |
| Mean CA ............... | 9–2.5 | 15–5.4 |
| Range of MA's (est. true).. | 10–8 through 12–6 | 10–8 through 12–6 |
| Mean MA .............. | 11–3.2 | 11–3.0 |
| Range of IQ's (est. true)... | 116 through 138 | 72 through 84 |
| Mean IQ .............. | 126.5 | 79.5 |

*Selection of Comprehension Abilities Investigated*

A survey of the professional literature, teachers' manuals accompanying series of readers, standardized tests, and reported results of factorial studies was made for suggestions of specific abilities involved in reading comprehension. Consideration was also given to availability of measuring instruments for these specific abilities, the possibilities of adapting available instruments to the purposes of this study, and the purported importance of given abilities. This resulted in the selection of the following abilities for inclusion in this investigation:

1. Word Recognition (the ability to recognize given words "on sight").

2. Word Meaning (the ability to understand or recognize the particular meaning of a word as it is used in context).

3. Memory for Factual Details (the ability to recall specific facts which have been definitely stated in a selection).

4. Location or Recognition of Factual Details (the ability to locate or recognize specific factual details which are explicitly stated in a given selection).

5. Perception of Relationships among Definitely Stated Ideas (the ability to recognize or to formulate an idea which is not explicitly stated in a selection but which is contained in the selection when two or more definitely stated ideas are considered together).

6. Recognition of Main Ideas (the ability to recognize the central thought or main idea of an entire selection, a paragraph, or a specific part of a paragraph).

7. Drawing Inferences and Conclusions (the ability to recognize, or to formulate, an idea which is not stated in a selection but which is dependent upon the combination of an idea (or ideas) which is (are) definitely stated in a selection and one which is outside the selection and within the informational or experiential background of the individual).

In addition to these abilities, measures of reading rate and listening comprehension were also obtained. Reading rate scores were secured not only because comparisons between the groups were of some interest in themselves, but also because marked differences in rate could be responsible for differences in comprehension abilities, even though the tests were untimed. The measures of listening comprehension were obtained in order to determine whether differences in general comprehension ability exist when unencumbered by possible difficulties with mechanical skills in reading.

*Criterion Tests Used*

Eighty words from the Flashed Word Recognition and Word Analysis Test of the *Durrell Analysis of Reading Difficulty,* and twenty more difficult words from various forms (Q through T) of Part II (Vocabulary) of the Reading Comprehension Test, Advanced Battery, of the *Iowa Tests of Basic Skills,* were included in the Word Recognition Test. These one hundred words were arranged in lists of twenty each and were presented tachistoscopically for a duration of approximately one second. Only results obtained with the last four lists (eighty words) were included in the analysis of results.

The Word Meaning Test was a multiple response test consisting of a representative sample of fifty items chosen from various forms (Q through T) of Part II (Vocabulary) of the Reading Comprehension Test, Elementary and Advanced Batteries, of the *Iowa Tests of Basic Skills*.

A test of Comprehension Abilities was made up of nine reading selections and one hundred and thirty items which were adapted from the Reading Comprehension Test of the Elementary and Advanced Batteries of the *Iowa Tests of Basic Skills*, Forms L through T. Five subtest scores, each based on from twenty-five to twenty-seven items, were obtained as measures of these five specific abilities: Memory for Factual Details, Location or Recognition of Factual Details, Perception of Relationships among Definitely Stated Ideas, Recognition of Main Ideas, and Drawing Inferences and Conclusions. The reading selections were chosen on the basis of relative difficulty, apparent interest value, and the extent to which items accompanying selections represented the specific abilities named above. To obtain subtests of approximately equal length and difficulty, a number of original items were eliminated and additional ones were constructed when necessary.

A Listening Comprehension Test was constructed in a manner similar to that for the Test of Comprehension Abilities, except that items for Location or Recognition of Factual Details were not included. The test consisted of four reading selections and forty-two items. The test booklets contained only the questions related to the selections. The selections and the test items were read aloud to the subjects by the examiner; and subjects marked their chosen responses to each question after it and its answer choices had been read.

The Reading Rate Test consisted of a selection of approximately fifteen hundred words of fourth- to fifth-grade level of difficulty. Subjects were instructed to read the selection once "at the same speed as you usually read." They were told before they began that there would be questions over the material read. A short comprehension test, consisting mainly of items measuring memory for details, followed the reading of the selection. The rate score was a complement of the number of complete ten-second intervals which had elapsed during the reading of the selection.

All of the criterion tests were administered by the writer during an eight-day testing period. All were administered as group tests, without time limits, with the exception of the Word Recognition Test, which was administered to each subject individually. All test items, except those for the Word Recognition Test, were of the four-choice multiple-response type. Except for the Reading Rate Test rate scores, all scores used in the analyses of results represented the number of items answered correctly.

*Analysis of Results*

An analysis of variance design, "group-by-levels", was employed in the analysis of results. The bright and dull children represent the "groups," and the intervals of six months in the two-year mental age range used in the study constitute the "levels." A schematic presentation of the groups-by-levels design as it applies to this study is shown below.

| MA Level | MA (Es'd True) | Criterion Scores | |
| --- | --- | --- | --- |
| | | Bright Group | Dull Group |
| I ............... | 12–1 to 12–6 | n = 7 | n = 7 |
| II ............... | 11–7 to 12–0 | n = 9 | n = 9 |
| III ............... | 11–1 to 11–6 | n = 7 | n = 7 |
| IV ............... | 10–7 to 11–0 | n = 5 | n = 5 |

In the case of each ability investigated, the null hypothesis was tested, *i.e.*, that the means of the populations of which the dull and bright groups were representative samples were the same. To test this hypothesis, the ratio of the mean square for groups to the mean square for within cells was employed. This ratio yields a value which is distributed as F, provided that the hypothesis is true and that certain conditions are met. A five per cent coefficient of risk, selected in advance of the analyses, was employed in rejecting the null hypothesis.

## Results

A summary of the obtained results is presented in Table II. The table includes the mean and standard deviations for each group, the differences between the means, and the F-values obtained in the tests of the significance of the differences between the means of the bright and dull groups. Positive differences favor the bright group.

Obtained differences between the mean scores of the two groups favored the bright group with respect to all of the abilities except Word Meaning. In the case of this one exception, the difference was not only nonsignificant, but also less than one raw score unit. The analyses of variance yielded significant differences with respect to the following five abilities: Location or Recognition of Factual Details, Recognition of Main Ideas, Drawing Inferences and Conclusions, Total Comprehension Abilities, and Listening Comprehension. While not significant at the required level, differences between the mean scores for Memory for Factual Details and for

## Table II

### Summary of Results: Mean Scores for Each Group, Differences between Means, and F-Values, for Each Ability

| Ability | Bright | | Dull | | Differences $(M_B - M_D)$ | F* |
|---|---|---|---|---|---|---|
| | Mean | SD | Mean | SD | | |
| Word Recognition ...... | 58.6 | 11.8 | 56.2 | 13.0 | +2.4 | 0.499 |
| Word Meaning ......... | 30.4 | 6.1 | 30.8 | 6.1 | −0.4 | 0.076 |
| Memory for Factual Details ............... | 17.4 | 4.0 | 15.1 | 4.8 | +2.3 | 3.678 |
| Location or Recognition of Factual Details .... | 15.8 | 3.6 | 12.7 | 3.3 | +3.1 | 10.126** |
| Perception of Relationships among Definitely Stated Ideas ......... | 15.4 | 3.6 | 14.0 | 3.6 | +1.4 | 2.058 |
| Recognition of Main Ideas | 16.3 | 4.1 | 13.9 | 3.9 | +2.4 | 5.319** |
| Drawing Inferences and Conclusions ......... | 14.9 | 3.1 | 12.9 | 3.7 | +2.0 | 4.628** |
| Total Comprehension Abilities ............ | 79.8 | 15.1 | 68.4 | 16.7 | +11.4 | 7.922** |
| Listening Comprehension. | 30.6 | 3.6 | 23.6 | 4.7 | +7.0 | 47.574** |
| Reading Rate (rate score) | 61.6 | 17.9 | 55.4 | 15.9 | +6.2 | 1.602 |
| Reading Rate (comprehension score) ....... | 10.7 | 2.4 | 9.8 | 3.4 | +0.9 | 1.444 |

* For each F-value, df = 1, 48; $F_{05}$ = 4.04.
** Significant at 5 per cent level.

Perception of Relationships among Definitely Stated Ideas were substantial, and further investigation with respect to these two abilities seems warranted. Differences with respect to Word Recognition, Word Meaning, and Reading Rate were not significant.

The Test of Listening Comprehension was included in anticipation of the possible event that the group which was found significantly poorer on most of the abilities would be found to be significantly better with respect to listening comprehension. Then such results might have been interpreted in terms of possible difficulty with mechanical skills in reading rather than in terms of differences in intellectual abilities or specific comprehension abilities. However, the bright group, which excelled on nearly all of the abilities, also excelled significantly on the Listening Comprehension Test. Similarly, if a significantly higher rate had been found for the group also found to be significantly poorer with respect to most of the abilities, the poorer showing might have been attributed, in part, to tendencies to read carelessly and too hastily. However, no significant rate difference was found between the two groups and analysis of the reading rate comprehension check indicated that the two groups had read the reading rate selection with comparable degrees of understanding. These findings with respect to reading rate and listening comprehension tend to further indicate that superiority in reading comprehension involves superiority in intellectual functions rather than in the more mechanical skills.

Tests for interaction between groups and levels were also made. No significant interaction effects were found for any of the abilities tested, thus satisfying one of the necessary conditions or underlying assumptions involved in the particular design of the study.

Inspection of the frequency distributions for the various abilities involved in this study revealed that, in general, obtained scores did not closely approach the maximum possible at the upper end of the distribution or the "chance" scores at the lower end. Thus, neither ceiling nor floor effects operated to bias the results.

### Conclusions

In the strictest sense, the sample studied may be regarded as a representative sample only of hypothetical populations that show the same relative distribution of MA's, IQ's, and CA's as the groups in the sample itself; and generalizations based upon obtained results should be restricted to these hypothetical populations. However, since no significant interaction effects between groups and levels were found, restrictions upon extending generalizations to real populations may be lifted to a considerable extent. Therefore, generalizing to a population of dull and bright children with widely differing IQ's but approximately equal MA's within the MA ranges found in this study and with reference to the various comprehension abilities as defined operationally, the following conclusions seem warranted:

1. Bright children are significantly superior to dull children of com-

parable mental ages with respect to total reading comprehension and the following specific abilities: locating or recognizing factual details, recognizing main ideas, and drawing inferences and conclusions.

2. It seems probable that bright children are also superior to dull children of comparable mental ages with respect to memory for factual details and perception of relationships among definitely stated ideas.

3. Bright children are superior to dull children of comparable mental ages with respect to listening comprehension.

4. Reading rates of bright and dull children of comparable mental ages appear to be approximately the same when comparable degrees of understanding of material read are attained, with a wide range in rate being found in both groups.

5. Bright and dull children tend to be alike with respect to ability in word recognition and word meaning. Bright children are significantly superior to dull children of comparable mental ages with respect to the relatively more complex, and intellectual, comprehension abilities.

6. It would seem that levels of expectation with respect to the more complex comprehension abilities should not be as high for dull children as for bright children of comparable mental ages.

## References

1. ALMACK, JOHN C. and JAMES L. ALMACK. "Gifted Pupils in the High School." *School and Society*. **14:**227–28 (September 24, 1921).

2. KOLSTOE, OLIVER P. "A Comparison of Mental Abilities of Bright and Dull Children of Comparable Mental Ages." *J. of Educ. Psychol.* **45:**161–68 (March 1954).

3. LEWIS, W. DRAYTON. *A Study of Superior Children in the Elementary School*. George Peabody College Contributions to Education, No. 266, George Peabody College for Teachers, Nashville, Tenn. (1940).

4. LINDQUIST, E. F. *Design and Analysis of Experiments in Psychology and Education*. Boston: Houghton Mifflin Co. (1952).

5. McGEHEE, WILLIAM A. *A Study of Retarded Children in the Elementary School*. George Peabody College Contributions to Education, No. 246, George Peabody College for Teachers, Nashville, Tenn (1939).

6. RAMASESHAN, RUKMINI S. "A Note on the Validity of the Mental Age Concept." *J. of Educ. Psychol.* **41:**56–58 (January 1950).

7. TERMAN, L. M. and M. A. MERRILL. *Measuring Intelligence*. Boston: Houghton Mifflin Co. (1937), p. 46.

8. THOMAS, G. I. "A Study of Reading Achievement in Terms of Mental Ability." *Elementary School Journal.* **47:**28–33 (September 1946).

9. UNSICKER, WILLARD D. *A Psychological Study of Bright and Dull Children with Comparable Mental Ages.* Unpublished Doctor's dissertation, State University of Iowa, Iowa City, Iowa (1950).

10. VAN WAGENEN, M. J. "A Comparison of the Mental Ability and School Achievement of the Bright and Dull Pupils in the Sixth Grade of a Large School System." *J. of Educ. Psychol.* **16:**186–92 (March 1925).

# 10

## ON THE THEORIES AND PROBLEMS OF ADOLESCENCE *

### Abraham S. Luchins

Adolescence has often been characterized as a period of storm and stress. From a biological standpoint it is defined as the period during which the individual attains sexual maturity. In psychological terms it may be regarded as the period of transition between childhood and adulthood. There is some disagreement among educators, psychologists, biologists, and anthropologists regarding the definition of adolescence. However it is defined, the author of this selection urges that more attention and study be focused on the individual adolescent and less on adolescents as a class or group. He illustrates this point of view with brief histories and analyses of three boys of age 14–15 who exhibited behavior which in one respect or another was quite inconsistent with some of the usual generalizations about adolescence. Dr. Luchins theorizes on the possible reasons for the turbulence and conflict which many adolescents seem to experience, and closes with some suggestions for helping the adolescent to handle such tensions in a satisfactory manner.

*Questions:*

1. Make a list of terms which seem to you to characterize the adolescent period. For example, teenager, puberty, etc. Compare your list with that of someone else.

2. In this article you will find the terms *genotype* and *phenotype*. Define them.

3. Explain and illustrate some of the social factors which may influence adolescent behavior.

4. What is your reaction to the point of view expressed in this selection? Is it sound? Or do you find it faulty? Defend your opinion.

* Reprinted from the *Journal of Genetic Psychology,* **85**:47–63 (September 1954), by permission of author and publisher.

### A. Disagreement Concerning the Meaning of Adolescence

When the man in the street speaks of "adolescence," he generally knows what he means by the term and is probably quite confident that the next fellow using the expression has the same referent in mind. The experts, however, are not in agreement concerning the meaning of adolescence.

### 1. The Period of Adolescence

Some psychologists refer to adolescence as the period between 12 and 17 years of age, but others refer to it as the teen age period, while still others regard it as the entire second decade of life, or as extending until the 25th year of life, or even later. There are psychologists who are opposed to this description in terms of age, maintaining that adolescence begins with biological puberty.

But there are psychologists who claim that the beginning of adolescence cannot clearly be characterized either in terms of biological maturity or chronological age but should be characterized in terms of when the individual faces adult adjustments. Adolescence itself is then regarded as the period of transition between childhood and adulthood. For example, in a recent text on adolescence, Kuhlen [8] * writes that regardless of actual chronological age or state of biological development, an individual is adolescent to the extent that he is engaged in the process of making sexual-social adjustments, ideological adjustments, vocational adjustments, and adjustments relating to achievement of freedom from parents. One is pre-adolescent in the years before he is concerned with such problems, and he is adult to the extent that he has successfully solved these difficulties and eliminated them as problems. It must be emphasized that even among psychologists who define adolescence as the period between childhood and adulthood, there are differences of opinion as to the criteria determining the cessation of childhood and those determining the onset of adulthood.

### 2. The Characteristics of Adolescence

*a. Storm and stress.* Not only is there a lack of agreement among psychologists as to when the period of adolescence begins and when it ceases, but there is not even general agreement concerning the *characteristics* of adolescence. One of the characteristics sometimes referred to is that of

* Figures in brackets apply to references at end of article.

emotional disturbance and instability. G. Stanley Hall, who pioneered in the study of adolescence, in 1904 described adolescence as a period of emotional storm and stress [4]. In line with Hall's theory of recapitulation—the theory that every individual in his development parallels the history of evolution of his species—he maintained that development in adolescence is suggestive of some ancient period of storm and stress for the species when old moorings were broken and a higher level attained. While the theory of recapitulation has largely been abandoned, the notion of adolescence as a period of storm and stress has persisted to the present day, exercising considerable influence not only on the layman's thinking but also upon that of many psychologists.

Yet this notion has not remained unchallenged. Psychologists and anthropologists, among them Ruth Benedict [1] and Margaret Mead [11], have emphasized the differences in adolescent behavior patterns prevailing in different cultures. They note that in some so-called primitive cultures, for example, Samoa, emotional disturbances do not seem to accompany biological puberty or the teen-age years or the second decade of life or the attainment of adult status. On the basis of such evidence it would not be valid to generalize that adolescence is everywhere an emotionally stressful period.

One might seek to limit this generalization to adolescence in our society but even this conception has been challenged. Thus Kuhlen, after assessing the available evidence, concludes that adolescence in our society does not seem to be an unduly stressful period, that it is not a period of general storm and stress [8, p. 282].

*b. Reinforcement of sex drives.* Another supposedly general characteristic of adolescence pertains to the reinforcement of sexual drives. This aspect is emphasized by psychoanalysts who relate adolescence to the reawakening of the sex drives, particularly the drive for heterosexuality which is assumed to be rather latent in the period from about 6 to 10 years of age. A recent text by Harsh and Schrickel [5] *defines* adolescence as that period during which sexual motivation reaches its peak, when psychosexual drives and emotions are probably more intense than at any earlier or later period of life. But actual observation and investigation do not support the contention that sex drives and emotions are for every individual necessarily more intense beginning with puberty or in the teens or during the second decade of life than at other periods. For some individuals, sex drives seem to become highly active before overt signs of puberty are noted or before the ages of 10 or 12 or 13 or any of the various criteria considered to mark the beginning of adolescence; while for other individuals sex drives and emotions seem to become active or to be particularly intense only long after puberty or even after the second or third decade of life.

Thus, in this area also it does not seem possible to draw a conclusion which is generally valid.

*c. Changes in personality development.* Consider now another characteristic sometimes attributed to adolescence. G. Stanley Hall emphasized that marked and rapid changes occur in all aspects of *personality development* during adolescence, the changes being so dramatic that he referred to adolescence as a rebirth or a new birth. This conception has been challenged on the grounds that personality development constitutes a gradual and continuous pattern which generally does not reveal any striking deviations at or about the time of adolescence. In Hollingworth's words, the notion that every child is a changeling who at puberty comes forth as a different personality is but a widespread myth [6, p. 17].

### 3. The Biological Origin of Adolescent Behavior

A particularly persistent belief exists that the characteristics of adolescence are biologically generated, that they result from the biological changes occurring at puberty. This point of view was set forth by Hall and has been reaffirmed by many other psychologists. For example, Blanchard, writing from a psychoanalytically oriented point of view, concludes that reinforcement of the drive for heterosexuality, of the drive for independence, and possibly, of the drive for aggression, are *direct results* of the physiological changes accompanying puberty [2, p. 710].

*a. Cross-cultural comparisons.* Evidence against this viewpoint may be found in the reports of certain cultural anthropologists and psychologists. They indicate that the same physiological changes tend to be accompanied by different behavior in different cultures. They have emphasized the influence of different culturally-determined attitudes toward the same physiological and morphological characteristics. Thus, in certain parts of Africa, females desirous of becoming attractive enter a fattening house whereas in our society females having the same desire go on a starvation diet. To cite another example: Among the Carrier Indians of British Columbia at the time of the first menstruation the girl is considered to be seized by evil spirits and is treated as a social pariah who must live apart from the others, whereas among the Apache Indians the girl at puberty is considered to be possessed by good spirits and is regarded as a direct source of supernatural blessing [1, pp. 28–29].

*b. Influence of socio-economic conditions.* The thesis of biological determinism becomes even more tenuous if we consider the results of studies of the effects of socio-economic conditions on adolescent behavior. In our own culture, the great grandfathers of our present day youth were generally considered adults, with adult responsibilities, at an age at which the youth of today often manifests so-called adolescent behavior. Surely the average chronological age of biological puberty has not advanced. As a matter of fact, the available evidence seems to indicate that the average age of physiological maturity of the studied samples tends to be somewhat lower nowadays than it was several generations ago [3, p. 643]. Another example may be found in the general differences among adolescent behavior in urban districts as compared to rural districts [8, p. 149–153] when presumably the same physiological changes occur in urban youth as in rural youth.

*c. Physical-behavioral correlations.* Finally, against the thesis that behavioral phenomena of adolescence are caused by pubertal changes, I should like to present the conclusions of a psychologist such as Wayne Dennis who is admittedly strongly biologically oriented. Dennis [3] defines the beginning of adolescence as coinciding with biological puberty and conceives the central aim and interest of the psychology of adolescence to be the portrayal of the effects of pubertal changes upon behavior. To study these effects, he examines what he describes as certain sets of mental-physical correlations, bearing on the relationship between physical maturity and such a variety of behavioral phenomena as: sexual behavior, various play activities and interests, religious activities and interests, delinquency, suicide, and so on. His finding is that the available studies are generally inconclusive with reference to the causal relationship between psychological phenomena and physiological changes accompanying puberty. It would seem that even a biologically-oriented investigator can at the present time find little evidence to support the thesis that biological changes accompanying puberty *cause* any given behavioral phenomenon.

*d. To summarize.* I have attempted thus far to show that there is a lack of agreement among psychologists with regard to the definition of the period of adolescence, the characteristics of adolescent behavior, and whether or not the behavior is biologically determined.

## B. Neglect of the Individual Case

Even after allowance is made for the varying definitions of adolescence, valid generalizations holding for all adolescents seem to be rare. Perhaps this is not as unfortunate a state of affairs as it may appear at first glance. Perhaps there has been an overemphasis on the attempts to derive generalizations valid for all or most adolescents and too little emphasis on the study of the adolescent as an individual. In support of this contention I should like to review some of the major approaches to the study of adolescence and to note how their very methodology involves a neglect of the individual case.

One of the approaches, which has already been referred to, seeks to correlate behavioral phenomena and physiological phenomena. Whatever else may be said for or against this approach, it seems to be clear that the individual is of necessity lost in the correlations, that the correlations may portray *trends* but cannot portray what actually occurs in a particular case. Another approach, sometimes described as culturally-oriented, seeks to compare prevailing patterns of adolescence in one culture with that in another culture. While the merits of this approach are not denied, it must not be overlooked that it concentrates on gross cultural differences, on general patterns and attitudes which seem most prevalent in a particular culture. But the approach thereby tends to neglect or to minimize individual differences within any one culture. A third approach is concerned with the influence of various social conditions and institutions in our society on adjustment to adulthood. Adherents of this approach may note that adjustment to adulthood was somewhat different several generations ago than it is today or that even today the adjustment is somewhat different in rural than in urban districts. Noteworthy as such observations are, they do not reveal individual differences in adjustment patterns which presumably existed for young people several generations ago and which exist today, even within any particular urban or rural district.

It seems to me that it is time to cease this rather futile chase after generalizations valid for all adolescents or for all adolescents of a particular culture or generation or locality. It is perhaps time to concentrate on intensive studies of individual adolescents. It may be time to cease attempting to explain the phenomena of adolescence exclusively in terms of biology or culture or society or psychoanalysis, or what have you. Rather, we should perhaps suspend judgment as to the how and why of adolescent behavior. We should momentarily put aside our theories and hypotheses, and seek to look as unbiasedly as possible at some examples of this behavior, permitting the behavior itself to suggest possible hypotheses for explanations.

## C. Some Observational Data

I shall now turn to some observations which I made during a seven year study of a group of boys of Brooklyn, New York. The techniques used included participation with the boys in some of their activities, naturalistic observations, individual and group discussions with the boys, and discussions with their parents, teachers, siblings, and others in the neighborhood who knew them, as well as analysis of diaries kept by the boys. All the boys were of bright normal or superior intelligence and of about the same socio-economic status.

In 1931, when the study began, their ages ranged from 10 to 14. Let us consider now the behavior manifested by three of the boys in the period between 1935 and 1936, when each of them was about 14 or 15 years of age.

### 1. Description of Behavior

When I first met Robert he seemed to be a happy, even-tempered youngster. But at the age of 14 he was displaying what has been described as typically adolescent behavior. He was depressed, moody, irritable, emotionally unstable, and difficult to get along with. His parents and other adults frequently attributed this behavior to his adolescence. In short, Robert seemed to fit the stereotype of the adolescent in our society.

Ted at 14 was well-poised, essentially happy, and emotionally stable, showing little of the turbulence manifested by Robert. His teachers and other adults commented on his social poise and maturity.

Lester's behavior was closer to that displayed by Robert. Lester was moody, irritable with parents, siblings, and almost everyone else. He was inclined to think deeply and often about his own misery and the world's misfortunes.

### 2. Attempts at Understanding the Behavior

Should the behavior of these three boys be attributed to pubertal changes or to adjustment to adulthood or to the culture in which they live?

Will any of these generalizations yield an understanding of the dynamics underlying each case? Will any of them give insight into the reasons for the differences and similarities in overt behavior?

To begin with, it should be noted that both Lester, the unhappy, brooding individual, and Ted, the happy, poised individual, were at 14 years of age manifesting an accepted sign of puberty, pigmented pubic hair, and were about equal in other signs of physical maturity. Robert, on the other hand, had at this age not yet shown any overt signs of pubertal change. Blond, slight of stature, and shorter than the others, he looked like a "kid," to use the label which members of the group sometimes applied to him in a derogatory manner.

Thus in two of the boys similar physical changes were accompanied by very different behavior patterns. Nor can the change in Robert's behavior from his earlier emotional stability to the storm and stress variety he manifested at the ages of 14 and 15 be correlated with any concomitant signs of overt physical maturity. Indeed, study of the relevant facts seem to indicate that Robert's change in behavior might more accurately be traced to his *lack* of physical maturity. Robert had previously been the acknowledged leader of the gang; but at 14 and 15, with the growing interest in females and social events, the group found him somewhat of a hindrance. They were afraid that his youthful appearance might hurt their chances with the girls and lessen their possibilities of making "pickups." Moreover, Robert's older brothers were prone to boast about their amorous exploits and Robert once told me that he wished that he were as manly-looking and attractive to girls as his older brothers.

What had happened to Robert? It might be said that he had lost status in the group, that he no longer had a sense of group-belongingness, that he no longer had a well-structured behavioral world, and that there were sharp discrepancies between his aspirations and his achievements. Incidentally, as Robert grew older and became physically mature, he joined another group, became their leader, and displayed considerably less behavior of the turbulent type. It would seem that physiological maturity in this case did not foster adolescent conflicts but was one of the factors helping to decrease emotional disturbance.

What about Lester? May his behavior be attributed to pubertal changes? As a matter of fact, acquaintance with Lester's life history reveals that he had for years been moody, irritable, concerned with the world's troubles. He had been struggling to find answers to such questions as: What is life? What is man? Who am I? He regarded as inadequate the answers given to him, directly or indirectly, by his teachers or by books he read. Although accepted and respected by members of the group, who were rather proud of his erudition, he often preferred being by himself and confided to me that he did not really feel that he belonged to the gang or that he could fully share the other members' interests. What is important to note here is that the behavioral patterns and emotional tone manifested by Lester at or about the time of puberty were not very different from those which he showed in the years preceding overt pubertal change or, for that matter, from those which he showed in the years which followed. Until his death in World War II at the age of 22, members of the group who were then with him later told me, he was always the same moody, irritable, philosophical Lester. And yet, a psychologist attempting to study Lester's behavior only at about the time of puberty might have concluded that the moodiness and concern with ideological matters which he then revealed were a unique development accompanying biological puberty. From the vantage point of a knowledge of Lester's history for several years prior and subsequent to pubertal change, it seems to me that he was seeking for a meaning in life, that he was attempting to develop a clearly structured world, and that there were sharp discrepancies between his ideals and reality as well as between his aspirations and achievements with regard to a purpose for man's existence.

Let us return to Ted, the third of the trio. Ted, the well-poised, emotionally stable youth was that way until about the age of 19 when a severe financial setback in his father's business necessitated his leaving college and obtaining a rather menial position to help support his family. He became irritable, argumentative, displayed extreme mood-swings and found it difficult to get along with his family and others. He was, in short, manifesting at 19 the kind of turbulent behavior which Robert had shown at 14. Analysis of my records on Ted made one thing clear. As early as his elementary school days, he had made definite vocational plans. He knew that he wanted to be a medical doctor, was confident of his mental ability and of the financial support required to achieve his goal. But the financial reverses made it impossible for him to reach his goal and frustrated his ambition.

### 3. Inferences from the Three Cases

What can be inferred from these three cases? Firstly, it would seem that youths living in the same locality and having similar socio-economic backgrounds may manifest strikingly different behavior patterns. Secondly, similar physiological changes may be accompanied by different behavior patterns. Also, individuals who are far apart with regard to physical maturity may display similar behavior patterns. While the issue of whether or not pubertal changes may directly induce some behavioral changes is still a moot one, it would seem that behavior may be a consequence of the *attitudes* possessed by the individual himself and others regarding physical changes or *lack* of such changes. Thirdly, the kind of emotional storm and stress which is sometimes considered as characteristic of adolescence may not be manifested at all, may occur long before or only long after pubertal changes, may be momentary or of rather limited duration, or may be generally characteristic of the individual.

As a hypothesis for future research it is suggested that emotional instability may tend to be manifested at any chronological age when the individual lacks a clear frame of reference with which to meet reality, when his behavioral world is not clearly structured, and when there are marked discrepancies between his aspirations and his achievements.

## 4. Conclusions Drawn from Study

The inferences drawn from the three cases are not sufficient to account for the behavior of the other 12 boys who were studied. Some of the boys, although behaving as typical adolescents, did not seem to have any serious emotional involvements. Rather, it seemed to me that they had simply adopted the characteristic *stereotype*. They were playing the rôle called for by this stereotype. They were exhibiting the kind of behavior which they and others expected of adolescents of this day and age. Still others of the boys behaved like impulsive children who were gorging themselves on new experiences in an irresponsible carefree manner. The behavior of one of the boys seemed to be related to a deficiency of social skills, such as the skills of dancing and getting along with girls. Once he acquired these skills, there was a noticeable change in his behavior.

In brief, adolescence does not seem to constitute one phenomenon. An analysis reveals a variety of different behavior patterns. Moreover, the different phenotypical patterns are not caused by one genotype. In other words, overtly similar behavior may be brought about by different conditions and overtly different behavior may be brought about by similar conditions. In view of this, it is not surprising to find a diversity of contemporary descriptions and explanations of adolescent behavior. One way to minimize the contemporary confusion of concepts and terminology may be to study the individual adolescent as a person instead of merely regarding him as a source of information which can confirm or infirm a hypothesis stemming from a general theory of adolescence.

### D. Some Social Factors Which May Influence Adolescent Behavior

Regardless of the shape which future studies or theories of adolescence may take, there is an immediate and practical problem which must be faced. It is obvious to parents, teachers, and even the youths themselves that many individuals go through an adolescent stage characterized by turbulence and conflict. On the basis of the data collected in the study referred to above I was led to conclude that there are certain social field conditions which operate to produce or aggravate such turbulence and conflict. It is not denied that temperamental and experiential factors may make one more or less susceptible to the influence of these conditions. What follows should be take as preliminary hypotheses to be tested by future research.

### 1. Uncertainty Concerning Adult Status

I have already hypothesized that emotional difficulties may tend to occur under conditions in which the individual lacks a clear frame of reference with regard to his status and function. There are factors in the social scene which are conducive to an unstable frame of reference concerning the achievement of *adult status*. Unlike what occurs in some other cultures, in our society there is no one initiation rite or ceremony or fixed pattern of activities in which one must participate in order to be regarded by himself and by others as having donned the mantle of adulthood. The physically mature youth may be treated as a child by those about him, either consistently or intermittently. At other times he may be reminded that he has no business behaving as a child. Indeed, there are individuals, regardless of chronological age, who are never quite certain of whether they have attained adult status.

Whether or not the individual ever attains adult status, either subjectively or objectively, depends on a host of socio-economic factors and on the nature of his inter-personal relations. Depending upon the individual circumstances and, to some extent, on such general conditions as whether it is a time of war or of peace, of depression or prosperity, there tend to be considerable differences with regard to the age of occurrence, the ease, and the mode of locomotion involved in the crossing of that nebulous threshold leading to adulthood. The existence of such differences may help to account for the various age limits which different authorities ascribe to the adolescent period. It may also help to account for the wide variety of behavior patterns observed during adolescence. Moreover the uncertainty which often accompanies the attainment of adulthood may help to account for the prevalency of emotional difficulties during adolescence.

Incidentally, I should like to refer here to the observation that adolescence in rural districts is by and large a less stressful experience than in urban districts. This may be related to the fact that the youth on the farm may be able to attain relative independence and other signs of adult status more readily than his urban cousin. Similarly, the observation that adolescence tended to be a less stressful experience several generations ago than it is today, may be related to the fact that adult status, including marriage, was generally attained at an earlier age in former years.

## 2. Institutional Complexity and Conflict

There are other factors which may contribute to an unstable frame of reference, to a lack of a clearly structured behavioral world. As the child becomes older, he may become more aware of contradictions between what is preached and what is practiced. He may realize that his parents and their beliefs are far from perfect. He may realize that his idols have clay feet.

Moreover, as he grows older, he comes into contact with more and more institutions and practices other than the primary institution of the home. Several generations ago the home was the center of life activities, with business, recreational, religious, educational, and vocational training activities centered in the home. Today there are separate institutions each specializing in an activity which was once the function of the home. By and large, these institutions lack the intimate, personal relationship which may have prevailed in the home. The very structure of these institutions may rule out the possibility of a warm, genuine interest in its members. The youth may be upset by what he regards as a cold, impersonal attitude towards him.

Each institution may think of the individual primarily as a tool for the fulfillment of the institution's goals and objectives. It may demand of him that he play a certain rôle regardless of the individual's own needs. Or it may be interested in the individual only in so far as he is capable of playing this rôle. A middling example of this is the practice of placing an individual into a vocational school because test results indicate that he has little chance of successfully playing the rôle of a student in an academic institution. This may occur in spite of the individual's desire to attend an academic school and in spite of social pressures exerted by family and friends that demand that he be an academic student.

The demands which one institution makes on the individual may conflict with the demands made upon him by other institutions. Moreover, the various demands may clash with the values and purposes learned in the home. Thus there may be a clash between what the home teaches and what the school teaches, what the church wants and what the street gang wants, and so on. Confronted by these conflicting demands, the individual may have some difficulty in meeting them and yet maintaining his integrity as an organized, whole being. He may have to struggle against becoming a mere collection of selves—a home self, a school self, a street self, a business self, and so on. He may be aghast at the thought that he is expected to play a rôle and be able to don and cast off rôles as one might change masks. Moreover, he may have difficulty in achieving a self-concept, in knowing just who he is. All this may contribute to adolescent conflict.

In short, the youth must learn to dance in harmony with many different tunes while still attempting to maintain some degree of harmony within himself. For some individuals, the conflicting demands may be extremely upsetting. They may find that the personal and rather clearly structured world of childhood is replaced by a cold, disorganized, and unstable world. They may not be quite certain of just who they are, whether they are being themselves or merely playing rôles, and just what rôle they are expected to play at any particular time. Herein may lie some clues to the emotional turbulence which has come to be associated with adolescence.

### 3. Gaps between Aspirations and Attainments

Reference was previously made to the possible effect on behavior of a discrepancy between aspirations and achievements. It seems to me that there are factors in our social fabric which, in some cases, make for a considerable discrepancy between the ideals and aspirations associated with adulthood and the actual achievements attained by the youth once he is "grown up." As a child he may have been led to believe that when he grows up he will be allowed entrance into the wonderland hitherto denied to him, the world of privileges, immunities, status, worthwhile responsibilities, independence, and fulfillment of numerous dreams. Yet, the physical signs of being grown up may be attained without the fulfillment of even one of the goals which had been intimately associated with being grown up.

For example, in our culture a premium is placed on economic independence. Yet, scarcity of positions, the need for lengthy educational training or lengthy apprenticeship may make it necessary to postpone such independence for many years. In some professions, economic independence cannot be secured until one is well past the second decade of life or well into the third.

Ideals and aspirations with regard to dating, romance, and marriage are fostered by the home, movies, and magazines. But these ideals may be quite impossible of attainment or may be interfered with by finances or physical unattractiveness or simply by the fact that the available candidates for romance are quite different from those portrayed in the movies.

Youth is bombarded by stimuli which arouse or intensify various kinds of needs, particularly those involving status and sex. The radio, television, movies, magazines, newspapers, and even the home serve to overstimulate certain needs. But at the same time there may be little or no opportunity for the youth to gratify these desires in socially accepted ways. For example, the boy or girl who is expected to abstain from sexual activity is at the same time exposed to stimuli which play up sex. The result may be that these overstimulated desires become central in the youth's view of the situation and that obstacles to these needs loom very large. Consequently, the youth may feel that he is blocked and hemmed in on all sides. One might draw an analogy between the situation he faces and that faced by the rat in Norman R. F. Maier's experiments on neuroses. Forces arousing and overstimulating the various needs may be compared to the airblast aimed at making the rat jump; but, like the rat, the youth may have no way of reacting to these forces without encountering punishment. It is therefore small wonder that what is akin to neurotic behavior may be noticed in some adolescents.

### 4. Some Other Hypotheses

Thus far I have suggested that the emotional difficulties often associated with adolescence in our culture may in part be the resultant of a gap between the youth's goals and achievements or of his lack of a stable frame of reference with which to view his rather disorganized world. It is also interesting to speculate to what extent the youth who is seemingly manifesting emotional storm and stress may simply have adopted the stereotype of behavior which he and others associate with this period. I should also like to refer to the interesting hypothesis advanced by Kuhlen [8]— namely, that the stress commonly attributed to the adolescent may in part be a projection of the emotional stress experienced by parents and other adults dealing with youth.

## E.   What Can Be Done About the Emotional Tensions of Adolescents?

I have described some social field conditions which may produce emotional tensions in the adolescent. The problem arises as to what can be done to minimize these tensions. Before dealing with this problem, I should like to draw a distinction between two kinds of tensions. Every living system experiences tensions; these are necessary for the life activities of the organism, for its development and growth, and for the attainment and maintenance of its equilibrium. The late Max Wertheimer, founder of Gestalt Psychology, used to refer to these as tensions with a small $t$. In contrast to the tensions with a small $t$, he referred to tensions with a capital $T$; by the latter he meant those tensions whose direction of operation is opposed to that of the organism, tensions which interfere with adequate functioning of the organism, hinder development, and even alter the organism's essential structure.

This distinction seems to me to be applicable to the tensions experienced by the adolescent. Some are related to the youth's striving toward equilibrium under changing conditions and are necessary to further his growth both as a physical organism and as a social being. Specifically, tensions may be said to have positive value insofar as they awaken the youth from a kind of lethargic slumber, arouse some self-analysis and introspection, and set him to seek for values and purposes in life. Because of tensions, the youth may be led to question, to evaluate critically, and perhaps to strike out in new directions, to find new ways of doing things. It might even be argued that the stresses and strains experienced by the younger generation help them to work for social change and social progress. To such tensions we may refer as those with small $t$'s. But there are tensions with capital $T$'s: tensions whose direction and nature of operation interfere with the youth's growth and development, which hamper his functioning at an adequate level, which keep him in continuous disequilibrium and may even create mental illness. These latter tensions are what I have in mind in what follows.

1. There is a need to decrease somewhat the gap between the youth's goals and desires, on the one hand, and what he can accomplish, on the other. Perhaps a step in this direction can be made by realistically evaluating the ideals and standards which our culture propagates with regard to adult status. For example, completion of education and economic inde-

pendence on the part of the male are often regarded as prerequisites for marriage. Scholarships, fellowships, and apprenticeships may require the single status. Under present-day conditions this often means late marriage which in turn makes more difficult the satisfaction of sexual needs within moral bounds. If our society holds that present day sex standards have definite and positive value, then something should be done to make it easier for the physically mature youth to live up to these standards. Somewhat less ballyhoo about sex in our movies, radios, magazines, may help to dim the spotlight currently focused on it and perhaps decrease the severity of youth's sex problems. Another solution might be earlier marriage. The success of married veterans who attended school after World War II seems to provide ample testimony that formal education and marriage are not necessarily incompatible. Undoubtedly early marriage will raise problems of its own, including the very pragmatic issue of finances; it may be necessary that financial assistance be given to the young couple by parents or perhaps private or government agencies. Notwithstanding the above something should be done to decrease the discrepancy between youth's sexual needs and his possibilities for gratifying them in a socially acceptable manner.

There is a broader issue involved here. Many of our ethical standards may be seen by youth primarily as taboos, as limitations. But just as a road facilitates travel even though it deters the traveler from other possible paths, so a social standard is not solely a taboo but often has a positive function. Greater emphasis on the positive function of social and ethical standards rather than emphasis on their limitations to actions, as well as greater opportunity for young people to realize the positive values of these standards in their own life situations, may help to make youth more willing to accept and comply with the moral standards of our society.

It is appropriate to refer here to the matter of independence, quite aside from financial independence. The mature individual in our society is expected to stand on his own feet, to make decisions on his own. But such intellectual and emotional independence, if I may refer to it as such, does not suddenly spring into being at any one time of life. Although the capacity for such independence may be related to personal endowment, the exercise of this independence hinges on previous training and on suitable conditions. Parents must be made aware of the importance of training for emotional and intellectual independence, of allowing and encouraging ever-increasing opportunities for independent judgment on the part of the child. They must, so to speak, allow for loosening of the proverbial apron strings.

Our schools can make an important contribution by placing an emphasis *not* on rote drill, memorization, and blind following, but on *understanding* and productive thinking. The child should not merely learn a collection of facts and skills but should learn to learn. Moreover, participation in the formation of value judgments in the school, as well as opportunities to evaluate these judgments, may help to create an individual who can make intelligent judgments outside of the school situation.

2. I have referred to the possible rôle of institutional conflicts in fostering emotional difficulties. Here there seems to be a decided need for discussion and coöperation among representatives of various institutions in the community, among parents, teachers, other educators, religious leaders, people who determine policies in recreational and advertising media, and so on. They should consider how they may contribute to the problems faced by adolescents. They should consider their goals and practices in relation to youth and the demands which they make of youth. The aim should be to minimize intra-institutional and inter-institutional conflict. This calls for community planning, for the utilization of social action research in the community as well as for the utilization of other group dynamic techniques which have been successfully applied by Kurt Lewin and his students to various community problems.

3. It is important to find socially useful functions for youth, socially productive uses of youth's vast sources of energies. Totalitarian movements have made use of the potential energy in youth and have taken advantage of youths' needs for group-belongingness, and need for a definite rôle and function in life. Democracies have yet to channelize youth's energies into socially productive paths so that the young person knows and feels that he belongs and is needed. The picture of groups of teenage youngsters, lolling idly about, seeking to kill time, seems to me to symbolize our tendency to be wasteful of our human resources.

In every community, worthwhile projects can be organized in which young people, either with their peers or together with other age groups, can serve in some worthwhile socially useful activity. Such experiences might help to develop a feeling of belonging and being useful. Since our social structure is of such a nature that there seems of necessity to be a long period between childhood and adulthood, we must learn to make those who are going through this period feel more than simply in-betweens, marginal individuals who are too old to be children and who are not yet adults. These young people are capable of dealing with certain community problems and projects, precisely because they are more mature than younger children and are not yet weighed down with all the time-consuming responsibilities of adulthood. In short, adolescence can be made into a worthwhile, socially productive period of life rather than being merely a waiting period.

## F. Concluding Remark

After criticizing others for talking in generalities rather than studying specific adolescents, I too have indulged in some generalizations and theorizing. Of course there is nothing intrinsically wrong in promulgating general hypotheses concerning adolescence. But, it seems to me, only by studying the individual case will we gain deep understanding of the particular field conditions which are operating to produce the specific kind of adolescent behavior. Theorizing should not be a substitute for observation and study of the particular individual. Nor should a theory or a hypothesis or a generalization predispose the investigator to look only for or at certain aspects of the phenomenon under study. In conclusion, I should like to stress the importance—for parents, teachers, clinicians, and others who deal with adolescents—not to allow any *theory of* adolescence to blur their vision of the particular youth with whom they are dealing.

## References

1. BENEDICT, R. *Patterns of Culture.* New York: Houghton Mifflin (1934).

2. BLANCHARD, P. "Adolescent Experience in Relation to Personality and Behavior." *In* J. McV. HUNT (Ed.). *Personality and the Behavior Disorders.* New York: Ronald Press (1944), pp. 691–713.

3. DENNIS, W. "The Adolescent." *In* L. CARMICHAEL (Ed.). *Manual of Child Psychology.* New York: Wiley (1946), pp. 633–666.

4. HALL, G. S. Adolescence: Its Psychology and Its Relation to Physiology, Anthropology, Sociology, Sex, Crime, Religion, and Education. New York: Appleton (1904), vols. I and II.

5. HARSH, C. M. and H. G. SCHRICKEL. *Personality: Development and Assessment.* New York: Ronald Press (1950).

6. HOLLINGWORTH, L. S. *The Psychology of the Adolescent.* New York: Appleton-Century-Crofts (1928).

7. HORROCKS, J. E. *The Psychology of Adolescence: Behavior and Development.* New York: Houghton Mifflin (1951).

8. KUHLEN, R. G. *The Psychology of Adolescent Development.* New York: Harper (1952).

9. LEWIN, K. *Resolving Social Conflicts.* (Ed. by Gertrude W. Lewin.) New York: Harper (1948).

10. MAIER, N. R. F. *Frustration: The Study of Behavior Without a Goal.* New York: McGraw-Hill (1949).

11. MEAD, M. *Coming of Age in Samoa.* New York: Morrow (1928).

# 11

## SEX DIFFERENCES IN THE LIFE PROBLEMS AND INTERESTS OF ADOLESCENTS, 1935 AND 1957 *

### Dale B. Harris

In 1935 a survey was made of problems and interests of 1,641 adolescents in New York City and Tulsa, Oklahoma. The survey was repeated twenty-two years later, under auspices of the Institute of Child Development, University of Minnesota, with 1,165 Minnesota junior and senior high school students. This report compares the findings of the two surveys. The results should be useful to parents, teachers, and counselors of adolescents. They reveal the concerns of young people then and now, and what changes have taken place during an interval of nearly a quarter century. It is interesting to find that the problems and interests of these boys and girls are, in many instances, the same today as before. At the same time it must be noted that changes have taken place. This is to be expected and it may be surprising to some that there have not been more of them and/or more drastic ones.

*Questions:*

1. What significant changes in interests of boys have taken place between 1935 and 1957? Of girls?
2. What significant changes in problems of boys have taken place during this period? Of girls?
3. What results reported in this study surprised you? Of what use as a teacher or counselor will this new information be to you?

\* \* \*

This is a study of interests and problems which uses the method of rank order rather than a check list as its research technique. The items ranked are 15 topics selected from the concerns of adolescents. High school students were asked first to consider the items as personal problems and to

* Reprinted and abridged from *Child Development,* **30**:453–459 (December 1959), by permission of author and the Society for Research in Child Development, Inc.

construct an order reflecting their own experience with the issues as personal problems. The students then reranked the same items in order of interest, considering the topics as things they would like to read about and discuss or hear discussed.

The problems and instructions for ranking were taken verbatim from a study published by Symonds [1, 2].[1] He had selected the issues from young people's own discussions and phrased the issues in terms used by young people themselves. His 1641 students attended junior and senior high schools in Tulsa, Oklahoma, and New York City. The 1165 youth in the present study came from the junior-senior high school in a Minnesota community. Twenty-two years and considerable social, cultural, and economic change separate the circumstances of the two studies. Whether geographic or regional differences also influence the data cannot be known. In both studies, the samples represented in general the socioeconomic distribution of the communities from which they were drawn. The comparability of samples drawn from different geographic areas without close control through a stratification procedure is questionable. But the comparability of samples is also problematical across long time intervals, in which social and cultural changes have occurred, even when stratification by some socioeconomic index has been attempted. Changing conditions may themselves affect the index.

The hypothesis of the present study is taken from Symonds' discussion [2]: "Change the social and economic structure of society and you immediately change the relative emphasis of these problems and interests" (p. 752).

In a ranking process as in any *system,* change in one feature or aspect may have widespread effects throughout the system. Thus, there are some limitations to the method. The elements are *relative* to one another. The resulting rank order is not a true *scale* of values. Each choice made removes a degree of freedom and relates to the choices already made and those yet to be made. The ranks accorded a series of stimuli are systematically affected by the order in which the stimuli are first presented. Symonds removed this effect in his study by presenting the items in reverse order to approximately half his subjects. This study used the same procedure. The sample of children was drawn randomly from the available supply to constitute groups of 100 boys and 100 girls at each grade; half of each sex responded to the items in the order Symonds presented them in his report, and the other half responded to a reversed order. . . .

---

[1] Figures in brackets indicate references at end of article.

But how do young people separated by almost a generation compare in the ordering of their problems and their interests? Boys' rankings of interests across the years are somewhat more consistent (+.76) than their rankings of problems then and now (+.47). For girls, there is little difference between relative positions accorded problems and interests over the years (problems, +.50; interests, +.55).

Do boys and girls accord the same order of importance to a set of adolescent problems? In both periods boys and girls rank their problems similarly. In 1935 the similarity of the rank order of the sexes is expressed by a correlation value of +.80. In the 1957 study the value is +.77. The similarity of boys and girls is as great, on the average, as the similarity of successive grade groups of boys, or of girls. When the items were ranked according to interest in 1935, a value of +.80 expresses the similarity of boys' and girls' judgments. The comparable figure in 1957 is +.58.

The changes described above become more interesting when we look at specific ranks in Tables 1 and 2. As problems (Table 1), three items change five ranks or more across time for both boys and girls (health,

**Table 1**

**Ranks Accorded Issues Considered as Problems by High School Boys and Girls in 1935 and in 1957**

| Issue | B O Y S | | | | G I R L S | | | |
|---|---|---|---|---|---|---|---|---|
| | 1935 | | 1957 | | 1935 | | 1957 | |
| | Mean Rank | Rank | Mean Rank | Rank | Mean Rank | Rank | Mean Rank | Rank |
| Health ................. | 6.7 | (2) | 9.1* | (12) | 6.6 | (2) | 8.7* | (12.5) |
| Love, marriage .......... | 10.8 | (15) | 9.2* | (13.5) | 11.0 | (15) | 8.5* | (10) |
| Safety .................. | 8.3 | (8.5) | 9.2* | (13.5) | 8.8 | (12) | 10.0* | (14.5) |
| Money ................. | 6.2 | (1) | 6.3 | (2) | 6.8 | (3) | 6.5 | (2) |
| Mental hygiene .......... | 8.7 | (13) | 8.2 | (8) | 8.2 | (9.5) | 6.9* | (3.5) |
| Study habits ............ | 6.8 | (3) | 5.0 | (1) | 7.4 | (6) | 6.3* | (1) |
| Recreation ............. | 8.3 | (8.5) | 10.1 | (15) | 8.4 | (11) | 10.0* | (14.5) |
| Personal, moral qualities .. | 7.1 | (4) | 6.6* | (3) | 7.3 | (4) | 7.1 | (5) |
| Home, family relationships. | 8.2 | (7) | 8.4 | (10) | 8.2 | (9.5) | 7.6 | (6) |
| Manners ................ | 8.5 | (11.5) | 7.6* | (5) | 7.4 | (6) | 8.6* | (11) |
| Personal attractiveness .... | 7.9 | (6) | 7.7 | (6) | 6.2 | (1) | 6.9* | (3.5) |
| Daily schedule .......... | 9.0 | (14) | 8.3* | (9) | 9.4 | (14) | 8.7* | (12.5) |
| Civic interest ........... | 8.5 | (11.5) | 7.9* | (7) | 9.0 | (13) | 8.4 | (9) |
| Getting along with other people ................ | 8.4 | (10) | 8.6 | (11) | 7.9 | (8) | 8.0 | (8) |
| Philosophy of life ........ | 7.5 | (5) | 7.5 | (4) | 7.4 | (6) | 7.7 | (7) |

* Change from 1935 significant at the 1 per cent level.

mental health, manners), three more for boys only (safety, recreation, schedule), and two more for girls only (love and marriage, and study habits). As interests (Table 2), three items change for both sexes across time (love and marriage, family relations, manners), and one more for each sex singly (recreation for girls, getting along with others for boys). There are as many sex differences now as in 1935. At that time seven topics sig-

**Table 2**

**Ranks Accorded Issues Considered as Interests by High School Boys and Girls in 1935 and in 1957**

| Issue | Boys | | | | Girls | | | |
|---|---|---|---|---|---|---|---|---|
| | 1935 | | 1957 | | 1935 | | 1957 | |
| | Mean Rank | Rank | Mean Rank | Rank | Mean Rank | Rank | Mean Rank | Rank |
| Health ................. | 5.6 | (2) | 6.4* | (2) | 6.6 | (4) | 7.0 | (6) |
| Love, marriage .......... | 9.3 | (13) | 7.7* | (8) | 9.4 | (12) | 6.5* | (4.5) |
| Safety .................. | 7.8 | (7) | 8.7* | (11) | 9.2 | (10) | 10.2* | (14) |
| Money ................. | 7.1 | (3) | 6.5* | (3) | 8.1 | (8) | 8.2 | (10) |
| Mental hygiene .......... | 9.6 | (14) | 9.5 | (13) | 9.8 | (13.5) | 8.0* | (9) |
| Study habits ............. | 8.7 | (11) | 9.4* | (12) | 9.3 | (11) | 9.9* | (12.5) |
| Recreation ............. | 4.9 | (1) | 5.6* | (1) | 5.6 | (2) | 7.8* | (8) |
| Personal, moral qualities .. | 7.7 | (5.5) | 7.3* | (6) | 7.6 | (7) | 7.1 | (7) |
| Home, family relationships. | 8.4 | (10) | 7.2* | (5) | 8.3 | (9) | 6.4* | (2.5) |
| Manners ................ | 7.5 | (4) | 8.6* | (10) | 6.3 | (3) | 8.5* | (11) |
| Personal attractiveness .... | 8.1 | (8) | 8.0 | (9) | 5.4 | (1) | 6.0* | (1) |
| Daily schedule ........... | 10.5 | (15) | 10.9 | (15) | 10.4 | (15) | 11.4* | (15) |
| Civic interest ........... | 9.0 | (12) | 9.6* | (14) | 9.8 | (13.5) | 9.9 | (12.5) |
| Getting along with other people ................ | 8.2 | (9) | 7.1* | (4) | 7.0 | (5) | 6.4* | (2.5) |
| Philosophy of life ........ | 7.7 | (5.5) | 7.4 | (7) | 7.3 | (6) | 6.5* | (4.5) |

* Change from 1935 significant at the 1 per cent level.

nificantly differentiated the sexes as problems at the .01 level of certainty.[2] Now eight topics satisfy the .01 level.

Sex differences in interests also are about the same. In 1935 boys and girls rated nine topics quite different. In 1957, 10 topics satisfied the .01 level.

Attention to item placements show that a number of topics are relatively high as sources of problems: *Money* is still high as a problem to both boys and girls (ranks 2 and 2, respectively). It is of considerably greater interest

[2] This index of statistical significance refers to the difference between mean ranks, interpreted in terms of the standard errors of these means. It does not refer to shift in rank order.

to boys than to girls (rank 3 as compared with rank 10.)[3] *Health* at rank 2 as a problem in 1935 is no longer seen as such (rank 12), though interest in it is still relatively high, especially among boys. *Study habits* are somewhat more of a problem now than in 1935, especially for boys, but the topic ranked quite low in interest value in both periods. *Moral qualities* and *philosophy of life* come next in position both as problems and as topics of interest and are of similar relative magnitude in both periods.

Of intermediate concern as problems are the following: Both sexes see *mental health* as somewhat more of a problem to them now than they did in 1935, and for girls it now appears in the top five ranks. It has, likewise, moved up significantly ($p = .01$) in rank of interest to girls, though it remains low on the boys' list. *Home and family relations* is likewise ranked higher as a problem by girls than by boys now ($p = .01$). Relative to 1935, boys rank it slightly lower and girls slightly higher as a problem, though in these intermediate positions such shifting is statistically meaningless. Both boys and girls rank this topic higher on the list of interests than they did in 1935, girls very considerably so (rank of 2.5 compared with 9, $p = .01$). *Manners and courtesy,* up somewhat ($p = .01$) as a problem for boys as compared with the earlier period, is significantly less a problem for girls now (rank 11 compared with rank 6, $p = .01$). As a topic of interest it is down sharply for both sexes. *Attractiveness,* of intermediate value both as a problem and as an interest for boys in both periods, ranks high in both interest value and as a problem for girls in both periods. Likewise, *getting along with others* was and is of considerable interest to girls and has risen (rank 4 compared to rank 9, $p = .01$) as a topic of interest to boys. It is of intermediate significance as a problem. *Civic affairs* was and is of about median significance as a problem to both boys and girls and is of even less relative importance as a topic of interest.

Of least concern as problems now are the following: *Recreation,* of intermediate significance as a problem to both boys and girls in 1935, is negligible now. It was and is number 1 in interest value to boys but has dropped from second to eighth place for girls ($p = .01$). *Health,* of high significance both as a problem and as a topic of interest to boys and girls in 1935, is now negligible as a problem to either sex. It is now only of intermediate interest to girls, though it remains high on the boys' list. *Safety* is of little interest and even less a problem to both boys and girls now than in 1935

---

[3] In 1935 Symonds attributed the high ranks accorded money to the current economic stress. Studies of allowances show that modern youth "never had it so good" from an economic point of view, but inflation and rising standards of living expectancy keep the teen age group keenly aware of the medium of exchange.

($p = .01$). *Love and marriage,* ranked low as a problem by boys in both periods, has risen to an intermediate rank as a problem for girls. Both sexes now give it an intermediate interest rating, some several ranks higher than 22 years ago. The change in both problem and interest values of this topic is statistically significant, highly so for girls. *Daily schedule* is of little significance then or now, both to boys and girls, as problem or as interest.

This observation concerning the specific rankings accorded the issues should be made. Both psychologically and statistically, the highest and lowest ranks are most differentiated in any ranking or scaling procedure. The method in this study called for the identification of the first three positions, and then positions 13, 14, and 15. The intermediate positions were assigned last and may, particularly in the ranking of interests, represent a state of psychological indifference or lack of discrimination more than a state of intermediate significance. Should this be the case, the significance attributed by Symonds to the "relatively high" rank of philosophy of life (6th in 15 issues) may be modified somewhat. He affirmed [1] that "values and goals are craved" by youth and challenged teacher and counselors by the rank accorded this topic. Symonds attributed the high rank of money as a problem to the depression years and observed "it is a pity" that money drops to a much lower rank in interest value. The problem significance of money was not just a function of depression years, it is now clear.

The lack of concern with love and marriage, identified by Symonds as "sex adjustments," puzzled him, and he explained the low ranks by reference to "repression." His own hypothesis concerning social change appears from the present data to be equally plausible. A similar point can be made about mental health as an issue in adolescence. Symonds dismissed the low ranks attributed to this issue in these words: "Mental health likewise is no concern of healthy, growing adolescents. The crest of life is before them. Their failures and thwartings have not yet turned them back upon themselves" [1, p. 517]. The changed cultural ethos apparently has made a difference in the significance accorded this issue in the adolescent years.

The shifts noted in the tables and in the brief discussion for the most part confirm what observers of recent social trends have noted. Today, youth marry younger and show an earlier interest in social relations, love, and marriage. Our culture appears to recognize more openly now than two decades ago the sex, love, and marriage problems of young people. Physical health is actually less a problem today, and possibly receives less attention in school and in the popular press, whereas mental health discussions, literature, and posters appear in every newspaper, magazine, and waiting room. An increase in informality and casualness in dress and behavior may reflect itself in the decline in concern with manners.

The student of adolescent behavior will not be surprised at the significance of money as a problem, high interest in recreation, lack of concern with and interest in safety, unconcern over daily schedule and civic affairs, considerable concern over study habits as a problem but lack of interest in the topic, nor will he be surprised by the greater interest of girls than boys in attractiveness, love and marriage, mental health, and philosophy and beliefs; of boys than girls in money, health, and recreation.

If adults wish to "view with alarm," they may attend to the adolescent's relative unconcern with safety and hazard, set over against the 'teen-age driving problem, and the young person's continuing unconcern with civic affairs, set over against the continued increased emphasis on "modern problems," and citizenship in the secondary school's curriculum theory and effort.

## References

1. SYMONDS, P. M. "Life Interests and Problems of Adolescents." *Sch. Rev.* **44:**506–518 (1936).

2. SYMONDS, P. M. "Sex Differences in the Life Problems and Interests of Adolescents." *Sch. and Soc.* **43:**751–752 (1936).

# 12

## THE DISCOVERY AND ENCOURAGEMENT OF EXCEPTIONAL TALENT *

### Lewis M. Terman

In this fascinating selection Dr. Terman, a pioneer in the development of the individual mental test and the leader in the identification and study of the gifted, tells of his experiences. He relates how he became interested in mental testing and in the study of exceptionally talented individuals while a graduate student. After joining the faculty at Stanford University he began his monumental project dealing with the characteristics and the life histories of 1,000 gifted children, which is still going on after nearly forty years.

In this article Dr. Terman also discusses such timely topics as the best ways for our society and our schools to stimulate and develop exceptionally able children; the importance of, and best procedures for, early identification of the gifted; and the differences that have been found between high achievers and what might be called low achievers among children of unusual ability. On the last point, consistent differences have been found in personality traits and family backgrounds that seem to be significantly related to accomplishment when ability is virtually the same.

*Questions:*

1. What were the two major purposes of the study of 1,000 gifted children?
2. Have the gifted in the study been found to bear out their early promise? What is the evidence?
3. Are there low achievers among the gifted? Aside from achievement how do they differ from high achievers?

\* \* \*

I have often been asked how I happened to become interested in mental tests and gifted children. My first introduction to the scientific problems posed by intellectual differences occurred well over a half-century ago when

* Reprinted and abridged from the *American Psychologist,* **9:**221–230 (June 1954), by permission of the American Psychological Association.

I was a senior in psychology at Indiana University and was asked to prepare two reports for a seminar, one on mental deficiency and one on genius. Up to that time, despite the fact that I had graduated from a normal college as a Bachelor of Pedagogy and had taught school for five years, I had never so much as heard of a mental test. The reading for those two reports opened up a new world to me, the world of Galton, Binet, and their contemporaries. The following year my MA thesis on leadership among children [10] * was based in part on tests used by Binet in his studies of suggestibility.

Then I entered Clark University, where I spent considerable time during the first year in reading on mental tests and precocious children. Child prodigies, I soon learned, were at that time in bad repute because of the prevailing belief that they were usually psychotic or otherwise abnormal and almost sure to burn themselves out quickly or to develop postadolescent stupidity. "Early ripe, early rot" was a slogan frequently encountered. By the time I reached my last graduate year, I decided to find out for myself how precocious children differ from the mentally backward, and accordingly chose as my doctoral dissertation an experimental study of the intellectual processes of fourteen boys, seven of them picked as the brightest and seven as the dullest in a large city school [11]. These subjects I put through a great variety of intelligence tests, some of them borrowed from Binet and others, many of them new. The tests were given individually and required a total of 40 or 50 hours for each subject. The experiment contributed little or nothing to science, but it contributed a lot to my future thinking. Besides "selling" me completely on the value of mental tests as a research method, it offered an ideal escape from the kinds of laboratory work which I disliked and in which I was more than ordinarily inept. (Edward Thorndike confessed to me once that *his* lack of mechanical skill was partly responsible for turning *him* to mental tests and to the kinds of experiments on learning that required no apparatus.)

However, it was not until I got to Stanford in 1910 that I was able to pick up with mental tests where I had left off at Clark University. By that time Binet's 1905 and 1908 scales had been published, and the first thing I undertook at Stanford was a tentative revision of his 1908 scale. This, after further revisions, was published in 1916. The standardization of the scale was based on tests of a thousand children whose IQ's ranged from 60 to 145. The contrast in intellectual performance between the dullest and the brightest of a given age so intensified my earlier interest in the gifted

* Figures in brackets apply to references at end of article.

that I decided to launch an ambitious study of such children at the earliest opportunity.

My dream was realized in the spring of 1921 when I obtained a generous grant from the Commonwealth Fund of New York City for the purpose of locating a thousand subjects of IQ 140 or higher. More than that number were selected by Stanford-Binet tests from the kindergarten through the eighth grade, and a group mental test given in 95 high schools provided nearly 400 additional subjects. The latter, plus those I had located before 1921, brought the number close to 1,500. The average IQ was approximately 150, and 80 were 170 or higher [13].

The twofold purpose of the project was, first of all, to find what traits characterize children of high IQ, and secondly, to follow them for as many years as possible to see what kind of adults they might become. This meant that it was necessary to select a group representative of high-testing children in general. With the help of four field assistants, we canvassed a school population of nearly a quarter-million in the urban and semi-urban areas of California. Two careful checks on the methods used showed that not more than 10 or 12 per cent of the children who could have qualified for the group in the schools canvassed were missed. A sample of close to 90 per cent insured that whatever traits were typical of these children would be typical of high-testing children in any comparable school population.

Time does not permit me to describe the physical measurements, medical examinations, achievement tests, character and interest tests, or the trait ratings and other supplementary information obtained from parents and teachers. Nor can I here describe the comparative data we obtained for control groups of unselected children. The more important results, however, can be stated briefly: children of IQ 140 or higher are, in general, appreciably superior to unselected children in physique, health, and social adjustment; markedly superior in moral attitudes as measured either by character tests or by trait ratings; and vastly superior in their mastery of school subjects as shown by a three-hour battery of achievement tests. In fact, the typical child of the group had mastered the school subjects to a point about two grades beyond the one in which he was enrolled, some of them three or four grades beyond. Moreover, his ability as evidenced by achievement in the different school subjects is so general as to refute completely the traditional belief that gifted children are usually one-sided. I take some pride in the fact that not one of the major conclusions we drew in the early 1920's regarding the traits that are typical of gifted children has been overthrown in the three decades since then.

Results of thirty years' follow-up of these subjects by field studies in 1927–28, 1939–40, and 1951–52, and by mail follow-up at other dates, show that the incidence of mortality, ill health, insanity, and alcoholism is in each case below that for the generality of corresponding age, that the great majority are still well adjusted socially, and that the delinquency rate is but a fraction of what it is in the general population. Two forms of our difficult Concept Mastery Test, devised especially to reach into the stratosphere of adult intelligence, have been administered to all members of the group who could be visited by the field assistants, including some 950 tested in 1939–40 and more than 1,000 in 1951–52. On both tests they scored on the average about as far above the generality of adults as they had scored above the generality of children when we selected them. Moreover, as Dr. Bayley and Mrs. Oden have shown, in the twelve-year interval between the two tests, 90 per cent increased their intellectual stature as measured by this test. "Early ripe, early rot" simply does not hold for these subjects. So far, no one has developed postadolescent stupidity!

As for schooling, close to 90 per cent entered college and 70 per cent graduated. Of those graduating, 30 per cent were awarded honors and about two-thirds remained for graduate work. The educational record would have been still better but for the fact that a majority reached college age during the great depression. In their undergraduate years 40 per cent of the men and 20 per cent of the women earned half or more of their college expenses, and the total of undergraduate and graduate expenses earned amounted to $670,000, not counting stipends from scholarships and fellowships, which amounted to $350,000.

The cooperation of the subjects is indicated by the fact that we have been able to keep track of more than 98 per cent of the original group, thanks to the rapport fostered by the incomparable field and office assistants I have had from the beginning of the study to the present. I dislike to think how differently things could have gone with helpers even a little less competent.

The achievement of the group to midlife is best illustrated by the case histories of the 800 men, since only a minority of the women have gone out for professional careers [15]. By 1950, when the men had an average age of 40 years, they had published 67 books (including 46 in the fields of science, arts, and the humanities, and 21 books of fiction). They had published more than 1,400 scientific, technical, and professional articles; over 200 short stories, novelettes, and plays; and 236 miscellaneous articles on a great variety of subjects. They had also authored more than 150 patents. The figures on publications do not include the hundreds of publications by journalists that classify as news stories, editorials, or newspaper columns; nor do they include the hundreds if not thousands of radio and TV scripts.

The 800 men include 78 who have taken a PhD degree or its equivalent, 48 with a medical degree, 85 with a law degree, 74 who are teaching or have taught in a four-year college or university, 51 who have done basic research in the physical sciences or engineering, and 104 who are engineers but have done only applied research or none. Of the scientists, 47 are listed in the 1949 edition of *American Men of Science*. Nearly all of these numbers are from 10 to 20 or 30 times as large as would be found for 800 men of corresponding age picked at random in the general population, and are sufficient answer to those who belittle the significance of IQ differences.

The follow-up of these gifted subjects has proved beyond question that tests of "general intelligence," given as early as six, eight, or ten years, tell a great deal about the ability to achieve either presently or 30 years hence. Such tests do not, however, enable us to predict what direction the achievement will take, and least of all do they tell us what personality factors or what accidents of fortune will affect the fruition of exceptional ability. Granting that both interest patterns and special aptitudes play important roles in the making of a gifted scientist, mathematician, mechanic, artist, poet, or musical composer, I am convinced that to achieve greatly in almost any field, the special talents have to be backed up by a lot of Spearman's *g,* by which is meant the kind of general intelligence that requires ability to form many sharply defined concepts, to manipulate them, and to perceive subtle relationships between them; in other words, the ability to engage in abstract thinking.

The study by Catharine Cox of the childhood traits of historical geniuses gives additional evidence regarding the role of general intelligence in exceptional achievement. That study was part of our original plan to investigate superior ability by two methods of approach: (*a*) by identifying and following living gifted subjects from childhood onward; and (*b*) by proceeding in the opposite direction and tracing the mature genius back to his childhood promise. With a second grant from the Commonwealth Fund, the latter approach got under way only a year later than the former and resulted in the magnum opus by Cox entitled *The Early Mental Traits of Three Hundred Geniuses* [1]. Her subjects represented an unbiased selection from the top 510 in Cattell's objectively compiled list of the 1,000 most eminent men of history. Cox and two able assistants then scanned some

3,000 biographies in search of the information that would throw light on the early mental development of these subjects. The information thus obtained filled more than 6,000 typed pages. Next, three psychologists familiar with mental age norms read the documentary evidence on all the subjects and estimated for each the IQ that presumably would be necessary to account for the intellectual behavior recorded for given chronological ages. Average of the three IQ estimates was used as the index of intelligence. In fact two IQ's were estimated for each subject, one based on the evidence to age 17, and the other on evidence to the mid-twenties. The recorded evidence on development to age 17 varied from very little to an amount that yielded about as valid an IQ as a good intelligence test would give. Examples of the latter are Goethe, John Stuart Mill, and Francis Galton. It was the documentary information on Galton, which I summarized and published in 1917 [12], that decided me to prepare plans for the kind of study that was carried out by Cox. The average of estimated IQ's for her 300 geniuses was 155, with many going as high as 175 and several as high as 200. Estimates below 120 occurred only when there was little biographical evidence about the early years.

It is easy to scoff at these post-mortem IQ's, but as one of the three psychologists who examined the evidence and made the IQ ratings, I think the author's main conclusion is fully warranted; namely, that "the genius who achieves highest eminence is one whom intelligence tests would have identified as gifted in childhood."

Special attention was given the geniuses who had sometime or other been labeled as backward in childhood, and in every one of these cases the fact clearly contradicted the legend. One of them was Oliver Goldsmith, of whom his childhood teacher is said to have said "Never was so dull a boy." The fact is that little Oliver was writing clever verse at 7 years and at 8 was reading Ovid and Horace. Another was Sir Walter Scott, who at 7 not only read widely in poetry but was using correctly in his written prose such words as "melancholy" and "exotic." Other alleged childhood dullards included a number who disliked the usual diet of Latin and Greek but had a natural talent for science. Among these were the celebrated German chemist Justus von Liebig, the great English anatomist John Hunter, and the naturalist Alexander von Humboldt, whose name is scattered so widely over the maps of the world.

In the cases just cited one notes a tendency for the direction of later achievement to be foreshadowed by the interests and preoccupations of childhood. I have tried to determine how frequently this was true of the 100 subjects in Cox's group whose childhood was best documented. Very marked foreshadowing was noted in the case of more than half of the group, none at all in less than a fourth. Macaulay, for example, began his career as historian at the age of 6 with what he called a "Compendium of Universal History," filling a quire of paper before he lost interest in the project. Ben Franklin before the age of 17 had displayed nearly all the traits that characterized him in middle life: scientific curiosity, religious heterodoxy, wit and buffoonery, political and business shrewdness, and ability to write. At 11 Pascal was so interested in mathematics that his father thought it best to deprive him of books on this subject until he had first mastered Latin and Greek. Pascal secretly proceeded to construct a geometry of his own and covered the ground as far as the 32nd proposition of Euclid. His father then relented. At 14 Leibnitz was writing on logic and philosophy and composing what he called "An Alphabet of Human Thought." He relates that at this age he took a walk one afternoon to consider whether he should accept the "doctrine of substantial forms."

Similar foreshadowing is disclosed by the case histories of my gifted subjects. A recent study of the scientists and nonscientists among our 800 gifted men [15] showed many highly significant differences between the early interests and social attitudes of those who became physical scientists and those who majored in the social sciences, law, or the humanities. Those in medical or biological sciences usually rated on such variables somewhere between the physical scientists and the nonscientists. . . .

I have always stressed the importance of *early* discovery of exceptional abilities. Its importance is now highlighted by the facts Harvey Lehman has disclosed in his monumental studies of the relation between age and creative achievement [8]. The striking thing about his age curves is how early in life the period of maximum creativity is reached. In nearly all fields of science, the best work is done between ages 25 and 35, and rarely later than 40. The peak productivity for works of lesser merit is usually reached 5 to 10 years later; this is true in some twenty fields of science, in philosophy, in most kinds of musical composition, in art, and in literature of many varieties. The lesson for us from Lehman's statistics is that the youth of high achievement potential should be well trained for his life work before too many of his most creative years have been passed.

This raises the issue of educational acceleration for the gifted. It seems that the schools are more opposed to acceleration now than they were thirty years ago. The lockstep seems to have become more and more the fashion, notwithstanding the fact that practically everyone who has investigated the subject is against it. Of my gifted group, 29 per cent managed to graduate from high school before the age of 16½ years (62 of these before 15½), but I doubt if so many would be allowed to do so now. The other 71 per cent graduated between 16½ and 18½. We have compared the accelerated with the nonaccelerated on numerous case-history variables. The two groups differed very little in childhood IQ, their health records are equally good, and as adults they are equally well adjusted socially. More of the accelerates graduated from college, and on the average nearly a year and a half earlier than the nonaccelerates; they averaged higher in college grades and more often remained for graduate work. Moreover, the accelerates on the average married .7 of a year earlier, have a trifle lower divorce rate, and score just a little higher on a test of marital happiness [14]. So far as college records of accelerates and nonaccelerates are concerned, our data closely parallel those obtained by the late Noel Keys [3] at the University of California and those by Pressey [9] and his associates at Ohio State University. . . .

Instruments that permit the identification of gifted subjects are available in great variety and at nearly all levels from the primary grades to the graduate schools in universities. My rough guess is that at the present time tests of achievement in the school subjects are being given in this country to children below high school at a rate of perhaps ten or twelve million a year, and to high school students another million or two. In addition, perhaps two million tests of intelligence are given annually in the elementary and high schools. The testing of college students began in a small way only 30 years ago; now almost every college in the country requires applicants for admission to take some kind of aptitude test. This is usually a test of general aptitude, but subject-matter tests and tests of special aptitudes are sometimes given to supplement the tests of general aptitude. . . .

Along with the increasing use of tests, and perphaps largely as a result of it, there is a growing interest, both here and abroad, in improving educational methods for the gifted. Acceleration of a year or two or three, however desirable, is but a fraction of what is needed to keep the gifted child or youth working at his intellectual best. The method most often advocated is curriculum enrichment for the gifted without segregating them from the ordinary class. Under ideal conditions enrichment can accomplish much, but in these days of crowded schools, when so many teachers are overworked, underpaid, and inadequately trained, curriculum enrichment for a few gifted in a large mixed class cannot begin to solve the problem. The best survey of thought and action in this field of education is the book entitled *The Gifted Child,* written by many authors and published in 1951 [16]. In planning for and sponsoring this book, The American Association for Gifted Children has rendered a great service to education.

But however efficient our tests may be in discovering exceptional talents, and whatever the schools may do to foster those discovered, it is the prevailing *Zeitgeist* that will decide, by the rewards it gives or withholds, what talents will come to flower. In Western Europe of the Middle Ages, the favored talents were those that served the Church by providing its priests, the architects of its cathedrals, and the painters of religious themes. A few centuries later the same countries had a renaissance that included science and literature as well as the arts. Although presumably there are as many potential composers of great music as there ever were, and as many potentially great artists as in the days of Leonardo da Vinci and Michaelangelo, I am reliably informed that in this country today it is almost impossible for a composer of *serious* music to earn his living except by teaching, and that the situation is much the same, though somewhat less critical, with respect to artists.

The talents most favored by the current *Zeitgeist* are those that can contribute to science and technology. If intelligence and achievement tests don't discover the potential scientist, there is a good chance that the annual Science Talent Search will though not until the high school years. Since Westinghouse inaugurated in 1942 this annual search for the high school seniors most likely to become creative scientists, nearly 4,000 boys and girls have been picked for honors by Science Service out of the many thousands who have competed. As a result, "Science Clubs of America" now number 15,000 with a third of a million members—a twenty-fold increase in a dozen years [2]. As our need for more and better scientists is real and urgent, one can rejoice at what the talent search and the science clubs are accomplishing. One may regret, however, that the spirit of the times is not equally favorable to the discovery and encouragement of potential poets, prose writers, artists, statesmen, and social leaders.

But in addition to the over-all climates that reflect the *Zeitgeist,* there are localized climates that favor or hinder the encouragement of given talents in particular colleges and universities. I have in mind especially two recent investigations of the differences among colleges in the later achievement of their graduates. One by Knapp and Goodrich [4] dealt with the undergraduate origin of 18,000 scientists who got the bachelor's degree between 1924 and 1934 and were listed in the 1944 edition of *American Men of Science.* The list of 18,000 was composed chiefly of men who had taken a PhD degree, but included a few without a PhD who were starred scientists. The IBM cards for these men were then sorted according to the college from which they obtained the bachelor's degree, and an index of productivity was computed for each college in terms of the proportion of its male graduates who were in the list of 18,000. Some of the results were surprising, not to say sensational. The institutions that were most productive of future scientists between 1924 and 1934 were not the great universities, but the small liberal arts colleges. Reed College topped the list with an index of 132 per thousand male graduates. The California Institute of Technology was second with an index of 70. Kalamazoo College was third with 66, Earlham fourth with 57, and Oberlin fifth with 56. Only a half-dozen of the great universities were in the top fifty with a productivity index of 25 or more.

The second study referred to was by Knapp and Greenbaum [5], who rated educational institutions according to the proportion of their graduates who received certain awards at the graduate level in the six-year period from 1946 to 1951. Three kinds of awards were considered: a PhD degree, a graduate scholarship or fellowship paying at least $400 a year, or a prize at the graduate level won in open competition. The roster of awardees they compiled included 7,000 students who had graduated from 377 colleges and universities. This study differs from the former in three respects: (a) it deals with recent graduates who had not had time to become distinguished but who could be regarded as good bets for the future; (b) these good bets were classified according to whether the major field was science, social science or the humanities; and (c) data were obtained for both sexes, though what I shall report here relates only to men. In this study the great universities make a better showing than in the other, but still only a dozen of them are in the top fifty institutions in the production of men who are good bets. In the top ten, the University of Chicago is third, Princeton is eighth, and Harvard is tenth; the other seven in order of rank are Swarthmore 1, Reed 2, Oberlin 4, Haverford 5, California Institute of Technology 6, Carleton 7, and Antioch 9. When the schools were listed separately for production of men who were good bets in science, social science and the humanities, there were eight that rated in the top twenty on all three lists. These were Swarthmore, Reed, Chicago, Harvard. Oberlin, Antioch, Carleton, and Princeton.

The causes of these differences are not entirely clear. Scores on aptitude tests show that the intelligence of students in a given institution is by no means the sole factor, though it is an important one. Other important factors are the quality of the school's intellectual climate, the proportion of able and inspiring teachers on its faculty, and the amount of conscious effort that is made not only to discover but also to motivate the most highly gifted. The influence of motivation can hardly be exaggerated.

In this address I have twice alluded to the fact that achievement in school is influenced by many things other than the sum total of intellectual abilities. The same is true of success in life. In closing I will tell you briefly about an attempt we made a dozen years ago to identify some of the nonintellectual factors that have influenced life success among the men in my gifted group. Three judges, working independently, examined the records (to 1940) of the 730 men who were then 25 years old or older, and rated each on life success. The criterion of "success" was the extent to which a subject had made use of his superior intellectual ability, little weight being given to earned income. The 150 men rated highest for success and the 150 rated lowest were then compared on some 200 items of information obtained from childhood onward [14]. How did the two groups differ?

During the elementary school years, the A's and C's (as we call them) were almost equally successful. The average grades were about the same, and average scores on achievement tests were only a trifle higher for the A's. Early in high school the groups began to draw apart in scholarship, and by the end of high school the slump of the C's was quite marked. The slump could not be blamed on extracurricular activities, for these were almost twice as common among the A's. Nor was much of it due to difference in intelligence. Although the A's tested on the average a little higher than the C's both in 1922 and 1940, the average score made by the C's in 1940 was high enough to permit brilliant college work, in fact was equaled by only 15 per cent of our highly selected Stanford students. Of the A's, 97 per cent entered college and 90 per cent graduated; of the C's, 68 per cent entered but only 37 per cent graduated. Of those who graduated, 52 per cent of the A's but only 14 per cent of the C's graduated with honors. The A's were also more accelerated in school; on the average they were six months younger on completing the eighth grade, 10 months younger at high school graduation, and 15 months younger at graduation from college.

The differences between the educational histories of the A's and C's reflect to some degree the differences in their family backgrounds. Half of the A fathers but only 15 per cent of the C fathers were college graduates, and twice as many of A siblings as of C siblings graduated. The estimated number of books in the A homes was nearly 50 per cent greater than in the C homes. As of 1928, when the average age of the subjects was about 16 years, more than twice as many of the C parents as of A parents had been divorced.

Interesting differences between the groups were found in the childhood data on emotional stability, social adjustments, and various traits of personality. Of the 25 traits on which each child was rated by parent and teacher in 1922 (18 years before the A and C groups were made up), the only trait on which the C's averaged as high as the A's was general health. The superiority of the A's was especially marked in four volitional traits: prudence, self-confidence, perseverance, and desire to excel. The A's also rated significantly higher in 1922 on leadership, popularity, and sensitiveness to approval or disapproval. By 1940 the difference between the groups in social adjustment and all-round mental stability had greatly increased and showed itself in many ways. By that time four-fifths of the A's had married, but only two-thirds of the C's, and the divorce rate for those who had married was twice as high for the C's as for the A's. Moreover, the A's made better marriages; their wives on the average came from better homes, were better educated, and scored higher on intelligence tests.

But the most spectacular differences between the two groups came from three sets of ratings, made in 1940, on a dozen personality traits. Each man rated himself on all the traits, was rated on them by his wife if he had a wife, and by a parent if a parent was still living. Although the three sets of ratings were made independently, they agreed unanimously on the four traits in which the A and C groups differed most widely. These were "persistence in the accomplishment of ends," "integration toward goals, as contrasted with drifting," "self-confidence," and "freedom from inferiority feelings." For each trait three critical ratios were computed showing, respectively, the reliability of the A–C differences in average of self-ratings, ratings by wives, and ratings by parents. The average of the three critical ratios was 5.5 for perseverance, 5.6 for integration toward goals, 3.7 for self-confidence, and 3.1 for freedom from inferiority feelings. These closely parallel the traits that Cox found to be especially characteristic of the 100 leading geniuses in her group whom she rated on many aspects of personality; their three outstanding traits she defined as "persistence of motive and effort," "confidence in their abilities," and "strength or force of character."

There was one trait on which only the parents of our A and C men were asked to rate them; that trait was designated "common sense." As judged by parents, the A's are again reliably superior, the A–C difference in average rating having a critical ratio of 3.9. We are still wondering what self-ratings by the subjects and ratings of them by their wives on common sense would have shown if we had been impudent enough to ask for them!

Everything considered, there is nothing in which our A and C groups present a greater contrast than in drive to achieve and in all-round mental and social adjustment. Our data do not support the theory of Lange-Eichbaum [6] that great achievement usually stems from emotional tensions that border on the abnormal. In our gifted group, success is associated with stability rather than instability, with absence rather than with presence of disturbing conflicts—in short with well-balanced temperament and with freedom from excessive frustrations. The Lange-Eichbaum theory may explain a Hitler, but hardly a Churchill; the junior senator from Wisconsin,* possibly, but not a Jefferson or a Washington.

At any rate, we have seen that intellect and achievement are far from perfectly correlated. To identify the internal and external factors that help or hinder the fruition of exceptional talent, and to measure the extent of their influences, are surely among the major problems of our time. These problems are not new; their existence has been recognized by countless men from Plato to Francis Galton. What is new is the general awareness of them caused by the manpower shortage of scientists, engineers, moral leaders, statesmen, scholars, and teachers that the country must have if it is to survive in a threatened world. These problems are now being investigated on a scale never before approached, and by a new generation of workers in several related fields. Within a couple of decades vastly more should be known than we know today about our resources of potential genius, the environmental circumstances that favor its expression, the emotional compulsions that give it dynamic quality, and the personality distortions that can make it dangerous.

## References

1. Cox, Catharine C. *The Early Mental Traits of Three Hundred Geniuses.* Vol. II of *Genetic Studies of Genius,* L. M. Terman (Ed.). Stanford: Stanford Univer. Press (1926).

2. Davis, W. "Communicating Science." *J. Atomic Scientists* 337–340 (1953).

* [At time of writing, Senator Joseph P. McCarthy.—V.H.N.]

3. KEYS, N. "The Underage Student in High School and College." *Univer. Calif. Publ. Educ.* **7:**145–272 (1938).

4. KNAPP, R. H. and H. B. GOODRICH. *Origins of American Scientists.* Chicago: Univ. of Chicago Press (1952).

5. KNAPP, R. H. and J. J. GREENBAUM. *The Younger American Scholar: His Collegiate Origins.* Chicago: Univer. of Chicago Press (1953).

6. LANGE-EICHBAUM, W. *The Problem of Genius.* New York: Macmillan (1932).

7. LEARNED, W. S. and B. D. WOOD. "The Student and His Knowledge." *Carnegie Found. Adv. Teaching Bull.,* No. 29 (1938).

8. LEHMAN, H. C. *Age and Achievement.* Princeton: Princeton Univer. Press (1953).

9. PRESSEY, S. L. *Educational Acceleration: Appraisals and Basic Problems.* Columbus: Ohio State Univer. Press (1949).

10. TERMAN, L. M. "A Preliminary Study in the Psychology and Pedagogy of Leadership." *Pedag. Sem.* **11:**413–451 (1904).

11. TERMAN, L. M. "Genius and Stupidity: A Study of Some of the Intellectual Processes of Seven 'Bright' and Seven 'Dull' Boys." *Pedag. Sem.* **13:**307–373 (1906).

12. TERMAN, L. M. "The Intelligence Quotient of Francis Galton in Childhood." *Amer. J. Psychol.* **28:**209–215 (1917).

13. TERMAN, L. M. *et al. Mental and physical traits of a thousand gifted children.* Vol. I of *Genetic studies of genius,* L. M. TERMAN (Ed.). Stanford: Stanford Univer. Press (1925).

14. TERMAN, L. M., and M. H. ODEN. *The gifted child grows up.* Vol. IV of *Genetic Studies of Genius,* L. M. TERMAN (Ed.). Stanford: Stanford Univer. Press (1947).

15. TERMAN, L. M. "Scientists and nonscientists in a group of 800 gifted men." *Psychol. Monogr.* **68:** in press (1954).

16. WITTY, P. (Ed.). *The Gifted Child.* Boston: Heath (1951).

17. *Bridging the Gap between School and College.* New York: The Fund for the Advancement of Education (1953).

18. *The Intelligence of Scottish Children.* Scottish Council for Research in Education. London: Univer. of London Press (1933).

# 13

## LOCATING GIFTED CHILDREN IN JUNIOR HIGH SCHOOLS— A COMPARISON OF METHODS *

### Carl V. Pegnato and Jack W. Birch

Recent years have brought greatly heightened interest in education of gifted children. Many educators feel that the gifted have been neglected in our schools, because, being competent and resourceful, they were known by teachers to be able to take care of themselves. However, taking care of themselves is not likely to create the most challenging and fruitful learning situation for them. Should we not give as much attention to educating our gifted children, from whom our leaders in science, art, business, and government will inevitably come, as we do to providing for the education of the handicapped? Sheer self-interest on the part of society would indicate that this would be a wise investment in our collective future. However, before special provisions can be made for educating the gifted, they must first be identified. How do we find out who among the children in our schools is so able as to deserve being called "gifted?" The authors of this article ask this question and, to answer it, investigate some six different methods that can be used for the purpose. The various methods are tested against a criterion taken by the authors as their standard, namely the I.Q. as determined by an individual intelligence examination.

*Questions:*

1. Who are the gifted? Before they can be identified it is necessary to define what we mean by the term. How would you define it?

2. Do you know of still other methods that have been used to identify gifted children? Do you know of any evidence on their value or usefulness?

3. After gifted children have been identified, what is the next step? What provisions have been made or tried? Do you know of any evidence on their value or success?

* Reprinted from *Exceptional Children,* **25**:300-304 (March 1959), by permission of senior author and publisher.

This is a report on a study of the relative efficiency and effectiveness of seven different means of locating gifted children in junior high schools. The major purpose of the investigation was to discover which procedure or which combination of commonly used procedures would prove best.

The importance of finding gifted children has long been acknowledged [2].* Only in the last quarter-century have the individual intelligence testing tools been shaped and sharpened sufficiently to allow psychologists to identify gifted children with a very high degree of certainty [4]. The international events of recent years have heightened the urgency for the prompt and early discovery of all gifted children—those who show their capacity through exceptional achievements and those in whom great potentialities are latent—in order that they may be given the best possible guidance toward self-realization through education and training [1].

The gifted children in a junior high school could be discovered if every child in the school were individually examined by a psychologist [3]. While some few schools in this nation have access to sufficient psychological service to provide for individual examination for all children, and while that amount of psychological service should ideally be available to all school districts, it is very rarely the case. In fact, it is the very shortage of psychological staff which makes it so necessary to find ways of choosing some small group of children from the total student body to refer for individual evaluation.

Several questions relating to locating children who might be gifted for referral to a psychologist seemed to need answers based on direct investigation.

1. Do teachers recognize the mentally gifted children in their classes?

2. Are the children who win Honor Roll status the gifted children of each class?

3. Are some gifted children to be found only through the interest and achievement they display in music or arts?

4. Are some gifted children identifiable primarily through the interest and ability they show in social, political, and other extra-curricular activities?

5. Does outstanding performance in mathematics call children to teachers' attention as gifted?

6. Can group intelligence tests be relied upon in the identification of gifted children?

7. Are group achievement test scores useful in selecting gifted children?

* Figures in brackets apply to references at end of article.

8. Are some gifted children overlooked even though all the criteria suggested above are employed in searching for them?

9. What screening method or combination of methods is most effective and efficient?

10. What is the magnitude of the problem of under-achievement among gifted children?

For the purposes of this inquiry, mental giftedness was defined in terms of a Stanford-Binet Intelligence Quotient of 136 or higher as determined from an examination by a school psychologist. This definition includes the most intelligent one percent of the general population, and, to that extent, is consistent with a number of current and widely used definitions.

As a setting in which to seek answers to these and other closely related questions, the junior division of a junior-senior high school in a large city (Pittsburgh, Pa.) was chosen. The school, in grades seven through 12, had 3600 students. The junior division enrolled 1400 students in grades seven through nine. In order to improve the prospect that a fairly large proportion of gifted children would be available for the study, the school chosen was not only a large one, but it was situated in and drew upon a very favored group of neighborhoods from a socio-economic standpoint.

## Methods of Screening for Referral

### Teacher Judgment

The first step in the investigation was to find which pupils the teachers considered mentally gifted. This was accomplished by circulating a simple inquiry form which read as follows:

"We are in process of identifying mentally gifted children at the junior high school level. We feel that teachers have recognized most of these children in their classes. It would be helpful to have a basic and general list that we can share and use in program planning. Will you please, therefore, use the attached form to name the children you consider mentally gifted in your home room and in any of your classes. Make a statement for each child as to why you judge the child to be mentally gifted."

The form referred to in the directions simply provided blanks for the child's name, grade, and room, as well as space for any statement the teacher wished to make. No definition was given; each teacher was free to interpret the term "gifted" in his own way. No limitation was placed on the teachers' access to records on the children. Except that the teachers had been informed in a general faculty meeting that their help would be

enlisted in finding all the gifted children in the schools, no further orientation was furnished. The forms returned by the teachers contained 154
different names.

## Honor Roll Listing

A second step was to collect the names of children on the Honor Rolls
for the different grades in the junior high school. An all-subject average of
"B" or higher on an "A-B-C-D-E" scale of relative excellence of achievement was necessary for placement on the honor roll. The letter grades
used in arriving at the average were assigned by the teachers, and each
teacher was free to use his own judgment in determining the child's letter-
grade. At the close of the report period from which this list of names was
taken, the 39 teachers involved had placed 371 children on the honor roll.

## Creative Ability in Art or Music

A third step in the investigation was aimed at locating mentally gifted
children who might be displaying creative ability through art or music.
The art and music teachers were asked to consider their students in terms
of creativity and talent, and to submit the names of outstanding children.
Teachers of vocal music, instrumental music, and arts contributed to a
list of 137 children, 71 from music and 66 from art.

## Student Council Membership

Social and political leadership might prove a special field of achievement for children who show mental giftedness in few or no other ways. It
was felt that students selected in each home room to represent their peers
in the Student Council would be classifiable as social and political leaders.
A review of records on this point yielded 82 names.

## Superiority in Mathematics

Because mathematical skill is considered closely associated with mental
giftedness, a fifth screening method was used. Arithmetic teachers were
asked to name children who were outstanding. This was done about a
month subsequent to the time all teachers were asked for the more general referrals. Again, there were no limitations placed on the teachers with
respect to what information they might use in making their selections. The
arithmetic teachers suggested 179 children's names.

## Group Intelligence Test Results

The investigation then turned to two somewhat more objective screening procedures which depended less upon professional judgment of teachers. These were group intelligence test scores and group achievement test scores.

The sixth step, then, was the review of cumulative records and the listing of children with group test intelligence quotients of 115 or higher. In the Pittsburgh school system the Otis Quick-Scoring Mental Ability Test, Beta Form, is administered at the end of the sixth grade and again at the end of the eighth grade. Scores were available on all the children at the school. The latest results were used. An IQ of 115 was chosen as the cut-off point for referrals for individual examination. This screening procedure produced 450 children with Otis IQ's 115 or higher.

*Group Achievement Test Results*

The final screening procedure used the results of standardized achievement tests. Metropolitan Achievement Tests are administered at the close of each school year in Pittsburgh. The latest scores available were used. Sub-test scores in two basic skill subjects, reading and arithmetic, were averaged. A list was compiled of the children with average scores at least three grade levels above grade placement. (Since the ceiling of the Metropolitan was 11th grade, the ninth graders who scored at the test ceiling were included.) This list contained 334 names.

## Procedure

When the lists from all of the seven screening methods were combined and analyzed, 781 different names appeared (394 boys and 387 girls). More than half of the total population of the junior high school grades (1400) had been recommended, by one or more screening method, for referral for individual examination to determine if they were actually mentally gifted.

At this point, the counselor and the vice-principal of the junior high school were asked to list the names of all children known to them to be emotionally or socially maladjusted and who might also be mentally gifted. When the names of those children were checked against the master list of 781, it was found that all had been included through some other screening procedure.

After the necessary individual psychological examinations were completed, the Stanford-Binet Intelligence Quotients of the 781 children were tabulated. The effectiveness and efficiency of the various screening procedures can be evaluated by reference to the material in Table 1, Effectiveness and Efficiency of Screening Procedures.

*Effectiveness* of a screening procedure is defined by the percentage of gifted children it locates. A screening procedure which includes all the gifted children among those it selects for referral to a psychologist is 100

**Table 1**

**Effectiveness and Efficiency of Screening Procedures**

| Screening Methods | No. Selected by Screening Method | No. Identified as Gifted by Stanford-Binet IQ | Effectiveness (Percent of Gifted Located; Total Gifted N = 91) | Efficiency (Ratio of No. Selected by Screening to No. Identified as Gifted, in Percent) |
|---|---|---|---|---|
| Teacher Judgment ... | 154 | 41 | 45.1 | 26.6 |
| Honor Roll ........ | 371 | 67 | 73.6 | 18.0 |
| Creativity ......... | 137 | 14 | 15.5 | 10.2 |
| Art Ability ....... | (66) | (6) | 6.6 | 9.1 |
| Music Ability ..... | (71) | (8) | 9.9 | 11.2 |
| Student Council ..... | 82 | 13 | 14.3 | 15.8 |
| Mathematics Achievement ........... | 179 | 50 | 56.0 | 27.9 |
| Group Intelligence Tests .......... | | | | |
| Cut-off IQ 115 .... | 450 | 84 | 92.3 | 18.7 |
| Cut-off IQ 120 .... | (240) | (65) | 71.4 | 27.1 |
| Cut-off IQ 125 .... | (105) | (40) | 43.9 | 38.1 |
| Cut-off IQ 130 .... | (36) | (20) | 21.9 | 55.5 |
| Group Achievement Tests ........... | 335 | 72 | 79.2 | 21.5 |
| Total ............. | 781 | | | |

percent effective. If it allows half of the gifted children to slip through its net and fails to refer them to the psychologist, it is 50 percent effective.

*Efficiency* of a screening procedure is defined by the ratio between the total number of children it refers for individual examination and the number of gifted children found among those referred. If the screening procedure refers 10 children and nine of them are found, upon individual examination, to be gifted, its efficiency is 90 percent.

The best screening method is one which combines high effectiveness and high efficiency, for that would result in most of the gifted being found with a minimum amount of wasted motion. Of course, if the main objective is to find as many of the mentally gifted children as possible, it may be necessary to use a highly effective screening method with less importance being placed on its efficiency.

## Results

Of the 781 children selected by screening methods, 91 had Stanford-Binet IQ's of 136 or higher. To find 6.5 percent of the population of a junior high school with Stanford-Binet IQ's of 136 or above is quite unusual. However, the school was selected in part because other information had suggested that an extraordinarily large number of gifted children attended. While individual psychological examinations on the other 619 students might have uncovered more children who would rank among the most intelligent one percent of the population, it is doubtful if many were missed. Since the findings are to be interpreted largely in relative terms, it was not essential that every gifted child be located.

Some of the questions which prompted this investigation can now be answered in quantitative terms.

1. Teachers do not locate gifted children effectively or efficiently enough to place much reliance on them for screening. The category *Teacher Judgment* in Table 1 indicates that only 45.1 percent of the gifted children actually present were included in the teachers' lists. Not only were more than half of the gifted missed, but a breakdown of those children referred as gifted by the teachers revealed that almost a third (31.4 percent) of those chosen by the teachers were *not in the gifted or superior* range but in the *average* intelligence range on the Binet.

2. Almost three-fourths (73.6 percent) of the 91 gifted children were on the Honor Roll. However 304 other children were rated Honor Roll status; therefore, the Honor Roll is among the less efficient screening methods.

3. Some gifted children do display unusual interest and achievement in music or art. However, these same children are noteworthy in other aspects of school work, too. All of the 14 gifted children among the 137 called outstanding in music or art were also screened for referral in at least two other ways.

4. The Student Council membership list contained no gifted children who were not among those already included by the group intelligence test

screening. All of the gifted children on Student Council appeared on at least two other lists also.

5. When mathematics achievement alone was the criterion used by teachers, the gifted children did not fare well. Almost half of them were overlooked, and for every mentally gifted child referred, more than two who were not mentally gifted were on the referral list.

6. Group intelligence tests like the one used in this study cannot be relied upon in the identification of gifted children in the junior high school grades. Reference to Table 1 indicates, when a cut-off point of IQ 130 is used that the group test located only 21.9 per cent of the gifted children. Almost four out of five were missed. Even if the cut-off point of IQ 125 were used, more than half of the gifted children would be missed. The important point seems to be that the group test does not discriminate well between children who are a little above and those who are a great deal above average in learning capacity. The group intelligence test does seem to possess the best combination of efficiency and effectiveness as a screen. Using IQ 115 as the cut-off point a little better than nine out of 10 of the gifted will be found among the group so chosen when they are examined by a psychologist.

7. Group achievement test scores run a fairly close second to group intelligence test scores in combined efficiency and effectiveness when used as they were in this situation.

8. Three gifted children were found who apparently did not make favorable showings in either group tests of intelligence or group achievement tests. One of these was located through the Honor Roll, and the other two were overlooked by all the screening procedures. The latter two were found because their cumulative records indicated that they had been examined by a school psychologist in the elementary grades and proved to be gifted.

9. By combining the group intelligence test list and the group achievement test list into one screening procedure, 88 of the 91 gifted children, or 96.7 percent of them, were found. Taken together, the two group tests resulted in the most effective screening procedure.

10. This investigation did not set out to obtain detailed information on underachievement among gifted children. However, analysis of the records of the 91 children with Binet IQ's 136 or higher showed six of them appearing on no list other than that of children with Otis IQ's 115 or higher. In addition, four others were on neither the Honor Roll or the list of children with achievement test scores three years above grade placement.

There is good reason to think, therefore, that 10 of the 92 gifted children might be under-achievers. The implication is strong that perhaps more than one out of 10 gifted children (10.8 percent in this study) is achieving markedly below an optimum level. Certainly the screening based on group intelligence test scores is helpful in locating gifted children who are not showing their potentialities either in letter-grades given by teachers or on group achievement tests.

## Summary

A major concern of our educational system is the identification and education of mentally gifted children. With reasonable certainty the identification of intellectually gifted students is now possible in the junior high school years through the use of individual intelligence tests administered by school psychologists. This identification procedure, though quite accurate, is both expensive and time consuming. Effective and efficient screening methods are necessary for choosing the children to be referred to the psychologist. Effective and efficient screening methods are those which make possible the identification of all the gifted children in a school while minimizing the total number of children who must be examined individually by the psychologist.

Seven kinds of screening procedures are considered. The use of group intelligence test results for screening is found to have advantages over other methods both in effectiveness and efficiency; they are of little value, however, for actual identification. The latter should be left to psychologists employing individual examination methods if measures of intelligence are to be the criteria used.

## Bibliography

1. *Education of the Gifted.* Washington, D. C.: Educational Policies Commission, National Education Association (1950).

2. HOLLINGWORTH, LETA S. *Gifted Children, Their Nature and Nurture.* New York: The Macmillan Company (1927).

3. PEGNATO, CARL. *An Evaluation of Various Initial Methods of Selecting Intellectually Gifted Children at the Junior High School Level.* Doctoral Thesis, Pennsylvania State College (1958).

4. TERMAN, LEWIS M. *et al. Genetic Studies of Genius, Volumes I-II-III-IV.* Stanford, California: Stanford University Press (1925 through 1947).

14

# CURRENT TRENDS AND PRACTICES IN THE EDUCATION OF THE MENTALLY RETARDED *

## Marion J. Erickson

The education of the mentally retarded was once considered the responsibility of the home or of special institutions. The point of view has been changing, however, and today schools are making more provisions for education of the retarded than was ever thought possible. It is no longer a question, generally speaking, of whether or not mentally handicapped children should be in school but rather that of what the best methods for helping them are. This is not to say that institutions for those who are uneducable no longer are needed, but our concept of what schools can do for children formerly considered fit only for an institution has been broadened. In the selection which follows, questions of philosophy and practice are discussed. Some of these are fairly well agreed upon by authorities in the field; others are matters of sharp controversy. Important research in this field is reviewed and need for further study, particularly on controversial issues where research is lacking or inconclusive, is pointed out.

*Questions:*

1. Distinguish between the terms "educable" and "trainable." Do the schools generally take responsibility for both? If not, which? Why?

2. What are the three usual types of programs in use for the mentally retarded? What does research say about the advantages and disadvantages of each?

\* \* \*

The education of the mentally retarded which was once considered the responsibility of the home or the institution is now generally recognized as a function of the public school system. Compulsory education laws have

\* Reprinted from *Educational Administration and Supervision*, **44**:297–308 (September 1958), by permission of author and publisher.

tended to bring into the schools children who previously would have been regarded as unfit and unable to profit from a public school education.

Studies have shown that while many mentally retarded children are unable to profit from the program offered to the normal child, they are able to benefit from a program adapted to their abilities and developmental patterns. It has been estimated that 1.5 or 2 per cent of the general population will fall into the category of educable mentally retarded and an additional 0.3 to 0.5 per cent will be classified as severely retarded. The educable mentally retarded child is generally defined as one who is potentially socially, economically and personally competent, while the severely retarded is considered as trainable but unable to profit from academic experiences. It has been recognized that the mentally retarded children cannot learn as much or as fast as the normal children and that an attempt must be made to offer them the experiences most essential to equip them to become contributing members of our society.

It has been shown by numerous studies that with appropriate education and guidance the mentally retarded have been able to achieve greater economic independence, to become more socially competent, to deal more adequately with personal problems and to develop more wholesome activities and interests leading to a fuller life. Providing an education that will enable the mentally retarded person to become partially or totally independent is a better investment for society than life-long care in an institution or home.

To facilitate the establishment of special programs for the mentally retarded all forty-eight states have passed legislation providing for special classes and forty-six states have provided some form of financial reimbursement.

Initiating new services into a school program requires considerable study to become acquainted with the research and the results of experimentation with different programs. A survey of the literature for the past twelve years reveals certain trends and practices that may prove helpful to the administrator who is considering a special education program. Some practices meet with widespread agreement; others are controversial. Where controversy exists, an attempt will be made to present the various viewpoints.

## Aims and Objectives

The universal acceptance of the aims and objectives of education for the mentally retarded establishes them as the basis for the organization and planning of special education programs. The goals listed by the Educational Policies Commission are:

(a) self realization or personal development embodying the individual's use of tools of learning, his health, his cultural and recreational interests and his personal philosophy.

(b) an understanding of human relationships as a member of the family and community.

(c) economic efficiency as a producer and consumer.

(d) civic responsibility in local, state and national government and the concern for people of other nations.

## Programs in Operation

At present there seems to be no conclusive evidence that any one program is best for the mentally retarded. Most of the programs described in the literature fall into three common types of organization: the special room, the consultant service and the regular grade.

The program which seems most adequate for the larger school system is that of the homogeneous special class which has been grouped in some way for more efficient instruction. The class is generally located in a regular school where pupils are given many opportunities to participate in the activities of the school. The classes are generally limited in size from twelve to eighteen pupils per teacher.

Organization of a complete program, according to Kirk and Johnson [1, p. 218] * should include the following groups:

(a) The pre-school class for children under age six with mental ages between two and four. The purpose of the pre-school class is to develop mental and social abilities during the formative years.

(b) The primary class for children whose ages are six to nine or ten, with mental ages of three to six and a half. The purpose of the primary group is to continue social and mental development and to provide readiness activities.

(c) The intermediate class should consist of children of ages ten, eleven, twelve and possibly thirteen, depending upon their mental and social abilities. Mental ages will range from six through eight or nine years. In this group emphasis is placed upon social growth and the development of skills.

(d) The secondary class for ages thirteen through sixteen or eighteen

* Figures in brackets apply to references at end of article.

with mental ages of eight to twelve. The program is designed to teach social living with the emphasis on home, vocational and social efficiency.

(e) The post-school period is to provide the guidance and supervision necessary to the individual's adjustment to society.

While many schools have organized classes to accommodate the different age levels, few report the complete program suggested above.

The special school for the purpose of handling all retarded children in one building is becoming obsolete. The reasons are obvious when we consider the pupil's need for participation in activities with non-handicapped children.

The ungraded special class in which all ages from six to sixteen are enrolled may be the only solution possible in the smaller school system where there are not enough pupils to group chronologically. The teacher in this situation will usually find it advisable to group the pupils within the class.

Ellsworth [2, p. 177] and Melcher [3, p. 207] describe county coöperative plans for communities too small to support separate programs. This arrangement has the advantage of providing more efficient services by serving a larger area.

Some systems report success with the consultant program in which a trained person may be employed who will act as a consultant to regular classroom teachers who may have mentally retarded children in their classes. The consultant is responsible for helping the classroom teacher set up an educational program for the retarded pupil and suggesting materials and methods to facilitate his learning.

Other schools are attempting to make adjustments to accommodate the mentally retarded pupils in the regular classroom. This program may operate in a number of ways. Retarded pupils may be assigned to a special teacher for part of the day and then returned to regular classes for the remainder of the time, or the pupil may be assigned to a regular teacher who is interested in his problems with the size of the class reduced to allow time for more individual help. The retarded children are sometimes placed in a group of educationally retarded children or others who are not adjusting to their school situations and are given remedial help and individual attention.

Within each type of organization are found variations to meet local situations. An evaluation of the different plans cannot be attempted without considering the many factors that enter into the organization and administration of the programs.

## Advantages and Disadvantages of Each Type of Program

Considerable controversy has arisen over the problem of segregated classes versus regular classes for the mentally retarded. Many of the arguments are based upon the social and psychological effects of segregation and are generally the result of personal opinion and observation rather than research. At the 1946 convention of the International Council for Exceptional Children the question of segregation was the subject of a panel discussion. While none of the panel members offered any supporting evidence other than personal opinion and observation, Shattuck [4, p. 235] reports that the general opinion of the group was that it is best not to segregate an individual if he can receive as good or better training in a normal group even though it may be necessary to give special help. The exception is encountered when the detriment to the interests of the group outweighs the benefit derived by the individual from his association with the regular group.

Studies to determine the social effects of placement for the mentally retarded have been conducted by Johnson [5, p. 60] and Johnson and Kirk [6, p. 65]. Johnson, in his study of the status of mentally retarded pupils in a regular class, concluded that the mentally retarded pupils are isolated and rejected and that social segregation is quite complete. In the follow-up study by Johnson and Kirk they sought to determine whether the same pattern of isolation and rejection would be present in a progressive school where social development was emphasized. The results of the study showed that the pattern was very similar to the first study.

Johnson [5, p. 60] reports that studies comparing school achievement and social development of special-class mentally-retarded pupils with those in regular classes have been inconclusive. He states that while there is agreement between those who advocate segregation and those who oppose it that, in order for the child to make a satisfactory adjustment, the school environment must be adjusted to the child's physical and mental limitations. There is disagreement on how to carry out such a program.

Mullen [7, p. 224] describes a three year study now being conducted in the Chicago Public Schools with one of its purposes that of studying the effectiveness of special class organization. A comparison of the progress of the educable mentally retarded pupils in special classes with an equated group who remain in regular classes is expected to provide further information on the subject of class organization for the retarded.

Arguments offered in favor of special classes are:

(a) They serve both the needs and the abilities by offering a more functional curriculum.

(b) The special class teacher is trained to understand the problems of the exceptional child.

(c) Mentally retarded pupils have greater opportunities for success when they are placed with pupils who are nearer their own level.

(d) Special equipment and facilities not generally found in the regular classroom are needed to facilitate learning for the mentally retarded.

(e) The regular classroom teacher can handle a larger class if the retarded children are removed.

In regard to the consultant program the following points should be considered:

(a) The consultant can serve the small school that does not have enough pupils for a special class.

(b) The consultant can serve a greater number of pupils than the special class.

(c) The consultant can tutor, but cannot offer the special curriculum needed by the retarded child.

(d) The success of the program depends too much upon the ability of the consultant to sell the program to the rest of the school.

The argument commonly offered regarding the expense of the special class is minimized by Wallin [8, p. 88] who considers that repeating grades is an expensive practice and also contends that from the standpoint of social and vocational returns the special class represents an economic investment for society. Kirk and Johnson [1, p. 123] suggest that when mentally retarded children are kept in the regular classes the class size should be reduced to about half the ordinary number which is also an expensive practice.

Before any conclusions can be drawn regarding the most advantageous placement of the mentally retarded, further studies must be made in all areas of the education of the retarded child.

### Selection of Pupils

Great care must be taken to admit only those children for whom the special class was intended. The only way to avoid errors in placement is to require adequate examinations before placement is authorized and to establish and enforce definite admission standards.

Most of the studies in the field of selection advocate a procedure similar to the one suggested by Kelly and Stevens [9, p. 238] in which the teacher makes the initial evaluation in terms of group standards. The second step is a group intelligence test which should be carefully selected and administered. The classroom teacher may need assistance in the selection of the test and the interpretation of the results. The educational and cumulative records should provide information concerning the child's past performance. A case history of pertinent data in the child's background is also of value in making a diagnosis. If the findings on the tests corroborate the school record of educational maladjustment, an individual examination by a qualified psychologist or diagnostician is advised. The psychologist, with the help of all available data, should be the one to make the diagnosis and recommend the program that will best fit the needs of the child. Some states furnish statewide diagnostic services for small communities.

Most programs make use of a screening committee composed of specialized school personnel such as the psychologist, the nurse, the curriculum consultant, the principal, the visiting teacher, the teacher and other appropriate personnel whose purpose is to develop an educational plan for each pupil and to decide when pupils are ready to be returned to regular classes.

### Range of Programs

Several significant trends in the direction of extending special services have been noted. The primary and intermediate classes have been the ones most commonly established in the past. In recent years there has been an increasing tendency to extend provisions to include pre-school and secondary school programs and classes for the severely retarded pupils. Kirk [10, p. 692] and Sloan [11, p. 755] have experimented with pre-school mentally retarded children in an effort to determine the value of early education for the mentally retarded. Both studies report encouraging results, especially in the area of social maturity.

While the problem of the mentally retarded has long been a concern of the elementary school, it is becoming increasingly acute in the secondary school. The present upward trend in holding power of students and the general increase in school population has awakened schools to the need for extending the program upward. Hegge [12, p. 190] presents arguments for continuing the special classes into the high schools. He contends that many of the retarded children continue to grow after age sixteen; others mature to the point of making better use of their learning. Remaining in school provides the opportunity to cultivate new areas of interest. The very slowness of the mentally retarded indicates the need for more time to educate them.

Dawe [13, p. 692] points out that the junior high school program should seek to improve basic skills and provide practical situations for their use, and should provide pre-vocational information to prepare the student for the more definitive instruction he is to receive in high school.

The attempts of high schools to adapt instruction to the mentally retarded pupils consist of various practices. Connelly [14, p. 262] summarizes the procedures as:

(a) Some schools attempt to meet all needs in a heterogeneous class.

(b) Some, using records of past performance and results of systematic testing to identify slow learners, group pupils for instruction.

(c) The intellectually slow group may be assigned to special sections in academic subjects with the balance of the day spent in regular classes.

Connelly states that there is a slowly emerging trend for the mentally retarded pupils to be assigned to one teacher for the major portion of the school day where they are taught by highly individualized methods.

A number of high schools such as those described by Borreca and others [15, p. 50], Lovell and Ingram [16, p. 574], Martens [17, p. 77], Kelly [18, p. 193] and others report well organized classes where skill subjects are integrated into units of experience and social living.

The District of Columbia reports [19, p. 77] a tailoring of instruction and curriculum to fit discovered needs by offering a four-track program in the senior high schools. The retarded pupils follow a program known as the basic curriculum which is designed for students who are below sixth grade level in reading and arithmetic. The basic sequence may be followed to graduation if the pupil is unable to remove his educational deficiencies. This system allows the mentally retarded student to complete four years of high school education.

The organization of classes for the severely retarded has gained impetus in recent years as a result of pressure brought about by parent groups whose children have been excluded from school because of low ability. The parents and some educators argue that although the child may be considered uneducable, he may still be trainable in a practical sense and should therefore be helped by the school to realize his potential. Several states have recently accepted this broader definition of their responsibility and have passed legislation providing public school facilities for the lower groups.

A number of studies have been conducted in the effort to discover more efficient ways of handling classes for the severely retarded. In 1951 a survey was conducted by a committee of the National Association for Retarded Children [20, p. 357] in the effort to determine the status of day classes for the severely retarded throughout the nation. Results of the survey revealed that classes have been supported by parent groups, local school systems, with or without state subsidy, or by private individuals who charge tuition. Criteria for selection generally was that the child be ambulatory, toilet trained, see and hear, show some readiness for training and be reasonably free from anti-social behavior. In a survey conducted in 1953 [21] of the status of classes for the severely retarded, the superintendents of major cities of the United States were requested to describe provisions in their schools for children with IQ's under 50. The practices were found to be so varied that no summary was made. Nisonger [22, p. 335] concludes from the study made by the American Association on Mental Deficiency in 1954 on the status of community training facilities for children with severe mental retardation that the establishment of facilities is a movement with great force and that statewide programs are expanding rapidly. He reports also that there is considerable uncertainty in areas concerning programs, public school participation and financing, and administrative responsibility.

Hill [23, p. 61] advises that in view of the many problems that are involved in establishing classes for severely retarded children and the limited experiences that may be drawn upon in planning new services that it may be desirable that the public schools should venture slowly into this field of education. He also suggests that a limited number of pilot or experimental programs be developed.

## Curriculum for Special Classes

The curriculum for the special class has tended to be functional and to place emphasis upon serving present and future needs of the pupil. Martens [17, p. 12] states that the aims of special education require that curriculum emphasis be placed upon:

(a) education in keeping with the capacities, limitations and interests of each child,

(b) education for some participation in the world's work,

(c) education for healthful living and wholesome social experiences, and that the education be so planned that at the time that a pupil leaves school at the age of sixteen or eighteen he will have had the type of practical experiences needed to help him to live better as a citizen, worker and parent.

While many of the reports indicate a "watered down curriculum," another group tends definitely to depart from this practice. Stress on social adjustment is reflected in many reports. Borreca and others [15, p. 364] report on a workshop project in living, practiced in a New York program of occupational education. Kelly [18, p. 193] describes a project in family living for retarded girls. Reports by Boland [24, p. 11], Hegge [12, p. 190], Kirk and Johnson [1, p. 206], Lovell and Ingram [16, p. 474], Martens [17, p. 20] and numerous others describe the core program or experience areas as suitable for the mentally retarded pupils.

## Parent and Community Relations

The rôles of the parent and the community should not be overlooked in the planning of special education facilities. Acceptance of the program can not be expected without the understanding that comes as a result of parent and public education. Coleman [25, p. 700], Drewry [26, p. 495], Weingold [27, p. 484], Grebler [28, p. 475], Levy [29, p. 19] and others discuss the need for parent study groups as a part of the education program. Coleman [25, p. 700] describes a program which is quite typical of the parent group programs in which the emphasis is upon home and school activities. Motion pictures and talks by local authorities on various phases of child development help to acquaint the parents with various aspects of their problem. Discussions aid in correcting many misconceptions concerning mental retardation and help parents to develop a realistic attitude toward the child. Weingold [27, p. 484] discusses the trend of parent groups to take the initiative in developing services for their children in the areas of clinics, preschool kindergartens, coöperative classes, sheltered workshops, after-school social activities, research projects and scholarships, and better state schools.

## Conclusions

While there is an abundance of material describing practices in the education of the mentally retarded, there is a paucity of research that provides conclusive answers to the problems of special education. There seems to be general agreement on the philosophy, goals, curriculum and methods of special education. The procedures for screening and placement are generally uniform.

Considerable controversy exists in the areas of class organization, social and academic effects of segregation, and the age and ability range to be included in the school programs.

Only through continued study and research with the coöperation of all agencies in the fields of education, psychology, medicine and social agencies can we hope to resolve these points of controversy and achieve an adequate program for the mentally retarded.

## References

1. KIRK, SAMUEL and ORVILLE JOHNSON. *Educating the Retarded Child.* Massachusetts: Riverside Press (1951).

2. ELLSWORTH, SHERIDAN. "Every School Can Have Specialized Services Through the Intermediate Unit." *National Education Association Journal.* **45:**177 (March 1956).

3. MELCHER, JOHN W. and K. R. BLESSING. "Special Education for Rural Retarded Youth." *Exceptional Children.* **28:**207–210 (February 1957).

4. SHATTUCK, MARQUIS. "Segregation Versus Non-Segregation of Exceptional Children." *Journal of Exceptional Children.* **12:**235–240 (May 1946).

5. JOHNSON, G. ORVILLE. "A Study of Social Position of Mentally Handicapped Children in the Regular Grades." *American Journal of Mental Deficiency.* **55:**60–89 (July 1950).

6. JOHNSON, G. ORVILLE and SAMUEL KIRK. "Are Mentally Retarded Children Segregated in the Regular Grades?" *Exceptional Children.* **17:**65–68 (December 1950).

7. MULLEN, FRANCIS A. "How Mentally Handicapped Children Learn." *Exceptional Children.* **24:**224–226 (January 1958).

8. WALLIN, J. E. WALLACE. *Education of Mentally Handicapped Children.* New York, Harper (1955).

9. KELLY, ELIZABETH and HARVEY STEVENS. "Special Education for the Mentally Handicapped." Forty-Ninth Yearbook of the National Society for the Study of Education: *The Education of Exceptional Children.* Chicago: The University of Chicago Press (1950), pp. 237–257.

10. KIRK, SAMUEL. "Experiment in the Early Training of the Mentally Retarded." *American Journal of Mental Deficiency.* **56:**692–700 (April 1952).

11. SLOAN, WILLIAM. "Pre-School Classes at Lincoln State School and Colony." *American Journal of Mental Deficiency.* **56:**755–764 (April 1952).

12. HEGGE, THORLIEF. "Education for Mentally Retarded Pupils of Senior High Age." *American Journal of Mental Deficiency.* **54:**190–191 (October 1949).

13. DAWE, ANNE. "Trends Toward the Extension of Special Services for the

Educable Mentally Handicapped at the Junior High School Level." *American Journal of Mental Deficiency.* **61:**692–697 (April 1957).

14. CONNELLY, GEORGE W. "What Are the Secondary Schools Doing to Develop a Program for the Slow Learner?" *National Association of Secondary School Principal's Bulletin.* **40:**262–263 (April 1956).

15. BORRECA, FRANK *et al.* "A Workshop in Developing Lessons for Retarded Adolescents in a Program of Occupational Education." *American Journal of Mental Deficiency.* **55:**23–59 (July 1950).

16. LOVELL, CATHERINE and CHRISTINE INGRAM. "A High School Program for Retarded Girls." *Journal of Educational Research.* **40:**574–582 (April 1947).

17. MARTENS, ELISE. *Curriculum Adjustments for the Mentally Retarded.* Bulletin No. 2. Washington, D. C.: U. S. Office of Education, Federal Security Agency (1950).

18. KELLY, ELIZABETH. "A Family Living Course for Mentally Retarded Girls at Pre-Vocational School for Girls." *American Journal of Mental Deficiency.* **53:**193–198 (October 1948).

19. HANSEN, CARL F. "How Can the Schools Best Provide for the Slow Learner?" Summary of Presentation. Proceedings of the Forty-First Annual Convention. *National Association of Secondary School Principals' Bulletin.* **41:**77–81 (April 1957).

20. "Day Classes for Severely Retarded Children; A Report of the Education Committee of the National Association for Retarded Children." *American Journal of Mental Deficiency.* **58:**357–370 (January 1954).

21. SCHINNERER, MARK C. "Status of Classes for Mentally Retarded Children as Reported by Superintendents of Schools in Major Cities of the United States." (Mimeographed Report) 21 p. (December 17, 1953.)

22. NISONGER, HERSHEL W. "Status of Community Training Facilities for Children With Severe Mental Retardation," *American Journal of Mental Deficiency.* **59:**335–337 (October 1954).

23. HILL, ARTHUR. "Special Education Serves Them Too." *School Life.* pp. 55–61 (January 1952).

24. BOLAND, RUTH. "High School Pupils With IQ's Below 75." *Understanding the Child.* **16:**11–14 (January 1947).

25. COLEMAN, JAMES C. "Group Therapy With Parents of Mentally Deficient Children." *American Journal of Mental Deficiency.* **57:**700–704 (April 1953).

26. DREWRY, HENRY. "Information for Parents of Mentally Retarded Children

in New York City." *American Journal of Mental Deficiency*. **57**:495 (January 1953).

27. WEINGOLD, JOSEPH. "Parent Groups and Problems of the Mentally Retarded." *American Journal of Mental Deficiency*. **56**:484–492 (January 1952).

28. GREBLER, ANNIE MARIE. "Parent's Attitudes Toward Mentally Retarded Children." *American Journal of Mental Deficiency*. **56**:475–483 (January 1952).

29. LEVY, JOSEPH. "A Study of Parent Groups for Handicapped Children." *Exceptional Children*. **19–20**:19–26 (October 1952).

# 15

## A COMPARATIVE STUDY OF ACHIEVING AND UNDERACHIEVING HIGH SCHOOL BOYS OF HIGH INTELLECTUAL ABILITY *

### Edward Frankel

A problem of serious concern today is the shortage of highly trained and competent scientists. There simply aren't enough of them to keep pace with needs in research and development. Moreover, this is true not only in scientific fields but in many others where scholarly competence and achievement are needed. The schools and colleges constitute by far the greatest source of trained manpower. It is a fact that many of our most intellectually capable students do not achieve in school what their measured capacity indicates they could, nor what other equally competent classmates do achieve. These so-called non-achievers represent a loss in that they could do much better. The reasons for such underachievement have not been clearly and unequivocally identified, although a good deal of research has been done on the question. In the study reported here two groups of very bright senior boys in a large city high school, matched on I.Q., entrance examination scores, and age, were chosen. The groups differed significantly in that one had a much higher record of achievement than the other. The author then compared these two groups on other criteria such as interests, personal problems, family background and the like. Some interesting differences were found which may help explain some of the differences in scholarship.

*Questions:*

1. Some students of this problem feel that there is little the school can do to change an underachiever to an achiever. What arguments, pro and con, with reference to this viewpoint, can you think of? Can you cite any evidence?

2. Are there any sex differences with respect to underachieving? Evidence?

*   *   *

This study was concerned with scholastic underachievement among intellectually superior high school students. The ever-broadening spectrum of

* Reprinted from the *Journal of Educational Research,* **53:**172–180 (January 1960), by permission of author and Dembar Publications, Inc.

our scientific and technological progress, from the harnessing of atomic energy to the conquest of outer space, has placed a special premium on talent and brainpower in all areas of human thought and endeavor. The young people whose scholastic performance lags far behind their intellectual ability represent a serious loss to society in terms of their potential contributions. In addition, failure to achieve at the level of their ability often leads to a depreciation of self-worth accompanied by unhappiness and frustration.

## Design of the Experiment

The purpose of this study was to find some answers to the general question, "Why do students of seemingly similar high intellectual ability perform so differently academically?" This investigation proposed to study achieving and underachieving boys of the same high intellectual ability to determine possible causes for the differences in their academic performance. The areas explored for possible significant differences between the two groups were: (1) aptitudes, (2) interests, (3) personal problems, (4) health, (5) home and family background, (6) socio-economic status, (7) reaction to school subjects, (8) reaction to school, (9) out-of-school activities, (10) vocational and college planning and (11) academic performance in junior high school.

### Instruments

The following instruments were used for gathering data related to each of these eleven areas: (a) Differential Aptitude Tests, (b) Kuder Vocational Preference Record, (c) Mooney Problem Check List, (d) school record, (e) a Student Questionnaire of 39 items prepared by the investigator, and (f) the Hamburger Scale for rating socio-economic class.

### The Experimental Group

The subjects participating in this study were selected from the male population of the senior class of June, 1957 at the Bronx High School of Science in New York City. The experimental group consisted of fifty pairs of boys, each pair composed of an achiever and an underachiever matched on the basis of equivalent I. Q., school entrance examination score, and age.

### Definition of Terms

Achiever was defined as a student in the top or first quartile of his class with a scholastic average of at least 89 per cent for the tenth and eleventh years. Underachiever was defined as a student in lowest or fourth quartile of the same class with a scholastic average of 79 per cent or less.

## Academic Environment of the Study

The study was limited to the Bronx High School of Science because not only was it an ideal source of high ability subjects for this study but also because the investigator has been a teacher and guidance counselor at the school since 1940. The school, which came into being in 1938, was designed to meet the needs of high ability students interested in science and mathematics. The school population is about 2400, one third of whom are girls. About 800 students are admitted annually, 150 from the elementary schools to the ninth year and 650 from the junior high schools to the tenth year. About 98 per cent of those who are graduated from the school enter college. The school has been described by Wolfle "as being the outstanding exception in this country in providing stimulation and training for bright youngsters with scientific interests."

About four to five times as many students as can be accommodated apply for admission to the school. A program for selecting students has evolved which includes a written examination administered at the school. It is an objective test consisting of two parts: (a) English, which includes reading comprehension and vocabulary, and (b) arithmetic. Ninety minutes are allowed for the entire test.

The curriculum of the school aims to prepare students of high ability to meet the admission requirements of liberal arts colleges as well as engineering and technical schools. The subjects are those usually offered in an academic high school. However, the curriculum is enriched by and supplemented with a broad program of elective courses in science and mathematics. In addition, opportunities for acceleration and advanced study are possible by offerings of college-level courses in English, mathematics, biology, chemistry, and physics.

## Selection of the Experimental Group

### Criteria for Selection

In matching an achiever with an underachiever, a maximum difference of five points in I.Q., five points in school entrance examination score, and twelve months in age, were used as a basis for obtaining equivalent groups.

The scholastic average which was used to define achiever and underachiever was obtained by calculating the mathematical average of the final grades received in all major subjects during the tenth and eleventh year. Ninth year subjects were not included in the calculations since eighty percent of the class were in junior high school during that year. Since one of the constant factors in this study was the school environment, marks received in other schools where differences in standards and marking systems might exist, would tend to introduce a variable not included in this study. To obtain equivalent groups optimally matched, only white boys were selected for this study. In addition, ninth grade entrants were matched only with ninth grade entrants, and those who came from junior high school and entered school in the tenth grade were matched with tenth grade entrants.

### Testing Criteria by Preliminary Study:

In May, 1956, a preliminary study, involving the class of June, 1956, was undertaken to test the criteria. It was found that forty-two pairs of boys could be matched, using the criteria selected.

### Criteria Characteristics of the Experimental Group:

In September, 1956, using the criteria established for matching, it was possible to select a maximum of fifty pairs of boys from the class of June, 1957, which had a male population of 468. (Table I)

The t-values for I.Q., entrance examination, score, and age indicated that there were no significant differences between the two groups for these

**Table I**

**A Comparison of Criteria for the Experimental Group: Fifty Pairs of Achieving and Underachieving Boys Selected from the Class of June, 1957**

| Criteria | Group [a] | Mean | S.D.[b] | Range | t-Value |
|---|---|---|---|---|---|
| Intelligence | A | 140.66 | 12.05 | 114–164 | |
| Quotient | U | 141.00 | 11.79 | 115–164 | 0.80 |
| Entrance Exam. | A | 161.70 | 13.60 | 137–190 | |
| Test Score | U | 161.80 | 12.27 | 142–187 | 0.21 |
| Age in Years | A | 17.00 | 0.60 | 16.00–18.34 | |
| | U | 17.00 | 0.55 | 15.83–18.34 | 0.03 |
| Scholastic | A | 91.24 | 1.69 | 89.0–96.2 | |
| Average | U | 74.13 | 4.07 | 59.0–79.5 | 23.76** |

[a] The letters "A" and "U" are used to identify the achievers and underachievers respectively.
[b] Standard Deviation.
** Significant at and beyond the .01 level.

criteria. On the other hand, the t-value of 23.76 for scholastic average clearly showed that the groups were significantly different in academic achievement, the mean difference being 17.1, with a minimum of 9.5 and a maximum of 37.2.

The entrance examination test score is a composite of the English and the arithmetic parts. In order to avoid inequalities in matching which might be masked by the composite score, the two groups were compared for the English and arithmetic scores separately. No significant differences were found between the two groups in English and arithmetic parts of the entrance examination. The two groups were matched not only for the composite entrance score but also for the English and arithmetic parts.

## Findings

*Aptitudes:*

The results which were obtained by the fifty pairs of boys on the four Differential Aptitude Tests which were administered in October, 1956, are shown in Table II.

### Table II
### Results of DAT Battery Taken by Experimental Group

| DAT Test | Group | Mean | S.D. | Range | t-Value |
|----------|-------|------|------|-------|---------|
| Space | A | 61.48 | 16.73 | 28–92 | |
| Relations | U | 62.93 | 18.90 | 26–99 | 0.43 |
| Abstract | A | 40.16 | 4.44 | 25–47 | |
| Reasoning | U | 39.36 | 4.86 | 25–46 | 0.75 |
| Verbal | A | 42.40 | 4.66 | 29–49 | |
| Reasoning | U | 39.85 | 4.98 | 31–50 | 2.83** |
| Numerical | A | 35.54 | 2.75 | 28.75–40.00 | |
| Ability | U | 31.95 | 4.48 | 16.00–37.50 | 5.15** |

** Significant at and beyond the .01 level.

The Numerical Ability test discriminated most sharply between the two groups with a highly significant t-value of 5.15. The achievers were definitely superior in their ability to understand numerical relationships and in handling numerical concepts.

In addition, the achievers showed definite superiority in Verbal Reasoning, the ability to understand concepts framed in words, the t-value being 2.83. Together these two tests are regarded as a measure of general learning ability. The Space Relations and the Abstract Reasoning tests revealed no significant differences between the groups.

The results of the Scholastic Aptitude Tests for May, 1956 and January, 1957 and the Scholarship Qualifying Tests for April, 1956, which half the subjects had taken, substantiated the DAT findings. The achievers showed significantly greater aptitudes than the underachievers in the verbal and mathematic areas.

*Interests:*

A comparison of the interests of the two groups as measured by the Kuder Vocational Preference Record administered in October, 1956 revealed the data shown in Table III.

### Table III

**Comparison of Areas of Interest of Experimental Group as Measured by the Kuder Vocational Preference Test**

| Area of Interest | Group | Mean | S.D. | Range | t-Value |
|---|---|---|---|---|---|
| Outdoor | A | 41.08 | 14.78 | 11–69 | |
| | U | 40.04 | 16.88 | 8–68 | 0.31 |
| Mechanical | A | 35.58 | 15.51 | 2–66 | |
| | U | 43.42 | 12.19 | 11–63 | 3.18** |
| Computational | A | 33.26 | 9.42 | 11–50 | |
| | U | 29.00 | 8.47 | 15–50 | 2.39** |
| Scientific | A | 54.76 | 12.50 | 20–70 | |
| | U | 45.64 | 13.60 | 15–66 | 3.01** |
| Persuasive | A | 38.20 | 13.41 | 11–69 | |
| | U | 42.84 | 13.40 | 21–72 | 1.88 |
| Artistic | A | 20.38 | 9.19 | 6–42 | |
| | U | 24.88 | 11.38 | 7–48 | 2.08* |
| Literary | A | 24.78 | 8.69 | 6–39 | |
| | U | 22.96 | 7.83 | 4–36 | 1.32 |
| Musical | A | 13.04 | 6.06 | 4–25 | |
| | U | 11.12 | 7.81 | 3–29 | 1.29 |
| Social Service | A | 38.94 | 12.70 | 18–71 | |
| | U | 34.92 | 13.29 | 12–62 | 1.55 |
| Clerical | A | 41.04 | 14.74 | 14–77 | |
| | U | 42.18 | 12.97 | 16–80 | 0.39 |

** Significant at and beyond the .01 level.
* Significant at and beyond the .05 level.

The interests of the U's were significantly greater in the mechanical area whereas those of the A's were in the scientific, the t-values being significant at the .01 level, 3.18 for the former and 3.01 for the latter. In addition, the A's were more interested in the computational and the U's in the artistic, the t-values being significant at the .05 level. The other six areas showed no significant differences.

*Personal Problems:*

The Mooney Problem Check List, administered in September, 1956, which was used as a measure of the personal problems of the two groups, showed no statistically significant difference in the total number of problems underscored although the A's underscored 723 and the U's 906 problems. An analysis by areas of the number of problems underscored is shown in Table IV.

"School" was the only area in which the U's presented significantly more problems than the A's. There were no significant differences in the other six areas.

Of the 210 items of the Mooney, differences in the frequency of responses of the A's and U's significant at and beyond the .05 level occurred

**Table IV**

**Distribution of Problems by Areas Underscored on the Mooney Problem Check List by Achieving and Underachieving Boys**

| Area | Group | Mean | S.D. | Range | t-Value |
|---|---|---|---|---|---|
| Health and Physical | A | 2.22 | 2.03 | 0–9 | |
| Development | U | 1.84 | 1.85 | 0–7 | 0.89 |
| School | A | 1.64 | 1.75 | 0–7 | |
| | U | 5.28 | 3.14 | 0–14 | 6.62** |
| Home and Family | A | 1.74 | 2.60 | 0–12 | |
| | U | 1.88 | 2.63 | 0–12 | 0.21 |
| Money, Work and | A | 3.32 | 2.94 | 0–15 | |
| Future | U | 3.30 | 2.75 | 0–11 | 0.04 |
| Boy-Girl Relations | A | 1.96 | 2.56 | 0–13 | |
| | U | 1.88 | 2.43 | 0–11 | 0.16 |
| Relations to People | A | 1.30 | 1.51 | 0–5 | |
| | U | 1.46 | 2.41 | 0–11 | 0.42 |
| Self-Centered Concerns | A | 2.28 | 2.46 | 0–12 | |
| | U | 2.50 | 2.85 | 0–12 | 0.46 |

** Significant at and beyond the .01 level.

for only ten items. Of these, nine were underscored by significantly more U's than A's. Eight of these were concerned with "School" and the other one was "being stubborn." "Family Quarrels" was the only item selected by more A's than U's. In answer to the free question "What problems are troubling you most?", the U's reiterated their concern with school and marks, whereas the A's were interested chiefly in the choice of college and vocation.

### Health

The information gathered by the Student Questionnaire regarding health showed no differences between the two groups in weight, height, hearing, speech, general state of health, and physical disabilities. The U's, however, reported significantly more days absent from school for health reasons, the t-values being 2.34. The A's, on the other hand, registered significantly more health complaints, chiefly acne and allergies; the t-value being 2.47.

### Family and Home Background

Questionnaire responses indicated no differences between the two groups with respect to (a) number of rooms in the home, (b) number of people living at home, (c) size of family, (d) number of disrupted family patterns, and (e) birth order of the subjects. Differences were found, however, in the education and occupation of the parents. Using the Edward's Scale for the classification of occupations, more of the fathers of the A's than U's were found in the top three groups—(1) professional, (2) semi-professional, and (3) proprietors, managers, and officials. With respect to number of years of schooling completed by parents of the two groups, it was found that the fathers of the A's had significantly more formal education than the mothers, the t-value being 2.33. No significant difference between the fathers and mothers of the U's in this respect was found; they had about the same amount of formal education. Significantly more working mothers were reported by the U's than A's, twenty-nine to seventeen, the chi-square value for the difference being 6.43 which is significant at and beyond the .05 level. More of the mothers of the U's than A's were in the lower three occupational groups. Almost two-thirds of them were typists, bookkeepers, secretaries, and saleswomen.

### Socio-Economic Status

Using the Hamburger Scale for determining socio-economic level, the A's came from families which were rated significantly higher than those of the U's.

## Reaction to School Subjects

In response to the Questionnaire items requiring the groups to name the major school subjects (a) liked best, (b) found easiest, (c) liked least, and (d) found most difficult, the following reactions were gleaned: The A's ranked mathematics as the easiest, and mathematics and science as the best liked, English as the most difficult and least liked. The underachievers, on the other hand, selected science as the easiest and best liked subject, and foreign language as the most difficult and least liked. Significantly more A's than U's selected mathematics as the easiest and best liked subject, and English as the most difficult. In contrast, the U's chose science as the easiest and mathematics as the most difficult school subject.

## Reaction to School

The criteria selected to measure reaction of the two groups to school were (a) attendance, (b) deportment, (c) participation in extra-curricular activities. These data were obtained from official school records: According to official attendance records, the U's were absent from school significantly more often than the A's, the t-value being 3.58, significant at the .01 level. School discipline records showed about four times as many offenses recorded against U's than A's, the t-value being 4.07, significant at and beyond the .01 level. With respect to extracurricular activities, the A's engaged in significantly more, the t-value being 5.35, significant at the .01 level. Twelve U's had records of no extracurricular activities. The A's engaged significantly more frequently in student government and publications, in science and mathematics clubs, and in the Social Studies club.

## Out-of-School and Leisure Time Activities:

The U's belong to significantly more athletic and social clubs and were somewhat more interested in the Scout movement. Insofar as leisure time activities were concerned the A's tended to spend more time reading whereas the U's were more interested in shop-work activities.

## Vocational and College Planning

Questionnaire responses with respect to vocational planning are shown in Table V. Significantly more A's planned to enter general fields of science such as mathematics, biology, chemistry and physics. The U's, in contrast, tended more in the direction of applied sciences and technical fields. Responses to a Guidance Committee questionnaire, in June, 1957, at the time of graduation, dealing with the choice of college program appear in Table VI.

Significantly more A's than U's planned to follow a liberal arts college program majoring in science, whereas more U's than A's expected to enter non-science fields such as business administration, accountancy, and the

### Table V

**Vocational Choices of Achievers and Underachievers**

| Group | Scientific | | Non Scientific | Undecided |
| | Technical | General | | |
|---|---|---|---|---|
| A | 14 | 22 | 0 | 14 |
| U | 22 | 9 | 4 | 15 |
| Chi-square | 1.36 | 4.64* | 2.25 | 0 |

\* Significant at and beyond the .05 level.

### Table VI

**Choice of College Program by the Experimental Group**

| Group | Technical | Liberal Arts | | Non-Liberal Arts | Undecided |
| | | Science | Non-Science | | |
|---|---|---|---|---|---|
| A | 14 | 27 | 5 | 0 | 4 |
| U | 18 | 12 | 7 | 8 | 5 |
| Chi-square | 1.47 | 5.03* | 0.08 | 6.13* | 0 |

\* Significant at and beyond the .05 level.

like. Of those who were undecided, as seen in Table V, more U's than A's selected non-science fields.

The Questionnaire also revealed that more U's than A's, as evidenced by the chi-square value of 4.11, significant at the .05 level, expected their parents to finance completely their college education.

### Junior High School Record

The records of forty-three pairs of boys who entered the school in the tenth year from junior high school were studied to determine whether their pattern of academic achievement was developed in the senior high school or had previously been established in the junior high school. It was found that twenty-eight achievers and thirty underachievers had been regarded as intellectually gifted and had been placed in Special Progress (S. P.) classes which had completed the three years of junior high school in two years.

In addition, the results of the reading and arithmetic achievement tests, which had been taken in the ninth year of junior high school, attested to their superiority. The Stanford Reading Test showed no differences between the groups. Approximately one third of each group made perfect scores and practically the entire group made grade equivalent scores above 10.0, a value derived by extrapolation. The mean grade equivalent score for the entire group was approximately 11 plus. On the other hand, on the New York Arithmetic Test, the equivalent scores of the A's was higher than

### Table VII

**Scholastic Average for the Ninth Year of Junior High School of Forty-Three Pairs of Achievers and Underachievers**

| Group | Mean | S.D. | Range | t-Value |
|-------|------|------|-------|---------|
| A | 90.98 | 3.00 | 97.00–84.00 | |
| U | 82.44 | 5.08 | 91.20–71.00 | 10.33** |

** Significant at and beyond the .01 level.

those of the U's, the t-value being 3.12, significant at the .01 level. Nine A's made perfect scores, and practically the entire group scoring above 9.4 also derived by extrapolation. The mean grade equivalent score of the A's was 11.59 and that of the U's was 10.84.

A comparison of the school grades received by the two groups in the ninth year of junior high school showed results set down in Table VII.

The scholastic record of the two groups for the ninth year indicated that they were performing distinctly differently. Three-quarters of the A's attained averages of 89 per cent or better, the lowest being 84. Half of the U's earned less than 80 per cent, fifteen were between 80 and 84, and only four were above 89 per cent. Three quarters of the U's had averages of less than 84 per cent.

## Conclusions

### 1. Aptitudes

Although the pairs were matched for equivalent I. Q. and school entrance examination, the achievers proved to be distinctly superior to the underachievers in mathematical and verbal aptitudes, particularly in the former.

## 2. Interests

The interest patterns of the two groups were distinctly different. The interests of the achievers were greater in mathematics and science whereas those of the underachievers were in the mechanical and artistic areas.

## 3. Personal Problems

While the chief concern of the underachiever appeared to be his present scholastic inadequacies, the achiever's was primarily thinking about the future, college and vocational choices.

## 4. Health

Although the U's reported twice as many days absent from school for health reasons, and official attendance records disclosed that the U's were absent from school significantly more frequently, they registered fewer specific health complaints on the Student Questionnaire, and underscored fewer items in the Health and Physical Development area of the Mooney. No evidence was found to lead one to believe that the two groups differed significantly in health. It seemed likely that the more frequent absence from school for health reasons reported by the U's might not necessarily have been the result of physical illness.

## 5. Home and Family Background

Although the physical aspects of the families of the two groups were very much alike, significant differences in the education and occupation of the parents existed. More of the fathers of the A's were in the top three occupational groups and they had more formal schooling than their wives. More of the mothers of the U's were working and they had at least as much schooling as their husbands.

## 6. Socio-Economic Status

As expected, the families of the A's were rated higher on the Hamburger Socio-Economic scale.

## 7. Reaction to School Subjects

The selection by the achievers of mathematics as the easiest, and science and mathematics as the best liked school subjects, was probably a reflection of their superior aptitude and greater interest in these areas. Similarly, the distaste of the U's for mathematics mirrored the difficulty which they had with this subject.

The negative reactions of the A's to English might be an expression of their science-mathematics preference. The selection of science as the easiest and best liked subject by the U's might be explained by the fact that the sciences with their concomitant laboratory opportunities offered an outlet for their mechanical interests.

## 8. Reaction to School

It was not surprising to find that the U's evidenced negative attitudes toward school, the major source of their personal problems, in terms of poorer attendance records, more recorded disciplinary offenses, and participation in fewer extra-curricular activities. In general, the U's were more recalcitrant, less conforming, and less happy at school. The achievers, in contrast, were more conforming, rarely broke school regulations, participated in more school activities, and assumed positions of leadership and responsibility.

## 9. Out-of-School and Leisure Activities

The greater participation of the U's in out-of-school organizations such as social and athletic clubs, and the Scouts, may have been a substitute for school activities.

## 10. Vocational and College Planning

The achievers appeared to regard college as preparatory for a career in science with the expectation of going on to graduate school for specialization. The underachievers tended to think of college in terms of direct vocational preparation; those going into the sciences were planning careers in applied and technical fields. However, a substantial number of U's planned to prepare for and enter non-science fields.

## 11. Junior High School Academic Performance

Notwithstanding the superior intellectual ability of the two groups, the ninth year junior high school record left little doubt that the two groups performed differently in terms of academic achievement. In general, the achievers maintained their high scholastic record while the performance of the underachievers deteriorated. The difference in the mean scholastic average of the two groups was twice as great in high school as in junior high school. It appeared probable that the factors relating to scholastic underachievement of this group may have been operating before these students entered the high school.

## References

I.  Books

1.  BRANDWEIN, PAUL F. *The Gifted Student as Future Scientist.* New York: Harcourt, Brace and Company, 1955.

2.  BRAY, DOUGLASS WESTON. *Issues in the Study of Talent.* New York: King's Press, Columbia University, 1954.

3.  COLE, CHARLES C., JR. *Encouraging Scientific Talent.* New York: College Entrance Board, 1956.

4.  HAVIGHURST, R. J., E. STIVERS, and R. F. DE HAAS. *A Survey of the Education of Gifted Children.* University of Chicago Press, November 1955.

5.  ROE, ANNE. *The Making of a Scientist.* New York: Dodd, Mead and Company, 1953.

6.  TERMAN, LEWIS and M. H. ODEN. *The Gifted Child Grows Up. Genetic Study of Genius, Vol. IV.* Stanford: Stanford University Press, 1947.

7.  WITTY, PAUL (ed.). *The Gifted Child.* New York: Heath and Company, 1951.

II.  Periodicals

1.  ARMSTRONG, MARION E. *A Comparison of the Interests and Social Adjustments of the Under-Achievers at the Secondary School Level,* Doctor's Thesis, University of Connecticut, 1955.

2.  BEASLEY, JANE. *Underachievement: Review of Literature.* Teachers' College, Columbia University (mimeographed) (March 1957).

3.  GOWAN, JOHN C. "The Under Achieving Gifted Child." *Exceptional Children.* **XXI**:247–249 (April 1955).

4.  GOWAN, JOHN C. *Underachievement of Gifted Children.* Los Angeles State College (mimeographed).

5.  GOUGH, HARRISON G. "Factors Related to the Academic Achievement of High School Students." *Journal of Educational Research.* **XL**:65–78 (1949).

6.  "Potential Use of Personality Tests in School and Colleges." *Fifth Annual Western Regional Conference on Testing Problems.* (April 13, 1956) Los Angeles: Educational Testing Service, pp. 2–19.

7.  HAMBURGER, MARTIN. *A Revised Occupational Scale for Rating Socio-*

*Economic Class.* Teachers' College, Columbia University (mimeographed) (May 1957).

8. HIERONYMUS, A. N. "A Study of Social Class Motivation: Relationship Between Anxiety for Education and Certain Socio-Economic and Intellectual Variables." *Journal of Educational Psychology.* **XLII:**193–205 (1951).

9. KIMBALL, B. "Completion Technique in a Study of Scholastic Underachievement." *Journal of Consulting Psychology.* **XVI:**353–358 (October 1952).

10. LAYTON, E. T. *A Study of the Factors Associated with Failure in the Ninth Grade at Hempstead High School.* Doctor's Thesis, New York University (1951).

11. MacCURDY, ROBERT D. *Characteristics of Superior Science Students and Some Factors that Were Found in Their Background.* Doctor's Thesis, Boston University (1954).

12. MacCURDY, ROBERT D. "Characteristics of Superior Science Students and Their Own Sub-Groups." *Science Education.* **XL:**3–24 (February, 1956).

13. MALPASS, L. F. "Some Relationships Between Students' Perception of School and Their Achievement." *Journal of Educational Psychology.* **XLIV:**475–482 (December 1953).

14. McQUARY, JOHN P. "Some Relationships Between Non-Intellectual Characteristics and Academic Achievement." *Journal of Educational Psychology.* **XLIV:**215–228 (April 1953).

15. MORGAN, H. H. "A Psychometric Comparison of Achieving and Non-Achieving College Students of High Ability." *Journal of Consulting Psychology.* **XVI:**292–298 (August 1952).

16. NASON, LESLIE J. *Patterns of Circumstances Related to Education Achievement of High School Pupils of Superior Ability.* Unpublished Ph.D. Thesis, University of Southern California (1954).

17. Portland Public Schools. *A Report Summarizing Four Years of Progress by the Cooperative Program for Students of Exceptional Talent.* Portland, Oregon (mimeographed) (March 1957).

18. RATCHICK, IRVING. *Achievement and Capacity; Study of Pupils with Low Achievement and High Intelligence Quotient with Pupils of High Achievement and High Intelligence Quotients in a Selected New York City High School.* Doctor's Thesis, New York University (1953).

19. RICCIUTI, N. N. and ROBERT SADACCA. *The Production of Academic Grades With a Projective Test of Achievement Motivation: II Gross Validation at the High School Level.* Princeton: Educational Testing Service (June 6, 1955).

20. ROE, ANNE. "A Psychologist Examines Sixty-Four Eminent Scientists." *Scientific American,* CLXXXVII, No. 5 (November 1952), 21–25.

21. Talented Youth Project, *Student Attitude Toward School Inventory.* Evanston, Illinois, Horace-Mann-Lincoln Institute of School Experimentation, Teachers' College, Columbia University (May 13, 1957).

22. TERMAN, LEWIS. "The Discovery and Encouragement of Exceptional Talent." *American Psychologist.* **IX:**221–230 (June 1954).

23. WOLFLE, DAEL. "Intellectual Resources." *Scientific American.* CLXXXV: **2:**42–46 (September 1951).

# 16

## AGE AND ACHIEVEMENT

### Harvey C. Lehman

The question of the relationship of age to achievement is of perennial interest. It is an established fact that mental and physical growth proceeds to maturity, usually considered to be attained by the late teens or early twenties. But what happens after that? Does the individual continue to increase in power and ability? When is the peak of achievement attained? As one grows older his powers begin to decline. This is most obvious in physical strength and endurance, as in athletics. There are few athletes over forty and most of them are in their twenties or early thirties. When does intellectual decline begin? Very old people often become senile. This does not happen suddenly but is the culmination of a long process of "slowing up." Dr. Lehman has devoted many years to the investigation of this question. As subjects he has used eminent men in many different fields of accomplishment. From history, biographies and other sources he has determined the ages at which such persons made their maximum achievements and has followed the course of their production in most cases to the end. The selection which follows is the concluding chapter of a detailed summary of Dr. Lehman's findings from many years of investigation.

*Questions:*

1. Do the findings reported here have any relevance to provisions for education of gifted children? Explain.

2. The outstanding exception to the general trend of the results of these studies occurs with political leaders. Dr. Lehman gives five possible reasons for this. Do all of them appear reasonable to you? If not, why not? Can you think of others?

\* \* \*

### Summary and Interpretation

By means of statistical distributions and graphs the preceding chapters show the ages (1) at which outstanding thinkers have most frequently made

\* Reprinted from *American Philosophical Society Memoirs,* chapter 20 (1953), p. 324–331, by permission of author and publisher.

(or first published) their momentous creative contributions, (2) at which leaders have most often attained important positions of leadership, and (3) at which high-salaried workers in several areas have most commonly received large annual incomes. A few data for professional athletes are included to show their similarity to the other findings.

The creative thinkers and the leaders whose lives were studied are mostly deceased persons. Because adequate data were not available for deceased recipients of large annual incomes and deceased athletes, living persons who fall in these two categories were studied. For all groups investigated proper statistical allowance was made for the fact that young men are more numerous than older ones.

Because dates of first publication rather than dates of actual achievement were usually available, the only thing that can be asserted with certainty is the fact that, as regards their most profound insights, our creative workers attained their highest average rate of productivity *not later than* certain specified age levels.

The most notable creative works of scientists and mathematicians were identified by experts in the various specialized fields of endeavor. For such fields as oil painting, education, philosophy, and literature, a consensus of the experts was obtained by a study of their published writings. In each field listed below the maximum average rate of highly superior production was found to occur not later than during the specified range of ages. For example, item 1 of this list, chemistry, 26–30, is to be interpreted as follows: in proportion to the number of chemists that were alive at each successive age level, very superior contributions to the field of chemistry were made at the greatest average rate when the chemists were not more than 26–30. The remaining items here and those in the tabular lists that follow are to be interpreted in similar manner.

| *Physical Sciences, Mathematics, and Inventions.* | *Biological Sciences.* |
|---|---|
| 1. Chemistry, 26–30 | 9. Botany, 30–34 |
| 2. Mathematics, 30–34 | 10. Classical descriptions of Disease, 30–34 |
| 3. Physics, 30–34 | 11. Genetics, 30–39 |
| 4. Electronics, 30–34 | 12. Entomology, 30–39 |
| 5. Practical Inventions, 30–34 | 13. Psychology, 30–39 |
| 6. Surgical Techniques, 30–39 | 14. Bacteriology, 35–39 |
| 7. Geology, 35–39 | 15. Physiology, 35–39 |
| 8. Astronomy, 35–39 | 16. Pathology, 35–39 |
| | 17. Medical Discoveries, 35–39 |

In this, and in succeeding tabulations, very precise cross comparisons should not be attempted because the maximum ages vary somewhat both with the era during which the workers were born and also with the quality of the output under consideration, and it was not possible to equate all these different kinds of contributions upon both these bases.

For most types of superior music, the maximum average rate of good production is likely to occur in the thirties. Here are the maxima.

18. Instrumental selections, 25–29
19. Vocal solos, 30–34
20. Symphonies, 30–34
21. Chamber music, 35–39
22. Orchestral music, 35–39
23. Grand Opera, 35–39
24. Cantatas, 40–44
25. Light Opera and Musical Comedy, 40–44

For the study of literary creativity, fifty well-known histories of English literature were canvassed. The works most often cited by the fifty literary historians were assumed to be superior to those cited infrequently. Best-liked short stories were identified similarly by use of 102 source books, and "best books" were ascertained by study of a collation of fifty "best book" lists. As is revealed by the following tabulation, literary works that are good and permanently great are produced at the highest average rate by persons who are not over 45 years old. It is clear also that most types of poetry show maxima 10 to 15 years earlier than most prose writings other than short stories.

26. German Composers of Note-worthy Lyrics and Ballads, 22–26
27. Odes, 24–28
28. Elegies, 25–29
29. Pastoral Poetry, 25–29
30. Narrative Poetry, 25–29
31. Sonnets, 26–31
32. Lyric Poetry, 26–31
33. Satiric Poetry, 30–34
34. Short stories, 30–34
35. Religious Poetry (Hymns), 32–36
36. Comedies, 32–36
37. Tragedies, 34–38
38. "Most Influential Books," 35–39
39. Hymns by Women, 36–38
40. Novels, 40–44
41. "Best Books," 40–44
42. Best Sellers, 40–44
43. Miscellaneous Prose Writings, 41–45

Fifty histories of philosophy, 49 histories of education, and 20 books dealing with the history of economics and political science were examined and the following maxima were obtained.

44. Logic, 35–39
45. Ethics, 35–39
46. Aesthetics, 35–39
47. "General" Philosophy, 35–39
48. Social Philosophy, 36–44
49. Metaphysics, 40–44
50. Contributions to Educational Theory and Practice, 35–39
51. Contributions to Economics and Political Science, 30–39

Although the maximum average rate of output of the most important philosophical books occured at 35–39, the total range for best production extended from 22–80, and for mere quantity of output—good, bad, and indifferent—the production rate was almost constant from 30–70.

In the body of this book mean ages, median ages, and modal ages are all set forth, but here in this summary, in order to save space, only modal ages are listed. Sixty books which contain lists of so-called "master paintings," one book on American sculpture, and one book on modern architecture yielded the following maxima.

52. Oil Paintings, 32–36
53. American Sculpture, 35–39
54. Modern Architecture, 40–44
55. Oil Paintings by Contemporary Artists, 40–44

Chapter 12 shows that a very large proportion of the most renowned men of science and the humanities did their first important work before 25, and that in general the earlier starters contributed better work and were more prolific than were the slow starters. In chapters 12 and 13 more than one hundred examples of outstanding creative achievements by youths not over 21 are described briefly. To avoid giving the false impression that *only* the young can do great things (Goethe's remark to Eckermann) . . . numerous outstanding accomplishments at advanced ages [have been cited].

For most types of creative work the following generalizations have been derived. Within any given field of creative endeavor: (1) the maximum production rate for output of highest quality usually occurs at an earlier age than the maximum rate for less distinguished works by the same individuals; (2) the rate of good production usually does not change much in the middle years and the decline, when it comes, is gradual at all the older ages—much more gradual than its onset in the late teens or early twenties; (3) production of highest quality tends to fall off not only at an earlier age but also at a more rapid rate than does output of lesser merit; and because the statistical distributions of age for the highest quality of work are skewed toward the older age levels, both the mean and the median ages are higher than the modal values.

The first item in the following list of high-salaried workers shows that, when taken in relation to the total population alive at successive age levels, leading movie actors attain their greatest box-office popularity not later than 30–34.

56. Movie Actors who are "best-money makers," 30–34
57. Movie Actresses who are "best money-makers," 23–27
58. "Best" Movie Directors, 35–39
59. Receivers of "Earned" Annual Incomes of $50,000 or more, 60–64
60. Outstanding Commercial and Industrial Leaders, 65–69
61. Receivers of Annual Incomes of $1,000,000 or more, 80–89

Item 62 in the following tabulation shows that, in proportion to the number of men who were still alive at each successive age level, presidents of American colleges and universities have served most often at 50–54. The other items in this tabulation are to be interpreted similarly.

62. Presidents of American colleges and universities, 50–54
63. Presidents of the U.S. prior to Truman, 55–59
64. U.S. Ambassadors to Foreign Countries from 1875 to 1900, 60–64
65. U.S. Senators in 1925, 60–64
66. Men in Charge of the U.S. Army from 1925 to 1945, 60–64
67. Justices of the U.S. Supreme Court from 1900 to 1925, 70–74
68. Speakers of the U.S. House of Representatives from 1900 to 1940, 70–74
69. Popes, 82–92

An analysis of age data for the most highly successful athletes reveals that their modal ages differ less from the norms for intellectual proficiency than is commonly supposed. The following comparisons are illustrative.

70. Professional Football Players, 22–26
71. Professional Prizefighters, 25–26
72. Professional Ice Hockey Players, 26
73. Professional Baseball Players, 27–28
74. Professional Tennis Players, 25–29
75. Automobile Racers, 26–30
76. Leading Contestants at Chess, 29–33
77. Professional Golfers, 31–36
78. Breakers of World Billiards Records, 31–36
79. Winners at Rifle and Pistol Shooting, 31–36
80. Winners of Important Bowling Championships, 31–36

To find out whether, with the passage of time, there has been any significant change in the modal ages at which important creative contributions have been made, data were isolated for noted achievers in such various fields as literature, practical invention, philosophy, geology, medicine, and the like. Two statistical distributions were then made for the workers in each field, one for those born prior to 1775, the other for those born between 1775 and 1850. In almost every instance the more recent workers exhibited their outstanding creative ingenuity at younger ages than did the workers of the earlier era.

In contrast with this age change for creative thinkers, the more recently-born 50 per cent of most kinds of leaders were found to be significantly *older* than were their predecessors who held the same nominal positions—both in the U.S.A. and also in certain other countries. Thus, for each of the following groups of non-American leaders, the more recently-born 50 per cent functioned at somewhat older ages than the earlier-born 50 per cent: the popes of the Roman Catholic church, the prime ministers of England, the archbishops of Canterbury, and hereditary rulers all over the world. The more recent leaders also were more nearly the same ages than were their predecessors.

When seven groups of earlier-born athletic champions were compared with seven groups of those more recently born, the field of sport being kept constant in each comparison, the later-born were found to be older than the earlier-born. The changes that have taken place in the modal ages of creative thinkers, leaders, and athletes all evidence the fact that these modal ages are not due solely to genetic factors. Whether the modal ages will continue to change and whether they can be subjected to some kind of human control are quite different questions.

A mere increase in man's longevity should not change greatly the modal ages at which man exhibits his greatest creative proficiency since, both for long-lived and for short-lived groups, the modal age occurs in the thirties. Although a part of the upward shift in the ages of leaders may be due to an increase in man's longevity, a possible alternative explanation is given [elsewhere].

*Possible Causes for the Early Maxima in Creativity*

At present we are in no position to explain these curves of creativity that rise rapidly in early maturity and then decline slowly after attaining an earlier maximum. Undoubtedly multiple causation operates in these complex behaviors and no discovered contributing condition is likely to be of itself a sufficient or necessary cause. Nevertheless, it is profitable here to list sixteen of the factors which have been suggested as contributing to these representative functions with their early maxima, for such factors indicate possible lines for further research. Here is the list.

(1) A decline occurs prior to 40 in physical vigor, energy, and resistance to fatigue. This decline is probably far more important than such normal age changes as may occur in adult intelligence prior to outright senility.

(2) A diminution in sensory capacity and motor precision also takes place with advance in age. For example, impaired vision and hearing handicap the older individual in many cumulative ways, and writing by hand also becomes more difficult with advance in age.

(3) Serious illness, poor health, and various bodily infirmities more often influence adversely the production rates of older than of younger age groups.

(4) Glandular changes continue throughout life. It is conceivable that

hormone research may some day reveal a partial explanation for the changes and especially for the early maxima.

(5) In some instances unhappy marriages and maladjustment in the sex life, growing worse with advance in age, may have interfered with creative work.

(6) The older age groups, more often than the younger, may have become indifferent toward creativity because of the death of a child, a mate, or some other dear one.

(7) As compared with younger persons, older ones are apt to be more preoccupied with the practical concerns of life, with earning a living, and with getting ahead.

(8) Less favorable conditions for concentrated work sometimes come with success, promotion, enhanced prestige, and responsibility.

(9) In some cases the youthful worker's primary ambition may not have been to discover the unknown or to create something new but to get renown. Having acquired prestige and recognition, such workers may try less hard for achievement.

(10) Too easy, too great, or too early fame may conceivably breed complacency and induce one to rest on his previously won laurels before he has done his best possible creative work.

(11) Some older persons may have become apathetic because they have experienced more often the deadening effect of non-recognition and of destructive criticism.

(12) As a result of negative transfer, the old generally are more inflexible than the young. This inflexibility may be a handicap to creative thinking, even though it is dependent on erudition.

(13) Perhaps in part because of the foregoing factors, some older persons experience a decrease in motivation which leads to a weaker intellectual interest and curiosity.

(14) Younger persons tend to have had a better formal education than their elders, they have grown to maturity in a more stimulating social and cultural milieu, and they have had less time to forget what they have learned.

(15) In some few cases outright psychosis has clouded what was previously a brilliant mind. Psychoses occur more often in the latter half of the normal life span.

(16) In other extreme cases, the individual's normal productive powers may have been sapped by alcohol, narcotics, and other kinds of dissipation. Here, as elsewhere, it is difficult to separate cause from effect.

*Possible Causes for the Older Ages of Leaders*

The factors that make for the older ages of leaders are also multiple, complex, and variable. The mere age of a country or of a people is not the determining factor. For example, from 1907 to 1939 only 7 per cent of the service of Chinese cabinet members was rendered by men of 60 or above, whereas, for England, France, and the U.S.A., the corresponding percentages were 41, 39, and 32 respectively. It is true also that from 1871 to 1918 the chancellors of the German empire had a median age more than 10 years older than the median age of the German chancellors who served from 1918 to 1945. This latter age difference could not be due to greater longevity on the part of the German people during the *earlier* era. Data . . . for some fifty other groups of leaders suggest that when a new group is being formed or when social unrest and dissatisfaction develop in a long-established organization, relatively youthful leaders are likely to emerge.

Consider next the possible contributory factors that cause leadership to occur usually at elderly ages. Examples of such factors are the following:

(1) Normally, for most kinds of leaders, the attainment of their leadership depends largely upon what the leader's potential followers think of him and his prospective leadership, a relationship that is probably less usual for the creative thinker even though the latter must act more or less in harmony with his *Zeitgeist*.

(2) Social institutions, like the church and the state, tend to be conservative; they are engaged primarily in the perpetuation of themselves and the existing cultural pattern. The leader is the instrument through which they act. Since older persons tend to be conservative more often than younger ones, the older are usually regarded as safer and saner leaders.

(3) For most kinds of leaders the recognition received, the prestige attained, and the honor achieved are likely to be far greater than for those who do creative work. Thus, other things equal, members of the older age groups are likely to be more strongly motivated in seeking and exercising various kinds of leadership than they are in pursuing creative work.

(4) The function of the leader differs from that of the creative thinker. Strictly speaking, leadership is less a personal attribute than a social relationship. An example of this is the fact that for many persons the leader serves as a father substitute, an important function which is, nevertheless, only one contributing factor, for there have been many young leaders.

(5) Nominal leaders have sometimes remained in office for years after they became incapacitated by illness or by other bodily infirmities for the routine performance of their duties. Thus, and especially at the uppermost age levels, some years of nominal leadership may represent merely the ages at which certain individuals have drawn their salaries. Needless to say, my creativity data are not vitiated by any analogous factor.

Upon the basis of all these statistics what is one to conclude? Whatever the causes of growth and decline, it remains clear that the genius does not function equally well throughout the years of adulthood. Superior creativity rises relatively rapidly to a maximum which occurs usually in the thirties and then falls off slowly. Almost as soon as he becomes fully mature, man is confronted with a gerontic paradox that may be expressed in terms of positive and negative transfer. Old people probably have more transfer, both positive and negative, than do young ones. As a result of positive transfer the old usually possess greater wisdom and erudition. These are invaluable assets. But when a situation requires a new way of looking at things, the acquisition of new techniques or even new vocabularies, the old seem stereotyped and rigid. To learn the new they often have to unlearn the old and that is twice as hard as learning without unlearning. But when a situation requires a store of past knowledge then the old find their advantage over the young.

Possibly every human behavior has its period of prime. No behavior can develop before the groundwork for it has been prepared, but in general it appears that the conditions essential for creativity and originality, which can be displayed in private achievement, come earlier than those social skills which contribute to leadership and eminence and which inevitably must wait, not upon the insight of the leader himself, but upon the insight of society about him.

## Bibliography

*Human Growth and Development—Individual Differences*

1. ALDRICH, C. ANDERSON and MILDRED A. NORVAL. "A Developmental Graph for the First Year of Life." *J. of Pediatrics.* **29**:304–308 (September 1946).

2. ANDERSON, ALICE and BEATRICE DVORAK. "Differences Between College Students and Their Elders in Standards of Conduct." *J. Ab. and Soc. Psychol.* **23**:286–292 (October–December 1928).

3. AUSTIN, MARY C. and G. G. THOMPSON. "Children's Friendships: A Study of the Bases on Which Children Select and Reject Their Best Friends." *J. Educ. Psychol.* **39**:101–116 (February 1948).

4. BALLER, WARREN R. "A Study of the Present Social Status of a Group of Adults Who, When They Were in Elementary Schools, Were Classified as Mentally Deficient." *Genet. Psychol. Monographs.* **18**:165–244 (June 1936).

5. BIENENSTOK, THEODORE. "The Peer Culture of Youth and the School." *Educ. Forum.* **18**:313–319 (March 1954).

6. BINGHAM, WALTER V. "Inequalities in Adult Capacity—From Military Data." *Science.* **104**:147–152 (August 16, 1946).

7. CAPEHART, BERTIS E., ALLEN HODGES, and ROBERT ROTH. "Evaluating the Core Curriculum: A Further Look." *Sch. Rev.* **61**:406–412 (October 1953).

8. COOK, LLOYD ALLEN. "An Experimental Sociographic Study of a Stratified Tenth-grade Class." *Amer. Soc. Rev.* **10**:250–261 (April 1945).

9. COOK, WALTER W. "Individual Differences and Curriculum Practice." *J. Educ. Psychol.* **39**:141–148 (March 1948).

10. COREY, STEPHEN M. "Designing a Curriculum for Student Development." *Bul. Nat'l Assoc. Sec. Sch. Prin.* **32**:101–110 (March 1948).

11. DENNIS, W. and M. G. DENNIS. "The Effect of Cradling Practice Upon the Onset of Walking in Hopi Children." *J. Genet. Psychol.* **56**:77–86 (March 1940).

12. FEIFEL, HERMAN and IRVING LORGE. "Qualitative Differences in the Vocabulary Responses of Children." *J. Educ. Psychol.* **41**:1–18 (January 1950).

13. FLESHER, M. A. and S. L. PRESSEY. "War-Time Acceleration Ten Years After." *J. Educ. Psychol.* **46**:228–239 (April 1955).

14. FRANK, LAWRENCE K. "The Fundamental Needs of the Child." *Ment. Hyg.* **22**:353–379 (July 1938).

15. FRENCH, JOHN E. "Children's Preferences for Pictures of Varied Complexity of Pictorial Pattern." *Elem. Sch. J.* **53**:90–95 (October 1952).

16. GARN, S. M. "Physical Growth and Development." *Amer. J. Phy. Anthrop.* N. S. **10**:169–192 (June 1952).

17. GATES, ARTHUR I. "The Nature and Educational Significance of Physical Status and of Mental, Physiological, Social and Emotional Maturity." *J. Educ. Psychol.* **15**:329–358 (September 1924).

18. ———. "The Necessary Mental Age for Beginning Reading." *Elem. Sch. J.* **37:**497–508 (March 1957).

19. ———. "Teaching Reading." *What Research Says to the Teacher.* No. 1. Washington, D. C.: Dept. of Classroom Teachers, Amer. Educ. Res. Assoc., N.E.A. (1953).

20. GOLDBERG, MIRIAM L. "Recent Research on the Talented." *Teach. Coll. Rec.* **60:**150–163 (December 1958).

21. GOODLAD, JOHN I. "Research and Theory Regarding Promotion and Non-promotion." *Elem. Sch. J.* **53:**150–156 (November 1952).

22. GRACE, HARRY A. and NANCY LOU BOOTH. "Is the 'Gifted' Child a Social Isolate?" *Peabody J. Educ.* **35:**195–196 (January 1958).

23. HAVIGHURST, ROBERT J. *Human Development and Education.* New York: Longmans, Green, and Co., Inc. (1953).

24. HILGARD, JOSEPHINE R. "Learning and Maturation in Pre-School Children." *J. Genet. Psychol.* **41:**36–56 (September 1932).

25. HINKELMAN, EMMET ARTHUR. "Relationship of Intelligence to Elementary School Achievement." *Educ. Adm. and Sup.* **41:**176–179 (March 1955).

26. HOLLINGWORTH, LETA S. *Children Above 180 IQ.* Yonkers, N. Y.: World Book Co. (1942).

27. HORROCKS, J. E. "The Relationship Between Knowledge of Human Development and Ability to Use Such Knowledge." *J. App. Psychol.* **30:**501–508 (October 1946).

28. ———. "What Is Adolescence?" *Educ.* **76:**218–221 (December 1955).

29. JANKE, LEOTA L. and ROBERT J. HAVIGHURST. "Relations between Ability and Social Status in a Midwestern Community." *J. Educ. Psychol.* **36:**499–509 (October 1945).

30. JERSILD, ARTHUR T. *Child Psychology,* 4th ed. New York: Prentice-Hall, Inc. (1954).

31. ———. "Self-Understanding in Childhood and Adolescence, *Amer. Psychol.* **6:**122–126 (April 1951).

32. JERVIS, GEORGE A. "Factors in Mental Retardation." *Children.* **1:**207–211 (November–December 1954).

33. JONES, HAROLD ELLIS and HERBERT S. CONRAD. "The Growth and Decline of Intelligence: The Study of a Homogeneous Group between the Ages of Ten and Sixty." *Genet. Psychol. Monographs.* **13:**223–298 (March 1933).

34. JONES, MARY C. "The Later Careers of Boys Who Were Early- or Late-Maturing." *Child Dev.* **28:**113–128 (March 1957).

35. ——— and NANCY BAYLEY. "Physical Maturing Among Boys as Related to Behavior." *J. Educ. Psychol.* **41:**129–148 (March 1950).

36. KOCH, HELEN L. "The Social Distance Between Certain Racial, National-
ity, and Skin-pigmentation Groups in Selected Populations of American
School Children." *J. Genet. Psychol.* **68:**63–95 (March 1946).

37. KUHLEN, R. G. and G. H. JOHNSON. "Changing Goals with Increasing
Adult Age. *J. Cons. Psychol.* **16:**1–4 (January–February 1952).

38. LATHAM, A. J. "The Relationship Between Pubertal Status and Leadership
in Junior High School Boys." *J. Genet. Psychol.* **78:**185–194 (June 1951).

39. LEVITT, EMMA. "Şeeking Parental Cooperation." *Health in the Elem.
School.* 29th Yearbook, Dept. of Elem. Sch. Principals of the N.E.A.
(1950).

40. LOHRMAN, H. P. "Minnesota Boy: His Parents' Child." *Minn. J. Educ.*
**34:**12–13, 37 (September 1953).

41. LORGE, IRVING. "The Influence of the Test Upon the Nature of Mental
Decline as a Function of Age." *J. Ed. Psychol.* **27:**100–110 (February
1936).

42. MACCOBY, ELEANOR E., PATRICIA K. GIBBS, and the Staff of the Laboratory
of Human Development, Harvard University. *Methods of Child-Rearing in
Two Social-Classes,* from *Readings in Child Development,* eds. W. E. Martin and C. B. Stendler. New York: Harcourt, Brace and Co. (1954), pp.
380–396.

43. MARPLE, CLARE H. "The Comparative Susceptibility of Three Age Levels
to the Suggestion of Group Versus Expert Opinion." *J. Soc. Psychol.*
**4:**176–186 (May 1933).

44. MARTINSON, RUTH A. "The California Study of Programs for Gifted
Pupils." *Excep. Child.* **26:**339–343 (March 1960).

45. McGRAW, M. B. "Later Development of Children Especially Trained
During Infancy: Johnny and Jimmy at School Age." *Child Dev.* **10:**1–19
(March 1939).

46. ——— "Neural Maturation as Exemplified by the Achievement of Bladder
Control." *J. Pediatrics.* **16:**580–590 (May 1940).

47. "Midcentury White House Conference on Children and Youth: The
School's Role in Personality Development." *A Healthy Personality for
Every Child—Fact Finding Report: A Digest.* Raleigh, N. C.: Health
Publications Institute, Inc. (1951).

48. MILLER, ROBERT V. "Social Status and Socioempathic Differences Among
Mentally Superior, Mentally Typical, and Mentally Retarded Children."
*Excep. Child.* **23:**114–119 (December 1956).

49. MILNER, E. A. "A Study of the Relationships between Reading Readiness
in Grade One Children and Patterns of Parent-Child Interaction." *Child
Dev.* **22:**95–112 (June 1951).

50. NEILON, PATRICIA. "Shirley's Babies After Fifteen Years: A Personality Study." *J. Genet. Psychol.* **73:**175–186 (December 1948).

51. OJEMANN, RALPH H. and FRANCIS R. WILKINSON. "The Effect on Pupil Growth of an Increase in Teacher's Understanding of Pupil Behavior." *J. Exp. Educ.* **8:**143–147 (December 1939).

52. OLSON, WILLARD C. and BYRON O. HUGHES. "Concepts of Growth—Their Significance to Teachers." *Childhood Educ.* **21:**53–63 (October 1944).

53. PRESSEY, SIDNEY L. "Concerning the Nature and Nurture of Genius." *Sci. Monthly.* **81:**123–129 (September 1955).

54. ROWLAND, THOMAS D. and CALVIN C. NELSON. "Off to School—At What Age?" *Elem. Sch. J.* **60:**18–23 (October 1959).

55. RUSK, HOWARD A. "Square Pegs in Round Holes." *N.E.A.J.* **47:**608 (December 1958).

56. SCHOEPPE, AILEEN and ROBERT J. HAVIGHURST. "A Validation of Developmental and Adjustment Hypotheses of Adolescence." *J. Educ. Psychol.* **43:**339–353 (October 1952).

57. SHANNON, DAN C. "What Research Says About Acceleration." *Phi Delta Kappan.* **39:**70–73 (November 1957).

58. SHIRLEY, MARY M. "Sequence of Motor Development from the First Two Years: A Study of Twenty-five Babies." *Intellectual Development,* Vol. 2. Mpls.: U. of Minn. Press. 1933.

59. SIEGEL, ALBERTA ENGVALL, *et al.* "Dependence and Independence in the Children of Working Mothers." *Child Dev.* **30:**533–546 (December 1959).

60. SMITH, M. E., *et al.* "The Effect of Race, Sex and Environment on the Age at Which Children Walk." *J. Genet. Psychol.* **38:**489–498 (December 1930).

61. STENDLER, CELIA BURNS. "Critical Periods in Socialization and Overdependency." *Child. Dev.* **23:**3–12 (March 1952).

62. STILES, F. S. "Developing an Understanding of Human Behavior at the Elementary School Level." *J. Educ. Res.* **43:**516–524 (March 1950).

63. STRANG, RUTH. "Gifted Adolescents' Views of Growing Up." *Excep. Child.* **23:**10–15, 20 (October 1956).

64. ———. "Guidance of the Gifted." *Pers. and Guid. J.* **31:**26–30 (October 1952).

65. STUART, HAROLD C. "Normal Growth and Development During Adolescence." *New England J. of Medicine.* **234:**666–672, 693–700, 732–738 (May 1946).

66. TERMAN, L. M. "Are Scientists Different?" *Sci. Amer.* **192:**25–30 (January 1955).

67. TYLER, L. E. "The Development of 'Vocational Interests': The Organization of Likes and Dislikes in Ten-Year-Old Children." *J. Genet. Psychol.* **86:**33–44 (March 1955).

68. ———. "The Relationship of Interests to Abilities and Reputation Among First-Grade Children." *Educ. Psychol. Measmt.* **11:**255–264 (Summer 1951).

69. TYLER, RALPH W. "Meeting the Challenge of the Gifted." *Elem. Schl. J.* **58:**75–82 (November 1957).

70. WAGNER, GUY. "What Schools Are Doing in Challenging the Rapid Learner." *Educ.* **78:**59–62 (September 1957).

71. WILSON, CHARLES C. "Planning Together for Good Health." *Health in the Elementary School.* 29th Yearbook, Dept. of Elem. Sch. Principals of the N.E.A. (1950).

72. WITTY, PAUL A. "Children's Interests in Comics, Radio, Motion Pictures and TV." *Educ. Adm. & Sup.* **38:**138–147 (March 1952).

73. WORCESTER, D. A. *The Education of Children of Above Average Mentality.* Lincoln, Neb.: U. of Neb. Press (1956).

## PART III

LEARNING—THE MAJOR
CONCERN OF
EDUCATIONAL
PSYCHOLOGY

It may be said that learning is the heart of educational psychology. In fact, some authorities have held that learning, broadly conceived, *is* educational psychology. Perhaps we should agree first on what the term *learning* stands for. As used here it means, first of all, human learning or learning by people, not by rats or monkeys or guinea pigs. Studies of animal learning have taught us much about simple kinds of learning such as running a maze, tripping a lever or a catch to get to food, but less about higher forms of learning such as thinking and attitudes. It is these as well as simpler types of learning that concern the educational psychologist. So we may say that he is concerned with all kinds of learning from the simplest, like learning to pick up a small object, to the most complex, like solving the problems of putting a man into orbit.

How do we define learning? A simple definition might be, *a change in behavior as a result of experience.* Note that the definition doesn't specify any judgment as to the desirability of the change, whether it is good or bad; it merely says "a change." Second, the change comes about as a result of experience. This rules out changes in behavior that are caused by maturation, innate or hereditary factors. Such changes are not learned, according to the definition. Most changes in behavior desired by the school are sought by means of changing the environment, that is, by providing certain experiences. There is little it can do about the process of maturation except to provide the best possible environment for it to take place.

One of the major concerns of educational psychology, then, is to determine by experiment, and by trial and error in many instances, how to bring about changes in behavior by manipulating the environment, that is, by providing the proper experiences. This is what the school attempts to do— to bring about or to facilitate changes in behavior, which society has agreed are desirable, by giving the learner certain experiences.

Implicit in the discussion so far is that the pupil wants to learn. In other words, he is motivated, or he has a goal which hopefully is the same as the teacher's or society's. It is often said that unless the pupil is motivated he will not learn. Getting him to want to learn what we want him to learn is sometimes difficult but nonetheless essential. This also is a field of study for educational psychology.

Another aspect of the problem of learning is transfer of training. By this is meant, *the improvement that takes place in one function as a result of practice (and improvement) in another related function.* More specifically, transfer of training involves such questions as, "How much improvement takes place in English vocabulary as a result of studying Latin?" or, "To what extent does the study of geometry improve general reasoning ability or ability to solve other kinds of problems?" or "Does the study of science improve one's attitudes of openmindedness, suspended judgment, and one's critical faculty?" Questions like these and similar ones are quite important from the educational point of view. Obviously, there must be some transfer, otherwise it would be necessary to teach everyone everything in minutest detail that he would ever need. The question becomes, then, not whether or not transfer of training occurs, but rather finding the ways of teaching which will result in the greatest possible amount of transfer. The greater the transfer, both in amount and in spread, the more efficient our teaching becomes.

In the selections which follow, the aspects of learning just referred to as well as some others are considered and the results of research are reported.

oκ

## 17

# EDUCATIONAL THEORY AND THE PSYCHOLOGY OF LEARNING *

## G. T. Buswell

In this thought-provoking article the author takes as his thesis that the psychology of learning can be useful to education only to the extent that it focuses its interest and experiments with awareness of current educational theory. He deplores the fact that so much research in the psychology of learning has been carried out with animal subjects in a laboratory and so little in the classroom with children. He urges that educational psychologists study problems of learning in the classroom setting rather than looking to general psychology for research findings based on sub-human subjects learning to run a maze. He goes on to suggest three important and potentially fruitful fields in the psychology of learning for educational psychology. These are the psychology of thinking, the psychology of personality, and the psychology of motivation.

*Questions:*

1. In general, are the problems of the educational psychologist more complex or simpler than those with which the laboratory psychologist deals? Why?
2. What is a fundamental problem for the teacher in the area of motivation? Do you know of any research bearing on it? If so, cite some.

* * *

. . . Any educational situation involves a purpose or objective, a content to be learned (a curriculum), and a process of learning. The over-all purpose or objective, what we are trying to do, is expressed as theory of education. The *process* of changing behavior in accordance with educational theory is expressed as the psychology of learning. Between these two is the content to be learned, whether substantive subject-matter or behavior traits. The thesis of this paper is that if the psychology of learning is

* Abridged and reprinted from the *Journal of Educational Psychology,* **47:**175–184 (March 1956), by permission of author and publisher.

to be effective in the schools, it must focus its interests and design its experiments with awareness of the theory of education that is currently accepted by the society in which the schools operate. As theory of education is modified, the direction of psychological study must be changed if its results are to influence educational practice. This is no different in the areas of education and psychology than in other areas. The current interest in nuclear physics has for a decade produced a new focus of attention for scientists of many fields. The movement from old issues to new characterizes a live science. Research in the field of educational psychology should reflect the movement of educational theory. In the 1920's, research on drill in arithmetic was in harmony with educational theory; in 1955, such studies would have far less significance because the purpose and theory of teaching arithmetic have undergone marked change. The ultimate objective, of course, is not merely to relate research to currently accepted educational theory, but rather, to do the kind of research that will help to formulate an educational theory that is *valid*.

I should like to illustrate this relationship between educational theory and the psychology of learning by reference to only two of the several theories of education which might be described. During the last century, and in some places still, education was considered as basically the acquisition of knowledge. The inscription, "Knowledge is Power," was found on many school buildings. Passing on the intellectual heritage of the race was considered the primary purpose of the school. Acquirement of knowledge, with some attendant skills, was the basic aim. Prior to the Civil War, the accumulation of knowledge was not so great as to constitute any considerable burden to the learner. Then the situation changed. Particularly in the field of science, a great expansion began. This increase in subject-matter to be learned was met by devising the elective system. This gave rise to the problem of what knowledge is of most worth and resulted in a fight for time among the different branches of the curriculum. By the twentieth century the situation began to be serious, particularly in the secondary school and junior college. Pupil programs, which at first were made up of a large common group of required subjects plus a few electives, began to show a progressively smaller group of required subjects and an increase in the electives. By the 1920's it became clear that any attempt to cover the field of essential knowledge was hopeless by the required and elective system. A new venture into general education, by means of survey courses, was tried, and now such courses are a part of the program at the junior college level in many institutions. Back of all these changes was the basic question,

"What is an education?" As long as it is defined as mastery of the body of knowledge, it must necessarily expand, although the individual learner's capacity to learn has undergone no corresponding change. The elective program was characterized as a specialization in depth in a few areas, with chasms of ignorance between. After thirty years of experimenting with survey courses, they are often subject to the charge of specialization in another axis; namely, specialization in superficialities. But if in theory a good education is defined in terms of knowledge and skill, what other alternatives are there, particularly in the face of a certain increase in the rate of accumulation of knowledge.

If some modification of the foregoing picture is accepted as a theory of education, then what type of psychological research in learning will likely follow? With so much to be learned, one would expect emphasis on the psychology of memory and retention. Problems of length and distribution of practice periods, whole and part methods of memorizing, prerequisites affecting the order in which different subject-matters should be learned would seem important. Major concern would be centered on subject-matter to be learned, rather than changes in the learner. One can find many specifics to illustrate both this theory of education and the kinds of learning studies mentioned.

However, one might conceive of a second very different theory of education. Rather than define a good education in terms of the knowledge and skills possessed, one might think of it in terms of certain changes brought about in the learner, by means of which he would develop abilities enabling him to respond successfully to the diverse and unpredictable situations that life will bring. Advocates of such a view would readily admit the necessity of a fairly large amount of basic knowledge and skill. Certainly they would not make a virtue of ignorance. But rather than conceive of education as an encyclopedic coverage of knowledge, they would deal with the heritage of knowledge in a highly selective way. They would probably agree on the necessity of certain knowledge and skill, for example, ability to read, knowing how to spell, knowing number facts and relations, and the skill of writing, plus other less well agreed upon additions. However, they would stress such general outcomes as learning how to think, learning how to use a library; how to design and carry out an experiment; how to meet people; how to control the emotions; how to adjust to frustrations. In the literature, the outcomes just enumerated are often dealt with in a very nebulous manner. However, if a person holding some such theory of education were asked to epitomize it, he might answer somewhat as follows: The expanding body of knowledge has already reached such proportions that an attempt by an individual to cover it is hopeless. Therefore, a better procedure might be to select carefully and coherently from racial experience a basic body of knowledge and skills which would serve as tools and background for whatever kinds of learning one might need to acquire. Using this carefully selected body of facts, concepts, skills, experiences, which would probably constitute the main load of early education, the learner would then test and enlarge his abilities through a rather thorough learning of some sample fields. The essence of such a theory of education is that it is the function of the school to help the pupil learn how to learn; that, beyond the acquiring of basic knowledge and concepts, the purpose of the school is to provide some excellent samples of learning experience in a number of fields and extending over the usual number of years devoted to general education. On completion of such a period of education, the graduate might say, "There are many things I do not know and many skills I do not have, but I know how to get them, I know how to learn what needs to be learned." This concept is the opposite from blueprinting and stereotyping the education of a child. It aims at giving him versatility and independence.

Now, supposing one held some such theory of education as has just been described, in what kind of a psychology of learning would he be most interested? Obviously, the crucial psychological problem for such a theory is that of transfer. How can the learning attained carry over and spread to other situations as they are encountered? How can the outcomes of education be generalized so as to be broad in scope? Certainly the early types of experiments on transfer, such as Thorndike's study of the effect of practice in judging the size of circles upon ability to judge the size of squares, would contribute little. The problem could not be met by studying the carry-over of one academic subject to another subject. Rather, the studies that have significance are those that deal with transfer at the general rather than the specific level; with the development of intellectual habits that may spread widely, rather than with narrow intellectual functions. Studies such as Harlow's experiments with chimpanzees in learning how to learn have high significance for such a theory of education, and they would have still higher significance if carried on with human subjects where the possession of language enhances the possibilities of transferring training.

The concept of transfer in learning how to learn applies both to subject-matter and to method and technique. The understanding embodied in the arithmetical generalization that "when both the numerator and denominator of a fraction are multiplied by the same number, the value of the fraction is not changed" is more transferable than the specific fact that two-thirds and four-sixths have equivalent value. Likewise, the acquisition of general techniques, such as how to use a library card catalogue, is of more general value than to learn the location on the shelves of a specific reference. The essential test of any theory of education is its transfer value, yet the design of most of our learning experiments dealing with transfer is feeble compared to the size of the problem to be studied.

The crux of my contention is that educational psychologists have been loath to strike out independently in solving problems in their own field. In the main, our problems deal with education in schools, with human subjects, and with higher mental processes involving language. Without the slightest criticism of experiments in general psychology, we cannot continue to be satisfied with implications for education from results of experiments with simple mental processes, with animals, and at the sub-language level. This past summer, parents of children from coast to coast were aroused by a recent book denouncing current methods of learning how to read and proposing that the schools go back to an earlier phonetic method as the sole way of learning to read. The answer to the place of phonics in learning to read will never come from animal experiments nor from the use of nonsense syllables. Nor will it come from half of the educational experiments on phonics which measure only the effect on the ability to pronounce words. If by reading one means the ability to get meaning from a printed page, there is little experimental evidence one way or the other at the present time regarding the value of phonics. The field of reading has without doubt been subjected to more careful research than any other area of learning in the school, yet here in the case of phonics is a prime example of an opportunity passed by to do research on an important transferable function.

I am proposing that educational psychologists take their cues for research from problems of learning in schools, where the processes are complex and where the learnings carried on are at the language level. May I try to indicate what, to me, seem to be three very fruitful fields for research.

I would suggest, first, research on the success, or lack of it, in teaching students how to think. For some years our schools, particularly at the high school and college level, have proclaimed this as one of their main objectives. Yet, a critical appraisal of available research on this problem gives little evidence that schools are accomplishing their objective. When allowance is made for constantly increasing mental maturity, and when pertinent variables are controlled, it is difficult to find evidence of any marked gains in ability to think due to the work of the schools. Our claims far outrun the evidence. Is it possible to learn how to think more effectively, or are the methods of the school wrong? There is plenty of evidence that students can learn to think within the area of the subject-matter being taught, but the real issue is whether or not they can transfer the ability to other areas. For example, in a study of problem-solving last year, we found that in one group of sixty-one college students, all of whom had had a course in algebra, only twenty of the sixty-one attempted to use algebra in solving a problem where the algebraic method was the most economical way to solution, and, of the twenty who attempted to use algebra, only one succeeded in getting the correct answer. Algebra had apparently failed to contribute a method of thinking to these students. Or, to illustrate further, it is probably true that most students, and some teachers, fail to sense that the high school course in geometry is in essence a course in deductive logical thinking, using space figures as the medium of operation. Rather, geometry is usually taught as a body of content, the learning of which is a sufficient outcome in itself. Here is a major problem in learning at the abstract language level, yet the bulk of the experimentation on it is with animals and at the sub-language level. Why do we so generally avoid experimenting on problem-solving with human subjects and in school situations where the real issues are?

I would suggest that a second area of research intimately related to current educational theory is in the learning of personality characteristics. The school expects its pupils to learn to be accurate, to carry responsibility, to be critical, to have good personal relations with others, and many more such traits. Here, clearly, is a problem in transfer of learning. Most schools deal with this problem of personal-social education in a loose, incidental manner. Whereas the school has a definite and coherent methodology, supported by a considerable body of research, for learning to read and to do arithmetic, there is little experimental evidence to guide the school in its program of personal-social education. In a widely used book on the subject, there is a bibliography of more than eleven hundred references dealing with personality; but less than a dozen of them report studies of learning personal-social traits in the schools. Admittedly, experimentation in schools is difficult, but can we not design studies with sufficient controls to take account of the difficulties?

Last, I would suggest the problem of motivation in school as of high importance for educational psychologists. Here, clearly, we are in difficulty if we rely on implications from studies of animal learning. In most animal studies, the motivation for behavior is hunger or punishment. Such incentives, obviously, are not applicable in the schools. In fact, the whole concept of tissue needs has little force for school learning. Most of the interests and motives that operate in the schools are learned, and it may well be that one of the main contributions of the school is to modify, through learning, the motivation that operates within the learner. If, for example, the school could succeed in making students intellectually curious, the operation of such a motive might have a broader effect than the mastery of any specific segment of subject-matter. The problem is, how and why do some students learn to be intellectually curious while others do not.

The three problems for research just suggested, namely, learning how to think, learning personal-social traits, and learning motivations, are not matters of great concern to a "Knowledge is Power" type of educational theory. However, to a theory of education based on the concept that the essence of education is learning how to learn, such problems are at the heart of the matter. With such a theory, the main concern is to find what curricular content and what intellectual tools are essential to carry on the kind of learning desired, and then, in turn, to what scope of subject-matter and to what depth and thoroughness should the school go in order to be sure that the student will be independent and versatile, and will feel confident that he knows how to learn as new occasions may require.

Educational psychologists must first of all be psychologists; there is no substitute for competence in the basic subject. But their field of operation is education and, in the main, is concerned with the schools which are society's principal agent for providing education. The main business of the school is learning, and psychologists should have something to say about learning. Whether what they say is understood and is useful to the school depends a great deal on whether or not the psychologist understands theories of education as well as theories of learning, and whether his research deals with problems which are important to the educational theory of the time or whether it deals with yesterday's issues. This dual rôle of the educational psychologist is not easy, but it is necessary.

The proposal of this paper in no sense suggests that educational psychologists do only applied research and leave basic research to the general psychologist. But basic research need not be restricted to simple mental processes, nor to subjects at the sub-language level. Basic study of motivation can deal with learned motives as well as physiological needs. Studies of transfer can deal with situations that operate through generalizations that are expressed in language symbols as well as with mazes and puzzle boxes. The designs of research will have to be more complex, but they can be made so. If educational psychologists can play their rôle at this higher level of research, they will be able to contribute significantly to the validaiton of educational theory.

## References

1.  GUTHRIE, E. R. "The Psychology of Learning," in *National Society for the Study of Education,* Forty-first Yearbook, Part II (1952).

2.  ————. *The Psychology of Learning,* Revised Edition. New York: Harper & Brothers, p. 310 (1952).

# 18

## HOW LEARNING THEORY IS RELATED TO CURRICULUM ORGANIZATION *

### Glenn Myers Blair

In this readable article, the author explains how some well-established principles of learning apply to the classroom and particularly to curriculum planning and organization. He suggests how the educational psychologist and the curriculum specialist can work together in building courses of study which will be more sound in terms of generally accepted learning theory, and therefore more effective. The concepts discussed and illustrated include readiness for learning, motivation, organization (meaning, organization and structure) and transfer of training. Findings of experimental studies and their application to curriculum development in each instance are clearly presented.

*Questions:*

1. How does the principle of readiness for learning apply in my teaching? Give specific illustrations.
2. What techniques are appropriate for me to use to make my pupils want to learn?
3. How can I teach so as to maximize the transfer that will take place?

\* \* \*

No one will dispute the statement that one of the fundamental bases of curriculum construction should be a knowledge of how individuals learn. But many confusions and cleavages exist among educators with respect to the nature of the learning process and how it specifically affects school curriculums. J. Paul Leonard in his recent book on the secondary-school curriculum apparently feels that psychology is partially responsible for the situation. He says: "Without doubt much of the great confusion in education today is due to the even greater confusion in psychology. We need a

* Reprinted from the *Journal of Educational Psychology,* **39:**161–166 (March 1948), by permission of author and publisher.

more acceptable and convincing explanation of human learning and behavior" [10].*

It is easy to understand such a feeling on the part of a curriculum builder. Psychology has never presented in any one place a complete, unified, coherent, and universally agreed upon account of the nature of learning. The science of psychology has not yet reached the stage of maturity which would make such a pronouncement possible. Despite this fact, much is known about learning, and a number of valid principles of great importance to curriculum builders have been established as the result of the efforts of psychological workers.

The purpose of the present paper is to set forth some of the concepts and findings from the field of learning theory which seem to have direct implications for curriculum development. This material will be presented under the following headings: (1) readiness for learning, (2) motivation and learning, (3) organization in learning, and (4) transfer of training.

## Readiness for Learning

Numerous studies [5, 12, 14] have shown that a sufficient stage of physical maturation is necessary before effective learning is possible. Equally important for learning is an adequate mental and educational readiness [18]. First-grade teachers are usually aware of the concept of 'reading readiness' and understand that until a child has reached a mental age of approximately six years, and has developed in certain other important ways he cannot profit from typical types of first-grade reading instruction. But teachers in the upper grades and high school, and curriculum builders in general all too often fail to recognize that readiness for learning is a prerequisite at all levels. A seventh-grade child who reads at the third-grade level is not ready to tackle seventh-grade reading materials. The child who has not as yet mastered the essentials of arithmetic is not ready for algebra. In building a defensible curriculum it is of utmost importance that for each grade or age group activities and materials be provided which will fit a great range of maturity levels. Courses of study which provide a given text for a given grade or a given set of exercises which all students must do, violate the principle of readiness for learning which is here being discussed.

Investigators who have tried to find the right grade placement for such topics as long division or improper fractions have really missed the point so far as maturation and learning are concerned. Regardless of the grade

* Figure in brackets apply to references at end of article.

at which such a topic is placed in the elementary school, there will be some children who are so immature in terms of experience backgrounds that the process will be too difficult for them and perhaps others so advanced in their educational development that the topic will be of no interest or concern to them.

Any type of curricular arrangement which is to be successful must provide experiences which begin where the child is. Any other plan not only eventuates in ineffective learning but inevitably produces frustration which may lead to behavior disorders [19].

## Motivation and Learning

Both Dashiell [3] and McConnell [11] have clearly shown that all major schools of psychology hold that the organism must be motivated to learn. Motivation has sometimes been termed the *sine qua non* of learning. Certain superficial types of learning have been produced when the organism is not fully ready from a maturational standpoint, but without some form of motivation there will be no response on the part of the organism and hence no learning whatsoever.

Careful investigations by Mowrer [13], and Hull [6], and others have suggested that all learning is contingent upon need reduction. The organism must have some need, drive, or goal set or there will be no learning. Every individual possesses a few basic drives or wishes that are constantly demanding satisfaction. Besides the physical needs, there are the personality or social needs. Thomas [15] has suggested that there are four fundamental drives of this latter type—the desire for recognition, security, response, and new experience. In addition to these more or less universal needs or drives, every individual develops his own personal needs and interests. These are undoubtedly based upon and related to the more elementary tissue needs of the body, but are so different from them that the connection is difficult to trace. Allport [1] in his discussion of the functional autonomy of motives has clearly shown that an endless variety of human wants can be developed.

The needs, wants, interests, and motives of children should be identified, and learning activities which take these into account should be provided by the school. The effective curriculum is one which is flexible enough to provide experiences which relate to the individual goals of children. Such an arrangement makes for effective learning and, at the same time, makes possible the development of new interests. The individual who attempts an activity because he believes it will help him reach one of his goals, not only learns the activity but in addition develops a liking for the activity.

## Organization in Learning and the Curriculum

A tremendous body of experimental evidence can be marshalled to support the hypothesis that learning proceeds much more rapidly and is retained much longer when that which is learned possesses meaning, organization, and structure. [17] Too often pupils in our schools are asked to learn isolated sets of facts and information which are either unrelated to significant problems facing the learner or appear to him to be unrelated. Under these conditions it is not surprising that forgetting takes place on a vast scale. In a study by Brooks and Bassett, [2] pupils in American history forgot within sixteen months' time approximately one-third of the facts they knew at the close of the semester. In a similar study conducted by Layton [9] it was found that pupils in elementary algebra classes forgot within a period of one year, two-thirds of the material they had known at the end of the course.

No such deterioration or drop in retention seems to occur, however, in those cases where the learner engages in activities which are organized in terms of his purposes and where his objective is to solve problems rather than to learn facts. Word and Davis [20] conclude from their significant study that "ability to apply principles, to explain phenomena, problem-solving procedures, and attitudes are retained over a long period with only slight loss."

In view of what we know about organization in learning and retention, it would appear that curriculum builders should design courses of study which make it possible for children to work on problems, projects, and units which possess a high degree of internal organization. Much has been written recently about the core curriculum. One of its greatest strengths is probably the fact that it cuts across subject-matter boundaries and draws upon materials from all fields for the solution of problems. In the selection of problems for the core curriculum, however, the greatest care must be taken to insure that a sufficient variety of problems are included to meet the differing maturity levels and interest patterns of individual children.

## Transfer of Training and the Curriculum

If the pupil possesses the necessary maturation and experience backgrounds for learning, is motivated, and if the material is properly organized, he will learn something. That something might be Latin, Sanscrit, or tiger-catching. According to the theory of formal discipline, anyone of these subjects might possibly sharpen the individual's mind and hence qualify for inclusion in the curriculum.

Scientific studies of transfer of training, [7] however, have repudiated the idea that the mind is composed of faculties which can be sharpened by almost any kind of abrasive material and hence made highly effective in dealing with all types of life's problems.

Thorndike's [16] theory of identical elements would seem to make it clear that the school curriculum should contain activities and problems which are very similar to those which the individual will encounter in life. Judd's [8] theory of transfer by generalization would likewise seem to support this same conclusion. What pupils learn to do in school is what they will be able to transfer to out-of-school situations. [4] The pupil who learns in the Latin class to say *hic, haec, hoc, huius, huius, huius* should be able to say this after his school days are over provided he has not forgotten it and has any occasion to do so. The pupil who learns to adjust a car carburetor in the school shop should be able to adjust the same or similar type of carburetor after he graduates. The pupil who develops a clear understanding of some principle in school should be able to apply this principle in life if a situation is ever found where the principle applies.

All that we know about transfer of training seems to indicate that those who would establish curriculums should have clearly in mind what it is they want children to learn. Only those materials, activities and problems should be selected which are directly related to these objectives.

## Summary

Principles from the field of learning theory which have a significant relationship to curriculum construction have been reviewed. It has been emphasized that the effective curriculum is one which: (1) makes provision for varying maturity and experience levels of pupils, (2) gears learning activities to the needs and goals of pupils, (3) provides projects, problems and units of experience which possess meaning and structure for the pupil, and (4) carefully selects and appraises projected pupil activities in terms of their transfer value to life's situations. The question might be raised as to whether a curriculum can do all four of these things at once. I believe the answer is—yes. The highly enriched and flexible curriculum will provide an almost limitless array of possible activities and learning experiences within certain broad areas. It should then be possible to select for a given pupil only those activities which satisfy these four criteria.

## References

1. ALLPORT, G. W. *Personality: A Psychological Interpretation*. New York: Holt, Rinehart & Winston, pp. 190–212 (1937).

2. BROOKS, FOWLER D. and S. J. BASSETT. "The Retention of American History in the Junior High School." *Journal of Educational Research*. **18**:200 (October 1928).

3. DASHIELL, J. F. "A Survey and Synthesis of Learning Theories." *Psychological Bulletin*. **32**:261–275 (1935).

4. GUTHRIE, E. R. "Conditioning: A Theory of Learning in Terms of Stimulus, Response, and Association." *The Psychology of Learning*. Forty-first Yearbook of the National Society for the Study of Education, Part II, pp. 24–26 (1942).

5. HILGARD, JOSEPHINE R. "Learning and Maturation in Preschool Children." *Journal of Genetic Psychology*. **41**:36–56 (1932).

6. HULL, C. L. *Principles of Behavior*. New York: D. Appleton-Century Co. (1943).

7. JAMES, WILLIAM. *Principles of Psychology*, Vol. 1. New York: Henry Holt and Co., pp. 666–668 (1890). E. L. THORNDIKE. "Mental Discipline in High-school Studies." *Journal of Educational Psychology*. Vol. 15, pp. 1–22, 83–98 (1924).

8. JUDD, C. H. *Educational Psychology*. Boston: Houghton Mifflin Co., p. 514 (1939).

9. LAYTON, E. T. "The Persistence of Learning in Elementary Algebra." *Journal of Educational Psychology*. **23**:52 (January 1932).

10. LEONARD, J. PAUL. *Developing the Secondary-school Curriculum*. New York: Holt, Rinehart & Winston, p. 84 (1946).

11. McCONNELL, T. R. "Reconciliation of Learning Theories," in *The Psychology of Learning*. Forty-First Yearbook of the National Society for the Study of Education, Part II, pp. 262–266 (1942).

12. McGRAW, M. B. "Neural Maturation as Exemplified in Achievement of Bladder Control." *Journal of Pediatrics*. **16**:580–590 (1940).

13. MOWRER, O. H. "Motivation and Learning in Relation to the National Emergency." *Psychological Bulletin*. **38**:421–431 (1941).
———. "The Law of Effect and Ego Psychology." *Psychological Review*. **53**:321–334 (1946).

14. SHIRLEY, M. M. *The First Two Years: A Study of Twenty-five Babies*.

Vol. 1: *Postural and Locomotor Development*. University of Minnesota Press (1931).

15. THOMAS, W. I. *The Unadjusted Girl*. Boston: Little, Brown and Co. (1923).

16. THORNDIKE, E. L. *Educational Psychology*. Vol. II, *The Psychology of Learning*. New York: Teachers College, Columbia University, pp. 358–359 (1913).

17. ———. *Human Learning*. New York: Century Company (1931). J. P. GUILFORD. "The Rôle of Form in Learning." *Journal of Experimental Psychology*. **10**:415–423 (1927). G. KATONA. *Organizing and Memorizing*. New York: Columbia University Press (1940). E. B. NEWMAN. "Forgetting of Meaningful Material During Sleep and Waking." *American Journal of Psychology*. **52**:65–71 (1939).

18. WASHBURNE, CARLETON. *Child Development and the Curriculum*. Thirty-Eighth Yearbook of the National Society for the Study of Education, Part I, (1939) pp. 299–324.
KAI JENSEN, *Ibid.*, pp. 325–360.

19. WICKMAN, E. K. *Childrens' Behavior and Teachers' Attitudes*. New York: The Commonwealth Fund, p. 151 (1928).

20. WORD, A. H. and ROBERT A. DAVIS. "Individual Differences in Retention of General Science Subject-matter in the Case of Three Measurable Teaching Objectives." *Journal of Experimental Education*. **7**:30 (September 1938).

# 19

# THE EFFECT OF TYPE OF TRAINING UPON TRANSFERENCE *

## Herbert Woodrow

The study reported below is a crucial one in the field of transfer of training. Although many earlier studies had revealed little transfer under conditions replicated here under the heading of "practice," little or nothing had been done previously to find out what might happen with a different kind of teaching or, as designated in this study, "training." Much of the earlier work on the problem showed that under the usual conditions of "formal discipline" where transfer was taken for granted, little or no transfer actually took place. However, Dr. Woodrow was not satisfied to let matters rest there. He felt there must be some effective methods for making transfer take place and for increasing the amount of it. The experiment reported here constitutes a milestone in the field, and its findings are still valid though reported more than a generation ago. Taking college sophomores as subjects, the experimenter devised and carried out a study which demonstrated that with the right kind of instruction, substantial transfer could be brought about and that the extent of transfer under such conditions was significantly greater than it was with groups who merely practiced.

*Questions:*

1. How could the findings of this study be applied in teaching your own subject? Explain with a specific illustration.

2. Does transfer of training ever take place automatically? If so, give an example. If not, explain why not.

3. Does this study shed any light on explanatory theories of transfer? If it does, give an example.

\* \* \*

When an experimental study has shown that practice in one operation, *e.g.,* memorizing poetry, fails to produce improvement in another, *e.g.,*

* Reprinted from the *Journal of Educational Psychology,* **18:**159–172 (March 1927), by permission of author and publisher.

memorizing prose [5],* does this mean that the same conclusion is valid no matter what type of practice is used? Does it hold for practice accompanied by explanation of methods and illustrations of how these methods should be applied in the performance of other tasks than the one in which the individual is drilled? It is worth while to know that an experimenter allowed his subjects practice of a sort which did not result in a large degree of transference; but is it not of at least equal value to know how training can be given so as to transfer, that is, so as to produce improvement in a number of related functions?

That training of the latter sort is possible has been indicated by various experimental findings. The experiments particularly referred to are not the great mass of transference experiments. These latter, however, it should be noted in passing, have shown that improvement resulting from almost any sort of practice yields, as a rule, some transference. The lack of transference has in the past sometimes been exaggerated. Pillsbury pointedly remarks that "A few men hold and more have held that the result indicates that there is no transfer of training whatsoever." [3] Stratton sums the matter up rather definitely when he writes that, "The experiments in clear support of this doctrine—that you train merely what you train—are few; most experiments contradict it." [6]

The experiments which are particularly important, however, are those which show that, while practice of a narrow, routine sort may produce very little improvement in activities other than the one practiced, practice differently directed may be of marked benefit. Only a few such experiments have ever been made, and even these few have not always been reported in an adequate statistical manner. Probably the most important of these experiments, though one for which detailed data were never published, is one described by Judd [2]. In this experiment, two groups of boys were given practice in shooting at a target beneath water and, in the case of one of the groups, this practice was accompanied by a full theoretical explanation of refraction. When the depth of the target was changed, the group which had been taught the theory showed a striking superiority over the other group. Mention should also be made of the experiments of Squire and of Ruediger. Squire, according to the report of her experiment by Bagley [1], found that the habit of producing neat arithmetic papers failed to produce the slightest improvement in the neatness of language and spelling papers. Such findings constitute a remarkable illustration of the utter inadequacy of certain methods of training. Ruediger [4], however, conducted an investigation through teachers which showed that, while teaching the habit of neatness in

* Figure in brackets apply to references at end of article.

one school subject, one could, by inculcating the *ideal* of neatness, obtain an improvement in the paper in other school subjects, even though the topic of neatness was scrupulously avoided in connection with these other subjects.

May not the general problem which is raised by these few citations be stated as the problem of the difference, with respect to the resulting transference, between unenlightened drill and intelligent teaching? It has been so conceived in the experiment to be described.

This experiment deals with the possibility of teaching a general technique of memorizing. Its object is to show that training in certain kinds of memorizing may be given in two such widely different ways that in the one case, the individual will benefit little or not at all and, in the other case, enormously, when he turns to new kinds of memorizing. The technique of memorizing was chosen largely because it is among those techniques concerning which we possess fairly adequate knowledge. It would, perhaps, have been more interesting to attempt to teach the proper technique of reasoning; but it was believed too hazardous to attempt to teach what is not yet known. The experiment which was carried out on memorizing has, however, its analogy in any field of teaching where training is given in the hope that it will result in a better ability to undertake activities related to, though different from, the particular performances in which the individual is trained.

Three groups of subjects were required in the experiment. These will be designated the control, practice and training groups. The control group, consisting of one hundred and six university sophomores, was given no practice or training in memorizing, but was tested in six different forms of memorizing at the beginning and end of a period of four weeks and five days. The two other groups, the practice and the training groups, numbering thirty-four and forty-two, respectively, were given at the beginning and end of this period the same tests as the control group. The analysis of the procedure employed with the practice and training groups will be postponed until these "end-tests," given to all three groups, have been described, and data presented on their degree of relationship as shown by their intercorrelations.

The final and initial forms of each end-test were similar in form, but the actual material to be memorized was entirely different. All the material, except that used in testing memory-span, was presented to the subjects for study on mimeographed sheets. The tests were given to the subjects in groups, each group consisting of a section of thirty to forty-five sophomore students in experimental psychology. The six end-tests were as follows:

1. *Rote Poetry.*—The time required for learning verbatim certain verses

was the measure used. The initial test consisted of four verses of "Mistress Gilpin" comprising twenty-eight syllables each. The final test consisted of five verses of "Alice Brand," of twenty-eight syllables each. This second poem was harder to memorize than the first, so that for all groups it required a longer time.

2. *Rote Prose.*—The initial test consisted of a passage of ninety-eight words from Benjamin Franklin's "Autobiography." The time required for verbatim learning was recorded.

3. *Facts.*—A test of memory for the substance of prose sentences. The initial and final tests each contained two lists of twenty miscellaneous items of information, gleaned from a dictionary of facts. The subjects were allowed six minutes for study of the facts, then after a thirty seconds' pause, were given fifteen minutes, a very liberal period, to write out all that they could remember. For purposes of scoring, the statement of each fact was divided into from four to eight parts, in such a way that each part, in the experimenter's opinion, was about equally important. The subjects' papers were scored by determining the number of these parts which, in substance, were correctly reported. Every effort was made to keep the subjective element in the scoring as uniform as possible. The maximum possible score in the intial test was ninety-nine, and in the final test, ninety.

4. *Turkish-English Vocabulary.*—Each end test consisted of a list of thirty Turkish words with their English eqiuvalents.* The subjects were allowed six minutes for study of the vocabulary. Then, after one minute of intermission the Turkish words, printed in large type, were shown at the rate of one every six seconds, and the subjects endeavored to write the corresponding English words.

5. *Historical Dates.*—Lists of twenty, little-known historical events, together with their dates, were given the subjects to study for a period of six minutes. One minute after the end of this period, the names of the events, printed on large cards, were shown at the rate of one every six seconds, and the subjects attempted to write the corresponding dates. Half credit was given when the last two figures of the date were correct but the century wrong. No credit was given when the century alone was right. The score was the total number of correct answers, including the half-credits.

6. *Memory span, for consonants,* presented orally at the rate of one per second. Both initial and final tests included two series of lists, each series extending from a list of four to a list of ten, inclusive. The series were treated as series of minimal changes given to determine the point at which

* This material was compiled by Dr. W. S. Foster for use in connection with his laboratory manual, "Experiments in Psychology," 1923.

the chances of getting the series right or wrong are equal. The scores made on the two series were averaged.

The above six tests, although they are all called tests of memory, do not show a particularly high degree of interrelationship. Some of them show a very low correlation with the others. This would indicate that any technique which benefits performance in all of these tests must possess a wide range of applicability. The degree of interrelationship between the tests is shown in Table I, which gives the coefficients of correlation between the six tests, together with their probable errors, as obtained with the one hundred and six subjects constituting the control group. These coefficients have been corrected for attenuation, so as to avoid the possibility of conveying an exaggerated impression of the degree of alienation between the tests, which is undoubtedly large. The calculations were made by the formula,

$r_{\infty\infty} = \dfrac{r}{\sqrt{r_{13}r_{24}}}$, in which $r$ is the average of the four Pearsonian coefficients of correlation obtainable between the two scores (initial and final) of any two end-tests, and $r_{13}$ and $r_{24}$ are the coefficients of reliability of those two end-tests. The coefficient of reliability of any end-test is the coefficient of correlation between its initial and final forms.

The obtained coefficients of reliability were as follows:

**Coefficients of Reliability**

| Test | $r$ | PE |
|---|---|---|
| Rote Poetry | +.67 | +.05 |
| Rote Prose | +.49 | +.07 |
| Facts (Substance) | +.48 | +.07 |
| Historical Dates | +.60 | +.06 |
| Turkish-English Vocabulary | +.70 | +.05 |
| Memory Span | +.55 | +.07 |
| (Auditory, for Consonants) | | |

These coefficients of reliability are not as high as one might expect. It should be remembered, however, that the initial and final forms of any test comprised entirely different material, and that the subjects constituted a rather homogeneous, highly selected group.

So far as the present experiment is concerned, Table I is of interest, primarily, as indicating the degree of heterogeneity of the end-tests. It is true that several of the coefficients of correlation in the table are rather high as, for example, that for prose with poetry (both of which tests require verbatim memorizing) and also that for dates with vocabulary (both of which demand the formation of paired associates). The average of all the coeffi-

## Table . I

### Intercorrelations of the End-tests, Corrected for Attenuation

Each Coefficient has Its Probable Error [1] Given Immediately below It

| Tests | Poetry | Prose | Facts | Dates | Vocab-ulary | Span |
|---|---|---|---|---|---|---|
| Poetry .................. | | +.91 ±.05 | +.46 ±.08 | +.28 ±.08 | +.34 ±.08 | +.15 ±.09 |
| Prose .................. | +.91 ±.05 | | +.45 ±.09 | +.34 ±.09 | +.31 ±.08 | +.14 ±.09 |
| Facts .................. | +.46 ±.08 | +.45 ±.09 | | +.55 ±.08 | +.52 ±.07 | +.39 ±.09 |
| Dates .................. | +.28 ±.08 | +.34 ±.09 | +.55 ±.08 | | +.73 ±.05 | +.12 ±.09 |
| Vocabulary .............. | +.34 ±.08 | +.31 ±.08 | +.52 ±.07 | +.73 ±.05 | | +.06 ±.08 |
| Span .................. | +.15 ±.09 | +.14 ±.09 | +.39 ±.09 | +.12 ±.09 | +.06 ±.08 | |

[1] Probable errors are calculated by the formula: $(PE\ (r^{\infty\ \infty}) = .6745 \frac{r^{\infty\infty}}{2\sqrt{N}}$

$\left(4r^2_{\infty\infty} + \frac{1}{r^2_{\infty\infty}} + \frac{1 + r_{13} + r_{24}}{r^2} + \frac{1}{r^2_{13}} + \frac{1}{r^2_{24}} - \frac{4}{r_{13}} - \frac{4}{r_{24}} - 2\right)^{\frac{1}{2}}$. See Kelley, T.L.: "Statistical Method." 1923, p. 210.

cients in the table, however, is only +.38, sufficiently low, considering that the coefficients have been corrected for attenuation, to indicate that the end-tests taken as a whole bring into play widely dissimilar activities.

The primary object of the present investigation is not to study the results obtained with the end-tests given the control group, but to compare the "practice" group with the "training" group. It is important therefore, to record exactly the procedure employed with these two groups. They were both given practice, between the initial and final end-tests, in two forms of memorizing, namely, learning poetry verbatim and learning nonsense syllables in columns of pairs. To the practice group this drill was given, as has been customary in experiments on transference, in a routine fashion without any explanation of principles, discussion of methods, or comparison of the methods to be used in different kinds of problems. To the training group some practice was given with the same materials utilized by the practice group but, in addition, instruction was given in the technique of memorizing. The total time consumed by each group, apart from the end-tests, was 177 minutes divided into periods occurring twice a week for four weeks.

The periods varied from 19 to 28 minutes and averaged 22 minutes. Of the total time, the practice group spent 90 minutes in memorizing poetry and 87 minutes in memorizing nonsense syllables. The members of the training group divided their time as follows: for a total of 76 minutes, they listened to an exposition of the technique of memorizing, including rules and illustrations of how these rules should be applied: for 76 minutes, they memorized poetry; and for 25 minutes, they studied nonsense syllables. In the practice periods, both groups were motivated by the assurance of the experimenter that such work would improve their memory. In the case of the training group, however, all the practice in memorizing was done with the purpose of attempting, as far as possible, to apply the rules that had been learned. Nothing was said to the practice group as to how they should memorize, except that they were told to memorize by heart, and when they finished one selection to begin another. With the training group, on the other hand, an attempt was made to give a thorough understanding of the technique of memorizing. No attempt was made to obtain a record of the improvement of the groups during the training periods. In view of the object of the experiment, such a record seemed unnecessary, and the testing required to secure it would have added a degree of similarity to the training of the two groups which it was preferred to avoid. Such testing, moreover, would have considerably reduced the time, already too short, that was available for practice. To both groups, the final end-tests were given five days after the last practice period.

The detailed program for the eight practice periods of each group is shown in Table II.

The rules which were taught to the members of the training group, and which they applied to the memorizing of poetry and lists of pairs of nonsense syllables, were the following:

1. Learning by wholes.
2. Use of active self-testing.
3. Use of rhythm and of grouping.
4. Attention to meaning and the advantage of picturing, or, depending upon the individual—otherwise symbolizing the meaning.
5. Mental alertness and concentration.
6. Confidence in ability to memorize.
7. Use of secondary associations.

Some of the methods which were taught may not be particularly valuable, but the experiment was not planned to determine their relative merit.

It should be emphasized that neither group was given practice in the

## Table II

### Program of Practice Periods

| Period | Practice group | Training group |
|--------|----------------|----------------|
| I | 20 minutes: memorizing poetry | 7 minutes: listening to exposition of rules<br>13 minutes: memorizing poetry |
| II | 25 minutes: memorizing poetry | 7 minutes: listening to exposition of rules<br>18 minutes: memorizing poetry |
| III | 28 minutes: memorizing nonsense syllables | 28 minutes: listening to exposition and illustration of rules |
| IV | 20 minutes: memorizing nonsense syllables | 5 minutes: listening to review of preceding period<br>15 minutes: memorizing nonsense syllables |
| V | 19 minutes: memorizing nonsense syllables | 9 minutes: attending to "black-board talk" on meaning of secondary associations<br>10 minutes: memorizing nonsense syllables |
| VI | 25 minutes: memorizing poetry | 25 minutes: memorizing poetry |
| VII | 20 minutes: memorizing poetry | 20 minutes: memorizing poetry |
| VIII | 20 minutes: memorizing nonsense syllables | 20 minutes: listening to review of methods, and the situations in which to use them |
| Total time.. | 177 minutes | 177 minutes |

forms of memorizing tested by any of the end-tests, with the exception of the practice in memorizing poetry. Methods were illustrated solely by the use of poetry and nonsense syllables, and practice was limited to the same materials. For example, after explaining what is meant by secondary associations, the experimenter wrote nonsense syllables on the black-board and pointed out numerous secondary associations which could be used to remember them in pairs. It was then explained that similar associations could readily be formed between a Turkish word and an English word and that such associations should be used when memorizing a Turkish-English vocabulary. The group was given practice, however, only in the use of secondary associations in memorizing pairs of nonsense syllables. Again, in illustrating the meaning of grouping, it was pointed out how, in the case of either nonsense syllables or a line of poetry, grouping could be secured by means of accent. It was then explained that when attempting to remember a list of consonants given orally, this same sort of grouping should be employed. Such exercises as these do not constitute practice in memorizing either Turkish-English vocabularies or lists of consonants, and no such practice was given. Likewise, practice in learning *poetry* by the whole-method, even though it be accompanied by information that the same method should be used in the case of prose, is a far different thing from practice in memorizing prose. It is not alleged that the exercises used with the training group were as effective as would have been a few moments of practice in the exact forms of memorizing for which these exercises prepared. This direct practice was avoided, however, as the whole object of the experiment was to determine whether, without such direct practice, marked improvement in ability could yet be secured.

The scores made on the end-tests by each of the three groups are summarized in Table III. This table shows the average score on both the initial and final forms of each end-tests. In the fifth column is given the difference between the average initial, and the average final score. It will be noticed that in two cases, namely, memory for prose and memory for facts, this difference, at least for the control group, is negative. The explanation of these negative differences is very simple. In the case of poetry, it is due to the fact that the final poetry test required memorizing of a longer, and possibly harder, poem than the initial test. In the case of memory for facts, it is undoubtedly due to the circumstance that the second list of facts was scored in units (phases or ideas) which were not identical with those of the first list of facts and which yielded a smaller maximum possible score. These negative differences, or losses, in no wise hinder a comparison between the groups. For example, while the control group required 172 seconds longer to master the final poem than to learn the first one, the training group took only 57 seconds longer. In other words, the training group did better than the control group by 172 minus 57, or 115 seconds.

A study of the entire column of differences between initial and final scores shows that the practice group sometimes improved more, and sometimes less, than the control group. In other words, the data indicate that the practice given this group sometimes helped, but in two cases interfered, with performance on the final tests. In the case of all the end-tests except one, however, the difference in improvement between the practice and con-

## Table III

### Differences between Initial and Final Performances on the End-tests

N, Control Group = 106; Practice Group = 34; Training Group = 42. For Units of Measurement, See Description of Tests

| Test | Group | Initial Average | Final Average | Differences | PE$_{diff}$ | Percentage of Gain or Loss |
|---|---|---|---|---|---|---|
| Rote Poetry ........ | Control | 524 | 696 | −172 | ±11 | −32.8 |
| | Practice | 571 | 737 | −166 | ±18 | −29.1 |
| | Training | 539 | 596 | − 57 | ±15 | −10.6 |
| Rote Prose ........ | Control | 637 | 454 | +183 | ±11 | +28.7 |
| | Practice | 654 | 487 | +167 | ±18 | +25.5 |
| | Training | 731 | 361 | +370 | ±22 | +50.7 |
| Facts (Substance) ... | Control | 67.5 | 64.2 | − 3.3 | ± 0.96 | − 4.9 |
| | Practice | 64.0 | 61.0 | − 3.0 | ± 1.68 | − 4.7 |
| | Training | 64.0 | 72.2 | + 8.2 | ± 1.28 | +12.8 |
| Dates ........... | Control | 7.6 | 9.8 | + 2.2 | ± 0.21 | +29.0 |
| | Practice | 7.2 | 9.9 | + 2.7 | ± 0.38 | +37.5 |
| | Training | 6.5 | 12.2 | + 5.7 | ± 0.38 | +87.7 |
| Vocabulary (Turkish-Eng.) .. | Control | 16.2 | 16.1 | − 0.1 | ± 0.32 | − 0.6 |
| | Practice | 14.6 | 15.1 | + 0.5 | ± 0.51 | + 3.4 |
| | Training | 13.6 | 21.1 | + 7.5 | ± 0.59 | +55.2 |
| Span (Consonants) . | Control | 6.6 | 7.0 | + 0.4 | ± 0.05 | + 6.7 |
| | Practice | 7.0 | 6.6 | − 0.4 | ± 0.06 | − 5.7 |
| | Training | 6.4 | 7.7 | + 1.3 | ± 0.10 | +20.3 |

trol groups is small and statistically unreliable. Just how significant the differences are is shown in Table IV. The training group, on the other hand, shows for every end-test a decidedly greater improvement than either the practice or the control group.

In the extreme right hand column of Table III, headed "Percentage of gain or loss," is given the difference between final and initial scores, reckoned as a percentage of the initial score. These percentages permit of a comparison of the various groups which is less affected by the size of the initial scores than one based upon the absolute differences between final and initial scores. That this is true was determined by sectioning the groups into those whose initial scores were above or below the average. The gains (or losses) shown by two such sections of a group usually differed little when calculated as a percentage of initial score. It should be observed, however, that the differences in the initial scores of the various sections are in no case large. Moreover, in all tests except "rote prose," the initial ability of the training group happened to be lower than that of the practice group.

Consequently, it is all the more convincing that the scores made by the training group are, in all the final tests, much better than those of the practice group. The average percentage of improvement in the end-tests, calculated from Table III, is, for the practice group, 4.5, and for the training group, 36.1. Thus, the difference in the average percentage of gain of the two groups is 31.6. In the separate tests, this difference, which is always in favor of the training group, varies from 17.5 (in memory for facts) to 51.8 (in the Turkish-English vocabulary test).

Any improvement, shown by either the practice or training groups in the final tests is, of course, due to two factors. One of these is the repetition in

### Table IV

**Gains, in the End Tests, of the Practice and Training Groups, after Subtraction of Gains of the Control Group; and Gains of the Training Group after Subtraction of Gains of the Practice Group**

| End-test | Practice Gain Minus Control | | | Training Gain Minus Control | | | Training Gain Minus Practice | | |
|---|---|---|---|---|---|---|---|---|---|
| | *Diff.* | *PE* | *D/PE* | *Diff.* | *PE* | *D/PE* | *Diff.* | *PE* | *D/PE* |
| Poetry ... | + 6 | ±21 | 0.3 | +115 | ±19 | 6.1 | +109 | ±23 | 4.7 |
| Prose .... | −16 | ±21 | 0.8 | +187 | ±26 | 7.5 | +203 | ±28 | 7.3 |
| Facts .... | + 0.3 | ± 1.9 | 0.2 | + 11.5 | ± 1.6 | 7.2 | + 11.2 | ± 2.1 | 5.3 |
| Dates .... | + 0.5 | ± 0.4 | 1.3 | + 3.5 | ± 0.4 | 8.8 | + 3.0 | ± 0.5 | 6.0 |
| Vocab. ... | + 0.6 | ± 0.6 | 1.0 | + 7.6 | ± 0.7 | 10.9 | + 7.0 | ± 0.8 | 8.8 |
| Span .... | − 0.8 | ± 0.1 | 8.0 | + 0.9 | ± 0.1 | 9.0 | + 1.7 | ± 0.1 | 17.0 |

the final tests of the same kinds of memorizing as those required in the initial tests. The other is the effect of the exercises given between the initial and final tests. In order to compare the effects of the latter in the practice and training groups (which is the main object of the experiment), it is helpful first to subtract from their improvement the improvement due simply to repetition of the end-tests, shown by the control group. In this way, one obtains a reasonably accurate measure of the gain (or loss) shown by the practice or training groups, in so far as this is due solely to the effect of the practice or training periods. The gains, or losses, of the practice and training groups, thus computed, that is, after algebraic subtraction of the gains or losses of the control group, are shown in Table IV.

It will be seen from Table IV that, in all cases but two, the practice given the practice group was beneficial. It appears to have been most beneficial in the case of memory for historical dates. The two exceptions, *i.e.,* cases in which the practice periods resulted in a detraction of ability, are those of rote prose and auditory span for consonants. Only in the case of memory span, upon which the effect of the practice periods was detrimental, is the effect great enough to be very significant. Noteworthy is the small improvement shown by the practice group in memorizing poetry—one of the forms of memorizing in which this group was given practice. Of course, the activities involved in memorizing any two poems are not the same, as is indicated by the fact that a coefficient of correlation of only $+.67$ was obtained between the initial and final poetry tests. And one may recall that the pioneer experiment of William James dealt with the question whether practice in learning one poem would help in learning a different poem. That it often does not is indicated, more reliably, than by the results of James himself, by the careful and widely cited study by Sleight. This investigator found that children who practiced learning poetry showed, not only no improvement, but actually a slight loss, in the poetry end-test, relative to the children of the control group, who were given no practice in memorizing. [6] In the present experiment, the final poetry test required the learning of a somewhat longer and probably harder poem than any used in the practice periods. In memorizing it the practice group showed an average gain over the control group of twenty-one seconds, a gain which is equal only to three-tenths of its probable error. Such a slight gain in one of the two forms of memorizing actually practiced suggests that the practice was of little value even for the purpose of memorizing the type of material with which the practice was conducted, and raises the question whether practice which fails to produce marked gain in the activity practiced could possibly show any considerable degree of transference. That it may do so is indicated by the results obtained by Sleight, which show that the group which practiced memorizing poetry fell slightly below the control group in the final poetry tests, but greatly excelled the control group (by a gain equal to six times its probable error) in the final tests of memory for nonsense syllables.

The training group shows results which stand in striking contrast with those obtained with the practice group. The improvement shown by the training group in the final tests is, in the case of every end-test, much greater than that of the control group. The difference in the gains of the two groups is in no case less than six times the probable error of the difference. The superiority of the gains of the training group over those of the practice group is hardly less pronounced. The differences in their gains, which are in all cases in favor of the training group, vary from 4.7 to 17.0 times the probable errors of those differences.

The facts given establish very definitely certain conclusions. They show unequivocally that the training group did much better than the practice group in every one of six end-tests, which were related to each other only to the extent of an average intercorrelation, after correction for attenuation, of 38.3 per cent. The percentage of gain in the end-tests averaged 31.6 higher for the training group than for the control group. This greater gain on the part of the training group was obtained in spite of the fact that drill in memorizing was given to the training group with no other material than that employed with the practice group. It was produced by using the drill material primarily as material with which to conduct practice in proper methods of memorizing and, further, by explaining these methods and calling attention to the ones which should be employed when new kinds of memorizing were undertaken. In short, the experiment shows that in a case where one kind of training—undirected drill—produces amounts of transference which are sometimes positive and sometimes negative, but always small, another kind of training with the same drill material may result in a transference, the effects of which are uniformly large and positive.

While the investigation that has been described has taken the form of a laboratory experiment, it is hoped that it shows sufficient analogy to schoolroom situations to have a definite bearing upon education. For example, it might be found that the study of some particular subject, such as algebra, produces little improvement in ability to reason about problems in other subjects. According to the present results, however, such findings would tell little with respect to the possible value of the aforesaid subject as a medium for the giving of drill in the technique of reasoning, or of the results which could be obtained by its study under a teacher who so used it. Naturally, such a teacher would need to know both the proper technique of reasoning and how to illustrate the use of this technique in many widely different fields. To determine the amount of transference of ability that did result from the study of a particular subject is one thing, to determine the amount of transference which *might* be secured from the study of that same subject is a different and far more difficult thing. The investigation of problems of the latter sort must constitute an important part of the program for establishing a scientific basis for methods of teaching.

## References

1. BAGLEY, W. C. *The Educative Process*. New York: The Macmillan Co., p. 208 (1916).
2. JUDD, C. H. "The Relation of Special Training to General Intelligence." *Educational Review*. **XXXVI**:36–37 (1908).

3. PILLSBURY, W. B. "Education as the Psychologist Sees It." New York: The Macmillan Co., p. 300 (1925).

4. RUEDIGER, W. C. "The Indirect Improvement of Mental Functions through Ideals." *Educational Review*. **XXXVI:**364–371 (1908).

5. SLEIGHT, W. G. "Memory and Formal Training." *British Journal of Psychology*. **IV:**417 and 431 (1911).

6. STRATTON, G. M. "Developing Mental Power." Boston: Houghton Mifflin Co., pp. 12, 422 (1923).

# 20

## LEVELS OF ASPIRATION IN PRESCHOOL CHILDREN *

### Pauline S. Sears and Harry Levin

The significance of the concept of "level of aspiration" in goal setting has been well established. In a pioneer study published in 1940 (see reference #7 in bibliography at end of this selection) the senior author reported an experiment with children in elementary grades demonstrating that those who had experienced consistent success in school (arithmetic and/or reading) tended to set realistic goals for themselves in these subjects; on the other hand, those who had a history of school failure often set goals unrealistically high or, in some instances, very low. Their choice of goals was much less predictable than that of successful children. In the following selection a similar investigation is reported using four- and five-year-olds as subjects. It is postulated that a child is motivated by two forces in his choice of tasks. One is the desire to investigate and master some aspect of the environment—a sort of "I want to see what I can do" motive. Second, is the desire for approbation of what he does by others—the "See what a bright boy am I" motive. The experiment was designed with two purposes in mind. One was to devise a standardized, quantitative procedure for measuring a child's reactions to a variety of unfamiliar tasks. The second purpose was to test certain hypotheses regarding the two motives mentioned, and goal-setting behavior using the standardized procedures. The student may find the report of the study somewhat challenging and perhaps difficult; a careful study of it will be interesting and rewarding.

### Questions:

1. Three hypotheses were stated and tested in this experiment. Restate each in your own words.

2. In each case were the hypotheses confirmed or rejected? Justify your answers with evidence from the report.

* Reprinted from *Child Development,* **28:**317–326 (September 1957), by permission of senior author and the Society for Research in Child Development, Inc.

3. What are some of the implications of this study, and of the work on level of aspiration in general, for the classroom teacher?

\* \* \*

Early childhood is a time of learning a great number of skills, of attempting and practicing a multitude of new tasks. In the course of normal development, most children progress at a moderately orderly rate from attempting and mastering first the more simple tasks and then the tasks having more taxing physical or mental requirements. The amount of striving, energy output, and the number of successes and failures experienced by the child during this period staggers the adult imagination. Furthermore, many, if not most, of the new activities tried by the baby and young child are in a very real sense self-chosen. The mother may place the child in a favorable setting for undertaking a new task, and she may try to entice him into new skills, but basically the choice of which tasks he will and will not undertake is the child's own.

There appear to be two kinds of motives for such choices, and for the tremendous amount of striving and sheer endeavor which go on during these early years. First, we can observe what seems to be an intrinsic curiosity about, and desire to master, the external environment. Woodworth [8]* has called this the problem of mastery. Achievement of goals, such as walking upright, pulling up to a standing position, or placing a block in a cup, seem to be attended by satisfactions which likely derive from an enhanced view of the self as able to manipulate and control the environment. Young children often make mistakes in judging how much they can accomplish (relation of probability of achievement to ability), but, on the other hand, it is surprising how well they are able to calculate their endeavors in terms of probability of success at the moment. It is a reasonable postulate that the tasks which are self-chosen by the young child are those for which he perceives a good chance of success and also some instrumental gratification in terms of mastery or control over interesting parts of the environment.

A second component appears to be the social facilitation provided when other people observe and react to the child's performances. Approval or adulation from parents is a common reaction to the baby's first steps, and the child may also receive disapproval or punishment for his attempts at new tasks which the parent deems inappropriate for him. Some children become hesitant in reaction to many unfamiliar undertakings, while some

* Figure in brackets apply to references at end of article.

appear deliberately to choose to try new tasks at very considerable levels of difficulty. It appears that through observation of the child's free choices of activities when varying degrees of difficulty are present, and of his effort in performance of the chosen activity, we have a good lead into an understanding of the beginnings of achievement motivation.

The level of aspiration technique has been widely employed as a method for study of such achievement-oriented behaviors. Ordinarily, subjects have been required to state verbally a goal or expectation for their future performance. Further, the subjects need to have at least a partial concept of levels of difficulty or a frame of reference for performance on the task. Tasks and techniques for studying aspirations of adults, and children older than eight years, have been rather widely used, but a standard method for study of younger children in this regard has not been so easy to discover. Two studies, those of Fales [3] and Anderson [1], have employed young children as subjects. Fales, who was interested in the developmental aspects of level of aspiration, observed "rudimentary aspirations" in two- and three-year-olds according to whether they accepted or refused help with putting on their wraps. Anderson used three-, five-, and eight-year-old subjects in a ring-throwing task. By various criteria, he found that "maturity" of level of aspiration, by adult standards, increased with age. Interestingly enough, he took the willingness of a subject to risk failure as an indication of a higher development of level of aspiration.

Neither of these studies employed a method which would permit observation and quantification of children's reactions to a variety of unfamiliar tasks. The problem is to develop a procedure in which young children's behavior in a variety of goal-striving situations is reasonably standardized as to forms of expression, is sufficiently explicit to be communicated to an observer, and is quantifiable to the extent that choices and performances can be compared from task to task and child to child. The present study has as its first purpose the development of such a procedure.

Secondly, a test was desired of certain predictions relative to modifiability of aspiration behavior under standard conditions, and of its consistency in individual subjects of preschool age. The child, after he chooses the level of a task for which he will try, can react to the consequent success or failure (achievement or nonachievement of the chosen level) in one of three ways. He may (a) set a still higher goal, (b) choose a lower goal, or (c) maintain the same goal. Following success, responses (b) and (c) are the "safer" ones, that is, they will make future success more probable. After failure, only response (b) increases the likelihood of later success; the other responses put him in line for recurrent failure experiences, provided other factors in the performance sequence remain constant.

It is postulated that the child reacts to this performance situation with motivation deriving from the two types of motivation previously described: the first component of desire for mastery, which instigates levels of endeavor likely to ensure successful performance; and the second component, which provides individual variation in predominant choice of level, depending on the child's experiences in gaining approval or social facilitation for his performances. For example, goal-setting responses may be influenced by the parents' previous treatments of successes or failures, and by their pressures on the child for independence, achievement, or competitiveness. We would expect that the child who has experienced reward for trying new and more difficult activities would react by setting a more difficult goal after success and persisting at the same goal after failure. Gratification has here been attached to achievement at a difficult level; the "success" experience is probably contingent upon this. With fewer rewards of this nature in his experience, the child is freer to choose goals which ensure some achievement with less effort, that is, to operate at the easier levels of tasks.

In the test situations that will be described here, the levels of difficulty were defined for the child in terms of "how many other children can attain" each level, the most difficult being possible for "only a very few children." Thus, the frame of reference given to the subjects was the abilities of a similar group; this is similar to the procedure used by Anderson and Brandt [2] with fifth grade children. Presumably, this frame of reference should influence upward the goal-setting choices of those children who have in the past gained social approval by performing better than the average; children whose parents have not made such comparisons should avoid the difficult tasks on the practical ground that success is less probable at the higher levels.

Further, the attitude of the experimenter, a friendly adult who was constantly present in the situation, was expected to influence the behavior of the children. The attitude adopted for the present experiment was a warm and nonevaluative one; the experimenter's reaction to the child's choices was equally friendly no matter whether their choices were high or low. It was predicted that as the child had continuing experience with this permissive situation, the forces in him which act to inhibit maximum success through repeated goal choices at difficult levels should be relaxed, permitting goal choices which maximize success.

In summary, it was hypothesized that (a) children will generally choose levels of difficulty so as to maximize achievement; (b) there will appear individual differences in the extent to which children elect to try for achievement at more difficult levels; (c) in an experimental situation in which social interaction with the experimenter is friendly and nonevaluative, it is expected that the child's original achievement pressures will gradually be relaxed so that he will be freer to choose tasks for which success is more likely.

## Method

There are certain requirements to the selection of tasks and procedures for use in connection with the level of aspiration technique [6]. When four- and five-year-olds are to be the subjects, special problems arise in the meeting of these requirements. The tasks must be absorbing and challenging to the children, yet not be ones with which they have had a great deal of prior experience. At the same time, instructions must be simple, and the tasks not so strange that the children cannot comprehend them. Success and failure must be apparent at the conclusion of each performance, and should be perceived by a child as a direct result of his own behavior, rather than as being imposed by definition of the adult experimenter.[1] Finally, the concept of a graduated order of difficulty, in each task, must be learned and transferred from task to task.

To meet the latter requisite, each task in the present instance had five levels of difficulty and each level was given a characteristic color which was the same for every task; for example, the green colored materials were the easiest level of each separate task and red always the most difficult. In addition, the child indicated his choice of level by putting a peg in a peg board which was divided into colored sections representing the five levels of difficulty. The board was carried from task to task and was a common element attached to all the tasks.

The concept of a graduated series of difficulty with different colors standing for different difficulties was introduced to the children by way of a motor task involving large muscle activity: jumping to hit balls hung at varying heights. Here, the child could see, for example, that a red colored ball was the highest of the five colored balls and could "feel" that it was harder to jump for. Attempts to teach the child this concept on tasks having less immediately apparent difficulty gradations were not so successful.

---

[1] Success and failure in this study are defined as the achievement or nonachievement of the goal which the child has previously set for himself.

*Equipment*

Six tasks were devised, each task having five levels of difficulty. The levels were indicated by colors; green being the easiest, then yellow, brown, blue, and red, which was the hardest. The five levels of difficulty were marked by the same colors for each of the tasks.

*Task 1—Jumping for balls.* Five sponge rubber balls were suspended on strings from a rod hung from the ceiling. They hung in a line, three inches apart. The easiest to reach (green) was just within fingertip reach of the child, and each was hung about three inches higher than the preceding so that the red was the highest and most difficult for the child to reach. The over-all height of the series of balls was adjusted to children of differing heights by raising or lowering the board on which they were fastened. The child was asked to choose the color of the ball which he would try to hit on his jump.

*Task 2—Designs.* Designs painted on cards in the appropriate colors were copied by the children, using small triangular parquetry blocks. The blocks were also appropriately colored to represent the difficulty level. The intricacy of the designs increased with each level of difficulty. Several series of designs were used so that when a child repeated any given level of difficulty, he could be given another design of the same level and color. The children were given two minutes to complete the design.

*Task 3—Pulling weights.* Five sash weights, appropriately colored, rode in five vertical tracks ranged a few inches apart along a wall. The top of the track was seven feet above the floor, and the child had to pull the weight from its resting place on the floor to the top of the track by pulling on a rope which rode over a pulley at the top of the track. The weights, in order of difficulty, were approximately 2½, 5, 10, 15 and 30 pounds. This was a very popular task.

*Task 4—Light up.* This is a commercial toy in which a page of designs with holes in the centers are mounted on a conductor plate so that when two appropriate holes are matched by inserting a metal stylus into each, a circuit is closed and a bulb lights up. The child's task was to find the design which matched the one in which the experimenter had inserted one stylus. The designs varied in difficulty from matching colors, to objects, simple geometric shapes, words, and finally, intricate designs. Each design sheet was appropriately colored, from the green, or easiest sheet, to red which was most difficult, and there were several in each series so that the child could repeat a color choice.

*Task 5—Broad jump.* Five squares were painted on the floor, green closest to the starting line and red farthest from it. The child had to reach the color of his choice by one jump from the starting line.

*Task 6—Remembering.* A number of small objects, such as a coin, light bulb, and miniature household objects, were concealed under each of five painted boxes. The child chose a box by naming the color and the experimenter lifted it. The child studied the objects until he announced that he was ready, and then the box was replaced. The child then tried to name the objects from memory. Levels of difficulty were varied by the number of objects under each box, starting with four objects under the green box and increasing by one for each color. Several series were necessary so that the child could repeat a level of difficulty.[2]

*Procedure*

The child was taken into a room in which all of the tasks were laid out. During the first session the order of tasks was as given above. The experimenter, pointing to the first task, said, "Every game we play has some easy ones and some hard ones. The brown is middling hard. Some children can do it and some can't. Now the blue is harder. Not many children can do it. Red is hardest of all. Just a very few children can do it. Green is very easy. Yellow is next hardest but not as hard as the brown. Do you understand? I wonder which one you are going to choose."

After the child made a choice, he was given the peg board and instructed to insert a peg into the color corresponding to his choice. After the child's performance, the experimenter said, in a nonevaluative manner, "You chose yellow and you got (did not get) yellow. Which are you going to choose next? You can choose yellow again, or brown, or blue, or red, or green." The instructions about the levels of difficulty were repeated several times during each task until it was certain that the child understood the set-up. There were *six trials* in each task.

In the second session, a few days later, the child was permitted to choose his own order of tasks. The directions about the colors and the peg board were repeated, as in the first session.

[2] It is our impression that the motor tasks (1, 3, 5 above) were more successful than the other three in involving the children and seeming meaningful to them. Task 2 (designs) did not completely fulfill our criterion that the outcome be apparent as resulting from the child himself, since it was a task timed by the experimenter. However, the children frequently looked at the watch wanting to know how much time was left, so we believe that they took the task seriously. The remembering task could be uncovered to show the children what objects he had forgotten. It appeared that the children, on the whole, were well motivated for all tasks.

The child's choices, whether he succeeded or failed, his comments and bodily tensions were recorded by a second observer from behind a one-way screen.

## Subjects

The subjects of this study were 19 four- and five-year-old children, 12 boys and 7 girls. The children were enrolled in the Harvard Preschool and came from middle-class, chiefly professional, families.

## Results

### Choices for Easy or Difficult Levels

A major problem in working with children of this young age is to ascertain that they are indeed reacting to the experimental situation rather than in some fortuitous fashion. If they were behaving randomly, we would expect their color choices to be the chance value (20 per cent) for each color. That this is not the case can be seen in Table 1. During the first

### Table 1
### Total Choices for Each Color

|  | Session 1 | | Session 2 | | | | |
|---|---|---|---|---|---|---|---|
|  | $N$† | % | $N$† | % | $\sigma_{diff.}$ | $t$ | $r$ |
| Green (Easy) .... | 177 | 27.95 | 237 | 35.42 | | | |
| Yellow .......... | 150 | 23.37 | 164 | 24.36 | | | |
| Brown .......... | 120 | 18.95 | 116 | 17.32 | | | |
| Blue ............ | 108 | 16.95 | 82 | 12.31 | | | |
| Red (Hard) ...... | 78 | 12.16 | 66 | 10.16 | | | |
| Green and Yellow . | 327 | 51.32 | 401 | 59.68 | 3.33 | 2.51** | .55** |
| Blue and Red ..... | 186 | 29.11 | 148 | 22.47 | 2.54 | 2.59** | .49* |

\* $p < .05$.
\*\* $p < .01$.
† Number of responses. The total possible number per session for all 19 subjects was 684. The total number of choices in this table is less than 684 since subjects occasionally refused to make all 36 choices required in a session.

session there are more easy and fewer difficult choices than might be expected by chance. The preponderance of easy choices is even more marked in the second session.

*Shifts with Increasing Experience in the Situation*

The percentages of all choices which are green and yellow, that is, at the easier levels of the tasks; and blue and red, the more difficult levels, are presented in the last two rows of Table 1. In the second experimental session, there was a significant mean shift of color choices toward the easier end of the series, and correlatively, away from the more difficult levels. This finding is in keeping with the hypothesis that the children's choices will change in the direction of ensuring more frequent success, when the situation is one that is nonevaluative and without external pressures or rewards for achievement.

### Table 2
**Responses after Success (Achievement of Goal)**

|  | Session 1 | | Session 2 | | $\sigma_{diff.}$ | $t$ | $r$ |
|---|---|---|---|---|---|---|---|
|  | N | % † | N | % † | | | |
| Up | 237 | 65.42 | 219 | 49.31 | 4.12 | 3.93** | .50* |
| Down | 91 | 23.78 | 128 | 29.84 | 3.10 | 1.95* | .65** |
| Same | 39 | 10.74 | 90 | 19.68 | 3.60 | 2.48** | .30 |
| Successes | 451 | 70.89 | 519 | 77.89 | 2.31 | 3.03** | .59** |

\* $p < .05$.
\*\* $p < .01$.
† Percentage of each type of response after success for each subject was calculated with the denominator equal to total number of successes minus the number of tasks whose final responses were successful.

We also hypothesized that with increasing experience in this situation the behaviors after success would change so as to maximize attainment of goals. Table 2 gives the proportions of choices upward, downward, and at the same level after success; *i.e.,* after the child has achieved his previously stated choice. In the second session, as compared to the first, there was a significantly greater proportion of successes which were followed by setting a lower goal or rechoosing the same goal. Correlatively, fewer successes in the second session were followed by setting of a higher goal, although in both sessions a higher choice after success was the most frequent response to reaching the previously set goal. In the first session the average number of successes (achievement of aspiration) was 70.89 per cent of all the trials, and in the second session, 77.89 per cent, so the changes in goal setting after success actually did result in a greater number of goals being reached.

If the child's purpose, after continuing experience in the level of aspiration situation, is to set goals which he has a high probability of reaching, the most adaptive response to failure is to set a lower goal for the next trial. That this is the most common response to failure in both sessions is seen in Table 3. The session-to-session increase in the proportion of failures followed by setting of a lower goal was in the expected direction, although not statistically significant. Likewise, there was a nonsignificant decrease in the proportion of failures which were followed by the child's setting a still

### Table 3
#### Responses after Failure

|  | Session 1 | | Session 2 | | | | |
|---|---|---|---|---|---|---|---|
|  | N | %† | N | %† | $\sigma_{diff.}$ | t | r |
| Up ............. | 37 | 24.17 | 24 | 17.15 | 5.19 | 1.35 | .25 |
| Down .......... | 95 | 63.84 | 76 | 66.47 | 7.18 | .37 | −.07 |
| Same .......... | 15 | 11.83 | 18 | 16.26 | 4.61 | .96 | .26 |
| Failures ........ | 182 | 29.11 | 146 | 22.11 | 2.30 | 3.04** | .60** |

** $p < .01$.
† See footnote to Table 2.

higher goal. The slight, though insignificant, increase in the second session in repeating a choice after failure was contrary to the hypothesis that the child will maximize successes. However, both repetition and going up after failure were rare responses.

Under what conditions will continued experience in a permissive and nonevaluative level of aspiration situation bring about a lowering in the goals set? Jucknat [5], for instance, found that the stronger the success (as judged by the experimenter) the more the subjects tended to increase their levels of aspiration. In the present situation, the external reward for reaching the stated goal was the same regardless of the level of the task at which the child was operating. The pressures to choose the more difficult absolute levels were intrinsic to the child rather than attached to adult approval offered by the experimenter. When these pressures could be relaxed through social interaction in this relatively permissive situation, the child was free to try for the "same" achievement at more likely levels. According to Anderson [1], the tendency for children to change their behavior so as not to risk failure might be interpreted as regression to a lower developmental level, *i.e.,* less stability for possibly internalized parental values toward achievement.

## Consistency of Aspiration

A major focus of interest in level of aspiration studies has been the generality, or consistency, of the levels set. Heathers' [4] work has shown that the generality of the level of aspiration is a function of the similarity of conditions under which levels are set. In Tables 1, 2, 3 are reported the correlations between sessions 1 and 2 on color choices, responses to success, and responses to failure.

The children tended to be consistent from session to session in the proportion of easy and difficult tasks they chose (*r*'s of +.55 and +.49). Also, they were consistent in their responses after success as to the proportion of trials in which they went up or down (*r*'s of +.50 and +.65). The correlation between the percentage of trials following success in which they chose the same level in the two sessions is .30, which, though positive, is not significant. These four- and five-year-old subjects, then, tended to show consistent responses in the levels of difficulty (colors) which they chose, as well as in the nature of their choices following successful trials.

On the other hand, the subjects showed no consistent pattern of choices from session to session in their choices after failure. One reason for this may be a lower reliability of the failure scores that may have resulted from the fact that there were considerably fewer of them than of the success trials. Secondly, this may represent the common finding that behavior following punishment or failure is more variable than behavior following reward. Sears [7], for example, found that children who had a history of school failure had more widely variable discrepancy scores in level of aspiration situations than did children who had habitual success, and also that induced failure increased variability of aspiration scores.

It is interesting to note that, although the group means for color choices and responses following successful trials changed in a predictable fashion, the individual children tended to retain their relative positions within the group, as shown by the *r*'s. This represents a consistency in behavior over the two experimental sessions.

## Summary and Conclusions

Nineteen four- and five-year-old children were observed in two sessions of a level of aspiration situation. There were six separate tasks, each of which was graded into five levels of difficulty. The following findings emerged from this study:

1. Children of these ages were able in the first session to discriminate among the levels of difficulty and tended to choose the easier levels of the tasks, *i.e.,* the levels at which success was more probable.

2. The choices of the levels of difficulty and the choices following success changed in the second session in the direction of ensuring more frequent success.

3. The children tended to be individually consistent from session to session in proportion of choices at given levels of difficulty and in their reactions to successful achievement at the level chosen.

4. There were no consistent patterns of responses following failure to achieve a previously set goal.

## References

1. ANDERSON, C. "The Development of a Level of Aspiration in Young Children." Unpublished doctor's dissertation. State Univer. of Iowa (1940).

2. ANDERSON, H. H. and H. F. BRANDT. "Study of Motivation Involving Self-announced Goals of Fifth Grade Children and the Concept of Level of Aspiration." *J. Soc. Psychol.* **10:**209–232 (1939).

3. FALES, E. "Genesis of Level of Aspiration in Children from One and One-half to Three Years of Age. Reported in Lewin *et al.* [6].

4. HEATHERS, L. B. "Factors Producing Generality in the Level of Aspiration." *J. Exp. Psychol.* **30:**392–406 (1942).

5. JUCKNAT, M. Leistung. "Anschpruchsniveau und Selbstbewusstsein." *Psychol. Forsch.* **22:**89–179 (1937).

6. LEWIN, K., *et al.* "Level of Aspiration." In J. McV. HUNT (ed.), *Personality and Behavior Disorders.* New York: Ronald Press (1944), pp. 333–378.

7. SEARS, PAULINE S. "Levels of Aspiration in Academically Successful and Unsuccessful Children." *J. Abnorm. Soc. Psychol.* **35:**498–536 (1940).

8. WOODWORTH, R. S. *Adjustment and Mastery.* Baltimore: Williams & Wilkins (1933).

# 21

# TO PROMOTE OR NOT TO PROMOTE? *

## John I. Goodlad

The controversy over promotion versus non-promotion has raged for years. Twenty-five years ago it was common practice to have pupils repeat one or more grades, especially the primary grades. So-called age-grade tables showed a large amount of retardation, that is, pupils who had repeated one or more grades and who therefore were overage. Gradually a change took place. Research on the question showed that pupils often did poorer work, or at least no better, when they repeated a grade than they had done the first time. Far fewer pupils are "retained" today than there were twenty-five years ago. But still the argument continues. Dr. Goodlad, who has studied the question intensively, reviews the arguments for non-promotion and those for promotion. Strangely enough they are very similar. In this article he seems to be saying that the argument is futile and that there should be none. He proposes a solution that he believes would eliminate the problem entirely.

*Questions:*

1. The author of this article surmises that there may be one million elementary school pupils retained in their present grades each year. Can you check this figure? See if you can find data on the question.

2. If grade barriers were eliminated below sixth grade what kind of grouping of pupils would be used? What new problems might arise?

\* \* \*

To promote or not to promote—That is the question that will plague teachers—several hundred thousand teachers—this coming June. And it is a question that has plagued them each year for decades. Had Rip Van Winkle been a teacher, and had he dozed off in 1934 while deliberating the fate of thirty youngsters, he might have resumed his deliberations quite

\* Reprinted from *Childhood Education,* **30:**212–215, No. 5 (January 1954), by permission of author and the Association for Childhood Education International, 3615 Wisconsin Avenue, N.W., Washington 16, D.C.

naturally on awakening in 1954. Not a soul would laugh; not a soul would consider his activities bizarre. Only the thankful thirty, spared through Rip's somnolent sojourn, might rejoice that the belated decisions would now have no bearing upon their lives.

Some claim that promotion scarcely can be considered a significant mid-century educational problem. "Why, I seldom find it necessary to retain more than three children," they may add. Three children out of, say, thirty? That's ten percent. And ten percent amounts to two and one half million elementary-school children in all of America. But it must be recognized that many schools promote all or nearly all pupils. Let's be very conservative, then, and say that only one million elementary-school children are retained in their present grades each year. Promotion an insignificant problem? One could hardly agree.

**Not to Promote**

Why retain a child? Let us think through some of the reasoning that must lie behind a million decisions not to promote. We may not agree with them, but the following are some of the reasons often given to justify non-promotion:

• When promotion is assured, pupils are unconcerned about their school work, developing poor work habits and careless attitudes.

• Bright children come to resent equal promotion rewards for work that is obviously inferior.

• Because of the need for teachers to spend a disproportionate amount of time with slow-learners, the presence of these children in the room serves as a hindrance to progress. The range of achievement is widened and group homogeneity reduced.

• Achievement levels are enhanced through the repetition of only partially learned material.

• Immature children, through grade repetition, are more likely to find suitable play and work companions at the lower grade level.

• The promoted slow-learner, unable to do the work of the grade, frustrated and discouraged, develops inferiority feelings which adversely affect his social relationships and personality development.

**To Promote**

There are many people who believe that slow-learning children should be promoted, regardless of present levels of attainment. Again, we may not agree with the arguments put forth to support this position but let's examine a few of them:

- The possibility of nonpromotion is a threat that constitutes negative motivation. Children learn best under conditions of positive motivation and therefore should be promoted.

- Children distribute themselves from poor to excellent on each of the many school endeavors in which they engage, usually with only slight variations from child to child on the continuum. To average these attainments is unrealistic. To determine arbitrary cutting points for passing or failing demands a refinement in judgment that defies human capacities.

- The presence of older, repeating children in a classroom decreases group homogeneity.

- Learning is enhanced when children move on to new endeavors instead of experiencing the dullness and boredom of repetition.

- Grade repetition results in over-ageness which, in turn, produces behavior problems requiring special disciplinary action.

- Promotion retains approximately equal chronological age as a common factor and results in improved personal and social relationships.

## What Are the Facts?

It is vividly apparent that the two sets of arguments are virtually identical. Each claims for itself the same virtues and, for the other, the same vices. Now for both to be right, obviously, is impossible. Either there is nothing to choose between the two practices or then one must be superior to the other on the questions in debate. What are the facts?

Fortunately, a considerable body of research is available. This research has been summarized elsewhere [1] and the reader is urged to go to the sources. On each of the arguments above, where there is research evidence in any acceptable form, that evidence points clearly to the fact that *slow-learning children profit significantly more from promotion than from nonpromotion*. They attain higher achievement levels when promoted, require less disciplinary action, display more positive attitudes toward school and teachers, and appear to enjoy more satisfactory social and personal lives. It should be clearly understood that promotion is no universal panacea for learning disabilities. It simply is the more defensible of two promotion alternatives.

## Neither Is the Answer

The crux of the promotion issue is that there ought not to be any alternatives. *There ought not be a decision to make.* Promotion and nonpromotion

[1] John I. Goodlad, "Research and Theory Regarding Promotion and Nonpromotion," *Elementary School Journal.* L 111, November 1952, 150–155.

are *both* inconsistent with certain significant insights into children and their learning:

• Neither promotion nor nonpromotion, in and of itself, can change a child's basic learning rate.

• Arbitrary grade norms for a field of study usually are approximated at a given time by less than half the children in that grade.

• A child seldom approximates arbitrary grade norms in all areas of endeavor. He may be significantly above in one and below in another, and only slightly above or below in still others.

• The spread in mental age among a group of children, already as much as four years in the first grade, becomes greater as these children progress through the elementary school. The spread in academic attainment, in turn, will tend to keep pace with the broadening spread in mental age, especially under conditions of good teaching.

In the light of these facts, how can concepts either of promotion or non-promotion be applied meaningfully? Susie is at third-grade expectancy in all areas except arithmetic where she lags behind at low second-grade level. Teddy's work spreads out from the second to the fifth grade but if all his attainments were averaged, his placement would be only three months into the third grade. Mary is very advanced. She is at the fifth-grade level in all her work but is very small for her age. All three are completing their third year at school. Should Susie be promoted and Teddy retained? Should Teddy be promoted and Susie retained? Should Mary be advanced to the sixth grade? Are these really the questions to which teachers' time should be devoted?

Neither promotion nor nonpromotion materially changes the natural heterogeneity ever-present in a group of six-year-olds, nine-year-olds, or twelve-year-olds. This statement has been amply documented. (See, for example, Walter W. Cook, *Grouping and Promotion in the Elementary Schools*. Minneapolis: University of Minnesota Press, 1941.) Miss Stevens must make provision for those children who read well or poorly, are large or small, get along well with others or have difficulty sharing. Keeping back two or three children each year doesn't help her or her colleagues. It may lull her into thinking, for a few blissful moments, that she has a homogeneous group. Alas, even groups of two aren't homogeneous! Promotion and nonpromotion are merely the trappings of an educational era that should be long past. They do absolutely nothing to ease or expedite the job of the teacher. They certainly do nothing for children.

**Several Answers—Not One**

To promote or not to promote— What is the answer? There are several answers rather than one.

First, it must be recognized that most teachers in America today work in a system of grade classification requiring that children move from step to step through it. It is recognized, further, that courses of study, textbooks, and even teachers are organized around the grade concept. When children are brought together in groups of thirty and more under such a grade classification system, it soon becomes apparent that some children deviate so markedly in certain characteristics that the desirability of retaining them in the group comes in for questioning.

Under such an organizational setup, retention of some children, while the group as a whole progresses to the next step, occasionally appears to be a logical solution. (The author deplores the circumstances over the act of retention itself.) In the face of ample research evidence, to the effect that nonpromotion less frequently than promotion results in favorable later adjustment of children, the teacher should be cautioned to ponder carefully each instance of doubtful promotion. When he cannot say with conviction, "Knowing this child as I do, the chances for successful school experience next year and in subsequent years are greater if he be retained," then he is advised to give the child the benefit of any existing doubt and promote him. We can ill afford to ignore the research that is before us.

But, under such circumstances, the act of promoting or retaining is only the beginning. The repeater must be provided for. Simply to do over work that was inadequately done before is not the answer. The year with younger classmates must be filled with exciting challenges; not dulled with the repetition of activities long since wrung dry of interest and stimulation. To promote the slow-learner to tasks far beyond his comprehension likewise is no kindness. Whether slow-progress children be regularly or irregularly promoted, adequate subsequent provision for their needs is essential.

These are short-term answers to the promotion question. In a sense, they constitute tardy treatment for a very sick horse. But now, let us go back to an earlier statement that neither nonpromotion nor promotion is the real answer. Needed is an educational organization that facilitates continuous progress of all children in each of the various facets of their development.

Is it not logical that children who are ready for more advanced work in reading should proceed to it, free from the artificial restrictions of grade barriers? Is it not logical that certain of these children, slow in arithmetic, should proceed slowly with appropriate work in this field?

These are the realities with which we are faced. Is it not time that we adapted organizational procedures to fit them? The time for us to abandon our Procrustean lock-step system that chops children to make them fit the norms is long past. Instruction has for too long been the handmaiden of organization.

The long-term answer, then, is the elimination of those grade barriers that have given rise to a host of fallacious notions about pupil progress, of which the fantasy that children should arrive precisely at a given "norm" each June is the most preposterous. Primary unit plans—such as those experimented with in Milwaukee, Wisconsin, and the Nathaniel Hawthorne School in University City, Missouri, to cite only two examples—constitute a step in the right direction.

Perhaps years of experimentation with such plans will show us at long last that grade barriers are as unreasonable above the third grade as they are for the first three grades.

The obvious result, of course, is that promotion and nonpromotion simply will disappear from school practice—yes, even from our vocabularies. With the philosophy of continuous progress—and there is a vast difference between "continuous progress" and "social promotion" or any other kind of one hundred percent promotion—firmly entrenched, and grade barriers no longer existent, to promote or not to promote no longer will be a question. Let us hope that this Utopia is so imminent that should any 1954 Rip Van Winkle doze off in the midst of his promotion meditations, continuation of his activities on awakening in 1974 would be absurd, indeed!

## 22

# THE EFFECT OF REPEATED PRAISE OR BLAME ON THE WORK ACHIEVEMENT OF "INTROVERTS" AND "EXTROVERTS" *

### George G. Thompson and Clarence W. Hunnicutt

A number of studies have been made of the effect of praise and blame on the work of children. The relations of these incentives to age, sex, intelligence, race and other factors have been investigated. In general, the results show that both incentives are effective as motivators but that indiscriminate or prolonged use of either tends to reduce its effectiveness. One study was concerned with the effects of blame or praise on different personalities, namely the extrovert and the introvert. However, the incentive was used only three times. The authors of the following selection, believing that the effects of more extended application of blame and praise should be investigated, set up an experiment with fifth grade pupils to do so. These pupils were classified as introverts or extroverts on the basis of their scores on a section of a personality test designed to measure this trait. Those whose scores were above the median were placed in one group, the extroverts, and those scoring below the median in the introvert group. Pupils worked on a cancellation test for six days. On the second and every succeeding day certain ones were told by the teacher that they had done well: the others that they had done poorly. Results are measured in terms of gains on the test and related to the incentive used and introversion-extroversion.

*Questions:*

1. As a teacher how would you decide whether to use praise (encouragement) or blame (reproof) with an individual pupil? Does this study help?

2. What do you predict the results of the experiment would have shown if it had been continued a week longer? Why?

\* \* \*

* Reprinted from the *Journal of Educational Psychology*, **35**:257–266 (May 1944), by permission of senior author and publisher.

An investigation by Forlano and Axelrod [1] has indicated that repeated applications of praise or blame have differential effects on the work performance of "introverts" and "extroverts." In the investigation conducted by them, praise or blame was repeated only two times. The present study was conducted to determine the effects of more extended applications of praise or blame on the work achievement of "introverts" and "extroverts." The methods employed, however, are quite similar to those used by Forlano and Axelrod.

If praise or blame has differential effects on children with different personality characteristics, teachers should be cognizant of the fact. It seems altogether possible that indiscriminate praise may be as detrimental to a pupil's school achievement and personality development as indiscriminate blame. It also seems possible that the skillful teacher could at times employ blame, as well as praise, to foster the child's general adjustment.

## Method

*Subjects*

Fifth-grade pupils from five classes in the Syracuse Public Schools were selected as subjects for this study. One class of twenty-seven pupils was used for the control group. The remaining four classes (comprising ninety-seven pupils) were subdivided into the various experimental groups in the manner described below.

Several days before the experiment proper was conducted the Introversion-Extroversion section of a Personality Test by Pintner and Others was administered to all of the one hundred twenty-four subjects employed in this study. On the basis of total scores obtained on this thirty-five-item test the children in each class were divided into two groups. Pupils with scores above the median were considered "extroverts," while those pupils with scores below the median were considered "introverts."

In the first class of fifth-grade pupils the "extroverts" were praised after each task, and the "introverts" were blamed. In the second class of pupils this procedure was reversed and the "extroverts" were blamed while the "introverts" were praised. By alternating this procedure in the remaining two classes it was possible to obtain approximately the same number of pupils in each of the four experimental combinations.

[1] Forlano, George, and H. C. Axelrod, "The effect of repeated praise or blame on the performance of introverts and extroverts." *J. Educ. Psychol.,* 1937, 28, 92–100.

*Introversion-Extroversion Scores*

The forty-seven subjects who were praised after each task (including both "introverts" and "extroverts") obtained a mean score on the Intro-version-Extroversion test of 21.2. The fifty subjects who were blamed after each task (including both "introverts" and "extroverts") obtained a mean score of 21.9. The Control Group of twenty-seven pupils obtained a mean score of 21.5. A statistical analysis of the introversion-extroversion scores obtained by these three groups resulted in an F of 0.317, which is not significant at any acceptable level of confidence. Hence, these three groups may be accepted as unbiased samples from the same population with respect to introversion-extroversion.

The mean introversion-extroversion scores obtained by the pupils in each of the four experimental combinations are shown in Table I.

**Table I**

| *Experimental Groups* | *Number of Subjects* | *Mean Score on Introversion-Extroversion Test* |
|---|---|---|
| Extroverts—Praised .......... | 23 | 24.4 |
| Extroverts—Blamed .......... | 28 | 23.8 |
| Introverts—Praised .......... | 24 | 18.2 |
| Introverts—Blamed .......... | 22 | 19.5 |

The results of a statistical analysis of the mean introversion-extroversion scores obtained by the subjects of the four experimental combinations are presented in Table II. It may be concluded from these results that the Extrovert-Praised and the Extrovert-Blamed groups are not significantly different in mean introversion-extroversion scores; and that the mean intro-

**Table II**

| *Experimental Groups* | *t* | *Level of Confidence* |
|---|---|---|
| E-P and E-B .......... | 0.47 | — |
| I-P and I-B .......... | 0.46 | — |
| E-P and I-P .......... | 7.95 | 1% |
| E-P and I-P .......... | 3.23 | 1% |
| E-B and I-P .......... | 4.20 | 1% |
| E-B and I-B .......... | 3.17 | 1% |

version-extroversion scores obtained by the Introvert-Praised and the Introvert-Blamed groups are also not significantly different. All of the other combinations within the four experimental groups are significantly different with respect to mean introversion-extroversion scores. The results of this analysis satisfy the requisite conditions for this experiment: (1) that the two extrovert groups be unbiased samples from a population of "extroverts," and (2) that the two introvert groups be unbiased samples from a population of "introverts." [2]

*Tasks and Procedure*

Six alternate forms of a cancellation test were constructed in order to measure each pupil's work achievement under the various experimental conditions. The different forms of this test were made sufficiently long so that no subject would be able to complete the task during any testing session. Each of these cancellation tests consisted of Arabic numerals from zero to nine presented in random sequences within each row. The pupils were instructed to draw a line through each of the 7's on the test sheet. Previous research has indicated that a cancellation test of this type has a low correlation with either intelligence or chronological age and has a substantially high reliability coefficient. In the present experiment employing one hundred twenty-four pupils a positive correlation of 0.87 was obtained between the combined scores of the three odd-tests and the combined scores of the three even-tests.

Before copies of the first test were distributed to any group of subjects an example of several numerals was placed on the blackboard and the experimenter demonstrated the manner in which a line was to be drawn through each of the 7's. The usual precautions were taken to insure each subject's readiness to start work on the "begin" signal and to cease work immediately after the "stop" signal.

The duration of each test period for both the control and the experimental groups was thirty seconds. A work period of such short duration seemed advisable because of the intrinsic dullness of the task. In thirty seconds it seemed unlikely that the subjects would become satiated with the

---

[2] The Control Group was not included in the comparisons because of its obvious overlap in introversion-extroversion scores with the two extrovert and the two introvert groups. A control group is not necessary to test the differential effect of praise or blame on 'introverts' and 'extroverts,' if the pupils in different experimental combinations do not differ significantly in their performance on the first assigned task. It will be shown later in this report that the subjects in the four experimental groups obtained essentially the same scores not only on the first task, but also on the second task (after the first differential incentives had been given).

task or that they would reach in six test periods a level of performance that would preclude any further improvement in work output. Analysis of the results has shown that test periods of thirty-seconds duration provide reliable scores; however there is some indication in the data that the experimental groups showing the greatest improvement in work achievement may have reached a level of performance that tended to make further improvement increasingly difficult.

In the control group no comments were made between any of the testing sessions. After the sixth and last task had been completed, the experimenter announced that all of the pupils had done satisfactory work.

In order to provide individual incentives to the subjects in the experimental groups the teacher passed around the room after each testing period, studied each pupil's paper for a few seconds and placed a "P" or a "G" on it. The pupils were asked to keep their marks secret. The teacher had been previously instructed as to which subjects were to receive marks of "P" (poor) and which subjects were to receive marks of "G" (good). After marking the first set of test papers, the teacher wrote a large "P" and a large "G" on the blackboard, and informed the pupils that those who had received "P's" had done very poorly and those who had received "G's" had done exceedingly well. After marking the papers for each of the subsequent tests the teacher reminded the subjects that "P" stood for poor work and "G" for good work.

It is assumed in this study that a mark of "G" represented to the subjects a form of teacher praise; and that a mark of "P" represented a form of teacher blame. The fact that the pupils had no assurance that their "good" or "poor" marks would not be made known to the entire class may also have been functioning as a form of motivation. The experimenters observed that some of the children who were blamed after each test became increasingly disturbed when they failed to obtain a "G" on their test papers. It was observed that some of the "blamed" pupils increased their efforts after receiving a poor mark, while other pupils who were blamed became distracted or sullen when the next test was given. One pupil who was continuously blamed became so resentful that he refused to try on the last test; his teacher reported that this was his typical reaction when he was reprimanded for poor school work.

At the end of the final test all children were marked "G." This could have no experimental effect and might leave the children with a pleasanter emotion. Most of the students who had been receiving "P" now showed marked signs of elation, indicating that the motivation had been functioning. This was particularly true of those "blamed" students who were normally accustomed to receiving good grades.

The "unfairness" of the experimental situation could not have been unusually disturbing. It was of short duration. More important, the customary pattern of assigning marks in school continues over a period of years to "blame" individuals for inadequacies beyond their control.

## Results

*Comparison of Blamed, Praised, and Control Groups*

To compare the work achievement of the Blamed (both introverts and extroverts), the Praised (both introverts and extroverts), and the Control Groups, the cancellation scores obtained by each subject on the first test were subtracted from the scores obtained on each of the succeeding five tests. This procedure was followed because the Control Group obtained somewhat higher scores on the first test than did the Blamed or the Praised Groups. The derived data are shown in Table III. It should be recalled that no extrinsic incentives were applied before the first test.

### Table III

| *Experimental Groups* | *Mean Gains in Cancellation Scores* | | | | |
|---|---|---|---|---|---|
| | *Test 2* | *Test 3* | *Test 4* | *Test 5* | *Test 6* |
| Total Blamed Group ........ | 18.1 | 16 3 | 17.9 | 20.3 | 21.1 |
| Total Praised Group ........ | 18.3 | 16.2 | 16.6 | 19.6 | 19.9 |
| Control Group ............ | 11.6 | 11.4 | 11.2 | 12.5 | 14.9 |

An analysis of variance was made of the gains shown by these three groups on tests 2, 3, 4, 5 and 6. F was found to be significant at the one-percent level of confidence for each of the five gains. Since F was found to be significant for each of the five gains, it was permissible to compare the mean gains of the three groups for each of the last five tests. The results of this analysis are presented in Table IV.

The values presented in Table IV show that there are no significant differences between any of the mean gains obtained by the Blamed and the Praised Groups on the last five tests. These values further show that all five of the mean gains obtained by the Control Group are significantly smaller than those obtained by either the Praised or the Blamed Group.

It may be concluded: (1) that either praise or blame was more effective than no external incentive in increasing the work output of these fifth-grade pupils: and (2) that praise and blame were equally effective in motivating fifth-grade pupils when "introverts" and "extroverts" were not differentiated.

**Table IV**

| Experimental Groups | t's for Differences Between Mean Gains * | | | | |
|---|---|---|---|---|---|
| | Test 2 | Test 3 | Test 4 | Test 5 | Test 6 |
| Total Praised Group vs. Total Blamed Group .......... | 0.23 | 0.10 | 1.07 | 0.50 | 0.69 |
| Total Praised Group vs. Control Group ............. | 6.45 | 4.14 | 3.72 | 4.55 | 2.86 |
| Total Blamed Group vs. Control Group ............. | 6.30 | 4.26 | 4.68 | 5.06 | 3.62 |

* $t$'s with the number of degrees of freedom available for these comparisons must be 2.75 or greater to be significant at the one per cent level of confidence and at least 2.42 to be significant at the five-per cent level of confidence.

However, it should be pointed out that the increased work output shown by the Praised and the Blamed Groups is almost entirely the result of the first incentive applied. The succeeding applications of praise or blame did not materially alter the pupils' mean scores, although the initial superiority attained by the Praised and the Blamed Groups after the application of the first incentives was maintained consistently during the later tests.

*Comparison of E-B, E-P, I-B, and I-P Groups*

The mean cancellation scores obtained on each of the six tests by the Extrovert-Blamed, the Extrovert-Praised, the Introvert-Blamed, and the Introvert-Praised Groups are presented graphically in Fig. 1.

An analysis of variance of the cancellation scores obtained by these four experimental groups on each of the six tests show that F was not significant for tests 1, 2 and 3; but was significant at the one per cent level of confidence for tests 4, 5 and 6. It may be concluded that there were no significant differences in work output between any of the four experimental groups on tests 1, 2 and 3, although the differences on test 3 showed a consistent trend toward the significant differences found for tests 4, 5 and 6. The results of this analysis permit a comparison of the mean cancellation scores obtained by these four experimental groups on tests 4, 5 and 6. The $t$'s for differences between mean scores are presented in Table V.

**Table V**

| | $t$'s for Differences Between Mean Scores | | | | | | | | |
|---|---|---|---|---|---|---|---|---|---|
| | Test 4 | | | Test 5 | | | Test 6 | | |
| | Diff. | $t$ | Level of Confidence | Diff. | $t$ | Level of Confidence | Diff. | $t$ | Level of Confidence |
| E-B minus E-P . | 5.9 | 2.80 | 1% | 6.3 | 3.01 | 1% | 6.4 | 2.83 | 1% |
| E-B minus I-B .. | 5.9 | 2.76 | 1% | 7.1 | 3.31 | 1% | 6.6 | 2.87 | 1% |
| I-P minus E-P .. | 4.8 | 2.21 | 5% | 5.8 | 2.71 | 1% | 5.4 | 2.32 | 5% |
| I-P minus I-B ... | 4.8 | 2.18 | 5% | 6.6 | 3.05 | 1% | 5.6 | 2.35 | 5% |
| E-P minus I-B .. | 0.0 | —— | — | 0.8 | 0.37 | — | 0.2 | 0.01 | — |
| E-B minus I-P .. | 1.1 | 0.53 | — | 0.5 | 0.25 | — | 1.0 | 0.45 | — |

These comparisons of mean scores substantiate what one could reasonably predict by examining Figure 1.

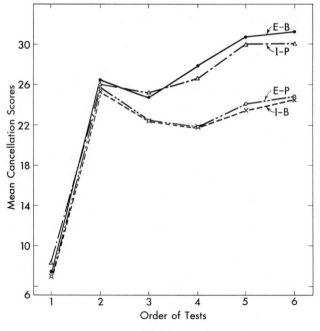

**Fig. 1.**

1) On tests 4, 5 and 6 the extroverts who were blamed (E-B) obtained significantly higher cancellation scores than either the E-P or the I-B Groups.

2) On tests 4, 5 and 6 the introverts who were praised (I-P) obtained significantly higher cancellation scores than either the E-P or the I-B Groups.

3) On tests 4, 5 and 6, as well as on tests 1, 2 and 3, the E-P and the I-B Groups did not differ significantly in mean scores. There were also no significant differences between the mean cancellation scores obtained by the E-B and the I-P Groups on any of the six tests.

In more general terms, it may be concluded from these results that applications of praise or blame, when repeated often enough in the form of school marks, have differential effects on the cancellation scores of introverted and extroverted fifth-grade pupils. Introverts achieve a higher level of performance when praised, and extroverts respond most favorably when blamed. The increasing divergence of the curves (Fig. 1) further indicates that there is a cumulative effect of repeated praise or blame on "introverts" and "extroverts."

**Summary and Conclusions**

The purpose of the present study was to determine the effects of repeated applications of praise or blame on introverted and extroverted fifth-grade pupils. One hundred and twenty-four fifth-grade pupils were selected as subjects. The Introversion-Extroversion section of a Personality Test by Pintner and Others was used to classify the pupils into two groups with regard to introversion-extroversion. Cancellation tests were employed to measure the effects of repeated praise or blame on the experimental groups. Praise or blame was administered by the teacher's placing a mark of "G" (good) or "P" (poor) on the subject's test paper. A control group was employed to test the effects of repeated applications of praise or blame on an unclassified population of fifth-grade pupils (introverts and extroverts grouped together).

The analysis of the data collected indicate that:

1. When introverts and extroverts are grouped together, praise and blame are equally effective in motivating the work achievement of fifth-grade pupils. Either praise or blame is more effective in increasing the work output of fifth-grade pupils than no external incentives.

2. If repeated often enough praise increases the work output of introverts until it is significantly higher than that of introverts who are blamed or extroverts who are praised.

3. If repeated often enough blame increases the work output of extroverts until it is significantly higher than that of extroverts who are praised or introverts who are blamed.

The results of this study indicate that praise, as well as blame, can be used unwisely by the elementary-school teacher if he does not fully appreciate and understand the different personalities present in his classroom. Praise and blame should not be judged on an either-or basis, but should be used to fit the case.

## 23

# A STUDY OF THE EFFECTS OF TEACHER KNOWLEDGE OF PUPIL CHARACTERISTICS ON PUPIL ACHIEVEMENT AND ATTITUDES TOWARDS CLASSWORK *

## Kenneth B. Hoyt

It seems reasonable to assume that the more teachers know about their pupils as individuals, the better they will understand them and the more effectively they will teach them. This assumption has been tested in some experiments and has been supported, in some cases at least, by the results. In a carefully planned and controlled experiment at the junior high school level the author of this article reports his findings. Using three different treatments or levels of teacher knowledge of pupils' ability, achievement, and personal information, he measures the achievement of the pupils in English, social studies and mathematics and pupil attitudes toward the teacher before and after the experiment, which lasted six months. The relationships of the different treatments to ability of pupils and their sex were also investigated. In addition every teacher was asked to fill out a blank designed to test his memory of characteristics of randomly selected pupils under each treatment. The findings of the study are clear and unequivocal but on the whole are at variance with those of other similar studies.

*Questions:*

1. The logical implication of the findings of this study might be that teachers can do just as effective teaching of subject matter with pupils about whom they know little as they can if they know a great deal about them. Do you think this is true? Why?

2. Can you offer any constructive suggestions for improvement of the techniques of Hoyt's study? If so, how would you defend them?

\* \* \*

* Abridged and reprinted from the *Journal of Educational Psychology,* **46:**302–310 (May 1955), by permission of author and publisher.

To say that individual differences exist in school children has little significance simply as an observation. The significance lies in the actions one can take as a result of having made this observation and the results which ensue in terms of changes in students.

Many people prominent in education have, over the last fifty years, urged teachers to discover the ways in which and the degrees to which school children differ in various characteristics [1, 2].* Some have been so bold as to state specifically such beliefs as "There is no doubt that better teaching results from supplying teachers with pertinent facts about all their pupils." [6].

## The Problem

One approach to the problem of the relative advisability or inadvisability of providing teachers with information concerning pupil characteristics is to study some of the effects resulting from such knowledge on the part of teachers. This investigation was concerned with studying the effects of teacher knowledge of pupil characteristics on pupil achievement and teacher-pupil relationships. Seven major questions were devised which served as the focus for the investigation. These were as follows:

1. What is the effect of providing teachers with systematic appraisal data relative to pupil characteristics on teacher knowledge of pupil characteristics?

2. What is the effect of teacher knowledge of pupil characteristics on pupil achievement?

3. Does the effect of teacher knowledge on pupil achievement act differentially for boys and girls?

4. Does the effect of teacher knowledge on pupil achievement act differentially on students from different learning ability levels?

5. What is the effect of teacher knowledge of pupil characteristics on pupil attitudes towards teachers?

6. Does the effect of teacher knowledge on pupil attitudes towards teachers act differentially for boys and girls?

7. Does the effect of teacher knowledge on pupil attitudes towards teachers act differentially on students from different learning ability levels?

The major experimental factors studied with reference to the treatment effect were teacher knowledge, sex, and ability level. The major experimental variables were pupil achievement and pupil attitudes toward teachers.

* Figures in brackets apply to references at end of selection.

## Populations Studied and Sampling Methods Employed

The experiment was conducted during the school year 1953–54 utilizing eighth-grade students in English, mathematics, and social studies classes from two public junior high schools in Minnesota. In School A, two hundred and ninety students were included on the roster and in School B, three hundred and fifty-six students. The actual experimental period was six months in length and all findings should be interpreted with this limitation in mind.

Individual students in each school were selected for and assigned to experimental sections by the method of random sampling within sex and scholastic aptitude sub-populations. Six sub-populations were formed from the roster in each school with boys and girls each being divided into highest, middle, and lowest ability groupings on the basis of obtained IQ scores on the *Otis Quick Scoring Mental Ability Test,* Beta level, Form Cm, which had been administered to all students in both schools during the school year 1952–53.

In School A, ninety students were selected and assigned at random, thirty to each of three experimental sections. Complete analysis data were available for eighty-five of these ninety students at the conclusion of the experimental period. In School B, one hundred and twenty students were selected and assigned at random, forty to each of three experimental sections, with complete analysis data being available for one hundred and nine students. The effects of the loss of these students as well as a graphical representation of the sub-populations involved can be obtained from an examination of Tables 1 and 2.

## Specification and Assignment of the Treatment Variables

Three distinct treatments were applied to each section during the experimental period. These were arranged for both schools in such a way that any one teacher was responsible for a different treatment with each section. Definitions of the three treatment variables are presented in terms of the amount of information concerning pupil characteristics given to teachers.

The treatment of "No Information" (N) is defined as the process of giving the teacher only the names of the pupils and no other systematic information.

The treatment of "Test Scores" (T) is defined as the process of giving the teacher the pupils' test scores. These consisted of converted IQ scores from the *Otis Quick Scoring Mental Ability Test,* Beta level, Form Cm. (which all students took during the school year 1952–53); scaled scores, by parts, for the *Coöperative English Test,* Lower Level, Form Z; the *Coöperative Social Studies Test for Grades 7, 8, and 9,* Form X; and the *Coöperative Mathematics Test for Grades 7, 8 and 9,* Form X (which each student took in September, 1953.) No other systematic information was given the teacher.

### Table 1

**Numbers of Students, by Sections, in Each Stratum for Which Complete Analysis Data Were Available in School A**

|  | Section 8A | | Section 8B | | Section 8C | | Totals | |
|---|---|---|---|---|---|---|---|---|
|  | Girls | Boys | Girls | Boys | Girls | Boys | Girls | Boys |
| High IQ | 5 | 5 | 5 | 4 | 5 | 5 | 15 | 14 |
| Middle IQ | 4 | 5 | 5 | 4 | 6 | 4 | 15 | 13 |
| Low IQ | 5 | 5 | 5 | 4 | 5 | 4 | 15 | 13 |
| Totals | 14 | 15 | 15 | 12 | 16 | 13 | 45 | 40 |

### Table 2

**Numbers of Students, by Sections, in Each Stratum for Which Complete Analysis Data Were Available in School B**

|  | Section 8D | | Section 8E | | Section 8F | | Totals | |
|---|---|---|---|---|---|---|---|---|
|  | Girls | Boys | Girls | Boys | Girls | Boys | Girls | Boys |
| High IQ | 7 | 5 | 7 | 5 | 7 | 6 | 21 | 16 |
| Middle IQ | 5 | 8 | 6 | 6 | 7 | 6 | 18 | 20 |
| Low IQ | 6 | 6 | 6 | 6 | 5 | 5 | 17 | 17 |
| Totals | 18 | 19 | 19 | 17 | 19 | 17 | 56 | 53 |

The treatment of "Tests Plus Other Information" (TO) is defined as the process of giving the teacher, for each student, all the information described for the Test Scores treatment plus a pupil information blank which was administered in September, 1953, and constructed by the experimenter.

## Description of Tests and Forms Used

In addition, each teacher was encouraged to discover all he possibly could about the characteristics of each student receiving this treatment.

These treatments were assigned to experimental sections by subject using a table of random numbers compiled by Fisher and Yates [3]. The resulting assignments for School A are shown in Table 3 and for School B in Table 4.

Table 3

**Assignment of Treatment Variables to Experimental Sections in School A**

| Section | Teacher 1 (English) | Teacher 2 (Mathematics) | Teacher 3 (Social Studies) |
|---------|---------------------|--------------------------|----------------------------|
| 8A | TO | N | T |
| 8B | T | TO | N |
| 8C | N | T | TO |

Table 4

**Assignment of Treatment Variables to Experimental Sections in School B**

| Section | Teacher 4 (English) | Teacher 5 (Mathematics) | Teacher 6 (Social Studies) |
|---------|---------------------|--------------------------|----------------------------|
| 8D | T | TO | N |
| 8E | TO | N | T |
| 8F | N | T | TO |

Student achievement was measured in September and again in April using the *Coöperative English Test,* Lower Level, Form Z, the *Coöperative Mathematics Test for Grades 7, 8, and 9,* Form X, and the *Coöperative Social Studies Test for Grades 7, 8, and 9,* Form X. While these tests measure recall and recognition, it is apparent that what some would regard as the relatively more important goals of retention and transferability of learned materials to new situations is not measured by these instruments. This serves to specify one limitation of the study.

Information relative to other pupil characteristics which were considered as important aspects of treatment TO were collected in September by administration of the pupil information blank.

Student attitudes towards particular teachers were measured by use of an inventory constructed by the experimenter. It consisted of items taken from the *Student Reaction Inventory* [4], contained in category 7, "Individualization of Instruction," which, on an item analysis, showed differences between "good" and "poor" teachers [5] significant at the 1% level. Forty such items were selected and five more non-discriminating items which had high face validity were added making forty-five items in all. Responses typical of those students make about "good" teachers were assigned a weight +1; those associated with "poor" teachers a weight of −1; and all items answered "undecided" were scored as zero. This instrument was administered to each student three times, once in each of the three experimental groups to which he was assigned.

Each teacher was asked to complete a blank consisting of questions designed to measure the degree to which he was able to recall specific characteristics of certain randomly selected pupils in the various experimental sections. Six students, one from each stratum, were picked at random from each experimental section in a given school and the three teachers involved were asked to complete the blanks for these eighteen students.

## Experimental Procedures

The experimental procedures employed in this investigation can perhaps be best described in terms of controls applied during the experimental period to the various treatment procedures. Rigid controls were also applied to the collection of data, but these are not described here.

*To maintain the limitations prescribed by treatment N* teachers were urged, for each member of the section where this treatment was applied, to: (a) Refrain from examination of the pupil's cumulative record folder; (b) Refrain from discussion of this pupil in conversations with other school personnel; (c) Refrain from discussing with the student any topics which might lead to information concerning his activities outside of the classroom; and (d) Refrain from seeking out parents of the student for consultation and discussion.

*To carry through the procedures prescribed by treatment T* teachers were urged, for each member of the section where this treatment was applied, to maintain the same limitations described for treatment N. They were given copies of all initial achievement test scores and IQ scores for individual students in this section. In addition, graphs of distributions of these scores were supplied as was a scattergram showing the relationships between intelligence and achievement test scores in the subject the teacher was teaching.

*To carry through the procedures prescribed by treatment TO* the teachers were supplied, for each member of the section where this treatment was applied, with all of the information described for the T treatment. In addition, they were given: (a) Individual record folders for each student in which they were encouraged to place records of all information learned regarding characteristics of the students; (b) The pupil information blanks which the student had completed and on which the experimenter had marked some interpretive suggestions; and (c) A four-page group analysis of the section made on the basis of information obtained from the pupil information blanks.

*To work towards a clear differentiation of treatments* individual conferences were held with teachers at least once every other week during the experimental period. Here, in addition to providing frequent reminders of the restrictions imposed by Treatments N and T, the experimenter worked with each teacher in interpreting the significance of the data compiled for students in the T and TO sections. No attempt was made to force the teacher to discuss every pupil; rather, the choice of pupils to be discussed was always left with the teacher.

*To work towards the prevention of gross changes in teaching method* teachers were asked to: (a) Use the same textual material for all experimental sections; (b) Cover the same units at approximately the same time with all experimental sections; (c) Use the same general approach in teaching method with all experimental sections, i.e., if a topic were presented by means of a student panel discussion in one section, this same approach should be used in all sections. Checks made during and at the conclusion of the experimental period satisfied the investigator that these restrictions were being carried out. . . .

## Summary of Findings

1. Teacher knowledge of pupil characteristics was increased through the use of appraisal data. Significant F ratios were obtained on this analysis for mean treatment differences, for mean teacher-subject differences, and for mean interaction differences of treatment with the various teacher-subject combinations. The mean square for the treatment effect provided a significant F ratio when compared with the mean squares for error, teacher-subject, and interaction thus establishing itself as probably constituting a

true effect. This finding indicates that the Treatment procedure did operate as intended.

2. Teacher knowledge of pupil characteristics was not found by itself to result in increases in pupil achievement in mathematics, social studies, or English. The application of the various treatment effects did not produce any significant differences in adjusted mean achievement test scores in mathematics and social studies. While significant adjusted mean differences in favor of Treatment N were found for adjusted achievement test scores in English, the complexities of the interaction effects present prevent one from regarding the observed differences as true treatment effects.

3. Teacher knowledge of pupil characteristics was not found to act preferentially on either sex in terms of its effect on increases in pupil achievement in mathematics, social studies, or English. There were no significant F ratios obtained for the interactions of the sex with the treatment factor.

4. Teacher knowledge of pupil characteristics was found to act preferentially on ability levels of pupils in terms of its effect on increases in pupil achievement in mathematics, social studies, or English. The interaction effects of ability level with the treatment factor were not significant in mathematics and social studies classes. A significant F ratio was found for the interaction between ability level and treatment in English classes. However, because of significant interactions also present between treatment and schools and between ability and schools plus significant main effects for school and treatments, the exact interpretation of the significant interaction of ability with treatment was not clear.

5. There was a definite tendency for increases in teacher knowledge of pupil characteristics to improve pupil attitudes towards teachers. Significant differences in favor of Treatment TO were found in School B. In School A, the F ratio of 1.461 was smaller than that of 3.04 required to reject the hypothesis of equality at the 5% level of significance. However, the mean of 8.37 for Treatment N, 8.77 for Treatment T, and 12.12 for Treatment TO were all in the direction indicated by the significant findings in favor of Treatment TO which were found in School B.

6. Teacher knowledge of pupil characteristics was not found to act preferentially on either sex in terms of its effect on pupil attitudes toward teachers. The interaction of sex with treatment was not significant in either school.

7. Teacher knowledge of pupil characteristics was not found to act preferentially on ability levels of pupils in terms of its effects on pupil attitudes

towards teachers. The interaction of ability level with treatment was not significant in either school.

## References

1. BALLER, WARREN, *et al.* "Essential Pupil-personnel Records." *Teachers College Record,* pp. 268–86 (January 1947).

2. BUSH, R. N. "A Study of Student Teacher Relationships." *J. of Educ. Res.,* pp. 645–656 (May 1942).

3. FISHER, R. A. and FRANK YATES. *Statistical Tables for Biological, Agricultural and Medical Research.* New York: Hafner Publishing Company, Inc. (1949).

4. GRIM, PAUL R. and CYRIL J. HOYT. "Appraisal of Teaching Competency." *Educational Research Bulletin,* pp. 85–91 (April 16, 1952).

5. ———. "Excerpts from Two Instruments for Appraising Teaching Competency." *J. of Educ. Res.,* pp. 705–710 (May 1953).

6. WADSWORTH, RALPH D. "Give Teachers the Facts about Pupils." *California Journal of Secondary Education,* pp. 84–87 (February 1946).

## 24

# TEACHER COMMENTS AND STUDENT PERFORMANCE: A SEVENTY-FOUR CLASSROOM EXPERIMENT IN SCHOOL MOTIVATION *

## Ellis Batten Page

A constant problem for teachers is that of motivating pupils. How do you get them to do "what they are supposed to do"? Do you praise them, scold them, punish them, give them rewards (marks, prizes, honors) ignore them, or what? There is little room to doubt that approval by the teacher is a strong motivating force, especially perhaps with younger pupils. They want the teacher to think well of them, to do what will bring approval from the teacher—a smile, a bit of praise perhaps, or a good report. In this interesting study, an attempt is made to assess the effect of three types of teacher response to pupils' examination or test papers: no comment, a specified comment, and free comment. One of the classes of each of seventy-four high school teachers served as subjects of the experiment. In each class pupils were assigned at random to one of the three types of comment groups. Care was taken that the three types of teacher response were assigned equally to all levels of ability. The effect of each type of response or treatment was measured on the very next objective test given by each teacher. If pupils receiving no comment did as well as either of the comment groups, the conclusion would seem to be that the comments had no measurable effect on achievement. The findings of the study which is very carefully conceived and executed will be of comfort to teachers, at least.

*Questions:*

1. In the paragraph headed "Previous Related Work" the author of this article criticizes other investigations for weaknesses in conception and/or technique. How well do you feel that his study meets these criticisms? Try to be specific in your analysis.

* Reprinted from the *Journal of Educational Psychology,* **49:**173–181 (August 1958), by permission of author and publisher.

2. Do the findings of this study tell us anything about the effect of teacher personality on pupil achievement? If you think so, tell why. If not, give reasons for your answer.

3. Can you think of other ways of measuring, that is, quantifying, the effect of teachers' comments on pupil achievement? Describe one.

\*  \*  \*

Each year teachers spend millions of hours writing comments upon papers being returned to students, apparently in the belief that their words will produce some result, in student performance, superior to that obtained without such words. Yet on this point solid experimental evidence, obtained under genuine classroom conditions, has been conspicuously absent. Consequently each teacher is free to do as he likes; one will comment copiously, another not at all. And each believes himself to be right.

The present experiment investigated the questions: 1. Do teacher comments cause a significant improvement in student performance? 2. If comments have an effect, which comments have more than others, and what are the conditions, in students and class, conducive to such effect? The questions are obviously important for secondary education, educational psychology, learning theory, and the pressing concern of how a teacher can most effectively spend his time.

### Previous Related Work

Previous investigations of "praise" and "blame," however fruitful for the general psychologist, have for the educator been encumbered by certain weaknesses: Treatments have been administered by persons who were extraneous to the normal class situation. Tests have been of a contrived nature in order to keep students (unrealistically) ignorant of the true comparative quality of their work. Comments of praise or blame have been administered on a random basis, unlike the classroom where their administration is not at all random. Subjects have often lacked any independent measures of their performance, unlike students in the classroom. Areas of training have often been those considered so fresh that the students would have little previous history of related success or failure, an assumption impossible to make in the classroom. There have furthermore been certain statistical errors: tests of significance have been conducted as if students were totally independent of one another, when in truth they were interacting members of a small number of groups with, very probably, some group effects upon the experimental outcome.

For the educator such experimental deviations from ordinary classroom conditions have some grave implications, explored elsewhere by the present writer [5].* Where the conditions are highly contrived, no matter how tight the *controls,* efforts to apply the findings to the ordinary teacher-pupil relationship are at best rather tenuous. This study was therefore intended to fill both a psychological and methodological lack by *leaving the total classroom procedures exactly what they would have been without the experiment,* except for the written comments themselves.

## Method

### Assigning the Subjects

Seventy-four teachers, randomly selected from among the secondary teachers of three districts, followed detailed printed instructions in conducting the experiment. By random procedures each teacher chose one class to be subject from among his available classes.[1] As one might expect, these classes represented about equally all secondary grades from seventh through twelfth, and most of the secondary subject-matter fields. They contained 2,139 individual students.

First the teacher administered whatever objective test would ordinarily come next in his course of study; it might be arithmetic, spelling, civics, or whatever. He collected and marked these tests in his usual way, so that each paper exhibited a numerical score and, on the basis of the score, the appropriate letter grade A, B, C, D, or F, each teacher following his usual policy of grade distribution. Next, the teacher placed the papers in numerical rank order, with the best paper on top. He rolled a specially marked die to assign the top paper to the *No Comment, Free Comment,* or *Specific Comment* group. He rolled again, assigning the second-best paper to one of the two remaining groups. He automatically assigned the third-best paper to the one treatment group remaining. He then repeated the process of rolling and assigning with the next three papers in the class, and so on until all students were assigned.

### Administering Treatments

The teacher returned *all* test papers with the numerical score and letter grade, as earned. No Comment students received nothing else. Free Com-

* Figures in brackets apply to references at end of article.
[1] Certain classes, like certain teachers, would be ineligible for *a priori* reasons: giving no objective tests, etc.

ment students received, in addition, whatever comment the teacher might feel it desirable to make. Teachers were instructed: "Write anything that occurs to you in the circumstances. There is not any 'right' or 'wrong' comment for this study. A comment is 'right' for the study if it conforms with your own feelings and practices." Specified Comment students, regardless of teacher or student differences, all received comments designated in advance for each letter grade, as follows:

A: Excellent! Keep it up.
B: Good work. Keep at it.
C: Perhaps try to do still better?
D: Let's bring this up.
F: Let's raise this grade!

Teachers were instructed to administer the comments "rapidly and automatically, trying not even to notice who the students are." This instruction was to prevent any extra attention to the Specified Comment students, in class or out, which might confound the experimental results. After the comments were written on each paper and recorded on the special sheet for the experimenter, the test papers were returned to the students in the teacher's customary way.

It is interesting to note that the student subjects were totally naive. In other psychological experiments, while often not aware of precisely what is being tested, subjects are almost always sure that something unusual is underway. In 69 of the present classes there was no discussion by teacher or student of the comments being returned. In the remaining five the teachers gave ordinary brief instructions to "notice comments" and "profit by them" or similar remarks. In none of the classes were students reported to seem aware or suspicious that they were experimental subjects.

## Criterion

Comment effects were judged by the scores achieved on the very next objective test given in the class, regardless of the nature of that test. Since the 74 testing instruments would naturally differ sharply from each other in subject matter, length, difficulty, and every other testing variable, they obviously presented some rather unusual problems. When the tests were regarded primarily as *ranking* instruments, however, some of the difficulties disappeared.

A class with 30 useful students, for example, formed just 10 levels on the basis of scores from the first test. Each level consisted of three students, with each student receiving a different treatment: No Comment, Free

Comment, or Specified Comment. Students then achieved new scores on the second (criterion) test, as might be illustrated in Table 1, Part A. On the basis of such scores, they were assigned rankings within levels, as illustrated in Table 1, Part B.

**Table 1**
**Illustration of Ranked Data**

| Level | Part A (Raw scores on second test) | | | Part B (Ranks-within-levels on second test) | | |
|---|---|---|---|---|---|---|
| | N | F | S | N | F | S |
| 1 | 33 | 31 | 34 | 2 | 1 | 3 |
| 2 | 30 | 25 | 32 | 2 | 1 | 3 |
| 3 | 29 | 33 | 23 | 2 | 3 | 1 |
| ... | ... | ... | ... | ... | ... | ... |
| ... | ... | ... | ... | ... | ... | ... |
| ... | ... | ... | ... | ... | ... | ... |
| 10 | 14 | 25 | 21 | 1 | 3 | 2 |
| Sum: | | | | 19 | 21 | 20 |

Note: N is No Comment; F is Free Comment; S is Specified Comment.

If the comments had no effects, the sums of ranks of Part B would not differ except by chance, and the two-way analysis of variance by ranks would be used to determine whether such differences exceeded chance. Then the *sums* of ranks themselves could be ranked. (In Part B the rankings would be 1, 3, and 2 for Groups N, F, and S; the highest score is ranked 3 throughout the study.) And a new test, of the same type, could be made of all such rankings from the 74 experimental classrooms. Such a test was for the present design the better alternative, since it allowed for the likelihood of "Type G errors" [3, pp. 9–10] in the experimental outcome. Still a third way remained to use these rankings. The summation of each column could be divided by the number of levels in the class, and the result was *a mean rank within treatment within class*. This score proved very useful, since it fulfilled certain requirements for parametric data.

## Results

### Comment vs. No Comment

The over-all significance of the comment effects, as measured by the analysis of variance by ranks, is indicated in Table 2. The first row shows results obtained when students were considered as matched independently from one common population. The second row shows results when treatment groups within classes were regarded as intact groups. In either case the conclusions were the same. The Specified Comment group, which re-

### Table 2
**The Friedman Test of the Over-all Treatment Effects**

| Units Considered | N | F | S | df | $\chi_r^2$ | p |
|---|---|---|---|---|---|---|
| Individual Subjects | 1363 | 1488 | 1427 | 2 | 10.9593 | < .01 |
| Class-group Subjects | 129.5 | 170.0 | 144.5 | 2 | 11.3310 | < .01 |

ceived automatic impersonal comments according to the letter grade received, achieved higher scores than the No Comment group. The Free Comment group, which received individualized comments from the teachers, achieved the highest scores of all. Not once in a hundred times would such differences have occurred by chance if scores were drawn from a common population. Therefore it may be held that the comments had a real and beneficial effect upon the students' mastery of subject matter in the various experimental classes.

It was also possible, as indicated earlier, to use the mean ranks within treatments within classes as parametric scores. The resulting distributions, being normally distributed and fulfilling certain other assumptions underlying parametric tests, permitted other important comparisons to be made.[2] Table 3 shows the mean-ranks data necessary for such comparisons.

### Table 3
**Parametric Data Based Upon Mean Ranks Within Treatments Within Classes**

| Source | N | F | S | Total |
|---|---|---|---|---|
| Number of Groups | 74 | 74 | 74 | 222 |
| Sum of Mean Ranks | 140.99 | 154.42 | 148.59 | 444.00 |
| Sum of Squares of Mean Ranks | 273.50 | 327.50 | 304.01 | 905.01 |
| Mean of Mean Ranks | 1.905 | 2.087 | 2.008 | 2.000 |
| S.D. of Mean Ranks | .259 | .265 | .276 | |
| S.E. of Mean Ranks | .030 | .031 | .032 | |

[2] It may be noted that the analysis of variance based upon such mean ranks will require no calculation of sums of squares between levels or between classes. This is true because the mean for any class will be $(k + 1)/2$, or in the present study just 2.00. . . . An alternative to such scores would be the conversion of all scores to $T$ scores based upon each class-group's distribution; but the mean ranks, while very slightly less sensitive, are much simpler to compute and therefore less subject to error.

The various tests are summarized in Tables 4 and 5. The over-all F test in Table 5 duplicated, as one would expect, the result of the Friedman test, with differences between treatment groups still significant beyond the .01 level. Comparisons between different pairs of treatments are shown in Table

### Table 4
#### Analysis of Variance of Main Treatment Effects
#### (Based on Mean Ranks)

| Source | Sum of Squares | df | Mean Square | F | Probability |
|---|---|---|---|---|---|
| Between Treatments: N, F, S | 1.23 | 2 | .615 | 5.69 | < .01 |
| Between Class-groups | 0.00 | 73 | .000 | . . . | |
| Interaction: T × Class | 15.78 | 146 | .108 | | |
| Total | 17.01 | 221 | | | |

Note: Modeled after Lindquist [3], p. 157 *et passim,* except for unusual conditions noted.

5. All differences were significant except that between Free Comment and Specified Comment. It was plain that comments, especially the individualized comments, had a marked effect upon student performance.

### Table 5
#### Differences Between Means of the Treatment Groups

| Comparison | Difference | S.E. of Diff. | t | Probability |
|---|---|---|---|---|
| Between N and F ...... | .182 | .052 | 3.500 | <.001 |
| Between N and S ....... | .103 | .054 | 1.907 | <.05 |
| Between F and S ....... | .079 | .056 | 1.411 | <.10(n.s.) |

Note: The *t* tests presented are those for matched pairs, consisting of the paired mean ranks of the treatment groups within the different classes. Probabilities quoted assume that one-tailed tests were appropriate.

### Comments and Schools

One might question whether comment effects would vary from school to school, and even whether the school might not be the more appropriate unit of analysis. Since as it happened the study had 12 junior or senior high schools which had three or more experimental classes, these schools were arranged in a treatments-by-replications design. Results of the analysis are shown in Table 6. Schools apparently had little measurable influence over treatment effect.

**Table 6**
**The Influence of the School Upon the Treatment Effect**

| Source | Sum of Squares | df | Mean Square | F | Probability |
|---|---|---|---|---|---|
| Between Treatments: N, F, S | .172 | 2 | .086 | . . .[a] | . . . |
| Between Schools | .000 | 11 | .000 | | |
| Between Classes Within Schools (pooled) | .000 | 24 | .000 | | |
| Interaction: T × Schools | 1.937 | 22 | .088 | . . . | . . . |
| Interaction: T × Cl. W. Sch. (pooled) | 4.781 | 48 | .099 | | |
| Total | 6.890 | 107 | | | |

Note: Modified for mean-rank data from Edwards [**1**, p. 295 *et passim*].
[a] Absence of an important main treatment effect is probably caused by necessary restriction of sample for school year (*N* is 36, as compared with Total *N* of 74), and by some chance biasing.

*Comments and School Years*

It was conceivable that students, with increasing age and grade-placement, might become increasingly independent of comments and other personal attentions from their teachers. To test such a belief, 66 class-groups, drawn from the experimental classes, were stratified into six school years (Grades 7–12) with 11 class-groups in each school year. Still using mean ranks as data, summations of such scores were as shown in Table 7. Rather

**Table 7**
**Sums of Mean Ranks for Different School Years**

| School Year | N | F | S |
|---|---|---|---|
| 12 | 21.08 | 22.92 | 22.00 |
| 11 | 19.06 | 23.91 | 23.03 |
| 10 | 20.08 | 23.32 | 22.60 |
| 9 | 22.34 | 22.06 | 21.60 |
| 8 | 21.21 | 22.39 | 22.40 |
| 7 | 22.04 | 22.98 | 20.98 |

Note: Number of groups is 11 in each cell.

surprisingly, no uniform trend was apparent. When the data were tested for interaction of school year and comment effect (see Table 8), school year did not exhibit a significant influence upon comment effect.

Though Table 8 represents a comprehensive test of school-year effect, it was not supported by all available evidence. Certain other, more limited tests did show significant differences in school year, with possibly greater responsiveness in higher grades. The relevant data [6, chap. 5] are too cumbersome for the present report, and must be interpreted with caution. Apparently, however, comments do *not* lose effectiveness as students move through school. Rather they appear fairly important, especially when individualized, at all secondary levels.

#### Table 8
#### The Influence of School Year Upon Treatment Effect

| Source | Sum of Squares | df | Mean Square | F | Probability |
|---|---|---|---|---|---|
| Between Treatments: N, F, S | 1.06 | 2 | .530 | 5.25 | <.01 |
| Between School Years | 0.00 | 5 | .000 | | |
| Between Cl. Within Sch. Yr. (pooled) | 0.00 | 60 | .000 | | |
| Interaction: T × School Year | 1.13 | 10 | .113 | 1.12 | (n.s.) |
| Interaction: T × Class (pooled) | 12.11 | 120 | .101 | | |
| Total | 14.30 | 197 | | | |

Note: Modified for mean-rank data from Edwards [1, p. 295 *et passim*].

One must remember that, between the present class-groupings, there were many differences other than school year alone. Other teachers, other subject-matter fields, other class conditions could conceivably have been correlated beyond chance with school year. Such correlations would in some cases, possibly, tend to modify the *visible* school-year influence, so that illusions would be created. However possible, such a caution, at present, appears rather empty. In absence of contradictory evidence, it would seem reasonable to extrapolate the importance of comment to other years outside the secondary range. One might predict that comments would appear equally important if tested under comparable conditions in the early college years. Such a suggestion, in view of the large lecture halls and detached professors of higher education, would appear one of the more striking experimental results.

#### Comments and Letter Grades

In a questionnaire made out before the experiment, each teacher rated each student in his class with a number from 1 to 5, according to the student's *guessed responsiveness* to comments made by that teacher. Top rating, for example, was paired with the description: "Seems to respond quite unusually well to suggestions or comments made by the teacher of this class.

Is quite apt to be influenced by praise, correction, etc." Bottom rating, on the other hand, implied: "Seems rather negativistic about suggestions made by the teacher. May be inclined more than most students to do the opposite from what the teacher urges." In daily practice, many teachers comment on some papers and not on others. Since teachers would presumably be more likely to comment on papers of those students they believed would respond positively, such ratings were an important experimental variable.

Whether teachers *were* able to predict responsiveness is a complicated question, not to be reported here. It was thought, however, that teachers might tend to believe their able students, their high achievers, were also

**Table 9**

**Mean of Mean Ranks for Different Letter Grades**

| Letter Grade | N | F | S |
|:---:|:---:|:---:|:---:|
| A | 1.93 | 2.04 | 2.03 |
| B | 1.91 | 2.11 | 1.98 |
| C | 1.90 | 2.06 | 2.04 |
| D | 2.05 | 1.99 | 1.96 |
| F | 1.57 | 2.55 | 1.88 |

Note: Each eligible class was assigned one mean rank for each cell of the table.

their responsive students. A contingency table was therefore made, testing the relationship between *guessed* responsiveness and letter grade achieved on the first test. The results were as predicted. More "A" students were regarded as highly responsive to comments than were other letter grades; more "F" students were regarded as negativistic and unresponsive to comments than were other letter grades; and grades in between followed the same trend. The over-all C coefficient was .36, significant beyond the .001 level.[3] Plainly teachers believed that their *better* students were also their more *responsive* students.

If teachers were correct in their belief, one would expect in the present experiment greater comment effect for the better students than for the poorer ones. In fact, one might not be surprised if, among the "F" students, the No Comment group were even superior to the two comment groups.

The various letter grades achieved mean scores as shown in Table 9, and the analysis of variance resulted as shown in Table 10. There was considerable interaction between letter grade and treatment effect, but it was caused almost entirely by the remarkable effect which comments appeared

[3] In a 5 × 5 table, a perfect correlation expressed as C would be only about .9 (McNemar [4], p. 205).

to have *on the "F" students*. None of the other differences, including the partial reversal of the "D" students, exceeded chance expectation.

These data do not, however, represent the total sample previously used, since the analysis could use only those student levels in which all three students received the same letter grade on Test One.[4] Therefore many class-groups were not represented at all in certain letter grades. For example,

### Table 10
#### The Relation Between Letter Grade and Treatment Effect

| Source | Sum of Squares | df | Mean Square | F | Probability |
|---|---|---|---|---|---|
| Between Treatments: N, F, S | 2.77 | 2 | 1.385 | 5.41 | <.01 |
| Between Letter Grades | 0.00 | 4 | 0.000 | | |
| Bet. Blocks Within L. Gr. (pooled) | 0.00 | 65 | 0.000 | | |
| Interaction: T × Letter Grades | 4.88 | 8 | .610 | 2.40 | .05>p>.01 |
| Residual (error term) | 32.99 | 130 | .254 | | |
| Total | 40.64 | 209 | | | |

Note: Modified for mean-rank data from Lindquist (**3**, p. 269). Because sampling was irregular (see text) all eligible classes were randomly assigned to 14 groupings. This was done arbitrarily to prevent vacant cells.

although over 10% of all letter grades were "F," only 28 class-groups had even one level consisting entirely of "F" grades, and most of these classes had *only* one such level. Such circumstances might cause a somewhat unstable or biased estimate of effect.

Within such limitations, the experiment provided strong evidence against the teacher-myth about responsiveness and letter grades. The experimental teachers appeared plainly mistaken in their faith that their "A" students respond relatively brightly, and their "F" students only sluggishly or negatively to whatever encouragement they administer.

### Summary

Seventy-four randomly selected secondary teachers, using 2,139 unknowing students in their daily classes, performed the following experiment:

[4] When levels consisted of both "A" and "B" students, for example, "A" students would tend to receive the higher scores on the second test, regardless of treatment; thus those Free Comment "A" students drawn from mixed levels would tend to appear (falsely) more responsive than the Free Comment "B" students drawn from mixed levels, etc. Therefore the total sample was considerably reduced for the letter-grade analysis.

They administered to all students whatever objective test would occur in the usual course of instruction. After scoring and grading the test papers in their customary way, and matching the students by performance, they randomly assigned the papers to one of three treatment groups. The No Comment group received no marks beyond those for grading. The Free Comment group received whatever comments the teachers felt were appropriate for the particular students and tests concerned. The Specified Comment group received certain uniform comments designated beforehand by the experimenter for all similar letter grades, and thought to be generally "encouraging." Teachers returned tests to students without any unusual attention. Then teachers reported scores achieved on the next objective test given in the class, and these scores became the criterion of comment effect, with the following results:

1. Free Comment students achieved higher scores than Specified Comment students, and Specified Comments did better than No Comments. All differences were significant except that between Free Comments and Specified Comments.

2. When samplings from 12 different schools were compared, no significant differences of comment effect appeared between schools.

3. When the class-groups from six different school years (grades 7–12) were compared, no *conclusive* differences of comment effect appeared between the years, but if anything senior high was more responsive than junior high. It would appear logical to generalize the experimental results, concerning the effectiveness of comment, at least to the early college years

4. Although teachers believed that their better students were also much more responsive to teacher comments than their poorer students, there was no experimental support for this belief.

When the average secondary teacher takes the time and trouble to write comments (believed to be "encouraging") on student papers, these apparently have a measurable and potent effect upon student effort, or attention, or attitude, or whatever it is which causes learning to improve, and this effect does not appear dependent on school building, school year, or student ability. Such a finding would seem very important for the studies of classroom learning and teaching method.

## References

1. EDWARDS, A. *Experimental Design in Psychological Research*. New York: Holt, Rinehart & Winston, 1950.

2. FRIEDMAN, M. "The Use of Ranks to Avoid the Assumption of Normality Implicit in the Analysis of Variance. *J. Amer. Statist. Ass.* **32:**675–701 (1937).

3. LINDQUIST, E. F. *Design and Analysis of Experiments in Psychology and Education.* Boston: Houghton Mifflin, 1953.

4. McNEMAR, Q. *Psychological Statistics.* (2nd ed.) New York: Wiley, 1955.

5. PAGE, E. B. "Educational Research: Replicable *or* Generalizable?" *Phi Delta Kappan.* **39:**302–304 (1958).

6. ——. The effects upon student achievement of written comments accompanying letter grades. Unpublished doctoral dissertation, Univer. of California, Los Angeles, 1958.

# 25

## COOPERATIVE VERSUS INDIVIDUAL EFFICIENCY IN PROBLEM SOLVING *

### Samuel F. Klugman

When children work in groups do they perform more efficiently than when they work alone? To put the question in another way, do they accomplish more? And do they take less time? These are interesting and significant questions, which the author of the study here reported attempts to answer. In addition, his experiment sheds some light on the relationship of such factors to sex, race, grade level, age, and I.Q. to the basic questions. Children in grades four, five, and six were used as subjects of the experiment, with arithmetic problems as the material on which they worked. Half the children worked a set of problems first as individuals, followed by a set of equivalent problems working in pairs. For the other half the order was reversed. Efficiency was measured in terms of number of problems solved correctly and in time required to complete the problems. The children were equated for sex, race, grade, age, and I.Q. The author seeks answers to a practical problem in a forthright, practical way; the results seem enlightening and convincing, though they may shake some rather widely held convictions.

*Questions:*

1. Are two heads better than one, as the saying goes? How would you answer in the light of available evidence?

2. Are there possible advantages in cooperative endeavor which the study reported here ignores? What might some of them be?

3. How would you proceed to test out your hypotheses, stated in answer to #2 above.

* * *

### A. Introduction

Coöperation has been defined by many writers [6, 7, 11, 16] ** as a kind of group competition or rivalry. Others [15, 18, 21, 27] interpret it as social

* Reprinted from the *Journal of Educational Psychology,* **35:**91–100 (February 1944), by permission of author and publisher.

** Figures in brackets apply to references at end of article.

facilitation in which individuals are stimulated to do better work simply because of the presence of other workers. Still others [3, 4, 8, 9, 13, 14, 20, 24] have thought of coöperation as pooled independent judgment, although Preston [20] (p. 471) speaks of "judgments which are a consequence of the interaction of viewpoints."

A definition of coöperation as employed in this paper has been stated briefly but effectively by Katz [12] (p. 119): "Coöperation . . . describes a joint coördinated effort by two or more individuals." Folsom [5] and Warren [26] hold to a similar point of view.

A number of studies exist which are concerned with the matter of coöperation as defined in this paper [1, 22, 23, 25, 27]. It might be stated, in passing, that perhaps it would be advisable, to avoid confusion, to make use of a word other than "coöperation." If so, this writer wishes to suggest the term "conplementation" as a possibility, since the members of a group are complementing each other's efforts.

Several investigators [2, 10, 17, 19, 22, 29] have sought to explain, on the basis of experimental data, the reasons for the improved results which seem to favor coöperative behavior over individual efficiency.

## B. Purpose

The purpose of this study was to determine whether, among children of average intelligence (IQ 90 to 109), two heads were better than one in the solution of twenty arithmetical problems graduated in difficulty; i.e., whether two children, working together, could do more problems correctly and in a shorter time than each child working alone. In order to overcome the matter of differences in speed of reading, all children were asked to complete all problems.

## C. Procedure

### The Subjects

In all there were one hundred thirty-six school children who took part in the experiment. They ranged in age from 108 to 155 months with a mean of 128.5 months. They were in Grades IV, V, and VI. There were seventy-two female and sixty-four male children. Seventy-six were white and sixty were Negro children.

### Equating the Pairs

The children were equated for sex, race, grade, age (within three months), and IQ (within four points).

## The Test

The children were required to take two forms—A and B—of the Otis Arithmetic Reasoning Test. The test is made up of twenty arithmetic problems graduated in difficulty and the directions call for a time limit of six minutes. However, as stated above, in this experiment a work limit plan was used in order to overcome the differences in speed of reading.

## Order of Testing

After the children in each classroom had been paired, the first pair was designated as I-P, the second as P-I, the third as I-P, etc. I-P means that the pair was to be tested individually with Form A, then paired on the following day at the same time and tested with Form B. P-I refers to paired testing with Form A followed by individual testing the next day with Form B. This procedure, of course, resulted in the elimination of any practice effect which would have occurred had all the children been tested as I-P or P-I.

## Directions

### To Paired Children

"Here is a test of arithmetic problems for each of you. You two are to work together in order to get the correct answers. That is, you are to talk over each problem until you feel that you have the correct answer. However, you must not waste time for you are to finish as soon as possible. You are to try every problem and I want an answer even if you have to guess. Write in the answers on only one test paper and when you finish you will return to me one paper with answers to all the problems and a clean paper with no answers on it. Now find the place on the test where it says, 'Sample Problem.' Listen while I read it." (When children indicated that they knew how to solve the problem, they were asked to turn over the forms and begin. They were timed with a stop-watch.)

### To Individual Children

"Here is a test of arithmetic problems. You are to find the answer to every problem and I want an answer even if you have to guess. Do not waste time for you are to finish as soon as possible. Now find the place on the test where it says, 'Sample Problem.' Listen while I read it." (When child indicated that he knew how to solve the problems, he was asked to turn over the forms and begin. He was timed with a stop-watch.)

## Scoring

When tests were scored for number of problems, the raw scores were used. The time was taken from the moment the children were asked to turn over the papers and begin until the moment the answer to the twentieth problem was put down.

## D.  Results

Table 1 gives an age and IQ picture of the group as a whole and of the several subgroups. Included are the means, standard deviations, and critical ratios. The mean age for the entire group of one hundred thirty-six was ten years eight and one-half months. The mean IQ for this group was slightly below 100. The means of the female group and of the white children were about one IQ point higher than the male and colored groups, respectively. Those in Grade IV had a mean IQ which was about one point higher than those in Grade V, while those in the latter grade had a mean which was about one point higher than those in Grade VI. It will be noted, however, that in no instance was there a statistically reliable difference in IQ between the various subgroups.

### Table 1
### Age and IQ Picture of the Group

|                | N   | Mean       | SD    | CR   |
|----------------|-----|------------|-------|------|
| Age            | 136 | 128.53[1]  | 11.30 | —    |
| Entire Group   | 136 | 99.09[2]   | 6.23  | —    |
| Sex:           |     |            |       |      |
| Male           | 64  | 98.41      | 5.90  |      |
| Female         | 72  | 99.58      | 6.08  | 1.14 |
| Grade:         |     |            |       |      |
| Four           | 38  | 100.47     | 5.74  |      |
| Five           | 44  | 99.20      | 6.20  | .89  |
| Six            | 54  | 98.00      | 6.41  | .94  |
| Race:          |     |            |       |      |
| White          | 76  | 99.79      | 5.99  |      |
| Negro          | 60  | 98.47      | 6.48  | 1.23 |

[1] Months.
[2] IQ.

Table 2 is intended to give a picture of how equally the entire group was divided into I-P and P-I halves. For age, for IQ of the whole group, and for

IQ of the various subgroups, no reliable differences were found between the means.

#### Table 2
#### Age and IQ Distribution of P-I and I-P Groups

| | | *P-I* | | | *I-P* | | |
|---|---|---|---|---|---|---|---|
| | *N* | *Mean* | *SD* | *N* | *Mean* | *SD* | *CR* |
| Age | 68 | 128.24[1] | 11.23 | 68 | 128.90 | 11.48 | .34 |
| Entire Group | 68 | 98.79[2] | 6.40 | 68 | 99.27 | 5.80 | .46 |
| Sex: | | | | | | | |
|   Male | 32 | 98.06 | 6.64 | 32 | 98.75 | 5.14 | .46 |
|   Female | 36 | 99.44 | 5.90 | 36 | 99.72 | 6.24 | .20 |
| Grade: | | | | | | | |
|   Four | 20 | 99.10 | 5.74 | 18 | 101.00 | 5.34 | 1.61 |
|   Five | 22 | 99.73 | 6.84 | 22 | 98.73 | 5.44 | .54 |
|   Six | 26 | 97.92 | 6.58 | 28 | 98.07 | 5.78 | .09 |
| Race: | | | | | | | |
|   White | 40 | 99.05 | 6.09 | 36 | 98.50 | 5.86 | .40 |
|   Negro | 28 | 98.50 | 7.00 | 32 | 98.31 | 5.85 | .11 |

[1] Months.
[2] IQ.

The results of the scores earned by the group as individuals and as members of a pair are presented in Table 3. Two sets of scores are given, one indicating the raw scores and the other the time scores in seconds. It will be

#### Table 3
#### Results of Individual and Paired Scores

| | *N* | *Mean* | *SD* | *CR* |
|---|---|---|---|---|
| I Scores | 136 | 6.18[1] | 2.49 | |
| | | | | 3.51 |
| P Scores | 136 | 7.29 | 2.77 | |
| I Time Scores | 136 | 1054[2] | 373 | |
| | | | | 3.61 |
| P Time Scores | 136 | 1238 | 462 | |

[1] Raw scores.
[2] Seconds.

seen from the data that the mean P raw score is slightly greater than one problem over the mean I score. That is to say, the entire group of one hundred thirty-six as individuals were each able to get about six problems correct out of the possible twenty. When working in pairs their mean score jumped to about seven. This difference is statistically significant.

When the means of the time scores are compared, it will be noted that the time taken to complete the twenty problems was 184 seconds less for the children when working as individuals than when working as members of a pair. The difference between the two means is a reliable one.

These results indicate, then, that when the children worked in pairs they earned reliably higher scores than when they worked independently. However, while the scores were higher it took them a reliably longer time. This longer time was primarily due to the presentation, discussion, rejection, and acceptance of a greater number of possible answers which occurred when the children worked in pairs.

Table 3 gives the results for raw scores and time scores for the entire group without indicating what effects pairing had upon the several subgroups. To supply these data, Table 4 was constructed to show the results for the raw scores and Table 5 was made to show the results for the time scores for the various subgroups. Each of these tables presents not only the subgroups as regards grade, race, and sex, but also upper- and lower-average intelligence groups and younger and older children.

A study of Table 4 reveals that in every instance and for every subgroup the mean P score is higher than the mean I score. In several instances, the differences are reliably significant; namely, for the children in Grade VI, for the white children, and for both the girls and boys. We may be fairly certain that the Negro children, those who are of upper- and lower-average intelligence (as measured by IQ scores), and both the younger and older pupils earned truly higher scores when paired than when working alone. For the children in Grades IV and V the critical ratio may be said to indicate a tendency in that direction.

Table 5 indicates that in every instance and for every subgroup the time scores for the P tests are greater than those time scores for the I tests. We may be reasonably certain that the differences are reliably significant for those in Grade VI, for the colored children, for the girls, for those in the lower-average group, and for the older individuals. We may be fairly certain of the reliability of the difference in the case of children in Grade V. A tendency may be said to exist in this direction among the white, the male, the upper-average intelligence, and the younger children. In the case of children in Grade IV, no difference existed.

The results have shown, thus far, that, when paired, children earned reliably higher scores and took a significantly longer time. Now it is entirely

**Table 4**

**Reliability of the Difference between Individual and Paired Raw Scores
for the Various Sub-groups**

|  | I Scores | | | P Scores | | |
|---|---|---|---|---|---|---|
|  | N | Mean | SD | Mean | SD | CR |
| Grade IV | 38 | 4.53 | 1.74 | 5.26 | 2.04 | 1.69 |
| V | 44 | 5.45 | 2 56 | 6.41 | 2.64 | 1.72 |
| VI | 54 | 6.67 | 2.49 | 8.19 | 2.59 | 3.10 |
| White | 76 | 5.97 | 2.32 | 7.18 | 2.51 | 3.09 |
| Negro | 60 | 5.13 | 2.52 | 6.30 | 2.99 | 2.31 |
| Male | 64 | 6.14 | 2.62 | 7.74 | 2.67 | 3.42 |
| Female | 72 | 5.21 | 2.30 | 6.30 | 2.62 | 4.01 |
| Lower Average [1] | 76 | 5.20 | 2.17 | 6.17 | 2.60 | 2.51 |
| Upper Average [2] | 60 | 6.26 | 2.77 | 7.39 | 2.87 | 2.19 |
| Younger [3] | 76 | 5.36 | 2.40 | 6.33 | 2.81 | 2 42 |
| Older [4] | 60 | 6.42 | 2.43 | 7.64 | 2.50 | 2.47 |

[1] 90–99 IQ.
[2] 100–109 IQ.
[3] Nine- and ten-year-olds.
[4] Eleven- and twelve-year-olds.

conceivable that the following situation may have arisen: Let us assume that of six children, five earned exactly the same score when paired as when working individually. The sixth child may have improved his score by six points. The average improvement for this group would indicate a gain of one problem as a result of pairing. Such a conclusion is rather a spurious one for, as a matter of fact, pairing improved only one subject's score while it did not affect that of the other five. Accordingly, a table (6) has been worked out to determine whether such a condition existed in this study.

Table 6 shows that not every subject improved his raw score and spent a longer time on the problems when paired. Over fifteen per cent obtained similar raw scores when paired as when working independently. Twenty-two per cent earned lower raw scores when paired. For the time scores, the table shows that thirty-six per cent took less time when paired than when working alone. When the critical ratio was determined between the percentage which earned higher raw scores and the combination of per-centages for the same and lower raw scores (i.e., 37.5 per cent) it was

**Table 5**

**Reliability of the Difference between Individual and Paired Time Scores for the Various Sub-groups**

| | *I Scores* | | | *P Scores* | | |
|---|---|---|---|---|---|---|
| | *N* | *Mean* | *SD* | *Mean* | *SD* | *CR* |
| Grade  IV | 38 | 1189 | 483 | 1221 | 556 | .27 |
| V | 44 | 1050 | 294 | 1262 | 416 | 2.78 |
| VI | 54 | 935 | 295 | 1230 | 421 | 4.21 |
| White | 76 | 1116 | 412 | 1216 | 472 | 1.39 |
| Negro | 60 | 983 | 308 | 1283 | 438 | 4.39 |
| Male | 64 | 1019 | 388 | 1156 | 422 | 1.91 |
| Female | 72 | 1072 | 366 | 1311 | 502 | 3.26 |
| Lower Average [1] | 76 | 1026 | 378 | 1284 | 478 | 3.69 |
| Upper Average [2] | 60 | 1077 | 376 | 1193 | 422 | 1.59 |
| Younger [3] | 76 | 1140 | 430 | 1224 | 455 | 1.35 |
| Older [4] | 60 | 920 | 288 | 1277 | 458 | 5.11 |

[1] 90–99 IQ.
[2] 100–109 IQ.
[3] Nine- and ten-year-olds.
[4] Eleven- and twelve-year-olds.

found to be 2.95. Similarly, when the critical ratio was obtained between the percentage of children who took a longer time when paired and the percentage who took less time, it was found to be 3.23.

These results indicate, then, that not only was there a reliable difference

**Table 6**

**Reliability of the Difference between the Percentage Earning Higher Raw and Time Scores and Lower Raw and Time Scores**

| | *Raw Scores* | | | *Time Scores* | | |
|---|---|---|---|---|---|---|
| | *N* | *Per Cent* | *CR* | *N* | *Per Cent* | *CR* |
| Higher Score | 85 | 62.50 | | 87 | 63.97 | |
| Same Score | 21 | 15.44 | 2.95 | . . . | . . . . . . | 3.23 |
| Lower Score | 30 | 22.06 | | 49 | 36.03 | |
| Total | 136 | 100.00 | | 136 | 100.0 | |

between scores, but that there also existed a significant difference between percentages of subjects obtaining higher raw and time scores and those getting the same and lower scores (those who showed no increase).

## E. Summary and Conclusions

The purpose of the study was to determine whether, among children of average intelligence (IQ 90 to 109), two heads were better than one in the solution of twenty arithmetical problems graduated in difficulty; i.e., whether two children, working together, could do more problems correctly and in a shorter time than each child working alone. In order to overcome the matter of differences in speed of reading, all children were asked to complete all problems.

The results indicated that children working together solved more problems correctly but took a longer time. The differences were statistically significant. This is true whether we think in terms of scores or percentages of cases. In addition, for the subgroups, the results of the raw scores showed with reasonable certainty that the sixth-grade children, the white children, and both sexes earned truly higher scores when working in pairs than when working independently. Mean time scores for all subgroups were higher for problem-solving when the children were paired than when working alone. The time scores for Negro, sixth-graders, female, lower-average intelligence, and older children were reliably longer.

The higher raw scores for the paired children and the longer time needed to solve the problems were both due to the presentation, discussion, rejection, and acceptance of a larger number of possible answers which occurred when the children were working together than when working independently.

## References

1. BARTON, W. A. "Group Activity versus Individual Effort in Developing Ability to Solve Problems in First-year Algebra." *Educ. Admin. and Supervis.* **12:**512–518 (1926).

2. BIRD, C. *Social Psychology.* New York: Appleton-Century, 1940.

3. BRUCE, R. S. "Group Judgments in the Fields of Lifted Weights and Visual Discrimination." *J. Psy.* **1:**117–121 (1935).

4. FARNSWORTH, P. R. and M. F. WILLIAMS. "The Accuracy of the Median and Mean of a Group of Judgments." *J. Soc. Psy.* **7:**237–239 (1936).

5. FOLSOM, J. K. *Social Psychology.* New York: Harper, 1931.

6. FORLANO, G. "An Experiment in Coöperation." *J. Ed. Res.* **25:**128–131 (1932).

7. FRYER, D. "Individual Mental Efficiency." *Fields of Psychology,* edited by J. P. GUILFORD. New York: Van Nostrand, chap. xvi, 1940.

8. GORDON, K. "Group Judgments in the Field of Lifted Weights." *J. Exper. Psy.* **7:**398–400 (1924).

9. ———— "Further Observation on Group Judgements of Lifted Weights." *J. Psy.* **1:**105–115 (1935–36).

10. GURNEE, H. "A Comparison of Collective and Individual Judgments of Fact." *J. Exper. Psy.* **21:**106–112 (1937).

11. HURLOCK, E. B. *Child Development.* New York: McGraw-Hill, 1942, pp. 473.

12. KATZ, D. "The Concepts and Methods of Social Psychology." *Fields of Psychology,* edited by J. P. GUILFORD. New York: Van Nostrand, chap. vi, 1940.

13. KELLEY, T. L. "The Applicability of the Spearman-Brown Formula for the Measurement of Reliability." *J. Ed. Psy.* **16:**300–303 (1925).

14. KNIGHT, H. C. *A Comparison of the Reliability of Group and Individual Judgments.* M. A. Thesis, Columbia University, 1921.

15. LEUBA, C. J. "An Experimental Study of Rivalry in Young Children." *J. Comp. Psy.* **16:**367–378 (1933).

16. MALLER, J. B. *Coöperation and Competition.* Teach. Col. Contr. Educ., 384 (1929), pp. 176.

17. MAY, M. A. and L. W. DOOB. *Competition and Coöperation.* New York: Soc. Sci. Res. Coun. (1937) Bull. 25, p. 191 ff.

18. MUKERJI, N. P. "An Investigation of Ability in Working in Groups and in Isolation." *Br. J. Psy.* **30:**352–356 (1940).

19. MURPHY, G., L. B. MURPHY, and T. M. NEWCOMB. *Experimental Social Psychology.* New York: Harper (1937), pp. 1121.

20. PRESTON, M. G. "Note on the Reliability and Validity of the Group Judgment." *J. Exper. Psy.* **22:**462–471 (1938).

21. RYAN, G. *An Experiment in Class Instruction vs. Individual Study at the College Level.* Baltimore: Author (1932), pp. 42.

22. SHAW, M. E. "A Comparison of Individuals and Small Groups in the Rational Solution of Complex Problems." *A. J. Psy.* **44:**491–504 (1932).

23. SOUTH, E. B. "Some Psychological Aspects of Committee Work." *J. Ap. Psy.* **11:**348–368 and 437–467 (1927).

24. STROOP, R. "Is the Judgment of the Group Better than that of the Average Member of the Group?" *J. Exper. Psy.* **15:**550–562 (1932).

25. THIE, T. M. "The Efficiency of the Group Method." *Engl. J.* **14:**134–137 (1925).

26. WARREN, H. C. *Dictionary of Psychology.* Boston: Houghton-Mifflin (1934), pp. 372.

27. WATSON, G. B. "Do Groups Think More Efficiently than Individuals?" *J. Abn. and Soc. Psy.* **23:**328–336 (1928).

28. WESTON, S. B. and H. B. ENGLISH. "Influence of the Group on Psychological Test Scores." *Am. J. Psy.* **37:**600–601 (1926).

29. YOUNG, P. T. *Motivation of Behavior.* New York: Wiley (1936), pp. 562.

# 26

## EFFECTS OF GROUP EXPERIENCE ON INDIVIDUAL PROBLEM SOLVING *

### Bryce B. Hudgins

In this excellent experiment, fifth grade pupils having been given experience in solving arithmetic problems in groups of four were compared with classmates who have worked at the same problems as individuals. In addition, half the groups were given some "specifications" or suggested steps to follow in solving problems. All pupils worked for three consecutive days at the problems, either individually or in groups as described. Following this, all pupils worked individually on another set of problems comparable in content and difficulty to those used during the first three days. The subjects of the experiment were matched on mental ability and arithmetic problem solving ability. The results of the investigation provided answers to the following questions:

Does problem solving experience in a group improve individual problem solving ability more than comparable individual experience does?

What is the effect on individual problem solving ability of experience in specifying the steps involved in arriving at a solution?

Would pupils who had group experience, including the specifying of steps involved in solving problems, do better as individuals than those who had group experience without specification?

*Questions:*

1. What do the results of this experiment indicate concerning the effects of group experience upon individual problem solving ability?

2. Should four pupils working in a group solve approximately four times as many problems in a given time as any one of them would solve working alone?

3. What are the advantages of group work as against individual work? Do the results of this experiment support your answer?

* Reprinted from the *Journal of Educational Psychology,* **51**:37–42 (February 1960), by permission of author and publisher.

4. Do the findings in Woodrow's experiment (Selection 19) have any bearing on the interpretation of the results of this one? Explain.

\* \* \*

A number of investigators [Gurnee, 1937; Klugman, 1944; Perlmutter & de Montmollin, 1952; Taylor & Faust, 1952] have examined the relative effectiveness of problem solving by groups and by individuals. In general, they have found that groups furnish more correct solutions to problems than comparable subjects do working as individuals. The present inquiry continues in this tradition, and attempts to extend knowledge in the area by providing experimental answers to two questions related to the problem solving behavior of elementary school children. First, do children working together in groups learn techniques of problem solving which they can apply later in similar situations, and, secondly, does interaction, as herein defined, contribute to the superiority of group problem solving? A casual inspection of elementary school principles of teaching texts would suggest that this transfer and the conditions under which it occurs are demonstrated facts rather than unanswered problems.

Answers to these questions hinged on the assumption that groups of children would be more successful in solving problems than their counterparts working individually. This result had been so well demonstrated in the past that there seemed little reason to doubt that it could be replicated in a school situation.

Additional significance of the study lies in the use of "natural groups." The use of *ad hoc* groups has been criticized in a survey of investigations of group and individual performance.

A common and dangerous practice is to generalize the principles valid for *ad hoc* groups to traditioned groups. The *ad hoc* group is treated as a microscopic model of the traditioned group. This might be true, but has not been experimentally validated. It is equally possible that *ad hoc* and traditioned groups behave in accordance with their individual principles (Lorge, Fox, Davitz, & Brenner, 1958).

The groups used in this study were *ad hoc* in the sense that they were organized for purposes of the investigation. It seems to the writer that what constitutes a traditioned group depends upon the context in which the group is found. It can be argued that groups which operate for three consecutive days, as in the present study, approximate traditioned groups as they exist in the classroom. The analogy here is between the experimental groups and others which are formed for a specific activity within the classroom.

## Hypotheses and Rationale

Three hypotheses were formulated to provide a basis for answering the questions asked above:

1. The first hypothesis was that problem solving experience in a group improves individual ability more than does individual experience.

It was hypothesized that when subjects (Ss) who had worked on arithmetic problems as members of a group were tested individually, their mean score would be significantly higher than the mean of Ss who had worked individually throughout the experiment. This answers the first question above, concerning the carry-over from the group situation to a subsequent individual one.

2. The second hypothesis was that individual ability to solve arithmetic problems improves as a result of specifying the steps involved in arriving at solution.

Specification consisted of providing written answers to a series of questions which were intended to lead Ss toward problem solution. There were four questions which specification subjects had to answer in connection with the solution of each problem:

1. What are you asked to find?
2. What information are you given that will help you find the answer?
3. What do you have to do to find the answer?
4. What is the answer?

It was predicted that the mean score of Ss who had worked under the condition of specification would be significantly higher than the mean of Ss who had not used specification.

Underlying this hypothesis was the reasoning that disagreement among group members about a solution initiates a review process during which the attention of individual members is directed to the various critical steps in problem solution. The group's contribution to successful problem solving, then, lies in "instructing" the participants in proper problem solving procedure. If this is true, the student working alone who is required to specify the steps by which progress is made toward problem solution will improve much as if he were exposed to the influence of the group. Thus, the group influence may be an artifact, seemingly important, but only because it invokes a process which one ordinarily would not use, but would be capable of using, in isolation.

3. A final hypothesis was that the improvement of problem solving ability as a result of group experience stems from the relevancy of intra-group communication to the processes involved in problem solution.

That is, students tested individually following a period of time in which they had worked as members of a group using specification would solve significantly more problems than subjects who worked initially in non-specification groups. By systematizing the "instruction" process in the group situation, presumably even greater gains in individual problem solving success will be realized.

In short, is there carry-over in the form of higher individual performance as a consequence of the group experience, and does a structuring of problem solving procedures account for a portion of the variation in pupil performance?

## Method

### Sample

The Ss of the investigation were 128 fifth-grade students selected in equal numbers from each of four public schools in the city of St. Louis.

### Controls

A measure of each S's general mental ability and arithmetic problem solving ability was made immediately prior to the experiment. The general mental ability test used was the California Test of Mental Maturity, Short Form. Arithmetic ability was measured by the California Arithmetic Test, Elementary, Grades 4–5–6, Form W.

The 32 Ss in each classroom were matched by fours on the basis of their general ability and arithmetic test scores, and assigned to one of four experimental groups. The assignment of the 8 Ss in each group to an experimental condition was done by reference to a table of random numbers. Following the final assignment there was no significant difference in either general mental ability or arithmetic ability among the groups prior to the experiment.

During the experiment, the groups from two of the classes were taken to a room other than their regular classroom. In the other two classes, Ss working individually were taken to another room, while the groups remained in their homeroom. This was done in order that the novelty of a new working environment would not exercise a systematic influence on any one of the experimental conditions.

## Tasks

The arithmetic problems from Forms J, K, L, and M of the Stanford Achievement Test, Intermediate, were used as experimental materials. The following are 2 problems out of the total 120 which Ss were asked to solve.

Bill jumped 13 feet, 5 inches on Tuesday. On Thursday he jumped 11 feet, 9 inches. How much farther did he jump on Tuesday than on Thursday.

The butcher says to cook a turkey 20 minutes for each pound. At what hour should a 15 pound turkey be started in order to be done at twelve o'clock noon?

## Procedures, Phase 1

The first phase consisted of three consecutive days of problem solving using Forms J, K, and L of the Stanford. The 128 pupils worked as follows: Thirty-two pupils (called A Ss) worked in subgroups of four students. Each subgroup had to agree on a single answer to each question in the specifications.

Another 32 pupils (B Ss) also worked in four-member groups. Within each group, members were free to develop their own methods for solving the problems. The only restriction imposed upon them was that the group must arrive at one answer to each problem.

Half of the 64 pupils working individually (C Ss) used the method of specification. The other half (D Ss) were simply instructed to solve the problems and to record each solution in the appropriate space on the problem sheets.

## Procedures, Phase 2

This portion of the experiment consisted of the 128 students solving individually the 30 problems in Form M of the Stanford. To ascertain the possible effects of differential retention, all the Ss from one classroom (i.e., one-fourth of the total sample) were tested on each of the following days after the completion of Phase 1—the first, second, fifth, and twelfth day. In this way, one-fourth of the A, B, C, and D Ss were tested on each day of Phase 2.

## Results

### Phase 1

Throughout the three days of Phase 1, Ss who worked in groups made higher scores than Ss working individually. On the first day the mean score of Ss working in groups (A and B) was 18.82; that for Ss working individually (C and D) was 12.80. The mean score for individuals rose on the second day to 13.13, while the groups' mean was only 17.69. On the final day, group *S*s had a mean of 20.81 correct responses as compared with 14.91 for individuals. The difference for each of the three days of Phase 1 was significant beyond the .01 level. If these differences had not occurred, there would have been no basis for testing the hypotheses in Phase 2. Any reason for expecting that transfer might result from the group experience, or that specification might be useful as an explanatory concept, would have been lacking. It is for these reasons that Phase 1, which simply demonstrated an already well established finding, was an essential part of the experiment. It confirmed the condition upon which the appropriateness of tests of the three hypotheses depended.

The mean of the *S*s using specification (Conditions A and C) was 13.88 for the first day. The mean of the B and D *S*s (conditions of nonspecification) for the same day was 17.74. This difference was significant beyond the .05 level. On the second and third days of the first phase, there was no significant difference between the specification and nonspecification conditions. However, the B *S*s (who worked in groups without specification) achieved higher scores during Phase 1 than *S*s working under any of the other three experimental conditions.

*Phase 2*

Table 1 gives the mean scores for Phase 2 of *S*s who had worked under each of the four experimental conditions, and the mean of each class which received Phase 2 on a given day, respectively. As revealed by Table 2, none of the differences among *S*s in Phase 2 was significant.

These findings indicated that, although groups of students working cooperatively solve more problems than comparable students working alone, there is no significant improvement in the problem solving performance of the former *S*s because of this group experience. Consequently, the first hypothesis was rejected. Nor were the other two hypotheses supported; that is, practice in specifying the steps used in solving a problem did not improve performance any more than in the case where such specification was not made. This was true whether specification was used by individuals or by small groups.

### Discussion

One problem undertaken by this investigation was an attempt to offer a valid explanation of the superiority of the group over individual problem

## Table 1

**Mean Score on Arithmetic Problems for Each Phase 1 Experimental Condition and Each Day of Phase 2**

| Phase 1 Experimental Condition | Day on Which Phase 2 Was Administered | | | | |
|---|---|---|---|---|---|
| | 1 (N = 32) | 2 (N = 32) | 5 (N = 32) | 12 (N = 32) | Mean |
| A: Groups with specification | 15.25 | 17.25 | 10.75 | 15.25 | 14.63 |
| B: Groups without specification | 17.38 | 19.88 | 14.25 | 13.75 | 16.19 |
| C: Individuals with specification | 16.25 | 14.63 | 16.38 | 13.25 | 15.13 |
| D: Individuals without specification | 19.13 | 15.75 | 12.88 | 12.75 | 15.13 |
| Mean | 17.00 | 16.75 | 13.57 | 13.75 | 15.27 |

## Table 2

**Summary Table of Analysis of Variance of Phase 2 Scores**

| Source | df | Mean Square | F | p |
|---|---|---|---|---|
| X: Group versus individuals | 1 | 2.53 | .09 | > .05 |
| Y: Specification versus nonspecification | 1 | 19.53 | .70 | > .05 |
| Z: Retention groups | 3 | 111.03 | 3.99 | > .05 |
| XY: Interaction | 1 | 19.54 | .70 | > .05 |
| XZ: Interaction | 3 | 48.28 | 1.73 | > .05 |
| YZ: Interaction | 3 | 19.87 | .71 | > .05 |
| XYZ: Interaction | 3 | 27.84 | .89 | > .05 |
| Within | 112 | 31.31 | | |
| Total | 127 | | | |

solving activity. It was hypothesized that this superiority must somehow grow out of the interaction among members working together in the group.

The results of the experiment are clearly opposed to the acceptance of such an hypothesis. However, it must be remembered that the interaction used in this investigation was of a particular type which has been designated specification. It cannot be said with certainty that interaction per se does not affect the quality of the group product. It is possible that, in another form, interaction may contribute to the group superiority.

For example, two interaction patterns were observed in the nonspecification groups during Phase 1. In some of the groups there was a tendency for one S to determine the answer and to communicate it to the other group members. If this person had status as a class leader, his solutions were accepted unquestioningly by the other group members. If he did not have such status, the correctness of his solutions had to be demonstrated before they were accepted.

The second pattern was a more cooperative one which approximated the pattern of the specification groups except for one difference. In these groups each S read the problem and solved it independently. The answers were then compared. If all the answers were identical, the solution was accepted; but if there was disagreement, one person usually took the initiative to demonstrate the appropriateness of the solution to the deviant member or members.

A point of interest arose from the way in which these solutions were determined. Suppose the problem under consideration to be the following: "Our team scored 16 points in the first game, 6 points in the second, and 14 in the third. How many points did we score in all three games?" If there was disagreement about the answer, one person would try to remove the confusion. The usual form of this was to say, "Sixteen and six are twenty-two and fourteen are thirty-six." Such unarguable logic was usually enough to convince the deviant member. On rare occasions the individual said, "You have to add to solve this problem." This remark was followed by the computation.

At no time was there any evidence of attention being given to the first two questions assigned to the specification groups. Such specification as occurred was related to the questions of deciding upon a process appropriate for the solution, and of finding the answer itself. No student was observed justifying his reason for selecting a particular process. Obviously when an incorrect process was selected and agreed upon, the resulting wrong answer tended to receive enthusiastic if misguided support.

Why did the group Ss fail to make higher scores than the C and D Ss on the final test? The answer to this question seems to lie in understanding how the Phase 1 tasks were approached by the members of both kinds of groups. Specification, which was used by half of the groups in Phase 1, provides a systematic means of attacking arithmetic problems. It was assumed that the correct answer to a problem would be found if Ss followed the prescribed steps and if the appropriate computational skills were known and could be used by them. It was also assumed that Ss who used specification in Phase 1 would see the applicability of the method when they were later confronted by similar problems, i.e., in Phase 2. The Phase 2 scores of "groups with specification" $S$s lead to the conclusion that there was no transfer from the group to the individual situation of the *steps* which were used in the training period.

As for members of nonspecification groups, it is probable that little if any problem solving skill was acquired in the training period. Their attention seems to have been focused upon accomplishing the task at hand with little regard for developing skills which would be useful in subsequent cases.

The importance for transfer of generalized experience has been demonstrated by Judd (1908) and by Hendrickson and Schroeder (1941). Furthermore, Kingsley and Garry (1957, p. 508) point out "that the mere knowledge of the principle will not insure transfer of training to new situations. Its general applicability must be realized, and the learner must be able to see the possibility of its application to the new situation."

This is a significant point for the present discussion. Prior to the experiment, $S$s were told the nature of the condition under which they would work. They were also informed that at a later time they would be asked to solve additional problems by themselves. Little emphasis was placed upon this statement, and no attempt was made to instruct specification $S$s that the task given them was one which might help them later in solving problems.

Despite the failure of specification to account for the superiority of groups over individuals, it is still possible, as indicated above, that interaction is related to this superiority. The most reasonable hypothesis at this point appears to be that the problem solving superiority of small groups depends upon the efforts of the most able member of the group to communicate his knowledge to others, and upon the degree to which he achieves acceptance of his solutions. If this hypothesis proves tenable, transfer from the group to the individual situation would not be expected to occur.

## Summary

This study inquired (*a*) whether specification (citing the steps leading to solution) is related to the problem solving superiority of small groups over individuals and (*b*) whether individual problem solving ability improves as a result of group experience.

Subjects were 128 fifth-grade girls and boys. The first phase of the study lasted three days during which subjects worked on sets of arithmetic problems under an experimental condition. Half worked as group members; half as individuals. Group members solved significantly more problems than subjects who worked alone.

In Phase 2, all subjects worked individually. No differences were found among subjects' scores in this second phase. It was concluded that specification is not related to group problem solving effectiveness and that group experience does not enhance individual problem solving.

## References

GURNEE, H. MAZE. "Learning in the Collective Situation." *J. Psychol.* **3**:437–443 (1937).

HENDRICKSON, G and W. SCHROEDER. "Transfer of Training in Learning to Hit A Submerged Target. *J. Educ. Psychol.* **32**:206–213 (1941).

JUDD, C. H. "The Relation of Special Training to General Intelligence." *Educ. Rev.* **36**:28–42 (1908).

KELLEY, H. H. and J. W. THIBAUT. "Experimental Studies of Group Problem Solving and Process." In G. LINDZEY (ed.), *Handbook of Social Psychology,* Vol. 2. *Special Fields and Applications.* Cambridge, Mass.: Addison-Wesley (1954), pp. 735–785.

KINGSLEY, H. L. and R. GARRY. *The Nature and Conditions of Learning* (2nd ed.). Englewood Cliffs, N. J.: Prentice-Hall, 1957.

KLUGMAN, S. F. Cooperative versus Individual Efficiency in Problem Solving." *J. Educ. Psychol.* **35**:91–100 (1944).

LINDQUIST, E. F. *Design and Analysis of Experiments in Psychology and Education.* Boston: Houghton Mifflin, 1953.

LORGE, I., D. FOX, J. DAVITZ, and M. A. BRENNER. "A Survey of Studies Contrasting the Quality of Group Performance and Individual Performance, 1920–1957." *Psychol. Bull.* **53**:337–372 (1958).

PERLMUTTER, H. V. and G. DE MONTMOLLIN. "Group Learning of Nonsense Syllables." *J. Abnorm. Soc. Psychol.* **47**:762–769 (1952).

TAYLOR, D. W. and W. L. FAUST. "Twenty Questions: Efficiency in Problem Solving as a Function of Size of Groups." *J. Exp. Psychol.* **44**:360–368 (1952).

# 27

## THE EFFECTIVENESS OF AN APPROACH TO THE PROBLEM OF VARYING ABILITIES IN TEACHING READING *

### Richard H. Hart

In this article some very serious instructional problems are brought to light and an experimental approach to their alleviation is described in simple, non-technical terms. The author first presents data revealing the wide range of reading ability in what may be assumed to be typical fourth, fifth, and sixth grade groups. The range in tested reading ability extends in these three grades from the primer to grade seven-plus, when the reading test results from nine intermediate grade classrooms are combined. The author's thesis is that the reading achievement of such pupils will be greater if they are taught in classes whose range of reading ability is considerably shortened by grouping than it would be if the classes were formed without any attempt to reduce the range. Two groups of pupils are used in the experiment, one taught reading in homogeneous classes, the other in classes without regard to the range of ability. The experiment was conducted over a period of one year with two fourth grade groups and with two fifth grade groups. The results are striking and convincing.

*Questions:*

1. How would you plan and conduct a similar experiment in your own subject? Can you think of any improvements that might well be incorporated?

2. Compare the standard deviations of the groups taught under the two plans. What do they suggest about the effect of the two plans on individual differences in reading achievement?

\* \* \*

### The Problem

The problem of providing for the needs of pupils of varying ability has long challenged the resourceful and conscientious teacher. In the field of

* Reprinted from the *Journal of Educational Research,* **52**:228–231, (February 1959), by permission of author and Dembar Publications, Inc.

language arts in the elementary school, the grouping of children within a classroom as the means of adjusting the instructional program to the needs of the pupils has been utilized with success [1].*

Such a developmental program had been in effect at Peter Boscow School for a number of years. Each teacher had at least three groups in reading. Each group was reading in a developmental basal text on their own level regardless of grade placement. If a fourth grade group was reading on an easy third grade level, difficult fourth grade level, etc., they were given reading materials at that particular level. Similar groupings were effected in other areas of the language arts—such as spelling

### Table I
### Results of Informal Reading Inventory
### (Grade 5-B)

| Reading Grade Placement | Number of Pupils |
|---|---|
| 8 plus | 2 |
| 7 | 4 |
| $6_2$* | 4 |
| $6_1$* | 3 |
| $5_2$ | 5 |
| $5_1$ | 4 |
| $4_2$ | 3 |
| $4_1$ | 4 |
| $3_2$ | 2 |

* $6_2$ indicates that the pupil is performing at the sixth grade, second semester level; $6_1$ indicates that the pupil is performing at the sixth grade, first semester level, etc.

The faculty at Peter Boscow School believed that such grouping was necessary in a heterogeneous, self-contained classroom, if a developmental program in reading was the objective. However, experience with standardized achievement tests and actual classroom performance of pupils had revealed that in the average classroom there is a very wide range in the reading achievement and ability of pupils. An Informal Reading Survey [2] given by each teacher in the intermediate grades revealed this range in ability to be greater than desirable in every 4th, 5th and 6th grade class.

A range in ability typical of the variation found in every class is outlined in Table I. The teachers readily perceived that to divide such a class into three groups for reading instruction would be far from adequate. The table reveals the need for nine such groups. To settle for less would result in some

* Figures in brackets apply to references at end of article.

pupils being asked to study skills already mastered while other pupils would be required to perform at a level beyond their capacity. And to have nine instructional groups in one classroom would be most unreasonable.

## The Plan

Table II is a composite of the results of the Informal Reading Inventory for the 4th, 5th, and 6th grades at Peter Boscow School. Whereas each

### Table II
### Composite Results of Informal Reading Inventory
### (Nine Intermediate Grade Classrooms)

| Reading Grade Placement | Number of Pupils |
|:---:|:---:|
| 7 plus | 27 |
| $6_2$* | 30 |
| $6_1$* | 33 |
| $5_2$ | 33 |
| $5_1$ | 32 |
| $4_2$ | 28 |
| $4_1$ | 19 |
| $3_2$ | 12 |
| $3_1$ | 19 |
| $2_2$ | 11 |
| $2_1$ | 5 |
| 1 basic | 6 |
| Primer | 2 |

* $6_2$ indicated that the pupil is performing at the sixth grade, second semester level; $6_1$ indicates that the pupil is performing at the sixth grade, first semester level, etc.

teacher in his own heterogeneous, self-contained classroom had seven to nine distinct groups, collectively the teachers had thirteen groups distributed among the nine teachers. If the children were grouped according to ability, each teacher would have one or two instructional groups in reading. The teachers concerned had believed that some form of ability grouping would help solve the problem. It was decided to experiment with a program similar to one reported in the February 1956 issue of Elementary English [3].

## Description of Program

Each pupil was given the Reading Battery of the California Achievement Tests, the Durrell-Sullivan Intermediate Reading Survey, and the 1950

S-Form California Short-Form Test of Mental Maturity. On the basis of the results of these tests, the pupils were divided into ability groups as follows:

| Teacher | Pupils | Reading Level |
|---------|--------|---------------|
| A | 27 | Grade 7 plus |
| B | 30 | " $6_2$* |
| C | 33 | " $6_1$ |
| D | 33 | " $5_2$ |
| E | 32 | " $5_1$ |
| F | 28 | " $4_2$ |
| G | 28 | " $4_1$ |
| H | 10 | " $3_2$ |
|   | 14 | " $3_1$ |
| I | 6 | " $2_2$ |
|   | 6 | " $2_1$ |
|   | 6 | " 1 basic |
|   | 2 | " Primer |

* See Table I or II for explanation of grade placement designations.

A block of time 85 minutes in length was set aside daily for the teaching of the language arts—reading, spelling, writing, and English. During this time grade level designations were dissolved. Pupils of similar ability from the 4th, 5th and 6th grades met with a particular teacher for language arts instruction. Each teacher used a developmental approach in the teaching of reading.

## Hypothesis

It was thought desirable to test, as part of an evaluation of the above program, the following hypothesis: Children's achievement in reading will be significantly greater in a reading instructional program where pupils are grouped homogeneously according to ability than in a heterogeneous situation, all other factors being equal.

## Procedures for Experimentation

The decision was made to compare the pupil achievement in reading under the experimental program (ability grouping) for a period of one year (Sept. to Sept.) with the pupil achievement for a similar period of time under the regular program (heterogeneously grouped, self-contained class).

It is most difficult to control all the factors in an experiment in the area of curriculum. However, it is the writer's opinion that the following factors were controlled to a significant degree in this experiment:

### 1. *Teachers*

This often is the most variable of all factors in experiments involving curriculum. However, five teachers taught reading to five fourth and fifth grade classes under the regular program, and the same five teachers taught reading to five fourth and fifth grade classes under the experimental program, with one exception. At the fourth grade level there was a turnover of one teacher. The principal of the building, the intermediate grade teachers, and the parents believed both teachers to be equally competent in the teaching of reading.

### 2. *Instructional Methods*

As was mentioned previously in this paper, a developmental approach was used in teaching reading to both groups. Since the same teachers were involved in teaching both groups, it is the writer's opinion that this factor was controlled.

### 3. *Pupils*

The pupils were comparable in every way—equal natural ability, equal home influence, etc., since they were drawn from the same identical community within a two-year period.

### 4. *Teaching Time*

Equal emphasis was given to the language arts in both the regular and the experimental program. An equal amount of time was given to the teaching of reading in the regular program as compared to the experimental program.

### 5. *Class Loads*

Class loads were very comparable under the two programs.

### 6. *Instructional Materials*

Instructional materials were not identical in every case, but were very similar in every case.

## Results

The achievement of the pupils from the fourth to the fifth grade (Sept. to Sept.) and from the fifth to the sixth grade (Sept. to Sept.) under the regular reading program and under the experimental program were compared as measured by the Reading Battery of the California Achievement Test. The comparison was analyzed statistically and produced the following results.

| *Fourth to the Fifth Grade* | | | |
|---|---|---|---|
| Regular Reading Program Sept. 1955 to Sept. 1956 | | Experimental Reading Program Sept. 1956 to Sept. 1957 | |
| *Group A* | | *Group B* | |
| Number of Cases | 47 | Number of cases | 49 |
| Median IQ | 111 | Median IQ | 102 |
| Mean gain | 10.2   mos. | Mean gain | 20.5   mos. |
| Standard Deviation | 6.90 | Standard Deviation | 7.67 |
| S. E. of the Mean | .982 | S. E. of the Mean | .903 |

T Ratio [4] equals 7.72. The difference is very significant and the null hypothesis can be rejected with confidence.

| *Fifth to the Sixth Grade* | | | |
|---|---|---|---|
| Regular Reading Program Sept. 1955 to Sept. 1956 | | Experimental Reading Program Sept. 1956 to Sept. 1957 | |
| *Group C* | | *Group B* | |
| Number of cases | 49 | Number of cases | 45 |
| Median IQ | 111 | Median IQ | 111 |
| Mean gain | 8.67   mos. | Mean gain | 18.0   mos. |
| Standard Deviation | 7.10 | Standard Deviation | 6.41 |
| S. E. of the Mean | .982 | S. E. of the Mean | .966 |

T Ratio equals 6.81. Again the difference is very significant.

## Conclusion

The results of this experiment indicate that reading achievement under the experimental program was significantly greater than the reading achievement under the regular program. All other factors being equal, it is this writer's opinion that this study gives strong support to those teachers and administrators who believe that ability grouping has merit and deserves serious consideration.

## References

1. BURTON, WILLIAM H. *Reading in Child Development*. New York: Bobbs-Merrill Company, Inc. (1956), pp. 505–519.

2. BETTS, ALBERT EMMETT. *Foundations of Reading Instruction*. New York: American Book Company (1946), pp. 438–87.

3. BARBE, WALTER B. and TINA S. WATERHOUSE. "An Experimental Program in Reading." *Elementary English*, XXXIII, pp. 102–104 (February 1950).

4. GUILFORD, J. P. *Fundamental Statistics in Psychology and Education*. New York: McGraw-Hill Book Company, Inc. (1950), pp. 208–210.

# 28

# WHAT WE KNOW AND CAN DO ABOUT THE POOR READER *

## Arthur I. Gates

Much has been said and written in recent years about the poor reader. Various plans or systems have been set forth as cure-alls. Teachers and reading specialists have been severely criticized because "Johnny Can't Read." It is as though there had suddenly been a great slump in the effectiveness of our methods of teaching reading and that all the research and experimentation that have been carried on in the teaching of reading for half a hundred years had been wasted. This article by Dr. Gates, though not directed primarily at critics of our reading programs, does point out some of the fallacies in the present loose thinking on the topic of teaching reading. But it does more—it identifies and discusses some of the real reasons why we have poor readers in the schools and it gives many practical suggestions for both parents and teachers to help Johnny to learn to read or to learn to read better. Implicit in the point of view presented is the idea that *every* teacher is a teacher of reading. If he isn't, he is doing only part of his job. No elementary or high school teacher can or should shirk his responsibility in this respect.

*Questions:*

1. List in outline form the suggestions in the article for (a) parents, (b) teachers, (c) both, (d) specialists (reading specialist, school diagnostician, psychiatrist).
2. What will be your "reading program" when you become a teacher?

\* \* \*

Like susceptibility to colds and other common bodily ailments, reading disabilities and failure have always been with us. The statements of certain

\* Reprinted from *Education,* **77:**528–533 (May 1957), by permission of author and by special permission of the publishers, the Bobbs-Merrill Company, Inc., Indianapolis, Indiana.

journalists to the contrary notwithstanding, retardation in reading is not a development of the last two or three decades. What has developed during this period is a vigorous program of study designed to correct and prevent reading difficulties. This intensive research enterprise was the result of the recognition of the extent and seriousness of difficulty and failure in reading which prevailed in 1920 and earlier. At that time, during the heyday of phonics and "meaty," primary material, one child in every five or six, as shown by Percival's study [2],* was required to repeat one or both of the first two grades primarily because of retardation or failure in reading. Difficulty in learning to read plagues the teachers and children of all nations, even those in which the relationship of letters and sounds is not so distressingly inconsistent and bewildering as it is in English [1]

## Learning to Read is Hazardous

It is important that parents and inexperienced teachers realize that learning to read is one of the most critical and difficult tests of a person's lifetime. For many it represents as serious a problem in adjustment as leaving home for the first time, going into the armed services or getting married. The seriousness of the task results from the fact that learning to read is for many a very difficult and subtle task. It comes at a time when the child is so young and inexperienced in learning in a new and often confusing group situation and one which demands so many other new adjustments. Difficulty springs, too, from the fact that his success or failure in learning to read is fraught with serious social consequences. If he learns to read well, all is well; if he does poorly or fails, the respect of his parents and acquaintances and his own self-esteem are threatened. When the test of learning to read becomes a test of a child's status as a total person, it becomes an ominous source of anxiety which increases the difficulty of learning and subtly induces many children to seek some sort of "escape" from the test. Unfortunately for the youngster, there is no satisfactory escape from learning to read, as there are from most of his other activities. If a child doesn't get on well in hopscotch or baseball or singing, he could turn to something else and save face. But there is in school and elsewhere today no satisfactory substitute for reading. The difficulty and cruciality of the learning-to-read period combine to make it a cauldron of anxiety and trouble, perplexing to child, parent and teacher. And herein lie the major "causes" of retardation and failure in reading.

* Figures in brackets apply to references at end of article.

After little more than three decades of study of the processes involved in learning to read in school, studies carried on by many specialists—teachers, educational diagnosticians, psychologists, neurologists, psychiatrists, oculists, anatomists, and others—it is recognized that to learn to read successfully a child must be pretty well equipped with aptitude for this type of symbolic learning; he must enjoy quite good health and vigor; he must be well taught; he must be well adjusted to the teaching mentally and emotionally, and he needs to be pretty lucky. Conversely, it is recognized that a deficiency in any of these areas may cause trouble in learning. There is nothing startling in this view. Every good physician knows that a similar situation exists in relation to keeping a person "in the pink" of physical condition, especially during a period of new and crucial adjustment. Whether a child's health and vigor are excellent, average or poor depends upon his general physical equipment, how he is nurtured and taught, the nature of his mental and emotional adjustment, the kind of habits he forms and, to some extent on his luck.

### Prevention and Correction

Efforts to improve the program for securing better development of reading interests and ability, of preventing difficulties and diagnosing and correcting those which appear are substantially the same in character as the corresponding approaches of medicine. All phases of the work depend upon achieving an understanding of all the factors which help and hinder improvement and of discovering and controlling their role in the case of each individual.

To prevent or cure reading difficulty, a teacher or reading specialist must determine the role of many factors quite as a physician must consider the effects of many influences if he is to prevent or cure indigestion, headaches or insomnia. Among the former are intelligence, or general aptitude for scholastic, especially symbolic learning, which may be gauged by using a "general intelligence" test. The reading specialist may use several tests of special abilities such as ability to perceive and recall word-like symbols; and ability to perceive similarity and difference in wordlike sounds. Such tests are similar in character to the physician's tests of blood pressure, pulse rate and temperature. A physician's or specialist's diagnosis of vision, hearing, and general physical condition are also often needed. The reading specialists, like the physician, will take a careful case history, giving the same attention to the psychological and educational factors that the physician gives to the physical, and both would take account of the character of the child's activities and relationships in the home, the neighborhood and the school.

## Emotionality

Reading difficulties, like indigestion, may be produced or aggravated by emotional factors existing in the home or playmate groups or the school. Indeed, both may arise from the same conditions—from such influences as overprotection, or overly severe discipline, or indifference of the parents or other older members of the family. The child who is "babied" too much may resent the inability of the teacher to lift him individually over every hurdle in learning to read and lack the initiative to learn by himself. Indeed, many children are dismayed to find that one cannot learn to read without effort. They may expect the story to come to them from the printed page as easily as it does from the movie or the television screen, and when it does not, they may become so discouraged or resentful as to seek to escape responsibility by refusing to try to learn or so jittery or apprehensive as to be unable to learn. Overanxiety of the parents or siblings or teacher may have the distracting effect that severe stage fright has for an adult. In such cases, urging the child to try harder or even trying inexpertly to help him learn may tighten rather than loosen the child's straight-jacket of doubt and tension. In all such cases—and they take many other forms—some sort of psychotherapy is essential.

By "psychotherapy" is not here meant special treatment by a psychologist or psychiatrist, although on rare occasions the help of such a specialist is indicated, nor is a separate period or provision of therapy necessarily required. What is suggested is that once the existence and nature of unfavorable emotional conditions and misleading personal relations are discovered, steps should be taken to relieve them. This may often be accomplished best by a shrewd teacher or reading specialist—who is or should be an exceptionally insightful teacher—in the course of normal classroom activities and often combined with suggested modifications of the pattern of family life. Usually, however, the demand for this type of therapeutic re-education of the child and his family or both calls for a considerable amount of extra time for diagnosis and individual counseling by the teacher. One of the tragedies is that a teacher who possesses the ability and desire to grapple successfully with such subtle problems simply does not have the time. She has many other problems, many other subjects and many other phases of instruction in reading to attend to.

## Reading Skills

Reading is probably the most difficult and subtle of all the scholastic abilities and skills to teach and the critical period comes at the very beginning of school life when the children are least experienced and most readily bewildered. It is very difficult to show a child, for example, all the tricks of working out the recognition and pronunciation of the weirdly artificial little hieroglyphic which printed words are. To be successful a child must catch on to good techniques. What is good for one word is often poor for another. To learn to recognize, sound, and blend the sounds of the letters may suffice for *hat* or *bag* but be utterly confounding for *haughty* or *hippopotamus,* the former because of phonetic inconsistence and the latter because the number of letters exceeds the child's immediate memory span. (The adult reader might try to blend the letter sounds of *zhljrpaufiom* from memory—it should be less puzzling because of his many years of experience with letters and their sounds).

The child must learn much by trial and error, and inappropriate techniques await at every hand to lead him astray quite as they do the adult who tries to learn to play golf or bridge or the violin without continual, expert, and individual instruction. Here is where "luck" enters. In learning to read, many children have the bad luck to hit off on faulty techniques which handicap them seriously. If a child, for example, begins to look first at the *end* or the *middle* of the word, rather than the beginning—a technique that works perfectly well in recognizing coins, insects, earrings, faces, and almost every object on earth except printed words—he is in for trouble. The woods of beginning reading are full of such treacherous pitfalls. Hence the need of a careful diagnostic inventory of the skills, insights, techniques and devices used by each learner.

Skill in using some one or a combination of several such diagnostic inventories now available is part of the equipment of every good reading specialist and an increasing number of teachers. They help the diagnostician discern the good and poor techniques used by a youngster. Using them gives no automatic insight; much depends upon the shrewdness of the teacher as, of course, it does in the case of the physician or music or golf instructor. The insightful diagnostician in all these fields uses the data from the diagnosis as a basis for planning a program of therapy or instruction tailored to fit the needs of the individual. This is called "corrective reading' or "remedial reading" but it differs in no important respect from the best types of everyday instruction. Indeed, the work of the reading specialist at its best differs from that of the regular classroom teacher only in being more expertly conceived, more skillfully conducted, and precisely adjusted to the needs of each child.

To teach such a subtle skill as reading to thirty to forty children is a formidable task for the best teacher and, of course, not all teachers are perfect. Some children are unlucky enough to get a relatively poor one— one who is so easy-going or unsympathetic that children become passive or aimlessly active, or one who is so autocratic as to make them jittery or fearful or angry, or one who is so uninspiring or inept, or one who is so blind to individual difficulties and needs as to leave children groping in uncertainty and confusion. Some children, moreover, are so unlucky as to miss school or change schools or teachers or encounter shifts in teaching methods or stumble into a change of interpersonal relationship in school or home at critical periods, and any gap not skillfully and individually bridged or any change not adequately guided may plunge the youngster into trouble. Emotionally unsettling events such as illness or misfortune or anger occurring to a member of the family or to the teacher or a playmate may be sufficient to reduce greatly the child's learning. The reaction of the teacher or pupils to a youngster on an "off day" may have a persistingly destructive effect. The writer recalls the occasion when one of the world's outstanding actors, who specializes in oral reading, made four or five "slips of speech" in each of a half dozen brief introductions of the artists participating in a program. If the most experienced and expert performers have such conspicuously bad spells, it is to be expected that a rank beginner will often have pathetically bad days. To offer crude, unsympathetic treatment at such a time is to sow the seeds of rebellion or failure.

### Panaceas

The considerations just presented should convince the parent that there can be no panacea for the troubled reader. There are unfortunately many panacea peddlers for poor reading, as there are for all sorts of physical ailments. Popular among them are various systems of formal phonics, most of which have appeared and reappeared for more than a century. Certain forms of psychiatric or psychoanalytic procedures have been advocated as sufficient for all cases. Recently popular are various mechanical gadgets such as rapid exposure apparatus, motion picture materials and various pacing machines. There are also a number of highly artificial and therefore novel forms of practice methods such as the kinesthetic method (tracing the outline of letters, etc.), flash card methods, experience story methods, reverse image exercises, visualization and other methods. None of these is good for all cases; to use any one in certain cases would be to add oil to the fire. Some of them are valuable for limited uses with certain cases. One should be suspicious of all panaceas, especially any rigid scheme of formal or freakish drills or mechanical gadgets.

### Parents and Reading

Parents often ask whether there is anything they can do to help a child learn to read or to improve his reading ability and interests. There are, indeed, many things parents can do. There is evidence that much of the basal equipment for reading is learned at mother's knee. Mother and father may contribute richly during all the pre-school years by helping the child engage abundantly and enjoyably in language activities. Answer the child's questions as fully and meaningfully as possible. Talk to him, tell him stories, report your daily experiences and encourage him to talk to you—the more the better. Take him on tours to the local stores, museums, factories, plants and other places and while doing so engage him in conversation, read the signs, placards, advertisements, and talk about them. Provide him at home with reading matter, signs, ads, picture cards, magazines and books—alphabet books, picture books, story and other books. Read them to him, observe the pictures and diagrams together.

Television programs, wisely selected, provide excellent opportunities for family enjoyment of great value. In using all these materials, read the words and text to the youngster, look at the pictures and talk about them together and *answer the child's questions,* listen to his comments, and respond as helpfully to them as you can. If he asks the name of a letter or a printed word, tell him. Run your finger along under the line of words you are reading as he observes. Put words and phrases on objects and pictures in his room and answer the questions he asks about them. Play word sound games. "What words begin with the same sound as *cat;* or end with the same sound as *sing?*" Should you teach him? No, not in a formal sense. Try, rather, to help him enjoy and engage at length in all kinds of verbal activity. If you can do that, you will have introduced a superior type of teaching. You will have helped your child enormously to make learning to read in school more certain and easy. If he learns to read before entering school, as many children with special aptitude will, so much the better. But don't undertake to teach him a heavy, formal system of phonics. This is a job for an experienced teacher.

The child will be helped enormously by the same pattern of family activity all through school, even into college. Let there be, at the appropriate level and in the proper areas, lots of conversation, reading aloud, reporting experiences and problems in which every person's contributions are welcomed and respected. Let there be a daily reading period, observed with the same regularity and conducted with the same spirit of enjoyment as the evening meal. Let each person read what he likes and feel free to talk about it to others.

Before a parent implies that his children's questions and comments are too silly and childish to merit respectful consideration, he might remind himself that in a few years his comments will seem equally naive and ignorant to the son or daughter who comes in fresh from study of up-to-the-minute knowledge in high school and college. The parent may expect to get, and deserves, the same treatment from his grown-up son or daughter as he gave them when they were children. Good readers, good students and good citizens tend to develop in homes in which good reading and good talk is a regular and enjoyable part of family life. A good reading specialist can spot in a few minutes a child who has suffered linguistic malnutrition in the home. And let no teacher or parent believe that a heavy dose of formal phonetics, or any other similar panacea, whether administered in the home or school, is a substitute for a wholesome diet of verbal food.

## References

1. KARLSEN, BJORN. "We Have Remedial Reading in Europe, Too." *California Teachers Journal* (May 1955).

2. PERCIVAL, WALTER E. *A Study of the Causes and Subjects of School Failure.* Unpublished Doctor's Dissertation, Teachers College, Columbia University, New York (1926).

# 29

## TEACHING MACHINES *

### B. F. Skinner

A development of great current interest to education is the so-called teaching machine. Coming as it does, out of the psychological laboratory, it is also more than mildly interesting to psychologists. It represents a promising application of a widely accepted principle of learning, namely immediate and unequivocal reinforcement. It is of interest to educators because of its potential use as an efficient aid to teaching. It holds the possibility of speeding up certain kinds of learning, thus making teaching more efficient and less demanding in terms of teaching time and effort. The result may be to aid materially in stretching out available teaching resources and in relieving the present and almost surely continuing shortage of qualified teachers. The article by Professor Skinner presents in condensed form the results of more than a quarter century of research and experimentation in this field. Pioneer work by Pressey in the 1920's and early 1930's was virtually abandoned and forgotten by all but a few psychologists until, as Skinner points out, the learning process was better understood and certain advances in technology came about. The future of the teaching machine looks bright, at least as long as enrollments continue to climb. Like television, it will undoubtedly find its proper place in education, in all probability, not as a substitute or replacement for the teacher but as a useful aid to instruction.

*Questions:*

1. In terms of the nature of subject matter what limitations of use of teaching machines and programmed learning do you see? Defend your answer.

2. What is the chief practical obstacle to programming learning? How is it to be overcome?

3. Could your own teaching subject—algebra, biology, American literature, woodworking—be adapted to teaching machines?

\* \* \*

There are more people in the world than ever before, and a far greater part of them want an education. The demand cannot be met simply by

* Abridged and reprinted from *Science,* **128:**969–977 (October 24, 1958), by permission of the author and publisher.

building more schools and training more teachers. Education must become more efficient. To this end curricula must be revised and simplified, and textbooks and classroom techniques improved. In any other field a demand for increased production would have led at once to the invention of labor-saving capital equipment. Education has reached this stage very late, possibly through a misconception of its task. Thanks to the advent of television, however, the so-called audio-visual aids are being reexamined. Film projectors, television sets, phonographs, and tape recorders are finding their way into American schools and colleges.

Audio-visual aids supplement and may even supplant lectures, demonstrations, and textbooks. In doing so they serve one function of the teacher: they present material to the student and, when successful, make it so clear and interesting that the student learns. There is another function to which they contribute little or nothing. It is best seen in the productive interchange between teacher and student in the small classroom or tutorial situation. Much of that interchange has already been sacrificed in American education in order to teach large numbers of students. There is a real danger that it will be wholly obscured if use of equipment designed simply to *present* material becomes widespread. The student is becoming more and more a mere passive receiver of instruction.

## Pressey's Teaching Machines

There is another kind of capital equipment which will encourage the student to take an active role in the instructional process. The possibility was recognized in the 1920's, when Sidney L. Pressey designed several machines for the automatic testing of intelligence and information. . . . In using the device the student refers to a numbered item in a multiple-choice test. He presses the button corresponding to his first choice of answer. If he is right, the device moves on to the next item; if he is wrong, the error is tallied, and he must continue to make choices until he is right [1].* Such machines, Pressey pointed out [2], could not only test and score, they could *teach*. When an examination is corrected and returned after a delay of many hours or days, the student's behavior is not appreciably modified. The immediate report supplied by a self-scoring device, however, can have an important instructional effect. Pressey also pointed out that such machines would increase efficiency in another way. Even in a small classroom the teacher usually knows that he is moving too slowly for some students and too fast for others. Those who could go faster are penalized,

* Figure in brackets apply to references at end of article.

and those who should go slower are poorly taught and unnecessarily punished by criticism and failure. Machine instruction would permit each student to proceed at his own rate.

The "industrial revolution in education" which Pressey envisioned stubbornly refused to come about. In 1932 he expressed his disappointment [3]. "The problems of invention are relatively simple," he wrote. "With a little money and engineering resource, a great deal could easily be done. The writer has found from bitter experience that one person alone can accomplish relatively little and he is regretfully dropping further work on these problems. But he hopes that enough may have been done to stimulate other workers, that this fascinating field may be developed."

Pressey's machines succumbed in part to cultural inertia; the world of education was not ready for them. But they also had limitations which probably contributed to their failure. Pressey was working against a background of psychological theory which had not come to grips with the learning process. The study of human learning was dominated by the "memory drum" and similar devices originally designed to study forgetting. Rate of learning was observed, but little was done to change it. Why the subject of such an experiment bothered to learn at all was of little interest. "Frequency" and "recency" theories of learning, and principles of "massed and spaced practice," concerned the conditions under which responses were remembered.

Pressey's machines were designed against this theoretical background. As versions of the memory drum, they were primarily testing devices. They were to be used after some amount of learning had already taken place elsewhere. By confirming correct responses and by weakening responses which should not have been acquired, a self-testing machine does, indeed, teach; but it is not designed primarily for that purpose. Nevertheless, Pressey seems to have been the first to emphasize the importance of immediate feedback in education and to propose a system in which each student could move at his own pace. He saw the need for capital equipment in realizing these objectives. Above all he conceived of a machine which (in contrast with the audio-visual aids which were beginning to be developed) permitted the student to play an active role.

### Another Kind of Machine

The learning process is now much better understood. Much of what we know has come from studying the behavior of lower organisms, but the results hold surprisingly well for human subjects. The emphasis in this research has not been on proving or disproving theories but on discovering and controlling the variables of which learning is a function. This practical orientation has paid off, for a surprising degree of control has been achieved. By arranging appropriate "contingencies of reinforcement," specific forms of behavior can be set up and brought under the control of specific classes of stimuli. The resulting behavior can be maintained in strength for long periods of time. A technology based on this work has already been put to use in neurology, pharmacology, nutrition, psychophysics, psychiatry, and elsewhere [4].

The analysis is also relevant to education. A student is "taught" in the sense that he is induced to engage in new forms of behavior and in specific forms upon specific occasions. It is not merely a matter of teaching him *what* to do; we are as much concerned with the probability that appropriate behavior will, indeed, appear at the proper time—an issue which would be classed traditionally under motivation. In education the behavior to be shaped and maintained is usually verbal, and it is to be brought under the control of both verbal and nonverbal stimuli. Fortunately, the special problems raised by verbal behavior can be submitted to a similar analysis [5].

If our current knowledge of the acquisition and maintenance of verbal behavior is to be applied to education, some sort of teaching machine is needed. Contingencies of reinforcement which change the behavior of lower organisms often cannot be arranged by hand; rather elaborate apparatus is needed. The human organism requires even more subtle instrumentation. An appropriate teaching machine will have several important features. The student must *compose* his response rather than select it from a set of alternatives, as in a multiple-choice self-rater. One reason for this is that we want him to recall rather than recognize—to make a response as well as see that it is right. Another reason is that effective multiple-choice material must contain plausible wrong responses, which are out of place in the delicate process of "shaping" behavior because they strengthen unwanted forms. Although it is much easier to build a machine to score multiple-choice answers than to evaluate a composed response, the technical advantage is outweighed by these and other considerations.

A second requirement of a minimal teaching machine also distinguishes it from earlier versions. In acquiring complex behavior the student must pass through a carefully designed sequence of steps, often of considerable length. Each step must be so small that it can always be taken, yet in taking it the student moves somewhat closer to fully competent behavior. The machine must make sure that these steps are taken in a carefully pre-scribed order.

Several machines with the required characteristics have been built and tested. Sets of separate presentations or "frames" of visual material are stored on disks, cards, or tapes. One frame is presented at a time, adjacent frames being out of sight. In one type of machine the student composes a response by moving printed figures or letters [6]. His setting is compared by the machine with a coded response. If the two correspond, the machine automatically presents the next frame. If they do not, the response is cleared, and another must be composed. The student cannot proceed to a second step until the first has been taken. A machine of this kind is being tested in teaching spelling, arithmetic, and other subjects in the lower grades.

For more advanced students—from junior high school, say, through college—a machine which senses an arrangement of letters or figures is un-necessarily rigid in specifying form of response. Fortunately, such students may be asked to compare their responses with printed material revealed by the machine. In such a machine, material is printed in 30 radial frames on a 12-inch disk. The student inserts the disk and closes the machine. He cannot proceed until the machine has been locked, and, once he has begun, the machine cannot be unlocked. All but a corner of one frame is visible through a window. The student writes his response on a paper strip ex-posed through a second opening. By lifting a lever on the front of the machine, he moves what he has written under a transparent cover and un-covers the correct response in the remaining corner of the frame. If the two responses correspond, he moves the lever horizontally. This movement punches a hole in the paper opposite his response, recording the fact that he called it correct, and alters the machine so that the frame will not appear again when the student works around the disk a second time. Whether the response was correct or not, a second frame appears when the lever is returned to its starting position. The student proceeds in this way until he has responded to all frames. He then works around the disk a second time, but only those frames appear to which he has not correctly responded. When the disk revolves without stopping, the assignment is finished. (The student is asked to repeat each frame until a correct response is made to allow for the fact that, in telling him that a response is wrong, such a machine tells him what is right.)

The machine itself, of course, does not teach. It simply brings the student into contact with the person who composed the material it presents. It is a labor-saving device because it can bring one programmer into contact with an indefinite number of students. This may suggest mass production, but the effect upon each student is surprisingly like that of a private tutor. The comparison holds in several respects. (i) There is a constant interchange between program and student. Unlike lecturers, textbooks, and the usual audio-visual aids, the machine induces sustained activity. The student is always alert and busy. (ii) Like a good tutor, the machine insists that a given point be thoroughly understood, either frame by frame or set by set, before the student moves on. Lectures, textbooks, and their mechanized equivalents, on the other hand, proceed without making sure that the student understands and easily leave him behind. (iii) Like a good tutor the machine presents just that material for which the student is ready. It asks him to take only that step which he is at the moment best equipped and most likely to take. (iv) Like a skillful tutor the machine helps the student to come up with the right answer. It does this in part through the orderly construction of the program and in part with techniques of hinting, prompting, suggesting, and so on, derived from an analysis of verbal behavior [5]. (v) Lastly, of course, the machine, like the private tutor, reinforces the student for every correct response, using this immediate feedback not only to shape his behavior most efficiently but to maintain it in strength in a manner which the layman would describe as "holding the student's interest."

## Programming Material

The success of such a machine depends on the material used in it. The task of programming a given subject is at first sight rather formidable. Many helpful techniques can be derived from a general analysis of the relevant behavioral processes, verbal and nonverbal. Specific forms of behavior are to be evoked and, through differential reinforcement, brought under the control of specific stimuli.

This is not the place for a systematic review of available techniques, or of the kind of research which may be expected to discover others. However, the machines themselves cannot be adequately described without giving a few examples of programs. We may begin with a set of frames (see Table 1) designed to teach a third- or fourth-grade pupil to spell the word *manufacture*. The six frames are presented in the order shown, and the pupil moves sliders to expose letters in the open squares.

The word to be learned appears in bold face in frame 1, with an example and a simple definition. The pupil's first task is simply to copy it. When he does so correctly, frame 2 appears. He must now copy selectively: he must identify "fact" as the common part of "manufacture" and "factory." This helps him to spell the word and also to acquire a separable "atomic" verbal operant [5]. In frame 3 another root must be copied selectively from "manual." In frame 4 the pupil must for the first time insert letters without

**Table 1**

**A set of frames designed to teach a third- or fourth-grade pupil to spell the word manufacture.**

---

1. **Manufacture** means to make or build. *Chair factories manufacture chairs.* Copy the word here:

   □ □ □ □ □ □ □ □ □ □ □

2. Part of the word is like part of the word **factory.** Both parts come from an old word meaning *make* or *build.*

   **m a n u** □ □ □ □ **u r e**

3. Part of the word is like part of the word **manual.** Both parts come from an old word for *hand.* Many things used to be made by hand.

   □ □ □ □ **f a c t u r e**

4. The same letter goes in both spaces:

   **m** □ **n u f** □ **c t u r e**

5. The same letter goes in both spaces:

   **m a n** □ **f a c t** □ **r e**

6. **Chair factories** □ □ □ □ □ □ □ □ □ □ □ **chairs.**

---

copying. Since he is asked to insert the same letter in two places, a wrong response will be doubly conspicuous, and the chance of failure is thereby minimized. The same principle governs frame 5. In frame 6 the pupil spells the word to complete the sentence used as an example in frame 1. Even a poor student is likely to do this correctly because he has just composed or completed the word five times, has made two important root-responses, and has learned that two letters occur in the word twice. He has probably learned to spell the word without having made a mistake.

Teaching spelling is mainly a process of shaping complex forms of behavior. In other subjects—for example, arithmetic—responses must be brought under the control of appropriate stimuli. Unfortunately the material which has been prepared for teaching arithmetic does not lend itself to excerpting. The numbers 0 through 9 are generated in relation to objects, quantities, and scales. The operations of addition, subtraction, multiplication, and division are thoroughly developed before the number 10 is reached. In the course of this the pupil composes equations and expressions in a great variety of alternative forms. He completes not only $5 + 4 = \square$, but $\square + 4 = 9$, $5 \square 4 = 9$, and so on, aided in most cases by illustrative materials. No appeal is made to rote memorizing, even in the later acquisition of the tables. The student is expected to arrive at $9 \times 7 = 63$, not by memorizing it as he would memorize a line of poetry, but by putting into practice such principles as that nine times a number is the same as ten times the number minus the number (both of these being "obvious" or already well learned), that the digits in a multiple of nine add to nine, that in composing successive multiples of nine one counts backwards (*nine, eigh*teen, twenty-*seven,* thirty-*six,* and so on), that nine times a single digit is a number beginning with one less than the digit (nine times *six* is *fifty* something), and possibly even that the product of two numbers separated by only one number is equal to the square of the separating number minus one (the square of eight already being familiar from a special series of frames concerned with squares).

Programs of this sort run to great length. At five or six frames per word, four grades of spelling may require 20,000 or 25,000 frames, and three or four grades of arithmetic, as many again. If these figures seem large, it is only because we are thinking of the normal contact between teacher and pupil. Admittedly, a teacher cannot supervise 10,000 or 15,000 responses made by each pupil per year. But the pupil's time is not so limited. In any case, surprisingly little time is needed. Fifteen minutes per day on a machine should suffice for each of these programs, the machines being free for other students for the rest of each day. (It is probably because traditional methods are so inefficient that we have been led to suppose that education requires such a prodigious part of a young person's day.)

A simple technique used in programming material at the high-school or college level is exemplified in teaching a student to recite a poem. The first line is presented with several unimportant letters omitted. The student must read the line "meaningfully" and supply the missing letters. The second, third, and fourth frames present succeeding lines in the same way. In the fifth frame the first line reappears with other letters also missing. Since the student has recently read the line, he can complete it correctly. He does the same for the second, third, and fourth lines. Subsequent frames are increasingly incomplete, and eventually—say, after 20 or 24 frames—the student reproduces all four lines without external help, and quite possibly without having made a wrong response. The technique is similar to that used in teaching spelling: responses are first controlled by a text, but this is slowly reduced (colloquially, "vanished") until the responses can be emitted without a text, each member in a series of responses being now under the "intraverbal" control of other members.

"Vanishing" can be used in teaching other types of verbal behavior. When a student describes the geography of part of the world or the anatomy of part of the body, or names plants and animals from specimens or pictures, verbal responses are controlled by nonverbal stimuli. In setting up such behavior the student is first asked to report features of a fully labeled map, picture, or object, and the labels are then vanished. In teaching a map, for example, the machine asks the student to describe spatial relations among cities, countries, rivers, and so on, as shown on a fully labeled map. He is then asked to do the same with a map in which the names are incomplete or, possibly, lacking. Eventually he is asked to report the same relations with no map at all. If the material has been well programmed, he can do so correctly. Instruction is sometimes concerned not so much with imparting a new repertoire of verbal responses as with getting the student to describe something accurately in any available terms. The machine can "make sure the student understands" a graph, diagram, chart, or picture by asking him to identify and explain its features—correcting him, of course, whenever he is wrong.

In addition to charts, maps, graphs, models, and so on, the student may have access to auditory material. In learning to take dictation in a foreign language, for example, he selects a short passage on an indexing phonograph according to instructions given by the machine. He listens to the passage as often as necessary and then transcribes it. The machine then reveals the correct text. The student may listen to the passage again to discover the sources of any error. The indexing phonograph may also be used with the machine to teach other language skills, as well as telegraphic code, music, speech, parts of literary and dramatic appreciation, and other subjects. . . .

It is not easy to construct such programs. Where a confusing or elliptical passage in a textbook is forgivable because it can be clarified by the teacher, machine material must be self-contained and wholly adequate. There are other reasons why textbooks, lecture outlines, and film scripts are of little help in preparing a program. They are usually not logical or developmental arrangements of material but stratagems which the authors have found successful under existing classroom conditions. The examples they give are more often chosen to hold the student's interest than to clarify terms and principles. In composing material for the machine, the programmer may go directly to the point. . . .

Whether good programming is to remain an art or to become a scientific technology, it is reassuring to know that there is a final authority—the student. An unexpected advantage of machine instruction has proved to be the feedback to the *programmer*. In the elementary school machine, provision is made for discovering which frames commonly yield wrong responses, and in the high-school and college machine the paper strips bearing written answers are available for analysis. A trial run of the first version of a program quickly reveals frames which need to be altered, or sequences which need to be lengthened. One or two revisions in the light of a few dozen responses work a great improvement. No comparable feedback is available to the lecturer, textbook writer, or maker of films. Although one text or film may seem to be better than another, it is usually impossible to say, for example, that a given sentence on a given page or a particular sequence in a film is causing trouble.

Difficult as programming is, it has its compensations. It is a salutary thing to try to guarantee a right response at every step in the presentation of a subject matter. The programmer will usually find that he has been accustomed to leave much to the student—that he has frequently omitted essential steps and neglected to invoke relevant points. The responses made to his material may reveal surprising ambiguities. Unless he is lucky, he may find that he still has something to learn about his subject. He will almost certainly find that he needs to learn a great deal more about the behavioral changes he is trying to induce in the student. This effect of the machine in confronting the programmer with the full scope of his task may in itself produce a considerable improvement in education.

Composing a set of frames can be an exciting exercise in the analysis of knowledge. The enterprise has obvious bearings on scientific methodology. There are hopeful signs that the epistemological implications will induce experts to help in composing programs. The expert may be interested for another reason. We can scarcely ask a topflight mathematician to write a primer in second-grade arithmetic if it is to be used by the average teacher in the average classroom. But a carefully controlled machine presentation and the resulting immediacy of contact between programmer and student offer a very different prospect, which may be enough to induce those who know most about the subject to give some thought to the nature of arithmetical behavior and to the various forms in which such behavior should be set up and tested.

## Can Material Be Too Easy?

The traditional teacher may view these programs with concern. He may be particularly alarmed by the effort to maximize success and minimize failure. He has found that students do not pay attention unless they are worried about the consequences of their work. The customary procedure has been to maintain the necessary anxiety by inducing errors. In recitation, the student who obviously knows the answer is not too often asked; a test item which is correctly answered by everyone is discarded as nondiscriminating; problems at the end of a section in a textbook in mathematics generally include one or two very difficult items; and so on. (The teacher-turned-programmer may be surprised to find this attitude affecting the construction of items. For example, he may find it difficult to allow an item to stand which "gives the point away." Yet if we can solve the motivational problem with other means, what is more effective than giving a point away?) Making sure that the student knows he doesn't know is a technique concerned with motivation, not with the learning process. Machines solve the problem of motivation in other ways. There is no evidence that what is easily learned is more readily forgotten. If this should prove to be the case, retention may be guaranteed by subsequent material constructed for an equally painless review.

The standard defense of "hard" material is that we want to teach more than subject matter. The student is to be challenged and taught to "think." The argument is sometimes little more than a rationalization for a confusing presentation, but it is doubtless true that lectures and texts are often inadequate and misleading by design. But to what end? What sort of "thinking" does the student learn in struggling through difficult material? It is true that those who learn under difficult conditions are better students, but are they better because they have surmounted difficulties or do they surmount them because they are better? In the guise of teaching thinking we set difficult and confusing situations and claim credit for the students who deal with them successfully.

The trouble with deliberately making education difficult in order to teach thinking is (i) that we must remain content with the students thus selected, even though we know that they are only a small part of the potential supply of thinkers, and (ii) that we must continue to sacrifice the teaching of subject matter by renouncing effective but "easier" methods. A more sensible program is to analyze the behavior called "thinking" and produce it according to specifications. A program specifically concerned with such behavior could be composed of material already available in logic, mathematics, scientific method, and psychology. Much would doubtless be added in completing an effective program. The machine has already yielded important relevant by-products. Immediate feed-back encourages a more careful reading of programmed material than is the case in studying a text, where the consequences of attention or inattention are so long deferred that they have little effect on reading skills. The behavior involved in observing or attending to detail—as in inspecting charts and the models or listening closely to recorded speech—is efficiently shaped by the contingencies arranged by the machine. And when an immediate result is in the balance, a student will be more likely to learn how to marshal relevant material, to concentrate on specific features of a presentation, to reject irrelevant materials, to refuse the easy but wrong solution, and to tolerate indecision, all of which are involved in effective thinking.

Part of the objection to easy material is that the student will come to depend on the machine and will be less able than ever to cope with the inefficient presentations of lectures, textbooks, films, and "real life." This is indeed a problem. All good teachers must "wean" their students, and the machine is no exception. The better the teacher, the more explicit must the weaning process be. The final stages of a program must be so designed that the student no longer requires the helpful conditions arranged by the machine. This can be done in many ways—among others by using the machine to discuss material which has been studied in other forms. These are questions which can be adequately answered only by further research.

No large-scale "evaluation" of machine teaching has yet been attempted. We have so far been concerned mainly with practical problems in the design and use of machines, and with testing and revising sample programs. . . . Material has been prepared to teach part of a course in human behavior to Harvard and Radcliffe undergraduates. Nearly 200 students completed 48 disks (about 1400 frames). The factual core of the course was covered, corresponding to about 200 pages of the text [7]. The median time required to finish 48 disks was 14½ hours. The students were not examined on the material but were responsible for the text which overlapped it. Their reactions to the material and to self-instruction in general have been studied through interviews and questionnaires. Both the machines and the material are now being modified in the light of this experience, and a more explicit evaluation will then be made.

Meanwhile, it can be said that the expected advantages of machine instruction were generously confirmed. Unsuspected possibilities were revealed which are now undergoing further exploration. Although it is less convenient to report to a self-instruction room than to pick up a textbook in one's room or elsewhere, most students felt that they had much to gain in studying by machine. Most of them worked for an hour or more with little effort, although they often felt tired afterwards, and they reported that they learned much more in less time and with less effort than in conventional ways. No attempt was made to point out the relevance of the material to crucial issues, personal or otherwise, but the students remained interested. (Indeed, one change in the reinforcing contingencies suggested by the experiment is intended to *reduce* the motivational level.) An important advantage proved to be that the student always knew where he stood, without waiting for an hour test or final examination.

### Some Questions

. . . Machines may still seem unnecessarily complex compared with other mediators such as workbooks or self-scoring test forms. Unfortunately, these alternatives are not acceptable. When material is adequately programmed, adjacent steps are often so similar that one frame reveals the response to another. Only some sort of mechanical presentation will make successive frames independent of each other. Moreover, in self-instruction an automatic record of the student's behavior is especially desirable, and for many purposes it should be fool-proof. Simplified versions of the present machines have been found useful . . . but the mechanical and economic problems are so easily solved that a machine with greater capabilities is fully warranted.

Will machines replace teachers? On the contrary, they are capital equipment to be used by teachers to save time and labor. In assigning certain mechanizable functions to machines, the teacher emerges in his proper role as an indispensable human being. He may teach more students than heretofore—this is probably inevitable if the world-wide demand for education is to be satisfied—but he will do so in fewer hours and with fewer burdensome chores. In return for his greater productivity he can ask society to improve his economic condition.

The role of the teacher may well be changed, for machine instruction will affect several traditional practices. Students may continue to be grouped in "grades" or "classes," but it will be possible for each to proceed at his own level, advancing as rapidly as he can. The other kind of "grade" will also change its meaning. In traditional practice a *C* means that a student has a smattering of a whole course. But if machine instruction assures mastery at every stage, a grade will be useful only in showing *how far* a student has gone. *C* might mean that he is halfway through a course. Given enough time he will be able to get an *A;* and since *A* is no longer a motivating device, this is fair enough. The quick student will meanwhile have picked up *A*'s in other subjects.

Differences in ability raise other questions. A program designed for the slowest student in the school system will probably not seriously delay the fast student, who will be free to progress at his own speed. (He may profit from the full coverage by filling in unsuspected gaps in his repertoire.) If this does not prove to be the case, programs can be constructed at two or more levels, and students can be shifted from one to the other as performances dictate. If there are also differences in "types of thinking," the extra time available for machine instruction may be used to present a subject in ways appropriate to many types. Each student will presumably retain and use those ways which he finds most useful. The kind of individual difference which arises simply because a student has missed part of an essential sequence (compare the child who has no "mathematical ability" because he was out with the measles when fractions were first taken up) will simply be eliminated.

## Other Uses

Self-instruction by machine has many special advantages apart from educational institutions. Home study is an obvious case. In industrial and military training it is often inconvenient to schedule students in groups, and individual instruction by machine should be a feasible alternative. Programs can also be constructed in subjects for which teachers are not available—for example, when new kinds of equipment must be explained to operators and repairmen, or where a sweeping change in method finds teachers unprepared [8]. Education sometimes fails because students have handicaps which make a normal relationship with a teacher difficult or impossible. (Many blind children are treated today as feeble-minded because no one has had the time or patience to make contact with them. Deaf-mutes, spastics, and others suffer similar handicaps.) A teaching machine

can be adapted to special kinds of communication—as, for example, Braille
—and, above all, it has infinite patience.

## Conclusion

An analysis of education within the framework of a science of behavior
has broad implications. Our schools, in particular our "progressive"
schools, are often held responsible for many current problems—including
juvenile delinquency and the threat of a more powerful foreign technology.
One remedy frequently suggested is a return to older techniques, especially
to a greater "discipline" in schools. Presumably this is to be obtained with
some form of punishment, to be administered either with certain classical
instruments of physical injury—the dried bullock's tail of the Greek
teacher or the cane of the English schoolmaster—or as disapproval or failure, the frequency of which is to be increased by "raising standards." This
is probably not a feasible solution. Not only education but Western culture
as a whole is moving away from aversive practices. We cannot prepare
young people for one kind of life in institutions organized on quite different
principles. The discipline of the birch rod may facilitate learning, but we
must remember that it also breeds followers of dictators and revolutionists.

In the light of our present knowledge a school system must be called a
failure if it cannot induce students to learn except by threatening them for
not learning. That this has always been the standard pattern simply emphasizes the importance of modern techniques. John Dewey was speaking for
his culture and his time when he attacked aversive educational practices
and appealed to teachers to turn to positive and humane methods. What he
threw out should have been thrown out. Unfortunately he had too little to
put in its place. Progressive education has been a temporizing measure
which can now be effectively supplemented. Aversive practices can not only
be replaced, they can be replaced with far more powerful techniques. The
possibilities should be thoroughly explored if we are to build an educational
system which will meet the present demand without sacrificing democratic
principles.

## References

1. The Navy's "Self-Rater" is a larger version of Pressey's machine. The items
   are printed on code-punched plastic cards fed by the machine. The time
   required to answer is taken into account in scoring.

2. PRESSEY, S. L. *School and Society*. **23:**586 (1926).

3. ———, *ibid*. **36:**934 (1932).

4. SKINNER, B. F. "The Experimental Analysis of Behavior." *Am. Scientist*. **45:**4 (1957).

5. ———. *Verbal Behavior*. New York: Appleton-Century-Crofts (1957).

6. ———. "The Science of Learning and the Art of Teaching." *Harvard Education Rev*. **24:**2 (1954).

7. ———. *Science and Human Behavior*. New York: Macmillan (1953).

8. MENGER, K. "New Approach to Teaching Intermediate Mathematics." *Science*. **127:**1320 (1958).

# 30

## RETENTION OF SUBJECT MATTER AS A FUNCTION OF LARGE GROUP INSTRUCTIONAL PROCEDURES [1] *

### Laurence Siegel, James F. Adams, and F. G. Macomber

Present enrolments in schools and colleges are the highest ever and even greater increases are expected in the years ahead. With the large numbers enrolled and anticipated, much attention is being given to methods of teaching large classes such as closed circuit television. A considerable body of research evidence suggests that students taught in large classes with the aid of television do as well on examinations in the course as those taught in small classes by conventional methods. However, it is not so clear as to how well such students retain what they know at the end of the course. In the following selection a study of this question is reported using college students in nine different courses as the subjects. The tests were administered one year and, in some instances, two years after the courses had been completed. Each student in these classes was matched with a student taught by conventional, small class methods. The results will not be particularly surprising to those who are convinced that instruction in large classes can be just as effective as that given in small classes.

*Questions:*

1. What proportion of the students in the original group of this study took the delayed tests? Is there any reason to suppose that this would affect the results? How have the authors guarded against any possible criticism?

2. What other outcomes, apparently not tested in this study, might be considered in a comprehensive evaluation program? Is there any reason to suppose that if these were included, the results might be different?

[1] This research was conducted under a grant to Miami University from the Fund for the Advancement of Education.

* Reprinted from the *Journal of Educational Psychology,* **51:**9–13 (February 1960), by permission of senior author and publisher.

3. In Table 2, although differences between mean scores are not great, eight out of nine mean retention scores favor the control groups. Do you think this might be significant?

* * *

Considerable research activity has been directed, during the past several years, to studies of the comparative achievement of students in televised classes, large (but not televised) classes, and smaller classes often designated as "conventional" instruction. Such research has been stimulated by the projected increases in college enrollments combined with an anticipated shortage of well qualified college teachers in many subject areas. Within this general context, closed circuit instructional television is regarded as potentially useful for simultaneously teaching large groups of students while overcoming some of the visual difficulties inherent in direct large class instruction.

The findings thus far reported for televised instruction indicate that students in TV classes tend to achieve about as well as those in conventional small classes, although they tend to prefer conventional to televised instruction (Carpenter & Greenhill: 1955, 1958; Macomber & Siegel: 1956, 1957). The same findings have been reported by Siegel, Macomber, and Adams (1959) when large group (not televised) instruction was compared with conventional instruction.

An outstanding feature of the studies of comparative achievement heretofore reported is that they have used a measure of immediate retention as the dependent variable. This measure has, in most cases, been the final examination administered in the course for the purpose of deriving course grades. A given level of performance on a final examination does not, however, guarantee a comparable level of subject matter retention after a lapse of time.

The present investigation was directed toward a comparative study of the effect of certain instructional procedures upon subject matter retention after a time lapse of from one to two years.

## Procedure

*Teaching Procedures*

Miami University's Experimental Study in Instructional Procedures has, since 1956, been investigating the comparative effectiveness of large group and small group (25 to 35 students) instruction. Three of the general approaches to large group instruction which have been investigated are designated TV (closed circuit television classes), LC (large classes with direct visual contact between student and instructor), and GS (instruction by graduate student assistants in classes of conventional size). The latter instructional procedure is classified as a large group technique because it increases the ratio of undergraduate enrollments to full-time faculty members.

Every comparison that has been made required a preliminary pairing of an experimental section (TV, LC, or GS) with at least one control (conventional) section. Students in both types of section were equated on the basis of tests of academic ability and measures of prior achievement. The control classes paired with the TV and LC sections were taught by the same instructor as taught the experimental sections. The control classes for GS sections, however, were taught by full-time faculty members rather than by graduate students.

## Subjects

The subjects (Ss) for the present investigation were those students who were enrolled in the experimental or control sections of nine different courses during the 1956–1957 and 1957–1958 academic years and were still in residence in April 1959. Since these nine courses are intended primarily for freshman and sophomore students, and since Miami University pursues a policy of nonselective admission of Ohio residents, there was considerable attrition in the number of available Ss. Contacts were made with a total of 1277 students who were still in residence of approximately 3000 students originally enrolled in the experimental and control sections of the nine courses. The proportion of students still in residence after the elapsed time corresponds roughly to the percentage of incoming students who are graduated.

Each of the 1277 Ss available for the retention study received a letter informing him of the fact that he was to report to a given room on campus at a specified time for research purposes. Although these students knew that the request came from the office of the Experimental Study in Instructional Procedures, they were not informed about the specific nature of the task they were to perform.

The letters were sent with a degree of trepidation lest an insufficient number of Ss appear at the scheduled time, and those who would appear would be poorly motivated. Both of these fears proved to be groundless. The retention tests were administered to 1022 students, representing 80%

of the group contacted. The tests were proctored by the instructors who had taught the course originally, and they reported a uniformly high level of student motivation. This was substantiated by the fact that a considerable number of students subsequently inquired about their performance on the retention test.

It was not possible to use the results of all 1022 Ss tested. The sample was a composite of students who had taken courses in two different academic years. It was necessary, therefore, to weight the experimental and control sections equally with respect to proportional representation of students who had taken the course during each of these years. This meant that certain of the Ss tested had to be deliberately eliminated from the sample. Eliminated cases were randomly determined by alphabetizing within each course and dropping every nth case. This procedure reduced the number of Ss actually used for the study to 744.

The number of Ss within each course who were tested and who were actually used for research purposes is shown in Table 1.

*Method*

The retention tests administered to the Ss consisted of selected objective items (primarily multiple choice in nature) from those that comprised the final examinations administered during the two previous academic years. These items were selected, in most cases, on the basis of item analysis data supportive of their discriminative power. The tests were suitable in length for administration during a 50-min. session, although the specific number of items in each retention test differed.

It was originally planned to analyze the retention test scores as a function of instructional procedure separately for the 1956–1957 group and the 1957–1958 group. This plan, which would have yielded information about retention after one year and after two years, had to be abandoned because many of the groups were insufficient in size. Consequently, an alternative procedure involving the pooling of data regardless of year the course was taken was followed. Thus the data presented herein are indicative of the retention test scores earned by students enrolled in the course both one and two years prior to the time they were tested.

## Results

Aside from the retention test scores, other data available for these Ss included their final examination scores earned at the time they were enrolled in the course, and their scores on the American Council on Edu-

**Table 1**
**The Samples**

| Course | Section | Students Enrolled in 1956–1957 | | Students Enrolled in 1957–1958 | | Total Ns Used |
|---|---|---|---|---|---|---|
| | | N Tested | N Used | N Tested | N Used | |
| Zoology | TV | | | 52 | 52 | 52 |
| | Control | | | 30 | 30 | 30 |
| Air Science | TV | 17 | 17 | 39 | 22 | 39 |
| | Control | 13 | 7 | 9 | 9 | 16 |
| Educational Psychology | TV | 36 | 35 | 59 | 43 | 78 |
| | Control | 15 | 13 | 17 | 16 | 29 |
| Introd. Psychology | LC | 20 | 17 | 29 | 19 | 36 |
| | Control | 18 | 8 | 11 | 9 | 17 |
| Freshman English | LC | 24 | 17 | 100 | 36 | 53 |
| | Control | 20 | 11 | 33 | 23 | 34 |
| Social Studies | LC | 10 | 8 | 29 | 28 | 36 |
| | Control | 10 | 8 | 29 | 28 | 36 |
| Geography | LC | 60 | 49 | 52 | 46 | 95 |
| | Control | 23 | 15 | 14 | 14 | 29 |
| Introd. Business | GS | 23 | 22 | 83 | 41 | 63 |
| | Control | 34 | 6 | 11 | 11 | 17 |
| Geology | GS | 27 | 27 | 51 | 38 | 65 |
| | Control | 12 | 8 | 12 | 12 | 20 |

cation Psychological Examination (ACE) and the Cooperative English test administered routinely to all incoming freshmen.

The final examination scores earned at the time the students were enrolled in the courses were analyzed to determine whether the $S$s from the experimental and control sections of these courses were comparable with respect to original level of achievement. This analysis took the form of computation of $t$ ratios to test the significance of the differences between the mean final examination scores of experimental and control group $S$s. The null hypotheses were not refuted. Original level of achievement was therefore not considered to be a factor of consequence with respect to retention scores.

The differences between mean retention test scores earned by subjects from the experimental and control sections of each course were tested for significance by analyses of covariance. The control variable in these analyses was the total ACE score for all courses with the exception of Freshman English. The control variable in this instance was the total score on the Cooperative English test. Scores on the control variables and the retention tests along with the appropriate $F$ ratios are summarized by course in Table 2.

### Table 2
### Summary of ACE and Retention Test Scores

| Course | Section | N | ACE | | Retention Test | | F Ratio[a] |
|---|---|---|---|---|---|---|---|
| | | | Mean | SD | Mean | SD | |
| Zoology | TV | 52 | 113.77 | 18.33 | 26.73 | 6.39 | 0.21 |
| | Control | 30 | 119.63 | 17.51 | 27.23 | 5.94 | |
| Air Science | TV | 39 | 112.26 | 17.23 | 46.62 | 7.63 | 0.36 |
| | Control | 16 | 111.69 | 21.82 | 47.44 | 6.02 | |
| Educational Psychology | TV | 78 | 111.19 | 18.97 | 31.19 | 4.53 | 1.11 |
| | Control | 29 | 107.79 | 15.96 | 31.69 | 5.12 | |
| Introd. Psychology | LC | 36 | 117.36 | 16.75 | 29.39 | 7.73 | 1.06 |
| | Control | 17 | 122.41 | 16.72 | 29.82 | 8.04 | |
| Freshman English | LC | 53 | 179.87[b] | 18.67 | 31.94 | 6.45 | 0.34 |
| | Control | 34 | 178.81[b] | 23.02 | 32.32 | 4.90 | |
| Social Studies | LC | 36 | 112.06 | 17.08 | 21.92 | 5.65 | 0.89 |
| | Control | 36 | 105.06 | 22.16 | 21.69 | 5.94 | |
| Geography | LC | 95 | 110.62 | 18.13 | 25.96 | 4.60 | 0.55 |
| | Control | 29 | 115.03 | 17.72 | 27.52 | 6.28 | |
| Introd. Business | GS | 63 | 112.12 | 18.96 | 24.71 | 4.67 | 0.40 |
| | Control | 17 | 109.41 | 20.17 | 25.47 | 4.23 | |
| Geology | GS | 65 | 113.86 | 19.15 | 23.03 | 5.25 | 0.20 |
| | Control | 20 | 113.10 | 12.90 | 24.45 | 4.83 | |

[a] Analysis of covariance controlling on ACE. The number of degrees of freedom for each $F$ ratio is 1: total $N - 3$

[b] Total score on the Cooperative Test of English Achievement was used as the matching variable instead of ACE

Since none of the $F$ ratios approach statistical significance, the null hypotheses cannot be rejected. It appears, within the scope of the present investigation, that retention of subject matter a year or two years after completion of a course is not adversely affected by increased class size or by the instructional procedures employed in this research.

## Summary

The purpose of this investigation was to determine the effect, if any, of instructional procedure upon subject matter retention one year or more after completion of a course. Retention scores of students who had received conventional instruction in nine courses were compared with the scores of students who had been instructed in the same courses by large group procedures: closed circuit television, large group (but not televised) instruction, and instruction by graduate student assistants rather than by full-time faculty members.

Of 1277 students, 80% (those who were still in residence of approximately 3000 students originally enrolled in the experimental and control sections) complied with a request to participate in the experiment. The retention test scores (based on objective items selected from the final examinations) were compared, with control on total ACE scores for eight of the courses and on the Cooperative English test score in the ninth course (Freshman English) being exercised by analysis of covariance.

None of the *F* ratios approached statistical significance. Hence, it appears within the limits of the present investigation, that retention of subject matter a year or more after completion of a course is not adversely affected by increased class size or by the particular instructional procedures used.

## References

1. CARPENTER, C. R. and L. P. GREENHILL. *An Investigation of Closed Circuit Television for Teaching University Courses: Rep. No. 1.* Univer. Park: Pennsylvania State Univer. (1955).

2. ———. *An Investigation of Closed Circuit Television for Teaching University Courses: Rep. No. 2.* Univer. Park: Pennsylvania State Univer. (1958).

3. MACOMBER, F. G. and L. SIEGEL. *The Experimental Study in Instructional Procedures: Rep. No. 1.* Oxford: Miami Univer. (1956).

4. ———. *The Experimental Study in Instructional Procedures: Rep. No. 2.* Oxford: Miami Univer. (1957).

5. SIEGEL, L., F. G. MACOMBER, and J. F. ADAMS. "The Effectiveness of Large Group Instruction at the University Level. *Harv. Educ. Rev.* (1959).

# 31

# THE POLITICAL PREFERENCES OF ADOLESCENTS *

## Norman Young, Frank Mayans, Jr. and Bernard R. Corman

A fundamental question for the social scientist has to do with the origins or sources of one's politics. How does one become a Republican or a Democrat? What part does education play in shaping one's political beliefs? Educators would probably like to believe that the social studies play a significant role in this matter. In order to shed some light on the question, 6,000 eleventh grade students were tested on interests, knowledge, attitudes toward politicians, and toward issues, and with personality and general ability tests. They were also asked to name their favorite political party and the party preferences of their parents. The results are analyzed for relationship between students' and parents' preferences; to determine the consistency between expressed preference and views generally held by the party of preference; to determine relationship between party preference and other factors such as religion, socio-economic status and occupation; and consistency of voting in a poll with party preference. The educational implications of the findings are discussed especially in relation to the teaching of social studies.

*Questions:*

1. How do the authors explain the finding that adolescents' political preferences are so similar to those of their parents? Does this mean that our young people do not think for themselves on political matters?

2. If, as the article suggests, political preferences of adolescents are established largely by influences outside the school, what role should the school, and especially the social studies, attempt to play?

3. Should the school attempt to change political preferences of students?

* Reprinted from *Teachers College Record,* **54**:340–344 (March 1953), by permission of the senior author and the publisher.

Much has been written about the importance of youth to the future of the nation. Whatever the tenor of the writing, there is emphasis on the fact that the youth of America will be influential in social, political, and cultural progress. This discussion is based on research into aspects of the political attitudes and interests of youth.

In an experimental program undertaken by the Evaluation Section of the Teachers College, Columbia University, Citizenship Education Project, more than 6,000 eleventh grade students were tested with a battery of six tests. These were: an interest test, a knowledge test, an attitude toward politicians scale, an attitude toward issues scale, a personality test, and a vocabulary test. The last of these we considered our intelligence test. In addition there was a political, scholastic, and personal background questionnaire. Except where otherwise indicated, the results are based on a 10 per cent sample of these students.

The adolescents' approach to political problems may be considered a function of a complex attitudinal set. For example, they may think of politicians as individuals basically beneficent to mankind or they may equate "politician" with "crook." They may favor the Democratic party or the Republican party or perhaps no party. Whatever their political attitudes may be, the existence of these attitudes is crucial to the character of their participation in adult political life.

The investigations reported in *The People's Choice* [3],* on the construction of an index of political predisposition for adults, lend support to the contention that cultural influences (or social characteristics, as the authors call them) determine political preference. One inference from their study is that the American adult is politically what he is socially.

We were interested in the same problem of political predisposition, but in terms of the future electorate, namely the adolescents. Since the adolescent has the same background characteristics as his parents, we would expect his selection of political party to be governed by the same factors, in addition to whatever identification relationship exists between him and his parents.

To test the foregoing hypothesis that adolescents are culturally predisposed in party reference, a tabulation was made of 6,000 responses to the section of the questionnaire requesting the adolescent's favorite political party and the party preference of his parents. Eighty-three per cent of the adolescents preferred the same party as their parents.†

* Figures in brackets apply to references at end of article.

† Less than ½ of 1 per cent of the students indicated a difference in party choice of father and mother.

Even without knowledge of parent choice, we could predict the adolescent's choice of party from his religion or the socioeconomic status of his family. Just as Lazarsfeld found for his adult group, our Protestant adolescents from higher socioeconomic levels tended to be Republicans, while Catholics from lower socioeconomic levels tended to be Democrats. In addition, we discovered that Republican adolescents tended to be more orthodox than the young Democrats.

The stratification of the electorate is nothing new to either politician or layman. The practicing politician is aware of what "types" of people (in terms of their background) are likely to be thoroughly imbued Republicans or traditional Democrats. The politician distinguishes a Republican from a Democrat by the same criteria a political scientist uses to predict party preference: Where does the citizen live? What is his religion? What sort of job does he have?

We find the same stratification possible with the adolescent. If we know where he lives, what his religion is, how often he goes to church, and how his father votes, we can predict with substantial confidence which party he prefers.

The adolescent's attitudes, including political attitudes, will be a resultant of the forces outside and inside the home. Within the family, interpersonal ties are strengthened by the specific experiences common to all of its members, resulting in a certain similarity of outlook.

The home as a factor in the inculcation of attitudes has been investigated by numerous workers in the field, including Hirschberg and Gilliland [2], who found that the home influences many kinds of attitudes. Helfant [1], working with adolescents, found high relationships between students' attitudes and parents' attitudes in some areas. Murphy, Murphy, and Newcomb [4] reported a series of correlation coefficients among pairs of siblings on a number of attitudes. The conclusion that may be drawn from these studies is that the core of experience in which a family shares, often results in an intrafamily community of attitude. This should be particularly true of adolescent-parent political attitudes.

Because politics is far from a leading interest of the student he pays relatively little attention to it. Thus, one may expect his exposure to an attitude such as political beliefs to be predominantly molded by what preference he perceives his parents to have. The adolescent does not generally see the choice of one party or another as answering any of his personal needs. The salient factor operating is the parents' political preferences. So strong are the familial bonds in forging attitudes that where there is no resistance by the adolescent to adoption of a political attitude, just knowing which party the parent prefers enables us to predict the adolescent's favorite party.

Political attitude in America is an expression of family loyalty as much as anything else. Political allegiance is often handed down from parent to child as if it were a legacy.

If people continue to select party more according to family allegiance than according to cognitive considerations, it will be the peculiar function of a comparatively small group to tilt the balance one way or another, because the great mass of the population is loyal to the saying "The Republican party (or the Democratic party) was good enough for my father and it's good enough for me."

At this point we asked ourselves: Is this adoption by the adolescent of his parents' favorite political party an empty selection of the label "Democratic" or "Republican" or is it a constellation of party preference along with attitudes toward particular issues consistent with party choice?

An independent research group ranked attitudes toward issues on a scale from a Democratic to a Republican position. Although there is wide acknowledgment of the fact that the range of opinion is tremendous within the parties, raters were able to agree as to the predominating party view. Using their ratings we found that Democratic adolescents had a significantly higher pro-Democratic score on issues; the Republican adolescents, a higher pro-Republican score. Apparently, then, the adolescent's party preference is not only a symbol which derives from his parents' loyalties, but is part and parcel of a syndrome of attitudes. This is consistent with the intra-family relationship of attitudes found in other areas by previous investigators.

Consistent with the viewpoint that adolescents have adopted a complex attitudinal set in the political area is the finding that the youngsters who selected the Democratic party were more favorably disposed toward politicians than were Republican youngsters. It is reasonable to suppose that the Democratic youngsters, having grown up in a period of Democratic ascendancy, will view the government policy makers with more favor, since these politicians are of the same party and, in the main, of the same political philosophy as the Democratic adolescents.

The question now arises: Are these statistically significant results politically significant? Does the close relationship between adolescents and their parents in party preference and attitudes hold in actual practice? We have evidence from our study and from recent research reported at Purdue University on this point [5]. Could adolescents be used to predict the election? Our study indicated that Eisenhower would get approximately 60 per cent of the adolescent votes and the Purdue University High School panel, involving 10,000 students, showed that Eisenhower got 58 per cent of the adolescent vote. Our results are not discordant with the findings which the pollsters published near the time of our testing. When we hear some wag remark that we need not poll the parents to predict election results—that all we have to do is poll the adolescents—it may be worth more than superficial consideration.

There are implications for education in these findings. Somehow the automaticity of choice is uncomfortable. This is not because political attitudes have correlates and are predictable with substantial confidence, but because the predictors are such comparatively stable factors as parents' choice, religion, socioeconomic status. It is as if we had a mass of political robots who were foreordained to react in a certain way, and the only reason not all react as predicted is that our mechanism for prediction is not 100 per cent efficient.

Where does this leave the teacher of social studies, whose objective is to train students so that their political attitudes will be based on a reasoned examination of the facts and conditions of each political issue? Perhaps the answer lies in a shift in emphasis. It may be that the task for educators must become one of making children understand why they act as they do, why they prefer one political party over another, why they have one set of attitudes rather than an opposite set. All too often social studies classes neglect to examine the motivations for their actions and beliefs. Behavior in the political area should be based on reason if the desideratum of an enlightened electorate is to be reached. Why people adopt the attitudes they express must be as much the concern of the teacher of social studies as the study of what the attitudes are.

Necessary, too, is further research into the developmental aspects of the problem. As stated earlier, our studies were made on an eleventh grade population. Here we find the matrix of political predispositions is already well defined. At what point on the school ladder does the choice of the parents' party carry with it a choice of the attitudes associated with that party preference? It may be that at an earlier age this association is not so stable. If this is the case, it may be that introduction of serious consideration of the student's future role as a citizen should come earlier than it does now.

The whole area of interest in political affairs has been given only passing attention in terms of finding the concomitants of political interest. That the interest of individuals may influence attitudes is fairly axiomatic with the proponents of the selective perception theory wherein people perceive according to their needs and values. On the basis of this theoretical formulation it would be expected that if we were to make a hypothesis concerning which adolescents would be most favorable to politicians, we would choose those for whom social studies is the favorite subject. This was precisely our finding: those who chose the social studies area had a significantly more favorable attitude toward politicians than the rest of the students. Those who favored mathematics were least favorable. Evidently, here minimal interest fostered stereotype reinforcement. We found that attitude toward politicians was not related to sex, religion, or frequency of church attendance.

The administration of our interest test and our question on favorite school subject revealed several points worthy of mention. Primarily, it was indeed gratifying for us to discover that those who selected social studies as their favorite school subject also scored high on our interest in political affairs test. Since this was expected it gave us validation material to support the interest test which we devised. We also learned that girls are more interested in political affairs than are boys, substantiation of their greater verbality and earlier maturity which have been reported in other studies.

When we compared our high political knowledge group, top 15 per cent, to our low political knowledge group, bottom 15 per cent, we discovered that the favorite school subjects in the high knowledge group were social studies and science, whereas in the low knowledge group we found a preponderance of those who chose vocational subjects, another substantiation of earlier reports found in the literature.

Findings which have been reported in other studies show that high knowledge is related to higher social class in the Warner sense [6]—at least as far as educational level of the parent correlates with social class—and those who selected science as their favorite school subject are most often among those with high intelligence. And finally, how regularly one goes to church is not related to political interest.

## Summary

Findings and inferences regarding the political interest, attitudes, knowledge, and personal background of adolescents as discerned from an experimental program originating in and administered by the Citizenship Education Project at Teachers College, Columbia University include the following:

Adolescents choose the same political party as their parents. Their attitudes on issues are related to the political party they prefer. Their attitude toward politicians varies with their interests and favored political party. Apparently their party choice is related to both religious affiliation and frequency of church attendance. Girls are more interested in political affairs than boys are.

Although these and our other findings may be statistically conclusive and apparently generalizable, there certainly remains the problem of integration of these segments of that mass of knowledge known as adolescent behavior.

There is a hint from this study and the literature that, for adults, being a Democrat or a Republican is a syndrome of characteristics involving levels of religion, socioeconomic status, intelligence, and so forth. Therefore, the study and ultimate understanding of political attitudes as resultants of various of the dynamic forces in life as we have delineated them would certainly be a "consummation devoutly to be wished."

## References

1. HELFANT, K. G. "Relationships Among Socio-Political Attitudes of Adolescents, Socio-Political Attitudes of Their Parents and Some Measures of Adolescent Hostility." Ph.D. Thesis, Columbia University, New York (1951).

2. HIRSCHBERG, G. and A. R. GILLILAND. "Parent-Child Relationships in Attitudes." *Journal of Abnormal and Social Psychology.* **37:**125–130 (January 1942).

3. LAZARSFELD, P. F., B. BERELSON, and H. GAUDET. *The People's Choice.* New York: Duell, Sloane and Pearce (1944).

4. MURPHY, G., L. B. MURPHY, and T. NEWCOMB. *Experimental Social Psychology.* New York: Harper & Bros. (1937).

5. Poll No. 33, Purdue Opinion Panel, Purdue University (1952).

6. WARNER, W. L. *et al. Social Class in America.* Chicago: Science Research Associates, Inc. (1949).

## Bibliography

*Learning—The Major Concern of Educational Psychology*

1. ANDERSON, RICHARD C. "Learning in Discussions: A Resume of Authoritarian—Democratic Studies." *Harv. Educ. Rev.* **29:**201–215 (Summer 1959).

2. ANGELL, G. W. "Effect of Immediate Knowledge of Quiz Results on Final Exam Scores in Freshman Chemistry." *J. Educ. Res.* **42**:391–394 (January 1949).

3. AUBLE, DONOVAN and E. VICTOR MECH. "Quantitative Studies of Verbal Reinforcement in Classroom Situations. 1. Differential Reinforcement Related to the Frequency of Error and Correct Response." *J. Psychol.* **35**:307–312 (April 1953).

4. AYER, FREDERIC L. and BERNARD R. CORMAN. "Citizenship Concepts Are Developed by Laboratory Practices." *Soc. Educ.* **16**:215–216 (May 1952).

5. BARKER, ROGER G. "Success and Failure in the Classroom." *Progressive Educ.* **19**:221–224 (April 1942).

6. BAVELAS, ALEX and KURT LEWIN. "Training in Democratic Leadership." *J. Ab. & Soc. Psychol.* **37**:115–119 (1942).

7. BAYLES, ERNEST E. "The Idea of Learning as Development of Insight." *Educ. Theory.* **2**:65–71 (April 1952).

8. BILLINGSLEA, F. and H. BLOOM. "The Comparative Effect of Frustration and Success on Goal-Directed Behavior in the Classroom." *J. Ab. & Soc. Psychol.* **45**:510–515 (1950).

9. BIRCH, HERBERT G. and HERBERT S. RABINOWITZ. "The Negative Effect of Previous Experience on Productive Thinking." *J. Exp. Psychol.* **41**:121–125 (February 1951).

10. BLACK, W. B. "How Can We Better Motivate the Underachiever and the Indifferent Student?" *Bul. Nat. Assoc. Sec. Sch. Prin.* **44**:174–180 (April 1960).

11. BLOOM, B. S. "Thought Processes in Lectures and Discussion." *J. Genet. Educ.* **7**:160–169 (April 1953).

12. ——— and L. J. BRODER. *Problem-Solving Process of College Students: An Exploratory Investigation.* Chicago: U. of Chicago Press (1950).

13. BOECK, CLARENCE H. "Teaching Chemistry for Scientific Method and Attitude Development." *Sci. Educ.* **37**:81–84 (March 1953).

14. BOLZAU, EMMA L. and ELIZABETH L. KELTZ. "What Shall We Do for the Slow Learner?" *Amer. Sch. Bd. J.* **133**:37–38 (November 1956).

15. BOVARD, E. W., JR. "The Psychology of Classroom Interaction." *J. Educ. Res.* **45**:215–224 (November 1951).

16. BRADLEY, BEATRICE E. "An Experimental Study of the Readiness Approach to Reading." *Elem. Sch. J.* **56**:262–267 (February 1956).

17. BREMER, NEVILLE. "Do Readiness Tests Predict Success in Reading?" *Elem. Sch. J.* **59**:222–224 (January 1959).

18. BRIGGS, L. J. and H. B. REED. "The Curve of Retention for Substance Material." *J. Exp. Psychol.* **32:**513–517 (June 1943).

19. BROHOLM, S. and G. HENDRICKSON. "Helping Children Learn Through Rational Decision Making." *Cal. J. Elem. Educ.* **27:**50–61 (August 1958).

20. BROYLER, CECIL R., E. L. THORNDIKE, and ELLA WOODYARD. "A Second Study of Mental Discipline in High School Studies." *J. Educ. Psychol.* **18:**377–404 (September 1927).

21. BURTON, DWIGHT L. "Spelling Can Be Taught to High-School Students." *Sch. Rev.* **61:**163–167 (March 1953).

22. CALABRIA, F. M. "Characteristics of Effective Teachers." *Educ. Res. Bul.* **39:**92–100 (April 1960).

23. CANTOR, G. N. "The Effects of Three Types of Pre-Training on Discrimination Learning in Pre-School Children." *J. Exp. Psychol.* **49:**339–342 (May 1955).

24. CANTOR, NATHANIEL. "Function and Focus in the Learning Process." *J. Educ. Res.* **45:**225–231 (November 1951).

25. COMBS, ARTHUR W. "Counseling as a Learning Process." *J. Counseling Psychol.* **1:**31–36 (Winter 1954).

26. COOK, RUTH CATHLYN. "Evaluation of Two Methods of Teaching Spelling." *Elem. Sch. J.* **58:**21–27 (October 1957).

27. CORY, N. DURWARD. "Incentives Used in Motivating Professional Growth of Teachers." *No. Central Assoc. Quarterly.* **27:**387–409 (April 1953).

28. CRONBACH, LEE J. "The Meaning of Problems." *Supplementary Educ. Monographs.* No. 66. Chicago: University of Chicago Press, pp. 32–43 (October 1948).

29. DANSKIN, D. G., and C. W. BURNETT. "Study Techniques of Those Superior Students." *Pers. & Guid. J.* **31:**181–186 (December 1952).

30. DAVIS, ALLISON. *Social-Class Influences Upon Learning.* Cambridge, Mass.: Harvard University Press (1948).

31. DAVIS, ROBERT A. "Applicability of Applications of Psychology with Particular Reference to Schoolroom Learning." *J. Educ. Res.* **37:**19–30 (September 1943).

32. DEGROAT, ALBERT F. and GEORGE THOMPSON. "A Study of the Distribution of Teacher Approval and Disapproval among Sixth-grade Pupils." *J. Exp. Educ.* **18:**57–75 (September 1949).

33. DILDINE, GLENN C. "Motivated to Learn." *NEA J.* **39:**356–357 (May 1950).

34. DRESSEL, P., J. SCHMID, and G. KINCAID. "The Effect of Writing Fre-

quency Upon Essay-Type Writing Proficiency at the College Level." *J. Educ. Res.* **46:**285–293 (December 1952).

35. DUNCKER, K. "Experimental Modification of Children's Food Preferences Through Social Suggestion." *J. Ab. & Soc. Psychol.* **33:**489–507 (1938).

36. EXTON, ELAINE. "Television at Work in the Schools." *Amer. Sch. Bd. J.* **134:**49–50, 70 (June 1957).

37. FREEBURNE, C. M. and M. S. FLEISCHER. "The Effect of Music Distraction Upon Reading Rate and Comprehension." *J. Educ. Res.* **45:**101–109 (October 1952).

38. GATES, A. I. "Recitation as a Factor in Memorizing." *Arch. Psychol.* No. 40 (September 1917).

39. GEBHARD, M. E. "Changes in the Attractiveness of Activities: The Effect of Expectation Preceding Performance." *J. Exp. Psychol.* **39:**404–413 (June 1949).

40. GERARD, H. B. "Some Factors Affecting an Individual's Estimate of His Probable Success in a Group Situation." *J. Ab. & Soc. Psychol.* **52:**235–239 (1956).

41. GOLDSTEIN, AVRAM. "Does Homework Help? A Review of Research." *Elem. Sch. J.* **60:**212–224 (January 1960).

42. GUILFORD, J. P., N. W. KETTNER, and P. R. CHRISTENSON. "The Nature of the General Reasoning Factor." *Psychol. Rev.* **63:**169–172 (May 1956).

43. HAIGH, G. V. and W. SCHMIDT. "The Learning of Subject Matter in Teacher-Centered and Group-Centered Classes." *J. Educ. Psychol.* **47:**295–301 (May 1956).

44. HASLERUD, G. M. and S. MEYERS. "The Transfer Value of Given and Individually Derived Principles." *J. Educ. Psychol.* **49:**293–298 (December 1958).

45. HENDRICKSON, GORDON and WILLIAM H. SCHROEDER. "Transfer of Training in Learning to Hit a Submerged Target." *J. Educ. Psychol.* **32:**205–213 (March 1941).

46. HILGARD, ERNEST R. "Aspirations After Learning." *Child. Educ.* **23:**115–118 (November 1946).

47. ———. "The Relation of Schools of Psychology to Educational Practices." *Cal. J. Elem. Ed.* **8:**17–26 (1939).

48. ———. "Success in Relation to Level of Aspiration." *School and Society.* **55:**423–428 (April 11, 1942).

49. ———, ROBERT P. IRVINE, and JAMES E. WHIPPLE. "Rote Memorization, Understanding, and Transfer: an Extension of Katona's Card-trick Experiments." *J. Exp. Psychol.* **46**:288–292 (October 1953).

50. HOWELL, WALLACE. "Work-Study Skills of Children in Grades IV to VIII." *Elem. Sch. J.* **50**:384–389 (March 1950).

51. HUMPHREYS, LLOYD G. "Transfer of Training in General Education." *J. Gen. Educ.* **5**:210–216 (October 1951).

52. HURLOCK, ELIZABETH B. "The Value of Praise and Reproof as Incentives for Children." *Arch. of Psychol.* No. 71 (July 1924).

53. ———. "An Evaluation of Certain Incentives Used in School Work." *J. Educ. Psychol.* **16**:145–159 (March 1925).

54. KASDON, LAWRENCE M. "Early Reading Background of Some Superior Readers Among College Freshmen." *J. Educ. Res.* **52**:151–153 (December 1958).

55. KEISTER, MARY E. and RUTH UPDEGRAFF. "A Study of Children's Reactions to Failure and an Experimental Attempt to Modify Them." *Child Dev.* **8**:241–248 (September 1937).

56. KILPATRICK, WILLIAM H. "We Learn What We Live." *N. Y. State Educ.* **33**:535–537 (April 1946).

57. KNAPP, CLYDE G. and W. ROBERT DIXON. "Learning to Juggle: I. A. Study to Determine the Effect of Two Different Distributions of Practice on Learning Efficiency." *Res. Quarterly.* **21**:331–336 (October 1950).

58. KOENKER, ROBERT H. "Arithmetic at the Kindergarten Level." *J. Educ. Res.* **42**:218–223 (November 1948).

59. LETSON, CHARLES T. "The Relative Influence of Material and Purpose on Reading Rates." *J. Educ. Res.* **52**:238–240 (February 1959).

60. LEVINE, J. and J. BUTLER. "Lecture Versus Group Decision in Changing Behavior." *J. App. Psychol.* **36**:29–33 (February 1952).

61. LEVINE, J. M. and G. MURPHY. "The Learning and Forgetting of Controversial Material." *J. Ab. & Soc. Psychol.* **38**:507–517 (October 1943).

62. LUCHINS, ABRAHAM S. "Mechanization in Problem Solving—The Effect of Einstellung." *Psychol. Monographs.* **54**:1–95, No. 6 (1942).

63. ———. "On Recent Usage of the Einstellung—Effect as a Test of Rigidity." *J. Consult. Psychol.* **15**:89–94 (April 1951).

64. MANDLER, GEORGE and SEYMOUR B. SARASON. "A Study of Anxiety and Learning." *J. Ab. & Soc. Psychol.* **47**:166–174 (1952).

65. MASLOW, A. H. "A Theory of Human Motivation." *Psychol. Rev.* **50**:370–396 (July 1943).

66. MAY, MARK A. "The Psychology of Learning from Demonstration Films." *J. Educ. Psychol.* **37:**1–12 (January 1946).

67. MITCHELL, JAMES V. "Goal-setting Behavior as a Function of Self-acceptance, Over- and Underachievement, and Related Personality Variables." *J. Educ. Psychol.* **50:**93–104 (June 1959).

68. MITNICK, LEONARD L. and ELLIOTT McGINNIES. "Influencing Ethnocentrism in Small Discussion Groups through a Film Communication." *J. Ab. & Soc. Psychol.* **56:**82–90 (1958).

69. MORSH, J. E. "The Development of Right-Handed Skill in the Left-Handed Child." *Child. Dev.* **1:**311–324 (December 1930).

70. MOWRER, O. H. "The Psychologist Looks at Language." *Amer. Psychol.* **9:**660–694 (November 1954).

71. MULFORD, HERBERT B. "TV for Education in Chicagoland." *Amer. Sch. Bd. J.* **133:**37–38 (October 1956).

72. MURPHY, LOIS BARCLAY. "Learning How Children Cope with Problems." *Children.* **4:**132–136 (July–August 1957).

73. NORBERG, KENNETH. "Perception Research and Audio-Visual Education." *Aud.-Vis. Communica. Rev.* **1:**18–29 (Winter 1953).

74. OTTO, H. J. and E. O. MELBY. "An Attempt to Evaluate the Threat of Failure as a Factor in Achievement." *Elem. Sch. J.* **35:**588–596 (April 1935).

75. PHILLIPS, B. N. and L. A. D'AMICO. "Effects of Cooperation and Competition on the Cohesiveness of Small Face-to-Face Groups." *J. Educ. Psychol.* **47:**65–70 (February 1956).

76. PRESSEY, S. L. "Development and Appraisal of Devices Providing Immediate Automatic Scoring of Objective Tests and Concomitant Self-Instruction." *J. Psychol.* **29:**417–447 (January 1950).

77. ———. "A Machine for Automatic Teaching of Drill Material." *Sch. & Soc.* **25:**549–552 (May 7, 1927).

78. ———. "A Simple Apparatus that Gives Tests and Scores—and Teaches." *Sch. & Soc.* **23:**373–376 (March 20, 1926).

79. ———. "A Third and Fourth Contribution to the 'Industrial Revolution' in Education." *Sch. & Soc.* **36:**668–672 (November 19, 1932).

80. RAPP, ALBERT. "The Experimental Background of the Problem of Learning." *Classical J.* **40:**467–480 (May 1945).

81. RINSLAND, HENRY D. "Readiness for Spelling." *Elem. Eng.* **27:**189–191 (March 1950).

82. RIVLIN, HARRY N. "The Classroom Teacher and the Child's Learning." *Amer. J. Orthopsychiatry*. **24:**776–781 (October 1954).

83. RUSSELL, DAVID H. "A Second Study of Characteristics of Good and Poor Spellers." *J. Educ. Psychol*. **46:**129–141 (March 1955).

84. SARNOFF, I. and D. KATZ. "The Motivational Bases of Attitude Change." *J. Ab. & Soc. Psychol*. **49:**115–124 (January 1954).

85. SCHMIDT, H. O. "The Effects of Praise and Blame as Incentives to Learning." *Psychol. Monographs*. **53:**1–56, No. 3 (1941).

86. SCHRODER, H. M. "Development and Maintenance of the Preference Value of an Object." *J. Exp. Psychol*. **51:**139–141 (February 1956).

87. ———— and J. B. ROTTER. "Rigidity as Learned Behavior." *J. Exp. Psychol*. **44:**141–150 (September 1952).

88. SCHWARTZ, BERNARD. "An Investigation of the Effects of a Seventh and Eighth Grade Core Program." *J. Educ. Res*. **53:**149–152 (December 1959).

89. SEARS, PAULINE SNEDDEN. "Levels of Aspiration in Academically Successful and Unsuccessful Children." *J. Ab. & Soc. Psychol*. **35:**498–536 (October 1940).

90. SILBERMAN, HARRY F. "Effects of Praise and Reproof on Reading Growth in a Non-laboratory Classroom Setting." *J. Educ. Psychol*. **48:**199–206 (April 1957).

91. SKINNER, B. F. "The Science of Learning and the Art of Teaching." *Harvard Educ. Rev*. **24:**86–97 (Spring 1954).

92. SMITH, H. P. "Do Intercultural Experiences Affect Attitudes?" *J. Ab. & Soc. Psychol*. **51:**469–477 (1955).

93. SMITH, NILA BLANTON. "What Research Tells About Word Recognition." *Elem. Sch. J*. **55:**440–446 (April 1955).

94. SPITZER, HERBERT F. "Class Size and Pupil Achievement in Elementary Schools." *Elem. Sch. J*. **55:**82–86 (October 1954).

95. ————. "Studies in Retention." *J. Educ. Psychol*. **30:**641–656 (December 1939).

96. STAIGER, RALPH C. and EMERY P. BLIESMER. "Reading Comprehension in the High School." *Educ*. **76:**563–567 (May 1956).

97. STORDAHL, K. E. and C. M. CHRISTENSON. "The Effect of Study Techniques on Comprehension and Retention." *J. Educ. Res*. **49:**561–570 (April 1956).

98. STRINGER, LORENE A. "Report on a Retention Program." *Elem. Sch. J*. **60:**370–375 (April 1960).

99. STROUD, JAMES B. and LOWELL SCHOER. "Individual Differences in Memory." *J. Educ. Psychol.* **50:**285–292 (December 1959).

100. SYMONDS, P. M. "What Education Has to Learn from Psychology: Motivation." *Teach. Coll. Rec.* **56:**277–285 (February 1955).

101. TAYLOR, D. W. and W. L. FOUST. "Twenty Questions: Efficiency in Problem Solving as a Function of Size of Group." *J. Exp. Psychol.* **44:**360–368 (November 1952).

102. THORNDIKE, E. L. "Mental Discipline in High School Studies." *J. Educ. Psychol.* **15:**1–22, 83–98 (January–February 1924).

103. TIEDEMAN, H. R. "A Study in Retention of Classroom Learning." *J. Educ. Res.* **41:**516–531 (March 1948).

104. TROW, WILLIAM CLARK, WILLIAM MORSE, and DAVID JENKINS, "Psychology of Group Behavior: The Class as a Group." *J. Educ. Psychol.* **41:**322–337 (October 1950).

105. TROW, WILLIAM CLARK. "When Are Children Ready to Learn?" *N.E.A. J.* **44:**78–79 (February 1955).

106. ULMER, G. "Teaching Geometry to Cultivate Reflective Thinking: An Experimental Study with 1,239 High School Pupils." *J. Exp. Educ.* **8:**18–25 (September 1939).

107. VINCENT, NICHOLAS M. P. and HELEN MERRILL. "Effective Classroom Motivation." *Peabody J. of Educ.* **38:**10–13 (July 1960).

108. WATSON, JOHN B. and ROSALIE RAYNER. "Conditioned Emotional Reactions." *J. Exp. Psychol.* **3:**1–14 (February 1921).

109. WEISS, A. H. "Decision-Making in Secondary Schools." *Phi Delta Kappan.* **37:**207–208, 210 (February 1956).

110. WESMAN, ALEXANDER G. "A Study of Transfer of Training from High School Subjects to Intelligence." *J. Educ. Res.* **39:**254–264 (December 1945).

111. WILLARD, RUTH A. "The Most Common and Least Common Learning Experiences Reported Present in Fifty-three Classrooms." *Educ. Adm. Sup.* **42:**72–77 (February 1956).

112. WOODRUFF, ASAHEL D. "Motivation Theory and Educational Practice." *J. Educ. Psychol.* **40:**33–40 (January 1949).

113. WORELL, LEONARD. "The Effect of Goal Value Upon Expectancy." *J. Ab. & Soc. Psychol.* **53:**48–53 (1956).

114. WRIGHT, H. F. "How the Psychology of Motivation is Related to Curriculum Development." *J. Educ. Psychol.* **39:**149–156 (March, 1948).

## PART IV

# MENTAL HEALTH, PERSONALITY AND ADJUSTMENT—THE DEVELOPMENT OF CHARACTER

In this section we find a variety of articles ranging from the teacher's responsibility for mental health of his pupils to the evasion of propaganda. The underlying theme is that of mental health, the well-being of the individual as an individual and in his relationship with others. Few aspects of educational psychology have had more attention in teacher education and in professional literature during the past two decades. Much time and effort have gone into the study of the "problem child" or the child who is not happy and successful in school. No less attention has been given to research on mental illness, juvenile delinquency, and other types of abnormality.

The extent to which educational institutions are responsible for these problems is a moot question. There is little reason to doubt that compulsory attendance laws, for example, keep children in school far longer than some of them would like to be. They simply don't like it, no matter what the school tries to do in the way of a broadened program and relaxation of standards. In the case of younger children, the slow learner or the child with tendencies toward emotional instability is likely to find school a frustrating experience. In this sense, the school creates emotional problems. In another sense, the question of the school's responsibility for mental health refers to the extent of the school's obligation for diagnosis and therapy. For years there has been a tendency to look to the school to take on more and more of the responsibility formerly assumed by the home and by other community agencies. As one article * puts it: "Is the divorce rate increasing? Let the schools teach family living. Is there death on the highway? Let the schools go in for driver education. Does annihilating war seem increasingly difficult to avoid? Let the schools give courses in international understanding. Do the churches fail to attract and hold young people? Let the schools purvey religious and moral teaching. Is emotional instability widespread and the incidence of mental illness high? Let the schools dispense mental health. . . . It is as though home, church, social and health agency, and all the other agencies and institutions by which mankind lives, or lives better than it otherwise might, had no existence, or no function to perform for the young. The young gather in the schools. Let the schools tend them in all aspects of their being."

To be sure, the schools are themselves partly to blame for this state of affairs. Well-meaning but misguided teachers attempt to assume responsibilities for which they are not qualified, by training or experience. Ambitious school administrators who wish to build an expanding program take on

* Ruth Kotinsky and Jules V. Coleman, Mental Health as an Educational Goal, *Teachers College Record*, **56**:267–276, February 1955.

responsibilities without adequately trained staff or facilities and then claim that the duties are forced on them by "the community." On the other hand, homes in which both parents are gainfully employed expect schools to be parent substitutes in every sense of the word. Community agencies like child guidance clinics have waiting lists that often make it impossible to get professional attention for months for a child that needs it immediately. The teacher is told to refer cases of all but the most superficial forms of maladjustment. But to whom? Smaller communities, which are obviously the most numerous, seldom have specially trained personnel or agencies, and those in larger places are too far away or too busy. The situation presents difficult and sometimes well-nigh insoluble problems, especially to the conscientious teacher. It seems as though in many instances it is all he can do to retain his own mental health, to say nothing of trying to save that of his pupils!

The articles in this section do not provide any panaceas. They do show that some changes in thinking about the problem are taking place, that we are moving in the direction of better understanding of it, and that those who have made a life-long study of the situation are rather conservative in what they expect of the classroom teacher and the school in general. This is not to say that they encourage the school to shrug off responsibility for mental health and socialization of its pupils, but that it is recognized that the school is but one of many organizations involved in the picture and that mental health is not its first and primary responsibility. The first responsibility of the school is instruction, not therapy. This is the job of the clinic, the psychiatrist, the psychiatric social worker, the school psychologist or diagnostician or even the counselor. It is through understanding and cooperation of these organizations and persons that progress must come. None can do the job alone.

# 32

## THE TEACHER AND MENTAL HEALTH *
### National Institute of Mental Health

In this brief article we find the distillation of experience and research by many persons regarding the functions and responsibilities of the classroom teacher for the mental health of pupils. Major human needs and drives are discussed briefly and practically. The teacher's role in helping the child to satisfy these needs in an acceptable manner is described. Resources available to teachers for learning more about mental health are listed. The particular advantages of the teacher's position for identifying children who need help in the area of adjustment and mental health are pointed out. Finally, a word of caution is given to teachers regarding their functions and limits of what may reasonably be expected of them in the area of mental health. Suggestions are made for referral of cases which require more technical and professional experience than teachers generally have in this area.

*Questions:*

1. Some writers suggest that a teacher's responsibility is to teach and that the mental health of pupils had best be left to psychiatrists or others with specialized training in this field. Do you agree? Why?

2. What is the position of the article reproduced here on the issue mentioned above? Is this a practical viewpoint? Give reasons for and, if possible, evidence to support your answer.

\* \* \*

Scientists and other workers in the mental health professions have elucidated basic principles of emotional growth and human relations which can make a direct contribution to the work of the classroom teacher. These disciplines have in common the basic concept that all human behavior is motivated by human needs and human drives.

* Reprinted from "The Teacher and Mental Health," *Public Health Service Publication No. 385,* U. S. Department of Health, Education and Welfare, Washington: U. S. Government Printing Office, 1959.

In the school-age child, these needs and drives are concentrated in the process of growing up. Modern psychiatry has taught us, in fact, that the dominant drive during childhood is the child's desire to grow up. Since a large part of the education process is aimed at constructive support and direction of this desire, some analysis and understanding of emotional needs and their manifestations are desirable.

## Meeting the Child's Emotional Needs

### Sense of Personal Worth

The child is not a miniature adult. He is a developing human being, and his need to grow up is a need to fulfill his own unique and individual endowment, to realize the gifts within himself. When this basic human drive is blocked, the child is not able to fulfill all of his capabilities. As a result, his confidence in himself and his self-respect suffer, and it becomes difficult for him to develop his potentialities. A crippling, "vicious circle" is thus set in motion.

As every teacher has reason to know, each child is unique. In spite of the fact that there are basic human needs common to everyone which are essential for growth, each person is a distinct and separate personality. One of the most important human needs is the need to be an individual, to be oneself. Belief in the worth and dignity of every individual is the cornerstone of both democracy and emotional health. For both to be realized, it is essential that every child feel he is important, and has something to contribute to his classmates, his school, his parents, and his community.

### Accepting Limitations

Every child needs to be aware of and accept his present or ultimate capabilities. A seven-year-old can't be expected to act like a small adult. When the people he likes do not expect too much from him, when they help him to find and achieve goals within his reach, he is able to keep his self-respect. Sometimes too-heavy burdens are put on his shoulders. If his elders go to the extreme and demand adult behavior, the child is likely to develop a sense of failure. Why should he even go on trying, he may ask himself, when he and everyone else know he is bound to fail?

What is the teacher supposed to do? One possibility is to accept some of the child's feelings of limitation temporarily and without fanfare. Pushing him at a pace that is faster than he is able to go or forcing him to compete unduly may produce highly destructive reactions, aimed either against himself or at his classmates.

## Need to Belong

Every child needs to feel that he belongs to a group of his peers. No matter how well he gets along with his elders, especially as he approaches adolescence, he must also believe he is accepted by his own age group.

A lot can be done to help the "shy" child—if he needs help. Some do not. There are children who like to be left alone to mull things over, or enjoy tinkering or working by themselves. But in most schoolrooms, withdrawn children who need help can be identified rather easily. Here, unobtrusive emotional first-aid may be offered after the child's problem is thoroughly understood.

Perhaps the shy child would like to work closely with a more extroverted classmate. Many children benefit when they are carefully paired off together. If Timothy is worried about going ahead with his assignments, he might be asked whether he would want to team up on a joint project with Robert who barges right into his work. The teacher knows and is able to apply the many other methods and techniques of modern pedagogy which reinforce this type of emotional support.

## Accepting and Taking Responsibility for Feelings

Every child needs to feel that he, too, can share in and enjoy relationships with others. In reaching out for life, children need to learn that their feelings are neither bad nor good, in and of themselves, but only in the way they are expressed. After all, human emotions cannot be divorced from the events that cause them.

For example, our society generally frowns on expressing feelings of hostility. Yet hostility usually arises as the reaction to a specific threat and, as such, can't be easily ignored or denied. But it's not the feeling of hostility that is damaging; it is the way these feelings are drained off, or as psychiatrists say, "acted out." Since destructive behavior is harmful, the teacher in each situation somehow must help the child admit his feelings and deal constructively with them—without forcing him to deny his true response. Paints, boxing gloves, a game of soccer, hammers and nails to build props for the new play—all these can help.

Emotions other than anger also are frequently rejected or suppressed, for other reasons; sometimes because they are regarded by our society as tending to be more masculine than feminine, or vice versa. The small boy may be ashamed to admit that he is scared when something frightens him badly.

Already he has absorbed the idea that to feel fear is to be a sissy—or that to have feelings of tenderness is unmanly. Yet all humans deserve to experience fully and honestly the total range of their emotions.

When children learn to accept basic human emotions—fear, anger, tenderness, etc.—as normal, it encourages them to seek more appropriate ways of solving problems. If, without being swayed by your own defensive responses to inappropriate behavior, you as a teacher can help children examine their actions and feelings, they will be more likely to seek healthier solutions. When serious behavior problems arise, a discussion of the "whys" and "wherefores" of acceptable behavior will usually evoke some thought even on the part of the most apparently thoughtless and inconsiderate child. Abrupt condemnation, on the other hand, may only provoke in him a blind stubbornness against what he might term injustice and persecution. Learning from the child what meaning his actions and feelings have for him can often help the teacher in influencing the child's behavior.

### Need for Direction

One of the child's basic needs—the need for security—is directly related to the subject of order and discipline. Since all children indulge in behavior which is neither beneficial to themselves nor to their group, boundary lines drawn by the teacher will help to establish a secure understanding of what is allowed and what is not. People who work with children have learned that all youngsters need to have and want to have limitations set for them. They want rules by which they can be guided, and they are confused if there are none. They will accept the fact that within certain bounds their desires and interests will be considered, but they also know that certain acceptable forms of behavior will be required of them, regardless of their individual desires.

Children can participate in formulating some of the guidelines, but unless additional guidelines are provided, they become puzzled about what is expected of them. Without these guidelines, they are given no fixed reality which they can come up against and with which they can freely interact to develop along their own individual lines.

### The Teacher's Attitudes and the Child's Emotional Health

Since each child is individual and his behavior, for better or for worse, stems from the interaction between his personality and his environment, "what-to-do-when" rules are impossible to formulate. Children differ in many ways, and so do teachers. Each situation must be met as it arises. It is for this reason that the teacher's attitudes toward feelings and behavior are so important for the security and development of the child. By learning from the child how he feels about himself and what has meaning to him in a given situation, the teacher is helped to establish a relationship with the child which fosters an atmosphere conducive to healthy growth.

The difference between attitudes that are helpful and those that are not is the difference between the rigid, authoritarian attitude that something "bad" is never permitted and an attitude of flexibility and reasonableness. The latter viewpoint admits that although certain acts are not acceptable, each incident is surrounded by a special set of circumstances and each child participating comes into it as an individual with a different past, different capabilities, and a different point of view.

Although children want rules, democratic planning pays good dividends. Let the child, therefore, have a voice in decisions that affect him. He will learn democratic ways by practicing them.

Because of the complexity of human interaction, it's impossible to understand oneself or one's pupils completely and with finality. But it is possible for all parents and teachers *to try to understand behavior better*. The more that you as a teacher understand of yourself and your motives, the causes of your own emotional responses, the better equipped you will be to help your pupils. Self-awareness is equally important in your relationships with school administrators, your colleagues, and in your life outside the classroom.

## Helping the Child Grow

Tolstoi wrote about the feelings of a little girl in *War and Peace,* describing her first visit to the Opera and how vividly the experience affected her. He tells how her immediate and natural reactions gradually are buried beneath the exclamations and comments of her companions. Her initial feelings become transmuted by her observation of the reactions of the adults in the audience and by what she eventually infers she is *supposed* to feel. Thus, this heretofore undiscovered continent of sound and color takes a new form in the eye of her mind, the form molded by the attitudes of the people in the opera box with her. This, in fact, is one aspect of the educative process at work—the shading which primary experience assumes as a result of the expressed feelings of others about that experience.

All teachers know how much the school contributes toward every child's psychological, intellectual, and social growth. They know that, along with the parents, teachers can offer not only protection and guidance but also supply some of a child's most lasting impressions of the way adults live in an adult environment. The teacher's values, the way she interacts with other persons, her ideals and goals, are watched by the child and absorbed by the child, especially if the teacher is trusted and admired.

In short, under his teacher's guidance, every child's school experience helps him to recognize his own individuality, provides him with achievable goals, gives him a sense of belonging and an opportunity to develop satisfying relationships with others.

### Resources for Learning More about Mental Health

The teacher's supportive role in helping the child meet his emotional needs presupposes knowledge of the dynamics of mental health principles. To provide this type of background for the teacher, many States are now offering in-service training in mental health through seminars, institutes, and conferences during summer months and vacation periods, through courses at local colleges or other graduate training centers, and through other types of psychiatric orientation. Many of these courses are offered through the State mental health agency or department of education or welfare.

In addition, school systems in many parts of the country are carrying on in-service education programs which help to bring about a better mental health climate in the schools and assist teachers in developing better understanding of their own personalities.

Some schools work on a local level with community agencies, bringing family service, health department officials, juvenile police officers, and welfare agency representatives together with teachers and school administrators. Sometimes a consultant-psychiatrist also attends these conferences. In one State, the psychiatrist on the staff of the department of public health comes once a month to consult with these representatives on the more effective utilization of existing community resources. When specialized mental health information is needed, he offers help in that area. In other schools, part-time or full-time mental health personnel are employed to help integrate mental health principles into the total school program.

### Handling the Special Problem

Of course, there will always be some children who will need special attention beyond what the teacher can give, and some who may require specialized services. Though the teacher herself cannot deal with these serious problems, she can help in their early recognition and, by prompt referral for treatment, can materially assist in a program of prevention.

The teacher is in an especially advantageous position to discover early signs of emotional disorders. She has many opportunities to learn about each child through direct observation in the classroom, on the playground, during lunch periods, and so on. Other opportunities are afforded by home visits, chats with the pupil himself, talks with his parents, or through staff conferences, discussions with the visiting teacher or school counselor, or athletic coach, school nurse, doctor, or principal. Cumulative records and the various sociometric and psychological tests are helpful tools, too— though ancillary to the personal understanding and interest of the teacher.

When the teacher discovers a child in her classroom who she feels needs a specialist's care, she can talk over the problem with her principal or other appropriate school official. Together they should be able to work out a plan for getting help to the child as soon as possible. In most communities, there is at least one person with the psychiatric know-how to give assistance; sometimes it is the school psychologist or social worker, sometimes a psychiatric social worker in a local agency, sometimes the public health nurse, and sometimes a private psychiatrist. Occasionally the trouble is not beyond the ability of the teacher or other school staff member to handle if special consultation is obtained from qualified psychiatric personnel outside the classroom. In this case, the teacher is guided in her approach by the outside consultant and the child is not referred to a special agency.

# 33

## TEACHERS' AND CLINICIANS' ATTITUDES TOWARD THE BEHAVIOR PROBLEMS OF CHILDREN: A REAPPRAISAL *

### Harry Beilin

In this timely and thorough survey Dr. Beilin reviews the research on the important problem stated in the title. The pioneer work of Wickman published in 1928 revealed a wide divergence between the attitudes of teachers and clinicians toward behavior problems. In fact, it showed little agreement on the seriousness with which certain such problems were regarded by the two groups. Wickman's study aroused a great deal of interest and some criticism, especially with respect to some of his procedures. A number of investigators have attempted to repeat his study, with or without modification. In the selection which follows all the studies including Wickman's are carefully reviewed and compared. Trends in the thinking of teachers and clinicians as revealed by them are discussed in relation to role theory and the changes that have taken place over the thirty years since the report of the first study was published.

*Questions:*

1. On the whole does the weight of evidence support the findings of Wickman's study? Cite evidence.
2. In what ways do the points of view of other investigators differ from that reported by Wickman?
3. Is there any evidence to suggest that both teachers and clinicians have changed their views with respect to this matter? If so, what is it?
4. What are the implications of these studies for the roles of the teacher and the clinician?

\* \* \*

The contrast between contemporary American education and that of 40 or 50 years ago is striking in at least one respect, the influence of psychol-

* Reprinted from *Child Development,* **30:**9–25 (March 1959), by permission of author and the Society for Research in Child Development, Inc.

ogy, in particular, clinical psychology.[1] It would require little effort to detail the many and diverse ways teacher training, parent education and child care reflect the consequences of psychology's influence. The future historian will undoubtedly dwell upon the part played by E. K. Wickman's 1928 Commonwealth Fund monograph, "Children's Behavior and Teachers' Attitudes" in this development [51].* Wickman's report, which contrasts teachers' and "mental hygienists' " attitudes toward the behavior problems of children evoked an assault upon the teacher's mode of dealing with children when it made evident that teachers' attitudes were widely at variance with those of clinicians. The effect of its publication is still felt. The contiguity of events might suggest to some a causal relationship between widespread knowledge of the Wickman findings and the emergence of clinical psychology as a force in contemporary education. However, a more temperate and realistic appraisal would accept the ubiquitous penetration of psychology into American life and not as a condition unique to education. The impact of the monograph was in actuality only one of a series of challenges to the values and attitudes of educational personnel. But irrespective of its true role—whether as reflection, or as initiator of a Zeitgeist—the place of the Wickman study in education and child psychology has been significant and will probably continue to be.

Wickman's results, in the main, suggested that mental hygienists were primarily concerned with *withdrawing* and other nonsocial forms of behavior in children of elementary school age, whereas teachers of these same children were more concerned with *classroom management, authority,* and *sex problems.* The results influenced many (starting with Wickman) to urge teachers to adopt a hierarchy of attitudes closer to that of the clinician. This view presumed that the clinician's judgment should be accepted as the criterion for adequate and inadequate behavior. Few have challenged this thesis.

The intent of the present review is to examine what the result of 30 years of research suggests for continued acceptance of this point of view. To anticipate, it will be suggested that Wickman's finding be reinterpreted and his prescription for change in educational policy modified.

[1] Although the period following the first World War saw the impact of the testing movement and the effects of Behaviorism, it was not till the 1930's and 1940's that clinical psychology became a part of the child development and educational scene in a major way.

* Figures in brackets apply to references at end of article.

## The Wickman Study

The Wickman studies were begun in Minneapolis in 1924, but a more ambitious program was undertaken in Cleveland in 1925–1926, where the following was done:

1. In a single pilot school, teachers' characterizations of undesirable behavior, with indications of "sensitiveness" to their occurrence, were elicited by questionnaire.

2. Teachers' attitudes toward various types of problems were obtained by three measures (detailed in part below).

3. On rating scales, teachers noted their reactions to problems themselves, then to pupils in whom the problems were observed, and finally to the total adjustment of their pupils.

4. Subsequently, the teachers from 13 schools in six communities and two additional teacher groups enrolled in graduate school were studied using the rating scale method developed for the pilot study. The most important feature of this involved the rating of a number of behaviors obtained from the teachers' original freely-given characterizations of problem behavior. The results are reported as mean ratings and rankings of mean ratings.

5. Finally, 30 "mental hygienists" (8 psychiatrists, 4 psychologists, 13 psychiatric social workers and 5 teachers with social work background) from child guidance clinics in three cities were studied for their attitudes toward 50 of the same behaviors rated by teachers. The mean ratings and rankings of ratings were then contrasted and correlated with those of teachers.

The rating instructions for teachers stressed: (a) *present* problems, (b) "seriousness" of the problems or "difficulties" created by them, and (c) rapid responses to the rating scale. With clinicians, the emphasis was on (a) relevance of the problem behavior for *future* adjustment, (b) though "seriousness" and "difficulty" were retained, the focus was on the "importance" of the behavior, and (c) no time limit was imposed for response to the rating scale.

The principal results can be summarized as follows:

1. Teachers were most aware of overt and aggressive behaviors, inattention to school tasks, and behaviors which violated their standards of morality. They were much less concerned with behaviors indicative of social or emotional maladjustment not directly related to school routine.

2. Boys were reported more frequently than girls for behavior problems.

3. Teachers preferred the less active, more compliant behavior of girls to the more aggressive behavior of boys. Desirable conduct for teachers, then, took on the distinguishing characteristics of girl behavior.

4. "Mental hygienists" considered withdrawing and other nonsocial forms of behavior most serious and discounted the teachers' stress on antisocial behavior and violations of school rules.

5. There was a rank order correlation of −.22 between the rankings by mental hygienists of 50 behavior problems and the original Cleveland teachers' ($N = 28$) rankings of the same behaviors. The correlation was −.11 when the full sample was used ($N = 511$).

These findings were interpreted by Wickman in Thorndikian stimulus-response terms. The teachers distinguish, he said, between the attacking and withdrawing types of behavior problems. Their attitudes are principally determined, however, by the attacking nature of the child's conduct. The aggressive behaviors are identified and considered more serious because the teacher is aroused to counterattack by virtue of the frustration in him. On the other hand, the responses to withdrawing forms of behavior are modified by sympathy and protective feelings.

On the basis of these findings Wickman then proposed that:

1. Teachers' attitudes should be influenced to become more like the "ideal" clinicians. (Clinicians' attitudes are considered ideal because their judgments are (ostensibly) based upon knowledge of research in child adjustment.)

2. Teacher attitudes should be changed not by exhortation but by (a) information about child behavior through seminars and other learning experiences; and (b) practice in therapy with children.

3. Teachers' functions be less concerned with intellectual learnings and more with life adjustment.

After the appearance of the 1928 monograph some serious limitations in method and conception were pointed out by G. Watson [50] in a critical note [2] which are as cogent now as when first offered. The majority of efforts to rectify the deficiencies have concerned only some of the criticisms. The others, however, may be of as great issue as those treated.

Watson's objections were:

_____

[2] One writer has even wondered how the study could have been so widely and uncritically accepted with these limitations. The answer probably rests in the fact that its thesis was part of a powerfully developing movement.

1. *The procedures themselves are open to criticism.*

   a. The directions given teachers and clinicians were not the same. Teachers were instructed to rank behaviors for *present* seriousness; clinicians, for *future* adjustment.

   b. The time given to respond to the questionnaires was not identical. Teachers were under the control of the experimenter; clinicians were allowed an extended period to respond.

   c. No definitions were given for the behavioral terms to be rated leaving to each subject the interpretation of the terms, and thus further reducing comparability of the results.

The issues raised by Watson's concern with methodology are intimately related to other criticisms.

2. *The choice of mental hygienists' attitudes toward the behavior problems of children as a criterion for evaluating teachers' attitudes toward the same problems is open to question.*

The Wickman study and others that follow (though not all) accept the clinicians' judgments as a criterion either implicitly or explicitly. Watson observes that there is no reason to suppose clinicians to be "correct" and teachers not, rather than vice versa. Wickman is questioned for not even considering this possibility.

3. *There has been too ready an acceptance of a causal relationship between withdrawing behavior in childhood and maladjustment in adulthood.*

In addition to questioning whether the term "withdrawing" means the same thing to teachers and clinicians, Watson questioned whether withdrawing behavior in childhood is causally related to, or predictive of, maladjustment in adulthood. Although this is contended in more than one theoretical position, there was very little evidence for the validity of this claim in 1928, and little more is available now. In Watson's paper there is reference to a pilot study which, for all its limitations, casts some doubt on the aforementioned assumption.

### The Literature

After the Watson critique there was concern for the validity of the results and replications were undertaken with one or another modification in design, ultimately making comparability difficult.[3]

[3] We shall consider all studies found that bear upon the problems focused on by Wickman and his critics in spite of the lack of comparability. Some studies are included which antedate Wickman because the data they offer are relevant.

The studies, in the main, fall into the following groupings according to procedures used:

A. *Studies employing descriptions of problem behavior.*

1. Teacher nomination of children with problems, followed by description and classification of problem behaviors [3, 5, 18, 29, 48].

   a. In addition to all or part of the above, some use is made of a rating scale of problem behaviors [8, 15, 24, 25, 37, 47, 53, 54].

2. Teacher description of problem behavior (with no reference to specific children) from which a rating scale is developed or the descriptions themselves are used [10, 11, 22, 36, 41, 45, 51].

3. Children identified and described as problems by a social or therapeutic agency [6, 33].

B. *Studies employing the Wickman rating scales.*

1. With Wickman's directions [1, 20, 35].

2. With modifications of Wickman's directions [14, 19, 26, 38, 39, 40].

### Confirmation of Wickman Findings

Early studies that made use of the Wickman scales "confirmed" what Wickman had found in that the rankings made by the teachers in other communities approximated those of Wickman's teachers. Boynton and McGaw [8] obtained a correlation of .87 between Wickman's and their own teacher ratings. Dickson [13], Laycock [22], Young-Masten [53] and Yourman [54] gave similar results as did the Epstein [15] and Snyder [37] studies. Thompson [45] offered the added information that teachers were more nearly in agreement with the rankings made by parents than with the rankings of child psychologists. In Young-Masten's study [53], in addition to securing conduct reports for nominated problem children, she observed a group of 28 problem children and a control group of the same number. From the classification of behavior records for each child observed, she obtained a statistically significant difference between the groups for behavior "which from the standpoint of the teacher, was annoying, and upset the order and peace of the classroom, and interfered with the other children" [p. 180].

Five years after the appearance of the Wickman report Bain [1] assessed the attitudes of teachers enrolled in graduate work using the original directions for teachers. The resulting rankings showed higher correlations with Wickman's mental hygienists than had been true for the original teacher sample. The correlations reflected greater teacher concern with *recessive, withdrawing behaviors* than with *active offenses* and *sex problems.*[4]

Replication of the Wickman study, employing the same directions, was undertaken in 1951 by Schruppe and Gjerde [35]. They concluded that teachers' attitudes in 1951 agreed more closely with the "ideal criterion" (clinicians' attitudes) than did 1927 teacher's attitudes (a correlation of .57 (1951) compared with −.04 (1927) using means of teachers' and clinicians' ratings). None of the traits listed as most serious by one group was listed as least serious by the other. Wickman had five such differences. Griffiths' study [16], although not a replication of Wickman's, was similar to some features of it. He found that behavior difficulties most reported by teachers relate to violations of classroom rules and work rules. However, he indicated that teachers have changed over the years as evidenced by their awareness that a child who is easy to manage is not necessarily well adjusted.

Del Solar's [11] study is a report of interviews with parents and teachers which details the joys and problems of child rearing. It was the shy and withdrawing, rather than aggressive, behaviors which concerned this group of teachers and parents. These findings contradict Wickman and most other investigators. Del Solar's findings may result however, from the nature of the questions asked in the interview (only one, concerning liabilities of students, is cited), the small size of the sample (6 teachers rating 28 children), and the atypical nature of the subjects (all teachers had advanced study and were employed in a school of above average socioeconomic status).

We would conclude from these studies (holding the question of the validity of Wickman's methodology aside for the moment) that there is considerable evidence to indicate agreement with Wickman's original findings. Furthermore, there has been an observable shift in the intervening years in the attitudes of teachers in the direction of being more like those of "mental hygienists." In spite of greater congruence, however, a sizeable difference remains between the attitudes of teachers and clinicians toward behavior problems of children.

## The Methodical Issue

Modifications as a rule have aimed at introducing uniformity in the administration of the problem rating scales. This has meant either modify-

[4] In another part of the study Bain reports that one semester of instruction had little effect in changing attitudes toward problem behaviors. Whether the differences reported in the Bain study result from the select character of the sample is not known.

ing the directions given clinicians or teachers so that both groups could respond under the same stimulus conditions.

In Ellis and Miller's 1936 investigation [14] the instructions used were those originally given clinicians. In this study they were administered to teachers. With this change in method ratings of teachers correlate .49 with Wickman's mental hygienists (and .65 with Wickman's teachers). Again, the change is the result of increased realization of the seriousness of *withdrawing* and *recessive* personality traits. The investigators note, however, that teachers "still consider" *violations of general standards of morality* and *transgressions against authority* as the most seriously rated types of behavior.

Sparks' investigation [38] made use of both the Wickman teacher and clinician directions and scales. These were administered to teachers and graduate students (in education). Teachers' ratings made in terms of seriousness for future adjustment (the mental hygienist form) were different from the kinds of ratings made when the directions stressed "troublesomeness" in the classroom, although in both cases they were still different from psychologists' ratings. The correlation of ratings (for teachers) between the original teacher form and the mental hygienist form of the scale was .05.

Mitchell's study [26] was conducted in the same cities where Wickman had done his 13 years earlier. The scales and directions were both modified, the scales but slightly. The directions given teachers and mental hygienists were the same: they were asked to rate behavior traits keeping in mind the behaviors of fifth and sixth grade children they had observed. (No such grade specification was made by Wickman.) The directions given the 1940 group were "almost" identical with those given by Wickman and these we presume were the instructions originally given clinicians. The correlation between means of ratings of 1927 and 1940 mental hygienists was .80. Some mental hygienists had apparently become more "conservative" in their ratings. They no longer considered *unsocial, withdrawing,* and other traits as extremely grave—in fact, no traits were now so considered. Whereas, the correlation in 1927 between the means of teachers and mental hygienists' ratings was .08 (by the rank difference method), the correlation in 1940 was .70. Mitchell interprets this to mean that either the identity in directions accounts for these results or teachers and clinicians have moved closer in their judgments.

In Stouffer's 1952 investigation [39] teachers were first given the original instrument for teachers; later, the original scale for mental hygienists. A group of mental hygienists were then administered the original mental hygienists' scale. Stouffer reports a correlation of .52 between the teachers' ranking of problem behaviors and mental hygienists' ranking of the same, employing different directions (the original Wickman procedure). A correlation of .61 was obtained when the instructions (those of mental hygienists) were the same for both groups. A rank order correlation of .87 was obtained between the rankings of Stouffer's and Wickman's mental hygienists.

Stouffer concluded that while teachers' attitudes toward the behavior problems of children have changed there has been little change in the attitudes of mental hygienists.[5] The changes in teachers' attitudes reflect again the reduced importance of problems related to *honesty, sex, truancy,* and *classroom order,* and increased importance of *withdrawing* and *recessive* personality traits.

Stouffer's 1956 study [40] is of particular interest because it recognizes that a difference may exist between teachers of different grade levels. In contrast to his 1952 study the later one deals with secondary school teachers. The instructions were those for clinicians. The results were contrasted with those of elementary teachers in the prior study and with Wickman's (elementary) teachers. The rank order correlation of secondary teachers' rankings and elementary teachers' rankings was .88; between the same secondary teachers' and mental hygienists' ratings, .49. As reported in the earlier study, the correlation between elementary teachers' and mental hygienists' rankings was .61. Elementary teachers are, then, in greater agreement with mental hygienists than secondary school teachers. In terms of children's behaviors, elementary teachers are more concerned with withdrawing tendencies; secondary school teachers, with classroom management and problems related to class work and school routines.

The findings that the criteria of adjustment and maladjustment differ depending upon age and grade level is given support in a study by Beilin [3]. In this instance, the procedure involves teacher nomination of maladjusted children, descriptions of their distinguishing characteristics, and content analysis of the descriptions. In general, an age trend (from elementary grades to young adulthood) was found with a concern (in elementary grades) for social-interpersonal aspects of adjustment (e.g., *withdrawal, aggressiveness, emotional instability*) to later concern (in high school) with character traits (e.g., *reliability, dependability*) and finally (young adulthood) with *achievement* and *integration into the community.*

[5] Note that Mitchell [26] suggests such a change although the correlation for the same relationship differs from Stouffer's by only .07.

In the 1957 study by Hunter [19], elementary and secondary school teachers were sent the Wickman mental hygienists' rating scale and instructions. His results are similar in direction to Mitchell's and Stouffer's though not in size of correlations. The correlation between teachers' and mental hygienists' rankings of mean ratings was .22. *Aggressiveness* is still rated more highly by teachers than by mental hygienists.

Using a procedure which raises some doubts, Ullmann [47] had teachers nominate well and poorly adjusted children who were then rated on a 144-item rating scale. Discrimination indices were computed for each item. The check list was then submitted to a group of mental hygienists who rated the extent to which each item was indicative of good or poor adjustment. The discrimination indices were correlated with the means of clinicians' ratings of the items. The correlation was .86. For favorable items it was .69; unfavorable, .50. These results are interpreted by Ullmann as confirming the Mitchell findings that teachers have moved closer to clinicians in their judgments (in spite of the considerable difference in procedure from Mitchell). Ullmann reports, however, that these correlations may be too high by virtue of some of his procedures.

At this point it appears that the differences in directions that were a part of the Wickman procedure quite clearly contributed to the differences demonstrated between teachers and mental hygienists. When this is controlled, however, differences still emerge and these are of the kind originally observed.

It is also apparent that there has been a change in the direction of greater congruence between the attitudes of teachers and clinicians. That that congruence is not consistent for all levels of teachers has been made explicit in recent studies. It is likely that differences between elementary and secondary teachers have always existed vis-à-vis the matters here reviewed, but, where teacher and clinician attitudes appear to be the same, differences in meaning may still attach to the behaviors.

## Teacher "Expertness"

The specific criteria employed by teachers and clinicians in assessing maladjustment in children have been mentioned. As already indicated, most investigators have shown teachers to be most concerned with children's behaviors that are *aggressive, disruptive of school routines,* or genererally reflecting *lack of interest in school activities.* In addition, teachers are, or have been, less concerned with *withdrawing* and other nonsocial behaviors. Some investigators have characterized this as indicative of a middle class value pattern; e.g., *stealing* is the teacher's consistent concern in MacClenathan's [24] study. The emphasis upon these school disrupting traits has not been unanimous, however. Peck [29] found *undesirable personality traits* to be the greatest concern of the teacher, *regressive* traits somewhat less so, and *aggressive* behaviors least. Of only moderate import were *violations of school work demands.* Clark [10] differs from the usual view, too, in concluding that teachers are actually more annoyed by children's behaviors which annoy other children than by behaviors which affect teachers themselves.

In most of the cited studies it is implied or explicitly stated that the teacher is "wrong" in reacting as she does to the problems of children. Teachers have been criticized as untutored in the scientific facts concerning child development and are thus seen as generally being incapable of assessing children's adjustment.

Stewart [42] rejects this thesis. With 184 boys and 193 girls as subjects, a comparison was made between ratings of problem students and non-problem students. Identification was also attempted of those with and without "whole life" problems. From ratings of these youngsters she concludes that teachers are capable of distinguishing between problems as school problems or "whole life" problems. She insists that teachers possess much more insight into children's behavior than they are credited with by some investigators.

In spite of the few studies that report different patterns of teachers' attitudes, the hierarchy of attitudes seems to be quite close to Wickman's formulation. The Stewart report is important not so much because it rejects this hierarchy but rather in its highlighting the difference between clinicians and teachers as not being a matter of ignorance. What the difference is attributable to remains to be discussed.

## Sex Differences

There seems to be universal agreement that boys are more likely to be identified as maladjusted or behavior problems than girls [6, 8, 15, 16, 18, 20, 25, 27, 29, 32, 37, 51, 53, 55]. The proportion of boys (in contrast to girls) so identified ranges in these reports from 66 to 88 per cent. Not only is there a difference in proportion but behaviors which form the bases for these identifications are in part different for each sex [5, 15, 51]. Ullmann's [47] interpretation is of some interest. It is *not,* he says, that "desirable conduct for teachers takes the distinguishing characteristics of girl behavior as suggested by Wickman but rather teachers assign girls more favorable ratings because they lack awareness of the manner in which girls are making their adjustment" [p. 39]. Ullmann explains that boys' patterns of adjustment are more manifest to the observer, whereas girls deal with problems on an intrapsychic level. This interpretation is in the tradition of imputing lack of insight to teachers. Stewart's [42] results are again cogent. Her data do not suggest that teachers lack insight into their adjustment, but rather that they distinguish a different *kind* of adjustment for girls. Another study with young adults suggests the same [5]. In this instance, sex differences in degree of adjustment are supplemented by differences in the types of behavior identified with the maladjustments of each sex.

Why should the nature of adjustment be different for boys and girls? Whatever the *ultimate* reasons (whether biological or social), the temptation is to say that the differences, in an *immediate* sense at least, result from different *expectations*. It is evident from the cited studies that boys and girls are expected to act in prescribed ways in our culture. The reasons girls are considered better adjusted by teachers is that teachers have certain expectations of what good adjustment in *school* should be and the prescription for girls' adjustment is more consistent with these expectations than the prescription for boys' good adjustment. As Wickman makes evident, the teacher is concerned with getting what she is teaching "across," and behaviors which facilitate this are more likely to be valued. The behaviors of girls are of this kind.

This approach is more acceptable to us, from the evidence, than the interpretation that teachers' attitudes are based on a lack of sophistication.

There is some evidence that men and women teachers evaluate the problems of children differently. Women are found by one investigator to rate problem behaviors as more serious than do men [14]. Another study [19] reports, however, that specific problem behaviors are treated differently by each sex. Men teachers consider *sex* problems as less serious than do women; women consider *appearance* and *destruction of property* as less serious than do men. Others [4, 41] report similar findings, although in the former case it is emphasized that the similarities are greater than the differences.

## Age and Grade Influences

The sixth grade appears to be modal for the nomination of children with problems, with the first and second grades offering the least. The fifth, seventh, and eighth grades also give the teacher some difficulty [18, 20, 25, 37]. Difference in maladjustments of elementary and secondary school youngsters were reported early in the literature [18] and somewhat neg-lected till recently. Hildreth [18] observed that maladjusted elementary school children are more likely to be identified as *unstable, nervous,* or *shy;* the secondary school pupils as *aggressive* or demonstrating *poor study habits.* Peck [29] finds the differential effect of sex of students in these identifications, however. Grade differences in problem type are reported by others as well [5, 40, 41]. The differences found by Stouffer [40] have already been described. Griffiths [16] states that certain behavior difficulties (as reported by teachers and parents) increase with age; others decrease.

## Socioeconomic Status

There are limited data relating socioeconomic status of the child to his identification as a problem. Levy [23] finds "socially high grade children have personality or emotional problems . . . children of lower classes have social problems" [p. 158]. Yourman [54] reports a larger proportion of problem children are of lower socioeconomic status. Snyder [37] found that schools differentiated by their level of socioeconomic status yielded different numbers of problems with more from the lower groups. There was no statistically significant difference, however, in socioeconomic status between a problem group and a control group.

The study by Griffiths [16] makes the most ambitious attempt to relate socioeconomic status to the identification of behavior problems. There were few significant differences among children of different socioeconomic levels in teachers' ratings of their problems. More differences appear, however, according to the parent's ratings and the child's own ratings. Griffiths concludes that some differences exist between middle socioeconomic level children and others. In particular, they are more submissive and less aggres-sive.

It is apparent that few data are available as to the relationship between socioeconomic status and the behavior problems of children.

## Discussion

The studies reviewed suggest strongly that differences in teachers' and clinicians' attitudes existed in 1927. From that time to the present changes appear to have taken place among teachers' attitudes so that they approxi-mate more closely those of clinicians. There is some possibility that clini-cians have tempered their evaluations as well.

Despite the shift toward congruence, teachers' attitudes remain different, and different in ways not dissimilar from what they were in Wickman's day. Why? First, let us recall that Wickman and others made much of this difference. It was suggested, even insisted, that the teacher should change. Such an injunction could rest only on the premise that the clinician's attitudes were more legitimate or more correct. This view was accepted though G. Watson was the first and not the last to question it. Watson's position was not that the clinician was necessarily incorrect or that he should not serve as a criterion. Rather, Wickman was chided for not even considering the alternatives to accepting the clinician as criterion. For Wickman, the virtue of choosing the clinicians' attitude as an ideal was recommended by his expert knowledge of children's adjustment. Let us examine this claim.

For one, Wickman asked clinicians to rate behaviors in light of their possible future consequences. Would the clinician, with any validity, know the future consequences of the appearance of a behavior in childhood? The answer is doubtful. In 1927 there were few if any studies which had indicated with even low degrees of certainty the outcome in adolescence or adulthood of a child's particular behavior (e.g., *withdrawing* behavior). In fact, if anything, there was some doubt that this could be done [30, 50]. Evidence since then leads to even greater uncertainty [2, 21]. According to some theories a withdrawn child is more likely to become maladjusted than one who is not. Yet the proof of how true this is and in what proportion for any population is almost nonexistent. Although it has been shown that in an adult *psychotic* group [52] there was a tendency for maladjustive behaviors to be present in childhood (information was obtained from retrospective reports), this tells us little about the prevalence of withdrawing behavior in a population of children or about the likelihood of such behaviors resulting in maladjustment, neurosis, or psychosis in adulthood.

However, there is a more important issue, in light of the functions of the therapist qua therapist: withdrawing behaviors present a problem to be dealt with at the time of their appearance. Such behaviors can be a basis for a visit to a therapist—in childhood as well as adulthood. The clinician is more likely to attempt some therapy than to postpone action till adolescence or adulthood (although, in some instances, this might reasonably be done). The clinician is often forced to act by immediate criteria; for he cannot wait for ultimate validation. It is thus part of his role as a therapist to be concerned about these behaviors. In essence, the behaviors with which a clinician is concerned are related to his status and the functions that accompany that status. If these behaviors were of equal relevance to the functions of the teacher, they would be equally valued. However, they are not. This has been so even in the period of "life-adjustment" programs and through the era of the "whole child," except possibly for some special groups of teachers. In spite of much pressure, teachers on the whole continue to be concerned with behaviors that facilitate or interfere with their teaching. A number of investigators recognize the difference in function between clinician and teacher [12, 18, 24, 35, 42, 50, 54] even though the teacher's role is not simple to define. It is, after all, a reflection of an educational philosophy. The prevailing philosophy of education in 1927, whether explicit or implicit, was oriented to the training of intellectual skills. In the interim the function of the teacher has broadened considerably to include training in social and other skills. There has been much pressure on the teacher to be a counselor and in some ways something of a psycho-therapist as well—but, at the least, to focus more on the emotional life and adjustment of the child. The question of which role is "better" is a question of values. At present, the trend is back again toward the training of intellectual skills. The trend of increasing teacher sophistication in psychology will probably continue, and will probably not revert to the level of 1927. To urge [e.g., 39, 40] that the teacher's attitudes approximate the clinician's is unrealistic unless the teacher's role becomes one with the clinician—and this seems unlikely.

Other considerations recommend themselves as well. The teacher has a vital role in the socialization of the child. She is, after all, a culture carrier and to some extent a parental surrogate. Her own behaviors are significant in the child's development of self-control, character traits, values, and work habits. These functions are certainly as important as any. There is no question that the teacher needs to be aware of withdrawing and other undesirable personality characteristics. What is questioned is the need for the teacher to concern herself with them to the same extent and in the same way as the clinician.

To summarize, the difference reported by Wickman in attitudes toward the behavior problems of children should be interpreted as reflecting differences in the roles of teachers and clinicians and the discharge of functions of the role incumbents [9, 34]. The efforts of many have been directed to alter the prescription of the teacher's role and performance in this role. This effort has in part been successful, as witnessed by the greater congruence in attitudes between teacher and clinician. In spite of the partial change in prescription, the teacher's role remains principally task-oriented;

the clinician's, more adjustment-oriented. It seems unrealistic and possibly even undesirable to expect the teacher's behaviors reflected in her attitudes and values to become congruent with those of clinicians. Other results reviewed here are consistent with this thesis. The reported disparity between elementary and secondary teachers results from differences in role. The high school teacher is even more subject matter-oriented than the elementary school teacher. The greatest impact of the "child-oriented" or "life-adjustment" philosophy in turn has been in the elementary school. This has resulted in a modification of role prescription for the elementary school teacher which is reflected in greater similarity between the attitudinal hierarchies of elementary teachers and clinicians. The observed differences are due not only to the teacher's role but result from the actions of the children themselves. The pupil's role-related behaviors change with progress through school as the youngster assumes new responsibilities and loses old ones. Behavior differences are not only bound to their age but also their sex. The same behavior is not expected or demanded of boys and girls. The attitudes of teachers in turn will reflect differences in age and sex role expectations.

## Summary and Conclusions

The studies concerning teachers' and clinicians' attitudes toward the behavior problems of children, which have emerged principally from the initiative of the Wickman 1928 monograph, are reviewed. The following conclusions are drawn:

1. Differences existed in 1927 between the attitudes of teachers and clinicians toward the behavior problems of children. This seems to have been true in spite of the methodological limitations of the Wickman study.

2. Since 1927 there has been a shift in the hierarchy of teachers' attitudes to approximate more closely those of clinicians. This shift is not due to an artifact of research methodology. Those studies which incorporate adequate controls and consistent instructions show even greater congruence between the attitudes of the two groups.

3. There has been some change in the attitudes of clinicians although this is based upon the conclusions of one study.

4. Criteria employed in evaluating the behavior problems of children differ for elementary and secondary school teachers.

5. More boys are identified as maladjusted than girls and the criteria of maladjustment (and adjustment) differ in part for each sex.

6. The sex of the teacher affects, in part, attitudes toward children's problems.

7. Studies of the relationship of socioeconomic factors to the evaluation of children's behavior problems are inadequately dealt with in the literature.

Differences in attitudes between teachers and clinicians are interpreted in the framework of role theory. The attitudinal hierarchies of teachers and clinicians are seen as reflecting their respective roles and the ways these roles influence the organization of their respective experiences. Wickman's findings of 1927 are interpreted as indicative of the role of the teacher in that era. The role expectations of teachers have changed. Replications of the Wickman study indicate these changes have resulted in greater congruence between teachers' and clinicians' attitudes. It is suggested by virtue of the teachers' essential task-orientation and the clinicians' adjustment-orientation that complete or nearly complete congruence is not likely to be achieved.

The relationship of sex and age to attitudes toward behavior problems is also explained in the light of role theory.

## References

1. BAIN, W. E. "A Study of the Attitudes of Teachers Toward Behavior Problems." *Child Develpm.* **5:**19–35 (1934).

2. BEILIN, H. "The Prediction of Adjustment over a Four Year Interval." *J. Clin. Psychol.* **13:**270–274 (1957).

3. ———. "Effects of Social (Occupational) Role and Age upon the Criteria of Mental Health." *J. Soc. Psychol.* **48:**247–256 (1958).

4. ——— and E. WERNER. "Sex Differences among Teachers in the Use of Criteria of Adjustment." *J. Educ. Psychol.* **48:**426–436 (1957).

5. ———. "Sex Role Expectations and the Criteria of Social Adjustment for Young Adults." *J. Clin. Psychol.* **13:**341–343 (1957).

6. BLANCHARD, P. and R. H. PAYNTER. "The Problem Child." *Ment. Hyg.* **8:**26–54 (1924).

7. BOWLES, H. H. "A Study of Nurses' Attitudes toward Behavior Problems in Children under Hospital Care." *Child Develpm.* **8:**282–288 (1937).

8. BOYNTON, P. L. and B. H. McGAW. "The Characteristics of Problem Children." *J. Juv. Res.* **18:**215–222 (1934).

9. BRIM, O. G. "The Parent-child Relation as a Social System: I. Parent and Child Roles." *Child Develpm.* **28:**343–364 (1957).

10. CLARK, E. J. "Teacher Reactions toward Objectionable Pupil Behavior." *Elem. Sch. J.* **51:**446–449 (1951).

11. DEL SOLAR, C. *Parents and teachers view the child; a comparative study*

*of parents' and teachers' appraisals of children.* New York: Bureau of Publications, Teachers College, Columbia Univer. (1949).

12. DAVIS, E. A. and E. McGINNIS. *Parent education; a survey of the Minnesota program.* Minneapolis: Univer. of Minnesota Press (1939).

13. DICKSON, V. E. "Behavior Difficulties that Baffle Teachers." *J. Juv. Res.* **16**:93–101 (1932).

14. ELLIS, D. B. and L. W. MILLER. "Teachers' Attitudes and Child Behavior Problems." *J. Educ. Psychol.* **27**:501–511 (1936).

15. EPSTEIN, L. J. "An Analysis of Teachers' Judgments of Problem Children." *J. Genet. Psychol.* **59**:101–107 (1941).

16. GRIFFITHS, W. *Behavior difficulties of children as perceived and judged by parents, teachers and children themselves.* Minneapolis: Univer. of Minnesota Press (1952).

17. HERTZMAN, J. "High School Mental Hygiene Survey." *Amer. J. Orthopsychiat.* **18**:238–256 (1948).

18. HILDRETH, G. "A Survey of Problem Pupils." *J. Educ. Res.* **18**:1–14 (1928).

19. HUNTER, E. C. "Changes in Teachers' Attitudes toward Children's Behavior over the Last Thirty Years." *Ment. Hyg.* **41**:3–11 (1957).

20. HURLOCK, E. B. and L. C. McDONALD. "Undesirable Behavior Traits in Junior High School Students. *Child Develpm.* **5**:278–290 (1934).

21. IVES, O. L. *A critique of teachers' ratings of high school boys as an indication of later neuropsychiatric rejection for the armed services.* New York: Bureau of Publications, Teachers College, Columbia Univer. (1949).

22. LAYCOCK, S. R. "Teachers' Reactions to Maladjustments of School Children." *Brit. J. Educ. Psychol.* **4**:11–29 (1934).

23. LEVY, J. "A Quantitative Study of the Relationship between Intelligence and Economic Status as Factors in the Etiology of Children's Behavior Problems." *Amer. J. Orthopsychiat.* **1**:152–162 (1931).

24. MACCLENATHAN, R. H. "Teachers and Parents Study Children's Behaviors." *J. Educ. Sociol.* **7**:325–333 (1934).

25. McCLURE, W. E. "Characteristics of Problem Children Based on Judgments of Teachers." *J. Juv. Res.* **13**:124–140 (1929).

26. MITCHELL, J. C. "A Study of Teachers' and Mental Hygienists' Ratings of Certain Behavior Problems of Children." *J. Educ. Res.* **36**:292–307 (1942).

27. NEUMEYER, M. H. *Juvenile delinquency in modern society.* New York: D. Van Nostrand (1949).

28. O'MALLEY, K. E. *A psychological study of the annoyances or irritations of teachers.* Unpublished doctoral dissertation, New York Univer. (1936).

29. PECK, L. "Teachers' Reports of the Problems of Unadjusted School Children." *J. Educ. Psychol.* **26:**123–138 (1935).

30. PRESTON, G. H. and W. McL. SHEPLER. "A Study of the Problems of 'Normal' Children." *Amer. J. Orthopsychiat.* **1:**245–256 (1931).

31. PULLIAS, E. V. "How Do You Behave when the Children Misbehave?" *Childh. Educ.* **10:**230–237 (1934).

32. ROGERS, C. R. "The Criteria Used in a Study of Mental Health Problems." *Educ. Res. Bull.* **21:**29–40 (1942).

33. ———. "Mental Health Findings in Three Elementary Schools." *Educ. Res. Bull.* **21:**69–79 (1942).

34. SARBIN, T. R. *Role Theory.* In G. LINDZEY (ed.), *Handbook of Social Psychology.* Cambridge: Addison-Wesley (1954), pp. 223–258.

35. SCHRUPP, M. H. and C. M. GJERDE. "Teacher Growth in Attitudes toward Behavior Problems of Children." *J. Educ. Psychol.* **44:**203–214 (1953).

36. SEIDMAN, J. M. and L. B. KNAPP. "Teacher Likes and Dislikes of Student Behavior and Student Perceptions of These Attitudes." *J. Educ. Res.* **47:**143–149 (1953).

37. SNYDER, L. M. "The Problem Child in the Jersey City Elementary Schools." *J. Educ. Sociol.* **7:**343–352 (1934).

38. SPARKS, J. N. "Teachers' Attitudes toward the Behavior Problems of Children." *J. Educ. Psychol.* **43:**284–291 (1952).

39. STOUFFER, G. A. W., JR. "Behavior Problems of Children as Viewed by Teachers and Mental Hygienists." *Ment. Hyg.* **36:**271–285 (1952).

40. ———. "The Attitudes of Secondary School Teachers toward Certain Behavior Problems of Children. *Sch. Rev.* **64:**358–362 (1956).

41. ——— and J. OWENS. "Behavior Problems of Children as Identified by Today's Teachers and Compared with those Reported by E. K. Wickman." *J. Educ. Res.* **48:**321–331 (1955).

42. STEWART, N. "Teacher's Concepts of 'Behavior Problems.'" In *Growing Points in Educational Research.* Washington: American Educ. Res. Ass. Rep., 1949.

43. STOGDILL, R. N. "Parental Attitudes and Mental Hygiene Standards." *Ment. Hyg.* **15:**813–827 (1931).

44. ———. "Experiments in the Measurement of Attitudes toward Children, 1899–1935." *Child Develpm.* **7:**31–36 (1936).

45. THOMPSON, C. E. "The Attitudes of Various Groups toward Behavior Problems of Children." *J. Abnorm. Soc. Psychol.* **35:**120–125 (1940).

46. UGER, C. "The Relationship of Teachers' Attitudes to Children's Problem Behavior." *Sch. & Soc.* **47:**246–248 (1938).

47. ULLMANN, C. A. *Identification of maladjusted school children.* Public Hlth Monogr. No. 7. Washington: U. S. Govt. Printing Office, 1952. (Rev. 1957)

48. WANDT, E. "Measurement and Analysis of Teachers' Attitudes." *Calif. J. Educ. Res.* **3:**10–13 (1952).

49. ———. "A Comparison of the Attitudes of Contrasting Groups of Teachers." *Educ. Psychol. Measmt.* **14:**418–422 (1954).

50. WATSON, G. "A Critical Note on Two Attitude Scales." *Ment. Hyg.* **17:**59–64 (1933).

51. WICKMAN, E. K. *Children's Behavior and Teachers' Attitudes.* New York: Commonwealth Fund, 1928.

52. WITMER, H. L. "Childhood Personality and Parent-child Relationships of Dementia Praecox and Manic Depressive Patients." *Smith Coll. Stud. Soc. Wk.* **4:**287–378 (1934).

53. YOUNG-MASTEN, I. "Behavior Problems of Elementary School Children: a Descriptive and Comparative Study." *Genet. Psychol. Monogr.* **20:**123–181 (1938).

54. YOURMAN, J. "Children Identified by Their Teachers as Problems." *J. Educ. Sociol.* **5:**334–343 (1932).

55. U. S. Children's Bureau. *Juvenile court statistics 1946–49.* Statistical Series No. 8. Washington: U. S. Govt. Printing Office, 1949.

## 34

# THE RELATION BETWEEN ACCEPTANCE OF SELF AND ACCEPTANCE OF OTHERS SHOWN BY THREE PERSONALITY INVENTORIES *

## Katherine T. Omwake

The relationship of self-concept to wholesome personality development and achievement is a matter of considerable significance and interest to teachers and counselors. A number of studies have been made of the relationship between the attitude of a person toward himself and his attitude toward others. Some persons seem generally accepting of others; some tend characteristically to underestimate or depreciate others. These attitudes affect the attitudes of other persons toward them and the relationships between them. Thus, the individual who is friendly, accepting and respectful of others is likely to engender similar attitudes toward himself; on the other hand, the individual who tends to depreciate others, to look down on them so to speak, is likely to engender similar feelings toward himself. The questions asked and investigated in the following article are: Do these attitudes toward others bear any relationship to attitudes toward the self? Does the person who thinks well of himself tend to be the person who thinks well of others, and vice versa? Dr. Omwake reviews some earlier studies and reports one of her own with college students using three different personality tests. The results are consistent and significant.

*Questions:*

1. Of what interest and significance is a pupil's attitude toward himself to a teacher or counselor? How can understanding of degree of self-acceptance possibly be of use to teachers in the elementary grades?

2. Inferiority feelings might be said to represent a low degree of self-acceptance. What is the bearing of this concept on such factors as (a) school failure, (b) accepting limitations, (c) sense of personal worth, (d) accepting respon-

* Reprinted from the *Journal of Consulting Psychology,* **18:**443–446 (December 1954), by permission of author and publisher.

sibility for feelings? (See Selection 32, *The Teacher and Mental Health* for other possible relationships.)

\* \* \*

In recent years psychiatrists and clinical psychologists have observed a relation between the attitude toward the self shown by the patient and his attitude toward other people. Adler [1] * noted a depreciation of others in those who themselves felt inferior. Horney [5] asserted that the person who does not love himself is incapable of loving others. Rogers [8] said that the person who accepts himself will for that very reason have better interpersonal relations with others. He also observed that, during therapy, as a person begins to accept himself he becomes capable of experiencing this attitude toward others. Changes in acceptance of the self and correlated changes in the acceptance of others occurring during client-centered therapy were studied by Sheerer [9]. Her study, and a similar one by Stock [10] also based on a small number of counseling cases, showed that perceptions of others, feelings toward others, and acceptance of others are significantly related to the perception of the self, feelings about the self, and acceptance of the self. These studies show that, in the course of therapy, with the increase in self-acceptance there is a corresponding increase in favorable attitude toward others.

Several attempts have been made to see to what extent these observations made by clinicians hold true for larger, more normal populations. Phillips [6] constructed a questionnaire on Attitudes Toward the Self and Others which he administered to several groups of students. In a university class composed chiefly of older students the correlation between attitudes toward the self and those toward others was .74, while with a younger group of college age it was .54. Berger [2] used the definitions of acceptance of self and acceptance of others which Sheerer [9] had made as the basis for the development of a questionnaire or scale. He found a correlation of .65 between acceptance of self and acceptance of others for evening students and of .36 for day students. This is in agreement with the study by Phillips [6], who also found a closer relation between acceptance of self and acceptance of others in the older group of college students than in the younger group. Bills, Vance, and McLean [4] devised an Index for Adjustment and values which measures self-acceptance, and a corresponding form which shows the individual's perception of how other people accept themselves.

.Phillips [6], Berger [2], and Bills, Vance, and McLean [4] have published

* Figures in brackets apply to references at end of article.

studies of the reliability and validity of their tests, and the results obtained from administration of them to college students and to some other groups, but they have not published the tests themselves. In the present study all three of these unpublished tests, by permission of their authors, have been administered to a group of over one hundred college students.

## Problem

This study is designed to test the assumption that, in a normal population, there is a positive relation between the acceptance of self and the acceptance of others, that those who are self-acceptant are also acceptant of others, and that those who reject themselves also tend to reject others.

A second hypothesis is that there should be agreement among tests designed to measure the same trait; that, therefore, various tests of acceptance of self should give similar results, and that various measures of acceptance of others, likewise, should agree.

## Method

Three unpublished personality inventories, made available to the investigator by their authors, were used in this study. They are: the scale for Self-Acceptance and Acceptance of Others by Berger [2], the questionnaire on Attitudes Toward the Self and Others by Phillips [6], and the Index of Adjustment and Values for self and for others, by Bills, Vance, and McLean [4]. Each was mimeographed without a title, so there was nothing to indicate what the inventory was designed to measure. These three personality inventories, described below, were administered to 113 students in the first course in psychology at Agnes Scott College. The students were told that the investigator wished to make a study of the personality tests, and that in order to make the study it was not necessary to know the identity of those taking the tests. Each student was assigned a number which she placed on each test. It was hoped that this method of preserving anonymity would increase frankness in answering the questionnaire.

The scale for measurement of Self-Acceptance and Acceptance of Others by Berger consists of 36 items concerned with acceptance of self and 28 with the acceptance of others, mixed in random order. The following is typical of the statements showing attitude toward the self: "I realize that I'm not living very effectively but I just don't believe I've got it in me to use my energies in better ways." "I believe that people should get credit for their accomplishments, but I very seldom come across work that deserves praise" shows attitude toward others. The person taking the test is to rate each item on a five-point scale.

The Attitudes Toward the Self and Others questionnaire by Phillips is basically similar to Berger's scale. It consists of 25 statements showing attitudes about the self and 25 showing attitudes toward others, mixed in random order. The person taking the test is to rate attitude on each statement on a five-point scale.

The Index of Adjustment and Values by Bills, Vance, and McLean consists of 49 adjectives, such as *acceptable, busy, calm, poised,* and *tactful.* The subject is asked to use each word to complete the sentence "I am a (an) . . . . . . . . . . . person," using a five-point scale to indicate how much of the time this is like him, and then to indicate, by rating, how he feels about himself as described in the first rating. The sum of these second ratings gives the measure of self-acceptance used in this study. The Index for others is similar. The subject uses the same 49 adjectives in turn to complete the statement "Other people are . . . . . . . . . . . . persons," with friends particularly in mind, and indicates how other people feel about themselves as they are, using a five-point scale as before. This gives a measure of the extent to which others are seen as accepting themselves.

### Results and Discussion

The three inventories measuring self-acceptance agree markedly, as shown by the correlations in Table 1. As might be expected, there is closest agreement between the tests which are most similar in form and content. Degree of acceptance of self given by Berger's scale correlates .73 with degree of self-acceptance in Phillips' scale. Bills's Index, which measures self-acceptance by a different technique, is in less close agreement with the other two scales, although even here the correlation of .49 with Berger's scale and .55 with Phillips' indicates a substantial correspondence. All three correlations are significant at the 1 per cent level of confidence.

There is slightly less agreement among the tests showing attitudes toward others. Here also the two tests which are similar in construction agree most closely. The correlation between the tests by Berger and Phillips is .60, significant far beyond the 1 per cent level, but lower than the correlation of .73 between the tests of acceptance of self by the same authors. Since Bills's Index for others show the individual's perception of how other people accept themselves, rather than the degree to which he is acceptant of others, it is understandable that it correlates less well with tests measuring the individual's attitude toward others. Bills's Index correlates .23 with Berger's scale, significant only at the 5 per cent level, while the correlation of .13 with Phillips' scale is not statistically significant.

There is a consistent tendency for those who accept themselves to be acceptant of others and to view others as being self-acceptant, and, on the other hand, for those who have a low opinion of themselves to reject others also, and to see others as rejecting themselves. This is seen in the correlations of .37, .39, and .41, significant at the 1 per cent level, between the acceptance of self and attitudes toward others as measured by the inventories by Berger, Bills, and Phillips.

**Table 1**

**Correlations of Measures of Acceptance of Self and Acceptance of Others**

| Tests | Correlation | Level of Significance |
|---|---|---|
| Acceptance of self vs. acceptance of self | | |
| Berger vs. Phillips | .73 | 1% |
| Bills vs. Berger | .49 | 1% |
| Phillips vs. Bills | .55 | 1% |
| Acceptance of others vs. acceptance of others | | |
| Berger vs. Phillips | .60 | 1% |
| Bills vs. Berger | .23 | 5% |
| Phillips vs. Bills | .13 | – |
| Acceptance of self vs. acceptance of others | | |
| Berger vs. Berger | .37 | 1% |
| Bills vs. Bills | .39 | 1% |
| Phillips vs. Phillips | .41 | 1% |
| Berger vs. Phillips | .25 | 5% |
| Berger vs. Bills | .23 | 5% |
| Bills vs. Berger | .23 | 5% |
| Bills vs. Phillips | .18 | – |
| Phillips vs. Bills | .30 | 1% |
| Phillips vs. Berger | .34 | 1% |

These correlations are similar to those obtained by Berger [2] and by Phillips [6] in groups of the same age as the group in this study. Berger's correlation is .37 as compared with .36 in the present study; Phillips' correlation of .54 shows a closer relationship than does the correlation of .41 obtained with the present group. Bills has not reported the correlation between self-other attitudes, so no comparison is possible.

As might be expected, each test of self-acceptance agrees more closely with the corresponding test of attitudes toward others made by the same author than it does with the scale for others made by another author. In every instance the correlation between the self-other parts of the same test is significant at the 1 per cent level of confidence, whereas Phillips' test of self-acceptance is the only one which gives correlations of this degree of statistical significance with tests of attitudes toward others made by another investigator. Three of the four other correlations between self-attitudes measured by one test and attitudes toward others obtained from another test are significant at the 5 per cent level. As shown by the correlations in Table 1, there is a consistent tendency for self-attitudes to be reflected in attitudes toward others.

A comparison was made of the attitude toward others held by those who represented the extremes of self-acceptance and of self-rejection. The self-acceptant group consisted of 19 subjects who were in the upper three deciles on all three tests of self-acceptance; the group who rejected themselves was composed of 12 individuals who were consistently in the lowest three deciles on all three tests. The larger number in the self-accepting group shows that a high degree of self-acceptance is more consistently shown than is a low degree; only a small number are extremely self-rejectant on all three tests, while a larger number consistently hold themselves in high esteem. On each test the mean score on attitude toward others made by the self-acceptant group is higher than the mean score made by the self-rejecting group. The difference between the means is significantly different from zero well beyond the 1 per cent level of confidence. This difference between the means on the tests by Berger and by Phillips indicates that those who are most self-acceptant also have a high degree of acceptance of others, while those who reject themselves also hold others in low esteem. The difference between the means on Bills's Index would indicate that those who are self-acceptant perceive others as accepting themselves, while those who are least self-acceptant perceive others as rejecting themselves. As had been assumed, there is a direct relation between the attitude an individual holds toward himself and that held toward others.

The data presented here, although based on personality inventories that do not probe very deeply into personality dynamics, verify in a fairly large group of college students the conclusions derived by clinicians from therapy sessions. There is evidence that in the normal population, as well as in those undergoing therapy, attitudes toward the self appear to be reflected in attitudes toward other people: the lower the opinion of the self, the lower the opinion of others. Only when the self is regarded with a fairly high degree of acceptance is it possible to relate effectively to others, to understand them, and to regard them as persons of worth.

## Summary

To test the hypothesis that in a normal population there is a positive relation between acceptance of self and acceptance of others, three unpublished tests measuring attitudes toward the self and toward others were administered to 113 college students who took them anonymously. The tests are: the scale for Self-Acceptance and Acceptance of Others by Berger, the questionnaire on Attitudes Toward the Self and Others by Phillips, and the Index of Adjustment and Values by Bills, Vance, and McLean. The three measures of self-acceptance agree closely; those for attitudes toward others agree less well. The results support the hypothesis in that there is a marked relation between the way an individual sees himself and the way he sees others; those who accept themselves tend to be acceptant of others and to perceive others as accepting themselves; those who reject themselves hold a correspondingly low opinion of others, and perceive others as being self-rejectant.

## References

1. ADLER, A. *The Neurotic Constitution*. New York: Dodd, Mead, 1926.

2. BERGER, E. M. "The Relation between Expressed Acceptance of Self and Expressed Acceptance of Others." *J. Abnorm. Soc. Psychol.* **47**:778–782 (1952).

3. BILLS, R. E. "A Validation of Changes in Scores on the Index of Adjustment and Values as Measures of Changes in Emotionality." *J. Consult. Psychol.* **17**:135–138 (1953).

4. BILLS, R. E., E. L. VANCE, and O. S. McLEAN. An Index of Adjustment and Values. *J. Consult. Psychol.* **15**:257–261 (1951).

5. HORNEY, KAREN. *New Ways in Psychoanalysis*. New York: Norton, 1939.

6. PHILLIPS, E. L. "Attitudes toward Self and Others: A Brief Questionnaire Report." *J. Consult. Psychol.* **15**:79–81 (1951).

7. ROBERTS, G. E. "A Study of the Validity of the Index of Adjustment and Values." *J. Consult. Psychol.* **16**:302--304 (1952).

8. ROGERS, C. R. *Client-centered Therapy*. Boston: Houghton Mifflin, 1951.

9. SHEERER, ELIZABETH T. "An Analysis of the Relationship between Acceptance of and Respect for Self and Acceptance of and Respect for Others in Ten Counseling Cases." *J. Consult. Psychol.* **13**:169–175 (1949).

10. STOCK, DOROTHY. "An Investigation into the Interrelations between the Self-concept and Feelings Directed toward Other Persons and Groups." *J. Consult. Psychol.* **13**:176–180 (1949).

# 35

## CHILDREN'S PERCEPTIONS OF THEIR TEACHERS' FEELINGS TOWARD THEM RELATED TO SELF-PERCEPTION, SCHOOL ACHIEVEMENT, AND BEHAVIOR [1] *

### Helen H. Davidson and Gerhard Lang

Recent work in social psychology and related fields has brought out the importance of the self-concept in human behavior and personality. A favorable self-concept tends to be associated with desirable behavior and good adjustment, a poor self-concept with less desirable performance and traits. The question naturally arises as to how the self-concept is formed. It is hypothesized that a child's self-concept is related to his perception of significant adults in his environment and their feelings toward him. In the interesting study reported here children's self-concept is compared with their perceptions of their teachers' feelings toward them. These in turn are also related to ratings of achievement and classroom behavior. The results show a significant correlation between pupils' self-concept and their perception of the teachers' feelings toward them. The relationships of such perceptions to achievement, classroom behavior, sex, and social class are all found to be positive and substantial. Some interesting possibilities for use of these findings in teacher selection and adjustment are suggested.

*Questions:*

1. What could I do as a teacher to help a child develop a more positive self-concept?

2. Does this study show the same results for the pupil's self-concept as for his perception of his teacher's feelings toward him?

[1] This study was supported by a grant from the James McKeen Cattell Fund.

* Reprinted from the *Journal of Experimental Education,* **29:**107–118 (December 1960), by permission of the senior author and Dembar Publications, Inc.

3. What is the viewpoint of the authors regarding the commonly expressed generalization that boys are by nature more aggressive than girls? Do you agree?

\*   \*   \*

## Introduction

The child's self-concept arises and develops in an interpersonal setting [30].* Feelings about the self are established early in life and are modified by subsequent experiences. Among the significant people believed to affect the child's feelings about himself are first, his parents, and, later his teachers. Ausubel [2] and Jourard and Remy [16] are among the few investigators who have reported results which support these theoretical contentions.

Rogers [24], Snygg and Combs [27], among others, assign the self-concept a central place in their personality theories and suggest that the individual's self-concept is a major factor influencing his behavior. Vigorous research in this area by Martire [17] and Steiner [28] has produced corroborative evidence for these views.

Only recently has the concept of the self been introduced into the school setting. Typical studies are those by Jersild [15], Reeder [23] and Stevens [29]. Jersild demonstrated the value of the self-concept theory in making the educative process more valuable. Reeder, using grade school children and Stevens, working with college students, explored the relation between self-concept and school achievement. Both of these investigators found that positive feelings about the self are associated with good academic achievement.

A series of studies dealing with teacher-pupil relations have sought to determine (a) how children see and feel about their teachers [11]; (b) how teachers see and feel about their pupils [5, 20]; and (c) how teachers think their pupils see themselves [22].

It has been widely recognized that teachers influence the personality development of their pupils [21]. Perkins, for example, found that teachers who had completed several years of child study were able to promote healthier personality growth in children, defined in terms of congruency between the self and the ideal self. For this reason, many researchers, among them, Barr and Jones [3] and Symonds [31] are engaged in the study of personality development of the teacher herself.

\* Figure in brackets apply to references at end of article.

Despite the abundance of research on these aspects of the school setting, an important dimension, not previously investigated, is how the child perceives his teacher's feelings toward him. In an investigation of this interaction, we not only may gain insight into the question of what qualities make for an effective teacher but also an understanding of how the child's perception of his teacher's feelings, irrespective of its accuracy, relates to his self concept, school achievement and classroom behavior.

It is the purpose of this investigation to determine what the relation is between children's perception of their teachers' feelings toward them and the variables: self-perception, academic achievement, and classroom behavior.

Specifically, three hypotheses were tested:

1. There exists a positive correlation between children's perception of their teachers' feelings toward them and children's perception of themselves. In behavioral terms it is predicted that the more favorable the child's perception of himself, the more positive will be his perception of teachers' feelings toward him.

2. There exists a positive relationship between favorable perception of teachers' feelings and good academic achievement.

3. There exists a positive relationship between favorable perception of teachers' feelings and desirable classroom behavior.

## The Instrument

To test the hypotheses proposed, it was necessary to develop an instrument to measure self perception and the perception of the feelings of others. It was decided to use an adjective checking method, since it is direct and simple. Adjective check lists have been used to measure adjustment [18], self acceptance [4], empathy [9], character traits [13], and to distinguish the self perceptions of persons classified according to some social and psychological variables [26]. In the main, these lists have been used with adults.

In developing the check list with children, words and phrases to be included were selected on the basis of the following three criteria:

1. The words should be those commonly used to describe how people feel toward and how people think of others, especially how teachers feel toward and think of children. An attempt was made to cover varied aspects of behavior and personality. For this purpose, lists already developed, like

those of Allport [1], Gough [12], and Hartshorne and May [13], were scanned for appropriate words.

2. The words should be easy enough for children in approximately the 10–16 year age range to read and comprehend. The Thorndike-Lorge Frequency Count [33] was used to eliminate words which would be too difficult.

3. The list should contain about an equal number of words connoting positive and negative feelings.

From an initial pool of 200 trait names, 135 remained after the application of criteria 1 and 2. The next step was to determine the feeling tone of the 135 words. Each of the words was then rated by 35 teachers and 50 junior high-school pupils as *favorable, unfavorable,* or *neutral.* Only those words were retained which were judged by more than 80% of the teachers and 80% of the pupils as being favorable or unfavorable. The words judged neutral were eliminated.

Fifty words remained after the teachers and students judged them as favorable or unfavorable. The 35 words finally used are listed below along with the F or U rating received. Fifteen words were dropped either because of the level of difficulty or because of some duplication in meaning.

| | | | |
|---|---|---|---|
| Fair | (F) | A hard worker | (F) |
| A nuisance | (U) | Bad | (U) |
| Afraid | (U) | A good sport | (F) |
| Cheerful | (F) | Considerate | (F) |
| A time waster | (U) | Not eager to study | (U) |
| Neat | (F) | Helpful | (F) |
| Not eager to learn | (U) | Careless | (U) |
| A leader | (F) | Sociable | (F) |
| Unhappy | (U) | Clever | (F) |
| Loving | (F) | Not alert | (U) |
| Outstanding | (F) | Smart | (F) |
| Loud | (U) | Silly | (U) |
| Generous | (F) | Kind | (F) |
| Nervous | (U) | Shy | (U) |
| Sensible | (F) | A sloppy worker | (U) |
| Polite | (F) | Dependable | (F) |
| Lazy | (U) | A day dreamer | (U) |
| Forgetful | (U) | | |

*Administration and Scoring of the Check List*

The children are instructed to decide how the teacher feels toward them with respect to each trait name, and then to rate it on a three-point rating scale: *most of the time, half of the time, seldom or almost never.* A favorable word is assigned a score of 3 when it is checked in the most of the time column; a score of 2 for half of the time, and 1 for seldom or almost never. For an unfavorable word the scoring is reversed.

The total score, the Index of Favorability, is obtained by adding the scores of all the words and dividing the total by the number of words checked. The higher the index, the more favorable is the child's perception of the teacher's feelings toward him. Theoretically, the index can range from 1.00 to 3.00.

*Reliability and Validity*

The Checklist of Trait Names was administered twice to four classes comprising 105 junior high-school children. The interval between the two administrations was from four to six weeks. A correlation of .85 was obtained (rank difference, $p < .001$).

The Checklist may be considered to have logical validity. However, it was desired to obtain a measure of empirical and concurrent validity. This was done by correlating the child's own perception of his teacher's appraisal of him with his classmates' perceptions of the teachers' feelings toward him. For this purpose, a modified version of the de Groat and Thompson *Teacher Approval and Disapproval Scale* [7] was administered along with Checklist to 93 children (3 classes). The de Groat and Thompson scale, as modified, consisted of 8 positive statements, such as, "Here is someone whom the teacher praises for trying hard," and 8 negative statements, such as, "Here is someone whom the teacher often points out as wasting too much time." For each statement, pupils were asked to name one to four of their classmates to whom these characteristics applied. They could also name themselves, if they so desired. Of the 93 children, 56 received 5 or more votes on one of the teacher approval and disapproval statements. For these 56 children, a teacher approval score was determined by subtracting the number of unfavorable statements on which five or more votes were received from the number of favorable statements on which five or more votes were received. A correlation of .51 was obtained (rank difference, $p < .001$) between the Index of Favorability and the teacher approval score.

The Checklist developed to assess children's perception of their teachers' feelings toward them appears to have satisfactory reliability and validity. Atlhough the estimate of reliability and validity was based on a sample of junior high-school students, the list was considered appropriate also for the upper grades of the elementary school because of the way the words were chosen.

## Experimental Design

### Subjects

The subjects of this study were 89 boys and 114 girls, attending 4th, 5th, and 6th grades of a New York City public school. These children were distributed in 10 different classrooms. In terms of reading ability, the classes selected were in the upper half of their respective grade level. Originally, it was planned to test all 4th, 5th, and 6th grade children, but after preliminary experimentation, it was found that several words were too difficult for children of limited language ability. It was therefore decided to test children in those classes which were known to have the better readers.

The children represented a wide range in socio-economic status. It was possible to divide them into three distinct groups on the basis of their fathers' and mothers' occupation. The upper group, consisting of 63 children, came from families of professional people, white collar workers and business men; the middle social class group of 57 children had parents who were skilled workers, policemen and firemen; the low group contained 83 children of semi-skilled and unskilled workers and a number of unemployed.

Table I presents the background information for the 203 children involved in the study.

### Procedure

The Checklist of Trait Names was administered twice to the children. At the first administration, the children were instructed to respond to the 35 adjectives comprising the list in terms of "My teacher thinks I am," and at the second testing, in terms of "I think I am." The first testing was done in the morning, the second in the afternoon. The "My teacher thinks I am" scale yields a measure of perceived teacher feelings, referrred to henceforth as the Index of Favorability; the "I think I am" scale yields a measure of self-perception.

The teachers, nine women and one man, rated their pupils on academic achievement, on a four-point scale: Very Well, Adequately, Below Average, and Very Poorly. In the analysis of data, the last two categories were combined due to the paucity of cases in the category Very Poorly. At the same time, the teacher also rated each child on 10 behavorial or personality characteristics. A weight of $+1$ was assigned to each of the traits judged to

**Table I**

**Distribution of Subjects in the Ten Classrooms by Sex and Social Class Status**

| | Socio-Economic Status | | | | | | Total | |
| | Upper | | Middle | | Lower | | | |
| Classroom | Boys | Girls | Boys | Girls | Boys | Girls | Boys | Girls |
|---|---|---|---|---|---|---|---|---|
| 4–1 | 8 | 5 | 3 | 8 | – | 2 | 11 | 15 |
| 5–1 | 1 | – | – | 2 | 7 | 8 | 8 | 10 |
| 5–2 | – | – | – | – | 3 | 5 | 3 | 5 |
| 5–3 | 7 | 10 | 7 | 2 | – | 1 | 14 | 13 |
| 5–4 | – | 2 | 3 | 1 | 9 | 8 | 12 | 11 |
| 5–5 | 2 | 4 | 6 | 3 | 3 | 7 | 11 | 14 |
| 6–1 | 5 | 5 | 4 | 3 | – | – | 9 | 8 |
| 6–2 | 2 | 5 | 4 | 2 | 1 | 6 | 7 | 13 |
| 6–3 | 3 | 3 | 5 | 3 | – | 9 | 8 | 15 |
| 6–4 | – | 1 | – | 1 | 6 | 8 | 6 | 10 |
| Total | 28 | 35 | 32 | 25 | 29 | 54 | 89 | 114 |

be desirable. The four desirable traits were: eager, obedient, cooperative, assertive. A weight of $-1$ was given to the characteristics judged to be undesirable: disorderly, destructive, hostile, defiant, unfriendly, and troublesome. The sum of the weights yielded a behavior rating score ranging theoretically, from $+4$ (very desirable) to $-6$ (very undesirable). Subjects who received the 0 and minus behavioral ratings were combined into one group due to the small number of cases in these categories.

## Results and Discussion

*Hypothesis 1*

There exists a positive correlation between children's perception of their teachers' feelings toward them and children's perception of themselves.

The two perceptual favorability indexes correlated .82 (product-moment, $p < .001$). The children who had a more favorable or a more adequate self-concept, that is, those who achieved a higher self-perception score also perceived their teachers' feelings toward them more favorably.

The finding of a significant correlation between the two kinds of perception lends support to the view that a child's assessment of himself is related to the assessment "significant people" make of him [30]. In two previous research investigations, a close relationship was found between self-appraisal and children's perception of their parents' feelings toward them [2, 16]. The present study for the first time has shown that a child's self-appraisal is significantly related to his perception of his teacher's feelings as well. Such a finding was anticipated in view of the fact that one role of the teacher, at least at the elementary level, is that of a "parent substitute." Several interesting questions may be raised: To what extent does a child's perception of his teacher's feelings resemble his perception of his mother's or father's feelings toward him? Does the child's perception of his present teacher differ from his perception of his previous teacher? Does favorability or perception decrease or increase with years in school?

*Hypothesis 2*

There exists a positive relationship between favorable perception of teachers' feelings and academic achievement. Table II presents the mean favorability scores and their standard deviations for the three levels of estimated achievement. The $F$ ratio of 15.61 was significant at less than the .001 level. The three $t$ tests were also significant at better than the .01 level.

**Table II**
**Index of Favorability as Related to Three Levels of Estimated Achievement**

|  | Achievement Category | | |
|  | *Very Well* | *Adequately* | *Below Average* |
|---|---|---|---|
| Mean Favorability Score | 2.68* (N = 53) | 2.57 (N = 111) | 2.40 (N = 39) |
| S. D. | .22 | .24 | .25 |

\* The higher the score, the more favorable the child's perception of his teacher's feelings toward him.

*Hypothesis 3*

There exists a positive relationship between favorable perception of teachers' feelings and desirable classroom behavior. The findings pertaining to the relationship between children's perception and their classroom behavior are shown in Table III.

### Table III
#### Index of Favorability as Related to Five Levels of Rated Behavior

| | Behavior Rating Category | | | | |
|---|---|---|---|---|---|
| | Very Desirable | | Desirable | | Undesirable (0 and |
| | (+4 | +3) | (+2 | +1) | Minus Scores) |
| Mean Favorability Score | 2.62* (N = 40) | 2.65 (N = 54) | 2.58 (N = 46) | 2.53 (N = 23) | 2.39 (N = 40) |
| S. D. | .26 | .19 | .27 | .27 | .28 |

* The higher the score, the more favorable the child's perception of his teacher's feelings toward him.

The overall $F$ ratio of 7.38 was significant at less than the .001 level. The only significant $t$ tests were those between the lowest category (0 and less) and all the other categories. In other words, the children who were rated as being disorderly, defiant, unfriendly, or troublesome, perceived their teachers' feelings toward them as being less favorable than the children who were rated as being eager, cooperative, assertive and the like.

One of the axioms of educational psychology is the statement that a child learns only when he is motivated to learn. Furthermore, the basic incentives which a teacher can furnish are her acceptance of the child on the one hand, and approval on the other. The findings of the present study furnish supporting evidence. The teacher's feelings of acceptance and approval are communicated to the child and perceived by him as positive appraisals. It is likely that these appraisals encourage the child to seek further teacher approval by achieving well and behaving in a manner acceptable to his teacher. We may also begin this cycle with the child's behavior. The child who achieves well and behaves satisfactorily is bound to please his teacher. She, in turn, communicates positive feelings toward the child, thus reinforcing his desire to be a good pupil. Which of these variables serves as the primary determiner is a fact difficult to ascertain. It seems rather that they reinforce each other. The implication is clear. It is essential that teachers communicate positive feelings to their children and thus not only strengthen their positive self-appraisals but stimulate their growth, academically as well as interpersonally.

It should be emphasized that these findings do not imply causality but rather suggest that certain pupil characteristics, such as self-perception, perceived teacher feelings, achievement and behavior in school are interrelated.

In addition to the results relevant to the tested hypotheses, other findings will now be reported.

*Sex Differences*

Sex differences were observed with regard to the three variables studied: index of favorability,[2] achievement, and behavior in school. Girls perceived their teachers' feelings toward them more favorably than did the boys (girls mean $= 2.60$; boys mean $= 2.52$; $t = 2.41$, p$<$.02). The behavior ratings of the girls were more favorable than those of the boys ($x^2 = 10.72$, df $=$ 4, p$<$.05); the girls were likewise rated more favorably in achievement, although this difference was not significant ($x^2 = 3.41$, df $= 2$, .10$<$ p$<$.20).

Past research has consistently shown that teachers report more problem behavior among boys [32]. One explanation, though not widely accepted, is that boys are naturally more aggressive. Another view, more plausible, holds that our society encourages aggressive behavior in men (and men to be) and submissive behavior in women. Teachers, most of whom are women, especially in the primary grades, therefore regard boys' classroom behavior as disturbingly different from the norms of behavior appropriate to their own female sex. The temptation is great to reward children of one's own sex. Meyer and Thompson's study [19] is pertinent here. Teacher-pupil interaction of sixth-grade pupils were studied over a one-year period and analyzed in terms of "approval" and "disapproval" contacts. In addition, children were asked to nominate by the "Guess Who" technique which of their classmates receive their teacher's approval and disapproval. Both approaches yielded the same finding. Classroom observers, as well as the children themselves, noted that teachers expressed greater approval of girls and greater disapproval of boys. The findings of the present investigation, which ascertained directly children's perceptions of their teachers' feelings, are in accord with the results of prior research. The suggestion has been frequently made that more men should be urged to teach at the primary level. Findings such as those discussed above suggest the urgency to establish a sexual balance in the teaching staff at the primary grades. Not only is it desirable for boys to have a male model with whom to identify, but conditions may then be created which may assure greater teacher approval for

---

[2] The index used in this and subsequent analyses is based on the Check List score of the child's perception of his teacher's feelings toward him.

boys and reduce teacher disapproval for behavior which is, to a large extent, culturally instigated.

## Social Class Differences

Because of the distinct differences found in social class status in this group of children, it was decided to investigate the relation of social class to the index of favorability, achievement and behavior in school. All three variables are related to social class in the direction one would predict. These data are shown in Table IV.

**Table IV**

**Social Class Status Related to Favorability Index, Achievement and Behavior**

| | Upper Social Class (N = 63) | Middle Social Class (N = 57) | Lower Social Class (N = 83) |
|---|---|---|---|
| Mean Favorability Index | 2.63 | 2.60 | 2.49 |
| S. D. | .26 | .22 | .26 |
| Achievement Rating Category: | | | |
| Very Well (N = 53) | 43%* | 34% | 23% |
| Adequately (N = 111) | 31% | 22% | 47% |
| Below Average (N = 39) | 15% | 36% | 49% |
| Behavioral Rating Category: | | | |
| Very Desirable (N = 94) | 41% | 29% | 30% |
| Desirable (N = 69) | 23% | 30% | 46% |
| Undesirable (N = 40) | 20% | 22% | 58% |

* These percentages are based on the N's of the Achievement and Behavior categories.

It may be observed from Table IV that there is a decline in mean favorability index from the upper to the lower social class. Two of the three *t* tests were significant at better than the .01 level; *t* was not significant between the upper and middle social class groups. Children in the two advantaged social class groups perceive their teachers' feelings toward them more favorably than do the children in the lower class group.

Social class and achievement in school are significantly related ($x^2 = 18.38$, 4df, $p < .01$). The differences in the percentage of children in the several categories may be pointed out, especially the difference between the two extremes; in the upper social class 43% of the children were rated by their teachers as doing very well in school while only 15% were rated as doing below average work.

Social class and behavior in school as rated by the teachers were not significantly related ($x^2 = 14.97$, 8df, $.05 < p < .10$). However, the distribution of children in the several categories reveal interesting differences. While the great majority of the children in the group were rated favorably by their teachers, there were 58% of the children in the lower class whose behavior was rated as undesirable while only 20% of the upper class children were so rated.

It has been suggested that teachers, as surrogates of middle class values, tend to give preferential treatment to the middle and upper social economic class pupils, and to withhold rewards from pupils who belong to the lower socio-economic class [6, 8]. Furthermore, previous research has shown that lower class children do not achieve as well as middle and upper class children [10, 14], in part due to lower motivation [25]. The data obtained in the present study corroborate these observations.

The interrelations found between children's perception of teachers' feelings, school achievement, behavior and socio-economic status are particularly significant since the majority of children in the public schools throughout the country come from families of low social class status. It is therefore likely that a lower class child, especially if he is not doing well in school, will have a negative perception of his teachers' feelings toward him. These negative perceptions will in turn tend to lower his efforts to achieve in school and/or increase the probability that he will misbehave. His poor school achievement will aggravate the negative attitudes of his teachers toward him, which in turn will affect his self-confidence, and so on. This vicious entanglement must be interrupted at some point. The point of attack may well be the teacher whose capacity to reflect feelings conductive to the child's growth should be of concern to educators.

*Analysis of Variance of Favorability Scores*

It was found that the index of favorability was positively related to achievement in school as well as to social class position. It is also evident from this and other studies that achievement in school is correlated with social class position. In order to study the influence of each of these factors on index of favorability, the favorability scores were re-analyzed first, for the three achievement levels within each social class and second, for the three social class groups within each achievement category. The mean favorability indexes for these separate groups are presented in Table V.

### Table V
**Mean Indexes of Favorability for the Three Achievement Categories and for the Three Social Class Groups**

|  | Achievement Category | | |
| --- | --- | --- | --- |
|  | Very Well | Adequately | Below Average |
| Upper Social Class | 2.71* (N = 23) | 2.61 (N = 34) | 2.51 (N = 6) |
| Middle Social Class | 2.71 (N = 18) | 2.60 (N = 25) | 2.44 (N = 14) |
| Lower Social Class | 2.59 (N = 12) | 2.52 (N = 52) | 2.34 (N = 19) |

* The higher the score, the more favorable the child's perception of his teacher's feelings toward him.

Reading Table V vertically, it may be observed that the mean favorability score declines from the upper social class to the lowest social class for each of the achievement categories; this decline is most noticeable between the two highest social class groups and the lowest social class group. It is apparent that the social class variable plays a part in the way a child perceives his teacher's feelings toward him regardless of his achievement in school. Similarly, reading Table V horizontally, the mean favorability score is observed to decrease from the highest achievement level to the lowest within each social class group. The evidence here suggests that achievement in school colors the child's perception of his teacher's feelings, regardless of his social class position. Analysis of variance of the data yielded two significant F ratios. These results indicate that both the factors of social class position and achievement are operating independently in affecting the way a child will perceive his teacher's feelings toward him.

These findings should arouse the educator for they imply that a teacher's reaction to a child is not solely influenced by the individuality of the child but also by his social class and achievement characteristics.

## Differences Among Teachers

It may be assumed that teachers reflect a variety of feelings toward children, either because of their own personality needs, or because of the way they use punishment or praise or for any other reason. These differences from teacher to teacher should be observable in the perceptions of the children affected by them. Table VI presents the mean favorability indexes for the 10 teachers in this study.

Table VI
The Index of Favorability for the Ten Classrooms

| Class | N | Mean | S. D. |
|-------|-----|--------|------|
| 4–1 | 26 | 2.61* | .26 |
| 5–1 | 18 | 2.25 | .21 |
| 5–2 | 8 | 2.45 | .29 |
| 5–3 | 27 | 2.62 | .17 |
| 5–4 | 23 | 2.45 | .23 |
| 5–5 | 25 | 2.62 | .22 |
| 6–1 | 17 | 2.57 | .08 |
| 6–2 | 20 | 2.64 | .23 |
| 6–3 | 23 | 2.64 | .19 |
| 6–4 | 16 | 2.70 | .10 |

\* The higher the score, the more favorable the child's perception of his teacher's feelings toward him.

It may be observed that the range in mean favorability score is from 2.25 to 2.70. Although the children generally perceived their teachers' feelings more favorably than otherwise, and the actual differences among the classrooms were not large, there were 3 or 4 classrooms with markedly low mean scores. The overall F ratio of 2.95 is significant at less than the .01 level. It should be remembered, at this point, that the classes were selected for better than average ability in reading, which makes the finding of significant differences even more compelling. Teachers do seem to vary in their inclination and/or their capacity to communicate favorable feelings. It seems urgent that teachers be helped to recognize the significance of the feelings which they express toward children, consciously or unconsciously. Some teachers, in addition, may need the help which can only come through a process of self-understanding, in order to avoid or to minimize the expression of negatively-toned feelings toward children, because of their sex, their socio-economic status, their behavior or achievement in school.

*Possible Uses of the Checklist*

The Checklist of Trait Names, in addition to its use as a research tool, may be adapted to practical school situations. Conceivably, it can be employed for the purpose of teacher selection and guidance. For instance, a principal might wish to select a teacher for a class comprised of under-privileged or troublesome children who are very much in need of accept-ance and approval. A good candidate for such a class would be a teacher who can easily project positive feelings. Supervisors of student teachers may find the checklist useful in evaluating the quality of teacher-student relations.

Teachers who are found to communicate largely negative feelings may be advised to participate in some kind of counseling or therapy. Similarly, children whose perceptions are primarily negative and/or distorted can be identified for personality diagnosis and thus be helped in self-understand-ing or in obtaining a more accurate perception of reality.

## Summary

The purpose of the study was to relate children's perception of their teachers' feelings toward them to self-perception, academic achievement, and classroom behavior. A Checklist of Trait Names, consisting of 35 descriptive terms, was administered to 89 boys and 114 girls in grades 4, 5, and 6 in a New York City public school. The children were rated by their teachers for achievement and on a number of behavioral characteristics.

The major findings were:

1. The children's perception of their teachers' feelings toward them correlated positively and significantly with self-perception. The child with the more favorable self image was the one who more likely than not per-ceived his teacher's feelings toward him more favorably.

2. The more positive the children's perception of their teachers' feelings, the better was their academic achievement and the more desirable their classroom behavior as rated by the teachers.

3. Further, children in the upper and middle social class groups per-ceived their teachers' feelings toward them more favorably than did the children in the lower social class group.

4. Social class position was also found to be positively related with achievement in school.

5. However, even when the favorability index data were re-analyzed

separately for each social class and for each achievement category, the mean favorability index declined with decline in achievement level, regardless of social class position and, similarly, the mean favorability index declined with social class regardless of achievement level.

6. Girls generally perceived their teachers' feelings more favorably than did the boys.

7. Finally, there were some significant classroom differences in the favorability of the children's perception of their teachers' feelings. These findings must be considered in light of the non-random selection of the sample. Nevertheless, it is reasonable to assume that these subjects are representative of the population of New York City elementary school children at these grade levels. . . .

## References

1. ALLPORT, G. and H. ODBERT. "Trait Names: A Psycho-lexical Study." *Psychological Monographs,* XLVII (1936).

2. AUSUBEL, D. P., *et al.* "Perceived Parent Attitudes as Determinants of Children's Ego Structure." *Child Development.* **XXV:**173–183 (1954).

3. BARR, A. S. and R. E. JONES. "The Measurement and Prediction of Teacher Efficiency." *Review of Educational Research.* **XXVIII:**256–264 (1958).

4. BILLS, R. E. *et al.* "An Index of Adjustment and Values," *Journal of Consulting Psychology.* **XV:**257–261 (1951).

5. COOK, W. W. "Significant Factors in Teachers' Classroom Attitudes." *Journal of Education.* **VII:**274–279 (1956).

6. DAVIS, A. *Social Class Influences Upon Learning.* Cambridge, Mass.: Harvard University Press (1952).

7. DE GROAT, A. F. and G. G. THOMPSON. "A Study of the Distribution of Teacher Approval and Disapproval Among Sixth-Grade Pupils." *Journal of Experimental Education.* **XVIII:**57–75 (1949).

8. DIXON, N. R. "Social Class and Education." *Harvard Educational Review.* **XXIII:**330–338 (1953).

9. DYMOND, ROSALIND F. "A Scale for Measurement of Empathic Ability." *Journal of Consulting Psychology.* **XIII:**127–133 (1949).

10. FRIEDHOFF, W. H. "Relationships Among Various Measures of Socio-Economic Status, Social Class Identification, Intelligence, and School Achievement." *Dissertation Abstract.* **XV:**2098 (1955).

11. GAGE, N. L., *et al.* "Teachers' Understanding of Their Pupils and Pupils' Ratings of Their Teachers." *Psychol. Monographs,* LXIX (1955).

12. GOUGH, H. G. *Reference Handbook for the Gough Adjective Check List.* Mimeographed. Berkeley, California: University of California, Institute of Personality Assessment and Research (1955).

13. HARTSHORNE, H. and H. A. MAY. *Studies in the Nature of Character, III: Studies in the Organization of Character.* New York: The Macmillan Co. (1930).

14. HEIMANN, R. A. and Q. F. SCHENK. "Relations of Social Class and Sex Differences to High School Achievement." *School Rev.,* **LXII:**213–221 (1954).

15. JERSILD, A. T. *In Search of Self.* New York: Bureau of Publications, Teachers College, Columbia University (1952).

16. JOURARD, S. M. and R. M. REMY. "Perceived Parental Attitudes, the Self, and Security." *J. of Consult. Psychol.* **XIX:**364–366 (1955).

17. MARTIRE, J. G. "Relationship Between the Self Concept and Differences in the Strength and Generality of Achievement Motivation." *Journal of Personality.* **XXIV:**364–375 (1956).

18. MERRILL, R. M. and L. B. HEATHERS. "The Use of an Adjective Checklist as a Measure of Adjustment." *J. of Consult. Psychol.* **I:**137–143 (1954).

19. MEYER, W. J. and G. G. THOMPSON. "Sex Differences in the Distribution of Teacher Approval and Disapproval Among Sixth-Grade Children." *J. of Educ. Psychol.* **XLVII:**285–296 (1956).

20. National Education Association, Research Division. "Teacher Opinion on Pupil Behavior." *Res. Bull.* **XXXIV:**51–107 (1956).

21. PERKINS, H. V ."Factors Influencing Change in Children's Self Concepts." *Child Develpm.* **XXIX:**221–230 (1958).

22. ———. "Teachers' and Peers' Perceptions of Children's Self Concepts." *Child Develpm.* **XXIX:**203–220 (1958).

23. REEDER, T. A. "A Study of Some Relationships Between Level of Self Concept, Academic Achievement, and Classroom Adjustment." *Dissertation Abstract.* **XV:**2472 (1955).

24. ROGERS, C. R. *Client-Centered Therapy.* Boston: Houghton Mifflin (1951).

25. ROSEN, B. C. "The Achievement Syndrome: A Psychocultural Dimension of Social Stratification." *Am. Sociol. Rev.* **XXI:**203–211 (1956).

26. SARBIN, T. R. and B. C. ROSENBERG. "Contributions to Role-Taking Theory: IV. A Method for Obtaining a Qualitative Estimate of the Self." *J. of Soc. Psychol.* **XLII:**71–81 (1955).

27. SNYGG, D. and A. W. COMBS. *Individual Behavior.* New York: Harper and Brothers (1949).

28. STEINER, I. D. "Self-Perception and Goal-Setting Behavior." *J. of Personality.* **XXV:**344–355 (1957).

29. STEVENS, P. H. "An Investigation of the Relationship Between Certain Aspects of Self-Concept Behavior and Students' Academic Achievement." *Dissertation Abstract.* **XVI:**2531–2532 (1956).

30. SULLIVAN, H. S. *Conceptions of Modern Psychiatry.* Washington, D. C.: W. A. White Psychiatric Foundation (1947).

31. SYMONDS, P. M. "Characteristics of the Effective Teacher Based on Pupil Evaluation." *J. of Exper. Educ.,* **XXIII:**289–310 (1955).

32. TERMAN, L. M. and L. E. TYLER. "Psychological Sex Differences." In L. CARMICHEAL, *Man. of Child Psychol.,* Second Edition. New York: Wiley and Sons (1954).

33. THORNDIKE, E. L. and I. LORGE. *The Teacher's Word Book of 30,000 Words.* New York: Bureau of Publications, Teachers College, Columbia University (1944).

# 36

## THE RELATIONSHIP OF SOCIO-ECONOMIC STATUS AND AGGRESSION TO THE COMPETITIVE BEHAVIOR OF PRESCHOOL CHILDREN *

### John P. McKee and Florence B. Leader

A question of considerable interest to psychologists and sociologists is the relationship of socio-economic status to competitive and aggressive behavior in children. This is surely a matter of relevance for teachers as well in that it may give them a better insight into behavior of this nature in their pupils. The authors differentiate between competition and aggression on the basis that the former is intended to excel, the latter to injure. One hundred twelve three- and four-year-olds were the subjects of this study. Half of them were from middle-class families and half from lower-class. Children were tested by being placed in a play situation, first alone and later paired with another child of the same age, sex and socio-economic status. In both instances the child's behavior and verbalizations were observed and recorded. The protocols were rated by two independent judges for competition and aggression. The judges did not know the age, sex or socio-economic level of the children. While the results of the study do not vary from those of earlier investigations, they shed light on some ancillary questions which have not previously been adequately considered or satisfactorily answered.

*Questions:*

1. What are the implications of this study for the classroom teacher? What could you do about competitive and/or aggressive behavior in your pupils?

\* \* \*

Although competition has interested psychologists and educators for

* Reprinted from *Child Development*, **26**:135–142 (June 1955), by permission of senior author and the Society for Research in Child Development, Inc.

years, only Greenberg [4]* and Leuba [7] have provided empirical data for the preschool years. And so far as the writers have been able to ascertain there is no empirical material concerning conditions responsible for the development of competitive behavior patterns. Nor is there adequate empirical information about the relationship of competition to other forms of social behavior during early childhood. Current textbooks, in fact—e.g., [5]—rather avoid this last question and progress from a discussion of competitive behavior through competitive motivation and the use of competitive incentives to sibling rivalry with no clear-cut indication that the last concept is frequently considered germane to the subject of aggression.

The investigation reported below attempts to fill some of these lacunae. First, it seeks to determine the role of socio-economic origin in the development of competition. The hypothesis is that competitive behavior will appear earlier and be more intense among children from lower socio-economic origins. This is suggested by the fact that in Leuba's American middle-class sample there was no competition among two-year-olds and very little among three- and four-year-olds while in Greenberg's underprivileged Viennese sample even some of the two-year-olds competed. Since the procedures, criteria and cultural background of the subjects differed considerably in the two investigations the evidence is only suggestive, but it agrees with the common sense notion that those who are deprived of status are likely to seek it more vigorously than those who are not so deprived. Another plausible possibility is that youngsters from lower socio-economic levels have learned the desirability of successful competition through having had to compete for a limited supply of material benefits. In short, the hypothesis is consonant with both reason and such facts as are available.

A second purpose of this experiment is to determine the relationship between competition and aggression. The lack of clarity mentioned above suggests that they may have much in common, or even that competition is simply a means of aggressing. In this case there ought to be a substantial positive correlation between measures of the two. On the other hand, it is possible that behavior which has no other purpose than simply to excel another (competition) may develop almost independently of behavior for which the aim is injury to another (aggression). Aside from these theoretical niceties there remains the question of whether the two categories of behavior can each be measured reliably enough to justify either point of view.

Beside the two preceding objectives this study has a number of explora-

* Figure in brackets apply to references at end of article.

tory aims. It makes a tentative examination of age and sex differences in both aggression and competition during the preschool years. And it attempts to extend to this period Davis' [1] finding with older subjects that aggression is more common among lower socio-economic groups.

## Subjects

One hundred twelve three- and four-year-old children divided equally as to sex, age, and socio-economic status served as subjects. Thus there were 14 children in each subgroup. Middle-class children were taken from three sources: the nursery school of the Institute of Child Welfare at the University of California, Berkeley; a Parent Co-operative Nursery School in El Cerrito, California; and a Parent Nursery School operated by the Berkeley School System in Berkeley, California. The parents of the Institute children were primarily University faculty or occupied in other professions. The El Cerrito school is financed entirely by the parents; tuition is charged and mothers must be free to participate in the school program. The Parent Nursery School is operated as an adult education class, requires tuition, maternal participation and attendance at a weekly class. Because of these parental characteristics and because of the residential areas involved, the children attending these three schools are considered to be of upper middle socio-economic origin. Children of lower socio-economic origin came from two sources in Berkeley: a Day Care Center and a Day Nursery for needy children. Attendance at the Day Care Center is contingent upon having a low family income (less than $330 per month for two parents and one child), or upon the mother's being employed in essential industry. Both financial status and the areas in which they live indicate that these subjects have considerably lower socio-economic origins than the upper middle-class sample, though they are not "Lower Class" in Warner's [8] sense.

## Procedure

To familiarize the subjects with the equipment each child was first brought into the test room alone for eight minutes. He found a small table with a chair at each end, a pile of small red and yellow toy construction bricks before each place, and two sample constructions in the center of the table. He was asked if he knew how to build with them, and if he did not, the experimenter helped him. The experimenter, who sat across from the child, built a stack of eight red bricks. After two minutes she left, commenting that she needed equipment from the next room. Six minutes later the experimenter returned and took the child back to his play group. After a few days the child was tested again. This time he was paired with another child of the same age, sex and socio-economic origin. Otherwise, the situation remained the same. Each child sat at one end of the table with a pile of blocks before him and two sample constructions in the center. The experimenter again remained for two minutes and then observed from another room for six minutes.

While observing, the experimenter recorded both the overt behavior of the children and their verbalizations. The written protocols were then rated on a four-point scale for both aggression and competition by two independent judges who did not know the age, sex or socio-economic status of the children. Each judge first made 112 ratings of competition, and then went through the protocols a second time to rate aggression.

Competition was defined as behavior of which the intent seemed to be to excel or to communicate the notion of one's own superiority to the partner. Aggression was defined as behavior of which the intent seemed to be to injure the partner.

Since the "intent" of a behavior can only be inferred, a number of denotative criteria were used to increase reliability and objectivity. Any remark about the relative size, beauty, excellence and so forth of the two children's products was considered very carefully in relation to competition, but both raters independently noted that occasionally such remarks seemed no more than statements of fact (e.g., "Yours is bigger") with, so far as could be determined, no overtones of feeling whatsoever. The criteria of aggression were such things as physical violence and derogatory remarks. While physical violence is pretty clear-cut, derogatory remarks not always are. Thus, the comment, "I'm going to make a bigger one than yours" may be purely informative, purely competitive, or may involve aggression as well. There were many instances of this kind and all that can be said is that the raters weighed the pros and cons and did their best. The final scores assigned to each child are the averages of the two independent ratings of competition and aggression.

## Results

Before analyzing the data in terms of the socio-economic factor there are two prior matters which were mentioned above. Can the same protocols be rated reliably for both competition and aggression? Assuming the answer to this question is "yes," then are the two categories of behavior independent enough to justify two analyses? For competition the reliability by the phi coefficient is $+.71$. For aggression it is $+.68$. While these coefficients are smaller than might be hoped for, they are high enough to permit analysis of the data. Furthermore, the phi for the relationship between competition and aggression is only $+.22$ which means that separate analyses are feasible.

Much of the remaining analysis will be made in terms of the number of *pairs* of children who showed competition or aggression. Bear in mind that there are 112 children, or 56 pairs, 28 pairs from each socio-economic level. The ultimate breakdown of pairs gives seven pairs in each subcategory (e.g., lower socio-economic, three-year-old girls).

### Competition

Table 1 gives the number of *pairs* of children in the lower and middle socio-economic groups in which neither child, one child, or both children

**Table 1**

**Number of Pairs in Which 0, 1, or 2 Children Showed Any Competition**

|  | 0 | 1 | 2 |
|---|---|---|---|
| Low status ........ | 7 | 6 | 15 |
| Middle status ...... | 15 | 8 | 5 |

$$\chi^2 = 8.19$$
$$.01 < p < .02$$

showed any competitive behavior (average rating greater than zero). The chi-square of 8.19 is significant at between the 1 and 2 per cent levels of confidence. Clearly, there is more competition among pairs from the lower social level. Since the behaviors of the members of a pair are not independent of each other, it is a little difficult to speak about individuals, but in passing it should be noted that 36 of 56 lower status children showed some competition while only 18 of the 56 middle status children showed any.

This preponderance of competition among the lower status children is found in each of the subgroup comparisons. They are summarized in Table 2. In all four comparisons there are more lower status pairs showing competition than there are middle status pairs. Assuming that a difference in either direction is equally possible gives a probability of only .0625 $(.5^4)$ that these results are due to chance. Similar results are obtained by comparing the individual children (as opposed to pairs) in each of the four sub-categories. In every instance more lower class children compete.

The means and medians are given in Table 3. The preponderance of zero ratings makes the distributions very skewed. Even so, all four sub-group comparisons yield somewhat higher means for the lower status group. This is not true for the medians, but this reflects only the fact that most medians are zero.

**Table 2**

**Number of Pairs in Which at Least One Child Showed Some Competition: Subgroup Comparisons**

|  | Low Status | Middle Status |
|---|---|---|
| 3-year-old boys ............. | 5 | 3 |
| 3-year-old girls ............. | 4 | 2 |
| 4-year-old boys ............. | 7 | 4 |
| 4-year-old girls ............. | 5 | 4 |

**Table 3**

**Mean and Median Ratings of Competition**

|  | Low Status | | Middle Status | |
|---|---|---|---|---|
|  | Mean | Median | Mean | Median |
| 3-year-old boys ............ | .92 | 0 | .25 | 0 |
| 3-year-old girls ............ | .36 | 0 | .30 | 0 |
| 4-year-old boys ............ | 1.24 | 1.50 | .70 | 0 |
| 4-year-old girls ............ | .80 | .75 | .42 | 0 |

In summary, every method of analysis confirms the hypothesis that competition is more frequent and more vigorous among the children with lower socio-economic origins. More individuals are involved and the average ratings are higher.

In addition to the socio-economic difference, Tables 2 and 3 yield important information about sex and age differences. In Table 2, three sex comparisons favor boys (middle status four-year-olds have the same number for both sexes) and all four age comparisons favor the older children. For the age differences the probability of obtaining such results by chance is .0625. Table 3 indicates almost the same thing, though of course the skewed distributions make the medians rather less informative than they might be and there is one contradiction in the sex difference between means (middle class three-year-old girls slightly exceed boys). All in all, though, the evidence strongly supports the generalization that competition is positively related to age and more common among boys than girls.

### Table 4
#### Number of Pairs in Which 0, 1, or 2 Children Showed Any Aggression

|  | 0 | 1 | 2 |
|---|---|---|---|
| Low status ........ | 5 | 5 | 18 |
| Middle status ...... | 12 | 8 | 8 |

$$\chi^2 = 7.44$$
$$.02 < p < .05$$

### Aggression

The results for aggression are similar in some respects to those for competition. Table 4 indicates more aggression among pairs with low status, and this general finding is confirmed in all but one instance in the subgroup comparisons in Tables 5 and 6, as well as by the fact that 41 individual lower status children showed at least some aggression while only 24 of the

### Table 5
#### Number of Pairs in Which at Least One Child Showed Some Aggression: Subgroup Comparisons

|  | Low Status | Middle Status |
|---|---|---|
| 3-year-old boys ............. | 7 | 3 |
| 3-year-old girls ............. | 6 | 4 |
| 4-year-old boys ............. | 5 | 4 |
| 4-year-old girls ............. | 5 | 5 |

### Table 6
#### Mean and Median Ratings of Aggression

|  | Low Status | | Middle Status | |
|---|---|---|---|---|
|  | Mean | Median | Mean | Median |
| 3-year-old boys .......... | 1.75 | 1.50 | .50 | 0 |
| 3-year-old girls .......... | .64 | .50 | .40 | .25 |
| 4-year-old boys .......... | .75 | 1.00 | .36 | 0 |
| 4-year-old girls .......... | .71 | 1.00 | .40 | 0 |

middle status children showed any. In brief, the evidence is strong that aggression is more common among children from the lower socio-economic level.

Unlike the results for competition, no clear-cut findings are evidenced with regard to sex and age differences. Jersild and Markey [6] report a similar lack of age trend while Green [3] and Dawe [2] report more complex age trends than this investigation was designed to yield. The failure to find a clear sex difference is puzzling, though the fact that the situation was one which elicited a great deal of verbal behavior may be relevant. Girls' well know verbal superiority may have given them a relative advantage not normally enjoyed in less structured free play situations.

## Discussion

While this investigation appears to shed some light on the development of competition it raises some new questions also. The first concerns just what feature of differential socio-economic status is responsible for the differences in competitive behavior. Presumably it is not due to more permissive child-rearing practices among the lower socio-economic group: the lower group in this study probably corresponds more closely to Warner's lower middle class than to his lower class. Is it a compensatory device for gaining status? Is it simply less parental supervision which permits children to learn competition by trial and error? Is it actually encouraged by parents from the lower sample and more or less ignored or even discouraged by the upper middle parents? The writers are inclined to favor a combination of the last two possibilities.

A second question concerns the low intercorrelation between competition and aggression. The writers' hunch about this fact is that it is due to the youth of the subjects who have learned to want to excel, but have just begun to learn to become angry when they are unsuccessful in this aim. If this is true, then the correlation between competition and aggression should be higher among somewhat older subjects. An investigation of this possibility will be undertaken shortly.

A last problem has to do with the failure to find more aggression among boys. It was suggested that the predominance of verbal responses may have increased the aggression score for girls. The hypothesis that girls' aggression is heavily weighted with language is not a new hypothesis with the writers, but good evidence on the matter seems to be lacking. It is a question well worth investigating.

## Summary

One hundred twelve three- and four-year-old children equally divided as to age, sex and middle or lower socio-economic status were pretested and then paired in an experimental play situation. The behavior and verbalizations of the children were recorded and the protocols then rated independently by two raters for the degree of competition and the degree of aggression.

Both competition and aggression could be rated with fair reliability and the association between the two kinds of behavior was very low (+.22). In this situation, significantly more competition was found among children from low socio-economic origins than among children from upper middle origins, and this finding was true of all subgroup comparisons. More instances of competition occurred among older children than among younger and among boys than among girls. Aggression was also more common among the lower status children and subgroup comparisons supported this finding almost without exception. Clear-cut sex and age differences in aggression did not appear.

## References

1. DAVIS, A. "Child Training and Social Class." In R. BARKER, J. KOUNIN, and H. WRIGHT (eds.), *Child Behavior and Development*. New York: McGraw-Hill (1943).

2. DAWE, HELEN C. "An Analysis of Two Hundred Quarrels of Preschool Children." *Child Develpm.* **5:**139–157 (1934).

3. GREEN, ELISE H. "Friendships and Quarrels among Preschool Children." *Child Develpm.* **4:**237–252 (1933).

4. GREENBERG, PEARL J. "Competition in Children: An Experimental Study." *Amer. J. Psychol.* **44:**221–248 (1932).

5. JERSILD, A. T. *Child Psychology.* (4th Ed.) New York: Prentice-Hall (1954).

6. JERSILD, A. T. and F. V. MARKEY. "Conflicts between Preschool Children." *Child Develpm. Monogr.* 21 (1935).

7. LEUBA, C. "An Experimental Study of Rivalry in Young Children." *J. Comp. Psychol.* **16:**367–378 (1933).

8. WARNER, W. L., M. MEEKER, and K. EELLS. *Social Class in America.* Chicago: Science Research Associates (1949).

# 37

## PSYCHOLOGICAL HEALTH AND CLASSROOM FUNCTIONING: A STUDY OF DISSATISFACTION WITH SCHOOL AMONG ADOLESCENTS [1] *

### Philip W. Jackson and Jacob W. Getzels

Many studies have been made of "drop outs" from school, especially high schools and colleges, to identify reasons for leaving. Most of them go at the problem directly, that is, the school leaver is asked why he left before finishing. Or perhaps we even give him a list of reasons and simply ask him to check the one or ones that apply in his case. By contrast, the study reported here is more indirect and more penetrating. It seeks to investigate the question of characteristics or traits which may differentiate the student who is dissatisfied with school from the one who is satisfied. Two groups, one whose responses to a check list indicated significantly more than average satisfaction with school, and the other indicating the opposite, were tested by various instruments. These included a series of tests of achievement and personality as well as ratings by their teachers on desirability as a student, leadership qualities, and ability to become involved in learning activities. The student also indicated his characteristic feelings while attending classes in particular subjects. Comparisons were also made between boys and girls in the two groups. The findings of the study are interesting and thought-provoking. They suggest that reasons for dissatisfaction with school may not be so much the fault of the school as they are within the student.

*Questions:*

1. The authors of this article suggest that a certain amount of dissatisfaction with school is normal and to be expected under any circumstances. Is this observation supported by conditions found in other types of activity, *e.g.* military service?

[1] This study was supported by a research grant from the United States Office of Education.
* Reprinted from the *Journal of Educational Psychology*, **50**:295–300 (December 1959), by permission of authors and publisher.

2. What implications do you see in the findings of this study for the classroom teacher? For the counselor? For the school principal?

* * *

The problem of dissatisfaction with school among children is of theoretical and practical significance to both psychologists and educators. At the theoretical level dissatisfaction with school becomes part of a broader area of inquiry which aims at an understanding of the individual's functioning in an institutional setting and which includes studies of staff morale, role conflict, productivity, and the like. At a practical level the question of why children like or dislike school is directly related to the immediate problems of school dropouts, grouping procedures, planning for the gifted child, and the like.

As might be expected, a social phenomenon as important as dissatisfaction with school is not without its explanatory hypotheses. Some of these spring from empirical findings, while others appear to be part of our cultural ethos. Educational studies that point to an empirical linkage between school failure and school dropouts, and industrial studies that demonstrate a relationship between low morale and decreased output, lead one to suspect that reduced effectiveness in school (i.e., low scholastic achievement) would be a natural concomitant of dissatisfaction with the institution. Thus one would expect to find heightened dissatisfaction among students who have low ability or who are unable for one reason or another to deal adequately with scholastic material.

More recently it has been suggested (although never adequately demonstrated) that many successful students with high ability are dissatisfied with their school experiences; the term "boredom" is often linked with the term "gifted child" in current expositions by educators. The boredom problem among "gifted" combined with the failure experiences of the low ability child suggests that the greatest number of dissatisfied students is to be found among extreme ability groups. Those who are low in ability and achievement would be expected to show dissatisfaction because of the numerous frustrations they experience in the classroom. Those who are high in ability and achievement would be expected to show dissatisfaction because of the relative lack of stimulation which they experience in the classroom.

Both of these explanations (or, more accurately, hypotheses) contain the implication that dissatisfaction with an institution arises out of the individual's interaction with that institution. An alternative explanation might be that the individual brings a set toward satisfaction or dissatisfaction *to* the institution—that it is a reflection of a more pervasive personal orientation and that success or failure experiences within the institution have a limited influence upon it. This hypothesis obviously places more emphasis than do the earlier ones upon psychological variables, as opposed to environmental variables, in understanding dissatisfaction with school. The research described here was designed to test the relative merit of these alternative views.

## Problem

The purpose of this investigation is to examine the differences in psychological functioning and classroom effectiveness between two groups of adolescents—those who are satisfied with their recent school experiences and those who are dissatisfied.

## Subjects and Procedure

The *S*s of this investigation were two groups of adolescents identified from among 531 students enrolled in a Midwestern private school. These students were divided into five class groups ranging from the prefreshmen to the senior year of high school. In this institution a single grade, the prefreshmen, is substituted for the usual seventh and eighth grades. The instrument used to select the experimental groups, called the Student Opinion Poll, was a 60-item opinionnaire designed to elicit responses concerning general satisfaction or dissatisfaction with various aspects of school—viz., the teachers, the curriculum, the student body, and classroom procedures. The following are sample items, one in each of the four areas.

3. While there are some differences among them, most teachers in this school are:
   *a.* Very inspiring
   *b.* Quite inspiring
   *c.* Somewhat inspiring
   *d.* Not inspiring
16. Most of the subjects taught in the school are:
   *a.* Interesting and challenging
   *b.* Somewhat above average in interest
   *c.* Somewhat below average in interest
   *d.* Dull and routine

14. From the standpoint of intellectual ability, students in this school are:

*a.* Too bright—it is difficult to keep up with them

*b.* Just bright enough

*c.* Not bright enough—they do not provide enough intellectual stimulation

5. The freedom to contribute something in class without being called upon by the teacher is:

*a.* Discouraged more than it should be—students do not have enough opportunity to have their say

*b.* Encouraged more than it should be—students seem to be rewarded just for speaking even when they have little to say

*c.* Handled about right

The instrument was scored by giving one point each time the $S$ chose the "most satisfied" response to a multiple-choice item. Thus, the possible range of scores was from 0 to 60. For the total school population the mean score on the Student Opinion Poll was 37.30; the standard deviation was 9.57. The experimental groups were chosen as follows:

Group I—the "dissatisfied" group—consisted of all students whose score on the opinionnaire was at least one and a half standard deviations *below* the mean of the entire student body. This group contained 27 boys and 20 girls.

Group II—the "satisfied" group—consisted of all students whose score on the opinionnaire was at least one and a half standard deviations *above* the mean of the entire student body. This group contained 25 boys and 20 girls.

The experimental groups were compared on the following variables:

1. *Individual intelligence tests.* In most cases this was the Binet. A small number of children were given the Henmon-Nelson, the scores of which were converted by regression equation into equivalent Binet scores.

2. *Standardized verbal achievement test.* The Cooperative Reading Test was used. Prefreshmen and freshmen were given Test $C_1$, Form Y; older students were given $C_2$, Form T.

3. *Standardized numerical achievement tests.* Because of differences in the curricula of the various grade groups it was not possible to administer the same test of numerical achievement to all $S$s. The following tests were given according to grade placement:

Prefreshman—Iowa Everypupil Arithmetic Test, Advanced Form O.

Freshmen—Snader General Mathematics Test.

Sophomores—Cooperative Elementary Algebra Test, Form T.

Junior—Cooperative Intermediate Algebra Test

Seniors—Cooperative Geometry Test, Form 2.

4. *California Personality Test.* Two forms of this instrument were used. The intermediate form was given to prefreshmen; the secondary form was given to

all of the older groups. Two subscores were obtained, "personal adjustment" and "social adjustment."

5. *Direct Sentence Completion Test*. Ss were asked to complete 27 sentences of the type: "When I saw I was going to fail I . . . . . . . . . . . .," or "I think my father is . . . . . . . . . . ." Each sentence was given a plus or minus score depending upon the presence or absence of morbid fantasy, defeatism, overt aggression, and the like. The total score was the summation of the individual sentence scores.

6. *Indirect Sentence Completion Test*. This instrument was identical with the Direct Sentence Completion Test except that proper names were inserted for the pronoun "I," thus changing it from a "self-report" to a "projective" instrument. Boys' names were used in the male form of the instrument and girls' names in the female form. The instrument was presented as a "thinking speed" test. To reinforce this notion Ss were asked to raise their hands when they were finished and the elapsed time was written on their test booklet. This instrument was administered approximately two weeks prior to the administration of the Direct Sentence Completion Test.

7. *Group Rorschach*. Cards III, IV, IX, and X were projected on a screen. For each picture the S was presented with 10 responses and was asked to choose the three which he thought to be most appropriate. Each list of 10 contained four "pathological" responses. The S's score was the number of nonpathologic responses among his 12 choices. This group technique follows that described by Harrower-Erikson and Steiner (1945).

8. *Teacher ratings*. Each student was given three ratings by his present teachers. These ratings included: (*a*) his general desirability as a student; (*b*) his ability to become involved in learning activities; and (*c*) his possession of leadership qualities. Teachers were required to place all of their students on a five-point scale so that Categories 1 and 5 each contained one-twelfth of the students; Categories 2 and 4 each contained one-fourth of the students; and Category 3 contained one-third of the students. The values 5, 8, 10, 12, and 15 were assigned to the categories and were used in quantifying the ratings.

9. *Adjective Check List*. From a list of 24 adjectives each student was asked to choose the 6 which best described his characteristic feelings while attending classes in particular school subjects. The list contained 12 "positive" (e.g., confident, happy, eager, relaxed) and 12 "negative" adjectives (e.g., bored, restless, misunderstood, angry). The use of the negative adjectives by the experimental groups was analyzed both quantitatively and qualitatively.

## Results

With the exception of the adjective check list the results of all comparisons are shown in Table 1. Contrary to popular expectations the "satisfied"

## Table 1

**Mean Scores, Standard Deviations, and t Statistics for Satisfied and Dissatisfied Adolescents on Dependent Variables** [a]

| | Boys | | | | | Girls | | | | |
| | Dissatisfied (N = 27) | | Satisfied (N = 25) | | t | Dissatisfied (N = 20) | | Satisfied (N = 20) | | t |
| | $\bar{x}$ | s | $\bar{x}$ | s | | $\bar{x}$ | s | $\bar{x}$ | s | |
|---|---|---|---|---|---|---|---|---|---|---|
| IQ | 134.85 | 14.58 | 136.44 | 14.59 | ns | 128.45 | 15.06 | 128.00 | 11.45 | ns |
| Verbal Achievement | 49.96 | 8.69 | 50.68 | 7.87 | ns | 50.63 | 9.11 | 52.28 | 6.76 | ns |
| Numerical Achievement | 50.35 | 9.75 | 52.17 | 10.52 | ns | 47.78 | 8.61 | 48.50 | 10.26 | ns |
| Calif. Personal Adjust. | 45.58 | 9.82 | 53.40 | 7.63 | 3.18** | 47.90 | 13.03 | 54.76 | 9.25 | 1.86* |
| Calif. Social Adjust. | 44.85 | 11.37 | 51.84 | 8.93 | 2.45** | 47.00 | 13.15 | 55.76 | 7.89 | 2.50** |
| Direct Sentence Comp. | 46.93 | 10.58 | 49.25 | 10.02 | ns | 46.65 | 12.01 | 54.00 | 5.73 | 2.53** |
| Indirect Sentence Comp. | 47.19 | 9.61 | 51.29 | 6.95 | 1.75* | 49.60 | 10.35 | 53.47 | 7.97 | ns |
| Group Rorschach | 48.35 | 10.66 | 47.44 | 10.30 | ns | 47.35 | 11.35 | 54.16 | 8.32 | 2.15** |
| Teacher Rating I: Desirability as a student | 8.94 | 1.83 | 10.35 | 1.70 | 2.85** | 9.84 | 1.91 | 10.05 | 1.59 | ns |
| Teacher Rating II: Leadership qualities | 9.01 | 2.08 | 10.13 | 1.96 | 2.00* | 9.91 | 2.37 | 10.04 | 1.24 | ns |
| Teacher Rating III: Involvement in learning | 9.09 | 2.14 | 10.23 | 1.69 | 2.14** | 9.67 | 2.32 | 10.33 | 2.11 | ns |

* Significant at the .05 level.
** Significant at the .01 level.
[a] With the exception of IQ, all scores were based upon parameters of the total student body from which the experimental groups were drawn. The scores of all tests were transformed to T scores with a mean of 50 and a standard deviation of 10. For the total population the teacher ratings have a mean of 10 and a standard deviation of 2. The mean IQs for the total school population are: boys, 132, and girls, 128.

420

and "dissatisfied" students did *not* differ from each other in either general intellectual ability or in scholastic achievement. Those differences which did appear were linked to psychological rather than scholastic variables. More specifically, each of the test instruments designed to assess psychological health or "adjustment" was effective in distinguishing "satisfied" from "dissatisfied" students within one or both sex groups.

For both sexes the experimental groups were differentiatd by their scores on the California Test of Personality. The experimental groups of boys were further differentiated by their responses to the Indirect Sentence Completion Test. For girls additional differences appeared in their responses to the Direct Sentence Completion Test and the Group Rorschach.

On all of these test variables the "satisfied" group attained the "better" score—i.e., the score signifying a more adequate level of psychological functioning. It is also worthy of note that whenever a significant difference appeared, the mean score of the total student population fell between the mean scores of the experimental groups. Thus, the variables that differentiate the experimental groups tend also to distinguish them from the total population of students.

In addition to showing differences on psychological health variables, "satisfied" and "dissatisfied" boys were perceived differently by their teachers. On all three of the teachers' ratings the "satisfied" boys received more favorable judgments than did "dissatisfied" boys. The fact that this result does not appear to be true for girls lends support to the popular expectation that boys are more likely to express their negative feelings publicly than are girls. This hypothesis receives some confirmation from the results of the adjective check list which are described below.

In Table 2 are shown the number of *S*s who chose negative adjectives when asked to describe their typical classroom feelings. As they are arranged in Table 2 the adjectives reflect the rankings of four judges who were asked to rank the words on the degree to which they involved an implicit or explicit criticism of others. The 12 adjectives were typed on separate cards and were accompanied by the following directions:

On the following cards are a number of negative adjectives which a person might use to describe himself. Rank these adjectives on the degree to which they involve an implicit or explicit criticism of others. For each adjective ask the question: If a person used this adjective *to describe himself* would he also be implicitly or explicitly criticizing others? Give a rank of 1 to the adjective which would be *least* critical of others and a rank of 12 to the adjective which would be *most* critical of others.

Four psychologists served as judges. The average rank order correlation among the four sets of judgments was .84. The adjectives are presented in Table 2 according to the ranked sum-of-ranks of the judges. The adjective "inadequate" was judged as being most free of criticism of others, while the adjective "restrained" was judged as involving the greatest amount of criticism of others.

**Table 2**

**Number of Subjects Choosing Negative Adjectives when Asked to Describe Typical Classroom Feelings**

| Adjective | Boys | | | Girls | | |
|---|---|---|---|---|---|---|
| | Dissatisfied (N = 27) | Satisfied (N = 25) | Chi Square | Dissatisfied (N = 20) | Satisfied (N = 20) | Chi Square |
| Inadequate | 19 | 16 | ns | 17 | 7 | 10.42** |
| Ignorant | 19 | 13 | ns | 15 | 3 | 14.54** |
| Dull | 25 | 16 | 6.36* | 16 | 9 | 5.60* |
| Bored | 24 | 13 | 8.61** | 20 | 13 | 8.48** |
| Restless | 20 | 15 | ns | 19 | 9 | 11.90** |
| Uncertain | 20 | 21 | ns | 17 | 13 | ns |
| Angry | 15 | 4 | 8.76** | 13 | 4 | 8.29** |
| Unnoticed | 19 | 5 | 13.25** | 7 | 4 | ns |
| Unhelped | 18 | 8 | 6.24* | 9 | 6 | ns |
| Misunderstood | 16 | 5 | 8.31** | 5 | 2 | ns |
| Rejected | 12 | 3 | 6.66** | 4 | 0 | ns |
| Restrained | 17 | 2 | 16.91** | 9 | 3 | 4.29* |

\* Significant at the .05 level.
\*\* Significant at the .01 level.

As might be expected, the use of negative adjectives was far more frequent among dissatisfied students than among satisfied students. Four adjectives seemed to discriminate equally well between the experimental groups for both sexes; these were: "bored," "angry," "restrained," and "dull."

An examination of Table 2 also suggests the existence of sex differences in the students' description of their typical classroom feelings. Remembering the classificatory scheme by which the adjectives are ranked in Table 2, it appears that dissatisfied girls are somewhat less likely than dissatisfied boys to use negative adjectives involving implicit criticism of others. Dissatisfied boys, on the other hand, are less likely than dissatisfied girls to be distinguished from their satisfied counterparts by the use of adjectives *not* involving implicit criticism of others. If one thinks of criticism directed towards others within Rosenzweig's schema of "intropunitiveness" and "extrapunitiveness" (Murray, 1945), then the observed sex differences may be conceptualized by saying that dissatisfied girls are more *intropunitive* than satisfied girls; dissatisfied boys are more *extrapunitive* than satisfied boys.

This difference in the direction of aggression may provide a context for the obtained differences in teacher ratings discussed earlier. If the dissatisfied boy is more likely than his female counterpart to lay the blame for his dissatisfaction upon others in his environment, particularly school authorities, it is reasonable to expect that he would be viewed as somewhat less than completely desirable by the classroom teacher. The dissatisfied girl, on the other hand, seems more willing to direct her negative feelings inward, thus avoiding the additional risk of counter-aggression by school authorities or by other adults.

## Discussion

Two major conclusions are suggested by the findings of this study. First, dissatisfaction with school appears to be part of a larger picture of psychological discontent rather than a direct reflection of inefficient functioning in the classroom. It is almost as if dissatisfaction were a product of a pervasive perceptual set that colors the student's view of himself and his world. Second, it appears that the "dynamics" of dissatisfaction operate differently for boys and girls. Boys seem to project the causes of their discontent upon the world around them so that adults are seen as rejecting and lacking in understanding. This tendency to blame adults may be one reason why these boys are seen as less attractive by teachers than are satisfied boys. Girls, on the other hand, are more likely to be self-critical, turning blame for their dissatisfaction inward. Feelings of inadequacy, ignorance, and restlessness more sharply differentiate satisfied and dissatisfied girls than is the case with boys. This tendency to be intropunitive may partially explain why teacher ratings fail to distinguish between our two experimental groups of girls.

The atypicality of the sample population used in this research places a number of limitations upon the inferential statements which can be made on the basis of these findings. Fortunately, however, the major portion of the investigation has recently been replicated using seventh and eighth grade lower-class Negro adolescents as *S*s (Spillman, 1959). The findings of the latter study are essentially the same as those reported here. Again the psychological rather than the intellectual or scholastic variables discriminated between satisfied and dissatisfied students. The findings with respect to the use of negative adjectives were not as clear-cut but, again, every intropunitive adjective was used more frequently by dissatisfied girls as compared with dissatisfied boys, while the latter exceeded the girls in their use of extrapunitive adjectives.

It should be noted that even the most satisfied students made some use of negative adjectives when asked to describe their typical feelings in the classroom. Also, the average member of the satisfied group expressed some dissatisfaction on one-sixth of the questions in the Student Opinion Poll. These two observations should serve as ample cautions against the danger of interpreting any sign of dissatisfaction with school as symptomatic of deeper psychological difficulties. Apparently, some degree of dissatisfaction is the rule rather than the exception. Nonetheless, the responses of the extremely disgruntled group of students leaves little doubt that dissatisfaction with school, like beauty, is frequently in the eye of the beholder.

## Summary

This investigation examines the differences in psychological functioning and classroom effectiveness between two groups of adolescents—those who are satisfied with their recent school experiences and those who are dissatisfied. The major findings point to: (a) the relevance of psychological health data rather than scholastic achievement data in understanding dissatisfaction with school; (b) the importance of differentiating the attitudes of dissatisfied girls from those of dissatisfied boys, the former being characterized by feelings of personal inadequacy, the latter by feelings critical of school authorities. Rosenzweig's concepts of intropunitiveness and extrapunitiveness are applied to these findings and a relevant theoretical framework is proposed.

## References

1. HARROWER-ERIKSON, M. R. and M. E. STEINER. *Large Scale Rorschach Techniques.* Springfield, Ill.: Charles C. Thomas (1945).

2. MURRAY, H. A. *Explorations in Personality.* New York: Oxford Univer. Press (1938).

3. SPILLMAN, R. J. Psychological and Scholastic Correlates of Dissatisfaction with School among Adolescents. Unpublished master's thesis. Univer. of Chicago (1959).

## 38

# THE EFFECTS OF AN ELEMENTARY SCHOOL FAST-LEARNER PROGRAM ON CHILDREN'S SOCIAL RELATIONSHIPS *

## Mary Goldworth

Among the provisions for exceptional children are special classes. These may be provided for handicapped or gifted. In the study reported here, fast-learners attended special classes in art, biological science, physical science, or social studies for two 90-minute periods per week. Pupils were combined into two levels or groups for these special classes, one including those from grades four through six; the other made up of pupils from grades seven and eight. The special classes were taught by teachers who were specialists in the respective subjects. Pre-tests and post-tests were given all pupils, both regular and fast-learner. They consisted of a sociometric questionnaire and a social distance scale. The experiment lasted five months. The results indicate that the children's social relationships remained relatively stable during the experimental period.

*Questions:*

1. There is one finding in this study that is at variance with the other results. What is it? Which of the author's possible reasons given seem most plausible to you? Why?

2. Compare the results of the study here reported with those of the study by Gallagher (selection 41). Do they differ or conflict in any respect? If so, what is it?

* * *

The recent mounting concern about the education of gifted children appears to be an appropriate one. Available studies suggest that intellectual potentialities of the gifted have been fulfilled inadequately [7; 16, p. 23;

* Reprinted from *Exceptional Children,* **26:**59–63 (October 1959), by permission of author and publisher.

18].* There are further indications that attention must be directed to socio-emotional factors in the school situation, in view of the relationships of such factors to achievement in school and in later life [5; 16, p. 132–62, 35–37]. A growing number of schools are attempting to implement more adequate programs [6], although educational efforts which take account of such findings have been considered seriously lacking [4, p. iii; 15].

Three basic schemes most commonly considered and upon which a variety of educational practices have been based are: acceleration, which involves faster-than-usual "promotion"; "enrichment" of pupil experience in the regular age-grade placement; and special grouping, involving the identification of gifted children and placing them together for instructional purposes. There has been much discussion of and disagreement about the desirability and effectiveness of these various approaches [13, 14, 17], and an examination of the arguments and evidence suggests that more information is needed to clarify the issues. One of the fears frequently voiced is that special grouping practices may promote attitudes of intolerance and may undesirably affect children's acceptance of each other [9, p. 403–404; 13, 39–41; 16, p. 205]. In this study an attempt was made to determine whether or not such negative attitudes may in fact be present by examining the effects on children's social relationships of a program for fast-learning children which involved part-time special grouping.

## Experimental Setting

The school district in which this study was conducted is located in a suburban community in the San Francisco Bay area. It provided a program whereby fast-learning children attended special classes held for 90-minute periods twice a week. Pupils admitted to this special program were those in the fourth through eighth grades whose IQ's were 130 or higher on the California Test of Mental Maturity or 120 or higher on the short form of the Revised Stanford-Binet. Four subject areas were offered for study: art, biological science, physical science, and social studies. Each child was assigned, as nearly as possible, to a class of his chosen interest, as determined by his responses to a questionnaire. In each area two groups were formed: pupils from grade levels four through six, and those from grades seven and eight. The number of children in each group was limited to fifteen. Since the building in which the special classes were held was located some distance away from the other schools in the district, all children were

* Figure in brackets apply to references at end of article.

transported to and from these classes by school bus. The early part of the 1955–56 school year was devoted to program planning and identification of fast-learners. The special classes were conducted during the five-month period beginning January 1956. The schools in this district do not practice mid-year promotions.

Four special teachers were employed on a half-time basis, one for each subject area. All of them were doctoral candidates in the School of Education at Stanford University, held a California Teaching Credential, and each was a specialist in one of the subject areas involved. Attempts were made to have the special and regular teachers work closely together in order that all might have a common understanding of the goals and activities of both the regular and the fast-learner program. Such coordination was achieved to only a limited extent during the experimental period because of circumstances within the school district.

In order to select an experimental and a control group for this study, the following procedures were used. Among grade levels four through eight in the eight schools throughout the district, 63 classrooms [1] were found to contain fast-learners. These classrooms were randomly divided by school and by grade level, into two groups, one of which was designated as experimental and the other as control. These two groups were comparable in size, IQ distribution, and number of fast-learners. They were also found to be comparable on the classroom index of "degree of acceptance," as indicated by an analysis of a set of data obtained from pre-measures at the beginning of the experimental period. The social distance scale and "degree of acceptance" will be discussed later. The fast-learners who were in the experimental group (N-204) participated in the special program; the ones in the control group did not (N-211). The following classification of groups was used:

1. *Experimental fast-learners,* who attended special classes

2. *Control fast-learners,* who did not attend special classes

3. *Non-fast-learner experimentals,* who were not designated as fast-learners but attended classrooms in which fast-learners were participating in the special program

4. *Non-fast-learner controls,* who were not designated as fast-learners and who attended classrooms in which fast-learners did not participate in the special program

5. *Experimental classrooms,* regular classrooms in which there were experimental fast-learners

---

[1] In these classrooms there was a total of 1,685 children, out of which 415 were identified as fast-learners.

6. *Control classrooms,* regular classrooms in which there were control fast-learners.

Pre-measures and post-measures were administered [2] to all children in experimental and control classrooms, using the Columbia Classroom Social Distance Scale [3, p. 401–402] and three sociometric tests. The former measure requires each pupil to rate each of his classmates on a five-point scale:

1. "I would like to have him as one of my best friends."
2. "I would like to have him in my group but not as a close friend."
3. "I would like to be with him once in a while but not for a long time."
4. "I don't mind his being in our room but I want nothing to do with him."
5. "I wish he were not in our room."

The sociometric test asked each pupil to indicate which three classmates he would most prefer to "work-with," "play-with," and "sit-with" (1, 2, 8, 10, 11, 12).

The experimental and control groups were compared, by grade levels, in terms of each of the following five variables:

1. change in children's acceptance of each other as friends
2. change in children's acceptance of fast-learners as friends
3. change in fast-learner's acceptance of classmates as friends
4. change in the degree of cohesion within regular classroom groups
5. change in the degree of fast-learner sub-group preferences within regular classroom groups.

The significance of differences between experimental and control groups with respect to these variables were tested by use of chi-square.

### Experimental Questions and Findings

**1. Is there a difference between children in the experimental classrooms and children in the control classrooms with respect to change in their acceptance of each other as friends?**

"Degree of acceptance" for each pupil was obtained from a raw score consisting of the number of ratings he received in the "best-friend" category of the social distance scale. However, this raw acceptance score could not be used directly for a pre- and post-comparison since the number of chil-

[2] Pre-measures were administered during the third week in January, 1956, and post-measures were administered during the last week in May. Thus, the attitudes studied reflect a period of four-and-a-half months.

dren in a classroom (and hence, the total number of ratings received by each child on all five points of the scale) often changed for the pre-period to the post-period. In order to eliminate this difficulty, each raw acceptance score was divided by the total number of ratings a child received from his classmates, thereby transforming it into percent. Change in degree of acceptance was then determined by comparing pre- and post-percents for every child. The proportions of children showing increases, decreases, and no change, were determined and the differences between those for experimental classrooms and those for control classrooms were tested for significance. At all grade levels, 4–6 and 7–8, it was found that the proportion of children showing an increase in the degree to which they were accepted as friends by their classmates was significantly greater (P<.001) in control groups than in experimental groups. These results may be explained by the fact that fast-learners were away from their classrooms for two periods a week. The way in which the program was implemented during this first year of experimentation suggests other possible explanations. Because of various practical considerations, regular classroom teachers did not participate in the planning of the program. In addition, there was no opportunity for organized coordination of effort between them and the special teachers, especially since the special classes were held in a school building some distance away from the other schools. These conditions may have limited the effectiveness with which the regular teachers could exploit the fast-learner program so as to maintain the most adequate social atmosphere possible for the pupils in the classrooms. Perhaps they found it difficult to make good use of the times during which fast-learners were out of the room attending special classes. Perhaps, too, lacking intimate knowledge of the progress that their fast-learner pupils were making in the special classes, they found it difficult to integrate special class experiences into the regular classroom activities. Obviously, such problems could affect the teachers' satisfaction with their work and consequently affect the degree to which children could enjoy their associations with one another within the context of their educational experience.

Another explanation of the results might be found in parental attitudes. It was hoped that parents would view the fast-learner program as an integral part of the regular school program and as a means of providing for the individual differences among school children. Unfortunately, no data on parent attitudes are available. However, since parents whose children were in the experimental classrooms were more directly in contact with the fast-learner program than parents whose children were in control classrooms, it seems likely that their opinions on this subject would have been not only more defined but also considerably more diverse. Some may have felt that the fast-learner classes offered better educational opportunities than the regular classes. Others may have felt that the special classes detracted from the effectiveness of the regular classes because they disrupted the school routine, or because they discriminated between children, giving special attention to some and not to others. In either case, children's enthusiasm for the regular classroom may have been dampened, thereby affecting their social relationships with classmates. The reader is reminded that this discussion pertains to a comparison between all children in experimental classrooms and all children in control classrooms.

**2. Is there a difference between experimental fast-learners and control fast-learners with respect to change in the degree to which they are accepted as friends by their classmates?**

Procedures for this question were identical to those used for the previous question except that, instead of considering all children in experimental classrooms, only fast-learners were compared. In grades 4–6, a greater proportion of controls showed an increase in the degree to which they were accepted as friends by their classmates. The difference was not significant $(.10 > P > .05)$ but warrants attention since it is in the same direction as that found above. The same reasons are offered in explanation. In grades 7–8, the difference between experimental and control fast-learners was not significant. $(.80 > P > .70)$. Possible reasons are that these children are older, more mature, and more stable in their feelings and that they are more accustomed to having their classmates leave the room for a variety of reasons.

**3. Is there a difference between experimental fast-learners and control fast-learners with respect to change in the degree to which they accept their classmates as friends?**

Procedures were identical to those described above with the exception that, instead of considering ratings made by classmates on each fast-learner, the analysis involved the ratings made by each fast-learner of his classmates. At all grade levels, 4–6 and 7–8, no significant differences were found between experimental and control fast-learners $(.50 > P > .30)$. Thus, the fast-learner program had no apparent effect on the feelings of fast-learners toward their classmates within the regular classroom setting. This finding seems to contradict the common view that special grouping fosters attitudes of intolerance.

**4. Is there a difference between experimental classrooms and control classrooms with respect to the degree of change in "group cohesion"?**

Each of the criteria on the sociometric test—"work-with," "play-with," and "sit-with"—was examined separately. A measure of group cohesion was determined for each regular classroom by dividing the actual number of mutual choices by the total possible number of mutual choices. The proportions of classrooms showing an increase, a decrease, or no change were determined and differences between experimental and control classrooms were then tested for significance. With one exception, no significant difference was found at any one of the grade levels or for any of the three sociometric test criteria. Significance levels ranged from $.20 > P > .10$ to $.90 > .80$. Thus, for the most part, the fast-learner program did not have any apparent effect on the volume of positive interaction (i.e., volume of mutual choices) within classroom groups with respect to any one of the educational settings referred to by the various sociometric criteria. These results seem to be in contradiction with the findings reported for question #1, where children in experimental classrooms showed a decrease in the degree to which they accepted each other as friends. However, the contradiction is more apparent than real. The explanation probably lies in the difference between the two measuring instruments and the ways in which the data were analyzed. The first question was concerned with the number of "best-friend" ratings, whereas the present one is concerned with the number of mutual choices. It is possible for the number of best-friend ratings to change while the number of mutual choices remains the same or even changes in opposite directions. The finding of these two questions indicate that, in the experimental classrooms, there was a decrease in the proportion of classmates who were accepted as best friends but no effect on the proportion of mutual friendships.

**5. Is there a difference between experimental and control classrooms with respect to the degree of change in the fast-learner "sub-group preference"?**

Data and procedures were the same as those for question #4. Sub-group preference was determined for each regular classroom by dividing the number of choices made by fast-learners of other fast-learner classmates by the total possible number of such choices that could have been made by fast-learners. At all grade levels, and for each of the three criteria, no significant difference was found between experimental and control fast-learners. Significance levels ranged from $.50 > P > .30$ to $.99 > P.98$. The fast-learner program did not result in the formation of identifiable subgroups or cliques among the fast-learners within their regular classroom groups.

## Implications

On the whole then, this study suggests that for regular classroom groups, the fast-learner program: ·(a) had a limiting effect on the number of classmates which children accepted as best friends, and (b) had no effect on fast-learners' acceptance of classmates as best friends, on group cohesion, or on sub-group preference. It is concluded that, despite the occurrence of some negative changes, these children's social relationships remained relatively stable.

Several precautions are necessary in interpreting these findings. The fact that this study was conducted under conditions which permitted only limited opportunities for coordination of effort between regular classroom teachers and special class teachers seems to constitute an important limitation on the experimental program. Another consideration is that the findings of this study are based upon an assessment of attitudes over a period of somewhat less than five months in duration, and that this period was in the latter part of the school year.

One must bear in mind that the use of sociometric instruments and of large number of subjects provides only limited information about social relationships and does not warrant specific generalization regarding the broad area of socio-emotional growth. Further, sociometric questions emphasize those educational objectives concerned with how well children like each other and get along together. Such objectives are not the only bases upon which the adequacy of an educational program should be judged, particularly if one is concerned with such dimensions as motivation, initiative, and creative thinking.

With regard to the educational program, a distinction must be made between administrative procedure (e.g., the organization of special classes) and actual learning experiences gained by the child. It is probable that two programs similar in procedure will differ qualitatively in their educational value.

It should be clear that this study did not examine the relative merits of different types of special provisions for the gifted. Rather, it compared a particular special grouping program with the kind of treatment ordinarily provided within a regular classroom setting. Although these two settings were found to be about equivalent in terms of most of the variables studied, the possibility that the special grouping program had positive or negative effects on other variables of interest to the school is yet to be explored.

## References

1. BRONFENBRENNER, URIE. "The Measurement of Sociometric Status, Structure and Development." *Sociometry Monographs*. No. 6: School of Education, University of Michigan: Beacon House, 1945.

2. CRISWELL, JOAN. "Measurement of Group Integration." *Sociometry*, X, No. 3, 1947, pp. 259–62.

3. CUNNINGHAM, RUTH, *et al. Understanding the Behavior of Boys and Girls.* New York: Bureau of Publications, Teachers College, Columbia University, 1951.

4. EDUCATIONAL POLICIES COMMISSION. *Education of the Gifted.* Washington, D. C.: National Education Association, 1950.

5. GOWAN, J. C. "The Under-achieving Gifted Child—A Problem for Everyone," *Exceptional Children*, XXI, April 1955, pp. 247–49; 270–71.

6. HAVIGHURST, ROBERT J., *et al.* "A Survey of the Education of Gifted Children." University of Chicago Press Supplement, *Educ. Monograph*, No. 83, November 1955.

7. HOLLINSHEAD, BYRON S. "Who Should Go to College in America." *College Board Review*, XVI, February 1952, pp. 248–53.

8. JAHODA, M., M. DEUTSCH, and S. COOK (eds.). *Research Methods in Social Relations.* New York: Dryden Press, 1953, Vol. II.

9. JUSTMAN, J. and J. W. WRIGHTSTONE. "Opinions of Junior High School Principals Concerning the Organization of Special Classes for Gifted Children." *Educational Administration and Supervision*, XXXVII, November 1951, pp. 296–404.

10. LINDZEY, GARDNER and EDGAR F. BORGATTA. "Sociometric Measurement," *Handbook of Social Psychology*, GARDNER LINDZEY (ed.). Cambridge: Wesley Publishing Company, 1954, Part II.

11. MORENO, J. L. *Who Shall Survive?* Washington, D. C.: Nervous and Mental Disease Publishing Company, 1934.

12. NORTHWAY, MARY L. *A Primer of Sociometry.* Toronto, University of Toronto Press, 1952.

13. PASSOW, A. H. *et al. Planning for Talented Youth: Considerations for Public Schools.* New York: Bureau of Publications. Teachers College, Columbia University, 1955.

14. SCHEIFELE, M. *The Gifted Child in the Regular Classroom.* New York: Bureau of Publications, Teachers College, Columbia University, 1953.

15. WILSON, FRANK T. "A Survey of Educational Provisions for Young Gifted Children in the United States, and of Studies and Problems Related Thereto," *J. of Genet. Psychol.*, LXXV, September 1949, pp. 3–19.

16. WITTY, PAUL (ed.). *The Gifted Child.* Boston: D. C. Heath and Company, 1951.

17. WORCESTER, DEAN AMORY. *The Education of Children of Above Average Mentality.* University of Nebraska Press, 1956.

18. WRENN, C. G. "Potential Research Talent in the Sciences Based on Intelligence Quotients of Ph. D's," *The Educ. Rec.*, XXX, January 1949, pp. 20–22

## 39

# THE EFFECT OF TEACHER-PUPIL CONTACTS INVOLVING PRAISE ON THE SOCIOMETRIC CHOICES OF STUDENTS *

## Ned A. Flanders and Sulo Havumaki

An experiment is reported in this article involving tenth grade boys and girls organized into seventeen groups of ten each for a discussion. The question to which the research was directed is: When a teacher praises a pupil before a group for his contribution to the discussion of an attractive activity in which the group may possibly participate, how does this affect the frequency with which the group chooses him to represent it in that activity? The participants did not know each other before the experiment so that there was no influence on their choices from previous experience. Their reactions to the teacher leading the discussion were, in the great majority of groups, favorable. Thus, whether or not they liked the discussion was also not a factor in making their choices. Your first reaction as you read the report may be that the results of the experiment could have been predicted in advance. On the other hand, more thoughtful consideration may make this conclusion seem less certain.

*Questions:*

1. Does the typical tenth grade pupil generally follow the teacher's lead in approving or disapproving his peers? Give evidence supporting your answer.

2. What factors do you think influenced the choices made by the students in this experiment?

\* \* \*

Many teachers have used sociometric data to assign a choice value to any individual in a group. The individual who receives the most choices has

* Reprinted from the *Journal of Educational Psychology,* **51**:65–68 (April 1960), by permission of senior author and publisher.

the highest choice value, and the rest of the group can be arranged in rank order. Very little has been said about how teachers can influence the choice value of a student.

The present study is an attempt to see if teacher-pupil contacts involving praise will affect the sociometric choices received later on. The hypothesis to be tested is that contacts involving praise, given by a prestige figure, will increase the choice value of the student.

The following conditions must be controlled to test this hypothesis:

1. The group situation must involve an attractive activity and the praise given by the prestige figure must be centered on the relationship between an individual's behavior and the major activity of the group; merely to talk about the individual per se would not be a fair test.

2. Information given to the group must be controlled by the teacher so that certain individuals can be singled out for attention.

3. Any acquaintanceship patterns existing in the group prior to the experimental discussions must be identified so that it can be demonstrated that the factor of personal acquaintance did not bias the results.

4. The criterion question used to elicit sociometric choices must be related to the major activity of the group and appear to have consequences in the future activities of the group. This eliminates such questions as, "Who contributed the most to this discussion?"

5. The prestige figure controlling the flow of information must be liked by the group, or at least not disliked.

## Procedure

In a study conducted at the University of Minnesota, Laboratory for Research in Social Relations, 33 groups of 10 subjects each (hereafter referred to as Ss) were involved in an experiment in which sociometric choices were made. In all groups the Ss consisted of approximately an equal number of boys and girls from tenth-grade classes of Minneapolis and St. Paul high schools. It was the belief of these groups that they were to appear in a Quiz Kid contest between schools from Minneapolis and St. Paul. Each group was to decide whether their group would appear on a radio or TV quiz program, either alternative being possible. This discussion was led by a teacher-trainer, not known to any of the students, whose function it was to help the students reach a decision and then train them for the performance. Elaborate arrangements were made to impress all Ss that the Quiz Kid contest was an attractive and exciting experience. Practically all Ss approached the problem of choosing between radio and TV programs seriously. At the very end of each experimental session when all Ss learned there would be no contest, sincere expressions of disappointment were displayed in each group. Judging from the manner in which all sessions were conducted and the behavior of the Ss, there is no doubt in the minds of the authors that the prospect of participating in the contest was attractive and stimulating to the Ss. Thus, these group discussions satisfactorily meet the first half of Condition 1 mentioned previously.

Besides the attractiveness of the group's activity, Conditions 1 and 2 refer to the nature of the teacher-trainer and the method of giving this information. The teacher-trainer's behavior for 17 groups was individually oriented, that is, he called on certain individuals by name and praised their contributions to the discussion. The teacher behavior thus served to provide praise for certain individuals in the group by focusing attention on these individuals in the individually oriented condition. The individuals attended to in this manner were always those who happened to sit in the odd numbered seats around a U shaped table. The original choice of seats was up to the Ss. The procedure of calling only on Ss seated in the odd numbered seats effectively restricted all verbal communication to these Ss and the teacher-trainer. While many Ss seated in the even numbered seats raised their hands indicating a desire to speak, they were not called on. Thus the teacher-trainer's praise reactions were clearly centered on Ss who were easily identified during the individual approach.

In the remaining 16 groups the teacher-trainer behaved in a group oriented fashion and praised the group as a whole for the ideas contributed by individual members. He called on no individuals by name and anyone who wished to talk was allowed to do so.

The verbal behavior of the teacher-trainer was categorized from voice recordings of all the group discussions. These categories consisted of a simple analysis of praise statements made by the teacher-trainer in response to student contributions. In the individually oriented condition most praise statements were made with reference to specific individuals; in the group oriented condition the praise statements were never coupled with an individual's name and were interpreted in terms of the group whenever this could reasonably be done.

Praise statements became standardized during pilot runs prior to conducting the discussions reported here. Examples of statements used in the individual approach are: "I'm glad John mentioned that point because it is very important for this group to consider in order to make a good decision"; "That's a very good suggestion, Mary"; "That's very true. I think Jim will be a big help to this team." During a group approach it was not always easy to turn a praise statement away from the individual toward the group, for example: "That's an important point. This team has good ideas"; "Good! A second good point; can anyone [looking at the group] add any more?" Occasionally, during the group approach only, the teacher-trainer would be interrupted after saying, "That's a good idea . . ." before praise could be turned toward the group. Thus, some praise statements during the group approach were classified as individual praise statements. An example of a praise statement that is clearly group oriented is: "This group is going to make a fine team."

The comparison of the praise statements of the teacher-trainer's individual and group oriented behavior patterns shown in Table 1 indicates that

### Table 1
### Distribution of Teacher Praise Statements

|  | Individual Condition (17 groups) | | Group Condition (14 groups)[a] | |
| --- | --- | --- | --- | --- |
|  | N | % | N | % |
| Praise to Individuals | 114 | 79.1 | 28 | 30.1 |
| Praise to Group | 30 | 20.9 | 65 | 69.9 |
| Totals | 144 | 100.0 | 93 | 100.0 |

[a] Two groups lost as recordings were inadvertently erased.

neither pattern is 100% consistent. Actually, the differences are greater than indicated in Table 1. For example, the data do not reveal such important aspects of the teacher-trainer's behavior as looking directly at an individual, calling on him by name, and praising his ideas in association with his name, as contrasted with looking generally at the whole group, not calling on any one individual, and never associating the name of an individual with praise. The two patterns of teacher behavior were clearly different to an observer and easily identified by the tape recording with 100% accuracy.

Thus far the discussion has dealt with the first two conditions necessary to the study; next, Conditions 3 and 4 will be considered. After each group was seated, they were first asked to list the names of all the Ss with whom they were acquainted and, in addition, place an "X" beside the name of any person who was a good friend. For all experimental groups the indication of friendship was so infrequent (a total of six friendship pairs) that they are not reported here. This was undoubtedly due to the cooperation of school authorities who were asked to choose $S$s for each group from separate homerooms. The pre-discussion acquaintanceship data show that 477 $S$s were acquainted with the 85 $S$s who sat in the odd numbered seats before the discussion started; similarly, 505 $S$s were acquainted with those $S$s who sat in the even numbered seats. Of the total (928) acquaintanceships reported, 48.6% involved $S$s in the odd numbered seats, 51.4% involved $S$s in the even numbered seats. The hypothesis that this difference is significant can be tested by chi square. Since chi square $= 0.012$, the difference is clearly not significant. In addition, the $S$s seated in the even numbered seats are slightly better known, so that a more rigorous test of the main hypothesis is possible.

**Table 2**
**Distribution of Choices for Program Participants**

|  | *Individual Treatment* *(17 groups)* | | *Group Treatment* *(16 groups)* | |
| --- | --- | --- | --- | --- |
|  | *N* | *%* | *N* | *%* |
| To Odd Seats | 496 | 59.3 | 384 | 48.6 |
| To Even Seats | 341 | 40.7 | 406 | 51.4 |
| Totals | 837* | 100.0 | 790** | 100.0 |

Note: Since some $S$s made only four choices, * does not equal $5 \times 17 = 850$ and ** does not equal $5 \times 16 = 800$.

After each discussion the teacher-trainer collected sociometric information in response to the statement, "List five members of the group whom you think would be good program participants." It was explained that two teams, size 10 each, would result in 20 $S$s being in the studio ready to answer the quiz questions, and this was far too many. Therefore, each team would have five program participants who would answer the questions and five helpers who could help the participants. The $S$s were told that their own group choices would be used to identify the program participants. The results of their selection are shown in Table 2.

## Results

The data in Table 2 follow the prediction that $S$s seated in the odd numbered seats in the individual treatment and given praise by the teacher-trainer would receive more choices than would occur by chance, and the same comparison in the group treatment would show no such trend. The significance of 59.3% distribution compared with a hypothetical 50–50 split can be calculated by using the standard error of correlated proportions. Testing the significance of a 59.3–40.7 split by this method yields a critical ratio of 2.98, indicating a 0.0028 probability that this difference could have occurred by chance. If one ignores the probable interdependence of the choice data and uses a chi square test on the data in Table 2, chi square = 19.063, indicating a probability of 0.001 for one degree of freedom.

The fifth condition. listed at the beginning of this article refers to the requirement that the $S$s like or at least not dislike the teacher-trainer. After the discussions, the teacher-trainer would leave, and the students were informed by the host-experimenter that it was not necessary for them to continue with the teacher-trainer who had led the discussions unless they

### Table 3
### Desire to Continue with Same Teacher-Trainer

|          | Individual Treatment | | Group Treatment | |
|----------|-------|-------|--------|-------|
|          | N     | %     | N      | %     |
| Yes      | 141   | 82.9  | 136    | 85.5  |
| Not Sure | 27    | 15.9  | 20     | 12.6  |
| No       | 2     | 1.2   | 3      | 1.9   |
| Totals   | 170   | 100.0 | 159[a] | 100.0 |

[a] One $S$ failed to answer this question.

wanted to. They were instructed to indicate their feelings toward the teacher-trainer by checking the item, "Would you like to continue working with the same teacher-trainer?"

Table 3 indicates that there is little difference between the two conditions of teacher behavior as to the degree of liking or of disliking of the teacher-trainer. The data for 329 $S$s are shown in Table 3.

The hypothesis that the distribution of answers for the individual treatment are not significantly different from the distribution of answers in the group treatment can be tested by chi square. A chi square = 0.966 for two degrees of freedom fails to reject this hypothesis.

### Summary

In a decision making experiment sociometric data were collected from 330 tenth-grade students after they had interacted with a teacher who praised their participation. In 17 10-man groups the teacher interacted only with *S*s seated in the odd numbered seats. In another 16 groups, all *S*s were allowed to talk and statements involving praise were directed to the group as a whole. In the former situation the *S*s in the odd numbered seats received significantly more choices than did the *S*s seated in the even numbered seats. In the latter situation, the difference between *S*s in the odd and even numbered seats was not significant.

There are undoubtedly many different ways to increase the choice value of students in a classroom. The results of this experiment indicate that teacher-pupil interaction involving praise that is supportive and constructive is likely to increase the choice value of a student indicating greater acceptance by his peers.

# 40

## SEX DIFFERENCES IN THE DISTRIBUTION OF TEACHER APPROVAL AND DISAPPROVAL AMONG SIXTH-GRADE CHILDREN *

### William J. Meyer and George G. Thompson

Most teachers in the public schools are women. In the elementary grades male teachers are comparatively rare; in secondary schools they are still outnumbered but by a much smaller margin. The effect of the predominance of female teachers on classroom climate, conventions, and procedures has been the subject of many studies. In the one reported here the authors attempt to answer the question of whether female teachers react differently to boys than they do to girls with respect to bestowing of approval and disapproval. Do boys receive more or less of each than girls? If so, what are the nature and direction of the differences? A related question also investigated has to do with the perception by pupils of such differences as may be found. Three sixth-grade classrooms were the subjects of the experiment. Each classroom was observed for a total of thirty hours spread in short periods over a school year. Interactions between teachers and pupils were recorded and classified according to whether the teacher verbally approved or disapproved a pupil's behavior. Observer agreement for both classifications was high. Pupils were also asked to list names of classmates who fitted situations described in which children typically receive either approval or disapproval. Results are discussed in relation to other studies, to the American culture, and as to the probable reasons for teacher responses to various kinds of behavior in boys and in girls.

*Questions:*

1. Do boys receive more disapproval from teachers as reported here? What about approval contacts? How do you account for this? Do the authors offer an explanation?

* Reprinted from the *Journal of Educational Psychology*, **47**:385–396 (November 1956), by permission of senior author and publisher.

2. Are boys just naturally more aggressive than girls? If they are, how can the school adjust to this so as to contribute to boys' adjustment to schools?

*   *   *

This study was designed to investigate the relative frequency of women teachers' approval and disapproval evaluations of sixth-grade male as contrasted with female pupils. The relevant data for this study were obtained by means of two independent techniques: thirty hours of direct observation of teacher-pupil interactions in each of three classrooms; and, the use of a modification of the "Guess Who?" technique to determine if the children themselves were aware of any sex differences in their teachers' approval and disapproval evaluations.

There is considerable agreement among psychologists that the use of approval by the teacher results in better learning and probably in better over-all adjustment [14, 18].* Some studies [19, 24] have shown that personal maladjustments in teachers have deleterious effects on the adjustment level of the children in their classes.

In a series of studies by Anderson *et al.* [1–3], using a sample of kindergarten-age children, the data indicate that teachers typically use statements of a dominative nature in their interactions with the children in their classes. Anderson further reports that the teachers in his study tended to levy most of their dominative and/or integrative overtures on only a few pupils to the relative neglect of the other children in the classroom. Further evidence of this nature is reported in a study by deGroat and Thompson using four sixth-grade classrooms [10]. In addition to reporting inequities in teacher approval and disapproval they also found that teachers give more praise to the youngsters who are brighter, better adjusted and higher achievers. The more poorly adjusted and the duller children were observed by these investigators to receive more disapproval from their teachers.

The purpose of the present investigation is to shed more light on the ways in which teachers respond toward the pupils in their classrooms. Extensive research findings have been reported in the literature [11, 12, 20, 21, 28] which consistently show that boys are more aggressive and generally more "unmanageable" than girls. It is our hypothesis that this "masculine" behavior will result in male pupils receiving a larger number of dominative, or punitive, contacts than girls from their teacher, who is usually a woman from the middle socio-economic stratum of our society. That is, we feel that

* Figure in brackets apply to references at end of article.

the behavior of boys in the typical classroom is of such a nature as to make it less acceptable to teachers who probably attempt to perpetuate certain middle-class standards of what "good" classroom behavior should be. We believe that girls usually display behavior more in conformity to the standards perceived as "good" by the average elementary school teacher and will therefore receive fewer disapproval contacts and more approval contacts from their teachers.

Assuming that the above hypotheses are supported by the data we would also predict that children of elementary school age will recognize, and take for granted, that boys receive more disapproval and blame from their teachers than girls.

### Experimental Procedure

In order to test the hypothesis that boys receive a larger number of dominative, or disapproval, evaluations from their teachers than do girls, teacher-pupil interaction within three sixth-grade classrooms were recorded for a total sample of thirty hours per classroom. These time samples of classroom behavior were spread over an entire school year. Among other things being studied, interactions between teachers and pupils were classified into two categories: (a) praise contacts (teacher initiated interactions with a child in which she verbally expressed approval of some behavior which the child had displayed), and (b) blame contacts (teacher initiated interactions with a child in which she verbally expressed disapproval for some bit of behavior which the child had displayed). Observer agreement for the praise classification ranged from eighty-four to one hundred per cent with a median of approximately ninety-two per cent. Observer agreement for the blame classification ranged from fifty-seven to one hundred per cent, with a median of approximately ninety-three per cent.

In an attempt to cast some light on children's perceptions of any sex differences in teacher disapproval, a modified "Guess Who?" approach was employed. The "Guess Who?" approach used in this study required each child to nominate fellow class members for a number of situations in which children are receiving approval or disapproval from their teacher for some behavior. (See deGroat and Thompson [10] for a more complete description of these scales and information about their reliabilities.) The behavior descriptions were selected on the basis of their familiarity to children and contain a fairly representative sample of situations in which children typically receive either approval or disapproval from their teachers. Each child was required to list the names of four of his classmates whom he thought fitted each of the behavior descriptions most adequately.

## Results

Fisher's *t* test was used to determine the reliability of the obtained sex differences.[1] The difference between disapproval contacts received by boys and by girls from their teachers was statistically significant in each of the three classrooms. As predicted, the boys received the larger number of disapproval contacts. These differences may be interpreted according to our

### Table I
**Sex Differences in Frequency of Teachers' Disapproval Contacts**

|  | *Classroom A* | | *Classroom B* | | *Classroom C* | |
|---|---|---|---|---|---|---|
|  | *Boys* | *Girls* | *Boys* | *Girls* | *Boys* | *Girls* |
| N | 10 | 9 | 12 | 14 | 17 | 16 |
| Mean | 11.10 | 2.67 | 10.75 | 2.79 | 10.06 | 1.44 |
| S.D. | 7.62 | 2.18 | 9.27 | 2.42 | 14.42 | 1.59 |
| *t* | 3.20** | | 3.11** | | 2.37* | |
| *F* | 12.22** | | 14.67** | | 130.36** | |
| $t_{01}$† | 3.30 | | 3.10 | | 2.92 | |

\* Significant at the five per cent level.
\*\* Significant at the one per cent level.
† See footnote 2.

hypothesis as supporting the notion that teachers are responding with counter-aggression to the greater expression of aggression by boys. The results obtained in analyzing the teachers' praise contacts with boys and girls are presented in Table II. The only statistically significant differences obtained for this variable was in school B. However, the boys received more praise than the girls in each of the classrooms. It may be that the teachers are attempting to reinforce any positive behavior that the boys may display. Or this tendency to praise boys more than girls may reflect compensatory behavior for guilt feelings created in the teacher by her excessive aggressiveness toward boys. Either interpretation, or any one of the several others that could be offered, is highly speculative.

[1] This test assumes that the samples being compared are homogeneous with respect to their variances. Frequently this assumption had to be rejected in some of the group comparisons. In such cases a more conservative test of significance was used which makes some allowance in the error term for heterogeneity of variance. This technique is presented in detail in Cochran and Cox [6].

## Table II
### Sex Differences in Frequency of Teachers' Approval Contacts

|  | Classroom A | | Classroom B | | Classroom C | |
|---|---|---|---|---|---|---|
|  | Boys | Girls | Boys | Girls | Boys | Girls |
| N | 10 | 9 | 12 | 14 | 17 | 16 |
| Mean | 9.90 | 9.67 | 10.50 | 5.50 | 3.71 | 2.69 |
| S.D. | 6.10 | 7.65 | 5.33 | 2.53 | 2.95 | 1.99 |
| t | 0.074 | | 2.50* | | 1.15 | |
| F | 1.57 | | 4.43** | | 2.19 | |
| $t_{05}$† | — | | 2.19 | | — | |

* Significant at the five per cent level.
** Significant at the one per cent level.
† See footnote 2.

## Table III
### Sex Differences in Children's Nominations for Teacher Disapproval

|  | Classroom A | | Classroom B | | Classroom C | |
|---|---|---|---|---|---|---|
|  | Boys | Girls | Boys | Girls | Boys | Girls |
| N | 10 | 9 | 12 | 14 | 17 | 16 |
| Mean | 21.60 | 5.33 | 42.33 | 9.71 | 33.82 | 5.18 |
| S.D. | 13.33 | 5.68 | 43.06 | 8.13 | 55.87 | 8.26 |
| t | 3.39** | | 2.79** | | 2.03 | |
| F | 5.51** | | 28.07** | | 19.21** | |
| $t_{01}$† | 3.26 | | 3.10 | | — | |

** Significant at the one per cent level.
† See footnote 2.

## Table IV
### Sex Differences in Children's Nominations for Teacher Approval

|  | Classroom A | | Classroom B | | Classroom C | |
|---|---|---|---|---|---|---|
|  | Boys | Girls | Boys | Girls | Boys | Girls |
| N | 10 | 9 | 12 | 14 | 17 | 16 |
| Mean | 11.00 | 34.33 | 23.58 | 31.42 | 23.71 | 21.60 |
| S.D. | 12.93 | 32.64 | 18.51 | 25.08 | 35.75 | 25.70 |
| t | 2.09 | | 0.856 | | 0.242 | |
| F | 6.376** | | 1.835 | | 19.35** | |
| $t_{01}$† | — | | — | | — | |

** Significant at the one per cent level.
† See footnote 2.

The data presented above are based on the extensive observations of an objective observer who played no functional rôle in the classrooms. The data presented in the following section reflect the teachers' approval and disapproval contacts as viewed by their pupils.

### "Guess Who?" Data

Analysis of the "Guess Who?" data was performed along the same lines as the data obtained by direct observation. A comparison of the pupils' nominations of their peers on the disapproval items revealed statistically significant differences between boys and girls for two of the three schools. This can be interpreted as showing that the boys are viewed by the girls as well as by their male peers as being involved in more situations which evoke disapproval from their teachers.

### Table V
#### Choices Made by Boys and by Girls on Teacher Disapproval Items

| | Classroom A | | | | Classroom B | | | | Classroom C | | | |
|---|---|---|---|---|---|---|---|---|---|---|---|---|
| | Boys Choosing | | Girls Choosing | | Boys Choosing | | Girls Choosing | | Boys Choosing | | Girls Choosing | |
| | B | G | B | G | B | G | B | G | B | G | B | G |
| N | 8 | 9 | 8 | 9 | 14 | 12 | 14 | 12 | 17 | 16 | 17 | 16 |
| % | 89.77 | 23.23 | 83.09 | 16.91 | 88.37 | 11.63 | 73.05 | 26.95 | 88.70 | 11.20 | 82.21 | 17.79 |
| CR | 5.60** | | 3.64** | | 6.10** | | 2.65** | | 7.03** | | 4.84** | |

** Significant at the one per cent level.

Analysis of the children's responses to the items related to teacher approval produced no significant differences between boys and girls.

A final analysis of the "Guess Who?" data was performed in an attempt to determine how boys as contrasted with girls perceived the teacher's approval and disapproval biases. The choices made by the boys and by the girls for the approval and disapproval items were separately analyzed. It seemed unreasonable to use the *t* test in this situation because of the unequal numbers of boys and girls in the classroom. Therefore the groups were equated by converting the frequencies of nominations to percentages and working with percentage differences.

The results of the statistical analysis of boys' nominations on the disapproval items show that boys respond as if they usually received more blame from teachers than do girls. It would appear that boys are quite sensitive to the disapproval of their teachers. Table V shows that the girls also respond as if boys receive more teacher disapproval.

### Table VI
### Choices Made by Boys and by Girls on Teacher Approval Items

| | Classroom A | | | | Classroom B | | | | Classroom C | | | |
|---|---|---|---|---|---|---|---|---|---|---|---|---|
| | Boys Choosing | | Girls Choosing | | Boys Choosing | | Girls Choosing | | Boys Choosing | | Girls Choosing | |
| | B | G | B | G | B | G | B | G | B | G | B | G |
| N | 8 | 9 | 8 | 9 | 14 | 12 | 14 | 12 | 17 | 16 | 17 | 16 |
| % | 36.98 | 63.01 | 34.07 | 65.92 | 56.95 | 43.04 | 24.58 | 75.42 | 57.56 | 42.43 | 46.22 | 53.77 |
| CR | 1.11 | | 1.38 | | 0.72 | | 3.01** | | 0.88 | | 0.44 | |

** Significant at the one per cent level.

There is little consistency in the nominations made by the boys for the praise items. In schools B and C the boys react as though they typically receive more praise than girls, although this difference is not statistically significant. In contrast to the boys' responses, the girls feel that they receive more praise, particularly in school B where the difference is statistically significant. These results might be interpreted as meaning that children fail to recognize any definite dichotomy in the teacher's distribution of praise contacts.

### Discussion

The general findings of this study support the hypothesis that the male pupil receives reliably more blame from his teacher than the female pupil. Moreover, the boys recognize that they are the recipients of a higher incidence of teacher disapproval. We feel that these data lend indirect support to the notion that "masculine" behavior is not tolerated by the typical teacher who in turn attempts to inhibit such behavior by means of punishment.

Davis and Havighurst [8] have discussed at length the divergence of cultural mores between lower-class children and their middle-class teachers. Their work may best be summarized in the assertion that the goals defined by the middle-class teacher do not receive reinforcement from the lower-class child's peer group or from his family. Teacher initiation of punishment for "misbehavior" only serves to reinforce an already existing dislike for school and further leads to peer group reinforcement. A similar (but by no means identical) interpretation appears relevant to the present discussion. Our society's definitions of acceptable male and female behavior are divergent particularly with respect to aggression. For example Radke [20] in her monograph on the relationship of parental authority to child behavior reports that the fathers in her sample felt that aggressive, assertive behavior on the part of boys was less undesirable than the identical behavior in girls (and in many cases was deemed highly desirable). The mothers felt that aggression was unacceptable behavior in either sex but in general they were in agreement that aggressive behavior is more unacceptable in girls. Another study specifically related to the notion that aggressive behavior is more unacceptable in the female culture is a study by Sears *et al.* [22]. These writers predicted that in father-absent homes, wherein the child is brought up by the mother, boys would be less aggressive than in father-present homes in which the boy models his behavior after the father. The results of their study support the "sex-typing" hypothesis as presented above. Bach [4] reports similar evidence in support of the "sex-typing" hypothesis.[2] Apparently the social mores of the typical female teacher, at least with respect to aggressive, assertive behavior, are in sharp contrast to the behavorial tendencies of the typical male youngsters. The behavorial tendencies of the female child are, however, in close agreement with those of her teachers. We feel that the above generalization accounts to a high degree for the data reported in this study. Our argument becomes somewhat stronger when the work of Wickman [29] and a follow-up study by Mitchell [17] are included in the discussion. These investigators found that teachers perceive aggressive nonconforming behavior as more serious than withdrawal behavior. More recently Kaplan [15] has reported that the aggressive child was deemed annoying to almost three-quarters of the teachers in his sample. The present investigation suggests that perhaps teachers react to the aggressive behavior of children with counter-aggression, a vicious circle for both pupil and teacher.

Consistent with the above interpretation is the larger amount of variation found among the male pupils as contrasted with the female pupils. In a culture such as ours in which the father is away from the home during most of the child's waking hours (and in some instances pays only cursory attention to the youngster when at home), it appears obvious that both the male and female child are more directly influenced by the mother. Many boys, however, will be influenced more by their fathers and peer culture than by

---

[2] Though there is insufficient evidence at this time the present writers feel that the factor of innate sex differences in aggressive tendencies should not be overlooked. See Beach [5] for suggestive findings.

the mother because of identification with the masculine rôle in our culture. Our belief is that these more "masculine" boys are the ones who receive the greater share of teacher disapproval. Such an interpretation appears consistent with the work of Sears [22] and Bach [4].

The foregoing discussion has certain implications for the student of child development and education. If our interpretation of the teacher and male-pupil relationship is accurate, then the fact that boys dislike school more than girls is understandable. The daily punishment received by the boy for behavior he really does not consider "bad" must certainly be anxiety producing. If the anxiety created in the school situation becomes sufficiently intense, it seems reasonable that tension reduction can be achieved by means of avoiding school. It is known that more boys leave school at an earlier age than girls [26].

Perhaps of even more importance is the effect of this teacher-disapproval generated anxiety on the general personality adjustment of male pupils. It is unfortunate that we do not have evidence on the changes in adjustment level of the children in our sample, but studies by Ojemann and Wilkinson [18] and others indicate that consistent teacher dominance has deleterious effects on the adjustment of children. We can only speculate as to the nature of these adjustment problems but such behavorial manifestations as nervousness, withdrawal and lack of self-confidence are a few of the known symptoms.

We feel that the consistent trends in our findings imply that teachers' negative attitudes towards their male pupils arise from a lack of appreciation for the term "normal" male child. In our culture, aggressive outgoing behavior is as normal in the male as quiescent nonassertive behavior is in the female. The teacher who attempts to thwart this behavior by means of threats and punishment can only meet with frustration since the boy is confronted with a conflicting social code. A more reasonable plan to follow would seem to be one in which the excess energy and tensions of the male child could be discharged on some constructive activity. Planned physical education classes will do much to dissipate aggressive needs in a socially acceptable manner. Perhaps most important of all, however, is the knowledge that some degree of aggressive behavior is a normal part of development in both boys and girls and should be treated not as a personal threat to the teacher but as sign of "normal" social and personality development.

## Summary

The purpose of this study was to investigate sex differences in teacher distribution of approval and disapproval among three sixth-grade classrooms. Data relevant to the children's perceptions of their teachers' attitudes towards boys and girls were also collected. Using the discrepancies in attitude between males and females in our culture toward aggressive behavior as the basic underlying variable, the hypothesis was offered that boys, who are more aggressive and nonconforming than girls, would receive more disapproval contacts from their teachers than girls. Girls being quiescent and more conforming than boys would as a consequence receive more approval from their teachers than boys. We further hypothesized that both boys and girls will be aware of the differences in their teachers' attitudes towards them.

In order to test the foregoing hypothesis three sixth-grade teachers and their pupils were directly observed for a total of thirty hours per classroom. All teacher initiated contacts of an approval or disapproval nature were recorded. The measurement of the children's perceptions of teacher attitude was accomplished by means of a variation of the "Guess Who?" technique. The pupils were asked to list the names of four students who best fitted a series of statements of a teacher approval nature and of disapproval nature. Analysis was made of the number of children of each sex chosen for the approval items and for the disapproval items.

Statistical analysis of the data clearly supports our hypothesis with respect to male pupils. In all three schools the boys received reliably more disapproval from their teachers than the girls. We also found that both the boys and the girls nominated more boys for the disapproval items than girls. This difference was statistically reliable. With respect to the second hypothesis concerning girls, the data did not yield any clear-cut differences. If any trend was present it was in a direction opposite to that predicted. These results indicated that the teachers in our sample tended to have fewer contacts with the girls in their classrooms.

The results of this investigation were interpreted as being consistent with the notion of a sex difference in attitude towards aggressive behavior. The conclusion was drawn that teachers attempt to "socialize" the male child by means of dominative counter-aggressive behavior. The negative consequences of this situation for the child are discussed.

## References

1. ANDERSON, H. H. and H. M. BREWER. "Dominative and Socially Integrative Behavior of Kindergarten Teachers." *Applied Psychol. Monograph No. 6.* Stanford, Calif.: Stanford University Press (1945).

2. ———— and J. E. BREWER. "Effects of Teachers' Dominative and Inte-

grative Contacts on Children's Classroom Behavior." *Applied Psychol. Monograph No. 8.* Stanford, Calif.: Stanford University Press (1946).

3. ———, J. E. BREWER, and M. F. REED. "Studies of Teachers' Classroom Personalities: III. Follow-up studies of the effects of dominative and integrative contacts on children's behavior." *Applied Psychol. Monograph No. 11.* Stanford, Calif.: Stanford University Press (1946).

4. BACH, G. R. "Father-Fantasies and Father-Typing in Father Separated Children." *Child Develpm.* **17:**63–80 (1946).

5. BEACH, F. A. *Hormones and Behavior.* New York: Paul B. Hoeber (1948).

6. COCHRAN, W. G. and G. M. COX. *Experimental Designs.* New York: Wiley & Sons, Inc. (1950).

7. DAVIS, W. A. *Social-Class Influences upon Learning.* Cambridge: Harvard University Press (1948).

8. ——— and R. J. HAVIGHURST. *Father of the Man: How Your Child Gets His Personality.* Boston: Houghton Mifflin Co. (1947).

9. ——— and J. DOLLARD. *Children of Bontage.* Washington, D. C.: American Council on Education (1940).

10. DeGROAT, A. F. and G. G. THOMPSON. "A Study of the Distribution of Teacher Approval and Disapproval among Sixth-Grade Pupils." *J. Exper. Educ.* **18:**57–75 (1949).

11. GOODENOUGH, F. L. "Anger in Young Children." *Child Welfare Monograph No. 9,* pp. xiii + 278. Minneapolis: University of Minnesota Press (1931).

12. HAYES, M. L. "A Study of the Classroom Disturbances of Eighth Grade Boys and Girls." *Teachers College Contributions to Education.* **871:**139 (1943).

13. HOLLENBERG, E. and M. SPERRY. "Some Antecedents of Aggression and Effects of Frustration on Doll Play." *Personality.* **1:**32–43 (1951).

14. HURLOCK, E. "The Value of Praise and Reproof as Incentives for Children." *Archives of Psychol.* **11:**71 (1924).

15. KAPLAN, L. "The Annoyances of Elementary School Teachers." *J. Educ. Res.* **45:**649–665 (1951–52).

16. LEEDS, C. and W. COOK. "The Construction and Differential Value of a Scale for Determining Teacher-Pupil Attitudes." *J. Exper. Educ.* **16:**149–159 (1947).

17. MITCHELL, J. C. "A Study of Teachers' and of Mental-Hygienists' Ratings of Certain Behavior Problems of Children." *J. Educ. Res.* **36:**292–307 (1942).

18. OJEMANN, R. and F. R. WILKINSON. "The Effect on Pupil Growth of an Increase in Teacher's Understanding of Pupil Behavior." *J. Exper. Educ.* **8:**143–147 (1939).

19. OLSON, W. and M. WILKINSON. "Teacher Personality as Revealed by the Amount and Kind of Verbal Direction Used in Behavior Control." *Educ. Adm. and Sup.* **24:**81–93 (1938).

20. RADKE, M. J. "The Relation of Parental Authority to Children's Behavior and Attitudes." *Child Welfare Monograph No. 22.* Minneapolis: University of Minnesota Press (1946).

21. SEARS, P. S. "Doll Play Aggression in Normal Young Children: Influence of Sex, Age, Sibling Status, Father's Absence." *Psychological Monographs.* **65:**42 (1951).

22. SEARS, R. R., M. H. PINTLER, and P. SEARS. "Effect of Father Separation on Preschool Children's Doll Play Aggression." *Child Develpm.* **17:**219–243 (1946).

23. SEARS, R., J. WHITING, V. NOWLIS, and P. SEARS. "Some Child-rearing Antecedents of Aggression and Dependency in Young Children." *Genet. Psychol. Monographs.* **47:**135–234 (1953).

24. SNYDER, W. "Do Teachers Cause Maladjustment?" *J. Excep. Children.* **14:**40–46 (1947).

25. SOLLENBERGER, R. T. "Some Relationships between the Urinary Excretion of Male Hormone by Maturing Boys and Their Expressed Interests and Attitudes." *J. of Psychol.* **9:**179–189 (1940).

26. TENENBAUM, S. "Uncontrolled Expressions of Children's Attitudes toward School." *Elem. Sch. J.* **40:**670–768 (1939–40).

27. TIEDEMAN, S. "A Study of Pupil-Teacher Relationship." *J. Educ. Res.* **35:**657–664 (1942).

28. TUDDENHAM, R. D. "Studies in Reputation: I. Sex and Grade Differences." *Psychol. Monographs.* **66:**58 (1952).

29. WICKMAN, E. K. *Teachers and Behavior Problems.* New York: Commonwealth Fund (1938).

30. WITHALL, J. "The Development of a Technique for the Measurement of Social-Emotional Climate in Classrooms." *J. of Exper. Educ.* **17:**347–361 (1949).

## 41

# PEER ACCEPTANCE OF HIGHLY GIFTED CHILDREN IN ELEMENTARY SCHOOL *

## James J. Gallagher

In the study of provisions for gifted children in our schools a number of questions persistently arise. One of these concerns the social adjustment of gifted children. Are they typically normal in their relationships with other children? Do they get along well with their peers? Are they well-balanced emotionally? and so on. One aspect of this matter reported in the present article has to do with peer acceptance of the highly gifted. Are such children well-liked by their classmates? Are they chosen as friends as often as children of less ability? Do they tend to avoid average children and keep to themselves? Such questions reflect the concerns of some people about the over-all welfare of gifted children, and the findings reported here are most reassuring, at least insofar as they can be generalized.

*Questions:*

1. Do the findings of the study here reported confirm the findings of other studies reviewed by the author in his article?
2. Can you think of any ways in which this study could be improved if it were to be repeated?
3. Read the section at the end entitled, "Further Questions." Does this weaken the study or strengthen it? Why?

\* \* \*

The variables associated with peer acceptance and rejection have been the subject of considerable investigation over the past few years. In a recent

* The article is reprinted from the *Elementary School Journal*, **58**:465–470 (May 1958), by permission of the author and the University of Chicago Press. Copyright 1958 by the University of Chicago.

review of the literature, Lindzey and Borgatta [5] * concluded that intelligence is positively related to social acceptance along with such variables as proximity in the classroom, socioeconomic status, and membership in religious and ethnic groups.

But do these findings hold for all levels of intellectual ability? Is there possibly a point high on the intellectual scale where the difference between the gifted and the average child becomes too great for peer acceptance or social interaction?

Terman's studies of gifted children [9] indicated that as a group they are socially accepted by their peers. Self-ratings as well as teacher-ratings supported this finding. However, the more highly gifted children had more problems of social adjustment than the less highly gifted. Hollingworth [3] supported this conclusion and suggested that gifted children whose intelligence quotients range from 125 to 155 showed the best peer adjustment. She felt that children who score higher have social difficulty because the complexity of their play behavior and the high level of their interests may alienate their peer group.

Kerstetter [4] studied twenty-five children whose intelligence quotients on the Stanford-Binet Scale ranged from 160 to 202. These boys and girls, who were in Grades II through VIII, had been placed in classes for gifted children in New York City. In these classes the highly gifted children were, on the whole, socially well adjusted, and there seemed to be no relation between increased intelligence and social adjustment.

Mann [6] investigated the social adjustment of 67 gifted children whose intelligence quotient on the Stanford-Binet Scale was 130 or above. These gifted pupils attended a workshop for a half-day and remained in the regular classroom for the other half-day. Mann found that the gifted children in Grades IV, V, and VI chose one another for friends more frequently than they chose from the 214 children of typical intelligence. Similarly, the children of typical intelligence tended to choose among themselves, generally ignoring the gifted children. It should be noted, however, that the children were asked to make their choice of friends while in their separate half-day programs. This may account in part for the few choices between the two groups.

Miller [7] compared the social status and the socioempathic differences between 40 mentally superior (intelligence quotient 120–140), 40 retarded children (intelligence quotient 60–80), and 40 randomly selected students in Grades IV and VI. He found that the gifted children in both grades were

* Figure in brackets apply to references at end of article.

significantly the most popular of the three groups. The gifted children were also able to predict the social status of other children more successfully than could the children in the other two groups.

## Problem and Hypotheses

The present study was designed to answer three questions: How socially accepted are highly gifted children in the elementary-school classroom? What is the intellectual level of the children whom they choose as friends? What is the intellectual level of children who choose gifted children for friends?

The study tested the following five hypotheses:

1. Gifted children are more socially accepted by their peers than are children of average intelligence in the classroom.

2. The popularity of children in the gifted group decreases as their intelligence reaches an extremely high level.

3. The popularity of gifted children is higher in schools where there are many other bright children than in schools where there are few bright children.

4. Gifted children are chosen by other bright children as friends more frequently than they are chosen by the less bright children in the classroom.

5. Gifted children choose children near their own intellectual level for their friends rather than children of lower levels of ability.

## Identifying the Gifted

The subjects in the study were 54 highly gifted children, 29 boys and 25 girls, in Grades II through V in a midwestern community. A large state university contributed materially to a population of less than 100,000. This study was part of a larger research program on the adjustment of gifted children in elementary-school classrooms. Other phases of the study are reported elsewhere [1].

Teacher referrals and results of group tests were used to identify potentially gifted children in Grades II through V. Each potential candidate for the study was given a Stanford-Binet intelligence test, Form L. All children who obtained an intelligence quotient of 150 or above were included in the group of highly gifted children.

The criterion of an intelligence quotient of 150 was chosen in order to identify more clearly the possible problems created by extremely high intellectual ability. Group tests of intelligence given earlier had indicated a high intellectual average for the school population under study. These results made it necessary to set up a high criterion for the gifted group.

## Tallying Friends

In each class where a highly gifted child was found, sociometric choices were obtained from all pupils. Each pupil was supplied with a standard form and given the following instructions by the teacher: "Write the names of the five people in the class who you feel are your best friends. Write your very best friend's name first." A number of other questions that were asked have no bearing on the present study.

The number of choices received by each child was tabulated classroom by classroom, and the distribution of these choices was divided into quarters. The 25 per cent of the class who received the largest number of choices made up the top quarter; the 25 per cent who received the fewest choices made up the lowest quarter.

To test Hypotheses 4 and 5, three classrooms were chosen at random from Grades II through V. Group intelligence scores were obtained for each child. The names of the children that each child chose for his friends were also listed. The group intelligence tests used were the California Test of Mental Maturity and the Otis Self-Administering Test of Mental Ability. Because of the differences between the standard deviation of intelligence quotients for these two tests, it was necessary to change the intelligence-quotient scores into $T$ scores with a mean of 50 and a standard deviation of 10. Thus, an intelligence quotient of 100 would be equal to a $T$ score of 50. An intelligence quotient equal to one standard deviation above the mean would be a $T$ score of 60.

Standard $t$ tests were used to determine the significance of the difference between intelligence scores of the children who chose a gifted child and the scores of children who did not choose a gifted child.

## Findings on Friendship

Table 1 shows the peer acceptance of highly gifted children in relation to sex and grade. The findings indicate the high popularity of the gifted children in this sample. Fifty-two per cent of the group were in the top quarter of their class in terms of social choice, while only 11 per cent were in the lowest quarter of their class. The Kolmogorov-Smirnov test [8], which measures differences in cumulative frequencies of distributions, was used to determine that the distribution of the gifted children on popularity exceeded chance expectations at the 1 per cent level of confidence.

This high level of acceptance was not affected significantly by the sex or the grade level of the child. Although there was no reason to believe that sex might be a determining factor, there was some expectation that the gifted child might have more and more problems of social acceptance as he moved into the higher grades. Difficulties, it was thought, might be prompted by increasing individual differences between the gifted and the

**Table 1**

**How Highly Gifted Children Rated as Friends with Their Classmates**

| Related Variable | Total Number of Gifted Children | Top Quarter | | Second Quarter | | Third Quarter | | Fourth Quarter | |
|---|---|---|---|---|---|---|---|---|---|
| | | Number | Per Cent | Number | Per Cent | Number | Per Cent | Number | Per Cent |
| Sex: | | | | | | | | | |
|   Boys ......... | 29 | 13 | 45 | 7 | 24 | 5 | 17 | 4 | 14 |
|   Girls ......... | 25 | 15 | 60 | 4 | 16 | 4 | 16 | 2 | 8 |
| Grade level: | | | | | | | | | |
|   Primary ...... | 23 | 13 | 56 | 2 | 9 | 5 | 22 | 3 | 13 |
|   Intermediate ... | 31 | 15 | 48 | 9 | 29 | 4 | 13 | 3 | 10 |
|   Total ....... | 54* | 28 | 52 | 11 | 20 | 9 | 17 | 6 | 11 |

\* Significant at .01 level of confidence.

average pupil. As Table 1 shows, the group in the intermediate grades received as much peer acceptance as did the group in the primary grades.

The six children who rated lowest in social acceptance were studied further. Three of these youngsters, it was learned, felt superior to their classmates and from time to time rejected their requests for help.

A fourth child in this group, described as popular by his teacher, may have received few choices because he was new in the class. The two other children in this group could be described as immature and withdrawn. One of them was having considerable difficulty with his teacher. Apparently the qualities that make a child of average ability unpopular can also prove a hindrance to a highly gifted child.

Table 2 shows the relationship of social popularity to the type of school attended and the intelligence of the gifted children. Two psychologists classified the schools in the study as high- or low-referral schools. High-referral schools were those where many children had been referred as potentially gifted, and group intelligence scores there were fairly high. If the psychologists were uncertain of the classification of a school, it was eliminated from this comparison.

Contrary to Hypothesis 3, there seemed to be no tendency for gifted children in low-referral schools to be less popular with their peers than gifted children in high-referral schools. Previous comparisons between high- and low-referral schools [1] had shown differences in the problems faced

**Table 2**

**The Popularity of Highly Gifted Children Related to Type of School Attended and Level of Intelligence**

| Related Variable | Total Number of Gifted Children* | Top Quarter | | Second Quarter | | Third Quarter | | Fourth Quarter | |
|---|---|---|---|---|---|---|---|---|---|
| | | Num- ber | Per Cent | Num- ber | Per Cent | Num- ber | Per Cent | Num- ber | Per Cent |
| Type of school: | | | | | | | | | |
| High referral . | 36 | 18 | 50† | 8 | 22 | 6 | 17 | 4 | 11 |
| Low referral .. | 11 | 7 | 64 | 2 | 18 | 1 | 9 | 1 | 9 |
| Intelligence quo- tient: | | | | | | | | | |
| 150–164 ..... | 39 | 22 | 57† | 9 | 23 | 6 | 15 | 2 | 5 |
| 165–205 ..... | 15 | 6 | 40 | 2 | 13 | 3 | 20 | 4 | 27 |

\* Seven children were not included in classification by type of school, since they attended schools that could not be classified as either high or low referral.

† No significant differences found on basis of type of school or level of intelligence.

by children in these schools. Children in the low-referral schools seemed to have more motivational problems in studying. These findings together with individual case studies indicated that highly gifted children in the low-referral schools may be obtaining social status at the expense of intellectual activity. To gain approval they conform to peer values, which are generally not intellectual.

Table 2 also compares the peer acceptance of children with intelligence quotients of 165 and above with children who scored between 150 and 164. According to Hollingworth and Terman, the higher group should have had more problems of social acceptance, and there did seem to be a trend in that direction. Although the number of pupils scoring above 165 was understandably small, more than 25 per cent of these pupils did appear in the lowest quarter of their class as compared with only 5 per cent of the group with intelligence quotients of 150 to 164. Although the Kolmogorov-Smirnov test failed to reveal differences of acceptable statistical significance, this trend needs further study.

Table 3 presents findings related to Hypotheses 4 and 5. It was suggested that highly gifted children would be more attractive to children of high

**Table 3**

**Mean Intelligence *T* Scores of Pupils Choosing and Being Chosen by Gifted Children ***

| | Choosing Gifted | Not Choosing Gifted | Chosen by Gifted | Not Chosen by Gifted |
|---|---|---|---|---|
| Grade II: | | | | |
| Number of pupils .... | 34 | 49 | 13 | 60 |
| Mean *T* score ....... | 54.7 | 55.2 | 56.6 | 54.7 |
| Standard deviation ... | 11.0 | 9.0 | 8.4 | 10.6 |
| Grade III: | | | | |
| Number of pupils .... | 21 | 56 | 17 | 61 |
| Mean *T* score ....... | 58.5 | 58.4 | 61.2 | 58.0 |
| Standard deviation ... | 8.4 | 7.5 | 7.7 | 7.6 |
| Grade IV: | | | | |
| Number of pupils .... | 23 | 65 | 14 | 74 |
| Mean *T* score ....... | 58.3 | 56.4 | 54.5 | 57.2 |
| Standard deviation ... | 7.6 | 8.2 | 6.9 | 6.1 |
| Grade V: | | | | |
| Number of pupils .... | 10 | 74 | 12 | 72 |
| Mean *T* score ....... | 53.0 | 52.8 | 55.8 | 52.4 |
| Standard deviation ... | 8.1 | 7.8 | 6.2 | 8.0 |
| Total: | | | | |
| Number of pupils .... | 88 | 244 | 56 | 275 |
| Mean *T* score ....... | 56.4 | 55.5 | 57.3 | 55.5 |
| Standard deviation ... | 8.6 | 8.8 | 7.8 | 8.5 |

* No significant differences found.

intelligence. Therefore, there would be a difference between the intelligence of children choosing the gifted child for a friend and the intelligence of children who did not choose the gifted child as a friend. As Table 3 clearly indicates, no support for this hypothesis was found at any grade level. Gifted children were chosen by children of all levels of intellectual ability.

It had been suggested, also, that gifted children would be attracted to children of high ability. Therefore the intelligence of children chosen by the gifted child would be higher than the intelligence of the children not chosen by the gifted child. Again the findings do not bear out this expectation. In Grades II, III, and V there was a slight but statistically insignificant tendency for gifted children to choose children who rated above the class average in intelligence. In Grade IV even this slight trend was reversed.

This result suggests that the gifted child is not concerned or unduly influenced in his choice of friends by their intellectual ability, nor is he chosen by other bright children more frequently than by classmates of average or below-average ability. The writer's previous research in this community [2] suggests that more important than intelligence in the choice of friends may be the distance between children's homes. The nearer one child lives to another, the better his chance of being chosen as a friend.

## Further Questions

This study of peer acceptance of highly gifted children seemed to indicate that, as a group, they were highly popular with their classmates. Far from isolating themselves in social cliques with other bright classmates, the gifted children extended their own friendships throughout the entire intellectual range in their classroom. On the other hand, children of all levels of intellectual ability valued the gifted as friends.

The study suggests that high intellectual ability seems to be related to high social popularity. However, intelligence is only one factor in social choice. Other variables, such as sex, type of school attended, or grade placement also influence friendships, though in this study they did not significantly alter the favorable peer acceptance of this group.

More research is needed on friendships of gifted children. Many questions remain unanswered. For example, are the favorable findings of this study maintained in junior and senior high school? Or do widening differences in interests produce differences in choices? Do children of astronomically high ability have difficulty in gaining acceptance by their classmates? If so, why?

The findings of the present study do not necessarily hold for every community. The environment, it should be remembered, was unusually favorable to gifted children. Intellectual interests enjoyed an exceptionally high place in the community. Also, the large number of children with above-average ability may have worked to the social advantage of the highly gifted children under study. Research in other communities might well produce different results.

Should parents, teachers, and others concerned with the growth and guidance of gifted children be pleased with the findings of this study? Superficially, the results seem encouraging, but we may well ask whether peer acceptance is being obtained at the expense of intellectual growth and stimulation. There is little doubt in the writer's mind that certain gifted pupils are paying a price for their popularity.

Despite the recent reaction against life-adjustment in the schools, the desire to be socially accepted and popular in a peer group is important to both children and parents. The question is not whether the gifted should enjoy social acceptance. The question that awaits an answer from teachers and other school personnel rather is this: How can we help gifted children to enjoy both the esteem of their classmates and the excitement of intellectual pursuits?

### References

1. GALLAGHER, J. J. and THORA CROWDER. "The Adjustment of Gifted Children in the Regular Classroom." *Excep. Child.* **XXIII:**306–312, 317–319 (April 1957).

2. ———. "Social Status of Children Related to Intelligence, Propinquity, and Social Perception." *Elem. School J.* **LVIII:**225–231 (January 1958).

3. HOLLINGWORTH, LETA. *Children above 180 IQ: Origin and Development.* Yonkers, New York: World Book Co. (1942).

4. KERSTETTER, LEONA. "A Sociometric Study of the Classroom Roles of a Group of Highly Gifted Children." Unpublished Doctor's dissertation, New York University (1952).

5. LINDZEY, GARDNER and E. F. BORGATTA. "Sociometric Measurement." *Handbook of Social Psychology.* Edited by GARDNER LINDZEY. Cambridge, Massachusetts: Addison-Wesley Publishing Co. (1954).

6. MANN, H. "How Real Are Friendships of Gifted and Typical Children in a Program of Partial Segregation?" *Excep. Child.* **XXIII:**199–201, 206 (February 1957).

7. MILLER, R. V. "Social Status and Socioempathic Differences among Mentally Superior, Mentally Typical, and Mentally Retarded Children." *Exceptional Child.* **XXIII:**104–119 (December 1956).

8. SIEGEL, S. *Non-parametric Statistics for the Behavorial Sciences.* New York: McGraw-Hill Book Co. (1956).

9. TERMAN, L. M., *et al. Mental and Physical Traits of a Thousand Gifted Children.* Stanford University, California: Stanford University Press (1925).

# 42

## THE EMOTIONALLY DISTURBED *
### Fritz Redl and Stanley Jacobson

For some time there has been evident a marked tendency to delegate more and more responsibilities to the schools. From human relations—international as well as personal—to teaching how to drive a car, many matters that formerly were regarded as the responsibility of the home, or the church, or other community agencies, the schools have been asked to take over. One of these is the education of exceptional children, especially the handicapped. Special schools, special classes, special equipment, and special teachers are provided in many communities for the mentally or physically handicapped. In a related category are the emotionally disturbed. Often such children appear and remain in the regular classroom for the regular teacher to cope with. It is perhaps to the credit of our classroom teachers that they have tried bravely and earnestly to handle this problem, often to the detriment of their primary responsibility as teachers and their value and service to the other pupils. In the article which follows a viewpoint on this problem is expressed by two writers who have had many years of experience working with and helping teachers in the problems of mental health. The article is sensible and realistic. It sets forth guidelines which should help conscientious but harried teachers to see their role in mental health in a practical and reassuring light.

*Questions:*

1. What are the "pros" and "cons" of keeping emotionally disturbed children in the regular classroom?

2. How can the classroom teacher find out what agencies are available for referral of emotionally disturbed children?

3. How can a teacher know when an emotionally disturbed child should be referred? Illustrate with an example.

\* \* \*

It isn't easy to become *an emotionally disturbed child*. We don't mean that it isn't easy to have an emotional disturbance—that's the easiest and

* Reprinted from the *National Education Association Journal*, **47**:609–611 (December 1958), by permission of senior author and publisher.

most natural thing in the world. All of us have to meet the frustrations and disappointments that are standard procedure in living, and all of us react with more or less disturbance.

We feel hurt or angry or anxious or depressed or some subtle variation of some unnamed emotion. We behave in ways we wouldn't approve of— hopefully not for long and with minimum damage to ourselves or others. Then we get over the disturbance, and maybe we even learn from it so that the next time we face the frustration we aren't thrown quite so fast or far.

For children, especially, this process is as regular as meals, only more frequent. And with good reason. Children are still busy learning to recognize feelings and urges that are an old story to us. To learn to cope with those emotions is one important job of the growing child, and to make it doubly hard, he can't do it alone. He has to depend on us to help him. We expect the process to be punctuated by an occasional "disturbance," just as we expect a healthy child to suffer an occasional cold.

Because school is a natural focus for so much of the growing, school is also bound to be the scene of some of the disturbances. We learn to recognize the symptoms—a sudden change from typical behavior, more fighting or more crying or more absence or less concentration. Six-year-old Johnny suddenly refuses to come to school. Twelve-year-old Bobby cries when he sees the "C" in math on his report card. Teen-age Sally, an "A" student, suddenly stops trying.

As we probe behind this behavior with parent, child, or school counselor, we find there is a reason:

"Ever since the baby came, Johnny hangs around me all the time."

"My father said he'd buy me a bike if I got an 'A,' and now he won't buy it."

"If I can't go away to college, I'm not going to do anything."

Then we apply the first aid that is usually all that is required. Johnny and his mother get some counseling about the meaning of the new baby. Bobby's father begins to look at his son's ability realistically. Sally learns the economic facts of life, and her parents learn about adolescent independency striving. And all is fixed.

But to become *an emotionally disturbed child* is another matter. For one thing, transient disturbances like the ones we mentioned above must have been repeatedly ignored, misjudged, or badly handled earlier in the game, before the child reached school age as well as afterward, so that anger or distrust or despair, a feeling of badness or wrongness in himself or in the world, has already begun to look like a permanent fixture in the personality.

By then, no one-sided, one-step remedy will work. By then, it isn't *simply* the chemistry of the glands or the focus of the eyes or the level of the IQ or what Papa said just before Johnny left for school this morning. By then, warmth and caring are not enough.

What is an emotionally disturbed child like? First of all, the term itself is much too broad. It covers illnesses as simple as measles and as serious as cancer, as different as tonsillitis and a broken arm.

For example, if little Johnny's screaming and vomiting and refusal to come to school continue even after ample demonstration that he is loved and appreciated as fully as the newly arrived infant, chances are that the baby is not the source of the problem, but only the last straw.

Johnny and his mother may need guidance deeper in focus and longer in duration. Mother may need to take an unsettling new look at her child-rearing attitudes, and Johnny may have to let off considerable steam in the safety of a therapist's office before he can take the risk of growing up.

There may be another Johnny in the same first-grade class who comes to school obediently day after day and goes robot-like through his classroom paces; but his teacher notices a mask-like quality about him, a pseudo-understanding. He's in another world.

Now it *may* be that this Johnny is by inheritance an especially slow child, as yet unequipped for the rigors of first-grade life. Or perhaps he is one of those unfortunate children so badly hurt by early experiences that his thinking is twisted, and he really *cannot* understand the world as we do. Both are certainly disturbed, but they are as different from each other as they are from our first Johnny.

As a fourth variety of disturbance, take the kind of child we have been studying at the National Institute of Mental Health. In the first grade, this Johnny would probably have the teacher threatening to resign, for he's the boy whose hand is quicker than his head, who wants but cannot share, who acts as if yesterday never happened and tomorrow's an eternity away. He's the acting-out boy, long on aggression and short on self-control.

All these children, and many more varieties, are emotionally disturbed. We could have added at least a fifth child—the wonderfully co-operative one whose private life is an anxious striving to meet self-imposed, perfectionistic goals—but we are not trying to list all the kinds of disturbance. That would be impossible in any case. Our point is that the term *emotionally disturbed* is too broad to have any practical meaning.

To say a child is emotionally disturbed is like saying that he has a fever: Both statements merely point out that something is wrong without indicating the nature of the illness, how serious it is, or what remedies are indicated to effect a cure.

Notice too, that there is a difference between *disturbed* and *disturbing*. The child who causes us most trouble may happen to be the most deeply troubled child in the room; but sometimes he is a normal child engaged in a temporary campaign—perhaps to overcome immigrant status in a new community or to prove he's "somebody" to the girl across the room. The opposite child, the quiet oasis of calm in a too easily distracted group, often needs our attention more, even though he does nothing to force it.

It is no doubt clear by now that emotional disturbances defy generalization. On the face of it, symptoms know no logic. Every situation requires its own analysis, every illness its own cure.

This means that general prescriptions for handling disturbed children in the classroom will have limited relevance for individual cases. It does not mean, however, that there are no guides for thinking about what to do. These there are, and many of them are already familiar to you. Here are only a few we would like to suggest:

### A Teacher Is to Teach

Children bring their emotional problems to the classroom, and the teacher has to find ways of helping them to cope with the problems while they are in school. When the emotional disturbances become entangled with classroom and learning situations, it is the teacher's job to try to disentangle them for the duration. It is not the classroom teacher's job to solve the child's difficulties for good and all.

### Disturbances Are Real

It may be true that a particular child "could" do the work if he "wanted" to, but this doesn't mean he isn't really disturbed. It only means that the trouble lies in the motivational machinery instead of in the cognitive machinery. We may call him stubborn, negative, resistant, or withholding; but whatever we call him, chances are the condition is beyond his control and as real a disturbance in its way as faulty vision.

This is also true of the child who promises but can't deliver, the one who has to keep his eye on everything but his assignment, and many others who try our patience day after day.

### It Isn't Personal

Not only are disturbances real; they also run deeper than the events of the day, as we have tried to indicate. The boy who continues his nasty disruptions in spite of your efforts to contain him probably has nothing against you personally, nor have you created the problem by failing to smile his way in the morning. You may symbolize all the adults who "do nothing but boss me around all the time," or you may be an innocent casualty in a battle to win prestige in the gang.

### The Exceptional Child Is an Exception

Although many disturbed children can be helped in a regular classroom, the fact remains that the disturbed child is exceptional, and the techniques that provide stimulating learning experiences for most normal children may only stimulate the disturbed child's pathology.

If a promising activities program leads to chaos in the classroom, the trouble may lie in one or two children with faulty control systems and not in the technique itself. Even in a very small class, with more than one teacher, some children cannot manage a program which depends on inner controls and self-maintained task-centeredness. On the other hand, one can see the very same activities producing significant learning in large classes of relatively normal children.

Is the answer to assign disturbed children to separate groups? Perhaps, but not for all of them. Some disturbed children need special classes or special schools and some cannot manage school at all, but the majority need the presence of a normal group in order to develop an image of constructive social behavior.

For these children, the answer lies in the kind of flexible planning that many schools are finding easier to achieve than they had imagined. Children are going to school part time, moving to different rooms and grades as their needs require it, staying home on bad days—and the schools are seeing the programs bear fruit.

What is right for any disturbed child still depends on an analysis of that case alone, but there are plenty of alternatives if a school is willing to be imaginative.

### You Can't Go It Alone

What we have just said is not meant to imply that a teacher has to find a way to teach every child on the class roster. In the first place, some *disturbing* children are unmanageable (and therefore unteachable) even if they are not seriously *disturbed*. Others who might be reached are all too frequently lost because of special school conditions.

When the teacher is hamstrung by a rigid curriculum, a dearth of special facilities, ragged equipment, and short supplies, he can only choose the path of sanity and admit his limitations. Too many teachers still stand like martyrs, alone and unprovided with necessary tools, struggling to accomplish a task which requires artistry even under the best of circumstances.

### Refer It

Tell somebody. The guidance counselor, the principal, the pupil personnel worker, the school social worker, the school psychologist—tell whichever person in your school has the job of knowing the resources for the troubled child and how to get child and resource together. And if the child you refer is lucky enough to arrive at the source of help, remember, specialists in helping troubled people can't go it alone either.

To be a specialist means to have special knowledge and skill in a specific area. It also means having less knowledge and skill in other areas. Psychiatrists, psychologists, and social workers may know as little about the classroom as teachers may know about the clinic. The helping specialist will depend on information from you to help him understand the case and plan the treatment *outside* the school.

As for the classroom program, that remains your area of specialty, and it will be up to you to translate findings about the child's personality and needs into classroom action. Education has perhaps done too little to develop specific educational techniques for the emotionally disturbed child, but that gap is being filled by a growing catalogue of literature and course work on the subject, and we urge you to take advantage of it.

### Speak Up

Disturbed children need special services, not only in the school but in the recreation, health, and welfare fields as well. For too many years, teachers have tried to provide services beyond their scope because those services were not available elsewhere in the community. It is time the teachers shoved back—not to get even, but because it is hard enough to be what classroom teachers are trained to be without also trying to be social workers, psychologists, and psychiatrists. Only if we speak up can the community understand the need and begin to meet it.

# 43

## DOES AN HONOR SYSTEM REDUCE CLASSROOM CHEATING? AN EXPERIMENTAL ANSWER *

### Ray R. Canning

A perennial question on college and university campuses is concerned with cheating. While not a pleasant topic for discussion it is generally recognized that it exists and "something should be done about it." Certainly it does not speak well for the efforts of the schools and colleges in developing character. It is probable that the extent of cheating varies from one situation to another, but not much is known about this. There is a good deal of knowing and often loose talk among students on the subject, but little actual evidence to look at. In this article a careful, objective study of some important basic questions is reported. The first has to do with the kinds and extent of cheating behavior indulged in by university students when they are placed in a situation where they can cheat with some feeling of assurance that they will not be detected. The study sheds some light on a related and most important question, namely, what happens when an honor system is introduced? The findings are encouraging on this point.

*Questions:*

1. Some students might say that a study such as this is "unfair." How would you answer?

2. According to the report of this study, cheating was measurably reduced under the honor system but still present. What might be done to reduce it still more? How would you test the efficacy of your suggestions?

\* \* \*

Opportunities for experimental research in the Behavior Sciences are severely limited. However, an occasional situation arises in which human beings can be manipulated either voluntarily or without their knowledge. The classroom offers such a research environment which, in this case, was used to determine cheating practices of university students.

\* Reprinted from the *Journal of Experimental Education,* **24**:291–296 (June 1956), by permission of author and Dembar Publications, Inc.

## The Technique

Previous studies of honesty among students have utilized a variety of techniques,[1] some of which were used in this study to test validity and reliability. However, for the experiment reported here, one simple technique was repeated five times over a period of six years:

1. After regular examinations were collected from lower division sociology students, duplicate copies of the students' answers were carefully recorded for later comparisons.

2. These duplicate test papers were then corrected and graded, but *no* markings were made on the original examination papers.

3. At the next class session the unmarked originals were returned to their owners with the implication that the instructor had not yet had time to correct them. "Aid" from the students was solicited, and each was "permitted" to "correct" his own paper.

4. At the end of this experimental period, the papers were again collected and any changes made upon the examination papers by the students were also recorded on the duplicate sheets.

5. Tabulated differences, then, became the data of this cheating experiment.

## The Time Period

In 1948, one year before an Honor System was established at the Brigham Young University, the first experiment was made upon what will be referred to as Class A. This group of students will be considered the "Before" part of the total experiment. During the years of introduction and revision of the Honor Code and System (1949–1953), three other classes (Classes B, C, and D) were studied. They constitute the "During" part of the experiment. Finally, five years after the inauguration of the System (1954), a follow-up study was made (Class E) which will be called the "Now" stage of the experiment.

## The Sample

Five lower division sociology classes were used in the experiment proper. Their 299 students were divided up as follows:

[1] For one example see: Harold T. Christensen. "An Experiment in Honesty." *Social Forces* (March 1948).

In the "Before" group there were 48 students, 181 in the "During" group, and 70 in the "Now" group. In addition to this research sample, three classes (X, Y, and Z) containing 71, 38, 96 students, respectively, were used in validity and reliability exercises. Similar experiments were made with 109 of these students but by different instructors.[2] Class Z (96 students) was experimented with by other techniques.[3]

Although a sample of 299 students is large enough for most statistical manipulations, it is well to note that in both the "Before" and "Now" groups the number is small.

## Standardization

Attempts were made to keep tests, samples, classroom conditions, and methods of conducting the experiment comparable throughout the "Before," "During," and "Now" periods. One instructor performed all experiments; classes had considered similar subject matter; the experiment was performed at the same time in the quarter; and the approach to the class was standardized. Throughout the six year period, no information was divulged which may have alerted the students to the nature of the experiment.

## Findings

### A. Changes in Incidence of Cheating

Of all students studied during the six years of experimentation, 45 percent cheated in the controlled examinations. The total percentage is not so important, however, as the change in percentage of students cheating before, during and after the instigation of the Honor System. The "Before" period had a high 81 percent of the students who cheated. This was reduced in the "During" period to 41 percent, and finally in the "Now" period to 30 percent. See Table I. The before-Honor System high was cut in half by the end of the first three years of the Honor System. In five years, it was reduced by nearly two-thirds (63 percent). Tests were made of these percentage reductions to determine if the differences were statistically significant.[4] There is less than one possibility in 1000 that such a difference could have

[2] In Class X (a lower division religion class of 75 students) and Class Y (a lower division sociology class of 38 students) 45 students or 41 percent cheated in the experiment.

[3] They were made to witness cheating in the classroom in order that their reactions might be recorded. This experiment will be reported in another paper.

[4] Chi square = 17.356; Df = 2; P ≤ .001.

resulted from chance factors. Of course, this does not prove a causal relationship between the Honor System and a reduction in cheating, but the likelihood should be noted.

## B. Male-Female Comparisons

It may be noted also from Table I that in every period more female students cheated than did the males. The comparative total was 78 to 57, respectively. Of the total cheating group, 58 percent were women and 42 percent were men. This statistic by itself, however, is misleading. The proportion of cheaters of either sex must be compared to the proportion within the total sample of members of that sex. Thus the 58 percent and 42 percent above should be compared respectively to 56 percent of the total group who are females and 44 percent who are males. Table II shows these relationships.

Although among the students who cheated in the "Before" group, 59 percent were women, of the *total* "Before" group they comprised 62 percent. The men in this group cheated out of proportion to their number in the total group. In the "During" period the proportions by sex in both the total and cheating groups were exactly the same. However, in the "Now" period of the experiment, the women cheated disproportionately, i.e., they comprised 62 percent of the cheating sample but only 53 percent of the total sample.[5] The rise and decline by sex should also be noted. The percentage among the cheaters who were male rose from 41 percent to 44 percent and then dropped to 38 percent, while among the cheaters the female percentage rose from 59 percent ("Before") to 62 percent ("Now").

Similarly, there were changes in the average number of points[6] cheated. In the "Before" period, the cheating males averaged 11.6 points with a range of 4 to 24 points, while the cheating females averaged 12.9 points and a range of 4 to 30 points. By the "Now" period the males had reduced their average to 9.1 (R = 3-17) but still had a higher average than the females who had dropped to an average of 7.6 points cheated per cheating-student (R = 3-17). Again, however, standard errors of these differences indicate that they are probably products of chance.

---

[5] These differences are not statistically significant. Chi-square test of the percent of women among the cheating population as compared to the percent among the total population, "Before", "During", and "Now" indicates that a greater difference could occur 40–50 times in 100 among other samples due to chance.

[6] "Points" hereafter will mean "points-per-100-possible." This designation is used in lieu of percent, inasmuch as the word "percent" is repeated so frequently in this paper.

**Table I**

**Number and Percent of Students Who Cheated, According to Sex**

| | Males | | | Females | | | Total | | |
|---|---|---|---|---|---|---|---|---|---|
| | No. in Sample | No. Who Cheated | % Who Cheated | No. in Sample | No. Who Cheated | % Who Cheated | No. in Sample | No. Who Cheated | % Who Cheated |
| Before | 18 | 16 | 89% | 30 | 23 | 77% | 48 | 39 | 81% |
| During | 80 | 33 | 41% | 101 | 42 | 42% | 181 | 75 | 41% |
| Now | 33 | 8 | 24% | 37 | 13 | 35% | 70 | 21 | 30% |
| Total | 131 | 57 | 44% | 168 | 78 | 46% | 299 | 135 | 45% |

**Table II**

**Percent of Total Group and Cheating Group, by Sex**

| | Percent of Total Group | | | | Percent of Cheating Group | | | |
|---|---|---|---|---|---|---|---|---|
| | Males | | Females | | Males | | Females | |
| | No. | % | No. | % | No. | % | No. | % |
| Before | 18 | 38% | 30 | 62% | 16 | 41% | 23 | 59% |
| During | 80 | 44% | 101 | 56% | 33 | 44% | 42 | 56% |
| Now | 33 | 47% | 37 | 53% | 8 | 38% | 13 | 62% |
| Total | 131 | 44% | 168 | 56% | 57 | 42% | 78 | 58% |

Significance is apparent, though, when the average points cheated of the total "Before" group (12.3 points) are compared to the average of the "Now" group (8.2 points).[7] Not only are there fewer cheating, but their cheating is of lesser magnitude.

### C. Methods of Cheating

Four methods of cheating were discernible in the experiment: (1) wrong answers were erased or crossed through and correct answers inserted, (2) previously-left blanks were filled with correct answers, (3) answers which were incorrect were not marked as such, and (4) arithmetical "mistakes" favorable to the students were made.

There were 427 individual cases of cheating divided among these four types as follows:

> 135 cases of "filled blanks" (32%)
> 125 cases of "changed answers" (29%)
> 95 cases of "'arithmetical' mistakes" (22%)
> 72 cases of wrong answers not checked (17%)

Although throughout the entire experiment "filling in blank answers" was the most popular form of cheating, this was not so in either the Before or During period. Before the Honor System, over half (53 percent) of the cheating cases were by "Changing-of-Correct-for-Incorrect-Answers," and during the first three years of the system, "Poor Arithmetic" was the most frequently used device (31 percent of the cases).

Sex differences are reflected in the most popular forms of cheating throughout the different periods studied. In the "Before" period "Changing Answers" was the most popular form of cheating of both sexes (M = 62 percent, F = 41 percent). In the "Now" period "Filling Blanks" (79 percent = M, 61 percent = F) was the most popular cheating technique used by students of both sexes.

The sexes "Changed Answers" and "Filled Blanks" proportionately, but the male students outdistanced the female students in "Not Checking Wrong Answers," while the women surpassed the men in "Making Favorable Arithmetic Mistakes."

### D. Cheating Related to Use of Pen or Pencil

Approximately 11 percent more people cheated among the students using pencils than among those using pen and ink (pens, 36 percent; pen-

---

[7] Significant beyond the .01 level of significance.

cils, 47 percent). Cheating students preferred pencils over pens by a ratio of 6 to 1; the non-cheating students, 4 to 1. A three-period comparison will show a decided change in this preference: Cheaters in the "Before" period when the rate of cheating was highest had a pencil-to-pen ratio of 19 to 1, as compared to 6 to 1 in the "During" period, and 3 to 1 in the "Now" period, typified by a relatively low cheating rate.

### E. Cheating as Related to High Scores on the MMPI

All students in the research population who had any score on the Minnesota Multiphasic Personality Inventory of 70 or above or 60 and above on the Lie score were classified according to their cheating-non-cheating behavior in the experiment. Fifty-seven students had T scores of 70 or up on one or more of the following scales: Hypochondriasis, Depression, Hysteria, Psychopathic Deviate, Interest, Paranoia, Psychasthenia, Schizophrenia, or Hypomania. Thirty-two students had Lie scores of 60 or above. Of the 57, 28 cheated and 29 did not. Of the 32, 15 cheated and 17 did not. Thus, cheating does not seem to be differentiated in terms of high MMPI students.

### F. Cheating and Academic Proficiency

The five highest and five lowest test scores were averaged for the cheaters and non-cheaters in each of the three periods of the experiment. A marked difference was noted in each case. The mean score of these fifteen highest cheaters was 70 compared to 88 for the fifteen highest noncheaters. The fifteen lowest scores averaged 47 for the cheaters, but 54 for the non-cheaters. Furthermore, the fifteen highest cheaters raised themselves an average of 15 points. It is clearly evident that points cheated are inversely related to test scores.

High school grade-point averages were computed for the cheaters and the noncheaters. The cheating students averaged 1.98 grade points before coming to the University while the noncheating students averaged 2.07 grade points.

### Verbalizations vs. Overt Behavior in the Cheating Experiment

Prior to the experiment, a situational questionnaire was administered to the students in order to find the relationship between verbalizations and cheating behavior, i.e., promised and actual behavior. Among other questions posed for the students' consideration was: "You have an opportunity to change your score on an examination; (you find the instructor's roll book, or discover some other technique) *What would you do?*" Twenty-six students did not answer. But of the 272 who did answer, 231 (85 percent) pledged that they would not cheat, while 41 (15 percent) said they would raise their grades. By comparison, in the experiment itself, 150 (55 percent) did not cheat and 122 (45 percent) did cheat. Thus a total of 89 people (31 men and 58 women) both cheated and lied—one-third of the total group who answered the questionnaire.

### Table III

**Students Who Answered Situational Questionnaire "Yes" or "No" According to Whether or Not They Cheated in the Experiment**

| | Number Who Answered "Yes" | Number Who Answered "No" | Total |
|---|---|---|---|
| **Cheated:** | | | |
| Males | 18 | 31 | 49 |
| Females | 15 | 58 | 73 |
| Both Sexes | 33 | 89 | 122 |
| **Did Not Cheat:** | | | |
| Males | 4 | 60 | 64 |
| Females | 4 | 82 | 86 |
| Both Sexes | 8 | 142 | 150 |
| **Total Group** | 41 | 231 | 272 |

Table III will show further that 33 students (12 percent) cheated as promised but did not lie about it; 142 students (52 percent) neither cheated nor lied; and 8 students (3 percent) did not cheat in the experiment although they had previously stated they would cheat.

### Summary and Limitations

After five years of testing under an Honor System at Brigham Young University, rates of cheating (of four specific types) were reduced by 63 percent in lower division sociology classes. Similarly, the average magnitude of cheating was less: Before the Honor System the average was 12.3 points per cheating student per test. After five years of the Honor System this average was reduced to 8.2 points.

Before the Honor System, male students cheated slightly out of proportion to their number in the total group, but after five years of the System, this proportion was reduced and the women students cheated disproportionately.

Although in general, the favorite method of cheating was by writing in correct answers for questions which during the examination had been left blank, prior to an Honor System the favorite device was through changing answers. Male students failed to check wrong answers more frequently than did women students who, in turn, were more adept at making favorable arithmetic "errors."

Pencil-users cheated more frequently than students who used pen and ink. And the decline in cheaters' preference for pencils is directly related to the reduction in cheating itself throughout the experiment.

No differentiations were noted between cheaters and non-cheaters who scored high on any of the scales of the Minnesota Multiphasic Personality Inventory. However, in terms of high school grade-point averages, the non-cheaters surpassed the cheaters with 2.07 to 1.98 grade points. They were also differentiated by average test scores, the cheaters consistently falling below the non-cheaters. Furthermore, the number of points students raised their scores was inversely related to their correct test scores, i.e., "poorer" students "raised" themselves more points than did the "better" students.

Verbalizing about honesty was relatively easy. Of the 272 students who answered a situational questionnaire designed to test the relationship between promised behavior and actual behavior, 33 percent cheated after promising that they would not; 12 percent cheated as they promised they would; 52 percent did not lie and did not cheat, and 3 percent promised to cheat but failed to do so.

The findings of this study must be interpreted only in view of its many limitations: the small number of people involved in some classes, the lack of further controls, the "temptation" conditions for certain types of cheating, and other unknown variables. It should not be considered as representative of larger groups or other conditions than those specifically described above.

## Bibliography

*Mental Health, Personality and Adjustment—*
*The Development of Characters*

1. AMATORA, MARY. "Case Study: A Method of Guidance." *Understanding the Child.* **23**:46–48 (April 1954).
2. ANDREW, GWEN and HILDA LOCKWOOD. "Teachers' Evaluation of the

Mental Health Status of Their Pupils." *J. Educ. Res.* **47**:631–635 (March 1954).

3. ———— and ESTHER L. MIDDLEWOOD. "The Goals of Mental-Health Education Commonly Selected by a Group of Experts." *Ment. Hyg.* **37**:596–605 (October 1953).

4. ARBUCKLE, D. S. "The Teacher as a Counselor." *High Sch. J.* **40**:285–289 (May 1957).

5. BAKWIN, HARRY. "Emotional Deprivation in Infants." *J. Pediatrics.* **35**:512–521 (October 1949).

6. BANNING, EVELYN I. "The Lonely Road of Unreality." *Sch. & Soc.* **72**:132–133 (August 26, 1950).

7. BLOS, PETER. "Aspects of Mental Health in Teaching and Learning." *Ment. Hyg.* **37**:555–569 (October 1953).

8. BONIME, W. "The Sense of Self in Children." *Child Study* **32**:31–34 (Winter 1954).

9. BRODHEAD, FRED C. "Pupil Adjustment in the Semi-Departmental Elementary School." *Elem. Sch. J.* **60**:385–390 (April 1960).

10. BRONFENBRENNER, URIE. "Socialization and Social Class Through Time and Space." In E. E. MACCOBY, T. M. NEWCOMB, and E. L. HARTLEY, *Readings in Social Psychology,* 3rd Ed. New York: Holt, Rinehart & Winston (1958), pp. 400–425.

11. CALVIN, A. D. and W. H. HOLTZMAN. "Adjustment and the Discrepancy Between Self-Concept and Inferred Self." *J. Consult. Psychol.* **17**:39–44 (February 1953).

12. CAMPBELL, ELISE HATT. "The Social-Sex Development of Children." *Genet. Psychol. Monographs.* **21**:461–552, No. 4 (1939).

13. CASTENEDA, ALFRED, BOYD R. McCANDLESS, and DAVID S. PALERMO. "The Children's Form of the Manifest Anxiety Scale." *Child Dev.* **27**:317–326 (September 1956).

14. CAVAN, RUTH SHONLE and GRACE BELING. "A Study of High School Marriages." *Marr. Fam. Lvng.* **20**:293–295 (August 1958).

15. CLARK, K. B. and M. K. CLARK. "The Development of Consciousness of Self and the Emergence of Racial Identification in Negro Pre-school Children." *J. Soc. Psychol.* **10**:591–599 (November 1939).

16. COREY, STEPHEN M. "Professed Attitudes and Actual Behavior." *J. Educ. Psychol.* **28**:271–280 (April 1937).

17. CRUIKSHANK, W. M. "The Relation of Physical Disability to Fear and Guilt Feelings." *Child Dev.* **22**:291–298 (December 1951).

18. DINEEN, M. A. and R. GARRY. "Effect of Sociometric Seating on a Class-room Cleavage." *Elem. Sch. J.* **56:**358–362 (April 1956).

19. DITTES, J. E. and H. H. KELLEY. "Effects of Different Conditions of Acceptance Upon Conformity to Group Norms." *J. Ab. & Soc. Psychol.* **53:** 100–107 (1956).

20. DUMPSON, JAMES R. "Gang and Narcotic Problems of Teen-Age Youth." *Amer. J. Psychotherapy.* **6:**312–328 (April 1952).

21. DURKIN, DOLORES. "Children's Acceptance of Reciprocity as a Justice-Principle." *Child Dev.* **30:**289–296 (June 1959).

22. FRANK, LAWRENCE K. *The Fundamental Needs of the Child.* New York: The National Association for Mental Health (1952).

23. FRANKLIN, ADELE. "Teachers—Not Therapists." *Nervous Child.* **10:**368–377, No. 3–4 (1954).

24. FRYMIER, JACK. "Acceptance and Rejection as Related to Length of School Attendance." *J. Educ. Res.* **53:**112–114 (November 1959).

25. GNAGEY, WILLIAM J. "Effects on Classmates of a Deviant Student's Power and Response to a Teacher-exerted Control Technique." *J. Educ. Psychol.* **51:**1–8 (February 1960).

26. GOUGH, HARRISON G. *et al.* "Children's Ethnic Attitudes: I. Relationship to Certain Personality Factors." *Child Dev.* **21:**83–91 (June 1950).

27. HARTSHORNE, HUGH and MARK A. MAY. "A Summary of the Work of the Character Education Inquiry." *Religious Educ.* **25:**607–619, 754–762 (September–October 1930).

28. HEALY, WILLIAM and AUGUSTA F. BRONNER. *New Light on Delinquency and Its Treatment.* New Haven: Yale University Press (1936).

29. HEISLER, FLORENCE. "Comparison Between Those Elementary School Children Who Attend Moving Pictures, Read Comics, and Listen to Serial Radio Programs to Excess, with Those Who Indulge in These Activities Seldom or Not at All." *J. Educ. Res.* **42:**182–190 (November 1948).

30. HILLSON, J. S. and P. WORCHEL. "Self-Concept and Defensive Behavior in the Maladjusted." *J. Consult. Psychol.* **21:**83–88 (February 1957).

31. JERSILD, ARTHUR T. "Understanding Others Through Facing Ourselves." *Childhood Educ.* **30:**410–414 (May 1954).

32. JOHNSON, ELIZABETH S. and CAROLINE E. LEGG. "Why Young People Leave School." *Bull. Nat'l Assoc. of Sec. Sch. Prin.* **32:**14–24 (November 1948).

33. JONES, EDWARD S. "Relation of Ability to Preferred and Probable Occupation." *Educ. Adm. & Sup.* **26:**220–226 (March 1940).

34. KOTINSKY, RUTH and JULES V. COLEMAN. "Mental Health as an Educational Goal." *Teach. Col. Rec.* **56:**267–276 (February 1955).

35. KUTNER, BERNARD. "Patterns of Mental Functioning Associated with Prejudice in Children." *Psychol. Monographs* **72:**1–48, No. 7 (1958).

36. LAYCOCK, S. R. "Effect of Teacher's Personality on the Behavior of Pupils." *Understanding the Child.* **19:**50–55 (April 1950).

37. LEVIN, HARRY, THOMAS L. HILTON, and GLORIA F. LEIDERMAN. "Studies of Teacher Behavior." *J. Exp. Educ.* **26:**81–91 (September 1957).

38. LEWIN, KURT, RONALD LIPPITT, and RALPH K. WHITE. "Patterns of Aggressive Behavior in Experimentally Created 'Social Climates'." *J. Soc. Psychol.* **10:**271–299 (May 1939).

39. MEYER, CHARLENE TRUMBO. "The Assertive Behavior of Children as Related to Parent Behavior." *J. Home Ec.* **39:**77–80 (February 1947).

40. MITTON, BETTY L., and DALE B. HARRIS. "The Development of Responsibility in Children." *Elem. Sch. J.* **54:**268–277 (January 1954).

41. MOWRER, O. H. "Authoritarianism vs. 'Self-Government' in the Management of Children's Aggressive (Anti-Social) Reactions as a Preparation for Citizenship in a Democracy." *J. Soc. Psychol.* **10:**121–126 (February 1939).

42. ———. "Discipline and Mental Health." *Harvard Educ. Rev.* **17:**284–296 (Fall 1947).

43. MUSSEN, PAUL H. "Some Personality and Social Factors Related to Changes in Children's Attitudes Toward Negroes." *J. Ab. & Soc. Psychol.* **45:**423–441 (1950).

44. MUSTE, MYRA J. and DORIS F. SHARPE. "Some Influential Factors in the Determination of Aggressive Behavior in Preschool Children." *Child Dev.* **18:**11–28 (March 1947).

45. OJEMANN, RALPH H. and FRANCES R. WILKINSON. "The Effect on Pupil Growth of an Increase in Teachers' Understanding of Pupil Behavior." *J. Exp. Educ.* **8:**143–147 (December 1939).

46. PATTERSON, C. H. "The Classroom Teacher and the Emotional Problems of Children." *Understanding the Child.* **21:**67–72 (June 1952).

47. PELLER, LILI E. *Significant Symptoms in the Behavior of Young Children: A Check List for Teachers.* New York: The National Association for Mental Health, Inc. (1952).

48. PORTER, ROBERT M. "Student Attitudes Toward Child Behavior Problems." *J. Educ. Res.* **52:**349–352 (May 1959).

49. RADKE-YARROW, MARIAN, HELEN G. TRAGER, and HADASSAH DAVIS. "Social

Perceptions and Attitudes of Children." *Genet. Psychol. Monographs.* **40:** 327–447 (November 1949).

50. READER, N. and H. B. ENGLISH. "Personality Factors in Adolescent Female Friendships. *J. Consult. Psychol.* **11:**212–220 (July 1947).

51. RECKLESS, WALTER C., SIMON DINITZ, and ELLEN MURRAY. "Self-Concept as an Insulator Against Delinquency." *Amer. Soc. Rev.* **21:**744–746 (December 1956).

52. REDL, FRITZ. "Pre Adolescents—What Makes Them Tick?" *Child Study.* **21:**44–48, 58–59 (February 1944).

53. REIMANN, MIRIAM. "How Children Become Prejudiced." *Commentary.* **11:**88–94 (January 1951).

54. ROGERS, CARL R. "Some Observations on the Organization of Personality." *Amer. Psychol.* **2:**359–368 (September 1947).

55. SCHRUPP, MANFRED H. and CLAYTON M. GJERDE. "Teacher Growth in Attitudes Toward Behavior Problems of Children." *J. Educ. Psychol.* **44:** 203–214 (April 1953).

56. SHOBEN, E. J., JR. "Toward a Concept of the Normal Personality." *Amer. Psychol.* **12:**183–189 (April 1957).

57. STENDLER, CELIA B. "Building Secure Children in Our Schools." *Childhood Educ.* **25:**216–220 (January 1949).

58. ———. "How Well Do Elementary School Teachers Understand Child Behavior?" *J. Educ. Psychol.* **40:**489–498 (December 1949).

59. ———. "A Study of Some Socio-Moral Judgments of Junior High School Children." *Child Dev.* **20:**15–28 (March 1949).

60. ——— and NORMAN YOUNG. "The Impact of Beginning First Grade Upon Socialization as Reported by Mothers." *Child Dev.* **21:**241–260 (December 1950).

61. STOCK, D. "An Investigation Into the Interrelations Between the Self Concept and Feelings Directed Toward Other Persons and Groups." *J. Consult. Psychol.* **13:**176–180 (June 1949).

62. STOUFFER, GEORGE A. W., JR. "Behavior Problems of Children as Viewed by Teachers and Mental Hygienists." *Ment. Hyg.* **36:**271–285 (April 1952).

63. STRANG, RUTH. "Characteristics of a Classroom Which Promotes Mental Health." *Nervous Child.* **10:**363–367, No. 3–4 (1954).

64. ———. "Guidance and Counseling and the Teacher." *J. Nat. Assoc. Women Deans & Counselors.* **22:**18–25 (October 1958).

65. SULLENGER, T. E., L. H. PARKE, and W. K. WALLIN. "The Leisure Time

Activities of Elementary School Children." *J. Educ. Res.* **46:**551–554 (March 1953).

66. SYMONDS, P. M. "Education for the Development of Personality." *Teach. Coll. Rec.* **50:**163–169 (December 1948).

67. ———. "Education and Psychotherapy." *J. Educ. Psychol.* **40:**5–20 (January 1949).

68. ———. "Is Frustration Compatible With Good Mental Hygiene?" *Prog. Educ.* **30:**107–110 (February 1953).

69. ———. "Teaching as a Function of the Teacher's Personality." *J. Teach. Educ.* **5:**79–83 (March 1954).

70. TALBOT, MIRA and ISABELLE HENSON. "Pupils Psychologically Absent from School." *J. Orthopsychiatry.* **24:**381–390 (April 1954).

71. TAYLOR, CHARLES and ARTHUR W. COMBS. "Self-Acceptance and Adjustment." *J. Consult. Psychol.* **16:**89–91 (April 1952).

72. THOMPSON, GEORGE G. and SAM L. WITRYOL. "Adult Recall of Unpleasant Experiences during Three Periods of Childhood." *J. Genet. Psychol.* **72:** 111–123 (March 1948).

73. TROW, WM. CLARK, *et. al.* "Psychology of Group Behavior: The Class as a Group." *J. Educ. Psychol.* **41:**322–338 (October 1950).

74. WAITE, R. R., *et al. "A Study of Anxiety and Learning in Children." J. Ab. & Soc. Psychol.* **57:**267–270 (1958).

75. WATSON, GOODWIN. "Some Personality Differences in Children Related to Strict or Permissive Parental Discipline." *J. Psychol.* **44:**227–249 (July 1957).

76. WICKMAN, E. K. *Children's Behavior and Teachers' Attitudes.* New York: The Commonwealth Fund (1928).

77. WIRT, ROBERT D. and WILLIAM F. BROEN, JR. "The Relation of the Children's Manifest Anxiety Scale to the Concept of Anxiety as Used in the Clinic." *J. Consult. Psychol.* **20:**482 (December 1956).

78. WRIGHTSTONE, J. WAYNE. "Measuring the Social Climate of a Classroom." *J. Educ. Res.* **44:**341–351 (January 1951).

79. Yearbook Committee. "Implications of the Yearbook for the Improvement of Mental Health in Our Schools." *Mental Health in Modern Education,* N.S.S.E. 54th Yrbk., 1955, chap. XVI.

80. YOUNG, L. R. "Delinquency From the Child's Viewpoint." In Vedder *The Juvenile Offender.* New York: Doubleday (1954).

## PART V

MEASUREMENT,
EVALUATION AND
REPORTING –
QUALITATIVE AND
QUANTITATIVE
APPRAISAL

An integral part of teaching is appraisal and reporting. There is no other way to judge the extent to which goals of instruction have been achieved and to relate this to interested persons. Unfortunately the responsibility is often passed over lightly and superficially in programs for the preparation of teachers. It sometimes seems to be assumed that measurement and evaluation are something which teachers come by just naturally and that they need no instruction. Or it may be assumed that the matter is too simple to require any special treatment. Whatever the reason for the neglect, it is safe to say that teachers often do a rather inefficient and careless job of it. The evidence for this is not hard to find. In the first place, teachers are usually reluctant to answer questions about their procedures of measurement and evaluation. This does not seem to be so about questions on methods or materials which they are usually ready and even proud to display and talk about. In the second place, the kinds of tests and examinations constructed by teachers, when copies of these can be obtained at all, typically leave much to be desired in relation to generally accepted standards of workmanship.

Teachers seldom spend the time and thought on their techniques and instruments for evaluation that they do on other phases of their work. It almost seems as though measurement and appraisal is an afterthought and often a distasteful one at that. They seemingly often prefer to rely also on very subjective and hazy judgments rather than to take the time and trouble to construct more efficient and accurate measures.

As stated above, appraisal and reporting are inescapable and important responsibilities of every teacher. Consequently, it seems reasonable to expect that they should be discharged as well as possible and not sloughed off or performed carelessly or superficially any more than is any other phase of the work.

In the matter of marking it is evident from the professional literature on the subject that a good deal of inquiry and thought has been directed at this problem. A number of systems of marking have been tried with varying degrees of success and acceptance. There has been a clear trend away from the percentage system to a system of letter grades. Also, there has been considerable experimentation with a reduced number of marks, such as "pass" and "fail"; with a differentiated marking system giving separate marks for achievement, effort, etc.; and with systems which attempt to give marks in relation to ability.

With regard to report cards, comments similar to those just made on marking apply. A good deal of experimenting has been done with different kinds of report cards and no report cards, particularly in elementary grades. Here letters to parents and parent-teacher conferences have been widely used. These methods have disadvantages as well as advantages, as those who have tried them have discovered. However, the trial of such methods of reporting has revealed a good deal about the comparative merits of the more conventional versus newer procedures. It has resulted in some definite improvements in the former and some useful information about the latter.

Our growing enrollments and increasingly complicated curriculums make the use and understanding of standardized tests more and more necessary. They provide measures that are skillfully planned and constructed, comprehensive, objective, and efficient. They are generally superior, technically at least, to what a local school system or individual can devise or has time and resources to construct. They provide a basis for important purposes such as diagnosis, counseling, comparison, placement, to name only a few. They do not take the place of measurement and evaluation locally devised, but provide a useful supplement to such procedures. Few teachers today can function effectively without some knowledge and understanding of such instruments. Thus it behooves the teacher, and even more the counselor and administrator, to have knowledge and understanding of modern standardized tests and testing programs.

In the section which follows, problems of measurement, evaluation, marking, and reporting are discussed. The selections are generally practical and down-to-earth; they deal with fundamentals of concern and interest to all professional school personnel, as well as to pupils and parents.

# 44

# TESTS AND WHAT THEY TEST *

## J. Wayne Wrightstone

There was a time in our schools when teachers and administrators seemed quite insensible to the fact that children differed in ability, aptitude, interests, and therefore in achievement. If a pupil did not learn well, it was assumed that this was a sign that he was lazy and the way to cure that was by application of the rod. Today we know that children do differ in almost every conceivable way and that these individual differences, very large in some cases, have much to do with school achievement as well as personal adjustment, and success in school as well as out. Modern tests and testing procedures have done much to bring out the fact of such differences and to quantify them. That is, tests not only reveal that the differences exist but also tell us their extent or size. In the selection which follows, we are given a brief overview of the major types of standardized tests used in the schools today and their particular uses and limitations. These are the ones every teacher and counselor should know about and understand so that he can use them properly and interpret results obtained from their use.

*Questions:*

1. The author lists and discusses four major types of tests. Can you name any important kinds not mentioned in the article? If so, what are they? What are their uses?

2. What is a test battery? What is its particular usefulness?

\*　　\*　　\*

Years ago, schools were concerned mostly with teaching facts and skills to children. Tests were given to find out how well Johnny had memorized his spelling or the date of Columbus' discovery of America. If Johnny made a poor showing on his tests, or if his conduct presented problems, he was punished with a bad report card, the disapproval of his teachers, and the

\* Reprinted from the *National Education Association Journal,* **47:**221–223 (April 1958), by permission of author and publisher.

disappointment of his parents. Often neither Johnny nor his parents nor his teachers knew just why he did not do well in school or just how he could be helped to do better.

Years of studying how children grow and what their needs are at different levels of development have brought important changes in educational goals. Modern educators know that children differ in their interests, their abilities, and the way they grow.

Teachers now stress the importance of knowing *what* each child is like and *why* he is that way, in order to help him develop to the best of his ability.

With the setting of new goals, emphasis in schools has shifted from merely pouring information into students to meeting their individual needs as well. Growing recognition of the importance of student counseling and guidance has stimulated the development of new and better tests to help us learn, for example, whether:

Nancy has enough talent to make her music lessons worthwhile.

Sam is bright enough to succeed in college.

Mike reads as well as he should for his age.

Bill's moody spells indicate serious abnormality or emotional disturbance.

Susan should be in a class for retarded pupils.

There is a test for almost every area of a student's life, and—properly used—these tests can be of great service in helping us answer questions about a child's ability, behavior, and special skills. Usually, we want answers to these questions for a particular purpose, such as to aid us in making a decision or to guide us in some kind of action. Increasingly, we realize that measurement, or testing, is a *means* to an end, not an end in itself.

Teachers should be familiar with the following types of tests and know what each is designed to test:

## Special Aptitude Tests

These are tests given to measure a person's capacity or talent for a given activity. To help decide about Nancy's music lessons, our test will probably measure her sense of pitch and time, her tonal memory or ability to distinguish between melodies, and her sense of rhythm.

A high score on these points does not *guarantee* Nancy's musical career because it takes more than aptitude to produce a Lily Pons. But the high score does tell us that Nancy is a good risk for special music instruction. Aptitude tests, therefore, are tests of *capacity*. They may be used to determine talent for clerical or mechanical work just as well as for artistic ability.

### Intelligence Tests

Intelligence tests are very specialized aptitude tests that answer questions about *learning ability*.

The two main types of intelligence tests are the IQ test and the multi-factor test.

The IQ (intelligence quotient) test provides a single score—a convenient numerical label which seems to speak with more authority than mere words like "bright" or "average." IQ is a useful concept if we remember that no single test tells the whole story about a child. We must be cautious, there-fore, in using the IQ test to predict achievement in specific school subjects, although it is a good guide to general school learning.

The multifactor test is based on the theory that intelligence is *not* a single trait, but is composed of several different abilities, such as understanding words and ideas about words, working quickly and accurately with num-bers, being able to plan ahead.

Both types of tests require a youngster to give evidence of logical think-ing, and test results on both provide a fairly accurate indication of how well he will do in school.

But here again, high scores do not *guarantee* success. Sam, a bright high-school student, may fail in college if he is not strongly motivated to succeed, or if he is undergoing some particular problems in adjustment or is otherwise emotionally disturbed. Special tests to analyze personality fac-tors, therefore, are often needed.

### Tests of Personal and Social Qualities

Measurements of personality are usually regarded as "tests," but more precisely they should be called *questionnaires, inventories, schedules,* or *records,* as there are no right or wrong answers to a personality measure.

When we wonder whether Bill is "normal," we are really wondering about his personality, a term that covers his interests, his abilities, his behavior patterns, his temperament, and often his aptitudes and capacities as well.

Probably no one test can accurately measure *all* aspects of his person-ality, but we may start by giving Bill a test which asks what kinds of activi-ties he enjoys, what moods he experiences in various situations, and whether he prefers to be with other people or by himself.

If his score is much like the average person's, we say Bill is normal. If not, we may administer several additional tests and conduct various interviews to see whether personality problems are keeping him from living effectively—and to find clues to ways to help him overcome his problems.

## Achievement Tests

The most common tests used in schools are achievement tests—tests to show how much a pupil knows about reading, writing, and arithmetic, and about social studies and sciences, too. When Mike's teacher wants to know if he's reading as well as he should for his age, chances are that a reading achievement test is in order.

This test will measure Mike's *vocabulary* and his *speed* of reading. The test may also contain short stories or reading passages followed by a set of questions to see if Mike understands what he reads—what his reading *comprehension* is.

Achievement tests show the teacher the facts, skills, and understanding pupils have absorbed—what level they *have* achieved. In this way, they differ from the aptitude tests mentioned earlier. Mike's score on a reading achievement test will tell his teacher how well he *is* doing rather than how well he *can* do. To tell how well he *should* be reading, we will need to know his capacity or aptitude for reading.

The preceding examples have been simplified to show what kinds of tests are used and why. Only rarely would we find just one test being used at a time. Usually, it takes a combination of tests—a *battery* of tests—to answer a question, or to make a decision about a person's abilities or aptitudes or personality. Combinations of tests help us to see the whole child more clearly and to avoid dangerous, one-sided judgments.

# 45

## ABCs OF TEST CONSTRUCTION *

### Julian C. Stanley

Most of the tests taken by pupils are of the home-made variety. Every teacher has the responsibility of measuring and evaluating the pupils in his classes. Principally, the teacher is concerned with evaluating achievement, that is, what the pupil has learned from instruction. Before this can be accurately determined, the teacher must decide what his goals or objectives are. In the light of these, he can construct a test to see how well pupils have progressed in the attainment of the goals set. Most teachers depend for such appraisal on tests they have made themselves. In the article below, Dr. Stanley discusses the importance of thinking about objectives before constructing a test. He then describes different types of tests and test items, and explains the advantages and disadvantages of each. Included in the discussion are all the well-known varieties: essay, short answer, true-false, multiple choice, and matching. The article presents practical suggestions for making better items of each kind and some general principles regarding the test as a whole.

*Questions:*

1. In what situations, subjects, or for what purposes would the essay test be most useful? Where would it be least useful?
2. The author uses the terms *reliable* and *valid* in his discussion. Define each and distinguish between them.
3. Construct a short set of matching items. Suggest some cautions to be observed in making such sets of items.

\* \* \*

Constructing a good test is one of the teacher's most difficult duties. Good tests do not just happen. Actual test construction, therefore, requires much thought and careful planning.

* Reprinted from the *National Education Association Journal,* **47:**224–226 (April 1958), by permission of author and publisher.

## Planning the Test

A well-planned test will provide the means for evaluating progress toward the expected outcomes of instruction, as expressed in the educational philosophy of the particular school and as defined in the objectives of the particular course.

If the school hopes to produce "good citizens" with "integrated personalities," for example, tests must measure the development of good social attitudes and a widening range of significant interests.

For any given course, instructional objectives must be expressed in terms of the specific changes in pupil behavior or growth which the teacher hopes to bring about.

A teacher, for instance, should be conscious that such an objective as the development of an appreciation of literature may express itself in various forms of student reaction. He sets out then to phrase test questions which will determine whether a particular piece of writing gave individual students a sense of satisfaction and enthusiasm, made them want to read more by the same author, stimulated their own creative expression.

The well-planned test will reflect the relative amount of emphasis each objective has received in the actual teaching of the course. The same test might not be equally valid for two teachers of general science if one has emphasized the memorizing of isolated facts, while the other was more concerned with the interrelation of facts. Each teacher would be helped by drawing up in outline form a kind of table of specifications to indicate not only the objectives of the course, but also the relative amount of time spent on each.

The content of the test should show a similar proportion in regard to the *number* of items to be included but not the *type,* for the type of item depends upon the nature of the objective to be measured.

The well-planned test must be designed to accomplish the purpose it is to serve. If the purpose is to give the basis for school marks or classification, it will attempt to rank the pupils in order of their total achievement. But if the purpose is diagnosis, its value will depend upon its ability to reveal specific weaknesses in the achievement of individual pupils.

Diagnostic tests would cover a limited scope, but in much greater detail than a test of general achievement, and would be arranged to give scores on the separate parts. The range of difficulty of items is relatively less important, also, in diagnostic tests. This is true, too, of mastery tests administered at the end of a teaching unit to see whether minimum essentials have been achieved.

The well-planned test will also fit the conditions under which it is to be administered, such as the time available for testing, facilities for duplicating the test copies, and cost of materials, as well as the age and experience of the pupils being tested.

## Preparing the Test

In actual construction of a test, these suggestions have helped:

1. Prepare a rough draft of the test as soon as possible. Many teachers jot down items day by day for possible inclusion to help ensure that no important points will be omitted, particularly those appearing in supplementary material that might be overlooked if the textbook itself is the chief basis of the test.

2. Do not make the test items too easy. Many teacher-constructed tests fail to make the items difficult enough. This, no doubt, is due in part to the influence of the "70% should be the passing grade" tradition. However, the test that is too easy is not an efficient instrument for measuring pupil progress.

3. Include more items in the first draft than will be needed in the final form. This will permit culling out of weak items and those not needed to produce proper balance.

4. Subject the test to critical revision some time after it is drafted by checking items against the table of specifications to see if they show the desired emphasis on various topics. If tests are submitted for criticism to other teachers of the subject, points of doubtful importance can be weeded out and ambiguous wording corrected.

5. Include more than one type of item in the test. A variety of test types is more interesting to students. The test situation may also require that three or four forms of objective items be used, or that these be combined with discussion or essay-type questions.

6. Place all items of one kind together in the test. Sometimes completion, true-false, and multiple-choice questions are thrown together in random order. This arrangement is rarely, if ever, desirable. When like items are grouped, the pupil can take full advantage of the mind-set imposed by a particular form, and the teacher will find scoring and interpretation of scores easier.

7. Arrange test items in an ascending order of difficulty. The placing of

very difficult items at the beginning is likely to produce needless discouragement for the average or below-average student.

8. Avoid a regular sequence in the pattern of responses. If items are arranged alternately true and false, or two true and two false, pupils are likely to catch on and answer correctly without considering the content of the item at all.

9. Make directions to the pupil clear, concise, and complete. Instructions should be so clear that the weakest pupil knows what he is expected to do, though he may be unable to do it.

It is better to tell young children to "draw a line under" than to "underline." In lower grades, teachers find it helpful to read instructions aloud while the class follows silently the written instructions. If the form of the test is unfamiliar or complicated, a generous use of samples correctly marked, or practice tests, is recommended.

Regardless of how carefully a test is planned and edited, it is impossible to know solely by inspection exactly how good it is, or which are the weak items. If possible, therefore, the test should be given some advance tryout which will approximate the conditions under which the real test will be given, show the actual length of time it will require, and indicate what scoring difficulties may result.

Because various studies have shown that a majority of teachers, especially at the high-school level, use a combination of essay and objective questions, the uses and limitations of both will be briefly examined here.

### The Essay Test

The essay test has both unique advantages and serious disadvantages. Some authorities claim that it calls forth less than half the knowledge the average pupil possesses on a subject, compared with results from an objective test, and takes twice the time to do it; that it overrates the importance of knowing how to say a thing and underrates the importance of having something to say; and that the score resulting from an essay test depends more upon *who* reads it and *when* than upon the student who wrote it.

Offsetting the serious scoring difficulties connected with essay tests and their frequently low degrees of validity, reliability, and usability, there is much to indicate that such tests have a legitimate place in the modern school.

Specifically, they are useful for measuring functional information, certain aspects of thinking, study skill and work habits, and an active social philosophy. These are educational objectives which emphasize the *functioning* of knowledge rather than its mere possession.

Such tests are especially valuable in courses in English composition and journalism, where the student's ability to express himself is a major instructional objective, and in advanced courses in other subjects where critical evaluation and the ability to assimilate and organize large amounts of material are important.

Essay tests have at least one other general merit: When pupils expect the test to be of that type, in whole or in part, they seem more likely to employ such desirable study techniques as outlining and summarizing, and to make a greater effort to recognize trends and relationships.

Despite popular opinion to the contrary, a high-quality essay test is more difficult to construct than is a good objective test. These three rules, however, should be helpful in improving the construction and use of essay tests:

1. Restrict such a test to those functions for which it is best adapted.

2. Increase the number of questions asked and decrease the amount of discussion required for each.

3. Make definite provisions for teaching pupils how to take such examinations.

### Types of Objective Tests

The simple *recall test* item employs a direct question, a stimulus word or phrase, or a specific direction to elicit from the pupil a response based on his previous experience. The typical response is short—hence its other name, the short-answer question.

The main problem is to phrase these test items so that they will call forth responses from a higher level than mere memory, and so that they can be readily scored.

Example: Eight is what percent of 64?

The *completion test* consists of a series of sentences in which certain important words or phrases have been replaced by blanks to be filled in by the students. This test has wide applicability, but unless very carefully prepared, it is likely to measure rote memory rather than real understanding, or to measure general intelligence or linguistic aptitude rather than school achievement.

Scoring is also more subjective, and complicated by the fact that the missing words are written in blanks scattered all over the page, rather than in a column. This difficulty can be avoided by a form such as this:

1. The man who headed the first expedition to circumnavigate the globe was ——————.

2. The Articles of Confederation were in force from 1781 to ——————.

An *alternative-response test* is made of items each of which permits only two possible responses. The usual form is the familiar true-false item and its cousins, the right-wrong, yes-no, same-opposite, and multiple-choice questions.

While the true-false type of question is popularly considered easy to prepare, experienced test-makers point out that this type of test requires great skill, and care must be taken in wording so that the *content* rather than the *form* of the statement will determine the response. The following suggestions may be useful in constructing such tests.

1. Avoid specific determiners, that is, strongly worded statements containing words such as "always," "all," or "none," which may indicate to pupils that the statement is likely to be false.

2. Avoid using the exact language of the textbook, with only minor changes to give the true-false pattern, because this puts too great a premium on rote memory.

3. Avoid trick statements which appear to be true but which are really false because of some inconspicuous word or phrase, such as "The Battle of Hastings was fought in 1066 *B.C.*"

4. Avoid "double-headed" statements, especially if partly true and partly false, as in this sentence: "Poe wrote *The Gold Bug* and *The Scarlet Letter.*"

5. Avoid double negatives lest pupils versed in grammar conclude that two negatives equal an affirmative, while others think such statements are emphatic negatives.

6. Avoid unfamiliar, figurative, or literary language and long statements with complex sentence structure—for reasons which should be obvious.

7. Avoid words that may have different meanings for different students. "Often" may mean once a week to one child; three times a year to another.

A *multiple choice test* is composed of items which require the student to select a correct or definitely better response from two or more alternatives (at least four whenever possible). This is one of the most useful test forms. It may be used to ascertain the ability to give definitions, identify purposes and causes, similarities and differences, or to ask many other varieties of questions.

In phrasing multiple-choice questions, it is essential to avoid giving irrelevant or superficial clues, and to assure that the question measures more than memory. The diagnostic value of this type of item depends as much on the skilful wording of the incorrect choices presented as upon correct statement of the right choice.

Scoring may be facilitated by arranging the items in groups, putting together all items with the same number of choices, and requiring the simplest possible method of recording the response.

Other useful rules are:

1. Make all responses grammatically consistent. For example, if the verb is singular, avoid plural responses.

2. Use direct questions rather than incomplete statements whenever possible. This helps eliminate irrelevant clues.

3. Arrange the responses so that the correct choice occurs about equally in all positions, and do not consistently make the correct answer longer or shorter than the others.

4. Make all the responses plausible, and when testing at higher levels, increase the similarity in the choices under each item in order to better test the powers of discrimination.

A *matching test* involves the association of two things in the mind of the learner by requiring him to pair the items in two columns: events and dates, events and persons, terms and definitions, laws and illustrations, and the like. Matching exercises are well adapted to testing in *who, what, where,* and *when* areas but not to measuring understanding as distinguished from mere memory.

Since most of the tests used in classrooms are teacher-made, it is highly important that teachers develop proficiency in the building of tests by discriminating use of what is now known, by keeping themselves informed on new studies of testing techniques and methods, and by careful evaluation of their own testing, day by day.

# 46

## EVALUATION—MORE THAN TESTING *

### Helen Heffernan

When modern objective tests came into existence and use about a half century ago, they seemed so superior to what had been available prior to that time that they were widely adopted and used, sometimes with much enthusiasm but little realization of the fact that they had limitations as well as advantages. In time this early uncritical attitude began to be replaced by a more thoughtful one. These new tests did have many uses and they were an improvement in many obvious ways over older measures. But they were not a cure-all, as indeed, no thoughtful person who knew them well ever claimed them to be. Nevertheless, a reaction set in and, as often happens, some persons went to extremes in their criticisms. It would have been better, some said, if these new-fangled tests had never been invented. Such an extreme denunciation is certainly quite unrealistic. It is just not possible to imagine schools, colleges, business, industry, or the military getting along today without the use of objective tests, considering the numbers they have to deal with and the complexity of their programs. In the selection which follows, Miss Heffernan calls attention to the need for a broad view of educational goals and their measurement. She points out that the full development of a child requires a thorough understanding of all phases of his development, including what tests reveal and much more that we learn by other means.

*Questions:*

1. The author says evaluation is more than testing. Discuss the meaning and significance of this distinction.

2. Are tests infallible? Have you ever read any professional literature which claimed that they were? If so, cite it.

3. What does the author mean by the last paragraph in the article?

\* \* \*

Our century has witnessed a nationwide effort to discover, through the application of scientific procedures, the effect of education on the behavior

* Reprinted from the *National Education Association Journal,* **47**:227–229 (April 1958), by permission of author and publisher.

of the learner. Tests have been devised in an effort to appraise various facets of a child's growth and development.

For their early attempts to create instruments to appraise the effectiveness of teaching and learning, the test-makers naturally selected those fields which appeared most likely to yield objective evidence of the outcomes of the educational program.

During the early decades of this century, professional educators directed much effort to making, standardizing, and using tests that are particularly applicable to the basic skills. School administrators were deeply interested in these devices and used them to classify children, to place them in different ability groups, and to make comparisons between children, teachers, grades, and schools.

At the same time that this great production and use of appraisal instruments was going forward, leaders in education and professional organizations throughout the country were carrying on studies and discussions designed to define more precisely the purposes of education in a democratic society such as ours.

From these efforts, there emerged a conviction that education must aim toward the development of personality, character, and active participating citizenship as well as toward the acquisition of knowledge and skills.

Experimentation in carefully controlled situations was also proving that basic knowledges and skills were best attained in lifelike experiences and situations in which the learner could put them to use rather than through formal drill.

The study of the purposes of education designed to meet the social needs of our times was greatly influenced by the contribution of the psychologists to our knowledge of individual differences. Reinforced by experimentation in measurement, the psychologists contributed to a widespread understanding that human beings differ from one another in every conceivable way.

Coupled with this knowledge and a growing acceptance of individual variation was our basic democratic commitment to the worth of the individual. Published statements of the purposes of education began to give a new emphasis to the importance of helping each individual to meet responsibility in all areas of life—family membership, community living, citizenship, the world of work.

To this acceptance, we can attribute the tremendous accomplishment during more recent years to meet the needs of children who deviate from normal in sensory acuity, physical adequacy, intellectual endowment, or emotional stability. Efforts to meet the needs of every child in our society have revealed the simple fact that the more we know about any child, the better we are able to serve him.

Finally, experimental schools have reinforced the principle that we learn what we do. Only through actual participation can learning take place. Children learn to share unselfishly only through their feelings of satisfaction in the outcomes of experiences in which they have behaved unselfishly. They learn to be responsible persons only as their nurture provides day-by-day opportunity for them to accept gradually increasing responsibility in situations that have meaning for them.

They learn to express initiative and creative ideas freely as the social situation provides acceptance and approval. They learn to be their honest selves as they come to understand how a group can frequently work together and through the diverse contributions of all its members produce something of value beyond that which could have been achieved by any individual alone.

Obviously, this broadened conception of the purposes of the school necessitates a shift in emphasis in measurement. As education has moved away from exclusive emphasis upon schooling as the acquisition of subject matter, the need for new types of measurement in terms of all the objectives of education has become apparent.

Teachers still want to know how well the children for whom they have responsibility have learned to read and spell and do arithmetic. They want to know the specific points at which their efforts to guide the child's learning have been successful or have failed to reach their goal. Only through such knowledge can the teacher modify the selection of materials and methods essential to the next step in the learning process.

But teachers want to know, too, what evidence is available that the child is maintaining and developing his physical resources; how well he is acquiring the major concepts in social studies and science; how well he is developing sound social attitudes and wholesome human relations; how well he is developing esthetic skills and appreciations.

Because certain of these purposes of education lend themselves less easily to objective measurement, a certain emphasis has been placed on the precise instruments which yield easily recorded and presumably comparable mathematical symbols. Mathematical symbols seem to convey an aura of authenticity.

In this situation, it becomes the urgent responsibility of the profession to see to it that education is not unduly dominated by devices which, at best, measure only part of what we are attempting to do in our schools and which, if improperly used, may make the teaching of the more easily measurable segment of the educational program the major focus of the schools. Educators must also take care that test-makers not be allowed to determine the curriculum.

Tests are but one of many different instruments which may be used effectively to assess pupil growth and development. Particularly do educators need to be watchful lest the use of tests unaccompanied by other evaluative procedures actually interfere with the achievement of the comprehensive purposes of education.

The aims of education in any school should determine the nature of the evaluation program in that school. The purposes of evaluation should be to improve learning, and, therefore, evaluation should be wide and diversified. Evaluation of the instructional program and the achievement of educational objectives as a whole should consist of much more than a testing program concerned with subject matter.

Good teaching emphasizes the importance of understanding and the ability to use intellectual processes, and especially the logical construction of ideas within a subject or experience as a basis for the child's dealing with his problems of living. These may be entirely overlooked in a testing program.

In *Education for Social Competence,* I. James Quillen and Lavone Hanna say that evaluation includes all the means of collecting evidence on pupil behavior.

In recent years, extensive use has been made of rating scales and growth records, pupil diaries, and the like. Pupil activities, questionnaires, checklists, interviews, reports from parents, and samples of pupils' work also provide us with useful evidence of pupil behavior.

Quillen and Hanna further point out that evaluation is more concerned with the growth of a pupil than with his status in the group, or with the status of the group, the school, or the program in relation to some national norm. Present-day concepts of child growth and development imply that the major point of reference shall be the child's former status, not a norm.

Too often the success of a school system's instructional program is determined by how well it compares with other school systems. Such an evaluation may have a certain usefulness, but it tends to draw the teacher's attention away from the individual child.

If teachers are to be judged in terms of the subject-matter achievement of their pupils, the test items really become the course of study. Teachers inevitably become more concerned with the total score than with the evidence revealed by performance on individual items which may indicate needed changes in the curriculum or increased individual guidance in learning.

Teachers need to understand the complexity of each individual, and for this we need inservice child-study programs as well as adequate preservice study of child growth and development; we need cumulative guidance records, tests of mental maturity as well as achievement tests, and knowledge of other reactions of each child. We do not need comparisons of classes and schools to achieve these purposes.

Evaluation is concerned with the total personality of the pupils and with gathering evidence on all aspects of personality development.

If the purpose of education is to change behavior of individuals, then the kinds of behavior desired become the educational objectives, and these include the knowing, the feeling, the thinking, and the doing aspects of behavior.

With a proper educational environment, we know that children will be motivated to grow and develop, but each will grow in accordance with his own individual growth pattern. If children do not grow, we can be certain that something is amiss with their environment or their physical makeup. To bring about growth, we must seek to discover the causes of the behavior which seems to be impeding expected development.

This is no easy process; the teacher must maintain a questioning attitude. Could the cause be found in physical or sensory maladjustment? In a failure of his environment to satisfy fundamental human needs? In anxiety or tension about his relationships with parents or teacher?

The chief function of measurement and diagnosis, then, is to find out how the child is growing and developing so that we may evaluate the adequency of his educational environment.

Testing is limited to the quantitative aspects of evaluation. Evaluation includes, in addition, the qualitative aspect. Good instruments of evaluation should help us to determine more than what the child is doing to his school work; they should help us to discover what the school program is doing to the child.

There is no way teachers can evaluate children unless they understand the pupils' individual differences.

The emphasis in education must be on securing a better understanding of children by making available to teachers the results of scientific study in child development. Part of this task involves a closer relationship between the home and the school.

Parents need to know that teachers value their friendly interest in the school and in the child's school life; teachers need to understand the cultures of the homes from which the children come and the relationships among the members of the family, because these relationships constitute the basis of the child's inner security.

Without this security, his learning will be ineffective; with it he will grow and develop in the way that is possible for him.

Providing children with understanding teachers is a serious educational task. It involves providing adequate opportunity for teachers to study children in order to make more accurate decisions concerning them. It involves training in scientific methods of arriving at judgments through the accumulation of a multitude of facts.

Looking at a child's total score on a test is almost meaningless unless the teacher knows specifically what the test actually measures and the values the child attaches to the particular learning.

Man's understanding of man is just beginning to keep pace with man's understanding of nature. In our scientific age, it is of the utmost importance to be aware of man's relationship to man. As teachers, we need to find out as much as we can about mental health and guide children in terms of our insight. As teachers, we need to know that if we induce anxiety in children, we must provide opportunity to release tension.

We know that thinking and doing and feeling are learned things; and learning takes place in relation to other people. No matter what a child is learning, he is also learning about getting along with other people.

Educators who have kept up with the progress that has been made in child study and the learning process are putting increased emphasis on *understanding* children as compared with *testing* them.

These educators are aware, for example, that when children first enter school, it may be a definitely traumatic experience for them to be subjected immediately to a testing program—whether it be reading-readiness tests or examinations by the school nurse. They know that children are already confronted with serious problems of adjusting to strange people, a new situation, and new demands.

Education must continue to become more personalized and humanized. We live in an age of automation, threatening to individual personality. But we live, also, in an age of awareness. We know the things that threaten the wholesome development of children and adults. We know the ways by which we may modulate the child's relationship to life.

We must be ever watchful not to sell the real values of education short because of the apparent infallibility of procedures which emphasize only a part of the far horizon of human realization toward which we move.

# 47

# RELIABILITY OF GRADING WORK
# IN MATHEMATICS *

## Daniel Starch and Edward C. Elliott

This pioneer study, now largely of historical interest, represents a milestone in the field of evaluation. One of several, it shows with simple and rather devastating technique the unreliability of teachers' marking even in so objective a study as plane geometry. The same paper, reproduced in its entirety as written by a high school student on an examination and graded by 138 teachers of geometry in as many different high schools was given marks on a percentage basis from 25 to more than 90. Similar results had been obtained in another study using an English paper. The authors thought that the great variability found in the grades of this paper could be explained by the fact that English is not as exact and therefore would result in more subjectivity. They were somewhat surprised at the findings with the paper in geometry, therefore. No one had demonstrated this fact so neatly and convincingly before, and it had a great impact particularly since it appeared at a time when objective or "new type" examinations were coming into general use.

*Questions:*

1. What reasons do the authors give for the finding that the variability of marks on the geometry paper is even greater than that found for the English paper? Can you think of any others?

2. Could the authors have reduced the variability of marks? How?

* * *

The present article is a sequel to the recent investigation of grading work in English [1] which revealed rather wide variations and differences among

---

\* Reprinted from *School Review*, **21**:254–259 (April 1913), by permission of senior author and the University of Chicago Press. Copyright 1913 by the University of Chicago.

[1] D. Starch and E. C. Elliott, "Reliability of the Grading of High School Work in English," *School Review*, XX, 442–57.

teachers in evaluating the same examination paper. It has been urged that marks in determining the merit of language work would necessarily vary considerably because of the personal and subjective factors involved, and that the situation would be very different in an exact science such as mathematics. Pursuant to this suggestion we have made a similar investigation with a geometry paper. This paper was written as a final examination by a pupil in one of the largest high schools in Wisconsin. Plates of this answer paper were made and several hundred copies were printed upon foolscap, thus exactly reproducing the original in every detail.

## Questions

Choose 8, including one selected from 4, 6, and 8.

1. Two triangles having the three sides of one equal, respectively, to the three sides of the other, etc. Prove.

2. Prove that every point in the bisector of an angle is equally distant from the sides of the angle.

3. An angle formed by two intersecting chords is measured by, etc. Prove.

4. If the middle points of two opposite sides of a quadrilateral be joined to the middle points of the diagonals, the joining lines form a parallelogram.

5. To construct a mean proportional to two given lines. Explain fully.

6. AM is a chord of a circle, $xy$ is a diameter perpendicular to AN and intersecting AM at O. XO is 10 in. and $ax$ is 20 in. Find the diameter of the circle.

7. The ratio of the areas of two similar triangles is equal to, etc. Prove.

8. Find the area of a right triangle whose hypotenuse is 1 ft. 8 in. and one of whose legs is 1 ft.

9. The sum of the interior angles of a triangle is equal to, etc. Prove.

10. If two circles are tangent, and two secants are drawn through the point of contact, the chords joining the intersections of the secants and the circumferences are parallel.

A set of questions and a copy of the answer paper were sent to approximately 180 high schools in the North Central Association, with the request that the principal teacher in mathematics grade this paper according to the practices and standards of the school.

One hundred and forty papers were returned. Twelve had to be discarded because some of the data called for were not given. Of the remaining 128, 43 came from schools whose passing grade is 70, 75 from schools whose passing grade is 75, and 10 from schools whose passing grade is 80. The papers show evidence of having been marked with unusual care and attention. Separate grades and comments usually accompanied the answer to each question.

The grades thus assigned are represented by the distribution charts in Figs. 1, 2, and 3. The scheme of these charts is self-evident. The range of marks is indicated along the base line and the number of times each grade was given is indicated by the number of dots above that grade. Thus in Fig. 1 the grade 70 was assigned by 5 teachers. The marks assigned by 10 schools whose passing grade is 80 are 72, 80, 83, 80, 58, 50, 50, 75, 73, 70.

Fig. 1 gives the values assigned by 43 teachers in schools whose passing grade is 70. Fig. 2 gives the values assigned by 75 teachers in schools whose

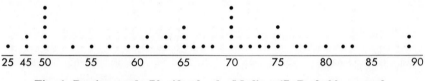

Fig. 1. Passing grade 70. 43 schools. Median 67. Probable error 8.

passing grade is 75. The median indicates the central measure. It is roughly, but not exactly, equivalent to the average. It is used here in preference to the average because it represents more correctly the central tendency than the average would. The probable error is roughly, though not exactly, equivalent to the average amount of error or deviation of the mark from the median.

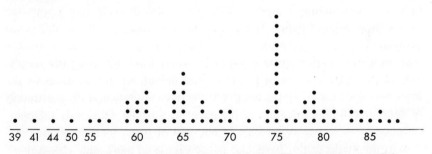

Fig. 2.    Passing grade 75. 75 schools. Median 70. Probable error 7.2.

Fig. 3 is a composite chart showing the values assigned by the entire group of teachers. The values assigned by the teachers in schools whose passing grade is 75 are represented as in Fig. 1, while the values assigned by the teachers in schools whose passing grade is 70 are all weighted by three points because the medians of the two groups differ by that amount.

The investigation shows the extremely wide variation of the grades even more forcibly than our study of English marks. The distribution considered purely from the statistical standpoint is a normal distribution just like that of any set of mental or physical measurements. But the alarming fact is the wide range of the distribution.

A geometry paper was used because of the current assumption that a mathematical paper can be graded with mathematical precision. Our inves-

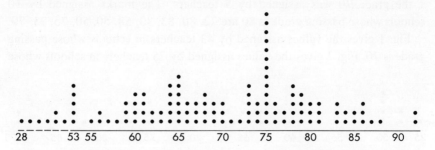

**Fig. 3. Passing grade 75. Marks assigned by schools whose passing grade is 70 are weighted by 3 points. Median 70. Probable error 7.5.**

tigation shows that the marks of this particular geometry paper vary even more widely than the marks of either English paper used in the former study. The probable error of the geometry marks is 7.5 (Fig. 3), whereas the probable error of the English papers was 4.0 and 4.8 respectively.

A little analysis, however, will show the absurdity of assuming greater precision in evaluating a mathematical paper than in evaluating a language or any other kind of paper. While it is true that there can be no difference of opinion as to the correctness of a demonstration, yet there are countless ways in which the demonstration may be worked out, involving the succession of the steps, the use of theorems and definitions, the neatness of the drawings, and most of all the relative value of each particular demonstration or definition in the evaluation of the paper as a whole. Obviously the complication of factors is as intricate in one sort of paper as in another.

Why the marks of this particular paper vary even more widely than those of the English papers is to be sought in the fact that this geometry paper allowed of two fairly distinct ways of evaluation. The form, make-up, and appearance of the paper were of decidedly poor quality. Some teachers entirely disregarded these elements while others imposed a heavy penalty upon the paper on their account. In many instances this was indicated by the comments on the papers. But even this difference in viewpoint alone does not explain the extremely high or extremely low marks. For example, one teacher gave the paper a mark of 50 and said that he had deducted 4 points for spelling. Another marked it 45 and stated that he had made no deduction for poor form. Still another one marked it 75 including a penalty for form, or 85 excluding a penalty for form. Furthermore the amount that was subtracted for careless make-up ranged from 3 points in the case of one teacher to 13 points in the case of another.

It is therefore fully evident that there is no inherent reason why a mathematical paper should be capable of more precise evaluation than any other kind of paper. In fact, the greater certainty of correctness or incorrectness of a mathematical demonstration or definition may even contribute slightly to the wider variability of the marks, because the strict marker would have less occasion to give the pupil the benefit of the doubt.

In the next place, the criticism might be offered that the wide variation of the marks is due to the fact that the paper was graded by schools scattered over a large area, each one having a different standard of attainment. A propos of this point we may note that the school from which the paper was obtained has five teachers of geometry, each of whom graded the paper independently as follows: 70, 65, 60, 70, and 59, average 64.8, mean variation 4.2. In a large high school in Ohio the paper was graded by four teachers of geometry as follows: 76, 75, 67, and 61, average 69.8, mean variation 5.8. In both of these schools the passing grade is 70.

Finally we may raise the question: How much variation is there in the marks assigned to the answer of any individual question? Sixty-two of the returns contained marks for the answer to each separate question. Forty-nine were graded on a scale of 0 to 12½, and thirteen on a scale of 0 to 10. The marks of the latter given to the answer for question ten . . . were as follows: 5, 5, 0, 0, 5, 3, 4, 2, 3, 2, 5, 6½, 5, average 3.5, mean variation 1.7.

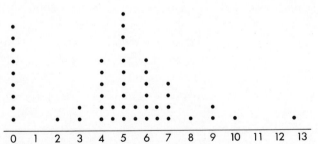

**Fig. 4. Grades of answer to question ten. Median 5.1. Probable error 1.1.**

Fig. 4 exhibits the distribution of the values assigned to the answer for question ten by the 49 teachers who graded on the scale of 0 to 12½. The median is 5.1 and the probable error is 1.1. If we transpose this probable error into terms of the usual scale of 0 to 100 by multiplying it by 8, we obtain a probable error of 8.8. This is nearly the same as the probable error of all the marks in Fig. 3, namely 7.5. Hence we see that the marks of the answer for a single question of the paper vary about as widely as those of the entire paper.

# WHAT DOES RESEARCH SAY ABOUT SELF-EVALUATION? *

## David H. Russell

A frequently-heard term in educational circles is "self-evaluation." Educational literature of the past decade contains many references to the process, usually with a laudatory or approving tone. Some advocates have gone "all out" in their commitment to self-evaluation by the pupil at every step of the evaluation process and in all phases of his work. It seems legitimate to ask what the reasons or values for such participation may be or may at least be assumed for it. One might be that in participating in the evaluation of his own assets and accomplishments, as well as his shortcomings and failures, the pupil learns a great deal not only about the process of evaluation but about himself. Another reason might be that the result of the evaluation will be more accurate, dependable, and valid if the pupil participates than it would be if the teacher does it independently. It appears that the bulk of the available research on the problem, both that dealing directly with it as well as that drawn from related areas such as level of aspiration studies, deals with the second supposed benefit, that is, to make the result more dependable. The following selection reports no new research but it presents a summary and interpretation of available studies at the time the article was written.

*Questions:*

1. In the studies reviewed in this selection what is the trend of correlations between self-ratings, ratings by peers, and ratings by teachers?

2. What areas of performance or traits are included in the studies reviewed? In which one do self-evaluations seem to be most dependable?

3. What bearing do socio-economic status and level of aspiration seem to have on self-evaluation? Explain.

\* \* \*

Self-evaluation is a "Johnny come lately" in educational research and

\* Reprinted from the *Journal of Educational Research,* **46:**561–573 (April 1953), by permission of author and Dembar Publications, Inc.

practice. In the past, teachers and evaluation experts have devoted more time to evaluating pupils' achievement than they have given to developing children's ability to evaluate their own growth. More recently, the rise of informal self-appraisal in the learning activities of many schools, plus the conviction that a major goal of education is to have pupils become increasingly independent in planning, executing and evaluating, necessitates a review of the evidence about self-appraisal as part of the total evaluation program. This report examines such evidence in a number of published and unpublished studies.

The importance of self-evaluation is suggested by a number of writers. Some ten years ago, in a summary of existing practices, Hamalainen concluded, "The extent to which a pupil should contribute to his own evaluation is not clear. It is certain that he should enter into the process; yet how and to what extent is only partially understood at present" [14:182].* In a description of theory and practices in evaluation Russell [28:190] suggested, "There seems little reason to doubt that, under guidance, pupils can appraise not only the work of a period or a day but also help in evaluating a whole unit or larger piece of work." Raths [25] also believed that pupils who have set up their own aims must consider their own progress, in terms of changing behavior, toward the goals they have set themselves. In a yearbook devoted to the measurement and evaluation of understanding, Findley and Scates stated, "Partly because of the fact that many of the subtler outcomes of learning (such as understanding) are difficult of appraisal and partly because it is desirable to educate pupils away from a goal of simply striving to please the teachers, it is important, certainly, by the middle of the elementary grades to begin the development of self-appraisal [9:62–63]. Grim was somewhat more specific when he said, "The pupil should share in every step in evaluation, just as he shares in the planning and carrying out of all phases of learning through problem solving both in and outside the classroom" [11:438]. Other writers have also stressed the importance of self-evaluation [6, 20].

Although self-evaluation has been commonly accepted at the verbal level, it seems to be rare at the action level [19, 33]. The comment of Orata illustrates this lag between theory and practice: "Evaluation as an integral part of the learning process, is much more talked about than practiced" [23]. This lack of emphasis upon self-evaluation in the school's appraisal program may be due to indifference, lack of knowledge, or difficulties in using a procedure unsuited to elementary and secondary school pupils and

* Figures in brackets apply to references at end of article.

to current school practices. In regard to the last point, one may inquire how practical and valuable self-evaluative practices are at various school levels. The following sections give some clues to the use and values of self-evaluation of personal-social competence and of academic learnings.

## Self-Rating of Personality

Any paper-and-pencil personality test is essentially a self-rating device for it asks the subject to rate himself on such items as keeping at his work until finished or what his classmates and friends think of him. Ellis [7] has pointed out that most personality self-rating devices have not been shown to have much validity in terms of correlation with external criteria. He states such disadvantages as the occurrence of a general over-estimation, or self-halo, effect where most people take the tests, and cites a long list of studies where the test results seemed quite unrelated to other ratings of personal-social competence.

An example of this difficulty is that of an early study by Rogers [26]. In the development of an instrument for measuring personality adjustment for children nine to thirteen years of age he used the pupil self-appraisal technique. In two forms, for boys and girls, he found correlations of only .39 between tested feelings of inferiority and clinician ratings, and of only .43 between social maladjustment and clinician ratings. Another correlation of .37 between family relationships and clinician ratings suggests that clinician's ratings may not be the best criterion against which to measure a child's self-rating of personality.

Another group of published studies related to self-evaluation are concerned with what the child or adolescent thinks are desirable traits in his peers. The criteria the child uses in judging himself may be related to standards used in judging classmates or acquaintances. For example, Mac-Farlane [17] has shown that, in one group of boys, "good at games" is a valuable characteristic in each of the first, third and fifth grades, whereas "quiet," which was desirable in the first grade, had no prestige value in the fifth grade. By this level "good looking," not mentioned in the lower grades, is associated with desirable social-personal status. Similarly Tryon [36] has shown that boys, and even more strongly, girls shift in their rating of desirable personality traits between the ages of 12 and 15. In a study more specifically related to the ideal self, Havighurst [15] obtained data from children and adolescents in the form of an essay on the subject, "The Person I Would Like to Be." A developmental trend was evident. In childhood, identification is with a parental figure; in middle childhood and early adolescence a romantic conception is prominent, and in late adolescence a composite picture is symbolized by an attractive young adult or an imaginary figure. The evidence seems clear that the normal child or adolescent will rate himself somewhat differently at different age levels in light of standards and values characteristic of a certain developmental level.

A comprehensive unpublished study utilizing personality tests is that of Stier [34]. He studied 325 children in five fifth grades and five eighth grades of various California schools. The investigation utilized sociometric measures, the California Test of Personality, a "Guess Who" test, a teacher rating scale of personality, an adapted form of the California Test of Personality used for peer rating, report card ratings by pupils, their peers, and their teachers, and results of standardized achievement tests. An interesting technique used by Stier was to get items on the "Guess Who" test, and the peer rating schedule comparable to certain items of the California Test of Personality. The results in terms of self-rating on the California Test of Personality indicate that girls are better adjusted than boys at both grade levels, that differences between grades five and eight are insignificant for each sex. Put another way, Stier found that girls consistently rate themselves higher on both self-adjustment and social adjustment on the California Test of Personality and a "Guess Who" test based on the same categories. Table I reveals that teachers and peer ratings of the group are more highly correlated with one another than with the self-rating of the California Test of Personality. This may mean that the influence of the teacher on peer ratings is considerable, especially at the fifth grade level. The correlations between teacher and peer rating on total adjustment for fifth grade girls ($r = .91$) and for fifth grade boys ($r = .80$) are considerably higher than other correlations. However, the ratings of eighth grade boys and their friends are in somewhat closer agreement ($r = .48$) than self and teacher ratings ($r = .30$). Stier found also that ratings of peers and teachers are closer to self-rating in the more overt personality traits but not so close in judgments of "Freedom from Withdrawing Tendencies" and "Freedom from Anti-Social Tendencies." Other findings from the Stier study are included in subsequent sections.

In another unpublished study Bullock [4] asked 139 pupils of grades four, five and six to predict their report card marks on both "Citizenship" and academic achievement at the end of either two or three report card periods. "Citizenship" was defined on the cards as a group of fifteen work habits, health and safety habits and social habits closely related to the usual

## Table I

**Correlations of Various Ratings of Personality for 162 Fifth Grade Pupils and 163 Eighth Grade Pupils in Terms of California Test of Personality Categories ***

| | Self-Adjustment | | | Social Adjustment | | | Total Adjustment | | |
|---|---|---|---|---|---|---|---|---|---|
| | Self-Peer | Self-Teacher | Peer-Teacher | Self-Peer | Self-Teacher | Peer-Teacher | Self-Peer | Self-Teacher | Peer-Teacher |
| Girls, Grade 5 | .55 | .64 | .81 | .49 | .61 | .86 | .59 | .66 | .91 |
| Boys, Grade 5 | .45 | .46 | .78 | .41 | .65 | .69 | .48 | .58 | .80 |
| Girls, Grade 8 | .47 | .60 | .81 | .22 | .53 | .65 | .40 | .62 | .74 |
| Boys, Grade 8 | .52 | .35 | .60 | .43 | .28 | .61 | .48 | .30 | .65 |

* Adapted from Stier, L. D., *A Comparison of Self-Evaluation, Peer Evaluation, Teacher Evaluation and Standardized Tests on Personality and Achievement Factors in the Fifth and Eighth Grades.* Unpublished Ph.D. dissertation (Berkeley: University of California, 1948).

concepts of personality. Bullock found that, without instruction, pupils did not improve their abilities of self-estimate in relation to teacher estimate or test results. He found a statistically significant tendency for these pupils to underestimate their citizenship marks. He found a small positive relationship between predicting tendencies in citizenship with personal adjustment $(r = .24)$ and with social adjustment $(r = .30)$ but obtained a zero correlation between these factors and predicting tendencies in academic achievements.

The findings of these studies on self-evaluation of personality tend to corroborate the earlier study of Tschechtelin [37] based on an extensive sampling. Using a twenty-two trait personality scale with over 1500 children and 485 teachers in grades four to eight, Tschechtelin found a tendency for girls to overestimate themselves and for boys to underestimate themselves, although the latter tendency seems to decline with age. An unpublished study by Tuddenham [38] agrees that girls tend to overestimate their adjustments on paper but disagrees with Tschechtelin by finding that self-judgment becomes less favorable with age for both boys and girls. Bonney [1] also agrees that fourth grade girls rate themselves more highly than boys rate themselves on a group of personality factors.

Two other unpublished studies are related to the problem of how well children can evaluate their own personal-social adjustments. Although it did not involve self-rating, Fehlman [8] made a comparison of parents' and teachers' appraisals of children. In thirty-six cases studied by means of personal interviews, school records, and checklists, she found an overlap of approximately one-third in items mentioned both by parents and teachers as satisfying qualities or problems in the same children. Teachers failed to mention a large number of traits which parents found desirable and, in the case of children having difficulty at school, teachers mentioned more problems than the child's parents. On the other hand, parents of the more maladjusted children mention more problems than these children's teachers do. Fehlman believes the child is more aware of what his parents think of him than of his teachers' attitudes in the matter. In the second study Gschwend [13] did not make direct use of self-evaluation but studied relationships between acceptance by the group, knowledge of selected concepts in democratic living, a test of democratic behavior and teacher ratings of citizenship in three fifth and sixth grade classes. Gschwend found correlations in the .60's and .70's between most of his sets of scores in this small group. For example, teacher ratings in citizenship correlate .75 and .69

with pupil acceptance and pupil recognition as measured by the Ohio scales. The children's knowledge of democratic behavior correlated .73 with teacher citizenship ratings, .63 with his social acceptance, and .74 with scores on a behavior test of the democratic thing to do. These figures need to be verified in a more complete study, but because of the relationships he found Gschwend believes the teacher should make much more use of peer ratings and of knowledge of democratic behaviors in evaluating children's growth in "citizenship."

In summary, research indicates that children's self-evaluation of their development of habits and attitudes contained in some of the usual concepts of personality or "good citizenship" in school bears a positive but slight relationship to two other criteria of adjustment, teacher and peer ratings. The makers of self-rating personality scales have established adequate reliability for their tests but we must conclude either that the tests have little validity in terms of teacher and peer judgments or that school children have little or no ability to evaluate their own personality development. The studies indicate also a tendency for girls to overestimate and for boys to underestimate their adjustments in light of these criteria. No consistent explanation of this phenomenon has appeared, although it may be related to the greater satisfaction and achievement of girls in the usual school activities.

## Self-Ratings of Academic Achievement

In the study described above, Stier [34] also attempted to determine the accuracy and realism of pupils in evaluating their academic achievement, in relation to their peers' and their teachers' estimates, and their actual scores on the Progressive Achievement Tests. He found that boys rated themselves lower than girls in achievement at both the fifth and eighth grade levels. This tended to be true of both self and peer ratings. In both grades both boys and girls showed a tendency to rate their own achievement higher than their peers rated it and significantly higher than their teachers rated it. As in the case of personality ratings, peer ratings and teacher ratings were in closer agreement than self-ratings and teacher ratings or self-ratings and peer ratings, except in the case of eighth grade boys. The relationships between the various ratings are shown in Table II. The table indicates clearly the close agreement between teachers' ratings and test results in the fifth grade only, and a tendency for self-rating to be less closely related to test marks than is teacher rating. It suggests, too, the importance of having junior high school teachers getting to know their pupils' achievements somewhat better or at least as well as the fifth grade teachers.

The Bullock study [4] also involved ratings of academic achievements. He also found that fourth, fifth and sixth grade pupils have a statistically significant tendency to rate themselves higher in reading, spelling and handwriting than their teachers rate them. He found, however, that there is a positive relationship between self-rating and test averages ($r = .52$) and self-rating and teacher rating ($r = .47$). Similarly in a group of 143 seventh and eighth grade pupils from an underprivileged community, and below average in intelligence, he found that the pupils tended to overestimate their achievement. However, these overestimates were rather cautious and the estimates showed a positive relationship with standardized test results

**Table II**

**Correlations of Various Ratings of Academic Achievement for 144 Fifth and 135 Eighth Grade Pupils ***

|                | Self-Peer | Self-Teacher | Self-Std. Test | Peer-Teacher | Peer-Std. Test | Teacher-Std. Test |
|----------------|-----------|--------------|----------------|--------------|----------------|-------------------|
| Girls, Grade 5 | .27       | .36          | .50            | .68          | .66            | .85               |
| Boys, Grade 5  | .53       | .54          | .54            | .67          | .47            | .72               |
| Girls, Grade 8 | .57       | .40          | .46            | .62          | .44            | .44               |
| Boys, Grade 8  | .46       | .61          | .35            | .41          | .21            | .43               |

* Adapted from Stier (34).

($r = .41$). The pupils of highest intelligence tended to underestimate their achievement; the pupils of lowest intelligence to overestimate it.

In a group of fifth and sixth grade pupils Bonney [2] found that the estimate of such matters as spelling score, library book withdrawals and absences from school were completely accurate in 27 percent of the cases and approximately correct in about 43 percent of the cases.

In a published study involving 95 college students in psychology, Sumner [35] found that students tended to overestimate their marks in direct proportion to their poorness as students, with the best students showing a definite tendency toward underestimating their accomplishments. The tendency toward overestimation or underestimation may be fairly consistent, not only in terms of previous achievement, but also in relation to certain personality traits. This third area of research is considered below. As in the case of personality rating, we must conclude that elementary school children who have received no special instruction do not appraise their academic progress much like their teachers or peers do, although they may be fairly consistent in overestimating or underestimating their achievements.

### Self-Evaluation and Socio-Economic Status

Two possible explanations of the consistent divergence between pupils' self-estimates and teachers' ratings may be found in the socio-economic status of pupils and in certain aspects of their personalities associated with their levels of aspiration.

In regard to the first factor, it has long been known that socio-economic status may affect school achievement. Shaw [31] summarizes seventeen studies published between 1911 and 1941, all of which show positive relationships between school achievements and socio-economic backgrounds. In his own study of children in the fourth to eighth grades, Shaw found correlations ranging from .27 to .41 between Sims scores of socio-economic status and various academic achievements. In addition to actual achievement, social class may influence a teacher's judgment of a child's achievement and his personality. In several studies Davis and Havighurst [5] have shown the effects of social class influence upon personality development such as the aggressive, negative behavior of some lower class children and the ambitious, conforming conduct of middle class children. The middle class standards of most teachers tend toward the approval of the middle class behavior [39].

Socio-economic background affects peer judgments as well as teacher judgments. This is an expected result because of the similarity of teacher and peer judgments in the elementary grades as outlined above. Other studies, some of them summarized by McGuire and Havighurst [18], confirm the result. In an investigation of relationships between selection-rejection, social status and personality among sixth grade children Grossman and Wrighter [12] found that social standing was related to popularity but that the association ceased for levels above the middle class. In another study Neugarten [22] found that fifth and sixth grade children also express class values in the evaluation of their peers. Upper and upper middle class children were rated high by all other children on such traits as liking for school, leadership and friendship.

There seems to be sufficient evidence to warrant the conclusion that socio-economic class not only affects a child's achievements in school but also the opinions about his achievements and personality of both his peers and his teachers. The development of any program of self-evaluation in a school system must undoubtedly take these facts into consideration.

## Self-Evaluation and Level of Aspiration

The studies quoted above deal with periodic rather than continuous self-evaluation and with group data rather than intensive study of individual self-appraisals. In the first area, little published research on the values of daily self-evaluation as part of the learning process seems available although an unpublished study by Schiesser [29], for example, indicates that emphasis upon pupil planning and evaluation pays dividends in the form of more democratic group behavior, and larger individual gains in language abilities. In the second area, Bullock [4] included a study of individual cases and found some evidence that individuals consistently overrate or underrate their achievements. In his study, 60 percent of the elementary pupils who made three estimates of scholarship on report cards were consistently high or low, and 80 percent were consistent in their predictions of "citizenship." He found some evidence that personality and adjustment are related to predicting tendencies, especially in "citizenship."

In an earlier study of the validity of self-estimate in a group of adults Shen [32] found evidence that the apparent inaccuracy of self-evaluation is due to a consistent error, peculiar to the individual, "a systematic tendency to over- or underestimate himself in all traits, according to the kind of delusion he has about himself." In explaining a negative correlation between self-estimate and achievement in his study of incoming high school freshmen Mitchell [21] reported a "defensive mechanism set up by slow pupils." In her detailed study of thirty-six elementary pupils Sears [30] measured differences in what children said they would like to achieve and their actual measured success in school subjects. To explain differences she used the "level of aspiration" hypothesis developed by Lewin and others, which seems to have so many implications for the self-evaluation program. She found that aspiration slightly above achievement was the characteristic pattern of the consistently successful and secure individuals. This pattern shifted, however, with changes in the pupils' patterns of successes. She found too that most unsuccessful pupils had aspirations far above their achievement, goals which were unresponsive to mild fluctuations in their successes. Aspiration below achievement was characteristic of some of the unsuccessful children. Sears concluded that "academic security" and "personality structure" are both associated with level of aspiration.

More recently Rotter [27] has advocated the use of the level of aspiration concept as a method of studying personality. Frank [10] has summarized studies involving the level of aspiration concept and Klein and Schoenfeld [16] have shown that level of aspiration operates only in "ego-involved situations" which have intense personal significance for the individual. Because of the pressures for academic success that many pupils face from both teachers and parents and the status needs of most elementary school children the self-evaluation situation, whether continuous or periodic, is a highly charged situation in which the child's ego is involved. It would seem, from these and other studies, that self-evaluation in the school can be accomplished only in a setting which considers the child's adjustments and needs. Because he is the kind of child he is, the teacher can help him in certain ways to arrive at more adequate and realistic evaluations of his personal-social and his academic achievements.

## Conclusion

The glib statement that self-evaluation is an important part of all evaluation programs would seem to need both further investigation and extreme caution in its application. This review of some published and unpublished studies indicates a lack of scientific study of the values of day-by-day evaluation in the learning activities of the modern school. It indicates further that the periodic evaluations of elementary school children, such as those sometimes used in reports to parents, bear little relation to the evaluations of peers and teachers in regard to both personality adjustments and academic achievements. This may mean that peers and teachers are wrong and the child is right. The evidence now available seems to indicate rather that the wise teacher can help children to improve their self-evaluations over a period of time, but that this help can be given only after consideration of a child's socio-economic status and aspects of his personality, particularly those factors associated with his level of aspiration.

## References

1. BONNEY, M. E. "Sex Differences in Social Success and Personality Traits." *Child Develpm.* **XV:**63–79 (March 1944).

2. ———. "The Validity of Certain Techniques of Gathering Psychological Data with Special Reference to Personality Questionnaires." *J. of Soc. Psychol.* **XIII:**103–122 (February 1941).

3. BOYER, P. A. "The Learner's Role in Evaluation." *Improving Educational Research.* Annual Report, American Educational Research Association (1948), pp. 71–74.

4. BULLOCK, H. *Some Aspects of Self-Evaluation by Pupils of Elementary School Age.* Unpublished Master's thesis. Berkeley: University of California (1948).

5. DAVIS, W. A. and R. J. HAVIGHURST. *Father of the Man: How Your Child Gets His Personality.* New York, Houghton-Mifflin (1947).

6. Elementary Classroom Teachers' Association and Elementary School Principals' Association. *Self-Evaluation in the Elementary School.* Elementary School Bulletin No. 11. Trenton: State of New Jersey Department of Education (1946).

7. ELLIS, A. E. "The Validity of Personality Questionnaires." *Psychological Bull.* **XLIII:**385–440 (September 1946).

8. FEHLMAN, C. *Parents and Teachers View the Child: A Comparative Study of Parents' and Teachers' Appraisals of Children.* Unpublished Ph.D. dissertation. New York: Teachers College, Columbia University (1946).

9. FINDLEY, W. G. and D. E. SCATES. "Obtaining Evidence of Understanding." Chapter IV of *The Measurement of Understanding,* National Society for the Study of Education 45th Yearbook, Part I. Chicago: University of Chicago Press (1946).

10. FRANK, J. D. "Recent Studies of Level of Aspiration." *Psychological Bull.* **XXXVIII:**218–226 (1941).

11. GRIM, R. R. "Youngsters Take a Hand." *Educ. Leadership.* **IV:**438–441 (April 1947).

12. GROSSMAN, B. and J. WRIGHTER. "The Relationship between Selection-Rejection and Intelligence, Social Status, and Personality Amongst Sixth Grade Children." *Sociometry.* **XI:**329–334 (November 1946).

13. GSCHWEND, P. R. *Relationships between Children's Group Status and Children's Knowledge of Democratic Behavior.* Unpublished Master's thesis. Berkeley, University of California (1947).

14. HAMALAINEN, A. E. "Existing Practices in the Evaluation of Pupil Growth in the Elementary School." *Elem. Sch. J.* **XLII:**175–183 (November 1941).

15. HAVIGHURST, R. J., M. Z. ROBINSON, and M. DON. "The Development of the Ideal Self in Childhood and Adolescence." *J. of Educ. Res.* **XL:**241–257 (December 1946).

16. KLEIN, G. S. and N. SCHOENFELD. "The Influence of Ego-Involvement on Confidence." *J. of Abn. and Soc. Psychol.* **XXXVI:**249–258 (1941).

17. MacFarlane, J. W. "Study of Personality Development." Chapter 18 of *Child Behavior and Development* edited by R. G. Barker, J. S. Kounin, and H. F. Wright. New York: McGraw-Hill (1943).

18. McGuire, C. and R. J. Havighurst. "Social Development." *Rev. of Educ. Res.* **XVII:**345–353 (December 1947).

19. Michaelis, J. U. "Current Practices in Evaluation in City School Systems." *Educ. and Psychological Measurement.* **XIX:**15–22 (Spring 1949).

20. ———. "Evaluation of Learning in the Social Studies." Chapter 15 of *Social Studies for Children in a Democracy.* New York: Prentice-Hall (1950).

21. Mitchell, C. "How Valid Are Pupils' Self-Evaluations?" *Clearing House.* **XIX:**486–488 (April 1945).

22. Neugarten, B. L. "Social Class and Friendship Among School Children." *Amer. J. of Soc.* **LI:**305–313 (January 1946).

23. Orata, P. T. "Evaluating Evaluation." *J. Educ. Res.* **XXXIII:**641–661 (March 1940).

24. Powell, M. G. "Comparisons of Self-Rating, Peer-Ratings and Expert's-Ratings of Personality Adjustment." *Educ. and Psychological Measurement.* **VIII:**225–234 (Summer 1948).

25. Raths, L. E. "Approaches to Measurement of Values." *Educ. Res. Bull.* **XIX:**275–282 (May 8, 1940).

26. Rogers, C. R. *Measuring Personality Adjustment of Children Nine to Thirteen Years of Age.* Teachers College Contributions to Education, No. 458. New York: Bureau of Publications, Teachers College, Columbia University (1931).

27. Rotter, J. B. "Level of Aspiration as a Method of Studying Personality." *Psychological Review.* **XLIX:**463–474 (September 1942). Also IV, "The Analysis of Patterns of Response." *J. Soc. Psychol.* **XXI:**159–177 (May 1945).

28. Russell, D. H. "Evaluation of the Elementary School Program." *Cal. J. of Elem. Educ.* **XIII:**182–192 (March 1945).

29. Schiesser, E. B. *Comparison of the Results of Teacher and Pupil Planning —Evaluating Procedures with Teacher Planning—Evaluating Procedures.* Unpublished Master's thesis. Berkeley: University of California (1947).

30. Sears, P. S. "Levels of Aspiration in Relation to Some Variables of Personality: Clinical Studies." *J. Soc. Psychol.* **XIV:**311–336 (November 1941).

31. Shaw, D. C. "Relation of Social Economic Status to Educational Achieve-

ment in Grades Four to Eight." *J. Educ. Res.* **XXXVII:**197–201 (November 1943).

32. SHEN, E. "The Validity of Self-Estimate." *J. Educ. Psychol.* **XV:**104–107 (February 1925).

33. SMITH, D. V. "Recent Procedures in the Evaluation of Programs in English." *J. Educ. Res.* **XXXVIII:**262–275 (December 1944).

34. STIER, L. D. *A Comparison of Self-Evaluation, Peer Evaluation, Teacher Evaluation and Standardized Tests on Personality and Achievement Factors in the Fifth and Eighih Grades.* Unpublished Ph.D. dissertation. Berkeley: University of California (1948).

35. SUMNER, F. C. "Marks as Estimated by Students." *Educ.* **LII:**429 (March 1932).

36. TRYON, C. M. "The Adolescent Peer Culture." Chapter XI of *Adolescence.* National Society for the Study of Education 43rd Yearbook, Part I. Chicago: University of Chicago Press (1944).

37. TSCHECHTELIN, SISTER M. A. "Self-Appraisal of Children." *J. Educ. Res.* **XXXIX:**25–32 (September 1945).

38. TUDDENHAM, R. D. *The Meaning of Differences in Reputation Among Elementary School Children.* Unpublished Ph.D. dissertation. Berkeley: University of California (1941).

39. WARNER, W. L., R. J. HAVIGHURST, and M. B. LOEB. *Who Shall Be Educated?* New York: Harper and Brothers (1944).

# 49

## STABILITY OF SOCIOMETRIC SCORES OF HIGH SCHOOL STUDENTS *

### Kenneth L. Cannon

In recent years sociometric questionnaires and their counterpart, the sociogram, have become well-known to teachers and counselors. Many have used them wisely and in a professional manner; others less so. One of the questions that concerns users of such devices is the stability or reliability of the results. How certain can one be that the responses of pupils are really dependable and that the same questions would be answered in the same ways tomorrow or next week? In the following selection a study is reported on the stability of sociometric choices of pupils in a small high school over periods of one, two, and three years. The significance of the findings and the possible effect of small enrollment in a high school in a "primary community" are discussed.

*Questions:*

1. Are the results of the study reported here consistent with those of similar studies?

2. What is the relationship of stability of sociometric scores to age and maturity of individuals?

3. Is there any evidence to justify the belief that the size and nature of the school and community have any bearing on the question posed by this study? If so, what is it?

\* \* \*

Moreno [6:13] ** has indicated the essential nature of the sociometric test by stating that it "consists in an individual choosing his associates for any group of which he is or might become a member." As commonly used, a sociometric test includes one or more situations in which the individual

\* Reprinted from the *Journal of Educational Research,* **52:**43–48 (October 1958), by permission of author and Dembar Publications, Inc.
\*\*Figures in brackets apply to references at end of article.

is asked to indicate the members of the group with whom he would prefer to associate.

Through the use of such tests the attempt is made to determine the feelings of the individual members toward each other. The test subjects may be asked with whom they prefer not to associate as well as to give their positive choices.

Sociometric type tests offer to the teacher or leader of the group or other interested persons a means of gaining increased understanding of the needs of the individual members as well as pointing toward more effective organization and cooperation among the members who comprise the group. Providing a basis for changing the social structure of the group may be one of the test's real contributions.

By enumerating the number of times each person is chosen by the others, a "social acceptance score" is determined for each individual. Marked differences may be found and often the results are surprising to the adult observer. Acceptance by the group is of particular importance to the adolescent as he is attempting to gain increased independence from parental and family control and is becoming more dependent upon the views of his peers.

One of the problems which is involved is that of the stability of the scores thus obtained. If the choices are capricious and subject to much change, little reliance can be placed upon such scores. If they remain relatively stable —over extended periods of time—their worth and the extent to which the teacher or other leader can rely on the results is greatly increased. However, if such tests and their results are valid, the scores should reflect actual changes in feelings of members of the group toward each other and hence in the relative acceptance of the individual by the group.

The sociometric type test has an advantage over other tests of the pencil-and-paper variety in that the individual can do little to affect his own score by his responses on the test—even though he may desire to place himself in a desirable light.

The stability of scores derived from sociometric tests has been considered in a number of studies. Jennings [5:51] correlated scores received by girls at the New York Training School for Girls on a one-item test with an interval of eight months between the times when the test was given. The coefficient was .65 which was significant at the 1% level. Bronfenbrenner [2:48] compared scores received in the autumn and the following spring by children attending a laboratory school at the University of Michigan. The correlation coefficients ranged from $.27 \pm .17$ in the nursery class to $.67 \pm .08$ in the kindergarten. The highest grade in the laboratory school, the V–VI class, had the next highest coefficient which was .59 ± .08. Bonney [1:413] also considered social acceptance scores of elementary school children and obtained the following correlation coefficients with a one year interval: .84 ± .02 between 2nd and 3rd grades (n = 48), .77 ± .04 between 3rd and 4th grades (n = 43), and .67 ± .05 (n = 57) between scores in the 4th and 5th grades. All the coefficients were significant at the 1% level and were obtained in spite of a turnover of approximately 30% in enrollment. Staker [7:158] correlated scores received in the 4th and 5th grades with an interval of a full year, and obtained a coefficient of .68. She also obtained a coefficient of .87 between scores received in December and May in the 5th grade.

In each of the studies, the correlations were statistically significant and indicated a tendency toward stability. However, only the study of Jennings [5] concerned youngsters of high school age and her study involved a very different situation from that of the public high school. Also the fact that the intervals were one year or less in each study, pointed toward a need for consideration of longer time intervals, and particularly at the high school level.

The basic problem of this study was: To determine the stability of the high school group's acceptance of its members over periods of one, two, and three years.

Theoretical considerations and the results of other studies suggested the hypothesis: That the high school group's acceptance of its members would show a tendency to remain stable over periods of one, two and three years.

## Procedures

### Test Used

The sociometric type test, *Fun, Work and Friends,* used in this study was developed by Staples at Nebraska for high school youngsters (not yet published). It included the following four items:

1. With what pupils would you enjoy working on a committee for putting on a school program?
2. With what people would you most enjoy going to a picnic?
3. What pupils would you vote to represent this school at an important state conference of schools?
4. Who are your very best friends in this school?

At the time the tests were given, the pupils were asked to make as many choices as they desired for each situation, but to limit their choices to pupils attending the same high school. A specific request was made that they do not sign their names to the test, but a concealed numbering device permitted identification of the subject in case of question (such as choosing his own name). In determining scores each pupil received one point for each time he was chosen regardless of whether it was a 1st or 10th choice.

The tests were given at yearly intervals for a period of four years beginning in January 1950. The subjects were pupils attending a rural high school with an enrollment of approximately 100 which was located in a small town in southeastern Nebraska. The town population was slightly under 1,000. The school drew about half of its students from farms located in the surrounding school districts. Practically all of the farm students had attended the first eight grades in one-room rural schools. Such schools are found in many parts of rural Nebraska.

A total of 14 comparisons were made between social acceptance scores for the members of different classes with intervals ranging from 1 to 3 years. The number of pupils in the classes varied from 14 to 29.

As indicated, other studies had used correlation to measure stability. Inasmuch as correlation is essentially a measure of position, stability, as used in this connection, has referred to the relationship between scores over various periods of time, rather than to the fixity of the scores. Thus, a high correlation coefficient may be secured where the scores change in the same direction and in about the same proportion.

### Findings

*Stability Over an Interval of One Year*

The length of the study made possible the comparison of scores for nine classes with an interval of one year. The mean scores received are given in Table I, along with the correlation coefficients which ranged from .61 to .91. As indicated in Table I, all coefficients were significant at the 1% level for the four items and the total scores.

*Stability Over a Period of Two Years*

Correlations were computed between social acceptance scores in the 9th and 11th grades for two classes and ranged from a low of .80 to a high of .90 (all significant at the 1% level). In contrast, the correlations obtained between the 10th and 12th grade scores for two classes were lower, ranging from .45 to .67 (all significant at the 1% level). These data are given in Table II.

## Table I
### Correlation of Social Acceptance Scores with an Interval of One Year

| Test | Number of Classes | Number of Pupils | Mean Social Acceptance Score | | r |
|------|------|------|------|------|------|
| | | | 9th grade | 10th grade | |
| Item 1 | 3 | 63 | 4.49 | 5.51 | .87** |
| Item 2 | 3 | 63 | 3.43 | 4.92 | .79** |
| Item 3 | 3 | 63 | 1.24 | 2.40 | .87** |
| Item 4 | 3 | 63 | 4.11 | 4.98 | .78** |
| Total | 3 | 63 | 13.27 | 17.81 | .91** |
| | | | 10th grade | 11th grade | |
| Item 1 | 3 | 73 | 5.69 | 6.82 | .81** |
| Item 2 | 3 | 73 | 4.99 | 6.40 | .82** |
| Item 3 | 3 | 73 | 2.34 | 3.80 | .80** |
| Item 4 | 3 | 73 | 5.25 | 6.01 | .85** |
| Total | 3 | 73 | 18.21 | 23.03 | .88** |
| | | | 11th grade | 12th Grade | |
| Item 1 | 3 | 69 | 6.64 | 6.38 | .74** |
| Item 2 | 3 | 69 | 6.03 | 5.45 | .75** |
| Item 3 | 3 | 69 | 4.22 | 7.00 | .85** |
| Item 4 | 3 | 69 | 6.20 | 5.61 | .61** |
| Total | 3 | 69 | 23.09 | 24.44 | .83** |

** Throughout these tables two asterisks (**) will be used to indicate significance at the 1% level.

## Table II
### Correlation of Social Acceptance Scores with an Interval of Two Years

| Test | Number of Classes | Number of Pupils | Mean Social Acceptance Score | | r |
|------|------|------|------|------|------|
| | | | 9th grade | 11th grade | |
| Item 1 | 2 | 47 | 4.96 | 7.87 | .82** |
| Item 2 | 2 | 47 | 3.98 | 7.17 | .82** |
| Item 3 | 2 | 47 | 1.26 | 4.57 | .80** |
| Item 4 | 2 | 47 | 4.32 | 6.51 | .84** |
| Total | 2 | 47 | 14.52 | 26.12 | .90** |
| | | | 10th grade | 12th Grade | |
| Item 1 | 2 | 39 | 5.59 | 5.97 | .64** |
| Item 2 | 2 | 39 | 5.31 | 5.23 | .64** |
| Item 3 | 2 | 39 | 2.28 | 6.69 | .60** |
| Item 4 | 2 | 39 | 5.10 | 5.74 | .45** |
| Total | 2 | 39 | 18.28 | 23.63 | .67** |

*Stability Over a Period of Three Years*

A comparison of scores for an interval of three years was possible for only one class—the group who were in the 9th grade when the study began. Of the 22 youngsters who were enrolled in the 9th grade, 17 of them were still in school for the 12th grade. Data are presented in Table III and indicate a relatively high level of stability—the lowest correlation is .66 for item 3 and the highest is .88 for item 1. All correlations were significant at the 1% level. The coefficients for the three year interval were higher than the coefficients obtained between the 10th and 12th grades (a two year interval) for two classes.

**Table III**

**Correlation of Social Acceptance Scores with an Interval of Three Years**

| Test | Number of Classes | Number of Pupils | Mean Social Acceptance Score | | r |
|------|-------------------|------------------|------------------------------|---|---|
| | | | 9th grade | 12th Grade | |
| Item 1 | 1 | 17 | 4.94 | 6.53 | .88** |
| Item 2 | 1 | 17 | 3.65 | 5.41 | .79** |
| Item 3 | 1 | 17 | 1.59 | 8.47 | .66** |
| Item 4 | 1 | 17 | 4.12 | 6.82 | .78** |
| Total | 1 | 17 | 14.29 | 27.23 | .84** |

**Discussion**

The high relative stability of social acceptance scores did not preclude rather marked changes in scores with the general trend being upward. This suggests the possible need for correction factors when the scores of students in different grades are to be compared.

In the cases of some individuals rather marked changes occurred in their scores. Such changes are to be expected and as Tryon [8] has suggested may be due in part to the possibility that behavior which the group approved in the 11th and 12th grades may be quite different from the approved behavior in the 9th grade. Not only may the group's approval of certain behavior change, but changes in the individual's behavior may enhance or detract from his acceptance. The acceptance scores and class rankings based thereon are given in Table IV for six pupils in each of the four high school grades. The data presented are examples of some of the changes which occur. Students A, C, and D are examples of individuals who maintain about the same relative position in the group, whereas students B and F represent students who make rather substantial gains in acceptance, and Student E illustrates the type of individual who becomes less acceptable to the group.

**Table IV**

**Individual Total Social Acceptance Scores and Rank of Six High School Students from the 9th to 12th Grades**

| | *Sex* | *High School Grade* | | | |
|---|---|---|---|---|---|
| | | *9th* | *10th* | *11th* | *12th* |
| Student A | Female | | | | |
| No. of times chosen: | | 38 | 62 | 64 | 72 |
| Rank in class: | | 2 | 1 | 1 | 2 |
| Student B | Male | | | | |
| No. of times chosen: | | 24 | 17 | 35 | 79 |
| Rank in class: | | 4–5 | 7–8 | 6 | 1 |
| Student C | Female | | | | |
| No. of times chosen: | | 1 | 0 | 1 | 7 |
| Rank in class: | | 18 | 19 | 17 | 16–17 |
| Student D | Male | | | | |
| No. of times chosen: | | 0 | 1 | 7 | 7 |
| Rank in class: | | 19 | 18 | 15 | 16–17 |
| Student E | Male | | | | |
| No. of times chosen: | | 24 | 41 | 51 | 15 |
| Rank in class: | | 4–5 | 5 | 3 | 11 |
| Student F | Female | | | | |
| No. of times chosen: | | 4 | 13 | 24 | 27 |
| Rank in class: | | 15–16 | 10 | 9 | 6 |

*Description of Individuals*

Student A—a girl—is an example of the student who maintains a very high rank through the four years of high school. In this particular case she was a very attractive girl who was nice and considerate of everyone and her work brought her into contact with all of the students. The girl successfully overcame the obstacle of having an alcoholic for a father and a relatively low socioeconomic status in the community.

Student B—a boy—is an example of the type of student who made a substantial gain in acceptance. He received fairly high scores during his first tnree years in high school, but during his last year he received more choices than any other student. In the 12th grade he developed into a very outstanding athlete. He was an excellent musician, his family socioeconomic status was high, and he had good prospects for the future.

Student C—a girl—is an example of the type who is relatively low in acceptance throughout her years in high school. She lived in a poorer part of the town, her family socioeconomic status was low, and she was a virtual isolate until her senior year when she acquired the friendship of some younger girls from her section of town. However, there was little increase in rank due to the increases which the other students had gained in acceptance.

Student D—a boy—is quite similar to Student C in that he was low in acceptance during each of the four years. He was from a well-to-do family and had attended grade school in town, but seemed to lack social skills. He found a few friends during his senior year, but his rank changed little.

Student E—a boy—is an example of the type of individual whose acceptance by the group decreases. In the 9th grade he stood out as the leader —boisterous, loud, full of mischief—with a good future in athletics in high school. Between the 11th and 12th grades he lost ground. His attitude became quite belligerent, he strongly opposed a change in the coaches at the high school, and he did not cooperate with the new coach who was generally liked. Other students turned from him, and from being tied for 4th in rank in the 9th grade in acceptance, he dropped to 11th in rank in the 12th grade. The only ones who chose him in his last year were two buddies and his girl friend, a very smart and likeable person. He showed little indication of having the ability to get along or to make something of himself in the adult world.

Student F—a girl—is an example of a student whose acceptance rank increased in each of the four years in high school. She was the daughter of a prominent town family, a good student, and a fine musician. The change in her acceptance may have been due to the added graciousness and kindness which she developed, and/or to the possibility that the qualities she possessed became more important to the group as they became older.

### Conclusions Regarding Stability of Scores

In this study, social acceptance scores were found to have a high level of stability over periods of one, two, and three years, thus providing support for the hypothesis that the high school group's acceptance of its members would show a tendency to remain stable over periods of one, two, and three years. These findings also tend to indicate that social acceptance scores tend to be reliable in such situations as that of the high school where this study was conducted. The reliability, however, takes into account a general tendency for the scores to increase from year to year as the youngsters progress through high school.

The high level of stability was maintained despite a turnover of approximately one-fourth of the students each year who comprised the student body—the group whose choices were analyzed to determine the social acceptance scores—as the 12th graders graduated and the new students entered in the 9th grade. It is very possible that the size of the student body —approximately 100 pupils—may have been a factor in causing the scores to be stable, as virtually all pupils were acquainted with each other. An additional factor may have been that the high school was located in what Fessler [4] terms a "primary community." Such a community has several of the characteristics of a primary group as set forth by Cooley, Angell, and Carr [3:55] including:

1. Face to face association
2. Unspecialized character of that association
3. Relative permanence
4. Small number of persons involved
5. Relative intimacy among the participants

Fessler [4:55–56] states with respect to the size of such a community that:

Practical considerations and experience in the field, rather than theoretical arguments, set the maximum population limits of the sample of primary rural communities in the Iowa study at two thousand for the community as a whole, or an average of one thousand for the trade center and a thousand for the outlying farm area. In Iowa, such a ratio of farm to village population has been found to exist.

It is very possible that in primary communities social acceptance scores may tend to be more stable than are such scores in larger communities. Further research might readily determine whether stability of social acceptance is related to the size of the community.

### References

1. BONNEY, MERL E. "The Constancy of Sociometric Scores and Their Relationships to Teacher Judgments of Social Success and to Personality Self-Ratings." *Sociometry.* **6**:409–424 (1943).

2. BRONFENBRENNER, URIE. "A Constant Frame Reference for Sociometric Research, Part II. Experiment and Inference." *Sociometry*, **7**:40–75.

3. COOLEY, C. H., ANGELL, and CARR. *Introductory Sociology*. New York: Charles Scribner's Sons (1933), p. 55.

4. FESSLER, DONALD R. "The Development of a Scale for Measuring Community Solidarity." *Rural Sociology*. **17**:144–152 (1952).

5. JENNINGS, HELEN H. *Leadership and Isolation*. New York: Longman's Green and Co. (1943), p. 51.

6. MORENO, J. L. *Who Shall Survive*. Monograph Series, No. 58. Washington, D. C.: Nervous and Mental Disease (1934), p. 13.

7. STAKER, ANNA MARIE. "Changes in Social Status of the Elementary School Pupils." *Educational Research Bulletin*. **27**:157–159 (1948).

8. TRYON, C. M. *Evaluation of Adolescent Personality by Adolescents*. Monograph Social Research, Child Development. **4**:4.

## 50

# A SCHOOL MARK—FACT OR FANCY? *

## S. Trevor Hadley

Although many teachers dislike it, marking is part of the job. By marking is meant some kind of appraisal or evaluation of each pupil's attainment. The mark may be a percent, or a letter mark, or a general statement in a letter or conference. No matter what form it takes, the responsibility for it rests primarily, if not entirely, on the teacher. There is and has been considerable dissatisfaction and experimentation with marking systems. No universally acceptable method has been found or devised, nor is there likely to be. In the present article a study is made of teachers' marks in twenty classrooms for fourth, fifth, and sixth grades. Variables considered were scores of 620 pupils in these classrooms on a standardized achievement battery of reading, arithmetic, language, and spelling; the pupils' marks in these subjects; and a teachers' rating indicating her acceptance or liking for each pupil in her room. With these data it was possible to make comparisons between measured achievement, teachers' marks, and teachers' acceptance rating. The results suggest that personal liking for, or acceptance of, the pupil by the teacher plays a substantial role in determining his mark in a subject. Other factors such as sex of teacher and pupil in relation to marks are also studied.

*Questions:*

1. Liking or acceptance of pupils by teachers is a broad concept. What specific elements might be covered by it?

2. Should a mark, say in arithmetic, be based upon achievement in arithmetic and nothing else? Give reasons for your answer.

\* \* \*

School marks have been used for many different purposes in public education. These purposes can be broadly classified as instructional and admin-

* Reprinted from *Educational Administration and Supervision,* **40:**305–312 (May 1954), by permission of author and publisher.

istrative. Teachers use marks as incentives for pupils to do better work and as warnings that present pupil work is not satisfactory. Administrators use them as criteria for promotion and to form the basis for permanent records of pupil progress. Both teacher and administrators consider marks to be evaluations of pupils' actual accomplishment in the many subject matter areas of the school and as such use them to report to parents.

Much of the confusion about school marks can be traced to the fact that marks are used for so many different purposes and that no one definition covers all factors involved. Teachers themselves do not agree on a standard meaning for a school mark. They admit that they use different criteria in evaluating pupil attainment [1].* Among the many factors reported in the literature to be included in the marks teachers assign their pupils are: actual attainment, the teacher-pupil relationship, deportment, sex, promptness and attendance, personal appearance, obedience, effort and attitude.

The one factor among these which is assumed to be common to all marks is the actual achievement of the pupil in the subject matter for which he received the mark. The other factors are either subjective appraisals or are factors that are difficult to translate directly into marks. The extent to which these factors help determine how well the teacher likes or accepts his pupils and indirectly help determine what marks he assigns is not known.

The literature provides much discussion relative to the influence many of these factors have on school marks. Much of it is conjecture, however, rather than actual findings of measurable relationships. C. C. Ross [2], for example, stated: "It seems too bad that the marks received by certain individuals are conditioned more by the contours of the face than by the contents of the head." R. A. Norsted [1] believed that these factors operated both on the conscious and the sub-conscious levels. He said that: "A large fraction of teachers, in some cases a considerable majority, consciously consider effort, attitude, and other factors in assigning marks in school subjects and many are affected by these factors without realizing it."

Other investigators reported that deportment, over-ageness, personality traits, and sex all had greater effect upon assigned marks than chance would allow in certain selected populations. C. C. Ross [2] further stated: "Pupils' handwriting, conduct, language ability, seating position in the class, and ratings on personality factors such as respect for authority and coöperativeness are significant factors in determining their marks, as well as the condition of fatigue or boredom the teacher happens to be in when the marks are awarded." Ross did not, however, offer any documentation for his state-

* Figures in brackets apply to references at end of article.

ment. Apparently, it represented his considered opinion, but no supporting research evidence was presented in his text.

The complex of components other than actual quality of performance which enters into marks such as sex, appearance, deportment, attendance, etc. has not been studied by any precise procedures. This is the point at which this study takes its departure.

## Design of the Study

Since actual attainment in subject matter could be conveniently and accurately measured with a valid battery-type achievement examination, it appeared desirable to seek for some quantifiable measure of these other components which enter into teachers' marks and then to determine the relative influence of each of these variables upon actual assigned marks. Accordingly, a rating scale was devised which led the teacher to assign rank positions to each of his pupils, positions which represented the degree of acceptance or liking which he as the teacher held for each child in his classroom. The purpose of this ranking process was disguised in a way that the teacher was really not aware that his own marking practices were being evaluated. For this ranking scale the stanine distribution was employed.\*\*

The sample population for the study was composed of six hundred and twenty pupils in twenty classrooms for fourth, fifth, and sixth grade self-contained classrooms all located in Indiana County, Pennsylvania. The classrooms were randomly selected from three school districts. The scores made by these six hundred and twenty pupils on the California Achievement Test, Elementary Battery, Form AA, closely approached national norms, thus supporting the assumption that the sample population of pupils was representative.

The three major variables employed then for the study were: (1) scores made on the California Achievement Test, Elementary Battery, Form AA, in four basic skill areas, reading, arithmetic, language, and spelling. Tests were administered during the last ten days of the school term; (2) a ranking on a liking or acceptance scale for each pupil indicating how well each teacher liked each of his pupils; (3) final, or term average, marks assigned

\*\* The stanine division of an assumed normal distribution of measures includes, respectively, 4, 7, 12, 17, 20, 17, 12, 7, and 4 per cent of the distribution of measures. The highest position is nine and the lowest, one. The variation in the size of the fractions at top and bottom provides a sharper discrimination of the highest and lowest measures in comparison with those intermediate. (See Lee Cronbach, *Essentials of Psychological Measurement*, Chapter 3, p. 35, New York. Harper and Brothers, 1949.)

each pupil at the end of the school year and representing his attainment in each of the four subjects measured by the California Test.

All three variables were then transposed into stanine rankings thus making direct comparisons and statistical treatment possible. For many of the purposes of the study rankings were distributed into three groupings: the highest twenty-three per cent on each variable comprising those assigned stanine rankings of 9, 8, or 7; the lowest twenty-three per cent comprising those assigned stanine rankings of 1, 2, and 3; and the larger middle or intermediate group comprising fifty-four per cent of the sample and including those assigned stanine positions of 4, 5, and 6.

This made possible the following kinds of statistical analysis: (1) The inter-correlations of each of the three variables both for the distribution of the whole sample and for individual class groups. (2) The biserial correlations for each pair of variables for the highest and lowest fractions of the distribution. (3) The interrelations of pairs of variables with the third held constant. (4) The comparison of the variables in relation to each of the sexes. (5) The examination of the marking practices of individual teachers.

## Findings

Results clearly demonstrated the tendency for most-liked pupils to be marked higher than their accomplishment would justify. Of the one hundred and fifty-eight pupils who were most liked by their teachers, fifty per cent were assigned marks higher than measured attainment. Only sixteen per cent were marked lower. Of the one hundred and eighteen pupils who were least-liked by their teachers, fifty per cent were marked lower than actual attainment, and only nineteen per cent were marked higher. Of the three hundred and seven who were assigned intermediate positions and were, therefore, neither most-liked nor least-liked, there was an even chance that they would be marked too high or too low. Table I presents these data in tabular form.

Space limitations prevent the inclusion of the master tables from which these percentages were taken. The large fraction of most-liked pupils marked above attainment and the large fraction of least-liked pupils marked below attainment only in part reveal the conditions found. The figures in Table I do not reveal the degree of over-marking or under-marking in individual cases, but only indicate the percentage of individuals so marked. When the extent of over- and under-marking is measured by the number of plus and minus displacements in stanine positions of marks in relation to actual accomplishment, the influence of teacher liking is much more pronounced. Only seven of the most-liked pupils had mark stanine rankings with downward displacement of more than one stanine position; thirty-five of them had mark stanine rankings with upward displacement of more than one stanine position.

Twenty-six of the least-liked pupils had mark stanine rankings with downward displacement of more than one stanine position; six of them had

**Table I**

**Association of Mark Rankings with Rankings on Accomplishment (in per cents)**

| Group | Marked Above Accomplishment | Marked Corresponding with Accomplishment | Marked Below Accomplishment |
|---|---|---|---|
| Most-Liked (Stanines 9, 8, 7) | 50 | 34 | 16 |
| Intermediate (Stanines 6, 5, 4) | 31 | 35 | 34 |
| Least-Liked (Stanines 3, 2, 1) | 19 | 31 | 50 |
| Total population | 31 | 35 | 34 |

mark stanine rankings with upward displacement of more than one stanine position. This, in brief, means that many most-liked pupils were marked far above actual attainment, and, similarly, many of the least-liked pupils were marked far below actual subject-matter attainment.

It might further be pointed out that those pupils neither most nor least liked had one chance in three of being assigned marks that fairly represented their subject-matter attainment—one chance in three of being assigned marks above this attainment, and one chance in three of being assigned marks below this attainment.

Sixteen of the twenty teachers, all of whom were women, assigned higher marks to girls. Fifteen of the twenty assigned higher liking rankings to girls. However, in only eleven of the twenty classrooms did the girls make higher attainment scores on the achievement test, and the over-all average of the boys and girls showed no significant difference in scores.

In every classroom where the boys were assigned higher acceptance rankings and made higher test scores, the teachers also assigned them higher marks. In five classrooms the teacher assigned the boys lower marks even though they made higher scores than the girls on the achievement tests.

Table II gives evidence of the favored position which the girls held in this sample of six hundred and twenty pupils when marked by twenty women teachers.

Forty-five per cent of the girls in the population of this study were marked higher than their test achievement as compared with twenty-three per cent of the boys. At the other end of the scale only twenty-two per cent of the girls were marked lower than test achievement while forty per cent of

### Table II
#### Comparison of Marks of Boys and Girls (in per cent)

| Sex | Marked Higher than Test Achievement | Marked Corresponding to Test Achievement | Marked Lower than Test Achievement |
|---|---|---|---|
| Boys | 23 | 37 | 40 |
| Girls | 45 | 33 | 22 |
| Total population | 31 | 35 | 34 |

the boys belong in this category. These data clearly demonstrate that in this sample the teachers, who happened all to be women, clearly favored the girls when it came to assigning their marks.

### Related Findings

1. Correlations between marks and teachers' acceptance rankings in the various classrooms ranged from .08 to .92.

2. Correlations between assigned marks and actual measured attainment in the various classrooms ranged from .20 to .94.

3. When the top and bottom ten per cent of the correlations were ignored, the range between marks and teacher acceptance was .47 to .85. The same procedure gave a range between marks and attainment in the individual classrooms of .58 to .90.

4. The correlation between marks and teacher acceptance was .58 when by biserial correlation the highest and lowest rankings for teacher acceptance were correlated with the marks assigned these pupils.

5. The correlation between marks and measured attainment was .59 when by biserial correlation the highest and lowest rankings for measured attainment were correlated with the marks assigned these pupils.

6. The correlation between teacher acceptance and measured attainment was .33 when by biserial correlation the highest and lowest rankings for teacher acceptance were correlated with the measured attainment of these pupils.

7. Seventeen of the twenty teachers assigned marks which were more closely related to measured attainment than to acceptance rankings; three teachers assigned marks which were more closely related to acceptance rankings than to measured attainment.

## Implications

These findings appear to suggest the following inferences:

1. Teacher acceptance of pupil and actual attainment are components, almost equally, in school marks assigned by teachers.

2. These two components in marks assigned are not mutually exclusive but the association between teacher acceptance of pupil and actual attainment is relatively low.

3. The findings suggest that for the large fraction of pupils whose acceptance and attainment are intermediate in degree, the marks below, above, or at attainment level were the result of chance.

4. Accidental factors influencing marks appear to be at a minimum for pupils distinguished by being highest or lowest in acceptance and attainment rankings, since the marks were consistently highest or lowest if either or both of the rankings for acceptance and attainment were at the highest or lowest extremes.

5. To be ranked highest in acceptance and/or attainment appeared to carry a reward in marks; to be ranked lowest seemed to involve a penalty in marks assigned. This was indicated by the large fraction of highest ranked pupils over-marked in relation to attainment and the large fraction of lowest ranked pupils who were given marks lower than actual attainment.

6. While this study was not designed to reveal the elements involved in teacher acceptance of pupils, it appears that some differences in the behavior pattern of girls from boys may influence relative acceptance. In general, the girls were given higher rankings in both acceptance and marks, notwithstanding relative equivalence in actual attainment as measured by standard tests.

7. The method used in this study may serve as one of the techniques of supervision and appraisal of teachers.

## Summary

It was not the purpose of this study nor do the results justify the conclusion that marking practices are uniformly bad and should be immediately revised. Marking procedures or methods are necessarily only as good or as weak as the individual who is trying to apply them. This study in no way indicates any particular direction that marking procedures can be changed or modified to improve the situation. It only tries to put the spotlight on one more facet of human dynamics. The teacher, who by the very demands of his job, must evaluate many children periodically should be made aware of the pitfalls and difficulties which surround interpersonal relationships. It is the belief of the writer that awareness of the situation should make for better marking practices. If the teacher knows that all teachers are prone to allow personal biases, attitudes, and reactions to enter into many of their marks, he may get some consolation from that fact; but even further, he should look upon the situation as one of the many challenges of good teaching—to strive for objective, accurate evaluations of pupils in learning situations.

The teacher most blind to the influence of such subtle factors in marking is most likely to assign marks supreme in his confidence that his marks are inviolate and therefore not to be questioned. Such an attitude is likely to lead to even grosser marking errors.

Our conclusion must be that marks are partly fancy and partly fact. Unfortunately, it would appear that for a very few teachers, they are more fancy than fact. Most teachers, however, mark as objectively as they can. Educators know of no better or easier method to evaluate and record pupils' scholastic progress. Every teacher should study his marking practices and strive for accurate objective evaluations of pupil work and progress. Only through such an approach, can we continue to convince both parents and students that our marks do mean something and that good scholastic records are worth the effort.

## References

1. NORSTED, R. A. "To Mark or Not to Mark." *J. of Educ.* **121**:81–84 (1938).

2. ROSS, C. C. *Measurement in Today's Schools,* 2nd Edition. New York: Prentice-Hall (1947), p. 405.

# 51

## AN EVALUATION OF THE DUAL GRADING SYSTEM *

### Irvin A. Keller

The author of the selection which follows was made responsible for the policies adopted in a campus high school beginning in 1944. Among the matters which concerned him was an improved marking system combining the best features of two systems used by the junior and senior high schools, respectively. After nearly six years of study and experimentation he reported on the system which he helped to develop and indicated in a preliminary way that it was working well. In this article he reports the results of attempts to make a more comprehensive and thorough evaluation after ten years. A study was made of the trends in marks from freshman to senior years, both in terms of over-all proportion of satisfactory and unsatisfactory marks, and in relation by years to required and elective courses. Further analysis of intelligence in relation to frequency of unsatisfactory marks is reported. Finally, results of an inquiry soliciting parents' reactions to the marking system are presented. It is not often that one finds so consistent and such continuous effort to improve a marking system and to evaluate it.

*Questions:*

1. To obtain a more thorough knowledge of the so-called "dual marking system," read the first article by Keller, mentioned at the end of the one below. Give your reactions to it.

2. Would the "dual system" be applicable in any school, elementary or secondary? Give reasons for your answer.

3. What is the essential or critical factor in using this system which distinguishes it from ordinary systems of marking? Do you see any problems here?

\* \* \*

Prior to the school-year, 1944–45, College High School consisted of a three-year junior high-school department and a three-year senior high-

* Reprinted from Bulletin of the *National Association of Secondary-School Principals,* **39:**38–45 (November 1955), by permission of author and publisher.

school department. It was decided in March, 1944, by the director of the College Training School and the College Administration that the two departments were to be re-organized into a six-year high school for the school year beginning September, 1944. The principal of the senior high school was retiring June 1, 1944, and the junior high-school principal was appointed to assume the duties as principal of the six-year high school. He was instructed to make whatever changes in policy and procedure that might be necessary to effect the reorganization.

One of the problems to be resolved was to decide what grade reporting system was to be used. The junior high-school department had been using letters to parents that informed them whether their children were making satisfactory or unsatisfactory progress. These reports were on an individualized basis. Whether a student was making satisfactory or unsatisfactory progress was determined by comparing his achievement to his capabilities as revealed by standardized intelligence tests. No comparative grade was given in the report. The senior high-school department had been reporting grades based on relative rank, which were comparative in nature. Both of these types of reports had their advantages and disadvantages, and it was not an easy matter to decide which one to use. As a basis for making the decision, a study was made of the history and development of the various types of marks used in high school and the kinds of reports made to parents. This study revealed that the development of the systems of grading had been from the percentage grade to a comparative mark based on relative rank; to an individualized mark of the satisfactory and unsatisfactory type; to attempts to combine both the comparative and individualized bases into a single mark. But no highly satisfactory system had been devised to accomplish this last step. After much study of the advantages that the combination of these two bases, comparative and individualized, would have, a dual system using both bases was proposed.

Since September, 1944, College High School has used this dual system and has reported dual grades to parents. Each student is given a letter grade of A, B, C, D, or E for the quality and quantity of his work as it compares with the work of other students. This mark is then studied in relation to the student's abilities, efforts, and other pertinent factors that might merit individual consideration. Standardized achievement and intelligence tests are used to help teachers determine what the student is capable of doing. If he had done as well as he could be expected to do in regard to his ability, *etc.,* he is given a second mark of "S." If it is evident that the student could have done better work, the second mark given will be a "U" to indicate that the student is capable of doing better work. All E's are reported unsatisfactory because it is assumed that any student who is promoted to a grade has the necessary background and is capable of doing passing work on that grade level.

An article describing this system of marking and reporting and its advantages was published in the January, 1952, issue of this publication.[1] This article attracted considerable attention and the author has had correspondence with a number of high schools about it. Copies of our report cards and other materials have been sent to forty-two high schools in twenty different states. An evaluation of this marking system has been made since that date from our records and from the opinions of parents. The purpose of this article is to present the results of that evaluation, and further to show the advantages of the dual grading and marking system.

## Evaluating the Marks

The first phase of the evaluation consisted of a careful study of the records of the 236 seniors who were graduated during the past nine years, and who were given dual grades for all four of their years of attendance in College High School. A tabulation was made of the marks they received to determine in what year in school the greatest and smallest number of unsatisfactory grades were made. Twenty-one of the 236 students made no unsatisfactory grade while in high school. The table below gives the distribution of unsatisfactory grades for the remainder of the students.

Because of the fact that College High School is small with an average senior class of approximately thirty students (transfer students who did not do all four years of their work in our school were not included in this study), the number of cases in the above table is insufficient to draw any final conclusions; however, the results show a need for further study.

It can be noted that no majority of students made the greatest or smallest number of unsatisfactory grades in any one school year, but that more of these students worked up to their capacities in the senior than in any other one single year. Both columns indicate that there wasn't a great change in the number of unsatisfactory grades made until the senior year. There may have been several reasons for the greater number of satisfactory grades on the senior level. Among the factors that have been considered and that need further study are:

[1] Irvin A. Keller, "A More Comprehensive and Significant Marking System," THE BULLETIN of the National Association of Secondary-School Principals, January, 1952.

1. Is the maturity of a student a significant factor in causing the student to make better use of abilities?

2. Do students make more satisfactory grades in elective subjects than in required subjects? (More elective subjects are taken in the senior year.)

### Table I
### Greatest and Smallest Number of Unsatisfactory Grades by School Year

| Year | Greatest Number | Smallest Number |
|---|---|---|
| Freshmen Year | 63  (29.3%) | 33  (15.3%) |
| Sophomore Year | 47  (21.9%) | 34  (15.8%) |
| Junior Year | 69  (32.1%) | 41  (19.1%) |
| Senior Year | 36  (16.7%) | 107  (49.8%) |
| Total | 215  (100%) | 215  (100%) |

3. Did the dual grading system have any effect upon the number of satisfactory and unsatisfactory grades made?

No attempt has been made to measure the effect of the maturity of students on the grades they make, because it would be pretty difficult to make such a study that would include only the factor of maturity. It is apparent in many cases that it does have much effect. In checking the prerequisites of young college men for practice teaching, the author has noted that the records of a large number of students who are veterans of World War II show that the grades made before going into service are much lower than the grades made after service. There may be several reasons for this fact, but, for many of these students, maturity seems to be an important cause. It is very reasonable to conclude that maturity plays a similar role in high school.

A study of the satisfactory and unsatisfactory grades reveals that students generally tend to make a higher percentage of satisfactory marks in elective subjects than in required courses; however, the difference is not as great as one might expect. Although a higher percentage of unsatisfactory grades are made by all students collectively in one year in all of the required courses than in all of the elective courses, a study of the marks made in English over a four-year period by the 1953–54 graduating class shows that the same students make a progressively higher percentage of satisfactory marks in this required subject. The percentages are given in the table below.

There is no other academic course that is required for four years in our school; hence, a study of the relative marks in required and elective courses is limited and no definite conclusions can be drawn at present. It does seem, however, that the election of courses plays a part in determining whether or not students work up to their capacities, but not as significant a part as might be expected. More significant is the fact that students who make a higher percentage of unsatisfactory marks in required courses also

### Table II

**Percentage of Satisfactory and Unsatisfactory Marks Made in English by 1953–54 Graduating Seniors**

| Year | Percentage of "S's" | Percentage of "U's" |
|---|---|---|
| Freshmen Year | 72.9 | 27.1 |
| Sophomore Year | 86.9 | 13.1 |
| Junior Year | 90.0 | 10.0 |
| Senior Year | 92.0 | 8.0 |

tend to make a higher percentage of unsatisfactory marks in elective courses than other students. This can be very easily seen by examining the permanent records of students making the most unsatisfactory grades.

It is difficult to determine exactly and how much effect the dual marking system had in causing students to work more nearly up to their capacities and, hence, earn a higher percentage of satisfactory grades. Our teachers and supervisors have observed that students appear to be as much concerned about whether their term grade is marked satisfactory as they are concerned about how high or low it might be. Many students have talked to their teachers, supervisors, and high-school principal about what quality of work they should do to be considered satisfactory for their abilities. Eighty-four per cent of the parents who answered a questionnaire on the dual marking system indicated that they thought the dual grades caused their children to improve their work. Although it cannot be accurately measured, it is reasonable to conclude from this evidence that the dual marks have caused many students to improve their work.

### Relationship of IQ to Unsatisfactory Marks

The second part of the evaluation of the records of the 236 seniors was a study of relationship between the intelligence quotients of students and the number of unsatisfactory marks that were made. Frequencies of ten were set up and a count of the unsatisfactory grades made in four years was made for each student who fell within each frequency. These were then totaled and the average number of unsatisfactory marks earned in four years per student was compared for each frequency. The results are given in the following table.

### Table III

**Average Number of Unsatisfactory Marks Received over a Four-year Period in Relation to Intelligence Quotients**

| No. of Cases | IQ Frequency | Average No. of "U" Marks |
|:---:|:---:|:---:|
| 8 | 81–90 | 8.5 |
| 44 | 91–100 | 8.18 |
| 84 | 101–110 | 7.71 |
| 73 | 111–120 | 9.15 |
| 22 | 121–130 | 11.5 |
| 5 | 131–140 | 16.8 |

It can be noted from the table that the students who most nearly worked up to their capacities fell in the IQ range of 101–110, and that the students who fell below this frequency worked up to their capacities better than the students who fell in the frequencies above 110. How typical the implications of this study might be in other schools is of course unknown, but there is reason to believe that these results are more general than is commonly realized. Perhaps some of the most retarded students in our schools are those who have superior ability but are only doing average work. Are the remedial programs providing help only for the inferior students? It would seem that it is equally as important to develop the potentials in above-average students.

The dual marking system was an important factor in causing the staff of College High School to realize that a number of the above-average students were not working up to their capacities before this formal study was made. In studying the reasons for this the following factors were considered as probable causes:

1. Most of the work in a typical class is geared to the average student.

2. Textbook materials are generally written for average students.

3. Standards are set up for average students and, hence, do not challenge the superior student.

4. Teachers tend to "teach to the average."

5. High-school teachers have not been given adequate training in

providing appropriate learning activities that will challenge students on several levels of ability and achievement in a mixed class.

6. Some superior students need better counseling in selecting elective courses that will more nearly challenge their abilities.

How far a school can go in getting all of its students to work up to the level of their abilities is yet to be determined. The following procedures are being used in College High School as possible means of improving the work of all students:

1. Sectioning students on the basis of both ability and achievement when possible. (This is done separately for each subject in which grouping is practiced.)

2. Differentiated assignments in mixed classes that encourage and require work of a different nature and degree of difficulty for superior, average, and below-average students.

3. Use of better motivating techniques.

4. More individual counseling of students by supervisors.

5. Improvement of standards for superior students.

6. (The use of the dual marking system also has the purpose of causing students to work more nearly up to capacity.)

There is nothing new in any of these approaches. They have been tried and proven as sound teaching procedures. The most significant fact is that, as a result of the dual marking system, our staff of supervisors and teachers were made more conscious of the need for applying them. Much concern has been shown when a student does not work up to his potential level, while, on the other hand, much satisfaction is expressed and praise is given when a student with below-average ability does the best that he can be expected to do. The high-school staff is continuing to study how better to allow for individual differences so that each student will more nearly do the type of work that he is capable of doing.

### Parent Reaction

Another phase of the evaluation of the dual marking system consisted of getting the reaction of parents to it. A simple questionnaire was sent to the parents of all students in the 1954–55 junior and senior classes. Our sampling was limited to these two classes to insure that a sufficient understanding would be had by the parents doing the evaluating on the questionnaires. They were instructed to return them unsigned unless they preferred to sign them. Thirty-one questionnaires were returned, which was slightly less than fifty per cent.

In the first item they were asked to check the type of report that they preferred for high-school students. The results are given in the table below.

### Table IV
### Type of Report Preferred

| *Type of Mark* | *No. Preferring It* |
|---|---|
| 1. A percentage mark | 0 |
| 2. A letter grade based on how one student's work compares with the work of other students. (A, B, C, D or E) | 1 |
| 3. An individualized mark or report that shows only whether a student is making satisfactory progress as compared with his own ability ("S" satisfactory, "U" unsatisfactory or a written statement to indicate either) | 0 |
| 4. The dual marks which show both how well the student's work compares with the work of others and whether he is doing satisfactory compared to his ability. (A, B, C, D, or E and "S" or "U.") | 30 |

One of the difficulties in reporting marks to parents is in furnishing a report that parents understand. A statement explaining the dual marking system accompanies the report card. Returns on the questionnaires showed that twenty-eight thought that they understood it sufficiently, three reported that they did not understand it very well, and none reported that they did not understand it.

In response to the question, "Did the dual grades help you better to understand what your child could do with a reasonable amount of effort?", four parents replied that dual marks gave *some* help; seven, that they gave *much* help; and none, that they gave *no* help. The parents were also asked to indicate the effect that they thought the dual marks had upon the work of their child. Three parents replied that the dual marks seemed to have no effect; two replied that they discouraged him; and 26, that they caused him to improve his work.

Twenty of the thirty-one questionnaires had statements by parents in the space reserved for comments. All twenty comments are highly favorable to the dual marks. Appreciation was expressed for the more complete understanding that it gave to the parents about the work of their children. The facts revealed in these statements correlate with oral comments from parents in discussing this marking system over a ten-year period. Although parents have asked questions of the staff from time-to-time about how the marks were determined, not a single criticism has been made of it and much satisfaction with the report has been expressed.

## Summary Evaluation

The following statements summarize the findings and observations we have made since the dual marking system was initiated:

1. The fact that teachers must examine the apperceptive background of students to give the dual marks has resulted in a better knowledge of individual differences and has caused the teachers to increase their attention to these differences. This has resulted in better teaching.

2. It insures better use of a standardized testing program.

3. It more nearly implements the accepted theories and principles of evaluation of secondary-school teaching than does any other system of marking.

4. Many students have improved the quality and quantity of their work after learning from the dual marks that the teachers thought they were capable of doing better.

5. The dual marks are a better basis for determining the probable future success of a student than are single marks.

6. The reliability of the marks given has been increased.

7. The dual marks help the student to understand himself better.

8. Parents have a better understanding of what their children are capable of doing and how well they are applying themselves in their studies.

9. The parental pressure has been diverted from expecting a student to "do as well as Johnnie does" to concern that he does as well as he is capable of doing.

10. Teachers consider it to be an improved marking system.

11. It has been well received and supported by parents.

Although the persons who have had experience with this system of marking as teachers and parents consider it an improved method of grading the work of students, it is very probable that it can be further improved by refinement of the techniques of administering it. Consideration is being given at present to using a three-step scale for the individualized mark by adding "Highly Satisfactory" to the Satisfactory (S) and Unsatisfactory (U) now given. This would better evaluate students who are "over achievers," or who work above what their apperceptive backgrounds indicate is their probable level. The report cards that are used (mid-term and term report cards) have a space for comment. Teachers need to be better trained to write statements that explain the reasons for satisfactory and unsatisfactory marks.

Our high school has found the dual marks both helpful and challenging and shall continue to work toward a better evaluation of the efforts of our students.

Persons who desire a better knowledge of the theory on which this system of marking is based and how it is administered are referred to the article, "A More Comprehensive and Significant Marking System," in the January, 1952, issue of THE BULLETIN.

# 52

# TRENDS IN JUNIOR HIGH-SCHOOL PROGRESS REPORTING *

## R. M. Roelfs

The preceding selection was concerned primarily with the improvement of the marking system. The one which follows reveals trends in a variety of aspects of reporting to parents at the junior high school level. An investigation was made of reporting practices in detail through a questionnaire sent to principals of junior high schools in every state. They were asked certain questions concerning practices and were also requested to return a copy of the report cards or forms currently in use in their respective schools. The results of the survey are based principally on the author's study and analysis of the 154 replies he received, including at least one from every state and the District of Columbia. The report includes information on such matters as types of reports in use, frequency of issue of reports, marking systems, behavior ratings, content, and general physical characteristics of reports. In addition, earlier studies of this question are reviewed and the findings compared to determine trends over a period of more than twenty-five years.

*Questions:*

1. Describe two or three significant changes in reporting taking place over the period covered in this report.
2. Would you expect to find different results from those reported here if a comparable survey of practice in elementary grades were available? What evidence can you cite to support your answer?
3. Look up the reference by Wrinkle in the listing at the end of the selection. Do you find any evidence relating to Question 2?

\* \* \*

* Reprinted from *Journal of Educational Research*, **49**:241–249 (December 1955), by permission of author and Dembar Publications, Inc.

## Introduction

Reporting procedures have been changed gradually and repeatedly in our public schools the past few decades. The amount of attention given this topic by educational writers in books and periodicals, by professors of education in their classes, and by participants in the various local, regional, and national professional programs affirms that reporting to parents is a popular subject with educators in general. That it is an area of particular concern to public school teachers and administrators is concretely evidenced by the vast amount of experimenting and innovating they have sponsored in the hope of improving the procedures and materials used in reporting.

Changes in reporting on pupil progress over the years have been in many directions and have resulted in a variety of forms and practices. From reading the literature one gets the impression that these changes are consistently in the direction away from the traditional report card and persistently toward more informal means of reporting. The question is raised: Is this an accurate interpretation of the prevailing tendency of current modifications in pupil progress reporting, or has the pendulum started its swing in the opposite direction?

## The Problem

This study is an attempt to identify recent significant trends in the reporting on pupil progress in junior high schools of the United States.

## Previous Studies

Only a few inclusive research studies are available that reveal practices in junior high schools. Four deserve special mention. In 1925, Chapman and Ashbaugh [2] * studied 842 report card forms from cities of all sizes over 10,000 population from every state in the Union. Only 70 of these forms were from junior high schools. Ten years later Hill [6] reported the results of an examination of 443 report forms, 58 of which were being used in junior high schools. A survey of 149 report forms from junior high schools in cities of 50,000 population or over was completed by Berman [1] in 1943. One hundred fifty-nine junior high schools representing every state and the District of Columbia were included in a survey of progress re-

* Figures in brackets apply to references at end of article.

porting practices made by this writer in 1948 [10]. This latter study was restricted to schools in cities of 10,000 population or over.

The current picture of how junior high schools are reporting to parents on pupil progress was obtained by studying the reporting forms that are being used in junior high schools in the current school year, 1952–53. Two hundred principals of junior high schools were requested to supply the writer with copies of the report form or forms that were being used in their respective schools. Anticipating that some schools may not have a formal system of reporting, a simple check sheet was included along with the request on which the respondent was asked to indicate which of the following methods of reporting were used in his school: (1) reporting by means of report cards or other printed or mimeographed forms, (2) reporting by means of informal letters, conferences with parents, or both, or (3) reporting by a combination of the two methods mentioned above.

Junior high schools from every state and the District of Columbia were included. An attempt was made to distribute the requests geographically, approximately four per state, and to include only those locations sufficiently large to support a junior high school as a separately-housed school attendance center.

In order to ascertain the status of pupil progress reporting in junior high schools prior to the present time, a review of statements, conclusions and opinions of various writers of the past quarter century was accomplished. However, the generalizations arising from this investigation are based primarily on the four studies by Chapman and Ashbaugh in 1925 [2], Hill in 1935 [6], Berman in 1943 [1], and this writer in 1948 [10]. Throughout the remainder of this paper, data associated with the above mentioned dates have been taken from the corresponding research study.

### Findings

Information was received from 154 or 77 percent of the total included in the original request. At least one reply was received from every state and the District of Columbia. Of the 154, seventeen or less than 12 percent reported an enrollment of less than 400. A distribution of the requests sent and the replies received is shown by regions in Table I.

### Types of Reports in Use

In 1925, all of the junior high school reports were reported to be a formal or traditional type. During the next ten years many people advocated the substitution of informal letters for report cards but there is little evidence of this being practiced in junior high schools in the middle thirties. Both the 1943 and 1948 data indicate that approximately two percent of the junior high schools were using letters to parents in lieu of reports. In the present study, not a single school indicated that it relied solely on informal methods in reporting. Apparently all 154 schools are accomplishing the reporting function by means of report forms of one kind or another. However, 38

**Table I**

**Distribution by Regions of Junior High Schools Included in Survey of Current Reporting Practices**

| Regions | Requests Sent | Responses Received | Percentage Return |
|---|---|---|---|
| New England (6 states) | 24 | 16 | 66.7 |
| Middle Atlantic (7 states and D. C.) | 29 | 24 | 82.8 |
| Southern (12 states) | 47 | 36 | 76.6 |
| North Central (12 states) | 57 | 45 | 78.9 |
| Western (11 states) | 43 | 33 | 76.7 |
| Totals | 200 | 154 | 77.0 |

percent of them are supplementing the periodic report with letters to parents, parent-teacher-pupil conferences, telephone calls and other informal methods.

*Frequency of Issuance of Reports*

Current writers report that many schools now report only once a semester or three times a year and no mention was found in recent accounts of schools reporting more frequently than six times a year. Neither the current survey nor the writer's 1948 study revealed any great tendency for junior high schools to report less frequently than on a quarterly basis. Table II gives the

**Table II**

**Frequency of Reporting on Pupil Progress in Junior High Schools**

| No. of Reports per Year | Percent of Schools Issuing Reports | | |
|---|---|---|---|
| | 1925 | 1948 | 1953 |
| More than six | 27 | 2 | 1 |
| Six | 39 | 54 | 49 |
| Five | 7 | 1 | 4 |
| Four | 27 | 42 | 45 |
| Less than four | 0 | 1 | 1 |

results of three studies on the frequency of reporting. Comparable data were not available in 1935 and 1943.

In addition to the regular report, it is now a practice in more than one-third of the junior high schools to send out notices between the regular reports to the parents of those pupils whose work is not satisfactory. A commendatory notice of those pupils who have shown outstanding improvement or special accomplishment is in use in approximately one-tenth of the junior high schools included in the 1953 survey.

## Marking Systems

Three systems of marking are identified for the purpose of this investigation: (1) the percentage system, (2) symbols explained or interpreted in terms of percentages, and (3) symbols interpreted by means of words or phrases. Table III shows the trend in the use of these three systems in junior high schools.

"ABCDF" marking in the subject matter areas appears to have been the most popular since the early days of the junior high school. The earlier studies did not determine the extent of the deviation from the usual five-

**Table III**

**Marking Systems Used in Junior High Schools**

| Marking System | Frequency of Use in Percentage | | | | |
|---|---|---|---|---|---|
| | 1925 | 1935 | 1943 | 1948 | 1953 |
| Percentage | 23 | 12 | 4 | 1 | |
| Symbols expressed as percentages | 28 | 28 | 27.5[a] | 15 | 17 |
| Symbols | 49 | 62 | 72.5 | 81 | 82 |

[a] Berman's study combined percentage marking and symbols expressed as percentages.

point marking scale. It was reported in 1943 that 56.1 percent of the junior high schools were using a five-point scale. The data collected in the two more recent studies and reported in Table IV point toward an even greater reliance on the five-step system.

Instructions advising that the marks were to be distributed according to the normal curve appeared on six percent of the forms studied in 1948 as compared to only four percent in 1953.

## Behavior Rating

The same system was used for marking behavior as in rating achievement by 48 percent of the junior high schools in 1935, by 31 percent in 1948, and by 40 percent in 1953. A two-point satisfactory-unsatisfactory scale was employed by 69.6 percent of the schools studied in 1943, by 21 percent in 1948 and by 28 percent in 1953. The next most common way of rating citizenship or character traits was a three-point scale which is now used in 26 percent of the junior high schools as compared to ten percent five years ago. The earlier studies revealed almost an unanimous use of one single term such as Conduct or Citizenship to be rated. In 1943 twenty percent were using a single term but by 1953 this increased to 42 percent, indicat-

**Table IV**

**Frequency of Use of Variations of Symbol Marking Systems
in Junior High Schools**

| No. of Steps in Marking Scale | Example | Frequency in Percent | |
|---|---|---|---|
| | | 1948 | 1953 |
| Six | ABCDEF | 3 | 9 |
| Five | ABCDF | 80 | 81 |
| Four | ABCF | 8 | 3 |
| Three | HSU | 3 | 2 |
| Two | SU | 3 | 1 |
| More than six | ABCDEFX | 3 | 4 |

ing a trend towards simplifying this phase of reporting. On many of the recent reports, behavior rating is accomplished by means of a checklist. As many as fifteen such items or statements were found on a card of a junior high school in 1948 and as many as twenty-four on a single card in 1953.

*Content of Reports*

About the only feature found common in all reports during the last twenty-five years is that all make some attempt to evaluate subject matter achievement. Recently though, instead of giving a single rating for each subject a few junior high schools are subdividing each subject into skills, habits or goals for evaluation purposes. The increase in this procedure of reporting achievement during the past decade is indicated in the comparison of the results of three studies. In 1943, only 3.4 percent of the junior high schools made an attempt to analyze subjects into goals and skills, while in 1948 there were 9 percent, and in 1953, 20 percent.

Some form of behavior was rated on 40 percent of the reports in 1925, on 86 percent in 1924, on 83 percent in 1948 and on 90 percent of the 1953 report forms.

Some aspect of attendance was reported on 96 percent of the 1925 and

1935 forms, 94 percent of the 1948 and 93 percent of the 1953 progress reports. All studies indicated that the item most frequently reported on was "days absent," with "times tardy" running a close second.

In 1925 a very few junior high schools provided space on cards for reporting on the health of pupils. Usually this consisted of blanks on the forms to indicate height and weight. By 1935, it was reported that 36 percent of the schools considered some phase of health. This figure is considerably above the findings of others so it is surmised that the ratings of health objectives in connection with other subjects had been included. Correctible de-

**Table V**

**Frequency of Providing a Space for Comments by Teachers or Parents on Junior High School Reporting Forms**

| Space on Report for Comment | Percentage of Report Forms in | | |
|---|---|---|---|
| | 1943 | 1948 | 1953 |
| By Teachers | 20.1 | 39 | 41 |
| By Parents | 10.1 | 18 | 22 |

fects were identified on 3.5 percent of the 1943 reports. Health traits, posture being the most frequently mentioned, appeared on 11 percent and 13 percent of the 1948 and 1953 forms respectively.

Table V shows the frequency of the occurrence of space for comments or remarks by teachers and parents. In no instance was a space for pupil comments found. The area of space provided in the 1948 forms varied from as little as three to as much as ninety-nine square inches.

*General Physical Characteristics*

In the analysis of the organization of the 1943 forms, 50 percent were found to be arranged in a 4-page folder as compared to 42 percent in 1948 and 39 percent in 1953. One-page or single-sheet reports were the most frequently used in 1935 and were found in 42 percent of the 1948 sample and 32 percent of the 1953 group. The use of individual cards for each subject has increased from 17 percent to 29 percent in the last five years.

Report cards have been issued in many different colors. Especially popular are some of the light hues such as tan, cream, yellow or salmon. White always has been and still is the most used color. Seventy percent of the 1925, 65 percent of the 1948 and 66 percent of the 1953 cards and forms were white.

The most popular size of reporting form through the years has been

4" x 6". Twenty percent of the 1925, 18.7 percent of the 1943, 24 percent of the 1948 and 28 percent of the 1953 progress reports were 4" x 6" in dimensions. The smallest and largest were of identical dimensions in the 1948 and 1953 surveys, the former being 2¾" x 4½" and the latter, 8" x 11". In 1953, 24 percent of the forms were larger than 5" x 8" as compared to 19 percent in 1948.

Junior high schools in both 1948 and 1953 used over thirty different designations in referring to their report forms. Several, approximately one-eighth, had no title or heading other than the name of the school system or school unit. The word appearing most often in the titles was "report," 75 percent in 1935, 83 percent in 1948 and 82 percent in 1953. One-fourth of both the 1948 and 1953 samples were designated as "report cards." The word "progress" is appearing more frequently in titles of 1953 reports, 20 percent of them, than in those five years earlier, 13 percent.

## Trends

The following trends appear to be evident in the reporting to parents on pupil progress in junior high schools:

1. There is continuing an intense interest in the subject of reporting pupil progress on the part of administrators, teachers and parents.
2. While reports have become less formal, the trend is not toward using diagnostic letters or conferences as the only means of reporting to parents on the child's work in school, but rather to use informal reporting procedures to supplement the periodic progress report.
3. There has been no significant change in the reporting of attendance during the last twenty-five years.
4. While the tendency has been to use the report form in giving to parents a wider variety of information, schools are not now further extending the scope of reporting but are endeavoring to improve the validity of the various phases on which evaluations are made.
5. There is a trend for schools to mark progress in academic subjects by subdividing each subject into goals, skills, or habits.
6. A few more schools are indicating correctible physical defects on pupil progress reports, but this is practiced by only a very small proportion of junior high schools.
7. More junior high schools are providing space on the report forms for comments by teachers and parents than in the past.

8. The percentage system of marking has all but disappeared and the trend toward the use of symbols is continuing.

9. There has been a return to "ABCDF" marking by many who were using various two-, three-, and four-step marking scales. During the past five years there has been a noticeable increase in the use of marking systems having more than five categories, the tendency being to add a qualifying passing mark for low-ability students.

10. The rating of behavior in junior high schools is now very much in a state of flux. Within the past few years, they have been returning to the practice of using the same rating device here as in subject-matter. Also there is a recent tendency to rely more on a single term such as "Citizenship" rather than on a series of traits in this evaluation.

11. Reports are made to parents either four or six times a year in most junior high schools. The Quarterly Report is continuing to gain in popularity.

12. There is a definite trend toward informing parents whenever their child is making unsatisfactory progress by means of a supplementary report between the regular reporting dates. The practice of sending commendatory or complimentary notes to parents concerning the accomplishment of pupils is increasing.

13. A 4" x 6" report form is in use by more schools than any other sized card, but there is a tendency for more schools to use a form approximately 5" x 8" or slightly larger, and for fewer schools to use cards smaller than 4" x 6".

14. The shift to employing color in progress reports appears to have stopped. Approximately two-thirds of the current reports are white.

15. A great variety of names are used to designate the report to parents. The word "report" is found in a large majority and the word "progress" is being used more frequently.

16. A decreasing number of progress reports contain instructions to teachers to distribute marks according to a fixed percentage based on the normal curve.

17. There is a slight trend away from organizing the progress report into a 4-page folder or single page card in favor of issuing separate cards or sheets for each of the individual subjects.

18. Teachers and administrators are expressing concern that reporting to parents is becoming too complicated and laborious, but progress in the direction of simplicity is not yet evident.

## References

1. BERMAN, SAMUEL. "Revising the Junior High School Report Card." *Bull. Nat. Assoc. Secondary-School Principals.* **27**:49–62 (May 1943).

2. CHAPMAN, H. B. and E. J. ASHBAUGH. "Report Cards in American Cities." *Educ. Res. Bull.* **5**:289–293 (October 7, 1925).

3. CROOKS, A. DURYEE. "Marks and Marking Systems: A Digest." *J. Educ. Res.* **27**:259–272 (December 1933).

4. EVANS, ROBERT O. *Practices, Trends, and Issues in Reporting to Parents on the Welfare of the Child in School.* New York: Bureau of Publications, Teachers College, Columbia University (1938) 98 pp.

5. GRUHN, WILLIAM T. and HARL R. DOUGLASS. *The Modern Junior High School.* New York: The Ronald Press Company (1947) 492 pp.

6. HILL, GEORGE E. "The Report Card in Present Practice." *Educ. Method.* **15**:115–131 (December 1935).

7. JOHNSON, LEMUEL R. "Are There Better Ways of Evaluating, Recording and Reporting Pupil Progress in the Junior High Schools?" *Bull. Nat. Assoc. Secondary-School Principals.* **34**:73–79 (March 1950).

8. MESSENGER, HELEN R. and WINIFRED WATTS. "Summaries of Selected Articles on School Report Cards." *Educ. Admin. and Sup.* **21**:539–550 (October 1955).

9. ODELL, C. W. "Marks and Marking Systems." *Encyclopedia of Educational Research.* New York: The Macmillan Company (1950) pp. 711–717.

10. ROELFS, R. M. *Trends in Reporting to Parents on Pupil Progress in Junior High Schools.* Unpublished Master's Thesis. Boulder: University of Colorado (1948) 90 pp.

11. WRINKLE, WILLIAM L. *Improving Marking and Reporting Practices.* New York: Holt, Rinehart & Winston (1947) 120 pp.

# 53

# HOW TESTS HELP US IDENTIFY THE ACADEMICALLY TALENTED *

## Henry Chauncey

Recent years have witnessed a greatly increased interest in academically talented or, as they are more often called, gifted children. Educators have come to realize in a way they did not before that these children are the potential leaders of the next generation and that from among them will come most, if not all, of our future scientists, statesmen, jurists, educators, and political leaders. Along with this realization has come the admission that, by and large, the gifted children in our schools have not been challenged to exert themselves to their fullest capacity, and that we have tended to let them drift along knowing that they would probably at least get by if left pretty much to themselves. Today there is a great deal of talk and activity about special provisions for the gifted. Indeed, there are some schools, particularly on the secondary level, that are set aside for children with I.Q.'s above a certain point, and there are classes or sections for academically talented youngsters in many places, something which could hardly have even been mentioned in some educational circles a few years ago. In the following selection, the use of tests in identifying the gifted is discussed and illustrated, pointing out the main advantages as well as the limitations of such instruments for the purpose.

*Questions:*

1. What other methods of identifying gifted children can you name? Is there any evidence regarding their efficiency?
2. What are the arguments "pro" and "con" for special classes or special schools for the gifted? Can you cite any evidence on the issue?

\* \* \*

There are many kinds of tests with many purposes and uses, but in this article, I am going to focus on the kinds of tests which have proved most

* Reprinted from the *National Education Association Journal,* **47:**230–231 (April 1958), by permission of author and publisher.

practical and effective for widespread use in identification of academic talent.

Such tests, whether labeled "intelligence," "aptitude," or "ability," consist usually of two chief components, generally called "verbal" or "linguistic," on the one hand, and "quantitative" or "mathematical," on the other. These two components do not measure all of the dimensions of academic talent, but what they do measure seems clearly and consistently related to academic achievement.

The verbal element is likely to involve word meaning, reading comprehension, analogy, sentence completion, and the like. The quantitative element most frequently involves numerical computations.

Now, what do such verbal and mathematical tests measure? Do they, dependent as they obviously are on learning and environmental influence, pretend to measure innate intelligence?

The answer is "No." To avoid any such implication, I prefer to speak of testing "developed ability." Whenever we test a student, we are dealing with him as he is—a product of certain interactions between his heredity and his environment. So far, it has proved impossible to isolate and measure separately these hereditary and environmental influences.

The present verbal and mathematical abilities of an individual—regardless of what may account for them—offer the best prediction of his future academic achievement.

Since such achievement depends on previous learnings, we must grant that different cultural backgrounds inevitably affect test performance. However, the same cultural factors which influence test scores also appear to influence the academic achievement which we want to predict by means of those test scores. Therefore, tests of developed ability actually gain in predictive effectiveness by tapping some basic verbal and mathematical learnings of the sort that all of our schools emphasize for all pupils.

Some may ask, "Why use a test at all? Why not depend entirely on previous school performance for prediction?" In brief, because we know that test scores and school marks together predict more accurately than either one separately.

In general, we have greatest expectancy of future academic success for those pupils who rank high on both predictors. Our expectancy of success is somewhat lower for those who rank high on one predictor but not on the other, and least for those who rank low on both. Also, each predictor identifies some potentially high achievers not identified by the other.

Test scores have certain advantages. They furnish—at any grade level—

a standardized, comparable set of observations of pupils who may have had different teachers and come from different schools with different marking systems.

They are unaffected by any disciplinary element such as may affect course grades. However, for purposes of identification and prediction, both marks and test scores, as well as such other data as may be accessible and relevant, can make significant contributions.

Tests, of course, have their limitations. We have no particular evidence that they measure potential creativity, original thinking, inventiveness. They certainly will not single out for us the individual who will discover new intellectual territory as distinct from the other individuals who will settle and cultivate that territory.

In short, we cannot feed results of a secondary-school standardized testing program into an electronic computer and expect a guaranteed roster of future Einsteins and Pasteurs to emerge. No matter how refined our techniques become, it is safe to say, with William James, that "individual . . . biographies will never be written in advance."

What tests can do for us is identify the larger number of students who are in the score ranges from which creative scientists, engineers, philosophers, historians, economists, psychologists, jurists, educators are most likely to emerge. Thus, if we are fishing for sizable intellectual talent, standardized testing will not single out the species or net the catch for us. But it will tell us which pools are most promising for the "big ones."

Hundreds of carefully conducted studies have produced convincing evidence of a substantial relationship between test scores and such criteria of intellectual achievement as high-school marks, college marks, college graduation, graduate degrees, and occupational "levels."

The specific amount of relationship has, of course, varied according to specific tests, criteria, populations, and other experimental characteristics. We cannot say categorically that a certain amount of statistical relationship is universally true and applicable to every situation. On the contrary, local research is required in order to derive the maximum benefit from testing for any given purpose, such as admission to X college, or prediction of success in first-year algebra at Z high school.

Even in less specific settings, however, predictions can be safely and helpfully expressed in terms of probabilities or expectancies. For example, the report of the Commission on Human Resources and Advanced Training was able to give the educational expectancies for 14-year-olds at various test-score levels, representing not a single "college, city, year, graduating class, or other . . . limited sample" but "estimates for the United States as a whole in the middle of the twentieth century."

Thus, 14-year-olds with a test score equivalent to 80 on the Army General Classification Test scale have about 60 chances out of 100 of entering high school and 23 chances out of 100 of graduating, about five chances out of 100 of entering college, and one chance (or less) out of 100 of graduating.

For 14-year-olds with a test score of 100 ("average" in respect to the total population of 14-year-olds) the expectancies are higher: 85 chances out of 100 of entering high school, 60 chances of graduating, 18 of entering college, and eight of graduating. For a higher score (AGCT-120) the respective chances would rise to 98 out of 100 for entering high school, 90 for graduating, 37 for entering college, and 25 for graduating.

Clearly, scores from tests given at age 14 can predict, with some degree of effectiveness, the educational level likely to be attained. Other studies have shown that scores on tests given at age 14 correlate very highly with scores on similar tests four years later.

How effective are typical scholastic-aptitude tests in the prediction of college success?

While the results of specific studies vary, we can say with confidence what is *usually* found. Typically, of the students in the top 20% on the test, about 45% will do honor work, 52% will do satisfactory work, and only about 3% will fail. Of the students in the bottom 20% on the test, only about 3% will do honor work, 52% more will pass, 45% will fail. When we take the middle 60%, we find that on the average, 17% will do honor work; 66%, satisfactory work; and 17% will fail.

Not a perfect record, obviously, but as actuarial forecasts go, reasonably good; especially when we consider that predictions are based only on aptitude-test scores and do not take into account such factors as interest and motivation.

The junior high-school years are an especially timely period for administering a standardized testing program. Prediction at this point is practical and appropriate in terms of both the psychological development of individuals and the organization of our schools.

The growth of intellectual abilities, as reflected by standardized test scores, has stabilized by this age period to the extent that an eighth-grade test is likely to be nearly as effective as a twelfth-grade test in predicting— let us say—college freshman marks.

Our educational system generally requires of pupils differential curriculum choices at the end of the eighth (or sometimes ninth) grade. Decisions made at this point are of vital importance for the educational and career choices of students. These decisions tend to close some doors or hold them open. School administrators also must often make, around this period, particularly significant decisions about the ability grouping of pupils in such subjects as English and mathematics.

Although the junior high-school years offer both an excellent opportunity and a pressing need to marshal efforts at identification of intellectual ability, I do not mean to imply that such efforts should be confined to these grades. On the contrary, identification should be a continuous process. The formal program directed at such critical choice-points as eighth and twelfth grades should, ideally, build upon previous activities and lead into future ones.

Test-score results not only correlate with future academic success, but appear to have a definite bearing on post-educational achievement as well.

An investigation was made several years ago of some 281 men in *Who's Who* and *American Men of Science* who had taken the Scholastic Aptitude Test of the College Entrance Examination Board when they applied to go to college. The individuals had achieved prominence in a variety of fields: government, writing, education, business, law, banking, engineering, the sciences, and a number of other vocations.

By relating the scores of these 281 men to known score distributions of those who had taken the test, it was found that a person with a score on the Scholastic Aptitude Test equivalent to 120–130 on the Army General Classification Test had two-and-a-half times as great a chance of being in *Who's Who* or *American Men of Science* as a person in the score range of 110–120. A person with a score equivalent to between 130–140 had four times as great a chance as a person scoring between 110–120; a person with a score between 140–150 had seven times as great a chance; a person with a score of over 150 had 14 times as great a chance.

These findings seem to me rather impressive, particularly in view of the fact that the Scholastic Aptitude Test in the early days contained only verbal questions—no quantitative material.

This, then, is the general picture of testing and its effectiveness at the present time. To me the results mean that tests are by no means infallible but that they provide a highly serviceable degree of accuracy. Properly understood and properly used, tests offer a potent aid in the selection, guidance, or placement of students.

## Bibliography

*Measurement, Evaluation and Reporting—Qualitative and Quantitative Processes*

1. BARBE, WALTER B. "Evaluation of Special Classes for Gifted Children." *Excep. Child.* **22:**60–62 (November 1955).

2. ———. "What Happens to Graduates of Special Classes for the Gifted?" *Educ. Res. Bul.* **36:**13–16 (January 1957).

3. DAVIS, W. ALLISON and ROBERT J. HAVIGHURST. "The Measurement of Mental Systems." *Sci. Monthly.* **66:**301–316; **67:**313–314 (April, October 1948).

4. DRESSEL, PAUL L. and JOHN M. GRABOW. "The Gifted Evaluate Their High School Experience." *Excep. Child.* **24:**394–396 (May 1958).

5. DUNNINGTON, MARGARET J. "Investigation of Areas of Disagreement in Sociometric Measurement of Preschool Children." *Child Dev.* **28:**93–102 (March 1957).

6. EBEL, ROBERT L. "The Forms of Objective Test Items." From *Educational Measurement,* ed. by E. F. LINDQUIST. Washington, D. C.: American Council on Education (1951), pp. 193–204.

7. ——— and DORA DAMRIN. "Tests and Examinations." *Encyclopedia of Educational Research.* New York: The Macmillan Co., Third Edition 1960), pp. 1502–1517.

8. EELLS, KENNETH. "Some Implications for School Practice of the Chicago Studies of Cultural Bias in Intelligence Tests." *Harvard Educ. Rev.* **23:** 284–297 (Fall 1953).

9. FLANAGAN, JOHN C., SHIRLEY S. PUMROY, and SHIRLEY A. TUSKA. "A New Tool for Measuring Children's Behavior." *Elem. Sch. J.* **59:**163–166 (December 1958).

10. FLANAGAN, J. C. "Testing Programs: Their Function in Education." *Cal. J. Sec. Educ.* **35:**41–45 (January 1960).

11. FREEMAN, FRANK S. "How the Curriculum Is Evaluated and Modified Through Educational Measurement." *J. Educ. Psychol.* **39:**167–169 (March 1948).

12. FLOTOW, ERNEST A. "Charting Social Relationships of School Children." *Elem. Sch. J.* **46:**498–504 (May 1946).

13. GAGE, N. L. "Explorations in Teachers' Perceptions of Pupils." *J. Teach. Educ.* **9:**97–101 (March 1958).

14. GATES, A. I. "A Study of the Role of Visual Perception, Intelligence and Certain Associative Processes in Reading and Spelling." *J. Educ. Psychol.* **17:**433–435 (October 1926).

15. GRACE, H. A. "Information and Social Distance as Predictors of Hostility Towards Nations." *J. Ab. & Soc. Psychol.* **47:**540–545 (1952).

16. GREENE, JAMES E. "The Role of Evaluation in the Improvement of Instruction in Institutions of Higher Learning." *J. Exp. Educ.* **25:**33–35 (September 1956).

17. GRONLUND, NORMAN E. and ALGARD P. WHITNEY. "The Relation Between Teachers' Judgments of Pupils' Sociometric Status and Intelligence." *Elem. Sch. J.* **58:**264–268 (February 1958).

18. HAGEN, ELIZABETH P. and ROBERT L. THORNDIKE. "Evaluation." *Encyclopedia of Educational Research.* New York: The Macmillan Co., Third Edition (1960), pp. 482–485.

19. HALL, E. C. "The Proper Use of Test Results." *Elem. Sch. J.* **54:**450–455 (April 1954).

20. Joint Committee, *Technical Recommendations for Psychological Tests and Diagnostic Techniques*, supplement to the *Psychol. Bul.* **51:**1–38. Washington: American Psychological Association (1954).

21. Joint Committee, *Technical Recommendations for Achievement Tests.* Washington: American Educational Research Association (1955).

22. KELLER, IRVIN A. "A More Comprehensive and Significant Marking System." *Bul. of Nat. Assoc. of Sec.-Schl. Prin.* **36:**70–78 (January 1952).

23. KORNHAUSER, ARTHUR. "Replies of Psychologists to Several Questions on the Practical Value of Intelligence Tests." *Educ. and Psychol. Meas.* **5:** 181–189 (Summer 1945).

24. LENNON, ROGER T. "Testing: Bond or Barrier Between Pupil and Teacher?" *Educ.* **75:**38–42 (September 1954).

25. MARTENS, CLARENCE C. "Educational Achievements of Eighth-Grade Pupils in One-Room Rural and Graded Town Schools." *Elem. Sch. J.* **54:**523–525 (May 1954).

26. MILLER, W. S. "The Variation and Significance of Intelligence Quotients Obtained from Group Tests." *J. Educ. Psychol.* **15:**359–366 (September 1924).

27. MOONEY, R. L. "Community Differences in the Problems of High School Students: A Survey of Five Communities by Means of a Problem Check List." *Educ. & Psychol. Meas.* **3:**127–142 (Summer 1943).

28. PARKER, BEATRICE F. "The Parent-Teacher Conference." *Elem. Sch. J.* **53:**270–274 (January 1953).

29. PRESSEY, S. L. and P. CAMPBELL. "The Causes of Children's Errors in Capitalization: A Psychological Analysis." *English J.* **22:**197–201 (March 1933).

30. RUSSELL, J. L. and W. A. THALMAN. "Personality: Does It Influence Teachers' Marks?" *J. Educ. Res.* **48:**561–564 (April 1955).

31. SILVEY, H. M. "Changes in Test Scores After Two Years in College." *Educ. & Psychol. Meas.* **11:**494–502 (Autumn 1951).

32. STALNAKER, JOHN M. "Suggestions for Improving Essay Questions." From *Educational Measurement,* ed. by E. F. LINDQUIST. Washington, D. C.: Amer. Council on Education (1951), pp. 516–528.

33. STRANG, RUTH. "Reporting Pupil Progress." *Sch. Exec.* **72:**47–50 (August 1953).

34. TRAXLER, ARTHUR E. "Twelve Current Trends in Testing." *Clearing House.* **28:**3–7 (September 1953).

35. ———. "The Use of Tests in Differentiated Instruction." *Educ.* **74:**272–278 (January 1954).

36. WALKER, HELEN M. "What Teachers Need to Know About Statistics." From *Statistical Understandings Every Teacher Needs—Improving Educational Research.* Washington, D. C.: Am. Educ. Res. Assoc. (1948), pp. 207–213.

37. WESTOVER, FREDERICK L. "A Comparison of Listening and Reading as a Means of Testing." *J. Educ. Res.* **52:**23–26 (September 1958).

38. WOMER, FRANK B. "Initiating a Testing Program." *Elem. Sch. J.* **57:**193–197 (December 1956).

39. WORBOIS, G. M. "Changes in Stanford-Binet I.Q. for Rural Consolidated and Rural One-Room School Children." *J. Exp. Educ.* **11:**210–214 (December 1942).

40. WRIGHTSTONE, J. W. "Evaluation of the Experiment with the Activity Program in the New York City Public Schools." *J. Educ. Res.* **38:**252–257 (December 1944).